Lecture Notes in Computer Science 12525

More information about this subseries at http://www.springer.com/series/7411

Olga Galinina · Sergey Andreev ·
Sergey Balandin · Yevgeni Koucheryavy (Eds.)

Internet of Things, Smart Spaces, and Next Generation Networks and Systems

20th International Conference, NEW2AN 2020
and 13th Conference, ruSMART 2020
St. Petersburg, Russia, August 26–28, 2020
Proceedings, Part I

 Springer

Editors
Olga Galinina (iD)
Unit of Electrical Engineering
Tampere University
Tampere, Finland

Sergey Balandin (iD)
FRUCT Oy
Helsinki, Finland

Sergey Andreev (iD)
Unit of Electrical Engineering
Tampere University
Tampere, Finland

Yevgeni Koucheryavy (iD)
Unit of Electrical Engineering
Tampere University
Tampere, Finland

ISSN 0302-9743   ISSN 1611-3349 (electronic)
Lecture Notes in Computer Science
ISBN 978-3-030-65725-3   ISBN 978-3-030-65726-0 (eBook)
https://doi.org/10.1007/978-3-030-65726-0

LNCS Sublibrary: SL5 – Computer Communication Networks and Telecommunications

This Springer imprint is published by the registered company Springer Nature Switzerland AG
The registered company address is: Gewerbestrasse 11, 6330 Cham, Switzerland

Preface

We welcome you to the joint proceedings of the 20th International Conference on Next Generation Teletraffic and Wired/Wireless Advanced Networks and Systems (NEW2AN 2020) and the 13th Conference on the Internet of Things and Smart Spaces (ruSMART 2020) held in St. Petersburg, Russia, during August 26–28, 2020.

Originally, the NEW2AN conference was launched by the International Teletraffic Congress (ITC) in St. Petersburg in June 1993 as an ITC-Sponsored Regional International Teletraffic Seminar. The first edition was entitled "Traffic Management and Routing in SDH Networks" and held by the R&D Institute (LONIIS). In 2002, the event received its current name, the NEW2AN. In 2008, NEW2AN acquired a new companion in Smart Spaces, ruSMART, hence boosting interaction between researchers, practitioners, and engineers across different areas of ICT. From 2012, the scope of ruSMART conferences has been extended to cover the Internet of the Things and related aspects.

Presently, NEW2AN and ruSMART are well-established conferences with a unique cross-disciplinary mixture of telecommunications-related research and science. NEW2AN/ruSMART are accompanied by outstanding keynotes from universities and companies across Europe, the USA, and Russia.

The NEW2AN 2020 technical program addresses various aspects of next-generation data networks, while special attention is given to advanced wireless networking and applications. In particular, the authors have demonstrated novel and innovative approaches to performance and efficiency analysis of 5G and beyond systems, employed game-theoretical formulations, advanced queuing theory, and stochastic geometry. It is also worth mentioning the rich coverage of the Internet of Things, cyber security, optics, signal processing, as well as business aspects.

ruSMART 2020 provided a forum for academic and industrial researchers to discuss new ideas and trends in the emerging areas of the Internet of Things and Smart Spaces that create new opportunities for fully-customized applications and services. The conference brought together leading experts from top affiliations around the world. This year, we have seen participation from representatives of various players in the field, including academic teams and industrial companies, particularly representatives of Russian R&D centers, which have a solid reputation for high-quality research and business in innovative service creation and development of applications. The conference was held virtually due to the COVID-19 pandemic.

We would like to thank the Technical Program Committee members of the two conferences, as well as the invited reviewers, for their hard work and important contributions to the conference. This year, the conference program met the highest quality criteria, with an acceptance ratio of around 35%. The number of submissions sent for peer review was 225, while the number of full papers accepted is 79. A single-blind peer-review type was used for the review process.

The current edition of the conference was organized in cooperation with IEEE Communications Society Russia Northwest Chapter, YL-Verkot OY, Open Innovations Association FRUCT, Tampere University, Peter the Great St. Petersburg Polytechnic University, Peoples' Friendship University of Russia (RUDN University), The National Research University Higher School of Economics (HSE), St. Petersburg State University of Telecommunications, and Popov Society. The conference was held within the framework of the "RUDN University Program 5-100."

We believe that NEW2AN 2020 and ruSMART 2020 conferences delivered an informative, high-quality, and up-to-date scientific program.

August 2020

Olga Galinina
Sergey Andreev
Sergey Balandin
Yevgeni Koucheryavy

Organization

Technical Program Committee

Torsten Braun	University of Bern, Switzerland
Paulo Carvalho	Centro ALGORITMI, Universidade do Minho, Portugal
Chrysostomos Chrysostomou	Frederick University, Cyprus
Roman Dunaytsev	The Bonch-Bruevich Saint-Petersburg State University of Telecommunications, Russia
Dieter Fiems	Ghent University, Belgium
Alexey Frolov	Skolkovo Institute of Science and Technology, Russia
Ivan Ganchev	University of Limerick, Ireland
Jiri Hosek	Brno University of Technology, Czech Republic
Alexey Kashevnik	SPIIRAS, Russia
Joaquim Macedo	Universidade do Minho, Portugal
Ninoslav Marina	UIST, North Macedonia
Aleksandr Ometov	Tampere University, Finland
Pavel Masek	Brno University of Technology, Czech Republic
Edison Pignaton de Freitas	Federal University of Rio Grande do Sul, Brazil

Publicity Chair

Nikita Tafintsev	Tampere University, Finland

Contents – Part I

Contents – Part II

New Generation of Smart Services

Identification of Abnormal Functioning of Devices of Cyber-Physical Systems

V. V. Semenov[1]([envelope]) [ID], M. E. Sukhoparov[2] [ID], and I. S. Lebedev[1] [ID]

[1] SPIIRAS, 14-th Linia, VI, No. 39, St. Petersburg 199178, Russia
v.semenov@iias.spb.su
[2] SPbF AO «NPK «TRISTAN», 47 Nepokorennykh pr., Saint Petersburg 195220, Russia

Abstract. This paper undertakes the task of determining the information security state of autonomous objects using information obtained through a side acoustic channel. The basic prerequisites for using externally independent monitoring systems to monitor the state of objects at risk of the influence of threats to information security are considered. An experiment to study the functioning parameters of unmanned vehicles in various functioning situations was performed. The appearance and statistical characteristics of the signals, which enable the identification of abnormal deviations during the operation of unmanned vehicles, are shown. Furthermore, an algorithm of two- and three-class classification of the states of the studied objects is presented. It was found that analysis based on the obtained sample is acutely sensitive to any changes in the software and hardware configuration. Simultaneously, with a minimum time of accumulation of statistical information using the proposed approach based on a given threshold, it becomes possible to determine the point at which the attack was begun. The proposed approach model implies the possibility of using various mathematical apparatus, statistical methods, and machine learning to achieve specified indicators for assessing the state of an object's information security.

Keywords: Information security · Side channels · Cyber-physical systems · Information security monitoring systems · Signal analysis

1 Introduction

An increasingly significant direction in the development of systems is the improvement of the theory and practice of managing, controlling, and using mobile remote autonomous objects that can independently solve individual problems using artificial intelligence tools [1]. This approach involves decentralized management, the dispersal of mobile systems objects, and the implementation of episodic interaction distributed on a spatio-temporal scale, which necessitates the implementation of many measures aimed at ensuring information security.

Decisions regarding the organization of distributed elements must be protected from intentional and unintentional destructive influences, which necessitates the introduction of not only protection systems but also state monitoring systems. Classical approaches

O. Galinina et al. (Eds.): NEW2AN 2020/ruSMART 2020, LNCS 12525, pp. 3–10, 2020.
https://doi.org/10.1007/978-3-030-65726-0_1

to the protection of information, expressed in countering unauthorized access to data, do not guarantee the achievement of a safe state.

In connection with the previous statement, one of the problematic issues is the development of models and methods for monitoring information security (IS) using additional sources that provide independent analysis of the status of remote autonomous systems.

2 Problem Statement

The effectiveness of information security solutions for computing devices located outside the controlled zone is associated with the development of a scientific and methodological apparatus designed to improve the quality indicators of identifying the state of security. Protecting cyber-physical systems from attacks is an important but challenging task [2]. As a result, it becomes necessary to develop models and methods for monitoring the information security of autonomous computing facilities [3, 4], taking into account the features of cyber-physical systems [5].

Side channels are one of the additional sources allowing for analyzing the state of information security. The authors in [6, 7] proposed a model for determining which key was pressed on a device based on acoustic information obtained through side channels. The work [8] provides an overview of some methods for determining the abnormal functioning of devices using side-channel information. The choice of the side channel depends on the specific application and the type of external monitoring system [9].

In [10–12], as applied to information security protection and monitoring systems, solutions were considered that make it possible to carry out the mainly binary classification that defines dangerous and safe states of elements of cyber-physical systems and computing devices. However, in some cases, for surgical intervention, it is important not only to analyze the state of the system or node as a whole, but also to identify the beginning of the destructive effect, to determine the point from which the deviation occurs.

Using side channels as a source, it is possible to describe the state of an object. For example, the state of an autonomous system object based on an electromagnetic (EM) or acoustic channel will be described by a sequence of amplitudes after the signal is sampled in time:

$$X = \{x_n\}; \ X = [x_{m_0}, x_{m_1}, x_{m_2}, \ldots, x_{m_{N-1}}], \ n = 0, \ldots, N-1. \tag{1}$$

For various nodes of an autonomous object, there can be several such channels where the signal amplitudes $X_0, X_1, \ldots, X_m$ are taken. It is necessary to assume that the latent state sequence $X_I = [x_{m_{I_1}}, x_{m_{I_2}}, \ldots, x_{m_{I_M}}]$ is the most probable state for abnormal behavior corresponding to a given EM signal sequence to implement training identification algorithms.

Deviation from the normal state is reflected in a sudden change in signal paths. A modified spectrum input will cause the corresponding latent state vector to depart from the expected vector in the state space.

3   The Proposed Approach

Being of an object of a computing system under attack causes various anomalies in the internal computing processes of the device, which entails a change in power consumption, signals, spurious emission parameters, an increase in the delay time, etc.

The suggested approach emphasizes statistical algorithms, where the first stage is self-training, which identifies the current parameters that describe the state of the object. Training is carried out on predetermined sequences that reflect the behavior of the device in a known state. The accumulated statistical data in the future allow the determination of the criteria based on whether it is possible to implement classifiers for the detection of anomalies.

As a result of the destructive effect, changes in the execution of control sequences occur. By determining the threshold value L for evaluation, abnormal states can be identified.

Let H_0 (H_1) indicate the permissible (invalid) execution of control sequences; then, the detection problem can be expressed as:

$$L \begin{matrix} H_0 \\ \lessgtr \\ H_1 \end{matrix} \varepsilon \tag{2}$$

where ε is the specified threshold.

When the threshold value is less than the specified threshold, the system is in a safe state, and in the opposite case, in a dangerous state.

4   Experiment

An analysis of the abnormality detection capabilities was carried out based on experimental data, where an unmanned vehicle was exposed to external forces during a maneuver. The preliminary stage of the experiment consisted of training an external control system based on the characteristics of signals recorded via secondary acoustic channels when performing maneuvers.

To improve the quality of the training sample, segmentation was applied based on a graph model of state transitions [13, 14], which allowed the implementation of various classification algorithms on predefined sets of states.

The scheme of the experiment is shown in Fig. 1.

The obtained data were converted into characteristics that describe the signal sequence. The duration of the recorded maneuvers was four seconds.

The use of a trained network and segmentation of a state model allows for classifying under conditions when unacceptable state transitions affecting the result are removed from consideration.

An "incorrect" command was occasionally introduced to simulate an attacking device during the execution of a maneuver. For example, with a "straight-ahead" command, a "turn right" or "turn left" command could occur. As a result, the form of the received

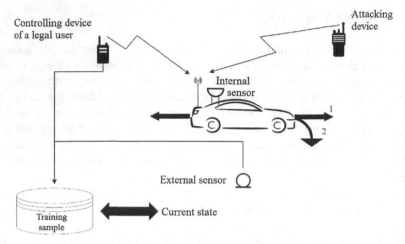

Fig. 1. Scheme of the experiment

signal along the side channel changed. Figure 2 shows an overlay of the timeline, which exhibits the normal state signal S_1 and the same signal when a command from the attacking device appeared. The arrows indicate the moments of exposure of the attacking device.

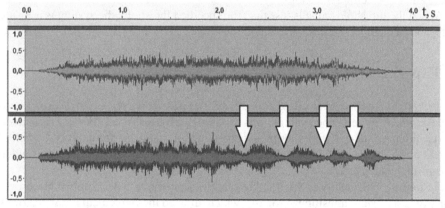

Fig. 2. Signals appearance for cases: movement directly without attacking influences (top), movement directly with commands "turn to the right" from the attacking device (bottom)

Figure 3 shows the appearance of the signals (the dependence of the amplitudes of the signals on time) for various states (two examples from the training sample for each studied state).

In the given experiment, differences in the sound range are visible for the spectra of states obtained by repeated sequential execution of commands. For example, Fig. 4 shows the spectra of signals for S_1 and S_3 states.

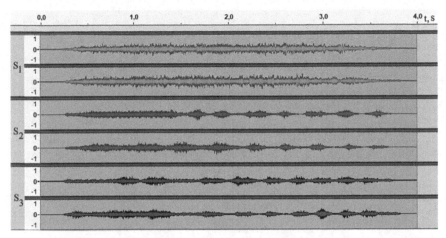

Fig. 3. Signals appearance. S_1 – movement directly without attacking influences, S_2 – movement directly with periodic commands "turn to the right" from the attacking device, S_3 – movement directly with periodic commands "turn to the left" from the attacking device

A two- and three-class classification was carried out, the algorithm of which is given below:

1. The ith spectral sequence Sp_Test was selected from the test sample.
2. For each kth frequency (Hz) of Sp_Test, its level (dB) was compared with the level of the kth frequency of the jth spectral sequence from the training sample Sp_Train;
3. The measure of similarity was the Euclidean distance and its comparison with the threshold value ε:

   Listing 1. A fragment of the program code in the Matlab programming language

```
r = zeros(length(Sp_Train(1,:)),length(Sp_Test(1,:)));

for i = 1 : length(Sp_Test(1,:))
    for j = 1 : length(Sp_Train(1,:))
        for k = 1 : length(Sp_Train(:,1))
            if sqrt((Sp_Train(k,j) - Sp_Test(k,i))^2) > ε
                r(j,i) = r(j,i)+1;
            end
        end
    end
end
```

4. If the deviation of the level of the kth frequency of the ith spectral sequence Sp_Test from the level of the kth frequency of the jth spectral sequence Sp_Train exceeded the threshold value ε, then an increment of 1 occurred in the cell (j, i) of the zero matrix r. There was a transition to the next step after the end of the cycle.
5. At this step, directly determined that each ith spectral sequence Sp_Test from the test set belongs to one of the state classes $S_1 - S_2$ (for two classes) or $S_1 - S_2 - S_3$ (for

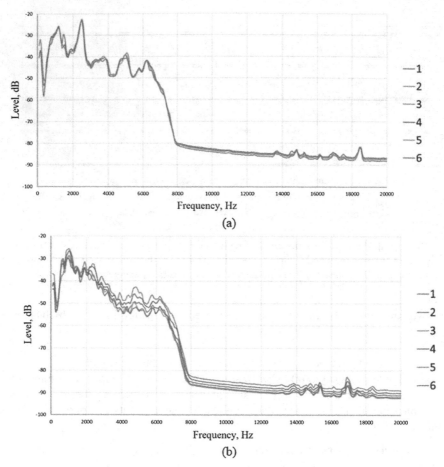

Fig. 4. Signal spectra for states S_1 (a) and S_3 (b) at repetitions from 1 to 6

three classes) by searching for the smallest value in the matrix column $r(:, i)$. If the smallest value was present in several classes, then the ith spectral sequence Sp_Test was recognized as being in one or the other states, from which the presence of an error of the second kind, consisting in the incorrectly accepted hypothesis about the similarity of the two spectral sequences from Sp_Train and Sp_Test, is obvious.

Figures 5, 6 show the percentage of correctly classified results and errors of the first kind for classifying states. Recognition of two and three classes indicates the presence of a range of threshold values in which detection occurs with acceptable error values.

Based on the given threshold and the digitized signal data received via the side channel, the point at which the attack began is determined.

The method used uses the information contained in the structure of the received signal, however, to improve the quality characteristics, reduce the likelihood of errors when solving errors, it is possible to use groups of external behavioral signs related to

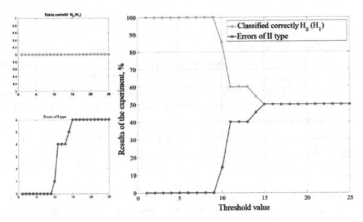

Fig. 5. Experimental results for S_1–S_2 states

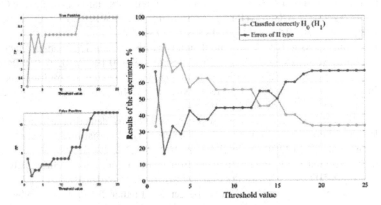

Fig. 6. Experimental results for S_1–S_2–S_3 states

vibration, changes in power consumption, and readings of various sensors of computing devices.

5 Conclusion

The proposed approach to monitoring the state of information security, using a symbiosis of machine learning methods and statistical data determined based on side channels, allows for not only assessing the state of information security but also determining the moment of occurrence of a destructive effect on the system.

At the same time, one of the drawbacks is the dependence of the obtained data samples for training with various software and hardware platforms. Analysis based on the obtained sample is very sensitive to any changes in the software and hardware configuration. The implementation of methods for recognizing the state of a computing device depends on the processing method and types of signals.

References

1. Meleshko, A., Desnitsky, V., Kotenko, I.: Machine learning based approach to detection of anomalous data from sensors in cyber-physical water supply systems. IOP Conf. Ser. Mater. Sci. Eng. **709**, 033034 (2020). https://doi.org/10.1088/1757-899X/709/3/033034
2. Wang, M., Huang, K., Wang, Y., Wu, Z., Du, Z.: A novel side-channel analysis for physical-domain security in cyber-physical systems. Int. J. Distrib. Sensor Netw. **15**(8) (2019). https://doi.org/10.1177/1550147719867866
3. Kosek, A.: Contextual anomaly detection for cyber-physical security in Smart Grids based on an artificial neural network model. In: Joint Workshop on Cyber-Physical Security and Resilience in Smart Grids (CPSR-SG), pp. 1–6 (2016). https://doi.org/10.1109/CPSRSG.2016.7684103
4. Viksnin, I., Komarov, I., Pantyukhin, I., Yuryeva, R., Maslennikov, O., Muradov, A.: An approach to detecting new cyberattacks on cyber-physical systems based on anomaly detection method. Autom. Ind. **2**, 48–52 (2018)
5. Faruque, M., Regazzoni, F., Pajic, M.: Design methodologies for securing cyber-physical systems. In: Proceedings of the 2015 International Conference on Hardware/Software Codesign and System Synthesis (CODES+ISSS), Amsterdam, 4–9 October 2015. IEEE, New York (2015). https://doi.org/10.1109/CODESISSS.2015.7331365
6. de Souza Faria, G., Kim, H.Y.: Differential audio analysis: a new side-channel attack on PIN pads. Int. J. Inf. Secur. **18**(1), 73–84 (2018). https://doi.org/10.1007/s10207-018-0403-7
7. De Souza Faria, G., Kim, H.: Identification of pressed keys by acoustic transfer function. In: IEEE International Conference on Systems, Man, and Cybernetics, Kowloon, pp. 240–245 (2015). https://doi.org/10.1109/SMC.2015.54
8. Spatz, D., Smarra, D., Ternovskiy, I.: A review of anomaly detection techniques leveraging side-channel emissions. In: Proceedings of SPIE - The International Society for Optical Engineering, vol. 11011 (2019). https://doi.org/10.1117/12.2521450
9. Hayashi, Y., Homma, N.: Introduction to electromagnetic information security. IEICE Trans. Commun. **1**, 40–50 (2019). https://doi.org/10.1587/transcom.2018EBI0001
10. Settanni, G., Skopik, F., Karaj, A., Wurzenberger, M., Fiedler, R.: Protecting cyber physical production systems using anomaly detection to enable self-adaptation. In: IEEE Industrial Cyber-Physical Systems (ICPS), pp. 173–180 (2018)
11. Semenov, V., Sukhoparov, M., Lebedev, I.: An approach to classification of the information security state of elements of cyber-physical systems using side electromagnetic radiation. In: Galinina, O., Andreev, S., Balandin, S., Koucheryavy, Y. (eds.) NEW2AN/ruSMART 2018. LNCS, vol. 11118, pp. 289–298. Springer, Cham (2018). https://doi.org/10.1007/978-3-030-01168-0_27
12. Ferragut, E., Laska, J., Olama, M., Ozmen, O.: Real-time cyber-physical false data attack detection in smart grids using neural networks. In: International Conference on Computational Science and Computational Intelligence, pp. 1–6 (2017)
13. Semenov, V.V., Lebedev, I.S., Sukhoparov, M.E., Salakhutdinova, K.I.: Application of an autonomous object behavior model to classify the cybersecurity state. In: Galinina, O., Andreev, S., Balandin, S., Koucheryavy, Y. (eds.) NEW2AN/ruSMART 2019. LNCS, vol. 11660, pp. 104–112. Springer, Cham (2019). https://doi.org/10.1007/978-3-030-30859-9_9
14. Semenov, V., Sukhoparov, M., Lebedev, I.: Approach to side channel-based cybersecurity monitoring for autonomous unmanned objects. In: Ronzhin, A., Rigoll, G., Meshcheryakov, R. (eds.) ICR 2019. LNCS (LNAI), vol. 11659, pp. 278–286. Springer, Cham (2019). https://doi.org/10.1007/978-3-030-26118-4_27

Energy-Aware Algorithm for LoRa Technology: Prototype Implementation

Abdukodir Khakimov[1]([✉]), Mohammed Saleh Ali Muthanna[2,3], Polovov Mikhail[1], Ibodulaev Ibodullokhodzha[5], Ammar Muthanna[4], and Konstantin Samouylov[1]

[1] Peoples' Friendship University of Russia (RUDN University), 6 Miklukho-Maklaya St., Moscow 117198, Russia
khakimov-aa@rudn.ru, lojka10@list.ru, ksam@sci.pfu.edu.ru
[2] School of Computer Science and Technology, Chongqing University of Posts and Telecommunications, Chongqing, China
muthanna@mail.ru
[3] Department of Automation and Control Processes, Saint Petersburg Electrotechnical University "LETI", Saint Petersburg, Russia
[4] St. Petersburg State University of Telecommunication, 22 Prospekt Bolshevikov, St. Petersburg, Russia
ammarexpress@gmail.com
[5] National Research University Higher School of Economics, 20 Myasnitskaya St., Moscow, Russia
iibodullah@gmail.com

Abstract. Internet of things (IoT) development has already become one of the main directions in the telecommunications and the information and communication system development as a whole. Promising solutions in the communication networks evolution, such as the latest LTE standards, concepts, and solutions for building 5G networks critical, include this component as an integral part of a promising communication network. There are various modern solutions for building IoT networks, and Long-Range Wide Area Network (LoRaWAN) is one of them. LoRaWAN is a technical solution for the physical and partially link network layers. The paper proposes an algorithm for ensuring traffic quality of service, latency, and data loss, as well as to provide an effective way of energy consumption. We impalement a prototype for Long Range (LoRa) based edge computing.

Keywords: LoRa · Latency · Energy · Prototype · Edge computing

1 Introduction

Recently, technology affects all aspects of human life. In a short period, there has been an unprecedented breakthrough in the development of information and communication technologies, which has changed the traditional way of life. The information society, where every person has access to information, knowledge, and also "generates" certain amounts of data into a common network, presents new requirements both to the network aspect of the issue and to the management of large amounts of data, the organization of

O. Galinina et al. (Eds.): NEW2AN 2020/ruSMART 2020, LNCS 12525, pp. 11–20, 2020.
https://doi.org/10.1007/978-3-030-65726-0_2

services and, as a result, new, challenging tasks for service providers. Every year, the volume of traffic generated by devices with Internet access increases hundreds of times. If, in 2010, there were about 5 billion such devices, then by 2025, it is predicted that the total number of Internet of Things (IoT) devices will grow to 50 billion [1].

LoRa is an example of a low-power wide-area network (LPWAN) technologies. LoRa technology guarantees radio coverage over a vast area but is known to be unsuitable for multimedia transmission due to its low data rate. LoRa technology involves the use of low-cost transceivers for IoT networks. The classic LoRaWAN network architecture is consists of the end device, gateway, network server, and application server, as shown in Fig. 1. Today, vendors offer the following architecture: where the operator places in its data center and all points of the network are placed LoRa gateways, and all of them are connected via a virtual MPLS or VLAN channel to the LoRaWAN server.

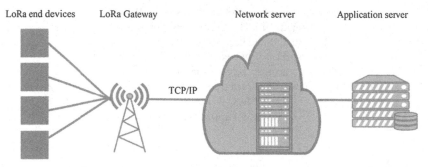

LoRa end devices   LoRa Gateway   Network server   Application server

TCP/IP

Fig. 1. LoRaWAN architecture

Power consumption and latency in LoRa technology are important issues that have not been resolved yet. To address these issues and in addition to achieving more important requirements, LoRa must deploy new communication paradigms such as mobile edge computing (MEC) [2]. The fundamental principle of MEC is to expand cloud computing capabilities at the edge of cellular networks. This will minimize network congestion and improve resource optimization, user interaction, and overall network performance. By using radio access networks (RANs), MEC will significantly improve latency and bandwidth utilization, making it easier for both application developers and content providers to access network services.

This paper proposes a prototype that consists of user devices. As in the case of Fog computing, it can be all kinds of IoT devices, such as sensors, mobile phones, smart vehicles, readers, etc. MEC servers are typically located in conjunction with a radio network controller or base station. The servers run multiple instances of the MEC host, which can perform calculations and storage on a virtualized interface. MEC servers are ignored by the MEC Orchestra, which processes information about the services offered by each host, available resources and network topology, and also manages MEC applications. MEC servers provide real-time information about the network itself, including network load and capacity, as well as information about the end devices connected to the servers, including their location and network information, the network core, and the public cloud - a cloud infrastructure located on the Internet.

Our paper presents a system using LoRa and Edge computing. To overcome limited bandwidth, power consumption and latency, an approach of placing the LoRa server at the edge is proposed. The remainder of this paper is outlined as follows. Related works will be introduced in Sect. 2. The problem statement will be presented in Sect. 3. The network model will be highlighted in Sect. 4. Experimental testbed and results will be described in Sect. 5, followed by a conclusion in Sect. 6.

2 Related Works

Edge and Fog computing is a paradigm [3] that relates to the concept of distributed computing, attracting the benefits of cloudy computing closer to the network edge [1]. This approach allows you to achieve benefits such as reducing the load in the cloud and using bandwidth. Besides, there is a relatively general overall delay system. While cloud computing plays a prominent role in IoT applications for smart cities, fog and edge computing are used to reduce the load on the network and the amount of raw data transfer, which provides a more balanced and intelligent solution with the distribution of computing tasks at different network levels. The authors in [4] presented the integration of edge and cloud computing, which minimizes the use of resources such as the network, cloud storage, and computing capabilities of cloud servers. In another work [5], the authors tested mobile edge computation (MEC) architecture using unmanned aerial vehicles (UAVs) to collect environmental data at different points in the city. Accurate and accurate data is required to obtain data. The advantages of using edge computing in the system allow us to study computing, network, and caching resources to improve the performance of various applications. Improving the quality of service (QoS) using mobile edge computing (MEC) through the implementation of the concept of "Follow Me Edge" was considered by the author in [6]. The proposed MEC network architecture has ultra-low latency. Another article [7] presented an architecture based on LoRa technologies for monitoring animal health. In this paper, to compress the data and extract features at the edge level, machine learning is used, and then the data is sent through LoRa for transmission to the Cloud servers. The protocols presented in [8] and [9] can transmit data with a data transfer rate of up to 250 Kbps in theory and 150 Kbps, while they consume about 70 mW of power. Accordingly, they are suitable for high data rate applications. When the number of sensor nodes increases significantly, additional hardware modules can be added to one or more edge gateways depending on the application. WiFi can be used as a basic wireless connection between sensor nodes and edge gateways. However, this leads to an increase in the power consumption of the sensor nodes. Data can be compressed using an algorithm. Approximately 10: 1, but the data can be correctly presented without prejudice to any information. It is suitable for critical applications such as video streaming. LoRa allows us to use the bandwidth effectively [10]. Also, data can be transmitted on gateways to provide LoRa bandwidth.

To the best of our knowledge, there are limited studies that have shown that edge computing is suitable for LoRaWAN technology in terms of latency [11, 14] and power consumption [12, 13]. Still, none of them have focused on LoRa physical layer in terms of how to increase battery lifetime and latency. In this paper, we demonstrate an algorithm for ensuring latency, and energy consumption, also several features, such as compressed data and data encryption.

3 Problem Statement

LoRaWAN architecture works perfectly and is already being put into operation by some operators. On average, the delay between the gateway and the server is 30–40 ms. Based on our research, we found that by reducing this delay, we can increase the longevity of the LoRa battery. In our work, we propose to use a distributed architecture of the server itself. We break up the server and stir it "close" to the gateways, thereby reducing the delay between the gateway and the server to 1 ms. The server is hosted at the MEC. For the experiment, LoRa silver was presented as a docker container for flexible installation at MEC hosts.

In Fig. 2, we see that after the end device sends the message, it waits for some time for the server to respond. It makes sense to reduce the response time by closing the receive window earlier. Experimentally, we got proof of our assumption and achieved a reduction in power consumption by the end device Fig. 2 shows the current consumption of the target device.

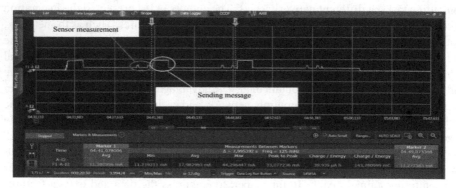

Fig. 2. End device required amperage

4 Network Model

In this work, we proposed system architecture for energy-aware LoRa based on edge computing and built a prototype to provide real experiments with the developed algorithm.

As we can see in Fig. 3, the system consists of 3 layers: access layer, network layer, and application layer.

Each layer solves its problem, together they provide a complete system for monitoring and controlling production processes.

The access layer consists of a wireless sensor network based on LoRa data technology. LoRa is a low-power broadband wireless network technology suitable for low-speed IoT applications over long distances. The advantages of this technology are low power consumption and low positioning costs. Several other parameters allow us to choose precisely the modulation method and LoRaWAN technology:

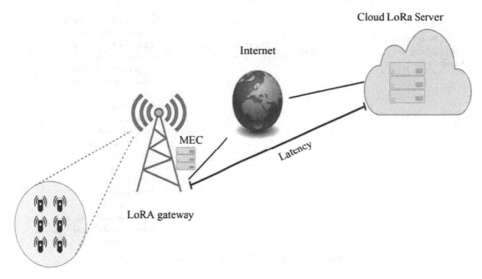

Fig. 3. Layer based architecture

- Long-distance and low power consumption: +14 dBm, 868 MHz. Up to 3.5 km in urban environments, up to 15 km in rural areas.
- Reliable communication: immunity of the interference from Bluetooth, WiFi, GSM, LTE, etc.
- High geolocation accuracy: the modulation format provides high geolocation accuracy, does not use a GPS receiver; it is possible to implement additional functions.
- Improved network capacity: the ability to connect a large number of devices, additional capacity for functions.

In our prototype, we add edge computing on LoRa gateway for resource allocation.

5 Evaluation

In this section, we will provide details on the experimental testbed and evaluation results.

5.1 Experimental Testbed

Our testing stand consisted of the following elements: 2x SDR NI USRP n2950, Deployed software-defined network (SDN) for building virtual channels on the LoRa-server gateway segment. One of the SDRs was used as a gateway, the second as an end device, upgrading the source code MyriadRF assembled a test bench based on GNURADIO (see Fig. 4). ChirpStack Network Server as a docker, was used as the LoRa network server. Using artificial interference input, the network simulated an Internet network with access to the cloud where the interference parameters were average latency, the probability of packet loss.

The average Delay - Normal distribution [avr = 30, $\sigma = 5$] ms

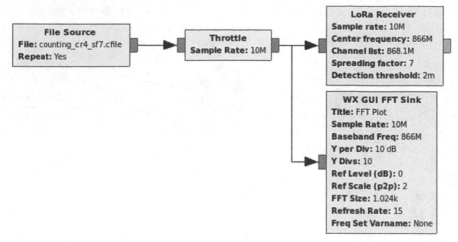

Fig. 4. Example of block' in gnu radio

The average packet loss is p = 0.001.

For the experiments, we have set up an experimental testbed (see Fig. 5). Our proposed structure for hosting the LoRa network server on MEC hosts was implemented without artificial interference imitating the Internet. However, we analyzed the average delay in packet delivery at the gateway server site. And it is a little over 1 ms. To prove the effectiveness of our proposed structure, we measured the response time at the end of the spectrum and approximated the positive results.

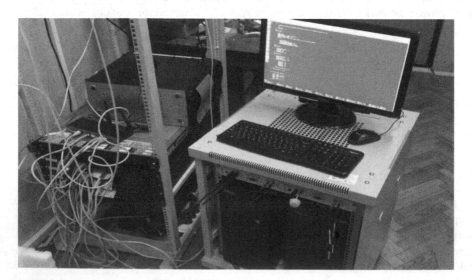

Fig. 5. Demonstration platform.

Figure 6 shows the sequence diagram of the proposed system.

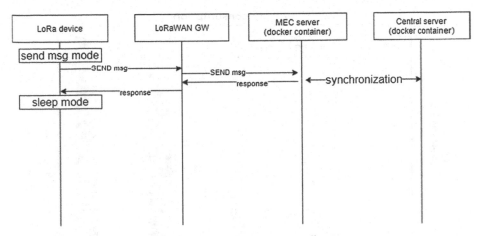

Fig. 6. Proposed system sequence diagram

This method of arranging LoRaWAN components can reduce the response delay from the server to the end device, thus reducing the power consumption of the end device.

5.2 Results Evaluation

Having carried out tests of our stand have received, a difference of total energy consumption for different intensity of sending messages by the end node to the server, as shown in Fig. 7 that the difference in duration of the end device with the intensity of 1/1000 min is more than 1.6 years.

Figure 8 shows the function of the dependence of energy consumption (J/Mbit) on the delay between the gateway and the server for each spreading factor (SF). Then, the Lagrange Polynomial was derived using the obtained point. The Lagrange polynomial works correctly for points related between the maximum and minimum points along the abscissa axis. Therefore, we derived a polynomial for all SF

$$SF7\_L(t) = -1,84 * 10^{-8}x^5 + 3.14 * 10^{-6}x^4 - 0,174 * 10^{-3}x^3 + 0,0032 * x^2 \\ - 0,0259x + 0.12455$$

$$SF8\_L(t) = 1,25 * 10^{-7}x^5 - 0,146 * 10^{-6}x^4 + 0,00063x^3 - 0,01032 * x^2 \\ + 0,0759x + 0.055$$

$$SF9\_l(t) = 2.75 * 10^{-8}x^5 - 2.59 * 10^{-6}x^4 + 0,000071x^3 - 0,00041 * x^2 \\ + 0,0159x + 0.16$$

$$SF11\_l(t) = -7.39 * 10^{-8}x^5 + 9.71 * 10^{-6}x^4 + 0,00034x^3 + 0,0075 * x^2 \\ - 0,024x + 0.2373$$

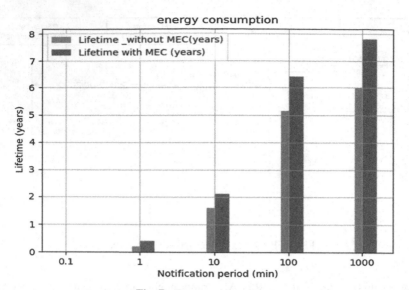

Fig. 7. Energy consumption

$$SF12\_l(t) = -1.98 * 10^{-7}x^5 + 0.251 * 10^{-6}x^4 - 0,0011x^3 + 0,022 * x^2$$
$$- 0,126x + 0.335$$

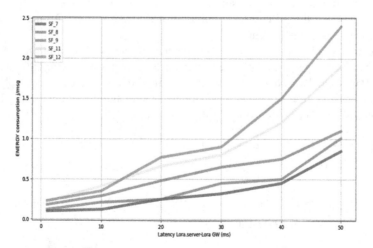

Fig. 8. LoRa server-LoRa gateway latency

By using these polynomials, energy consumption can be estimated for commissioning LoRaWAN networks.

6   Conclusion

In this paper, we proposed the implementation and prototype of the efficient use of LoRaWAN networks based on edge hosts. We proved that reducing delays in the gateway-server segment depends on the duration of the end nodes. Given that our architecture will be developed and available in most nodes of base stations, our proposed architecture will play a key role in building private LoRa networks. In future works, we plan to study the effectiveness of our proposed architecture in conditions of high and medium collision.

Acknowledgment. The publication has been prepared with the support of the "RUDN University Program 5-100" (recipient Abdukodir Khakimov). The reported study was funded by RFBR, project number 18-00-01555(18-00-01685) (recipient Konstantin Samouylov). For the research, infrastructure of the 5G Lab RUDN (Russia) was used.

References

1. General Electric. What is edge computing? https://www.ge.com/digital/blog/what-edge-com puting. Accessed 18 Apr 2019
2. He, Y., Richard Yu, F., Zhao, N., Leung, V.C.M., Yin, H.: Software-defined networks with mobile edge computing and caching for smart cities: a big data deep reinforcement learning approach. IEEE Commun. Mag. **55**(12), 31–37 (2017). https://doi.org/10.1109/MCOM.2017. 1700246
3. Khakimov, A., Muthanna, A., Muthanna, M.S.A.: Study of Fog computing structure. In: Proceedings of the 2018 IEEE Conference of Russian Young Researchers in Electrical and Electronic Engineering (EIConRus), Moscow, Russia, 29 January 1 February 2018, pp. 51–54 (2018)
4. Perera, C., Qin, Y., Estrella, J.C., Reiff-Marganiec, S., Vasilakos, A.V.: Fog computing for sustainable smart cities: a survey. ACM Comput. Surv. **50**(3) (2017). https://doi.org/10.1145/ 3057266
5. Chen, L., et al.: A lora-based air quality monitor on unmanned aerial vehicle for smart city. In: 2018 International Conference on System Science and Engineering (ICSSE), pp. 1–5, June 2018
6. Taleb, T., Dutta, S., Ksentini, A., Iqbal, M., Flinck, H.: Mobile edge computing potential in making cities smarter. IEEE Commun. Mag. **55**(3), 38–43 (2017). https://doi.org/10.1109/ MCOM.2017.1600249CM
7. Pyattaev, A., Johnsson, K., Surak, A., Florea, R., Andreev, S., Koucheryavy, Y.: Network-assisted D2D communications: implementing a technology prototype for cellular traffic offloading. In: IEEE Wireless Communications and Networking Conference, WCNC, art. no. 6953070, pp. 3266–3271 (2017)
8. Gia, T.N., Thanigaivelan, N.K., Rahmani, A.M., Westerlund, T., Liljeberg, P., Tenhunen, H.: Customizing 6LoWPAN networks towards Internet-of-Things based ubiquitous healthcare systems. In: NORCHIP 2014 - 32nd NORCHIP Conference: The Nordic Microelectronics Event. Institute of Electrical and Electronics Engineers Inc. (2014). https://doi.org/10.1109/ NORCHIP.2014.7004716
9. Nguyen Gia, T., et al.: Energy efficient wearable sensor node for IoT-based fall detection systems. Microprocess. Microsyst. **56**, 34–46 (2018). https://doi.org/10.1016/j.micpro.2017. 10.014

10. Ometov, A., et al.: Toward trusted, social-aware D2D connectivity: bridging across the technology and sociality realms. IEEE Wireless Commun. **23**(4), pp. 103–111 (2016). Art. no. 7553033
11. Muthanna, M.S.A., Wang, P., Wei, M., Ateya, A.A., Muthanna, A.: Toward an ultra-low latency and energy efficient LoRaWAN. In: Galinina, O., Andreev, S., Balandin, S., Koucheryavy, Y. (eds.) NEW2AN/ruSMART -2019. LNCS, vol. 11660, pp. 233–242. Springer, Cham (2019). https://doi.org/10.1007/978-3-030-30859-9_20
12. Dongare, A., et al.: Charm: exploiting geographical diversity through coherent combining in low-power wide-area networks. In: Proceedings of the International Conference on Information Processing in Sensor Networks, pp. 60–71 (2018)
13. Galinina, O., Tabassum, H., Mikhaylov, K., Andreev, S., Hossain, E., Koucheryavy, Y.: On feasibility of 5G-grade dedicated RF charging technology for wireless-powered wearables. IEEE Wirel. Commun. **23**(2), pp. 28–37 (2016). Art. no. 7462482
14. Gerasimenko, M., Petrov, V., Galinina, O., Andreev, S., Koucheryavy, Y.: Energy and delay analysis of LTE-Advanced RACH performance under MTC overload. In: 2012 IEEE Globecom Workshops, GC Wkshps 2012, pp. 1632–1637 (2012). Art. no. 6477830

Methods for Reducing the Amount of Data Transmitted and Stored in IoT Systems

Alexander Anufrienko$^{(\boxtimes)}$

Department of Electronic Engineering, Higher School of Economics, 20 Myasnitskaya Ulitsa, Moscow 101000, Russia
alexanuf@gmail.com

Abstract. In this paper presented method for reducing the amount of data transmitted and stored in IoT systems. Instead of expensive and complex network devices, developers can use cheap and proven low-speed solutions (ZigBee, NB IoT, BLE). This approach focuses on sensor processing. Correlation and auto-correlation methods for event detection depending on waveform are described in detail and implementation of endpoint architecture is proposed. Novelty and another feature of this approach is the use of not the full waveform, but their components and processing on the device. This significantly reduces the number of operations and complexity of implementation. Other methods focus on the cloud computing paradigm. The results of the simulation show that at the data transfer rate from the sensor ~10 MSample/s, the proposed method allows you to transmit and store 280 bytes in 70 min instead of 157 GB using the bypass method. Reducing data transfer and storage requirements will simplify and reduce the cost of IoT systems, improve performance, and apply additional precision sensors to provide more accurate data.

The solutions are focused on low-power and FPGA/ASIC implementations.

Keywords: Internet-of-Things · Industrial IoT · Cross-correlation · Autocorrelation · Storage · Platform · Streaming

1 Introduction

THE modern Internet-of-Things systems operate with huge data generated from IoT devices. The amount of data generated by sensors, devices, social networks, medical applications, temperature sensors, and various other software applications and digital devices that continuously generate large amounts of structured, unstructured, or semi-structured data is increasing significantly. This mass data generation results in "big data." The architectural concept of the Internet of Things has several definitions based on abstraction and identification of the Internet of Things domain. As a rule, the structure of the IoT is divided into five levels: the level of perception, the level of network, the level of middleware, the level of applications and the level of business. Some IoT architectures are designed for cloud computing at the center and a model of end-to-end interaction between different stakeholders in the IoT cloud [1]. IoT reference architecture

© Springer Nature Switzerland AG 2020
O. Galinina et al. (Eds.): NEW2AN 2020/ruSMART 2020, LNCS 12525, pp. 21–31, 2020.
https://doi.org/10.1007/978-3-030-65726-0_3

handles these requirements and builds a superset of functionality, information structures, and mechanisms. Additional consideration of entities and their interaction leads to a reference model. This model integrates aspects of related entities, such as human users, device implementations, and server structures, and provides a more complete view or template for the overall installation and its implementation in the domain [2]. Cloud computing frees the enterprise and end user from the specification of many details. This bliss becomes a problem for latency-sensitive applications that require nodes in close proximity to meet their latency requirements. Cloud computing extends the cloud computing paradigm to the boundaries of the network. Hazy vision was designed to solve problems with applications and services that don't fit well into the cloud paradigm [3]. The typical architecture and components of an IoT system [1–4] are shown in Fig. 1. The System includes modules consisting of sensors, actuators, and modems – devices that generate and transmit data. The number of sensors reads and reports the status of the connected tools. Industrial equipment can have thousands of points for generating data. The module can also have Executive mechanisms for influencing the logical state of the tool. The modem passes data to the next level – the gateway. Gate is usually a hardware component that interacts with a number of modules. Gate also interacts with the platform where data is stored, processed, and shared with end users. The platform (mainly a web platform) has a number of core components, such as DRM, network protocols, streaming (adaptive streaming), storage systems, databases, AI and BI tools, and app engine support. Thus, one of the specific devices in the system is a module, since the quality of primary data depends on this device. A typical case for an IoT system is data transfer from modules to the IoT platform (cloud) as it is, and deep processing.

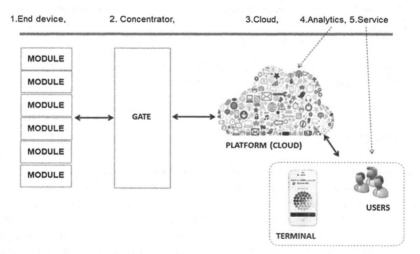

Fig. 1. Typical IoT system architecture.

There are two key issues:

1) Loss of events.

Typically, IOT systems are configured for a low sample rate: 1 sample/min – 1 sample/10 min for some industrial applications, and 1 sample/day – 1 sample/ month for smart home applications. But in this case, the system may lose valuable events, as shown in Fig. 3A in simple cases, when the characteristics of the monitored object are known, the data transfer rate generated by the sensors is low, and the network bandwidth is sufficient, we can assume that there is no data loss. But in real cases you need to get as much information about the object as possible.

2) Limited bandwidth of the Internet of things network and a large amount of data.

Very often, the amount of data transferred is so large that it is not possible to transfer it from an IoT device to the cloud, but it is necessary. Also, most wireless technologies used for building IOT networks have a typical bandwidth of 10-200 Kbit/s, and end devices can be autonomous (have an autonomous power source) and low-power. In addition, there are not enough storage systems for terabytes and petabytes of raw data. There are many applications (industrial, connected cars, Smart city, assessments) where several groups of sensors are used in tests or operations. In aviation, an aircraft engine can have up to 250 sensors. A twin-engine aircraft can produce up to 844 TB of data in 12 h of flight [5]. As already mentioned, not all data must be transmitted and stored for further processing. An example of an industrial application is shown in Fig. 2. For a deep and accurate analysis, critical modes are most important, especially in the evaluation process.

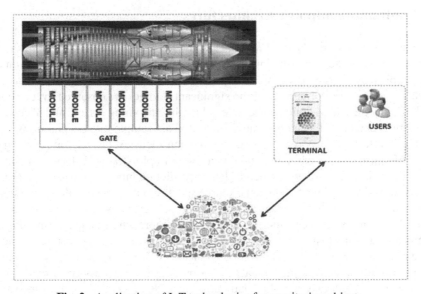

Fig. 2. Application of IoT technologies for monitoring objects.

As the sample rate increases, new events can be detected that can bring completely new information to end users (Fig. 3b).

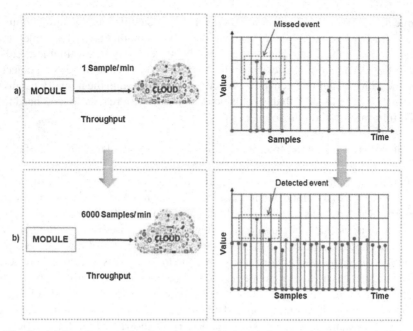

Fig. 3. a) Missed event when low data rate; b) detected event when data rate is high.

2 Clouds and Endpoint Architectures

One of the most commonly used approaches for IoT systems is to adapt the sample rate [6–9]. The sample rate is the rate at which a new sample is taken from a continuous signal supplied by the sensor Board. This speed can be adapted according to the input data received from the monitoring zone. If no significant changes are observed over a certain period of time, the sample rate can be reduced for the upcoming period, and Vice versa, if an event is detected, the sample rate increases. This sample rate adaptation is based on event detection [7]. Approaches to data reduction focus exclusively on reducing the number of transmissions while maintaining a fixed sampling rate [9]. The most popular of them is the double prediction scheme [10]. A prediction model that can predict future values is trained and shared between the source and destination, which allows the source sensor node to transmit only those samples that do not match the predicted value.

Another option is a space-time correlation-based approach to adapting sampling and transmission rates in cluster sensor networks [11]. The correlation between sensor nodes and the new sampling rates of each sensor is calculated. This approach does not require the implementation of any algorithm at the sensor level, the only tasks performed by the sensors are unambiguously sampling and transmitting data. All work is performed at the Cluster-Head (CH) level, where at the end of each round (the duration is determined by the user); CH runs an algorithm that finds a spatial correlation between data reported by sensors that belong to the same cluster. It then passes one of them its new sample rate for the next round according to its level of correlation with other neighboring sensors in the cluster. Sample rate planning follows a strict Protocol that keeps the sample rate of sensors showing high correlation with a large number of nodes at the optimal maximum level [11].

In [12], the authors propose to record such changes in the correlation of sensor data to improve the performance of detecting anomalies of IoT (Internet of Things) hardware. In our feature selection method, we first combine correlated sensors together to recognize duplicated deployed sensors according to sensor data correlations, and track data correlation changes in real time to select sensors with correlation changes as representative features for anomaly detection. Curve alignment and dynamic time warping (DTW) [13] are methods used to measure similarity between two sequences of time series data. However, DTW methods do not make assumptions about sequential time lag, but rather calculate the optimal match between two given time series of data with certain restrictions in order to maximize the measure of their similarity [12]. But these methods involve working with big data at the gate or cloud level.

The typical architecture of the end device used is shown in Fig. 4. The main components of the module are the sensor and a wired or wireless modem. The drive and battery are additional parts in this architecture. Thus, the processor is part of a modem (8051, ARM, etc.) and has relatively low performance. All data from the sensor is transmitted by the modem to the cloud over a wireless and wired channel. In this case, the intensity of data streaming is not as high.

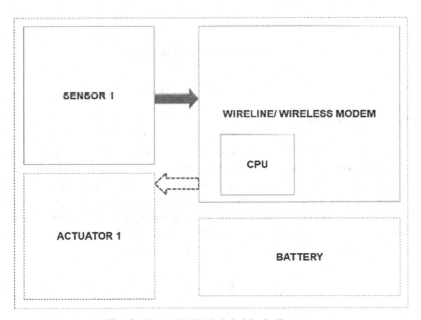

Fig. 4. Typical IoT Module block diagram.

In Fig. 5 shows a more advanced approach-processing data on-the-module (on- the-sensor) as an effective way to overcome the above problems. First, there are several sensors and actuators that can be controlled. The architecture includes an additional part-the processor, which is responsible for reducing the data flow. A managed object can have only one processor that interacts with multiple sensors and actuators. It is not necessary to transmit a complete data stream, but it is important to detect and transmit significant signal deviations. But the most effective case is when each sensor has an individual processor block.

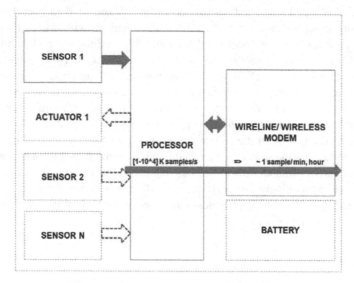

Fig. 5. Proposed IoT Module Block diagram.

3   Design and Results

Correlation methods can be effectively applied to solve topical issues. Applications for radar and sonar systems for determining range and position have already been found, in which transmitted and reflected signals are compared. In robotic vision, remote sensing by satellite is used to compare data from different images. Because of the system of Internet of things are digital, we will work with digital signals and values. The cross-correlation [14] between two digital sequences $x_1(n)$ and $x_2(n)$, each containing N data and normalized to the number of samples might be written as:

$$r_{12} = \frac{1}{N} \sum_{n=0}^{N-1} x_1(n) * x_2(n) \tag{1}$$

Since the sequences are shifted relative to each other, the correlation should be calculated with lags and Eq. (1) thus becomes:

$$r_{12}(j) = \frac{1}{N} \sum_{n=0}^{N-1} x_1(n) * x_2(n+j) \tag{2}$$

In case when sequence $x_1(n) = x_2(n)$, process is known as autocorrelation and can be written as:

$$r_{11}(0) = \frac{1}{N} \sum_{n=0}^{N-1} x_1^2(n) = S \tag{3}$$

where S – normalized energy of signal.

The cross-correlation values computed according to above equations depend on the absolute values of the data. But it is often necessary to measure cross-correlations in the fixed range $[-1; +1]$. This can be achieved by normalizing the values by an amount depending on the energy content of the data. And the normalized expression for $r_{12}(j)$ becomes:

$$\rho_{12}(j) = \frac{r_{12}(j)}{\frac{1}{N}\sqrt{[\sum_{n=0}^{N-1} x_1^2(n) * \sum_{n=0}^{N-1} x_2^2(n)]}} \tag{4}$$

Where "+1" means complete coincidence (correlation), and "−1" - complete mismatch, the signals are in antiphase. Despite the fact that the result in the range $[-1; +1]$ is convenient for understanding and analysis, the computational complexity of the denominator (4) is high and requires relatively large computational resources, especially the division operation.

To simplify we define $x_1(n) = x_2(n)$, so denominator of "(4)" might be written as:

$$\frac{1}{N} * \sum_{n=0}^{N-1} x_1^2(n) = \text{constant} \tag{5}$$

In this case, the denominator does not require dynamic calculation and simplifies the system, and the denominator can change.

One of application of correlation is the correlation detection implemented by the matched filter, which maximize S/N ratio at its output. And output result of the matched filter is the autocorrelation at lag zero of input signal and its locally saved copy. Chirp modulation for correlation processing in radar systems has proven its effectiveness. But opposite to radar applications, in IoT systems the Processing unit and Cloud can process only received signals. Using the methods proposed in the [14, 15] when calculated FFT and IFFT, for current conditions is associated with high computational complexity (Fig. 6).

In this paper, we propose an event detection method based on the slope level of the waveform. It is more important to have information about the rate of increase. Figure 5 shows simple examples of envelopes: 60°, rectangular, triangular, and 30° (slow-growing). The system of correlators was developed in accordance with models (2), (4) and (5). The System consists of two correlators, the first of which C1 is focused on processing a triangular waveform, and the second C2-a rectangular one. The length of correlation sequences was determined to be asymmetric and equal to 7. Based on the model, a sequence of data from 200 samples was taken for the experiment. The data sequence includes several events: rectangular events and several triangular events. The

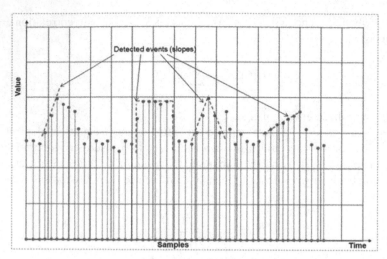

Fig. 6. Types of detectable events.

results of processing after correlators are shown in Fig. 7. The Upper graph shows the output of C1, when the maximum value is equivalent to a copy of the signal, and the second triangular shape has a value of 0.81. The square shape gave a value of 0.89.

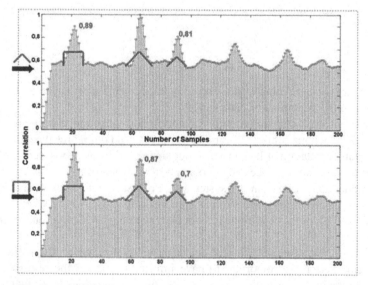

Fig. 7. Results of processing one data sequence with two correlators.

The lower diagram shows the result at output C2, when the rectangular signal corresponds to the correlation level 1, and the triangular waves had values of 0.87 and 0.7, respectively. Setting the threshold level to 0.95 our system allows us to distinguish the types of signals.

In the second example, the system also consists of two correlators, the first of which (C1) is focused on processing a semi-triangular waveform, and the second (C2) - a semi-square one. The length of the correlation sequences was determined to be asymmetric and equal to 3. The output results after the correlators are shown in Fig. 8.

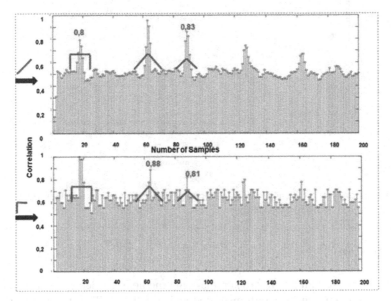

Fig. 8. Results of processing one data sequence with two half-shaped correlators.

The upper graph shows the result at output C1, when the maximum value is equivalent to a copy of the signal, and the second triangular form has a value of 0.83. the Square form gave a value of 0.8. As in this example $x_2(n)$ was not full copy of $x_1(n)$ the final correlation < 1 (0.98). The lower diagram shows the output from C2, when the rectangular signal corresponds to the correlation level 1, and the triangular shapes had values of 0.88 and 0.81, respectively. Setting the threshold level to 0.95 our system also allows us to distinguish the types of signals. But the number of multiplications was reduced compared to the previous example.

Let's assume that the sample rate is 10 Mbit/s and the sample size is 4 bytes. In the case of direct transmission (bypass), you will need 23 GB to store information after 10 min, and 202 GB after 90 min. When using correlation processing under the assumption that 4 events occur per minute, we need to transmit 40 bytes in 10 min, and only 360 bytes in 90 min.

The results are systematized in Fig. 9. When transmitting data over the network, as a rule, 50% of the data packet is service information and 50% is content [16]. In the calculations presented, we only take content. If the sample rate, sample size, or number of sensors is increased, the amount of data required for transmission and storage will automatically increase. The higher the sample rate, the higher the system gain. It is obvious that at a low sampling rate (1 sample per day – 1 sample per month), this approach is ineffective.

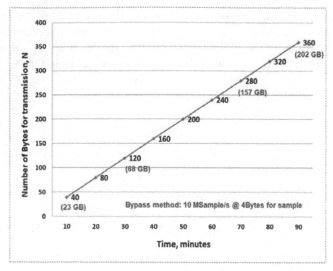

Fig. 9. Number of bytes for transmission and storage: correlation processing method (black) and bypass method (red). (Color figure online)

4 Conclusion

The main results presented here are summarizing methods for detecting critical events and reducing the amount of data transmitted and stored in IOT systems. Applications are particularly important in industrial systems (Industrial IoT).

Correlation and autocorrelation processes are described in detail, and the architecture of endpoints for the processing method is proposed. The presented model of the system is based on correlators, which store a copy of the signal with the full and reduced length of the correlation sequence. The simulation results show the effectiveness of event detection in combination with the establishment of a threshold level of the system that allows you to distinguish the types of signals. Implemented models are focused on low-power and FPGA/ ASIC implementation. Instead of expensive and complex network devices, developers can use cheap and proven low-speed solutions (ZigBee, NB IoT, etc.), particularly for rotating objects. Thanks to data processing on the sensor, additional precision sensors can be used to obtain additional information about the object being monitored. For future designs it is important to increase the accuracy of event detection for different amplitude levels and optimize computational complexity.

References

1. Khan, R., Khan, S.U., Zaheer, R., Khan, S.: Future internet: the internet of things architecture, possible applications and key challenges. In: Proceedings of the 10th International Conference on Frontiers of Information Technology (FIT 2012), pp. 257–260, December 2012
2. Weyrich, M., Ebert, C.: Reference architectures for the internet of things. IEEE Softw. **33**(1), 112–116 (2016)

3. Bonomi, F., Milito, R., Natarajan, P., Zhu, J.: Fog computing: a platform for internet of things and analytics. In: Bessis, N., Dobre, C. (eds.) Big Data and Internet of Things: A Roadmap for Smart Environments. SCI, vol. 546, pp. 169–186. Springer, Cham (2014). https://doi.org/10.1007/978-3-319-05029-4_7

4. Marjani, M., et al.: Big IoT data analytics: architecture, opportunities, and open research challenges. IEEE Access **5**, 5247–5261 (2017)

5. Engines in the Data Cloud. https://www.digitalcreed.in/engines-data-cloud/. Accessed 10 Apr 2018

6. Bhuiyan, M.Z.A., Wu, J., Wang, G., Wang, T., Hassan, M.M.: E-sampling: event-sensitive autonomous adaptive sensing and low-cost monitoring in networked sensing systems. ACM Trans. Auton. Adapt. Syst. **12** (2017)

7. Harb, H., Makhoul, A.: Energy-efficient sensor data collection approach for industrial process monitoring. IEEE Trans. Ind. Informat. **14**(2), 661–672 (2018)

8. Tayeh, G.B., Makhoul, A., Laiymani, D., Demerjian, J.: A distributed real-time data prediction and adaptive sensing approach for wireless sensor networks. Perv. Mob. Comput. **49**, 62–75 (2018)

9. Tayeh, G.B., Makhoul, A., Demerjian, J., Laiymani, D.: A new autonomous data transmission reduction method for wireless sensors networks. In: Proceedings of IEEE Middle East North African Communication Conference (MENACOMM), pp. 1–6, April 2018

10. Braten, A.E., Kraemer, F.A., Palma, D.: Adaptive, correlation-based training data selection for IoT device management. In: 2019 Sixth International Conference on Internet of Things: Systems, Management and Security (IOTSMS), Granada, Spain, pp. 169–176 (2019)

11. Tayeh, G.B., Makhoul, A., Perera, C., Demerjian, J.: A spatial-temporal correlation approach for data reduction in cluster-based sensor networks. IEEE Access **7**, 50669–50680 (2019)

12. Su, S., Sun, Y., Gao, X., Qiu, J., Tian, Z.: A correlation-change based feature selection method for IoT equipment anomaly detection. Appl. Sci. **9**(3), 437 (2019)

13. Kim, S., Lee, H., Ko, H., Jeong, S., Byun, H., Oh, K.: Pattern matching trading system based on the dynamic TimeWarping algorithm. Sustainability **10**, 4641 (2018)

14. Ifeachor, E., Jervis, B.: Digital Signal Processing: A Practical Approach, 2nd edn., pp. 184–245. Prentice Hall, Upper Saddle River (2001)

15. Oppenheim, A.V., Schafer, R.W., Buck, J.R.: Discrete-Time Signal Processing, 2nd edn., pp. 746–753. Prentice Hall, Upper Saddle River (1998)

16. Kurose, J.F., Ross, K.W.: Computer networking : a top-down approach, 7th edn. Pearson Education Limited, London (2017). 6th edn., pp. 264–266

Analysis of IDS Alert Correlation Techniques for Attacker Group Recognition in Distributed Systems

Artem Pavlov$^{(\boxtimes)}$ ⓘ and Natalia Voloshina ⓘ

ITMO University, St. Petersburg, Russia
artempavlov1@gmail.com

Abstract. Intrusion Detection Systems are widely used for detecting attacks based on network traffic and host events. However, the raw data they provide are not suitable for manual analysis due to information overload problem. Alert Correlation Systems are used for Intrusion Detection System data enhancing. They can reduce false positives, eliminate duplicate entries, correlate events, analyze attacker strategy and find attacker groups. In this paper, we are focused on the latter. Classification of existing algorithms according to the methods they use is performed. Then we analyze the categories for the compliance with the attacker group recognition requirements. We conclude by highlighting opportunities for further dataset analysis and supplementation options.

Keywords: Information security · Intrusion detection · Alert correlation · Attacker groups

1 Introduction

Intrusion Detection Systems (IDS) are widely used as a solution for attack detection, both based on network traffic and device events. Despite the significant development of the technology from the moment of its appearance, many solutions still have unsolved problems. Often the use of such systems is possible only with the involvement of an additional specialist for the analysis of IDS events. Thus, such systems can be considered as auxiliary rather than independent solutions in the field of information security.

The limitations of current IDS include the following [1]:

- Large amount of false positives [2–4]. An excessive number of false alerts leads to the complication of further analysis and the appearance of a phenomenon known as "alert fatigue"
- Skipping real attacks [5, 6]. As actual threats bypass defense solutions, full attack reconstruction becomes harder to accomplish
- Duplication of events in distributed systems [4, 7]. If the network data are analyzed by several IDS, they can cause multiple alerts to appear

© Springer Nature Switzerland AG 2020
O. Galinina et al. (Eds.): NEW2AN 2020/ruSMART 2020, LNCS 12525, pp. 32–42, 2020.
https://doi.org/10.1007/978-3-030-65726-0_4

- The heterogeneity of the information provided. Various IDS solutions provide alerts in different formats with nonidentical fields. This issue is of current interest for large-scale networks and collaborative IDS
- Large amount of low-level data [8]
- Lack of prioritization and alert connections

To solve these problems, the Alert Correlation Systems are used. They can be aimed at achieving the following goals [9]:

- Normalization
- Aggregation
- Correlation
- False Alert Reduction
- Attack Strategy Analysis
- Prioritization

Several approaches, for instance, attacker-centric network attack behavior analysis [10], are also aimed at the task of attacker group recognition.

In general, a group of attackers can be defined as an organization consisting of related attackers, united by tools, the purpose and status of attacks, and information obtained during the attacks. In the context of intrusion detection tools, it is important that attackers will be considered by the resources used in attack rather than the people conducting the attack.

From the perspective of information security, the identification of attacker groups may allow the defensive side to take more accurate countermeasures [11]. Some researchers consider, that "it is not the attack but rather the attacker against which networks must be defended" [12]. Several methods of group identification are able to determine those resources of the attackers that were not involved in known attacks, thus, it is possible to identify or destroy attackers using such methods.

Reviews of various event correlation methods have already been made previously. Pouget and Dacier [13] are considered to be pioneers. They classified the correlation methods existing at that time and outlined the development paths of the area. Sadoddin and Ghorbani [9] presented an analysis of the tasks that different approaches are capable of, and examined the focus on these tasks of the existing approaches. Among further works, following can be noted: Siraj [14] explored the possibility of using event correlation in Intrusion Detection and Response System; Mirheidari et al. [1] analyzed strengths and weaknesses of existing approaches; Chahira and Kiruki [15] highlighted the requirements for a modern correlation system; Zhou et al. [16] defined the limitations of existing approaches.

However, researchers did not consider the task of identifying attacker groups, only analyzing the possibility of reconstructing specific attack scenarios. This work aims to fill the gap.

The paper is organized as follows: in Sect. 2 algorithm classification is presented and examples are described. In Sect. 3 the requirements for group recognition are presented. Different categories are checked for compliance with these requirements. In Sect. 4 the conclusion of this work is given and further directions of research are evaluated.

2   Algorithm Classification

To date, several approaches have been proposed for classifying event clustering algorithms based on the type of data processing, the task to be performed, the chosen dataset and the methods used. A generally accepted approach has not been developed for the latter, and a new one based on the methodology for comparing these events is proposed in this paper. It is reasonable to distinguish two major types of techniques:

1. Attribute-based
2. Step-based

Attribute-based algorithms compare several events based on data present in events or supplemented using third-party data systems. Algorithms based on steps track the state of systems at the time of operation and work by compiling chains of events. Various approaches consider parameters such as the previous stages of attacks, the fact of capture, and so on.

It is worth noting that complex frameworks often combine both types. Therefore, the division into categories is based on what type the major part of the algorithm belongs to Fig. 1 illustrates the classification:

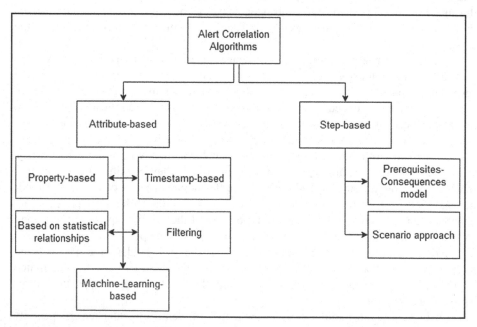

Fig. 1. Algorithm classification

The subsections below provide an analysis of the subcategories of correlation techniques.

2.1 Attribute-Based Algorithms

This category is based on a comparison of the data that came from the intrusion detection system, or these data after being supplemented using third-party systems. The following data types can be used as sources for supplementation:

- DNS records
- DNS history
- WHOIS records
- Open ports and service probes, etc.

In order to speed up some of the algorithms in this category combine similar events into meta-events containing the main characteristics of the group, after which new events are compared with them. A graph model is usually used to represent data, so the task is to search for clusters inside the graph by a certain weight function, which determines the differences in the algorithms.

Such type of algorithms is less expensive to prepare and set up and more versatile compared to step-based [1]. Often there is the possibility of parallel computing, which significantly improves the operating time of the system.

This group can be divided into the following subcategories:

- Property-based
- Timestamp-based
- Based on statistical relationships
- Filtering
- Machine Learning-based

Property-Based Algorithms. To correlate events, this algorithm type uses methods defined by the authors of the algorithm and comparing the resources included in the attack. The White Box method of operation allows to accurately determine the properties of events that contribute to the overall similarity function and to allocate similar resources. Such algorithms, as a rule, cannot detect complex attacks, but are able to determine the use of similar resources in various attacks.

Valdes and Skinner [17] proposed the correlation method based on EMERALD Framework [18]. In their algorithm, the authors proposed combining event groups into meta-events containing intersections of the properties of their events. For each new event, the weighted average function of the sum of the similarity of properties is considered. If it exceeds the required threshold by the sum, and for each property the minimum similarity threshold is overcome, then the event is added to the meta-event. On the next step the meta-events are combined into incidents based on a comparison with different attack classes.

Debar and Wespi [19] developed an algorithm for event aggregation and correlation, consisting of three stages:

1. Raw data preprocessing. Normalization of events received from different sources is performed. Data is reduced to one format: signatures of well-known ports are

replaced by their numbers, host names by IP addresses, and so on. In total, three types of data are used: information about the type of sensor, about the target and source of the attack.

2. Analysis of relationships. At this stage, duplicates are identified, then they are either removed from the final sample or, when a certain quantitative threshold is reached, are combined into meta-events. A sequence of events is also analyzed. A sequence is a predefined group of events that occurred during a specified time interval.

3. Joining in situations. Objects obtained at Stage 2 are examined in the framework of the concept of the situation: various options for intersecting the source, target and attack class are considered.

Cuppens [20] presented a method based on a set of expert rules. For such properties of events as the attack class, time, target and source of the attack, a set of functions is defined that measures the similarity of events and allows them to be combined. The author proposes approaches to combining data clusters and resolving conflicts; the work is also interesting in data presentation concepts.

Julisch [21] considers the separation of the values of certain types of properties into categories having a hierarchical structure. Clustering is based on distance of properties in the hierarchy of categories. Then the root causes of events are identified. Author proposes that fixing misconfigurations can significantly reduce the total number of IDS events.

Timestamp-Based Algorithms. This algorithm type uses event timestamp as the main property for correlation. It is mainly targeted at false alert reduction. CMRAF framework [22], proposed by Al-Saedi et al., reduces the number of events by identifying the similarities between them, collapsing events close in time and comparing CVE classification and clipping by CVE Score.

Fuzzy approach, proposed by Maggi et al. [23], allows to reduce the amount of data, based on the proximity of the detection time, with the ability to correct small errors in the data.

Algorithms Based on Statistical Relationships. This type of algorithm is based on determining the normal type of system operation and identifying suspicious events - attacks, as well as the connections between attacks. An example such technique implementation is the paper by Viinikka et al. [24], which estimates time series relationships and events that occur periodically.

Another application of the approach are algorithms that highlight the relationships between certain types of events in the system. The example of such works is an algorithm, proposed by Lee and Qin [25].

NoDoze algorithm, proposed by Hassan et al. [26], reduces false alert rate and prioritizes alerts based on anomaly score chains of events.

Filtering Algorithms. The basis of this algorithm category is the approach that determines the possibility of a detected attack in a particular network topology or information system. Thus, the approach is primarily focused on cutting off false positives [16].

Gula [27] considered the possibility of assessing whether the system is vulnerable to a specific type of attack contained in the IDS event to filter out false positives.

Desai [28] proposed an approach event management, based on the manual configuring of the services used for subsequent confirmation of IDS events.

Real-Time Network Awareness system, presented by Sourcefire [29], is based on passive scanning of traffic in the network and observing changes in the state of information systems to confirm events detected by IDS.

An active approach was proposed by Kruegel and Robertson [30]. Their modification for the Snort system extracts the CVE identifier from IDS events and uses special scanning software to confirm the vulnerability.

M-Correlator Framework [31] builds the network topology using the nmap utility. It then compares the success requirements of a particular attack with the following parameters:

– OS version and type
– Hardware type
– Service package
– Enabled network services
– Application

Based on the totality of compliance of these event parameters, an assessment is given in the range from 0 to 255; according to the results of the assessment, the event can be filtered. Then the events are prioritized and clustered into groups according to the applied policies.

Machine Learning-Based Algorithms. This category includes algorithms that automatically create comparison functions either base on already clustered data or unsupervised. Techniques using machine learning methods belong to the category of Black Box methods.

A good example is an algorithm developed by Dain and Cunningham [32, 33], which is based on DEF CON 8 CTF data. It combines events into a sequence of scenarios based on a comparison function, the parameters of which are obtained by machine learning methods. The decision tree of the algorithm is built on the basis of information obtained earlier.

Approaches based on the unsupervised learning method were proposed by Julisch [34], Zanero and Savaresi [35], Smith et al. [36] and Aminanto et al. [37].

Machine Learning-based alert clustering algorithms can be used both for defining similarity functions and for weighting of characteristics.

2.2 Step-Based Algorithms

The second major category of algorithms consists of approaches based on attempts to reconstruct the attacker's actions, as it is believed that an attacker usually needs to take several steps to achieve the goal of the attack [38].

A category can be divided into two subcategories:

1. Scenario approach
2. Prerequisites-Consequences model

Scenario Approach. In the framework based on that approach, the expert describes the known attack patterns using a formal language, then the system correlates existing sets of events with known scenarios. This approach cannot detect new types of attacks, since it is limited to a predefined set of rules, but it can detect more complex attacks than the attributive approach. However, for algorithms of this type, the significant presetting complexity remains.

The already mentioned techniques by Dain and Cunningham [32, 33] can also be classified as scenario approach. Among the formal languages used in the description of the scenarios, the following can be noted: LAMBDA [39], STATL [40], ADeLe [41] and CAML [42].

Prerequisites-Consequences Model. The Prerequisites-Consequences model is based on highlighting the prerequisites for the onset of events and assessing their possible consequences. The author of the algorithm constructs a graph of such dependencies, after which the algorithm compares a set of events with it.

Early work in this area includes the algorithm proposed by Templeton and Levitt [43], as well as a series of works by Ning et al. [44–47], including approaches that allow recovering some of the missing IDS events [5]. Peng and Xuena [10] proposed adding success tracking and attack capture to the algorithm to identify attacker groups.

JIGSAW [43] was proposed as a language for determining the prerequisites and consequences of attacks.

Methods of this category are difficult to implement, since they require a description for a very wide range of possible attacks, however, their accuracy is notably high [1].

3   Results

The identification of attacker groups can be aimed at achieving two goals:

1. Identifying the Tactics, Techniques, and Procedures used by a group of attackers to determine the level of threat and protective measures.
2. Forensic analysis aimed at identifying patterns of group action.

Based on these goals, a list of requirements for event correlation algorithms for use in identifying groups of attackers is formed:

3. Ability to put events related to common resources or attack steps into clusters.
4. Ability to explicitly represent the causes of connection between events.
5. Low error rate of type I and II.

The following Table 1 shows the analysis of the compliance of the categories of algorithms with the requirements:

Table 1. Applicability of correlation algorithms.

Category	Compliance	Comment
Property-based	Yes	–
Timestamp-based	No	The main area of application of these algorithms is the reduction in the number of duplicate events recorded in a short time period. They are not aimed at identifying resources or sequences of actions of attackers
Statistical relationships	Limited	It is possible to use a subgroup of algorithms that evaluate the causal relationships between events if they satisfy Requirement 3
Filtering	No	Algorithms of this type are aimed at reducing the number of false positives, rather than determining the relationships between events
Machine learning	Limited	Algorithms that define similarity function by the Black Box method do not allow to explicitly show the reasons for connecting events. However, algorithms that select the weight values of similarity of various properties by machine learning can be considered
Scenario	Yes	–
Prerequisites-Consequences	Yes	–

The data presented in the table determine only the applicability of those algorithms that are to be directly involved in the process of identifying attacker groups. Creating a framework for extracting groups from raw IDS data requires using other techniques aimed at achieving other goals: normalization, reducing the number of false and duplicate events, etc.

4 Conclusion

The paper examined the possibility of using various classes of IDS event correlation algorithms to identify attacker groups. Property based, scenario and Prerequisites-Consequences approaches are considered suitable for that goal, as well as some machine learning and statistical approaches. Based on the requirements for modern correlation systems [15], a comprehensive framework should include algorithms that belong to different categories. To select certain algorithms, a comparison of the approaches within the specific categories should be made.

Only a small part of the observed techniques uses event data supplementation systems. Future studies should consider the data obtained directly from IDS, and analyze what supplementation can be applied to them, and how extended data is more effective in terms of correlation of events.

Among the common problems inherent in event correlation algorithms, the use of artificial data sets to confirm effectiveness, such as DARPA 99/2000 [9], should be noted. Even if the data were obtained on the basis of real data, their depersonalization could entail the loss of significant features of the events. Algorithms based on honeypot and small organization datasets also cannot be considered proven effective. The nature of the systems used in them can significantly distort the output and patterns of attacks. Thus, research in the area of event correlation can be aimed at creating algorithms based on data from real malicious campaigns and Advanced Persistent Threat. An alternative could be checking the effectiveness of existing techniques on such data.

Methods based on steps often require a complex description of attacks by an expert, the skill of which determines the effectiveness of the system. Further research should consider the possibility of obtaining data on scenarios, prerequisites and consequences from existing expert databases such as MITRE ATT&CK and CARET.

Acknowledgements. This work was supported by the Government of the Russian Federation (grant 08-08).

References

1. Mirheidari, S.A., Arshad, S., Jalili, R.: Alert correlation algorithms: a survey and taxonomy. In: Wang, G., Ray, I., Feng, D., Rajarajan, M. (eds.) CSS 2013. LNCS, vol. 8300, pp. 183–197. Springer, Cham (2013). https://doi.org/10.1007/978-3-319-03584-0_14
2. Tjhai, G.C., Papadaki, M., Furnell, S.M., Clarke, N.L.: Investigating the problem of IDS false alarms: an experimental study using Snort. In: Jajodia, S., Samarati, P., Cimato, S. (eds.) SEC 2008. ITIFIP, vol. 278, pp. 253–267. Springer, Boston, MA (2008). https://doi.org/10.1007/978-0-387-09699-5_17
3. International Cyber Benchmarks Index[TM], January 2020. https://www.niscicb.com/
4. The Numbers Game: How Many Alerts are too Many to Handle? https://www.fireeye.com/offers/rpt-idc-the-numbers-game.html
5. Xu, D.: Correlation analysis of intrusion alerts. Ph.D. Thesis, North Carolina State University, North Carolina, USA (2006)
6. International Cyber Benchmarks Index[TM], May 2020. https://www.niscicb.com/

7. Husák, M., Kaspar, J.: AIDA framework: real-time correlation and prediction of intrusion detection alerts. In: Proceedings of the 14th International Conference on Availability, Reliability and Security (ARES 2019), New York, NY, USA, pp. 1–8. Association for Computing Machinery (2019). Article 81

8. Valeur, F., Vigna, G., Kruegel, C., Kemmerer, R.: Comprehensive approach to intrusion detection alert correlation. IEEE Trans. Depend. Secure Comput. **1**(3), 146–169 (2004)

9. Sadoddin, R., Ghorbani, A.: Alert correlation survey: framework and techniques. In: Proceedings of ACM International Conference on Privacy, Security and Trust: Bridge the Gap Between PST Technologies and Business Services (2006)

10. Xuena, P., Hong, Z.: A framework of attacker centric cyber attack behavior analysis. In: IEEE International Conference on Communications, Glasgow, 2007, pp. 1449–1454 (2007)

11. Xuena, P., Hong, Z.: An "attacker centric" cyber attack behavior analysis technique. In: The 9th International Conference on Advanced Communication Technology, Okamoto, Kobe, 2007, pp. 2113–2117 (2007)

12. Burroughs, D., Wilson, L., Cybenko, G.: Analysis of distributed intrusion detection systems using bayesian methods. In: 2002 Conference Proceedings of the IEEE International Performance, Computing, and Communications Conference, Phoenix, AZ, USA, pp. 329–334 (2002)

13. Pouget, F., Dacier, M.: Alert Correlation: Review of the state of the art. EURECOM, Technical report (2003)

14. Siraj, M.: Survey and comparative analysis of alert correlation systems in information security. In: The 3rd Brunei International Conference on Engineering and Technology 2008 (BICET 2008) (2008)

15. Chahira, J., Kiruki, J., Kemei, P.: A review of intrusion alerts correlation frameworks. Int. J. Comput. Appl. Technol. Res. **5**, 226–233 (2016)

16. Zhou, C., Leckie, C., Karunasekera, S.: A survey of coordinated attacks and collaborative intrusion detection. Comput. Secur. **29**(1), 226–233 (2010)

17. Valdes, A., Skinner, K.: Probabilistic Alert Correlation. In: Lee, W., Mé, L., Wespi, A. (eds.) RAID 2001. LNCS, vol. 2212, pp. 54–68. Springer, Heidelberg (2001). https://doi.org/10.1007/3-540-45474-8_4

18. Porras, P., Neumann, P.: Emerald: event monitoring enabling responses to anomalous live disturbances. In: Proceedings of the 20th National Information Systems Security Conference, pp. 353–365 (1997)

19. Debar, H., Wespi, A.: Aggregation and correlation of intrusion-detection alerts. In: Lee, W., Mé, L., Wespi, A. (eds.) RAID 2001. LNCS, vol. 2212, pp. 85–103. Springer, Heidelberg (2001). https://doi.org/10.1007/3-540-45474-8_6

20. Cuppens, F.: Managing alerts in a multi-intrusion detection environment. In: Proceedings of the 17th Annual Computer Security Applications Conference (ACSAC 2001), New Orleans, LA, USA, pp. 22–31 (2001)

21. Julisch, K.: Clustering intrusion detection alarms to support root cause analysis. ACM Trans. Inf. Syst. Secur. **6**(4), 443–471 (2003)

22. Al-Saedi, H., Ramadass, S., Almomani, A., Manickam, S.: Collection mechanism and reduction of IDS alert. Int. J. Comput. Appl. **58**(4), 40–48 (2012)

23. Maggi, F., Matteucci, M., Zanero, S.: Reducing false positives in anomaly detectors through fuzzy alert aggregation. Inf. Fus. **10**(4), 300–311 (2009)

24. Viinikka, J., Debar, H., Mé, L., Séguier, R.: Time series modeling for IDS alert management. In: ASIACCS 2006: Proceedings of the 2006 ACM Symposium on Information, Computer and Communications Security, New York, NY, USA, pp. 102–113. ACM Press (2006)

25. Qin, X., Lee, W.: Statistical causality analysis of INFOSEC alert data. In: Vigna, G., Kruegel, C., Jonsson, E. (eds.) RAID 2003. LNCS, vol. 2820, pp. 73–93. Springer, Heidelberg (2003). https://doi.org/10.1007/978-3-540-45248-5_5

26. Hassan, W.U., et al.: NoDoze: combatting threat alert fatigue with automated provenance triage. In: Network and Distributed Systems Security (NDSS) Symposium (2019)
27. Gula, R.: Correlating IDS alerts with vulnerability information. Technical Report. Tenable Network Security, p. 10 (2002)
28. Desai, N.: IDS Correlation of VA Data and IDS Alerts. Security Focus (2003)
29. Real-Time Network Awareness white paper. Sourcefire (2003)
30. Kruegel, C., Robertson, W.: Alert verification: determining the success of intrusion attempts. In: Proceedings of the Conference on Detection of Intrusions and Malware & Vulnerability Assessment (DIMVA) (2004)
31. Porras, P., Fong, M., Valdes, A.: A mission-impact-based approach to INFOSEC alarm correlation. In: Proceedings of Recent Advances in Intrusion Detection (RAID), pp. 95–114 (2002)
32. Dain, O., Cunningham, R.: Building scenarios from a heterogeneous alert stream. In: Proceedings of IEEE Workshop on Information Assurance and Security (2001)
33. Dain, O., Cunningham, R.: Fusing a heterogeneous alert stream into scenarios. In: Proceedings of ACM Workshop on Data Mining for Security Applications, vol. 6, pp. 1–13 (2001)
34. Julisch, K., Dacier, M.: Mining intrusion detection alarms for actionable knowledge. In: Proceedings of SIGKDD 2002, The 8th International Conference on Knowledge Discovery and Data Mining, Edmonton, Alberta, Canada, pp. 366–375. ACM Press (2002)
35. Zanero, S., Savaresi, S.: Unsupervised learning techniques for an intrusion detection system. In: Proceedings of the 2004 ACM Symposium on Applied Computing, Nicosia, Cyprus, pp. 412–419. ACM (2004)
36. Smith, R., Japkowicz, N., Dondo, M., Mason, P.: Using unsupervised learning for network alert correlation. In: Bergler, S. (ed.) AI 2008. LNCS (LNAI), vol. 5032, pp. 308–319. Springer, Heidelberg (2008). https://doi.org/10.1007/978-3-540-68825-9_29
37. Aminanto, M.E., Zhu, L., Ban, T., Isawa, R., Takahashi, T., Inoue, D.: Automated threat-alert screening for battling alert fatigue with temporal isolation forest. In: 17th International Conference on Privacy, Security and Trust (PST), pp. 1–3 (2019)
38. Cuppens. F., Miege, A.: Alert correlation in a cooperative intrusion detection framework. In: Proceedings of the 2002 IEEE Symposium on Security and Privacy (SP), pp. 202–215 (2002)
39. Cuppens, F., Ortalo, R.: LAMBDA: a language to model a database for detection of attacks. In: Debar, H., Mé, L., Wu, S.F. (eds.) RAID 2000. LNCS, vol. 1907, pp. 197–216. Springer, Heidelberg (2000). https://doi.org/10.1007/3-540-39945-3_13
40. Eckmann, S., Vigna, G., Kemmerer, R.: STATL: an attack language for state-based intrusion detection. J. Comput. Secur. **10**(1–2), 71–103 (2002)
41. Totel, E., Vivinis, B., Mé, L.: A language-driven IDS for event and alert correlation. InSEC, pp. 209–224 (2004)
42. Cheung, S., Lindqvist, U., Fong, M.: Modeling multistep cyberattacks for scenario recognition. In: Proceedings of the Third DARPA Information Survivability Conference and Exposition (DISCEX), pp. 284–292 (2003)
43. Templeton, S., Levitt, K.: A requires/provides model for computer attacks. In: Proceedings of the Workshop on New Security Paradigms, pp. 31–38 (2001)
44. Ning, P., Cui, Y., Reeves, D.: Constructing Attack Scenarios through Correlation of Intrusion Alerts. In: Proceedings of the 9th ACM Conference on Computer and Communications Security, pp. 245–254 (2002)
45. Ning, P., Cui, Y., Reeves, D., Xu, D.: Techniques and tools for analyzing intrusion alerts. ACM Trans. Inf. Syst. Secur. (TISSEC) **7**(2), 274–318 (2004)
46. Ning, P., Xu, D.: Learning attack strategies from intrusion alerts. In: Proceedings of the 10th ACM Conference on Computer and Communications Security (CCS), pp. 200–209 (2003)
47. Ning, P., Cui, Y., Reeves, D.: Analyzing intensive intrusion alerts via correlation. In: Recent Advances in Intrusion Detection (RAID), pp. 74–94 (2002)

Explaining Android Application Authorship Attribution Based on Source Code Analysis

Ivan Murenin[1], Evgenia Novikova[1,2(✉)], Roman Ushakov[2], and Ivan Kholod[2]

[1] Laboratory of Computer Security Problems, Saint Petersburg Institute for Informatics and Automation, Saint-Petersburg, Russia
imurenin@gmail.com, Novikova.evgenia123@gmail.com
[2] Department of Computer Science and Engineering, Saint Petersburg Electrotechnical University "LETI", Professora Popova Str. 5, Saint-Petersburg, Russia
romik75263@gmail.com, iiholod@etu.ru

Abstract. Source code authorship attribution is a process of source code authorship identification based on set of known code samples belonging to the given author. One of practical applications of code attribution is a malware analysis and detection. In the paper we explore attribution of Android applications based on classification of source code data with particular focus on explanation of the role of selected features and their impact on the final classifier decision. The proposed solution uses Local Interpretable Model–Agnostic Explanations (LIME) technique to explain decisions produced by classifiers. We explored this approach on several types of classifiers such as SVM, Random Forrest and neural network and dataset containing applications belonging to more than 20 different authors.

Keywords: Code authorship attribution · Explainable code attribution · LIME · Android application · Source code, support vector machine · Random forest · Neural network

1 Introduction

The task of code authorship attribution is associated with an ability to determine the author of the program code based on their coding style. This task has many practical application and is used when implementing copyright investigation, authorship verification, establishing de-anonymized code writer [1]. Another interesting application is a software forensics when analyst having a set of malware samples tries to identify possible malware author. Usage of authorship attribution techniques in this problem provides an alternative approach to malware analysis. Instead of focusing on a particular malware sample an analyst creates a set of specific features describing all malware samples created by a particular malware developer [2]. This idea is based on the assumption that all malware authors like software developers have their distinct coding style that can be used to generate a set of specific features describing all malware samples created by a particular malware developer. This assumption has solid practical basis. For example, the authors of the Ginp banking Trojan developed its modification called Coronavirus

O. Galinina et al. (Eds.): NEW2AN 2020/ruSMART 2020, LNCS 12525, pp. 43–56, 2020.
https://doi.org/10.1007/978-3-030-65726-0_5

Finder that was disguised as legitimate application targeted to locate people nearby infected with COVID-19, however the primary goal of the application was to steal user's bank credentials [3].

In general case code authorship attribution is a classification problem that requires thorough selection of features reflecting individual programming style. This problem has been widely studied and there are a number of approaches varying in extracted features and classification techniques utilized. But in major cases the suggested approaches represent themselves a black box as their decisions could hardly be explained due to the origin of analysis models being used. In this paper we apply Local Interpretable Model–Agnostic Explanations (LIME) technique to explain the result of author attribution. As LIME produces explanation in form of text and image artifacts, we investigate the problem of authorship attribution based on analysis of the source codes extracted from Android application. It has been shown that some syntactical features in source code recovered during decompilation of binary are robust against optimization techniques [2].

Thus, our contribution is the assessment of the applicability of source code decompiled from Android application for authorship attribution, we also investigated parameters for transforming texts into vector space and tested three different classification algorithms – algorithms based on random forest, support vector machine and artificial neural network. Our experiments showed that the highest accuracy is demonstrated by random forest classifier. To understand the decision of classifiers, we applied LIME technique and assess its abilities in interpreting results of authorship attribution. The experiments allowed us to conclude that in major cases similar features contribute to final decisions of different classifiers. We also showed that this technique is not enough to understand how the writing style of some authors differs from others because this technique is based on explainable models that produce local explanations focusing on features that are locally important.

The remainder of the paper is structured as follows. Section 2 presents related works in the field of code authorship attribution and techniques used to explain results of the author attribution. Section 3 gives general description of the suggested analysis process and Sect. 4 describes results of experiments. Conclusions sum up the results obtained and define the directions of the future research.

2 Related Works

2.1 Code Authorship Attribution

Previous research work on authorship attribution has focused on a wide variety of issues and practical application. In major cases it is a classification problem that is depending on type of task – authorship verification, copyright investigation, malware forensics –either two class or multiclass classification. For example, when attributing malware author, a forensics expert solves multiclass classification problem, in case of copyright investigation this problem is a two class one. The most crucial issue in code authorship attribution is the choice of analyzed features describing unique software developer coding style [1]. This set of features depends on type of source data – source code or binary, and programming language.

In [1] authors discuss problem of authorship attribution based on analysis of the source code written in C++ programming language, they propose to use three types of features – lexical, layout and syntactic features. Lexical features are built up based on analysis of word unigram frequency, layout features describe code-indention and length functions, syntactic features are language dependent ones, and represented by abstract syntax tree, and keywords. The authors also suggest a feature set adopted to the peculiarities of Python language. Similar features extracted from the analysis of simple word unigrams and abstract syntax trees are used when analyzing binaries. For example, in [4] authors derive lexical and syntactical features from disassembled executable binary. They analyze such features as abstract syntax tree node unigrams, labeled edges, node average depth etc.

Kalgutkar et al. [5] investigated the problem of Android authorship attribution through string analysis. They analyzed the accuracy of classification problem depending on type of source date. They used strings extracted from DEX file as a list of identifiers, extracted from strings.xml. As the primary focus of the research paper is malware analysis, the authors applied the proposed technique to attribute benign, malicious and obfuscated applications, and demonstrated that accuracy for malware author attribution has 96.03% when analyzing all types of string data. In [2] authors analyzed the possibility to establish authorship based on usage of specific data structures such as arrays and classes definitions. They extracted attributes related to classes, their methods and fields and array operations from bytecode, and the feature vector consisted of numerical values describing usage of classes, statistic values from size of array definitions, such as average, mean, median, and n-grams describing both array operations and data structures detected.

E. Karbab et al. [6] proposed an attribution framework that relies on dynamic analysis of sequence of API method calls using deep neural network. The authors constructed benign and malicious patterns of API calls that could be used to identify a malware author.

In [7] authors surveyed techniques used to attribute authorship of malicious code, and highlighted challenges inherent to this problem, they are the following: scarcity of data set, code obfuscation, usage of code generation techniques etc. However among these problems it should be noted a problem of lack of explainability of the machine learning techniques used to identify application author. In case of malware analysis it is necessary to understand that this problem relates to an open world classification problem, as new samples and new malicious code writers are constantly appearing, there is no baseline for writing malware that could be used to classify authors, and attributing rare and unknown malware is a challenging task. The ability to understand the similarity between sets of malware samples and to explain classification results could significantly help in solving this task.

There are only few works devoted to the problem of making malware analysis interpretable. One of the most well-known approaches to explain decision of malware detection model is described in [8]. The authors proposed a framework explaining solutions of the support vector machine (SVM) classifier. Firstly, they determined different types of static features such as permissions, API, network addresses used to classify malware, and assigned each type a textual explanation. Then they evaluated the contribution of each feature to the classification function $f(x)$, it is done by storing the largest k weights that determine the application position on malicious side of the hyperplane during computations. In [9] authors generalized this approach for explaining SVM and Random Forrest (RF) classifiers by evaluating features contribution to the classifier decision. Thus, there is a need to develop novel approaches to malware authorship attribution and explanation of existing solutions.

In the paper we use approach to explain decisions made by classifiers based on application of local linear models that could be easily interpreted and evaluate it applicability to malware author attribution.

3   Methodology

The analysis workflow is presented in Fig. 1. Firstly, we decompile Android application to extract source code, then we apply text vectorizer to generate vector based on decompiled source code, and then we determine the author profile using classifier trained earlier and explain results using local interpretable model agnostic explainable technique. We discuss these steps in detail in this section.

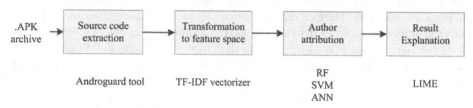

Fig. 1. Scheme of proposed author attribution process

Source Code Extraction. The decompiled source code is extracted from APK file of the application. This is done using androguard tool [10]. All *.java source codes are merged into one source_code.txt.

Feature Vector Generation. To form numerical features on the basis of the source code for each application, we represent text as a set of n-grams. The numerical representation of the text is then constructed using vectorization based on TF-IDF measure (term frequency and inverse document frequency). Application of this approach requires setting two main parameters - length of n-grams and the length of the dictionary, which is a set of n-grams, ordered by a number of words found. These parameters were investigated during experiments. Another important parameter for creating numerical presentation of the text is usage of stop words. Stop words in natural language processing represent very common words in language, and they are usually removed from the analysis as they do not contribute to text semantic analysis or classification. In our approach we decided to form two vocabularies with stop words, one *Var_Vocabulary* vocabulary contains words that represent automatically generated variable names, such as v0_0, v1_1_1, another *Key_Vocabulary* vocabulary contains a set of key words of Java programming language, they represent data types (byte, int, float, etc.), access modifiers (public, private, protected, final, static, etc.), and information flow control elements (if, while, else, break, for, etc.). In the experiments we evaluated impact of these vocabularies on classifiers accuracy and interpretability level of the classifier explanations generated by LIME.

Authorship Identification. The code authorship is established using pre-trained classifiers, we evaluated the accuracy of three types of classification algorithms – random forest algorithm (RF), support vector machine (SVM) and artificial neural network (ANN). To evaluate the efficiency of the analysis models, we applied 10-fold cross-validation of the random permutation of sample elements, the initial set was divided into the training and test set in the ratio of 80% to 20%.

Classification Results Explanation. In this approach we evaluated approach called Local Interpretable Model agnostic Explanations (LIME) technique that explains the predictions of any classifier in form of text or image artifacts [14]. It uses linear interpretable models such as decision trees of small depth, falling rule lists to create local explanation. Local explanation means that explanation considers features that are locally important for a particular sample but they may not be important in global context. For text classification the interpretable representation of meaningful features is a binary vector that indicates presence or absence of a word, and this representation does not depend on complex feature extraction procedures such as word embeddings.

4   Experiments

4.1   Data

To train the classification models, we used dataset of benign Android applications described in [5]. The archive provided by the authors contains more than 40 archives and includes labeled applications belonging to different authors. We excluded archives that did not contain apk files, or contained small number of apk files. After this procedure, 28 archives with applications authored by different software developers remained, the number of applications per one author varied from 13 to 77 apk-files, with total number of files equal to 817.

As it was stated above, only files with decompiled source code of the application written in the Java language were used; during archive processing the vector containing class labels for each author was generated.

The experiments conducted could be divided into two parts – identification of the optimal parameter for text vectorizer and classifiers and explanation of the classifying results using LIME for different types of classifiers.

4.2   Classification Performance Evaluation

The classification task was performed using three machine learning methods: random forest, support vector machine and artificial neural network. The last classification technique is based on the use of feed-forward artificial neural network with two hidden layers. The network architecture is shown in Fig. 2. The network was trained using the Adam optimizer with a learning rate coefficient of 0.005. To reduce overfitting, the method of batch normalization was used on each layer of the network. The network trained in 100 epochs showed accuracy 0.86957 ($\pm$0.00463) on cross-validation, which was not significantly improved during experiments, the authors suppose that this is due to lack of data for complete training.

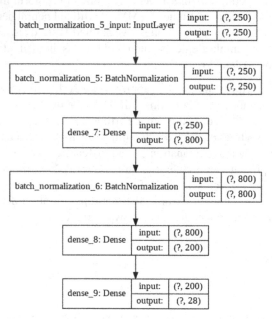

Fig. 2. The architecture of the proposed fully connected neural network

The accuracy of the rest classifiers assessed using cross validation is given in Table 1, it shows that the best accuracy is achieved by RF classifier.

Table 1. Classifiers accuracy and optimal values for hyper parameters

Classifier	Hyper parameters	Accuracy
RF	Ntrees = 250, Depth = 28	0.96257 ($\pm$0.00567)
SVM with radial kernel	Regularization C = 10000, Gamma = 1.022	0.93622 ($\pm$0.00585)
ANN	Epoch number = 100 Learning rate = 0.005	0.86957 ($\pm$0.00463)

In order to produce numerical representation of the text, we applied vectorizing procedure based on TF-IFD measure. Its application requires setting two parameters

−length of n-grams and the length of the dictionary. To assess these parameters, we conducted a series of experiments using RF classifier with optimal parameters (ntrees = 250, depth = 28). Table 2 shows classification accuracy for different values of the vectorizer parameters. The best results were obtained with a dictionary length of 250 words and the use of bigrams, but since the results did not differ much, unigrams were also added to evaluated explainable capabilities of LIME.

Table 2. Dependence of RF classification accuracy on TF-IDF vectorizer parameters: number of n-grams and dictionary length

n-gram range	Vocabulary length				
	25	50	100	250	1000
(1, 1)	0.93750 (±0.01017)	0.95024 (±0.00759)	0.95368 (±0.00703)	0.95547 (±0.00845)	0.95876 (±0.00521)
(1, 2)	0.93472 (±0.00953)	0.94614 (±0.00780)	0.95408 (±0.00670)	0.95928 (±0.00690)	0.96081 (±0.00684)
(1, 3)	0.93491 (±0.01477)	0.94427 (±0.01288)	0.95320 (±0.01334)	0.96059 (±0.01055)	0.96250 (±0.01122)
(2, 2)	0.93699 (±0.00623)	0.94753 (±0.00423)	0.95536 (±0.00644)	0.96257 (±0.00567)	0.96235 (±0.00620)
(2, 3)	0.92938 (±0.01089)	0.94640 (±0.01135)	0.95320 (±0.00968)	0.95997 (±0.01090)	0.96293 (±0.01080)
(3, 3)	0.92638 (+0.01329)	0.94929 (±0.01317)	0.95554 (±0.01162)	0.95924 (±0.01061)	0.96026 (±0.01081)

4.3 Data Splitting and Oversampling

Further experiments related to increasing the interpretability of classification results using the LIME. In the process of research, the authors encountered two problems that did not allow proper interpretation of the results obtained during classification. The first problem is that each data element has a very large size, the length of the source code examples for one application exceeded 5×10^6 characters, while the experiments showed that interpretation of a local text sample using LIME is resource consuming task starting with text length exceeds 10^5 characters, and with higher values it becomes almost impossible in practically meaningful time. The second problem relates to the imbalance of classes in the original data set, which can negatively affect the interpretation of classification results, the ability of the classifier to correctly interpret objects from small classes, while the accuracy as a whole remains high.

To balance source data set and reduce the size of each specific sample, we propose following procedure. Firstly, we divide each object into separate parts, considering each part as a separate independent sample element with a label of the corresponding class, and within each class, use a different partition length in order to balance the training set. Another advantage of this approach is that it allowed us to artificially increase the amount of data, which can positively affect the performance of the neural network.

In the process of splitting, it is necessary to determine a number of partitions individually for each class. To do this, we calculate length of the samples of the source code *data(lbl)* for each *lbl* author from the *classes,* where *classes* is a set of authors labels, then we calculate their average, and divide the obtained value by the average for each class and multiply by the coefficient of the expected length *scale*, where *scale* is chosen in such manner that sample with target *scale* is easily interpreted using LIME. After that, we split each sample of the source code into the obtained number of parts within each class and assign it a corresponding label. The number of *ksplit* parts for splitting within each *lbl* class can be calculated by this formula, where N is the number of classes:

$$ ksplit(lbl) = round \left(\frac{\sum\limits_{lbl \in classes} data(lbl) \cdot N \cdot Scale}{\sum\limits_{lbl \in classes} data(lbl)} \right). $$

Figure 3 shows distribution of samples per author in the source data set before and after application of the proposed procedure. The total size of the new data set increased up to 37910 source code samples, and the matrix of attributes submitted to the classifiers had a dimension (37910, 250). For this novel dataset the training procedure for all classifiers was repeated.

4.4 Classification and LIME Performance Evaluation on Extended Dataset

We constructed LIME interpretation for an arbitrary data element for each classifier. The visualization of the results is shown in Fig. 4. The bar charts in upper part of figure shows the probability of the sample class, the vertical bar charts in lower part of the figure show the list of words with corresponding probabilities, that contribute to the decision of the classifier.

It is clear, that the distribution of words which define the decision of the classifier is more likely to demonstrate the syntactic features of the program code than the individual features of the application or the author's coding style.

When creating a numerical representation of text data using TF-IDF in the first experiment, we did not use any stop words. In order to understand the impact of different features describing program flow, access modifiers, etc., we applied two vocabularies - *Var_Vocabulary* and *Key_Vocabulary*, as they are defined in Sect. 3. In total, the *Var_Vocabulary* included 5514 words and *Key_Vocabulary* - 28 keywords.

Table 3 presents the results for evaluating the accuracy of three algorithms with previously selected hyperparameters with and without use of stop words in the text vectorizing process for new data set consisting of 37910 samples. The neural network was trained twice, in the first case the best accuracy value was selected for 100 epochs automatically using the callback checkpoint in the keras library, in the second case the network was trained for 200 epochs, and 10% of the training sample was used for checking the accuracy of the network for each epoch. Figure 5 shows a graph of accuracy in the training and validation set for each epoch, one can see that after the 100th epoch,

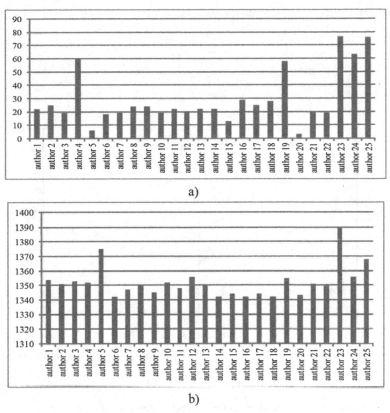

a)

b)

Fig. 3. Samples distribution per author a) for initial data set and b) after application of splitting procedure with scaling parameter $scale = 10^5$

accuracy does not significantly increase, therefore, further training does not make much sense, in addition, the effect of overfitting may occur.

Thus, usage of stop words had impact on the quality of classification. The neural network turned to be the most stable to usage of vocabularies, its accuracy does not decrease during training for 200 epochs. The random forest turned to be the most sensitive to the usage of stop words, its accuracy decreased by more than 1%. At the same time, the accuracy of the neural network when using *Var_Vocabulary* or *Key_Vocabulary* only as a vocabulary of stop words increased. This at first glance allowed us to assume that syntactic features do not contribute much to the final decision of the neural network in global context.

We also evaluate the prediction of which classes the classifier makes with higher confidence using confusion matrix. Digits on diagonal present the number of correctly predicted elements from the test set, and at the edges are the numbers of false predictions for the corresponding class. The confusion matrix for the random forest classifier with stop words is shown in Fig. 6.

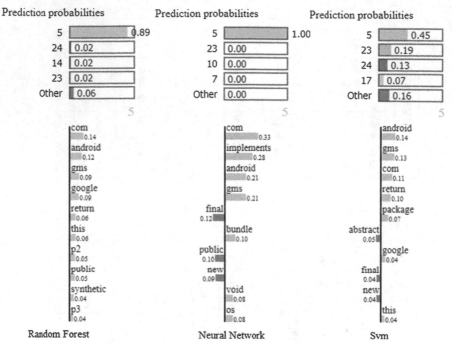

Fig. 4. Visualization of LIME interpretation results for three classification methods without stop words.

Table 3. Classification results on a new dataset using stop words

Stop-words	Random forest	Neural network 100 epochs	Neural network 200 epochs	SVM
None	0.9402	0.9143	0.9146	0.8984
Key_Vocabulary	0.9358	0.9183	0.9250	0.8996
Var_Vocabulary	0.9356	0.9249	0.9266	0.8857
Key_Vocabulary and *Var_Vocabulary*	0.9277	0.9092	0.9151	0.8902

Based on this visual interpretation, we can conclude that, for example, class objects with labels 3, 4, 7, 9, 11 are classified more correctly in comparison with objects belonging to classes 1, 23, 24, 25. Let us consider class 3, according to the confusion matrix, we see that the classifier makes a confident decision about whether this object belongs to this class.

Let us analyze the interpretations produced by LIME for any object of class that has either high prediction confidence or low prediction confidence, in order to explain these results. The LIME interpretation for the sample belonging to the class (class 3) with high classification confidence is shown in Fig. 7. We see that now many words are specific

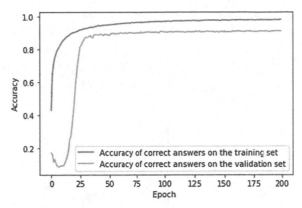

Fig. 5. Neural network accuracy on test and validation set

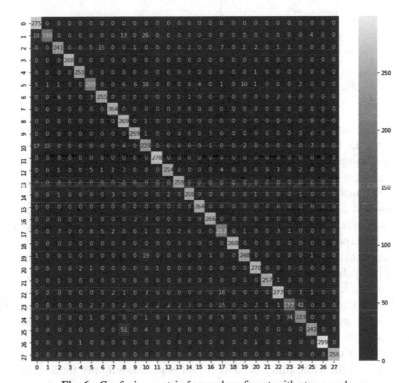

Fig. 6. Confusion matrix for random forest with stop words

methods for modifying data structures, and the signs that have the greatest weight, such as `ggbook` and `tencent`, do not belong at all to java syntax. Thus, they may contain a semantic characteristics of a particular application.

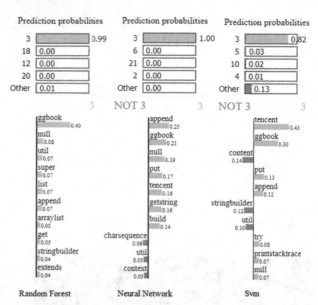

Fig. 7. Visualization of LIME interpretation results for three classification methods with stop words for a class object with a minimum classification errors.

Then we take an element belonging to a class that is classified with less accuracy, for example, class 25. Figure 8 presents a visualization of the explanation obtained using LIME for this sample.

In this case, the classifiers have no such clear decision-making boundaries, while the support vector machine does not change significantly compared to the first case, random forest and neural network with some significant probability tend to choose an object from another class, but at the same time, each classifier forms the right decision. In addition, the interpretation shows that all three classifiers rely more on the same words when making decisions, only the probability distribution differs. Thus, the decision is made more likely due to the structure of the words distribution in the program code than due to the unique features specific to a particular application.

Based on the experiments performed to interpret the classification results, the following conclusions can be drawn. LIME allows interpreting the contribution of the attribute to the decision of the classifier, to show the probability distribution of the object belonging to a particular class, the difference between the values of individual attributes for each class. But at the same time, the assessment is performed only for a specific data sample. LIME does not allow generalizing and building profiles of typical characteristics for each class and does not make it possible to conduct a comprehensive assessment.

In the task of explaining the attribution of program code, LIME allows one to evaluate the most significant words, to understand the style of writing the code of a particular application, and to understand how much the distribution of words affects the decision. In addition, experiments with removal of words that represent Java key words from analysis allowed us to focus on the details that may contain individual features of the application and its semantics. Since the method is based on local explanations, it does

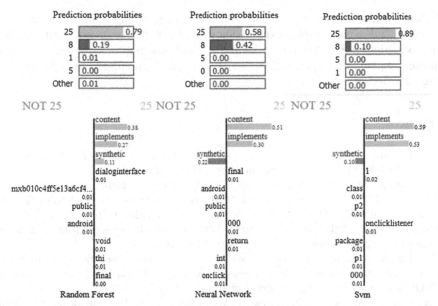

Fig. 8. Visualization of LIME interpretation results for three classification methods with stop words for a class object with significant classification errors.

not allow us to understand how the writing style of some authors differs from others and whether the decision of the classifier depends on the writing style or only on the distribution of the most significant features (words) in the program code.

5 Conclusion

The paper presents an approach to Android source code authorship attribution based on analysis of decompiled source code and its explanation using LIME technique. We evaluated three types of classification algorithms to solve this problem – random forest, support vector machine and artificial neural network. We obtained more than 95% classification accuracy on dataset consisting of more than 800 applications from 28 developers.

Our experiments also showed that application of LIME technique to explain source code classification is very resource consuming task, and to be able to apply this algorithm as well as to avoid overfitting and to increase test data volumes, an approach based on dynamic data partition was proposed. To construct input vectors for classification and explanation, we applied TF-IDF vectorization procedure and experimented with usage of stop words.

We explained feature contribution and class distribution for two data samples with various error dispersion for three different classification algorithms, and showed that in major cases similar features contribute to final decisions of different classifiers. We also showed that this technique is not enough to understand how the coding style of some authors differs from others as this technique is based on explainable models that produce local explanations.

Future works is related to the classification and explaining malware application, experiments with more complex explanation models with higher generalization ability, feature extraction from different sources like a control flow graphs, strings and file headers, more complex feature preprocessing techniques, and training and tuning classifiers on large amounts of data.

References

1. Caliskan-Islam, A., et al.: De-anonymizing programmers via code stylometry. In: Proceedings of the 24th USENIX Security Symposium. pp. 255–270 (2015)
2. Gonzalez, H., Stakhanova, N., Ghorbani, A.A.: Authorship attribution of android apps. In: CODASPY 2018 - Proceedings of the 8th ACM Conference on Data and Application Security and Privacy. pp. 277–286 (2018) https://doi.org/10.1145/3176258.3176322
3. Chebyshev, F., et al.: IT threat evolution Q1 2017. Statistics. https://securelist.com/it-threat-evolution-q1–2020-statistics/96959/Accessed 15 June 2020
4. Caliskan, A., et al.: When coding style survives compilation: de-anonymizing programmers from executable binaries. In: Proceedings of Network and Distributed Systems Security (NDSS) Symposium (2018) https://doi.org/10.14722/ndss.2018.23304
5. Kalgutkar, V., Stakhanova, N., Cook, P., Matyukhina, A.: Android authorship attribution through string analysis. In: ACM International Conference Proceeding Series, pp. 1–10 (2018) https://doi.org/10.1145/3230833.3230849
6. Karbab, E.M.B., Debbabi, M., Derhab, A., Mouheb, D.: MalDozer: Automatic framework for android malware detection using deep learning. In: DFRWS 2018 EU - Proceedings of the 5th Annual DFRWS Europe. pp. S48–S59 (2018) https://doi.org/10.1016/j.diin.2018.01.007
7. Kalgutkar, V., Kaur, R., Gonzalez, H., Stakhanova, N., Matyukhina, A.: Code authorship attribution: Methods and challenges. ACM Comput. Surv. (2019). https://doi.org/10.1145/3292577
8. Arp, D., Spreitzenbarth, M., Hübner, M., Gascon, H., Rieck, K.: Drebin: effective and explainable detection of android malware in your pocket. In: Proceedings of Network and Distributed Systems Security (NDSS) (2014). https://doi.org/10.14722/ndss.2014.23247
9. Melis, M., Maiorca, D., Biggio, B., Giacinto, G., Roli, F.: Explaining black-box android malware detection. In: European Signal Processing Conference (2018). https://doi.org/10.23919/EUSIPCO.2018.8553598
10. AndroGuard. Reverse Engineering. https://github.com/androguard/androguard Accessed 15 June 2020

Next Generation Wired/Wireless Advanced Networks and Systems

The Method of Forming the Digital Clusters for Fifth and Beyond Telecommunication Networks Structure Based on the Quality of Service

A. Paramonov[1,2]([✉]), N. Chistova[1], M. Makolkina[1,2], and A. Koucheryavy[1]

[1] St. Petersburg State University of Telecommunication,
22 Prospekt Bolshevikov, St. Petersburg, Russia
alex-in-spb@yandex.ru

[2] Peoples' Friendship, University of Russia, RUDN University, 6 Miklukho-Maklaya St.,
Moscow 117198, Russia

Abstract. The paper presents the results of an analysis of the impact of requirements on the quality of service and traffic on the structure of the telecommunication networks of the fifth and beyond generations. Given the crucial role of the network in building an effective digital economy, the concept of a digital cluster is introduced. A model is proposed that allows you to choose the size of a digital cluster, taking into account the requirements for the quality of service of subscriber traffic and the distribution of users on the territory. The proposed model allows you to create a network structure of digital clusters, taking into account various requirements and user traffic. A method for the location of service delivery points is also proposed, using the proposed model to select the sizes of digital clusters. The results can be used in modeling and planning telecommunication networks of the fifth and beyond generations.

Keywords: Telecommunication network with ultra low latency · Digital cluster · Quality of service · Latency · Traffic · Service model · Service provision point

1 Introduction

Over the course of its evolution, telecommunication networks have changed both in terms of technologies for implementing channels and switching methods, and in terms of the structure of their construction. Historically, the first telecommunication networks had a fully connected peer-to-peer structure, and in the course of their technological development and penetration, this structure was transformed into a multi-level hierarchical structure, including nodes and communication lines. Until recently, these elements were the elements of telecommunication networks. However, further development led to the integration of the telecommunication networks and computing systems, which led to the formation of an integrated infocommunication system (environment) [1].

© Springer Nature Switzerland AG 2020
O. Galinina et al. (Eds.): NEW2AN 2020/ruSMART 2020, LNCS 12525, pp. 59–70, 2020.
https://doi.org/10.1007/978-3-030-65726-0_6

The convergence, and frequently integration, of application-level implementation tools (services) and data delivery tools is so significant that it is often difficult to distinguish both hardware and software that belong to only one of these levels. The introduction of data centers (DCS) and software-defined network (SDN) technology is the next step in this integration [2].

Naturally, new elements, technologies and capabilities are reflected both the number of implemented services and the structure of the infocommunication system as a whole.

In particular, the introduction of data centers and information services on their basis is a significant factor that affects the redistribution of traffic and, as a result, the need to make structural changes to existing networks.

Potentially, data centers in the modern structure can act as centers that provide a variety of services, and are points of concentration of traffic. The choice of the number and geographical location of these points determines the redistribution of traffic in the communication network, and therefore its structure.

The desire to create high-performance data centers and the concentration of all functionality in a small number of geographical locations perhaps in part justified by economic considerations, but frequently contradicts the requirements for the stability of functioning, as well as the requirements of modern services.

Moreover, it is the requirements from the service side that have already led to the emergence of new structural solutions, in particular, to the emergence of so-called "cloud" services and various ways to implement them, both as part of the data center and as part of other elements of the infocommunication system, for example, as part of the nodes of the base station network and even as mobile nodes of land or air based [3–7].

The variety of modern solutions and approaches is due to the diversity of different services and requirements. Consequently there is a need to systematize them and determine the main requirements for structural solutions.

This paper is devoted to the analysis of modern requirements to the structure of fifth and beyond telecommunication networks [8–10] from the service side and the choice of the method of its construction taking into account the variety of requirements.

2 Problem Statement

Let's define the main factors that affect the network structure. It is known that the main task in building a communication network is the solution of compromise between subscriber traffic (demand for the service), the quality of its service and the volume of network resources. Since the network is built on a certain territory, while solving this problem, it is also necessary to take into account geographical features, which often play a leading role and determine the structure of the network.

Currently, in the field of fifth and beyond telecommunication networks the concept of ultra Reliable and Low Latency Communications (uRLLC) [11, 12], based on the concept of the Tactile Internet that appeared a little earlier [13, 14] is beginning to play a main role. Fundamental changes in the amount of delay, according to the requirements of the Tactile Internet and uRLLC, the delay can not exceed 1 ms, lead to physical restrictions on the distances at which the corresponding service can be provided. This factor has an impact not only on the telecommunication network itself, but also on the construction of an effective digital economy, since it leads to the decentralization of the network and creates prerequisites for the decentralization of the economy [3]. In view of the above, in papers [16, 17] it was suggested such a concept as digital agglomerations, within which it is possible to provide users with appropriate services. We will continue to use a slightly different concept – digital cluster, because in our opinion this concept more accurately reflects the structural characteristics of the network, which have a direct impact on the possibility of forming certain services in a particular territory (territories). Note that a digital cluster cannot be separate, because it appears in the process of clustering the network based on fairly strict mathematical representations, and its location in the network depends, of course, on the location of other digital clusters.

The main factor affecting the network structure is subscriber traffic [18]. We will talk about traffic as a process of data entering the network. This process depends on the type of service, its relevance (demand) and the number of users. In a network, traffic is usually transmitted between the user's connection point and the service delivery point, the latter can be either the user's connection point or the service servers. Between these points, traffic can be transmitted over different sections, depending on the accepted route selection rules. Therefore, traffic on the network element (channel) will also depend on the physical and logical structure of the network.

The second factor is the distribution of users across the territory that the network should serve. Naturally, most of the resources of modern communication networks are concentrated in those geographical areas where users are localized. And, as a rule, the degree of their penetration is higher, the greater the number and density of users. A feature of modern communication networks is that they can be used not only by people, but also by various devices, such as the Internet of things [19, 20]. Their distribution also has a significant impact on the network structure, especially if their number is comparable to or exceeds the number of human users.

The third factor is the quality of service requirements. Quality of service requirements are the main factor that determines the requirements for network resources and its structure. These requirements are expressed in the definition of normative values for the main features of the network operation. The main parameters selected are those that most affect the quality of perception of the service, if the consumer of the service is a person. In the case of data transfer between automatic devices (Internet of Things, Tactile Internet), the defining requirement is the implementation of the necessary functionality for which the data is transmitted.

The main quality parameters for modern communication services are probabilistic-time indicators of traffic service [21–23]. Here we will consider such indicators as the probability of losing a data packet and the delay in its delivery. These parameters are crucial for most services. As part of this paper, we will consider the services that have the most stringent requirements for these parameters.

In the way, when building fifth and beyond telecommunication networks, it is necessary to form a structure that can potentially ensure the quality of modern and promising services.

3 Network Model

We assume that the main parameter that characterizes the quality of the service is the delay in data delivery τ. This approach determines the ability to build uRLLC networks, and by and large the effectiveness of building a digital economy. The amount of delay depends on many factors. First, it depends on the size of the unit of quantity (volume) of data that is being transmitted, and the speed of data transmission over the communication line for each of the route sections, if the route consists of several sections. Second, from the possible delays in the route nodes associated with waiting in the buffer due to busy line transmission of the next data packet. Third, the time of signal propagation between data exchange participants.

Given this it is possible to write the following.

$$\tau = \bar{t} + \bar{w} + t_p \tag{1}$$

where $\bar{t} = \bar{L}/\bar{b}$ - average transmission time; $\bar{L}$ - average amount of data transmitted; $\bar{b}$ - the average transfer speed; $\bar{w}$ - average waiting time; t_p - the propagation time of the signal. For a route under certain assumptions the average delay can be estimated as the sum of the delays for each of the sections

$$T = \sum_{i=1}^{k} \tau_i \tag{2}$$

where τ_i is the delay for the i-th section, defined according to (1).

Let's assume that the network between the user and the point of service provision consists of two sections: the access section and the connection line to the point of service provision. The structure of the network model is shown in Fig. 1.

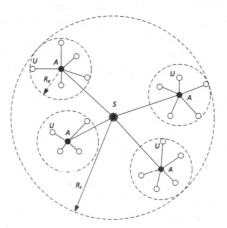

Fig. 1. Network structure.

The model consists of service users U, access points A, and the point of service provision S. The accepted assumptions are that the access points are connected to the point of service provision by communication lines whose length is equal to the length of a straight line segment passing through the corresponding points. The maximum distance from the user to the access point is Ra, and the maximum distance from the point of service provision to the access point is Rs. Then the max distance covered by the signal will be

$$d_{\max} = R_S + R_a \tag{3}$$

With the assumptions made above

$$R_a \ll R_s \tag{4}$$

Under the assumption (4), the distance between the user and the point of service provision can be assumed to be equal to R_a.

The propagation time of a signal is determined by the speed of light propagation in the transmission medium. We believe that between the access point and the point of service provision a fiber-optic communication line is used. So, taking into account the recommendation [24]

$$t_p = t_o R_S \tag{5}$$

where t_o - delay in propagation per unit length.

According to [15], the propagation time $t_0 = 5$ us/km.

We also assume that users are randomly distributed over the territory and their distribution can be described by a Poisson field

The probability of entering n users in the service area by the point of service provision will be defined as

$$p_n = \frac{\left(\pi R_S^2 \eta\right)^n}{n!} e^{-\pi R_S^2 \eta} \tag{6}$$

where η - density of users on the territory ($1/m^2$)

The number of users in the service area will be

$$v = \pi R_S^2 \eta \tag{7}$$

Intensity of requests (flow) in the service area

$$\lambda = \lambda_0 v \tag{8}$$

Intensity of requests (flow) in the service area

where λ_0 - request intensity created by a single user.

Let's assume that traffic can be described by a flow model with a coefficient of variation in the time interval between Ca requests. Let's define the waiting delay (for one network segment) using the model for the GI/G/1 Kramer and Langenbach-Baltz system [25]

$$\bar{w} \approx \frac{\rho \bar{t}}{2(1 - \rho)} \left(C_a^2 + C_t^2\right) g\left(C_a^2, C_t^2, \rho\right) \tag{9}$$

$$g\left(C_a^2, C_t^2, \rho\right) = \begin{cases} e^{-\frac{2(1-\rho)}{3\rho}\frac{\left(1-C_a^2\right)^2}{C_a^2+C_t^2}}, & C_a^2 \le 1 \\ e^{-(1-\rho)\frac{\left(C_a^2-1\right)^2}{C_a^2+4C_t^2}}, & C_a^2 > 1 \end{cases} \tag{10}$$

where

$\rho = \lambda \bar{t}$ - the use of the channel (the intensity of the load);

C_a.- coefficient of variation of the interval between requests (packages);

C_t.- coefficient of variation in service time.

Let's estimate the dependence of the packet delay at the node using an example when the data transfer rate is 10 Gbts and the packet length is 1518 bytes. the package length is selected maximum from the list of possible lengths offered for Ethernet testing in [26].

Figure 2 shows the dependence of the wait delay on the traffic intensity ρ and the coefficient of variation for the C_a stream.

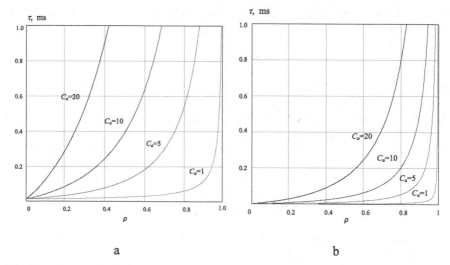

a   b

Fig. 2. Delay dependence on flow properties for transmission rates of 1 (a) and 10 (b) Gbts.

As you can see from the figure, the waiting time depends significantly on the properties of traffic and its intensity. The data transfer rate of 1 Gbts can be considered typical for 5G networks, and 10 Gbts - for communication lines between elements of such a network.

Comparing the graphs in Figs. 2a and 2b, you can see that the dominant value for equal line usage is the access section, and the difference between delays is determined by the ratio of transfer rates.

Given that the length of the access section is significantly less than the communication line, there is reason to believe that the dominant value of the propagation time is the propagation time over the communication line.

In [15] it is shown that the area of service provision can be described like a circle with a radius that is determined mainly by the time of signal propagation, i.e. the distance. This is actually the defining value and the results presented in this paper can be considered as the limit bounds of the digital cluster.

In this paper, we intend to refine this value by taking into account the traffic generated by the digital cluster. Increasing the radius of the digital cluster RS according to (7) and (8) leads to the growth in the intensity of requests, which according to (9) and (10) leads to the growth in latency due to waiting, Fig. 2b. Taking into account this dependence, the limit value of RS will be slightly less than [3].

The second task is to take into account the different requirements for delayed delivery from different services. Suppose that the network serves traffic of m services, and for each of the services the maximum allowed average delay value is defined. Then a limit value RS can be defined for each of the services. In planning the telecommunication networks of the fifth and beyond generations when implementing the concept of ultra-low latency communications uRLLC, the delay requirements can be taken from [27].

The third task is to choose the method of organizing the network structure, in which it is necessary to ensure the quality of m services.

4   Method of Forming Digital Clusters for the Telecommunication Networks of the Fifth and Beyond Generations

4.1   Cluster Size

First, determine the value of R_S for the service to which is made requirement for the time of delivery of the message. Then the limit value of R_S can be found from the solution (1) with respect to R_S, taking into account (4) and (5).

Based on (7) and (8) solution (1) can be expressed using R_S.

$$\tau = \bar{t} + \bar{w}(\rho, C_a, C_t) + t_p \qquad (11)$$

where

$$\rho = \lambda\bar{t} = \lambda_0\pi R_S^2\eta\bar{t} \qquad (12)$$

Figure 3 shows the results of the calculation according to (11) for several values of user density η. The user density was selected based on the population density data for Moscow, Saint Petersburg, and the Moscow region [28]. The traffic intensity was selected to be equal to $\lambda_0 = 0, 01$ packets per second. These data don't claim to be accurate estimates of traffic for any particular service, but they clearly demonstrate the qualitative nature of the change in delivery delay from the radius of the digital cluster.

As a results, we can say that the delay dependence on the size of the digital cluster is linear only for relatively small traffic intensity values. When approaching the value that corresponds $\rho \to 1$, there is drastic increase in the delay value.

We can conclude that while planning the placement of digital clusters in the telecommunication networks of the fifth and beyond generations for services with strict requirements for the amount of delay, it is necessary to take into account the amount of traffic intensity, which is proportional to the population density, along with the delay introduced by the time of signal propagation.

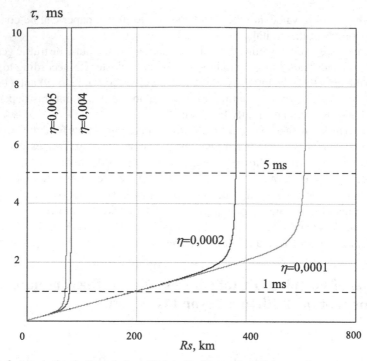

Fig. 3. A figure caption is always placed below the illustration. Short captions are centered, while long ones are justified. The macro button chooses the correct format automatically.

It is expected that for cities with a high population density, the Ra value will be significantly less than for localities with a low population density.

As can be seen from the graphs in Fig. 3 limiting the value of RS with traffic is much earlier than without it.

Given the size of the territory and the fact that the population density in the Russian Federation varries significantly in different localities, it makes sense to use the refined model proposed above when choosing the size of a digital cluster (11).

4.2 Cluster Type

Different types of services have different requirements for the amount of delay in data delivery. For example, the highest latency requirements are imposed on the part of production automation and Tactile Internet services (1 ms) [27, 29]. Somewhat less stringent requirements (5 ms) exist on the part of augmented reality and virtual reality services. There may also be new groups of services with increased requirements for the amount of delay. This is due to the development of various types of automated and remotely controlled robotic tools, vehicles, etc.

Therefore, it is advisable to solve the problem presented above of choosing the size of a digital cluster for each such group of services. In this case, the network structure must contain points of service provision (servers) differentiated by various service groups.

Figure 4 shows an example of coverage of the territory by points of provision of two services with different requirements for the quality of service. One of the points combines the functions of providing both services, the others only one service. This example illustrates the possible structure of organizing digital clusters in the telecommunication networks of the fifth and beyond generations with an even distribution of users across the territory.

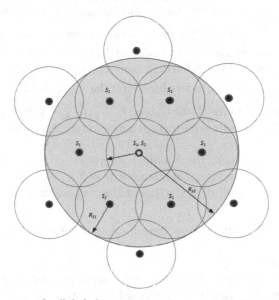

Fig. 4. Example of a digital cluster structure for two uRLLC network services.

This is an ideal case, which is the task of covering the territory with digital clusters of the same radius. The solution to this problem is known, the optimal coverage (the minimum number of digital clusters) is achieved when their centers are located at the vertices of an equilateral triangle. This approach is applicable when you need to build a network on a territory with an even distribution of users.

However, in practical tasks, you need to cover a certain number of points (users, buildings, localities, etc.). This is quite obvious, since users are concentrated in localities, and the size of the digital clusters in question can be commensurate with the size of localities and the distances between them.

This problem can be formulated as an optimization problem, in which it is necessary to ensure the minimum coverage of a given number of points by digital clusters (circles). The analytical solution to this problem is unknown.

The simplest approach to solving this problem is to use clustering algorithms, in particular the FOREL algorithm [30], as was done in [15].

Using this algorithm, you can find a particular solution to the problem of selecting points for providing a single service (covering the same radius with digital clusters). However, in this case, you need to place points for providing multiple services (covering digital clusters with different radius).

To implement the task in this case, we propose a method based on several stages of executing this algorithm for each of the services separately.

Below is a representation of the proposed method.

0. The initial data for solving the problem are: the number of services m; requirements for the amount of delay for each of the services $\{\hat{\tau}_1, \ldots \hat{\tau}_m\}$; coordinates of points corresponding to localities and other elements that need to be covered by a digital cluster $\{x_1, \ldots x_g\}$, where g is the total number of specified points; the number of users at specified points $\{n_1, \ldots n_g\}$; the specific traffic intensity for each of the services $\{\lambda_0^{(1)}, \ldots \lambda_0^{(m)}\}$; the data transfer rate on network sections and the average packet size for each of the services, which allows to estimate the transmission time c.

1. At this stage, based on the initial data, according to the model (11), are calculated the values of the size of digital clusters for each of the services, $\{R_S^{(1)}, \ldots R_S^{(m)}\}$, $i = 1$.

2. Preparing source data for clusterization: $X = \{x_1, \ldots x_g\}$, $R_S^{(i)}$, $Y = X$.

3. Then the FOREL algorithm is executed in a metric space, and the space is bounded by the set $M = Y$.

If the algorithm is complete, the solution is received.

If the algorithm is incomplete, it continues at $M = X$.

The solution is a set of points where the service servers are located $S^{(i)} = \{s_1^{(i)}, \ldots s_k^{(i)}\}$, $k_i \leq g$

4. If i = m, then all solutions are obtained, output of solutions, stop.

If not, $Y = S^{(i)}$, $i = i+1$

Go back to point 3.

The method proposed above performs step-by-step clusterization of a given set of X points. At each stage, clusterization is performed with the corresponding radius defined according to the model (11). Moreover, clusterization begins with the smallest R_S values in ascending order.

Clusterization uses a modified FOREL algorithm. The modification is that the range of permissible provisions of the digital center of the cluster is limited by many M. This modification allows you to ensure that the points provide a variety of services, whenever possible, coincide, which gives the possibility of reducing the length of the lines.

This method allows to get a particular solution to a multi-criteria optimization problem. The quality of this solution can be characterized by the volume of resources (entered service delivery points) and the quality of service.

By setting different initial conditions for solving the clustering problem, you can get another solution. This gives you an additional opportunity to choose the most appropriate decision for multiple solutions to the problem.

5   Conclusions

1. The introduced model makes it possible to estimate the size of digital clusters in the telecommunication networks of the fifth and beyond generations, taking into account the user traffic produced in them. The proposed model, in view the dependence on traffic, allows us to consider the specifics of territories with different user densities. The latter

is necessary when planning networks in the Russian Federation, since the population density in various territories changes from 0.07 to about 5000 people per km^2.

2. Using this model and differentiated estimation of the size of digital clusters for services with various latency requirements makes it possible to form the structure of the telecommunication networks of the fifth and beyond generations, namely, to choose the positions and size of digital clusters for multiple services, taking into account the concept of uRLLC networks.

3. The developed method of placing digital clusters is based on the application of the models and modified clustering algorithm FOREL developed in this paper. The method allows to get a close to optimal solution, which is choosing the placement of digital clusters.

Acknowledgement. The publication has been prepared with the support of the "RUDN University Program 5-100".

References

1. Senkina, N.S.: Analysis of the development of modern communication services and their impact on traffic redistribution. In: Senkina N.S., Paramonov A.I., Okuneva D.V., Distributed Computer and Telecommunications Networks: Management, Computing, Communication (DCCN-2016) Materials of the Nineteenth International Scientific Conference: in 3 volumes. Under the General editorship of Vishnevsky V.M., Samuylova, K.E. pp. 149–155 (2016)
2. Muthanna, A., Khakimov, A., Ateya, A A , Paramonov, A., Koucheryavy, A.: Enabling M2M communication through MEC and SDN. In: Vishnevskiy, V.M., Kozyrev, D.V. (eds.) DCCN 2018. CCIS, vol. 919, pp. 95–105. Springer, Cham (2018). https://doi.org/10.1007/978-3-319-99447-5_9
3. Hu, Y.C., Patel, M., Sabella, D., Sprecher, N., Young, V.: Mobile edge computing A key technology towards 5G. ETSI White Paper. 11(11), 1–16 (2015)
4. Ateya, A.A., Vybornov, A.I., Koucheryavy, A.E.: A layered cloud architecture for the services of the Tactile Internet. Telecommunications 2, 26–30 (2017)
5. Solomitckii, D., Gapeyenko, M., Semkin, V., Andreev, S., Koucheryavy, Y.: Technologies for efficient amateur drone detection in 5G millimeter-wave cellular infrastructure. IEEE Commun. Magaz. 56 (1), 43–50 (2018)
6. Petrov, V., et al.: Vehicle-based relay assistance for opportunistic crowdsensing over narrowband Iot (NB-IoT). IEEE IoT J. 5(5), 3710–3723 (2018)
7. Ometov, A., et al.: Feasibility characterization of cryptographic primitives for constrained (wearable) IoT devices. In: 2016 IEEE International Conference on Pervasive Computing and Communication Workshops, PerCom Workshops (2016)
8. Ateya, A.A., Muthanna, A., Koucheryavy, A.: 5G framework based on multi-level edge computing with D2D enabled communication. In: 2018 20th International Conference on Advanced Communication Technology (ICACT). pp. 507–512. IEEE (2018)
9. Devyatkin, E.E., Bochechka, G.S., Tikhvinsky, V.O., Borodin, A.S.: 6G at the start. Telecommunications, (2020)
10. Koucheryavy, A.E.: Communication Networks (2030)
11. Koucheryavy, A.E., Borodin, A.S., Kirichek, R.V.: Elektrosvyaz. pp. 52–56 (2018)
12. Koucheryavy, A.E.: Communication networks with ultra low latency. In: Proceedings of FSUE NIIR, Anniversary issue (2019)

13. Popovski, P., et al.: Wireless Access for ultra-reliable low latency communications. IEEE Network. **32**(2), pp. 16–23 (2018)
14. Fettweis, G.P.: The tactile internet: Applications and challenges. IEEE Veh. Technol. Magaz. **9**(1), 64–70 (2014)
15. Koucheryavy, A.E., Makolkina, M.A., Kirichek, R.V.: Tactile internet communication networks with ultra-low delays. Telecommunications. (1), 44–46 (2016)
16. Borodin, A.S.: Fifth-generation communication Networks as the basis of the digital economy. In: Borodin, A.S., Koucheryavy, A.E., Elektrosvyaz. no. 5. pp. 45–49 (2017)
17. Blanutsa, V.I.: Digital agglomeration of urban settlements in Siberia based on ultra low delays in telecommunication networks. Geographical Bulletin. **1** (48), 5–14 (2019)
18. Blanutsa, V.I.: Territorial structure of the digital economy of Russia: preliminary delimitation of "smart" urban agglomerations and regions. Spatial Econ. **2**,17–35 (2018)
19. Livshits, B.S., Pshenichnikov, A.P., Harkevich, A.D.: Theory of teletraphy. M., Svyaz, p. 224
20. Koucheryavy, A.E., Prokop'ev, A.V.: Self-organizing networks. Saint Petersburg, "Lubavitch". p. 312 (2011)
21. Koucheryavy, A.E.: Internet Of Things. Telecommunications. (1), 21–24 (2013)
22. Kuznetsov K.A.: Tactile Internet and its applications
23. Kuznetsov, K.A., Muthanna, A.S.A., Koucheryavy, A.E.: Information technologies and telecommunications. 7(2), 12–20 (2019)
24. Makolkina, M.A.: the Distribution of resources in the provision of augmented reality services. In: Makolkina, M.A., Paramonov, A.I., Gogol, A.A., Koucheryavy, A.E., Telecommunications. (8), pp. 23–30 (2018)
25. Makolkina, M.A., Paramonov, A.I.: Characteristics of communication networks and applications of augmented reality
26. Koucheryavy, A.E.: Problems of equipment and technologies of telecommunications Ptitt-2016 First scientific forum "telecommunications: theory and technology" 3T-2016. pp. 137–138 (2016)
27. Recommendation ITU-T Y.1542 Framework for achieving end-to-end IP performance objectives. Switzerland Geneva, (2010)
28. Kramer, W., Langenbach-Belz, M.: Approximation for the delay in the queueing systems GI/GI/1. In: Congressbook 8th International Teletraffic Congress, Melbourne. pp. 235–235 (1976)
29. Recommendation ITU-T Y.1564 Ethernet service activation test methodology. Switzerland Geneva (2016)
30. Li, Z., Uusitalo, M., Shariatmadari, H., Singh, B.: 5G URLLC: Design Challenges and System Concepts. In: 15th International Simposium on Wireless Communication Systems (ISWCS), Tokio, Japan. p. 6 (2018)
31. Federal state statistics service. www.statdata.ru Accessed 01 March 2020
32. The Tactile Internet. ITU-T Technology Watch ReportAugust 2014. https://www.itu.int/dms_pub/itut/oth/23/01/T23010000230001PDFE.pdf, свободный – (01.03.2020)
33. Mandel, I.D.: Cluster analysis. M. "Finance and statistics". p. 176 (1988)

Analyzing the Effectiveness of Dynamic Network Slicing Procedure in 5G Network by Queuing and Simulation Models

Irina Kochetkova[1,2,3]([⊠])(iD), Anastasia Vlaskina[1], Sofia Burtseva[1],
Valeria Savich[1], and Jiri Hosek[3]

[1] Applied Mathematics and Communications Technology Institute, Peoples'
Friendship University of Russia (RUDN University), Moscow, Russian Federation
gudkova-ia@rudn.ru
[2] Institute of Informatics Problems, Federal Research Center "Computer Science
and Control" of the Russian Academy of Sciences, Moscow, Russian Federation
[3] Department of Telecommunication, Brno University of Technology,
Brno, Czech Republic

Abstract. In this paper, we propose three metrics that could be used
for accessing the effectiveness of a dynamic Network Slicing. On the
one hand re-slicing could result in more adaptive resource allocation for
different virtual network operators (VNO), but could arise the signaling
overhead. On the other hand an insufficient amount of re-slicing could
significantly decrease the quality of service for VNO users, but reduce the
signaling delays. Proposed metrics could be used for analyzing the above-
mentioned effect. We illustrate the metrics by the simulation model for
a simple dynamic network slicing algorithm. We also propose a queuing
system approach for analyzing dynamic network slicing for 2 VNOs.

Keywords: Impatient elastic traffic · Two-service QS · Dynamic
system · Efficiency indicators

1 Introduction

Nowadays there is an increase in the number of devices and users of various
mobile network services. In an effort to meet the needs of users in terms of
quality of service, mobile operators are developing new software and hardware

The publication has been prepared with the support of the "RUDN University Program 5–100" (recipients I. Kochetkova, A. Vlaskina, Sect. 4). The reported study
was funded by RFBR, project number 20-37-70079 (recipients I. Kochetkova, A.
Vlaskina, V. Savich, Sect. 3). The reported study was funded by RFBR, project
number 18-00-01555(18-00-01685) (recipients I. Kochetkova, Sect. 2). This article is based as well upon support of international mobility project MeMoV, No.
CZ.02.2.69/0.0/0.0/16_027/00083710 funded by European Union, Ministry of Education, Youth and Sports, Czech Republic and Brno University of Technology.

O. Galinina et al. (Eds.): NEW2AN 2020/ruSMART 2020, LNCS 12525, pp. 71–85, 2020.
https://doi.org/10.1007/978-3-030-65726-0_7

introducing new principles for building a network architecture based on new standards [1]. The most common way to reduce operating costs in fourth generation (4G) networks is sharing a Radio Access Network (RAN) between two or more mobile operators. The Multi-Operator Core Network (MOCN), LTE-operators with dedicated frequencies, and Multi Operator RAN (MORAN), 3G-operators with dedicated frequencies, are solutions for RAN sharing. The new technologies of 5G networks have fundamental advantages allowing to maintain high data transfer speeds and a larger number of users [2–4]. One of the most important concepts of fifth-generation networks is Network Slicing, which provides the ability to logically divide the operator's resources into slices depending on the tasks [5], for example, by type of service: one for cellular, the other for the Internet of things [6,7]. Slicing is crucial in resource management to provide ultra-fast and reliable communications in segments of the fifth generation networks such as Enhanced Mobile Broadband (eMBB), Critical Communications (CriC), Massive Internet of Things (MIoT) [8], Enhanced Vehicular to Everything (eV2X), which impose different and often conflicting performance requirements [9]. The tasks that arise as part of the implementation of this technology are now being actively investigated. The development of network slicing technology led to the task of designing a theoretical communication model that takes into account the heterogeneous requirements and various characteristics of three services – Ultra-Reliable Low Latency Communication (URLLC), eMBB and Massive Machine-Type Communications (mMTC) [10]. It is important to note that this approach ensures the implementation of guarantees on the quality of service, delay and the number of supported devices. For efficient resource management in network slicing scenarios, a comparison of two schemes is presented in [11] – separation based on the developed forecasting algorithm and equal resource sharing in each slice. The first implies one reasonable option, and the second saves a lot of computational cost. In [12], a mixed-justice scheme is considered when slices are further scaled based on a large class of utility functions in real time. Such a scheme is a network slicing game in which each slice tenant responds to the distribution of users of other tenants in order to maximize their own utility [13,14]. To ensure the specified parameters of Quality of Service (QoS), dynamic resource allocation is used [15–17]. The possibility of deploying a car network, taking into account the priority of requests from transport, classifying flows, and grouping such scenarios as applications for safe driving, infotainment applications, or applications responsible for the operability of comfortable driving indicators, as well as the possibility of programmed multiple access, was studied in [18,19]. Autonomous driving applications are also considered in [20]. Here is a model of a system for dividing services into a four-level logical architecture. An analysis of propagation delay and processing latency is presented based on the $GI/M/1$ queuing system. The construction of queuing systems for solving network slicing tasks is also used, for example, to create a new business model Slice-as-a Service (SlaaS). The authors in [21] solve the problem of access control using the Markov model with several queues for heterogeneous requests. Queuing systems with a buffer, repeated calls [22], minimum guaranteed data rate [23] and different types of service-level agreement [24] were built to solve the problem of efficient slicing. The dynamic sharing of network segments supporting inelastic users with minimal speed requirements and denial of service for users whose requirements cannot be met is presented in [25].

In this paper, we investigate the problem of efficient use of network resources. Slices are formed taking into account the features of the services provided to users, or are grouped by mobile network operators. A distinctive feature of the studied model is dynamic redistribution performance analysis (how often we need to do it), taking into account the workload of the system. With this approach, it can be not only achieve high performance and avoid downtime of resources, but also ensure that the minimum guaranteed requirements are met. This problem is solved by simulation methods, and the analysis of a particular scenario for two slices is carried out using the methods of queuing theory.

The paper is organized as follows. The next section presents the system model and metrics for dynamic network slicing. Section 3 presents the algorithm for resource allocation and its illustration. Queuing system for case with 2 slices dedicated in Sect. 4. Appendix, containing the technical details, conclude the paper.

2   System Model and Metrics of Interest

We are interested in understanding how some slices should efficiently share the same radio resources. onsider a set of network slices $\mathcal{K} - \{1, 2, \ldots, K\}$, which virtual operators (VNO) can use. The total number of slices is $K = |\mathcal{K}|$. The aggregate bit rate that could be reached on the available resources C is allocated between K slices. So, in the initial moment of time resource slicing is $\frac{C}{K} = N_1(t_0) = N_2(t_0) = \ldots = N_k(t_0) = \frac{N}{K}$, where N – total size of K slices. In other words, the maximum number of users that could be served simultaneously. This allocation is fixed in the Service Level Agreement (SLA) – $(N_1(t_0), N_2(t_0), \ldots, N_K(t_0))$. Slices receive some user requests, for each of which the virtual operator allocates one of $N_k(t)$ positions corresponding to the amount of resources of slice (Fig. 1).

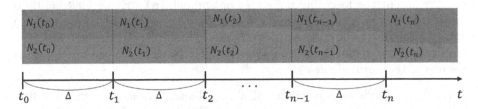

Fig. 1. Scheme of resource slicing in time with a cutting interval Δ

At time moments t_l the resource is reallocated, therefore the first moment of slicing $t_0 = 0$ and the rest are produced at intervals: $t_{l+1} = t_l + \Delta$,

$l = 0, 1, \ldots$; $\Delta = $ const. From here, $N_k(t_l)$ – size of k-slice as a result of real-location algorithm. At t some number of users $(n_k(t))$ are allocating the k-slice resources and some $(m_k(t))$ – wait in buffer with a maximum size M_k for k-users. The Table 1 reflects the main parameters that describe the system model.

Table 1. System parameters for simulation model

Parameter	Description
K	Number of slices (operators, types of users)
C	Aggregate bit rate that could be reached on the available resources (PRBs) for K slices [bps]
N	Total size of K slices (i.e. maximum number of users that could be served simultaneously) [user]
Δ	Time interval between the moments of time for dynamic resource reallocation between slices [s]
t_l	Moment of time for dynamic resource reallocation between slices [s]
$N_k(t)$	Size of k-slice at moment t [user]
$N_k(0)$	Default size of k-slice at moment $t_0 = 0$ (specified in the SLA) [user]
M_k	Size of k-buffer (i.e. maximum number of k-users waiting for service to start) [user]
$n_k(t)$	Number of k-users allocating the k-slice resources at moment t [user]
$m_k(t)$	Number of k-users waiting for service to start in k-buffer at moment t [user]

2.1 Metrics of Effectiveness of Dynamic Network Slicing

For optimal dynamic network slicing, it is necessary to introduce some conditions. We accept the following points for our model: (a) striving for conditions contained in the SLA; (b) minimum system load by service messages; and (c) exclusion of resource "downtime" in conditions of buffering on other slices. Therefore, for resource management the following indicators have been developed as measures of the optimal slicing:

(a) $\alpha \in [0, 1]$ – coefficient describing SLA compliance. We assume that the first allocation of the resource contained in the SLA is our initial state, which our system is committed. Thus the average value among all slices is:

$$\overline{\alpha} = \frac{1}{K} \sum_{k \in K} a_k, \tag{1}$$

where $\alpha_k \in [0,1]$ – the ratio of the value of the SLA compliance in the interval (t_l, t_{l+1}) to the total value of whole simulation time. It is determined as:

$$a_k = \lim_{T \to \infty} \frac{\sum_{l=1}^{L(T)} ((t_l - t_{l-1}) \min (N_k(t_l), N_k(t_0)))}{T N_k(t_0)}, \qquad (2)$$

where T – full time simulation of the system, $L(T)$ – entire number of calls of slicing. Using the law of total probability for the selected resource $N_k(t_l)$ for k-slice with initial slicing $N_k(t_0)$ at t_l: $P(A \mid H_i) = P\{N_k(t_0) \leq N_k(t) \mid t = t_l - t_{l-1}\}$. This can be expressed as $\frac{N_k(t_l)}{N_k(t_0)}$, which shows how close is the amount of resources to the initial. However, $N_k(t_l)$ may have a greater numerical value than $N_k(t_0)$, therefore, for the correct calculation of this probability it is necessary to choose the minimum value from these two quantities: $P(A \mid H_i) = P\{N_k(t_l) = N_k(t_0)\} = \frac{\min(N_k(t_l), N_k(t_0))}{N_k(t_0)}$. The probability of an event being at the required time interval can be written as $P(H_i) = P\{t = t_l - t_{l-1}\} = \frac{t_l - t_{l-1}}{T}$. In total there is $L(T)$ such events. Then we obtain:

$$P(A) = \sum_{l=1}^{L(T)} \frac{(t_l - t_{l-1}) \min (N_k(t_l), N_k(t_0))}{T} \frac{}{N_k(t_0)}.$$

Further it remains only to find the limit of this expression for $T \to \infty$, and sum it over all slices and divide by the number of such slices. We get the formula for calculating SLA compliance coefficient (2).

(b) $\beta \in [0,1]$ – coefficient of useful slicing calls :

$$\beta = \lim_{T \to \infty} \frac{\sum_{l=1}^{L(T)} \max_{k \in K} 1\{N_k(t_l) \neq N_k(t_l - 0)\}}{L(T) + 1}. \qquad (3)$$

At the time of reallocation of resources the system sends a service message. However, if there are too many messages it will be overload. Consider all the calls of the resource redistribution algorithm and calculate the number of those for which the value of $N_k(t)$ has changed for (useful slicing). Find the number of useful slicing: $\max_{k \in K} 1\{N_k(t_l) \neq N_k(t_l - 0)\}$, where $t_l - 0$ – point in time before l-th slicing. The result of this function will be 0 if there is no changes and 1 – otherwise. Sum these values over the entire number of slices $L(T)$ to get the number of favorable outcomes and to find the number of slicing moments $L(T) + 1$.

(c) $\overline{UTIL} \in [0,1]$ – the average value of the coefficient of employment of resources of virtual operators. We try to reduce downtime of system when one of the slices is overloaded, but on the other there is free resources:

$$\overline{UTIL} = \frac{1}{K} \sum_{k \in K} UTIL_k, \qquad (4)$$

where $UTIL_k \in [0,1]$ – the ratio of sum of periods of device employment to full model time:

$$UTIL_k = \lim_{T \to \infty} \frac{\sum_{i=1}^{I(T)} (t_i - \tau_i)}{T}, \qquad (5)$$

where τ_i and t_i are the beginning and end of the resource busy interval, and $I(T)$ – number of this intervals.

3   Numerical Illustration of Metrics

3.1   Simplified Algorithm for Dynamic Network Slicing

To summarize the main assumptions discussed so far, we assume that such system can be represented as a model with a fixed number of users, the behavior of each is determined in accordance with the following principle. The user sends a request for the service, receives a resource and utilize it for a while, then waits and loads it again. Clearly, for the l-th slicing at t_l: $N(t_l) = (N_1(t_l), N_2(t_l), \dots, N_K(t_l))$.

The system operation is described by three situations:

1. $\forall\, m_k(t_l) = 0$, $k \in \mathcal{K}$ – the buffers of all operators are empty $\rightarrow$ leave the resource allocation unchanged: $N(t_l) = N(t_{l-1})$.
2. $\forall\, m_k(t_l) > 0$, $k \in \mathcal{K}$ – all buffers have at least one request. $\rightarrow$ leave the resource allocation unchanged: $N(t_l) = N(t_{l-1})$.
3. $\exists\, k \in \mathcal{K}$: $m_k(t_l) > 0$; $\exists\, j \in \mathcal{K}$: $m_j(t_l) = 0$ – there is at least one non-empty queue $\rightarrow$ reallocation needed. Find the amount of free resource units available for redistribution for each operator and the number of requests in all buffers. Further find the smallest difference between free resource and buffer fullness. And finally, we allocate the free resource between the busiest buffers until either the resource runs out or all the buffers become empty. All these actions are described in the Algorithm 1. We omit the parameter t_l for convenience.

3.2   Simplified Algorithm for Two Slices

In the case when there are two virtual operators in the system the following simplifying assumptions can be made. If all the buffers are empty or busy as for K-operators, the resource allocation remains unchanged: $N(t_l) = N(t_{l-1})$. But if at least one buffer is not empty, there are two different events:

(a) $m_1(t_l) > 0, m_2(t_l) = 0$ – the first buffer is not empty and all resources of the 1-operator are busy;
(b) $m_1(t_l) = 0, m_2(t_l) > 0$ – the second buffer is not empty and all resources of the 2-operator are busy.

We consider these events (a) and (b) in more detail. In each of them different development options of events are possible, depending on the parameters that determine the state of events. In the reallocation in (a) there can be two orthogonal situations, (i) and (ii). Similar conditions can be presented for event (b). The new amount of slice resources is given by (6).

Algorithm 1. Cycle

1: **for** k, K **do**
2:     $\overline{n}_k = N_k - n_k$
3: **end for**
4: **Sort**
5:     $\mathcal{K} = \{i_1, i_2, \ldots, i_K\}, i \in \mathcal{K}, \overline{n}_{i_1} \geq \overline{n}_{i_2} \geq \ldots \geq \overline{n}_{i_K},$
6: **EndSort**
7: **for** k, K **do**
8:     $\overline{n}. = \overline{n}. + \overline{n}_k$ ▷ sum of available resource units for slicing
9:     $m. = m. + m_k$ ▷ sum of all requests in buffers
10: **end for**
11: $i := \min(\overline{n}., m.)$
12: **repeat**
13:     $s = \operatorname{argmax}(\overline{n}_k), k \in \mathcal{K}$
14:     $q = \operatorname{argmax}(m_k), k \in \mathcal{K}$
15:     $N_s := N_s - 1$
16:     $N_q := N_q + 1$
17:     $m_q := m_q - 1$
18:     $\overline{n}_s := \overline{n}_s - 1$
19:     $i := i - 1$
20: **until** $s > 0$ and $i > 0$

(i) $m_1(t_l) \leq N_2(t_{l-1}) - n_2(t_l)$ – the free resource of 2-operator is enough to cover the number of pending requests in the 1-queue;

(ii) $m_1(t_l) > N_2(t_{l-1}) - n_2(t_l)$ – the free resource of the 2-operator is not enough.

$$N_1(t_l) = \begin{cases} N_1(t_{l-1}) + m_1(t_l), & m_1(t_l) \leq N_2(t_{l-1}) - n_2(t_l), \\ N_1(t_{l-1}) + N_2(t_{l-1}) - n_2(t_l), & m_1(t_l) > N_2(t_{l-1}) - n_2(t_l), \end{cases} \quad (6)$$

$$N_2(t_l) = \begin{cases} N_2(t_{l-1}) - m_1(t_l), & m_1(t_l) \leq N_2(t_{l-1}) - n_2(t_l), \\ n_2(t_l), & m_1(t_l) > N_2(t_{l-1}) - n_2(t_l). \end{cases}$$

3.3   Numerical Example

To carry out simulations, we consider network slicing scheme with $C = 60$ [Mbps] available resources. As network traffic, a File Transfer-service was chosen, which is characterized by the volume of the transmitted file (exponential distribution with a mean $s = 2$ [Mb]). $K = 5$ slice are defined in five scenarios of user behavior. Assume that the amount of time between file download requests is exponentially distributed with a means $\lambda_1 = 2$ for 1-slice and $\lambda_2 = 5$, $\lambda_3 = 8$, $\lambda_4 = 10$, $\lambda_5 = 15$ for other slices, respectively. Herewith, the same minimum guaranteed bit rate are provided inside each slice, $b_{min} = 0.1$ [Mbps]. The queue length for each slice is $r = 50$. Note that users can departure from the queue due to impatience (losses) with intensity $\gamma = 0.000001$.

The choice of such system parameters is determined by the desire to demonstrate the operation of the resource slicing algorithm described above. Furthermore, with an increase in the number of slices, the number of studied characteristics, such as the average time for servicing requests, the average number of requests in a system (device or queue), increases directly, because it is necessary to calculate these characteristics for each slice separately and construct their own confidence intervals.

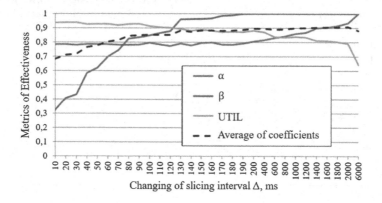

Fig. 2. Dependence of resource employment on the number of users for the first and second systems

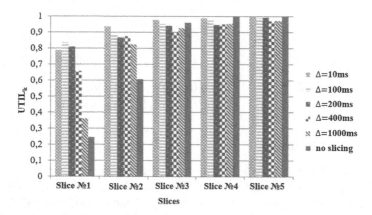

Fig. 3. Comparison of the resource employment coefficient for each operator for different lengths of the slicing interval

The graph (Fig. 2) shows the dependence of each of the selected performance indicators on the value of the gap between the cuts (the interval Δ), as well as the average value for them, made in black dotted line. Taking into account the basic principles laid down in the Algorithm (2.1), we choose a segment in which the green dot and the black dotted line take values close to 1 at the same time. As a solution, we suggest any value of the δ in the interval $150 - 200$ ms. A sample result is shown in Fig. 3,which shows the values of resource employment coefficients separately for slices. It is easy to notice that significant changes from initial slicing occur for the first two slices (in 1-slice the allocated resource is used only for a quarter of the volume, and in 2-slice more than 40% of the resources are not used). Accordingly, the graphs show that the value of δ that gives a significant increase in resource load is 200 ms. The results of modeling for $\Delta = 200$ ms are illustrated in Fig. 4. It can be observed that significant jumps in available resource volumes occur for slices with a higher intensity of requests.

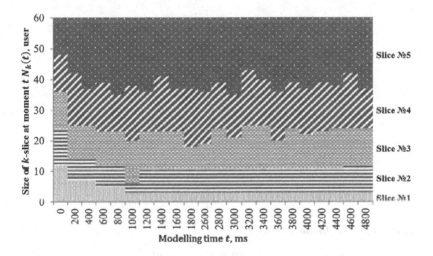

Fig. 4. Slice dynamics at $\Delta = 200$ ms

4   Queuing Model for Two Slices

4.1   Model Description

Here, we describe the model with two operators ($K = 2$) in the form of queuing system. Let N – the total size of slices, then M_1 and M_2 are sizes of the corresponding buffer. So, a three-dimensional Markov process represents as:

$$\mathbf{X(t)} = (N_1(t), N_2(t), M_1(t), M_2(t))_{t \geq 0}, \tag{7}$$

where $N_k(t)$ – the total number of users on the slice of k-operator at time t. $M_k(t)$ – the total number of users of k-operator in the buffer at t.There are two buffers in the system, m_1 and m_2. The number of users of the first slice is n_1 and the second slice is n_2 (see Table 2). Consequently, the state-space representation for this system is:

$$\mathcal{X} = \{(n_1, n_2, m_1, m_2) : n_1 \geq 0, n_2 \geq 0, m_1 \geq 0, m_2 \geq 0;$$
$$(n_1, n_2, 0, 0) : n_1 + n_2 \leq N; \qquad (8)$$
$$(n_1, n_2, m_1, m_2) : n_1 + n_2 = N, m_1 \leq M_1, m_2 \leq M_2\},$$

Let λ_1 and λ_2 is the Poisson arrival rate of the first and second type users. The minimum guaranteed bit rate for the user we denote by b_{min} and the average exponential file size by s_1 and s_2. Users can departure from the queue due to impatience with exponential reneging rate with means γ_1 and γ_2. The dynamic reallocation of resources is indicated by dashed line on the device. Figure 5 shows the scheme of the queuing system.

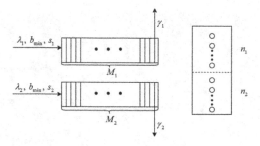

Fig. 5. Queuing model for two slices

4.2   Infinitesimal Generator

We write the system of equilibrium equations in a matrix form $\boldsymbol{p}^T = \mathbf{A} \cdot \mathbf{0}$, where $\mathbf{A}$ – infinitesimal generator, $\boldsymbol{p}^T$ – row-vector of stationary probability states. The equation is solved together with the normalizing condition $\sum_i p_i(x) = 1$, where $p_i(x)$, $x \in \mathcal{X}$ – various states of queuing system. To express the formulas that show the effectiveness of the system, it is necessary to create a infinitesimal generator. The simulation showed that a system with two slices has 15 states. Table 3 presents the system states in general, where n_1 and n_2 are the number of users allocating corresponding slice, the m_1 and m_2 are the number of users in corresponding buffer.

4.3   Performance Characteristics

In order to evaluate the effectiveness of slicing, we introduce the following indicators:

1. The average number of users on slices:
   $\overline{L_k} = \sum_{(n_1, n_2, m_1, m_2) \in \mathcal{X}} n_k p(n_1, n_2, m_1, m_2)$, where $\mathcal{X}$ – space-state (see Formula 8)

Table 2. System parameters for queuing model

Parameter	Description
$K = 2$	Number of slices (operators, types of users, types of files)
C	Aggregate bit rate that could be reached on the available resources (PRBs) for $K = 2$ slices [bps]
b_{min}	Minimum guaranteed bit rate to transfer one file [bps]
$N = \frac{C}{b_{min}}$	Total size of $K = 2$ slices (i.e. maximum number of users that could transfer files simultaneously) [user]
M_k	Size of k-buffer (i.e. maximum number of k-users waiting for file transfer) [user]
λ_k	Poisson arrival rate of requests for file transfer from k-users [1/s]
s_k	Average exponential file size from k-users [bit]
γ_k	Exponential reneging rate for k-users (waiting users are impatient and decide to interrupt the waiting process with the reneging rate) [1/s]
n_k	Number of k-users allocating the k-slice resources [user]
m_k	Number of k-users waiting for file transfer in k-buffer [user]

2. The average number of users in the buffer:
$\overline{Q_k} = \sum_{(n_1,n_2,m_1,m_2)\in \mathcal{X}} m_k p(n_1, n_2, m_1, m_2)$.

3. Blocking probability:
$\overline{B_k} = \sum_{(n_1,n_2,m_1,m_2)\in \mathcal{B}} p(n_1, n_2, m_1, m_2)$, where $\mathcal{B} = \{(n_1, n_2, m_1, m_2) : (\sum_{k=1}^{K} n_k = N) \cap (m_k > M_k)\}$.

4.4 Numerical Example

We present numerical simulation results for the following initial data: $N_1 = N_2 = 5$ [users], $M_1 = M_2 = 10$ [users], $C = 10$ [Mbps], $b_{min} = 1$ [Kbps], λ_1 from 1 to 10 [users/min], $\lambda_2 = 5$ [users/min], $\gamma_1 = 0.1$, $\gamma_2 = 0.1$, $s_1 = s_2 = 1$ [b]. Models with a strict resource sharing and with dynamic slicing were considered.

As we can see (Fig. 6) for a model with dynamic resource sharing, the average number of users for each slice will vary depending on the needs of the system. For a model with strict resource sharing, such a re-slicing will not occur and the maximum number of users for each slice will be fixed.

It can be seen from the Fig. 7 that due to slicing, the number of users in the buffer in the model with dynamic slicing of resources will tend to balance. This

Table 3. States of transition rate of a system with dynamic segmentation.

State	Intensity	Comment
$(n_1 + 1, n_2, 0, 0)$	λ_1	There is no queue. User of the 1st operator comes to the 1st slice.
$(n_1, n_2 + 1, 0, 0)$	λ_2	There is no queue. User of the 2nd operator comes to the 2nd slice.
$(n_1 - 1, n_2, 0, 0)$	$\frac{C}{s_1}$	There is no queue. The user of 1st operator is served.
$(n_1, n_2 - 1, 0, 0)$	$\frac{C}{s_2}$	There is no queue. The user of 2nd operator is served.
$(n_1, n_2, m_1 + 1, m_2)$	λ_1	All resources are busy. The user of 1st operator has entered the queue.
$(n_1, n_2, m_1, m_2 + 1)$	λ_2	All resources are busy. The user of 2nd operator has entered the queue.
$(n_1, n_2, m_1 - 1, m_2)$	$\frac{C}{s_1} + m_1\gamma_1$	On slices users of two operators. In the queue of each there are users. 1) The user was served. In its place there is a user from the 1st queue. 2) Impatient user.
$(n_1, n_2, m_1, m_2 - 1)$	$\frac{C}{s_2} + m_2\gamma_2$	On slices users of two operator. In the queue of each there are users. 1) The user was served. In its place there is a user from the 2nd queue. 2) Impatient user.
$(n_1, n_2, m_1 - 1, 0)$	$\frac{C}{s_1} + m_1\gamma_1$	On slices users of two operator. The 2nd type queue is empty. 1) The user is served from the queue of the 1st type. 2) Impatient user.
$(n_1, n_2, 0, m_2 - 1)$	$\frac{C}{s_2} + m_2\gamma_2$	On slices users of two operator. The 1st type queue is empty. 1) The user is served from the queue of the 2nd type. 2) Impatient user.
$(n_1 - 1, n_2 + 1, 0, m_2 - 1)$	$\frac{C}{s_1}$	On slices users of two operator. The 1st queue is empty. The user of 1st operator was served, the user of 2nd operator was received on the slice, since its queue isn't empty.
$(n_1 + 1, n_2 - 1, m_1 - 1, 0)$	$\frac{C}{s_2}$	On slices users of two operator. The 2nd queue is empty. The user of 2nd operator was served, the user of 1st operator was received on the slice, since its queue isn't empty.
$(n_1 - 1, n_2 + 1, m_1, m_2 - 1)$	$\frac{C}{s_1}$	On slices users of two operator. In the queue of each there are users. The user of 1st operator is serviced and user of 2nd operator comes in its place from the queue.
$(n_1 + 1, n_2 - 1, m_1 - 1, m_2)$	$\frac{C}{s_2}$	On slices users of two operator. In the queue of each there are users. The user of 2nd operator is serviced and user of 1st operator comes in its place from the queue

phenomenon occurs due to the user selection algorithm for service. In a model with strict resource sharing, the number of users will depend on the maximum buffer capacity.

The blocking probability for a model with dynamic resource sharing (Fig. 8) for users of the first and second operators will increase when the intensity of the arrival of the first operator users increases, since resources will be re-slicing

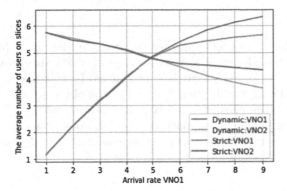

Fig. 6. The average number of users on slices.

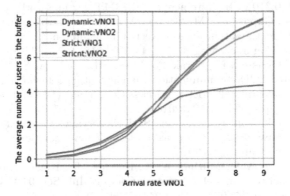

Fig. 7. The average number of users in the buffer.

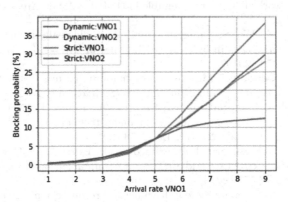

Fig. 8. Blocking probability.

between the two operators in a timely manner. However, for a model with strict resource sharing, re-slicing will not occur and, accordingly, the blocking probability in the first operator will be noticeably higher than in the second.

5   Conclusion

The Network Slicing concept plays a key-role in the development of fifth-generation networks. However, it involves a number of issues related to the fair and efficient sharing of resources between slices. In this paper, we have proposed the method of dynamic slicing, based on the obtained slicing performance indicators, the lengths of slicing intervals are determined. As a special case of network configuration, a mathematical model is constructed in the form of a queuing system for two slices, formulas for calculating performance indicators are obtained.

References

1. ITU-T Rec. Y.0.3101 - Requirements of the IMT-2020 network, January 2018
2. Solomitckii, D., Gapeyenko, M., Semkin, V., Andreev, S., Koucheryavy, Y.: Technologies for efficient amateur drone detection in 5G millimeter-wave cellular infrastructure. IEEE Commun. Mag. **56**(1), 43–50 (2018)
3. Pyattaev, A., Johnsson, K., Surak, A., Florea, R., Andreev, S., Koucheryavy, Y.: Network-assisted D2D communications: implementing a technology prototype for cellular traffic offloading. In: IEEE Wireless Communications and Networking Conference, WCNC, pp. 3266–3271 (2014)
4. Pyattaev, A., Johnsson, K., Andreev, S., Koucheryavy, Y.: Proximity-based data offloading via network assisted device-to-device communications. In: IEEE Vehicular Technology Conference (2013)
5. Muhizi, S., Ateya, A.A., Muthanna, A., Kirichek, R., Koucheryavy, A.: A novel slice-oriented network model. Commun. Comput. Inf. Sci. **919**, 421–431 (2018). https://doi.org/10.1007/978-3-319-99447-5_36
6. Ni, J., Lin, X., Shen, X.S.: Efficient and secure service-oriented authentication supporting network slicing for 5G-enabled IoT. IEEE J. Sel. Areas Commun. **36**(3), 644–657 (2018)
7. Wu, D., Zhang, Z., Wu, S., Yang, J., Wang, R.: Biologically inspired resource allocation for network slices in 5G-enabled Internet of Things. IEEE Internet Things J. **6**(6), 9266–9279 (2019)
8. Trivisonno, R., Condoluci, M., An, X., Mahmoodi, T.: mIoT slice for 5G systems: design and performance evaluation. Sensors (Switzerland) **18**(2), 635 (2018)
9. Afolabi, I., Taleb, T., Samdanis, K., Ksentini, A., Flinck, H.: Network slicing and softwarization: a survey on principles, enabling technologies, and solutions. IEEE Commun. Surv. Tutorials **20**(3), 2429–2453 (2018)
10. Popovski, P., Trillingsgaard, K.F., Simeone, O., Durisi, G.: 5G wireless network slicing for eMBB, URLLC, and mMTC: a communication-theoretic view. IEEE Access **6**, 55765–55779 (2018)
11. Li, R., et al.: Deep reinforcement learning for resource management in network slicing. IEEE Access **6**, 74429–74441 (2018)
12. Leconte, M., Paschos, G.S., Mertikopoulos, P., Kozat, U.C.: A resource allocation framework for network slicing. In: IEEE INFOCOM, April 2018, pp. 2177–2185 (2018)
13. Caballero, P., Banchs, A., De Veciana, G., Costa-Perez, X.: Network slicing games: enabling customization in multi-tenant mobile networks. IEEE/ACM Trans. Netw. **27**(2), 662–675 (2019)

14. Jia, Y., Tian, H., Fan, S., Zhao, P., Zhao, K.: Bankruptcy game based resource allocation algorithm for 5G cloud-RAN slicing. In: IEEE Wireless Communications and Networking Conference, April 2018, WCNC, pp. 1–6 (2018)
15. Lee, Y.L., Loo, J., Chuah, T.C., Wang, L.-C.: Dynamic network slicing for multi-tenant heterogeneous cloud radio access networks. IEEE Trans. Wireless Commun. **17**(4), 2146–2161 (2018)
16. Raza, M.R., Fiorani, M., Rostami, A., Ohlen, P., Wosinska, L., Monti, P.: Dynamic slicing approach for multi-Tenant 5G transport networks. J. Optical Commun. Netw. **10**(1), A77–A90 (2018)
17. Dighriri, M., Alfoudi, A.S.D., Lee, G.M., Baker, T., Pereira, R.: Resource allocation scheme in 5G network slices. In: 32nd IEEE International Conference on Advanced Information Networking and Applications Workshops, WAINA, pp. 275–280 (2018)
18. Tayyaba, S.K., et al.: 5G vehicular network resource management for improving radio access through machine learning. IEEE Access **8**, 6792–6800 (2020)
19. Campolo, C., Fontes, R.R., Molinaro, A., Rothenberg, C.E., Iera, A.: Slicing on the road: enabling the automotive vertical through 5G network softwarization. Sensors (Switzerland) **18**(12), 4435 (2018)
20. Chekired, D.A., Togou, M.A., Khoukhi, L., Ksentini, A.: 5G-slicing-enabled scalable SDN core network: toward an ultra-low latency of autonomous driving service. IEEE J. Sel. Areas Commun. **37**(8), 1769–1782 (2019)
21. Han, B., Sciancalepore, V., Feng, D., Costa-Perez, X., Schotten, H.D.: A utility-driven multi-queue admission control solution for network slicing. In: IEEE INFO-COM, April 2019, pp. 55–63 (2019)
22. Markova, E., Adou, Y., Ivanova, D., Golskaia, A., Samouylov, K.: Queue with retrial group for modeling best effort traffic with minimum bit rate guarantee transmission under network slicing. In: Vishnevskiy, V.M., Samouylov, K.E., Kozyrev, D.V. (eds.) DCCN 2019. LNCS, vol. 11965, pp. 432–442. Springer, Cham (2019). https://doi.org/10.1007/078 3 030 36614-8_33
23. Vlaskina, A., Polyakov, N., Gudkova, I.: Modeling and performance analysis of elastic traffic with minimum rate guarantee transmission under network slicing. In: Galinina, O., Andreev, S., Balandin, S., Koucheryavy, Y. (eds.) NEW2AN/ruSMART -2019. LNCS, vol. 11660, pp. 621–634. Springer, Cham (2019). https://doi.org/10.1007/978-3-030-30859-9_54
24. Ageev, K., Garibyan, A., Golskaya, A., Gaidamaka, Y., Sopin, E., Samouylov, K., Correia, L.M.: Modelling of virtual radio resources slicing in 5G networks. Commun. Comput. Inf. Sci. **1109**, 150–161 (2019). https://doi.org/10.1007/978-3-030-33388-1_13
25. Caballero, P., Banchs, A., De Veciana, G., Costa-Perez, X., Azcorra, A.: Network slicing for guaranteed rate services: admission control and resource allocation games. IEEE Trans. Wireless Commun. **17**(10), 6419–6432 (2018)

Space Division Multiple Access Performance Evaluation in Ultra-Dense 5G Networks

Vadim Davydov[1], Grigoriy Fokin[2], Vitaly Lazarev[2(✉)], and Sergey Makeev[1]

[1] Peter the Great Saint Petersburg Polytechnic University, Saint-Petersburg, Russia
davydov_vadim66@mail.ru, st_makeev@mail.ru
[2] The Bonch-Bruevich SPbSUT, Saint-Petersburg, Russia
grihafokin@gmail.com, laviol.94@gmail.com

Abstract. The fifth-generation (5G) wireless networks will utilize higher frequency mmWave bands with wider bandwidth to increase system capacity in Ultra-Dense Network (UDN) scenarios. Massive multiple-input multiple-output (mMIMO) and beamforming (BF) technology have attracted much attention to compensate for path-loss at higher frequency bands. Using new protocols and procedures, e.g. spatial beam management, motivates to evaluate 3D Beamforming (3DBF) and Full-Dimensional MIMO (FD-MIMO) performance for Space Division Multiple Access (SDMA) with spatial separation of user equipment (UE) in UDN 5G wireless networks. Intelligent SDMA should take into account UE location and include preliminary positioning procedures to steer the transmitted signal of interest (SOI) toward the desired direction and simultaneously, avoiding signal of no interest (SNOI) transmission or reception from the unwanted direction. The purpose of this work is to evaluate the performance of interference suppression rate (ISR) as a relation of SOI to SNOI levels in 5G UDN using MISO (Multiple Input Single Output) when Base Station (BS) implements Adaptive Beamforming (AB) for two neighboring UE angular and distance separation scenarios. SOI to SNOI rate is evaluated for linear and planar antenna array patterns with several elements and contribute to the development of recommendations for UE separation in 5G UDN for spatial multiplexing and SDMA.

Keywords: Ultra-dense radio networks · Beamforming · Antenna pattern · Preliminary positioning

1 Introduction

5G wireless networks introduce several enabling technologies, among which millimeter-wave (mmWave) transmission and three-dimensional (3DBF) beamforming are expected to solve challenges for increasing demands in data rate and a number of users.

On the physical layer, smart antenna utilization in RAN should consider following: adaptive beamforming includes creating and controlling the beam with a different configuration of antenna arrays to focus energy in the desired direction; antenna training protocols to align transmitter and receiver beam direction pair; angle of arrival estimation for the transmitter to point at the receiver direction [1].

© Springer Nature Switzerland AG 2020
O. Galinina et al. (Eds.): NEW2AN 2020/ruSMART 2020, LNCS 12525, pp. 86–98, 2020.
https://doi.org/10.1007/978-3-030-65726-0_8

On the MAC layer, smart antenna utilization in RAN should consider following: spatial beam patterns formation for successful SDMA support; directional MAC protocols, including directional CSMA protocols with RTS/CTS transmissions in directional and omnidirectional modes and TDMA channel time allocation [1].

Beamforming is a signal processing method that generates directional antenna beam patterns using multiple antennas at the transmitter [2]. From the layer of the wireless network, its ability to steer the transmitted signal of interest (SOI) toward the desired direction and simultaneously, avoiding signal of no interest (SNOI) transmission or reception from unwanted direction enables interference suppression and thus, leads to spatial multiplexing or space division multiple access (SDMA), which is of great importance for next-generation 5G ultra-dense network (UDN) architecture [2].

Comparing the models for beamforming control schemes on the plane, where beam radiation pattern is adapted only in the horizontal plane, and termed two-dimensional beamforming (2DBF), 3DBF utilizes beam radiation pattern adaptation in both elevation and azimuth planes to provide more degrees of freedom in supporting users. Higher user capacity, less intercell interference, higher energy efficiency, improved coverage, and increased spectral efficiency are some of the advantages of 3DBF [2].

The mathematical framework for elevation beamforming with full dimensional MIMO architecture in 5G systems is proposed in [3]. Transmit beamforming technique for MISO downlink systems with three-dimensional antennas where a transmit antenna is determined in three-dimensional coordinates is investigated in [4]. However, works [3, 4] consider only a single-user case and do not take into account interference evaluation. 3D beamforming scheme based on the spatial distribution of user location is proposed in [5] and provides a 3D beamforming model where beam steering depends on the random spatial distribution of UE. In contrast to the random spatial distribution of UE, it is obvious, that preliminary positioning of UE could substantially increase spatial multiplexing and SDMA network capabilities [6–10]. Moreover, distortions of the antenna pattern shape can lead to significant changes in the direction-finding of UE [11–14]. Thus, the aim of this work is to account for linear and planar antenna array during performance evaluation of interference suppression rate (ISR) as a relation of SOI to SNOI levels in 5G UDN for two neighboring UE with preliminary angular and distance positioning and contribute to the development of recommendations for UE spatial multiplexing and SDMA.

The material in the paper organized in the following order. Mathematical models of linear and planar antenna arrays, essential for ISR performance evaluation, are presented in the second part. Direction of arrival (DOA) estimation as a part of preliminary positioning and adaptive beamforming cases in 5G UDN are formalized in the third part. UE angular and distance separation scenarios for interference suppression in 5G UDN simulation are presented in the fourth part. Finally, we draw conclusions about UE spatial multiplexing and SDMA in the fifth part.

2 Mathematical Models of Antenna Arrays

In this part mathematical models of linear and planar antenna arrays, essential for ISR performance evaluation, are presented. As shown in [14], it is more convenient to use planar antenna arrays for wireless communications, since linear arrays are not intended for scanning in 3D space. Also, planar arrays can form a beam in any direction: by θ (elevation) and ϕ (azimuth). However, linear arrays are a well-studied and convenient framework to compare results, thus we consider basic principles and expressions for linear and planar antenna system (AS) arrays. For all of the array types, we will denote the array factor (AF) metric, which refers to pattern multiplication and is a function of the antenna height and the observation angle [14].

2.1 Linear Antenna Array System

The first of AS array types we will consider a linear AS (LAS), consisting of M (even) identical elements with uniform spacing, where all elements are positioned symmetrically along the y-axis, as shown in Fig. 1, and the AF for this type of array is [14]:

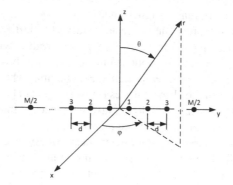

Fig. 1. Linear array with elements along the y-axis.

$$(AF)_M = w_1 e^{+j(1/2)\psi_1} + w_2 e^{+j(3/2)\psi_2} + \ldots + w_{M/2} e^{+j[(M-1)/2]\psi_{M/2}}$$
$$+ w_1 e^{-j(1/2)\psi_1} + w_2 e^{-j(3/2)\psi_2} + \ldots + w_{M/2} e^{-j[(M-1)/2]\psi_{M/2}} \qquad (1)$$

Normalizing the expression (1), the AF for an even number of elements with uniform spacing along the y-axis reduces to:

$$(AF)_M = \sum_{n=1}^{M/2} w_n \cos[(2n-1)\psi_n] \qquad (2)$$

where

$$\psi_n = \frac{\pi d}{\lambda} \sin\theta \sin\phi + \beta_n \qquad (3)$$

In (2) and (3), w_n and β_n represent, respectively, the amplitude and phase excitations of the individual elements. The amplitude coefficients w_n control the shape of the pattern and the major-to-minor lobe level while the phase excitations control primarily the scanning capabilities of the array [14].

2.2 Planar Antenna Array System

As we mentioned before, LAS array lacks the ability to scan in 3D space, and since it is necessary for portable devices to scan the main beam in any direction of θ (elevation) and ϕ (azimuth), planar antenna system (PAS) arrays are more efficient in such cases. Let us assume that we have M × N identical elements (M and N are even), with uniform spacing positioned symmetrically in the XY-plane as shown in Fig. 2.

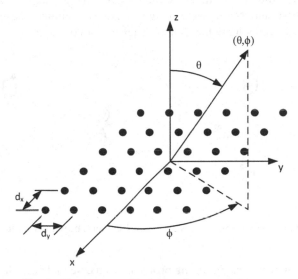

Fig. 2. Planar array with uniformly spaced elements

The AF for this planar array with its maximum along θ_0, ϕ_0, for an even number of elements in each direction can be written as:

$$[AF(\theta, \phi)]_{M \times N} = 4 \sum_{m=1}^{M/2} \sum_{n=1}^{N/2} w_{mm} \cos[(2m-1)u] \cos[(2n-1)v] \qquad (4)$$

where

$$u = \frac{\pi d_x}{\lambda}(\sin\theta \cos\phi - \sin\theta_0 \cos\phi_0) \qquad (5)$$

$$v = \frac{\pi d_y}{\lambda}(\sin\theta \sin\phi - \sin\theta_0 \sin\phi_0) \qquad (6)$$

In (4), w_{mn} is the amplitude excitation of the individual element. For separable distributions $w_{mn} = w_m w_n$. However, for nonseparable distributions, $w_{mn} \neq w_m w_n$. This means that for an M × N planar array, only M + N excitation values need to be computed from a separable distribution, while M × N values are needed from a nonseparable distribution [14]. Considered mathematical models of linear and planar antenna arrays will be uses further for ISR performance evaluation in the fourth section.

3   DOA and Adaptive Beamforming Scenarios in 5G UDN

Adaptive beamforming (AB) is one of the main tools of the 5G radio networks and includes beamforming and control procedures, adaptive antenna systems (AAS) training protocols, and DoA signal angle/direction determination methods [15, 16].

AAS training protocols with adaptive beamforming are designed to solve the problem of preliminary beam alignment of the transmitting and receiving radio stations and are a feature of the directional radio communications (Fig. 3a). In contrast to non-directional receptions and transmissions (Fig. 3b), AAS preliminary beam alignment of the transmitting and receiving radios is a prerequisite for communication sessions.

a)   b)

Fig. 3. Preliminary beamforming a) with beam alignment, b) without beam alignment.

DOA together with the AAS training protocols is an essential procedure for adaptive beamforming. Preliminary DoA procedures can be helpful to the radio communications organization both in the presence of LOS and in the absence of line of sight (NLOS); in the last case, the beams of the receiving devices work with reflected signals. The objectives of a digital signal processing unit are to estimate: a) the direction of arrival (DOA) of all incoming signals; b) the appropriate weights to steer the maximum radiation of the AP toward the SOI and to place nulls towards the SNOI.

AAS with beam switching is the evolution of traditional sectorized antennas and represents an alternative option of directional radio communication with partially over-lapping sectors [6]. In AS with beam switching, transmission and reception are carried out using predefined AP from a finite set that is implemented in current AS. In contrast to adaptive AS with the capabilities of the current situational beamforming based on CSI, SOI, and SNOI parameters, both optimistic and pessimistic scenarios are possible in AS with beam switching. In the optimistic scenario (Fig. 4a), the user equipment (UE), which is the receiver of the useful SOI signal, is located at the maximum of the AP of the switched beam, and other UEs, which are SNOIs, are located in some local minima of the switched beam. In the pessimistic scenario (Fig. 4b), the UE, which is the receiver of the useful SOI signal, is shifted in azimuth from the maximum of the AP of the switched beam, while other UEs, which are SNOI, are at the local maxima of the side lobes of the switched beam, which causes an increased level of intra-system interference. The advantage of AS with beam switching over adaptive systems is the lower overhead of the communication protocol based on situational parameters CSI, SOI, and SNOI [14].

AS with beam switching can significantly increase the budget of the mmWave radio channel and can be used when the rapid collection of CSI, SOI, and SNOI parameters is difficult.

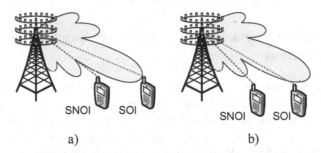

a)   b)

Fig. 4. Radio communication directions in antenna systems with beam switching when a) SOI is in a local maximum of AP and SNOI is in a local minimum of AP, b) SOI is not in the main lobe maximum of AP and SNOI is in a side lobe maximum of AP

Massive MIMO is the evolution of MIMO systems with the number of elements significantly exceeding the number of subscriber terminals in the coverage area of a BS or UE. In mMIMO antenna arrays, the number of antenna elements can reach 128, 256, or more. With a certain configuration of the elements of the antenna array, spatial 3D diagram formation is possible both horizontally and vertically and we can talk about the Full Dimensional MIMO systems, that includes beam steering in space (Fig. 3) (Fig. 5).

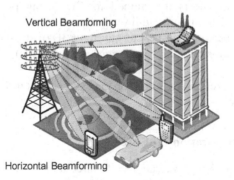

Fig. 5. 3D vertical and horizontal beamforming in FD-MIMO systems

When operating in spatial multiplexing mode and corresponding processing on the transmitting and receiving sides, mMIMO systems can increase the radio link bandwidth by a factor comparable to the number of antenna elements, as well as implement multiuser spatial detection of signals from different devices [15, 16].

4   UE Separation Scenarios for Interference Suppression in 5G UDN Simulation

As mentioned before, to determine how to separate UE in 5G UDN for SDMA, we need to analyze the different initial conditions that can be set on a case-by-case basis. In [17–19] different potential performance requirements of the positioning use cases are listed. For example, for augmented reality value of spatial angle resolution is 10° (for 2 m/s velocity), but for UAV connections spatial angle resolution is 2°. (for 0.5 m/s velocity). Also, in [20] angle accuracy better than 5° for the 3-Dimension direction of travel is set. Previously, in [12] it was shown that for a given distance between UE (i.e. a cell radius), a certain angular accuracy of beamforming is achieved, but paying attention to UDN concept it is more convenient to use minimum requirements, performed in the ITU-R report: 1 000 000 devices per km^2 [18]. Also, in [21] it is shown that the cell radius in UDN networks can be greatly reduced, down to values less than 100 m. For the purpose of recommendations development for UE separation in 5G UDN for spatial multiplexing and SDMA, let us set up the three main approaches for investigation:

1. An azimuth angle between UE is determined for 2D (using preliminary AOA/DOA, positioning information and angle separation requirements);
2. A distance between UE is determined for 2D (using preliminary positioning information and IMT minimum requirements);
3. An elevation angle between UE is determined for 3D (using preliminary AoA/DoA, positioning information and angle separation requirements);

Analysis of all the cases above is built on the ISR using SOI/SNOI estimation based on AF for a 2-user case.

4.1   Azimuth Angle Separation 2D Case

Using requirements in [19, 20] we can specify three main cases for the UDN concept using angle separation: 2°, 5°, and 10°. The assumed scenario for all angle separation cases is shown in Fig. 6. Model results for 2D using LAS array are presented in Tables 1 and 2 (Fig. 7).

Analysis of the azimuth angle separation 2D case shows that in the worst-case of 2° UE separation minimum number of AS elements are 32 to provide required ISR.

4.2   Azimuth Distance Separation 2D Case

Using requirements in [18] we can specify three main cases for the UDN concept: distance is below 1 m, is equal 1 m, and above 1 m. It was investigated, that average

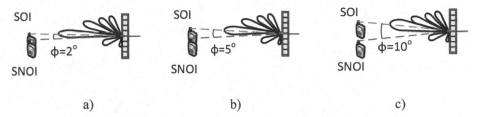

Fig. 6. UDN angle separation 2D case illustration when the angle between UE is a) 2°, b) 5°, c) 10°.

Table 1. Antenna factor for SOI, SNOI and total SOI/SNOI in 2D for azimuth angle $= 2°$ between UE ($d = 0.5\lambda$, $\mu = 0.01$, 500 samples, AF null $= -40$ dB, w/o AWGN)

Number of AA elements	Azimuth angle between UE, deg		
	SOI, dB	SNOI, dB	SOI/SNOI, dB
8	−3.3	−6.8	3.5
16	−4.5	−26.5	22
32	−1	−40	39
64	0	−40	>40
128	0	−40	>40

Table 2. SOI/SNOI in 2D for different angles between UE ($d - 0.5\lambda$, $\mu - 0.01$, 500 samples, AF null $= -40$ dB, w/o AWGN)

Number of AA elements	Azimuth angle between UE, deg		
	2	5	10
8	3.5	17.7	39.6
16	22	39.6	>40
32	39	>40	>40
64	>40	>40	>40
128	>40	>40	>40

intersite distance (ISD) for UDNs is reduced to around or less than 100 m in contrast to the 400 m distance in the traditional 4th-generation (4G) deployment [21]. For our purposes, we will take a radius of 20 m, which is near to the femtocell radius of 4G and can be one of the frequent cases for 5G. The assumed scenario for all distance cases is shown in Fig. 8. Model results for 2D using LAS array are presented in Tables 3 and 4.

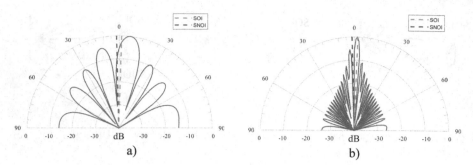

Fig. 7. Beamforming pattern for 2D angle separation case (2°) with antenna elements number a) N = 8, b) N = 32

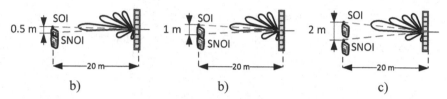

Fig. 8. UDN distance separation 2D case illustration when the distance between UE is a) 0.5 m, b) 1 m, c) 2 m.

Table 3. Antenna factor for SOI, SNOI and total SOI/SNOI in 2D for distance = 1 m between UE (d = 0.5λ, μ = 0.01, 500 samples, AF null = −40 dB, w/o AWGN)

Number of AA elements	Angle between UE, deg		
	SOI, dB	SNOI, dB	SOI/SNOI, dB
8	−3.6	−16	12.4
16	−1	−40	39
32	0	−40	>40
64	0	−40	>40
128	0	−40	>40

Analysis of the distance separation 2D case shows that in the worst-case scenario of 0.5 m UE separation minimum number of AS elements are 32 to provide required ISR.

Table 4. SOI/SNOI in 2D for different distances between UE (d = 0.5λ, μ = 0.01, 500 samples, AF null = −40 dB, w/o AWGN)

Number of AA elements	Distance between UE, m		
	0.5	1	2
8	3.9	12.4	11.1
16	20.8	39	>40
32	39	>40	>40
64	>40	>40	>40
128	>40	>40	>40

4.3 Elevation Angle Separation 3D Case

To evaluate the case with the elevation angle separation, we use the model shown in Fig. 9. With a fixed azimuth, based on the requirements in [19, 20], using the cell radius from a previous case and antenna array height that equals 8 m (e.g. billboards and lampposts), three elevation angle cases are considered: elevation difference equals 2°, 5°, and 10°. The assumed scenario for 10 degrees elevation angle separation is shown in Fig. 10. Model results for 3D using PAS array are presented in Tables 5 and 6.

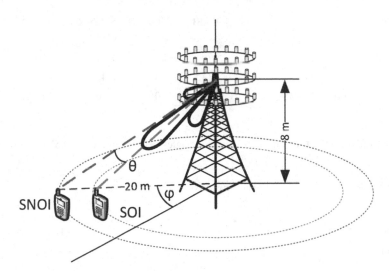

Fig. 9. UDN elevation angle separation 3D case illustration.

Analysis of the elevation angle separation 3D case shows that in the worst-case scenario of 2° UE separation the minimum number of antenna elements is 256 to provide required ISR.

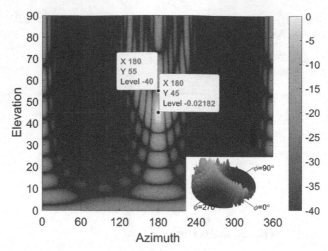

Fig. 10. Beamforming pattern for 3D elevation angle separation case (10°) with antenna elements number N = 256

Table 5. Antenna factor for SOI, SNOI and total SOI/SNOI in 3D for elevation angle = 10° between UE (d = 0.5λ, μ = 0.01, 500 samples, AF null = −40 dB, w/o AWGN)

Number of AA elements	Elevation angle between UE, deg		
	SOI, dB	SNOI, dB	SOI/SNOI, dB
(4 × 4) 16	−5.76	−21.01	15.3
(8 × 8) 64	−2.145	−40	>40
(16 × 16) 256	0	−40	>40

Table 6. SOI/SNOI in 3D for different elevation angles between UE (d = 0.5λ, μ = 0.01, 500 samples, AF null = −40 dB, w/o AWGN)

Number of AA elements	Angle between UE, deg		
	2	5	10
(4 × 4) 16	1.0	5.1	15.3
(8 × 8) 64	12.5	>40	>40
(16 × 16) 256	>40	>40	>40

5 Conclusion

In this paper, we investigated UE angular and distance separation scenarios for interference suppression in 5G UDN. Spatial separation cases were formalized and various antenna array models and 5G UDN scenarios were considered. Simulation results show, that in worst-scenario cases 32 antenna elements for linear antenna array and 256 antenna elements for planar antenna array are required for assured interference suppression, especially, spatial multiplexing and SDMA capabilities with 2° azimuth/elevation angular and 0.5 m distance UE separation using FD-MIMO are verified for 5G UDN scenarios.

References

1. Agiwal, M., Roy, A., Saxena, N.: Next generation 5G wireless networks: a comprehensive survey. IEEE Commun. Surv.Tutorials **18**(3), 1617–1655 (2016)
2. Razavizadeh, S.M., Ahn, M., Lee, I.: Three-dimensional beamforming: a new enabling technology for 5G wireless networks. IEEE Signal Process. Mag. **31**(6), 94–101 (2014)
3. Nadeem, Q., Kammoun, A., Alouini, M.: Elevation beamforming with full dimension MIMO architectures in 5G systems: a tutorial. IEEE Commun. Surv. Tutorials **21**(4), 3238–3273 (2019)
4. Wookbong, L., Lee, S., Kong, H-B., Lee, I.: 3D beamforming designs for single user MISO systems. In: 2013 IEEE Global Communications Conference (GLOBECOM), Atlanta, GA, pp. 3914–3919 (2013)
5. Rachad, J., Nasri, R., Decreusefond, L.: A 3D beamforming scheme based on the spatial distribution of user locations. In: 2019 IEEE 30th Annual International Symposium on Personal, Indoor and Mobile Radio Communications (PIMRC), Istanbul, Turkey, 1–7, (2019)
6. Stepanets, I., Fokin, G., Müller, A.: Beamforming techniques performance evaluation for 5G massive MIMO Systems. In: CEUR Workshop Proceedings, vol. 2348, pp. 57–68 (2019)
7. Lazarev, V., Fokin, G.: Positioning performance requirements evaluation for grid model in ultra-dense network scenario. In: 2020 Systems of Signals Generating and Processing in the Field of on Board Communications, Moscow, Russia, pp. 1–6 (2020)
8. Lazarev, V., Fokin, G., Stepanets, I.: Positioning for location-aware beamforming in 5 g ultra-dense networks. In: 2019 IEEE International Conference on Electrical Engineering and Photonics (EExPolytech), St. Petersburg, Russia, pp. 136–139 (2019)
9. Fokin, G., Lazarev., V.: Location accuracy of radio emission sources for beamforming in ultra-dense radio networks. In: 2019 IEEE Microwave Theory and Techniques in Wireless Communications (MTTW), Riga, Latvia, pp. 9–12 (2019)
10. Fokin, G., Lazarev, V.: 3D location accuracy estimation of radio emission sources for beamforming in ultra-dense radio networks. In: 2019 11th International Congress on Ultra Modern Telecommunications and Control Systems and Workshops (ICUMT), Dublin, Ireland, pp. 1–6 (2019)
11. Sinitsyn, M., Podstrigaev, A., Smolyakov, A., Davydov, V.: Analysis of the sea surface influence on the shape of microwave spiral antenna radiation pattern. In: 2019 Proceedings of the 2019 Antennas Design and Measurement International Conference, St. Petersburg, Russia, pp. 72–74 (2019)
12. Podstrigaev, A.S., Smolyakov, A.V., Davydov, V.V., Myazin, N.S., Grebenikova, N.M., Davydov, R.V.: New method for determining the probability of signals overlapping for the estimation of the stability of the radio monitoring systems in a complex signal environment. In: Galinina, O., Andreev, S., Balandin, S., Koucheryavy, Y. (eds.) NEW2AN/ruSMART -2019. LNCS, vol. 11660, pp. 525–533. Springer, Cham (2019). https://doi.org/10.1007/978-3-030-30859-9_45
13. Podstrigaev, A.S., Smolyakov, A.V., Davydov, V.V., Myazin, N.S., Slobodyan, M.G.: Features of the development of transceivers for information and communication systems considering the distribution of radar operating frequencies in the frequency range. In: Galinina, O., Andreev, S., Balandin, S., Koucheryavy, Y. (eds.) NEW2AN/ruSMART -2018. LNCS, vol. 11118, pp. 509–515. Springer, Cham (2018). https://doi.org/10.1007/978-3-030-01168-0_45

14. Balanis, C.: Antenna Theory, 4th edn. Wiley-Interscience, Hoboken (2016)
15. Rappaport, T., et al.: Broadband millimeter-wave propagation measurements and models using adaptive-beam antennas for outdoor urban cellular communications. IEEE Trans. Antennas Propag. **61**(4), 1850–1859 (2013)
16. Rajagopal, S.: Beam broadening for phased antenna arrays using multibeam subarrays. In: 2012 IEEE International Conference on Communications (ICC), Ottawa, ON, pp. 3637–3642 (2012)
17. Report ITU-R M.2410-0: Minimum requirements related to technical performance for IMT-2020 radio interface(s) (2017)
18. TR 22.872 V16.1.0: (Study on positioning use cases; Stage 1, Release 16), 3GPP (2018)
19. TS 22.261 V17.1.0: (Service requirements for the 5G system, Stage 1, Release 17) 3GPP (2020)
20. Wei, Y., Hwang, S.-H.: Optimization of cell size in ultra-dense networks with multiattribute user types and different frequency bands. Wireless Commun. Mobile Comput. **2018**, 10 (2018)

Analysis of the Response Time Characteristics of the Fog Computing Enabled Real-Time Mobile Applications

Eduard Sopin[1,2]([✉])(iD), Zolotous Nikita[1], Kirill Ageev[1], and Sergey Shorgin[2](iD)

[1] Peoples' Friendship University of Russia (RUDN University),
6 Miklukho-Maklaya Street, Moscow 117198, Russian Federation
{sopin-es,1032162867,ageev-ka}@rudn.ru
[2] Institute of Informatics Problems, FRC CSC RAS,
Vavilova 44-2, Moscow 119333, Russia
sshorgin@ipiran.ru

Abstract. Fog computing brings computing infrastructure to the edge of the network. This enables resource-greedy real-time mobile applications by offloading them to the fog, which provides enough computing resources and reduces the response time in comparison with cloud computing-based solutions. In the paper, we analyze the two-parameter offloading mechanism that takes into account both the computing complexity and the data size to be transferred in case of offloading. We derive the cumulative distribution function of the response time in terms of Laplace-Stieltjes Transform. It is used for the analysis of the probability that the response time exceeds a predefined threshold, which is specified based on the type of application.

Keywords: Fog computing · Computing offloading · Response time · Laplace-Stieltjes transform

1 Introduction

Fog computing has received attention in recent years, as the Internet of Things (IoT) paradigm is expected, bringing a number of new use case scenarios [1]. Fog infrastructure is placed at the edge of the network and work as intermediate nodes for mobile computing tasks offloading, which are closer to the end-user than remote data centers with high-performance servers, thus enabling new 5G-grade applications [2,3]. The physical limitations associated with the response times of remote high-performance servers lead to the emergence of fog computing concept [4].

The publication has been prepared with the support of the "RUDN University Program 5–100" (recipient E.Sopin). The reported study was funded by RFBR, project numbers 18-07-000576 (recipient S. Shorgin) and 20-07-01052 (recipient K. Ageev).

© Springer Nature Switzerland AG 2020
O. Galinina et al. (Eds.): NEW2AN 2020/ruSMART 2020, LNCS 12525, pp. 99–109, 2020.
https://doi.org/10.1007/978-3-030-65726-0_9

A lot of research is done on the tradeoff between the energy-efficiency and the response time in offloading of mobile application tasks to fog computing infrastructure. Authors of [5] compare the effectiveness (in the context of the trade-off) of cloud-based and edge-based deployments for IoT applications using extensive simulations. In [6,7], the authors consider a fog computing network with three layers with computing resources: mobile devices, fog nodes and remote cloud. By queuing theory methods, energy consumption, execution delay and payment cost of offloading processes are analyzed. Authors in [8] used the similar approach but proposed more complex offloading criterion, which implies that only heavy (in terms of the required computational resources) tasks should be offloaded to the fog or remote cloud. The paper [9] is focused on the offloading decision parameters that grants reasonable delays and optimized energy consumption of mobile devices.

All these papers analyze only average response time of the offloaded task. However, the majority of delay-sensitive applications require that response time is lower than the predefined threshold. Thus, more relevant performance indicator is the probability that the response time exceeds some value. In our work, we use the two-parameter offloading model proposed firstly in [10]. We carefully indicate all delays that occur during offloading and processing of tasks, derive their cumulative distribution functions (CDF) and finally obtain the CDF of the total response time. The CDF of the response time gives better insight to the system performance and allow estimating the probability that the response time exceeds some threshold.

The paper is organized as follows. Section 2 presents the system model, Sect. 3 is devoted to the analysis of the response time CDF. The case study is presented in Sect. 4, and conclusions are drawn in Sect. 5.

2 System Model

We consider a distributed computing system that consist of mobile devices (MDs), a fog node and a remote cloud. MDs run real-time applications that require significant amount of computational resources. For each task, a MD makes a decision, whether it will be offloaded to the fog node or processed locally. The performance of the fog node is limited, which means if there are too many tasks offloaded, then some of the offloaded tasks are redirected to the remote cloud to prevent the fog node congestion. The considered system is shown on Fig. 1.

Assume there are M MDs, each of them generating a Poisson flow of tasks with intensity λ_i, $i = 1, 2, ..., M$. Each task is characterized by the amount of processing volume required and the data size to be transferred in case of offloading. We assume that the processing volume (measured in millions of instructions, MI) and the data size (measured in MB) are independent random variables with CDFs $W_i(x)$ and $S_i(x)$, probability density functions (PDF) $w_i(x)$ and $s_i(x)$ respectively. MDs process locally served tasks in the FCFS mode with constant serving rate μ_i, $i = 1, 2, ..., M$ (measured in MIPS).

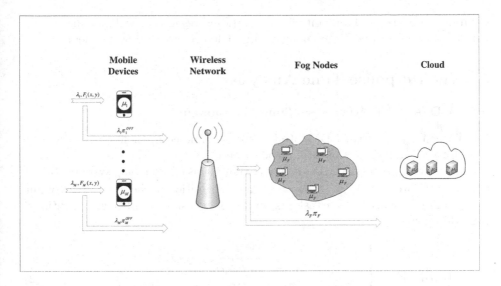

Fig. 1. Simulated fog system.

The proposed offloading mechanism implies offloading of "heavy" tasks in terms of processing volume and "light" - in terms of data size. Splitting to "heavy" and 'light" tasks are done by the threshold O_w on the processing volume and the threshold O_s on the data size. Consequently, the offloading probability $\pi_{i,O}$ on the i-th MD is evaluated according to the following formula:

$$\pi_{i,O} = \int\limits_{O_w}^{+\infty} w_i(x)dx \int\limits_{0}^{O_s} s_i(y)dy = (1 - W_i(O_w))\, S_i(O_s). \tag{1}$$

If the task is processed locally, then the response time is equal to the local serving time. If a task is offloaded, then the total response time is the sum of task transmission time to the fog node through wireless network, the processing time on the fog node and the transmission time back to the MD. If the fog node is overloaded, then the processing time at the fog is replaced by the transmission time between the fog node and the remote cloud, the processing time on the cloud and the transmission time back to the fog node.

We assume that the wireless network provides total bitrate R, which is used to transmit the data of tasks one-by-one in FCFS order, so the transmission time is obtained as the fraction of the data size of a task and total bitrate R. On the other side, the transmission time between the fog node and the cloud is assumed constant.

The fog node provide computational resources by means of virtual machines (VMs), each of them having the constant serving rate μ_F. The total number of VMs at the fog node is N. The constant serving rate μ_C of VMs at the cloud is greater than mu_F, and amount of computational resources (VMs) at the remote cloud is assumed to be large enough, so that it is cannot be overloaded.

3   The Response Time Analysis

3.1   CDFs of the Response Time Components

In this paper, we derive CDFs of all response time components, which will be used for the analysis of the total response time.

The service process at MD i is modeled in terms of a queuing system $M/G/1$ with arrival intensity λ_i, $\sum_{i=1}^{M} \lambda_i = \lambda$. The distribution of the processing volume $W_{MD,i}(x)$ of locally served tasks is obtained by using well-known conditional probability rules:

$$W_{MD,i}(x) = \begin{cases} \dfrac{W_i(x)}{1 - \pi_{i,O}}, x \leq O_w, \\ \dfrac{W_i(O_w) + (W_i(x) - W_i(O_w))(1 - S_i(O_s))}{1 - \pi_{i,O}}, x > O_w. \end{cases} \tag{2}$$

As the service time is the processing volume divided by the service rate μ_i of MD i, its CDF is simply

$$T_{MD,i}(x) = W_{MD,i}(\mu_i x) \tag{3}$$

With the CDF of service times, the waiting time distribution is obtained from [11].

If a task is offloaded to the distributed computing infrastructure, it is first transferred through the wireless network to the fog node. The delays in wireless networks are obtained analogously, by employing $M|G|1$ queue. Note that the arrival process is not actually Poisson, but may be approximated by Poisson process as the aggregated flow from a number of independent sources. The arrival intensity λ_F is the sum of the offloading intensities from all MDs:

$$\lambda_F = \sum_{i=1}^{M} \lambda_i \pi_{i,O} \tag{4}$$

The CDF of data size of an offloaded task is also derived using conditional probability rules:

$$S_{tr,i}(x) = \begin{cases} \dfrac{1}{\pi_{i,O}}(1 - W_i(O_w))S_i(x), x \leq O_s, \\ 1, x > O_s, \end{cases} \tag{5}$$

And the service time distribution in the wireless network is

$$T_{tr,i}(x) = S_{tr,i}(Rx). \tag{6}$$

At the fog node, there are N VMs to serve offloaded tasks, so the service process may be modeled by $M|G|N|0$ queue, where the blocked customers are redirected to the next layer - remote cloud. The arrival intensity is the same as for wireless network - λ_F. The service time is determined by the required processing volume of a task, whose distribution is also obtained by using well-known conditional probability formula:

$$W_{F,i}(x) = \begin{cases} 0, x \leq O_w, \\ \dfrac{1}{\pi_{i,O}}(W_i(x) - W_i(O_w))S_i(O_s), x > O_w \end{cases} \tag{7}$$

The service time is simply processing volume divided by the service rate μ_F, so the CDF of the service time at the fog node is

$$T_{F,i}(x) = W_{F,i}(\mu_F x), \tag{8}$$

$$T_F(x) = \frac{\lambda_i \pi_{i,O}}{\lambda_F} T_{F,i}(x), \tag{9}$$

Denote τ_F - the average serving time at the fog node, which can be easily evaluated from the CDF $T_F(x)$. The overloading probability (the probability that a task is redirected to the remote cloud) π_F is obtained from Erlang formula for $M|G|N|0$ queues:

$$\pi_F = \frac{(\lambda_F \tau_F)^N}{N!}\left(\sum_{k=0}^{N} \frac{(\lambda_F \tau_F)^k}{k!}\right)^{-1}. \tag{10}$$

The fog overloading probability π_F does not depend on the processing volume of a task, so the service time distribution $T_C(x)$ at the cloud is

$$T_{C,i}(x) = W_{F,i}(\mu_C x), \tag{11}$$

Then, after processing in the cloud, the task returns to the mobile device with a constant delay between the fog nodes and the cloud and the wireless network. The task is considered completed.

3.2   Analysis of the Total Response Time

In this subsection we derive the Laplace-Stieltjes Transforms (LST) for all delay components, and obtain the LST of the total response time.

The LST of a function strongly depends on its type. So, for simplicity, we assume that both processing volume and data size have Gamma-distribution with $k = 2$:

$$w_i(x) = x^{k-1}\frac{e^{-\frac{x}{\delta_w}}}{\delta_w{}^k \Gamma(k)} \tag{12}$$

$$s_i(x) = x^{k-1}\frac{e^{-\frac{x}{\delta_s}}}{\delta_s{}^k \Gamma(k)} \tag{13}$$

The LST $\tilde{T}_{MD,i}$ of the service time at the MD i is found directly from (3):

$$\tilde{T}_{MD,i}(s) = \int\limits_0^{+\infty} e^{-sx} d(T_{MD,i}(x)) = \frac{1}{1-\pi_{i,O}} \left[\frac{\mu_i^2}{(s\delta_w+\mu_i)^2} \right.$$

$$\left. - \left(1 - e^{-\frac{O_s}{\delta_s}} \left(1 + \frac{O_s}{\delta_s}\right)\right) e^{-\left(\frac{sW_O}{\mu_i} + \frac{W_O}{\delta_w}\right)} \frac{\mu_i W_O(s\delta_w+\mu_i)+\mu_i^2\delta_w}{\delta_w(s\delta_w+\mu_i)^2} \right]. \tag{14}$$

Next, we find the LST $\omega_{MD,i}$ of the waiting time distribution according to [11] as the waiting time in a $M|G|1$ queue, and the LST of the sojourn time distribution on mobile device i, formulas (15) and (16) respectively.

$$\omega_{MD,i}(s) = \frac{s(1 - \rho_i)}{s - \lambda_i + \lambda_i \tilde{T}_{MD,i}(s)} \tag{15}$$

$$\phi_{MD,i}(s) = \tilde{T}_{MD,i}(s) \cdot \omega_{MD,i}(s). \tag{16}$$

Note that ρ_i is the offered load on the MD i.

The same steps are done for transmission time through the wireless network. First, we obtain the LST $\tilde{T}_{tr,i}(s)$ of the transmission time distribution directly from (6):

$$\tilde{T}_{tr,i}(s) = \int\limits_0^{+\infty} e^{-sx} d(T_{tr,i}(x))$$

$$= \frac{e^{-\frac{O_w}{\delta_w}}(O_w+\delta_w)R^2}{\pi_{i,O}\delta_w\delta_s^2} \left(\frac{e^{-\frac{O_s}{R}}\left(s+\frac{R}{\delta_s}\right)}{s+\frac{R}{\delta_s}} \left(\frac{O_s}{R} + \frac{1}{s+\frac{R}{\delta_s}}\right) - \frac{1}{\left(s+\frac{R}{\delta_s}\right)^2} \right) \tag{17}$$

Since the wireless network is also modeled in terms of the $M/G/1$ type queue, the LST $\omega_{tr,i}(s)$ of the waiting time distribution and the LST $\phi_{tr,i}(s)$ of sojourn time in the wireless network are:

$$\omega_{tr,i}(s) = \frac{s(1 - \rho_{tr})}{s - \lambda_F + \lambda_F \tilde{T}_{tr,i}(s)}; \tag{18}$$

$$\phi_{tr,i}(s) = \tilde{T}_{tr,i}(s) \cdot \omega_{tr,i}(s). \tag{19}$$

Here ρ_{tr} is the offered load in the wireless network and is equal to the product of λ_F and the average data size transferred, which is obtained from the CDF (5).

In the similar way, the LST $\tilde{T}_{F,i}$ of the service time distribution at the fog node is derived from CDF (8):

$$\tilde{T}_{F,i}(s) = \int\limits_0^{+\infty} e^{-sx} d(T_{F,i}(x)) = e^{-\frac{sO_w}{\mu_F}} \frac{\mu_F O_w(s\delta_w + \mu_F) + \mu_F^2\delta_w}{(b + O_w)(s\delta_w + \mu_F)^2} \tag{20}$$

Note there is no waiting queue both at the fog node and the remote cloud. And the LST $\tilde{T}_{C,i}(s)$ of the service time distribution in the cloud is obtained from CDF (11):

$$\tilde{T}_{C,i}(s) = \int\limits_0^{+\infty} e^{-sx} d(T_{C,i}(x)) = e^{-\frac{sO_w}{\mu_C}} \frac{\mu_C O_w(s\delta_w + \mu_C) + \mu_C^2\delta_w}{(b + O_w)(s\delta_w + \mu_C)^2} \tag{21}$$

It remains to get the LST $\tilde{T}_{FC}(s)$ of the constant transmission time between the fog node and the cloud:

$$\tilde{T}_{FC}(s) = e^{-t_{FC}s}, \tag{22}$$

where t_{FC} is the constant transmission time between the fog node and the cloud.

Finally, we can proceed to the LST of the total response time. Having received the LST of all delay component distributions, we apply the convolution formula and obtain the LST $\tilde{\tau}(s)$ of the response time distribution of a task from MD i:

$$\begin{aligned}
\tilde{\tau}_i(s) = (1 - \pi_{i,O})\phi_{MD,i}(s) + \pi_{i,O}(1 - \pi_F)\tilde{T}_{F,i}(s)\phi_{tr,i}^2(s) \\
+ \pi_{i,O}\pi_F\tilde{T}_{C,i}(s)\phi_{tr,i}^2(s)\tilde{T}_{FC}^2(s).
\end{aligned} \tag{23}$$

Further we employ numerical Reverse Laplace-Stieltjes Transformation to the $\tilde{\tau}_i(s)$ to obtain the CDF $\tau(x)$ of the response time. This allows to evaluate the probability $\Pi(T)$ that the response time is lower than a threshold T:

$$\Pi(T) = \tau(T). \tag{24}$$

4   Numerical Analysis

In this section, the results of the case study are presented. The main metric of interest here is the probability $\Pi(T)$ that the response time for a task does not exceed the threshold T.

We consider a scenario with homogeneous MDs that run the same applications, so the distributions of processing volume and data size of tasks are also the same. All values of parameters used in the section are gathered in Table 1.

Table 1. Parameter values for the numerical analysis.

Parameter	Value
M	20
N	8
R	150 Mbps
λ_i	2 tasks/s
μ_i	4 MIPS
μ_F	6 MIPS
μ_C	10 MIPS
δ_s	0.25
δ_w	0.75
t_{FC}	0.5 s

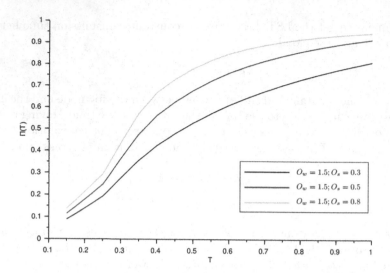

Fig. 2. Probability $\Pi(T)$ as a function of the response time threshold for different values of O_s

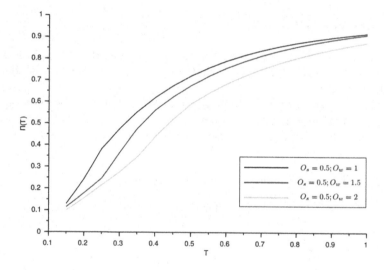

Fig. 3. Probability $\Pi(T)$ as a function of the response time threshold for different values of O_w

First, we analyze the behavior of the $\Pi(T)$ as a function of T for various offloading threshold parameters. In Fig. 2, the offloading threshold on the processing volume O_w is fixed and equal to 1.5 MI, which is the average value of the processing volume. So, from the processing volume point of view, the offloaded tasks are nearly half of the whole number. Then, with the increase of the data size threshold O_s, the offloading intensity is also increased. The plots show that more intensive offloading leads to better performance of the system for the considered scenario.

In Fig. 3, the offloading thresholds are replaced. Here we fix the data size threshold $O_s = 0.5$ MB, which is the average data size in the scenario, and vary the processing volume threshold. However, the increase of the processing volume threshold leads to the decrease of task offloading according to the considered offloading criterion. Again, as in the previous figure, one can conclude that the more tasks are offloaded, the better.

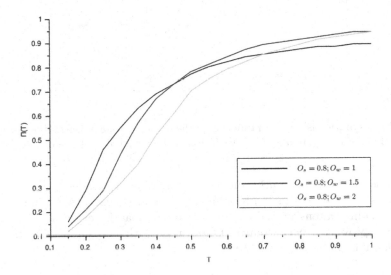

Fig. 4. Probability $\Pi(T)$ as a function of the response time threshold for different values of O_w with increased O_s

However, if the data size threshold is fixed on greater value $O_s = 0.8$ MB, the results are not so straightforward (see Fig. 4. For low values of T, the results are similar to those on Fig. 3, but with increase of T the situation changes. The reason of such behavior is increased load on the fog node, which causes more often rerouting of tasks to the remote cloud and the increase of the response time. For example, if $O_s = 0.8$ MB and $O_w = 1$ MI, more than 80% of the tasks are offloaded to the fog.

Figure 5 shows the probability $\Pi(T)$ as a function of processing volume threshold with the fixed response time threshold $T = 1$ s and various data size thresholds. Note that according to the considered offloading criterion, the increase of processing volume threshold O_w on the X-axis leads to the decrease of the offloading intensity. The reason for the different behavior of different curves is load balancing between MDs and the fog node. For small values of data size volume, the offloading probability is rather small and the majority of the incoming load is served locally. So, if the offloading probability is decreased further, the system performance goes down. But for $O_s = 0.8$ MB, the offloading

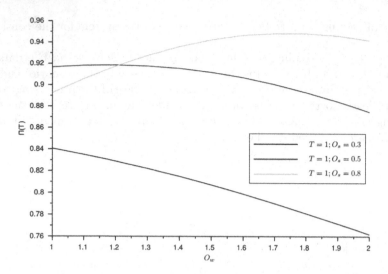

Fig. 5. Values of the distribution function of the response time of the system for a fixed response time of the system and the variation of the threshold volume of çalculations.

intensity is bigger significantly and the fog node is overloaded, which leads to the increase of the rerouting probability π_F. Consequently, with the decrease of the offloading intensity, the bigger part of the load is served at MDs, which helps to improve the performance. One can note that at $O_w = 1.75$ the ideal load balance is obtained.

5   Conclusion

In the paper, we focused on the analysis of the response time of real-time mobile applications that use fog computing infrastructure to increase the performance and to improve the battery life of mobile devices. We carefully defined all delay components and derived their CDFs. Using the LST technique, we obtained the CDF of the total response time and formula for the probability that the response time is lower than a predefined threshold. Further, we presented the extensive numerical analysis of this performance metric. The analysis showed that on the different intervals of the response time threshold the probability $\Pi(T)$ may have completely different behavior.

References

1. Petrov, V., et al.: Vehicle-based relay assistance for opportunistic crowdsensing over narrowband IoT (NB-IoT). IEEE Internet Things J. 5(5), 3710–3723 (2018). Art. no. 7857676
2. Solomitckii, D., Gapeyenko, M., Semkin, V., Andreev, S., Koucheryavy, Y.: Technologies for efficient amateur drone detection in 5G millimeter-wave cellular infrastructure. IEEE Commun. Mag. 56(1), 43–50 (2018). Art. no. 8255736

3. Galinina, O., Tabassum, H., Mikhaylov, K., Andreev, S., Hossain, E., Koucheryavy, Y.: On feasibility of 5G-grade dedicated RF charging technology for wireless-powered wearables. IEEE Wireless Commun. **23**(2), 28–37 (2016). Art. no. 7462482

4. De Donno, M., Tange, K., Dragoni, N.: Foundations and evolution of modern computing paradigms: cloud IoT, Edge, and Fog. IEEE Access **7**, 150936–150948 (2019)

5. Casadei, R., Fortino, G., Pianini, D., Russo, W., Savaglio, C., Viroli, M.: A development approach for collective opportunistic Edge-of-Things services. Inf. Sci. **498**, 154–169 (2019)

6. Chang, Z., Zhou, Z., Ristaniemi, T., Niu, Z.: Energy efficient optimization for computation offloading in fog computing system. In: GLOBECOM 2017–2017 IEEE Global Communications Conference, Singapore, pp. 1–6. IEEE (2017)

7. Liu, L., Chang, Z., Guo, X., Mao, S., Ristaniemi, T.: Multi-objective optimization for computation offloading in fog computing. IEEE Internet Things J. **5**(1), 283–294 (2018)

8. Sopin, E., Daraseliya, A., Correia, M.: Performance analysis of the offloading scheme in a fog computing system. In: 10th International Congress on Ultra Modern Telecommunications and Control Systems and Workshops (ICUMT), Moscow, pp. 1–5. IEEE (2018)

9. Jiang, Y., Chen, Y., Yang, S., Wu, C.: Energy-efficient task offloading for time-sensitive applications in fog computing. IEEE Syst. J. **13**(3), 2930–2941 (2019)

10. Sopin, E., Samouylov, K., Shorgin, S.: The analysis of the computation offloading scheme with two-parameter offloading criterion in fog computing. In: Montella, R., Ciaramella, A., Fortino, G., Guerrieri, A., Liotta, A. (eds.) IDCS 2019. LNCS, vol. 11874, pp. 11–20. Springer, Cham (2019). https://doi.org/10.1007/978-3-030-34914-1_2

11. Bocharov, P., D'Apice, C., Pechinkin, A.: Queueing Theory, p. 460. Walter de Gruyter, Heidelberg (2011)

Efficiency of RF Energy Harvesting in Modern Wireless Technologies

Sviatoslav Iakimenko[✉] 🆔 and Daria Ikonnikova 🆔

HSE Tikhonov Moscow Institute of Electronics and Mathematics (MIEM HSE), Moscow, Russia
{syakimenko,dmikonnikova}@miem.hse.ru

Abstract. The paper investigates the effectiveness of wireless power collection of electromagnetic energy emitted by LPD433 and Wi-Fi transmitters as well as by the base stations of the LTE and 5G mobile network. The legal regulations of the Russian Federation that affect wireless energy collection (sanitary zone range, maximum transmitter power and antenna gain, etc.) have been taken into consideration. The efficiency of options for wireless energy collection at various free and cellular frequencies has been compared according to such parameters as collected power, maximum charging range and energy replenishment coefficient. Based on the results of the comparison, the most promising RF bands which can be used for wireless harvesting in Russia have been proposed.

Keywords: Wireless charging · RF energy harvesting · LPD433 · Russian law regulations · Power collection effectiveness

1 Introduction

The rapid spread of technologies for radio frequency (RF) energy collecting can be explained by the wide availability of electromagnetic signals in human life: base stations, Wi-Fi routers, TV and radio broadcast stations. However, radio frequency energy sources are relatively low-power compared to other types of energy (solar, wind, ocean waves, etc.) In addition, the maximum level of electromagnetic radiation from transmitters is limited by the legislation of a particular country. Despite this, a huge advantage of RF energy sources is that the collection can be carried out continuously and does not impact the environment negatively.

In the future the amount of radio frequency energy in the environment will significantly increase. It is caused by the transition to ultra-dense 5G and IEEE 802.11ac networks with the support of massive MIMO and beamforming technologies. The RF energy can be used to charge electronic devices which have low energy consumption.

In addition, the recent challenges humanity is faced with, such as the Covid-19 outbreak, have markedly changed the patterns of people's workflow. It is becoming increasingly important to work from any convenient place rather than being restricted to the workplace. The wearable electronic devices (for example, smart rings, Bluetooth-headphones), which allow an employee to always be in touch with their colleagues and managers, are important attributes of working remotely. At the same time, the capacity

© Springer Nature Switzerland AG 2020
O. Galinina et al. (Eds.): NEW2AN 2020/ruSMART 2020, LNCS 12525, pp. 110–118, 2020.
https://doi.org/10.1007/978-3-030-65726-0_10

of wearable devices is small, and to ensure stable connectivity, the issue of finding alternative ways of recharging them is of utmost importance.

This work evaluates the efficiency of radio frequency energy harvesting at various frequencies which are typical for modern wireless technologies. The regulatory constraints of Russian Federation legislation have been considered. They include the limitations of the maximum transmit power and antenna gain for different radio technologies, which impact the conducted efficiency assessment.

2 Background of the Study

In terms of the industry, most of the developments in the field of wireless harvesting are based on the Qi standard [1], which was elaborated in 2009 by the Wireless Power Consortium. Qi is designed to transmit energy at a maximum distance of 4 cm. The tangible results have also been achieved in the usage of energy emitted by Wi-Fi devices. The scientists from the University of Washington have presented PoWiFi technology [2], which uses wireless routers to transmit power of RF signal without special equipment or damage to data transmitted. This technology is mostly based on emitting energy by Wi-Fi router when no data is transferred.

The ready-to-sell solutions have already been developed in the UK. For example, the created air quality sensor uses Freevolt technology [3], which allows harvesting from radio frequency waves of wireless networks. This sensor is capable of accumulating energy from two RF bands: 1800 MHz (GSM) and 2.4 GHz (Wi-Fi).

Although Qi and PoWifi are patented technologies, they are insufficiently known in Russia and their effective range is short.

For a long time, academia researchers have also demonstrated the feasibility of powering sensors and devices, focusing primarily on the effectivity and design of rectennas. In [4], the authors present a wearable device operating at GSM 900 and GSM 1800. The antenna of the device reaches RF-to-DC conversion efficiency of 84%. In [5], the authors demonstrate collecting energy at a distance of 110 m from the GSM base station with receiving dual-band antenna. The works [6, 7] investigate the integration of wireless radio-frequency charging technology into the 5G and urban crowd sensing ecosystem. They focus on the impact of network, the density of users and behavior on wireless charging, as well as Federal Communications Commission (FCC) regulatory issues.

However, none of the existing papers emphasize the Russian Federation legislation restrictions in the context of wireless harvesting. These regulations are strict in comparison with those of the EU, which could significantly affect the efficiency of wireless energy collection in this country. Therefore, the research topic has not been profoundly considered yet.

3 Restrictions Imposed by the Legislation of the Russian Federation

Sanitary epidemiological rules and standards (SanPiN's in Russian terminology) are developed in the specialized research institutes and institutions of the Ministry of Health of Russia. The control over their implementation is assigned to The Federal Service for

Surveillance on Consumer Rights Protection and Human Wellbeing (Rospotrebnadzor), which is subordinate to the Government of Russia.

The permissible levels of radiation of transmitting radio engineering objects for uncontrolled exposure to the population are established by SanPiN 2.1.8/2.2.4.1383-03 [8]. The electromagnetic fields (EMF) of the frequency range 30 kHz–300 GHz, affecting the population, are limited in Appendix 1 of [8] and are shown in Table 1.

Table 1. Maximum permissible levels of electromagnetic fields in the frequency range 30 kHz–300 GHz for the population in Russian Federation (source: [8])

Frequency range	30–300 kHz	0.3–3 MHz	3–30 MHz	30–300 MHz	0.3–300 GHz
Normalized parameter	Electric field strength, E (V/m)				Energy flux density $(\mu W/cm^2)$
Permissible level	25	15	10	3*	10 25**

* – Except for radio and television broadcasting (frequency range 48.5–108; 174–230 MHz).
** – For cases of radiation from antennas operating in the circular view or scanning mode.

Generally, with a view to preventing negative biological effects, in Russian Federation the reference levels or exposure limits for electromagnetic fields for the public are one of the most stringent requirements among the countries of Eurasia. The public exposure limit for power frequency magnetic fields is 5–20% of the reference levels in the EU recommendations for different types of areas and institutions [9].

The power of the base station transmitters and their maximum gain are determined and assigned by the State Commission on Radio Frequencies (SCRF) under the Ministry of Telecommunications of Russia. This state body is responsible for the regulation of the radio frequency spectrum in the Russian Federation, solves the problems of introducing new radio communication technologies and other tasks in this field.

Technical characteristics for the radio-electronic means of cellular networks of LTE and UMTS standards are defined in the SCRF decisions [10, 11] and are shown in Table 2.

Table 2. Transmitter power and antenna gain for electronic equipment of the LTE standard and subsequent modifications in Russian Federation (source: [10, 11])

Parameter name	Parameter value	
	User equipment	Base station
Maximum transmitter power, dBm	25	46
Maximum antenna gain, dB	7	24

Clause 3.17 of [8] limits the restriction zone around the emitter antennas as follows: "the impossibility of people's access and the absence of neighboring buildings at a distance of at least 25 m from any point of the antenna should be ensured, regardless of its type and direction of radiation".

4 Constants and Methodology

In general, the performance comparisons can be made according to many characteristics, although they are all interrelated (through the Friis formula [12]) and follow the same trends. Therefore, it is easier to estimate the collected power, which is the basis of the other parameters:

$$P_{coll} = \frac{P_{tx} G_{tx} G_{rx} \eta}{r^2} \left(\frac{\lambda}{4\pi}\right)^2 \tag{1}$$

where P_{tx} – transmitting antenna power, G_{tx} – transmitting antenna gain, G_{rx} – receiving antenna gain, λ – wavelength, η – RF-to-DC conversion efficiency, r – reference distance.

The power of the transceivers P_{tx} is limited by the documentation considered earlier: 0.1 W [13] for wireless access devices, including devices operating on the IEEE 802.11 standard, 0.01 W for the free LPD433 frequency [13]; 20 W is half of the maximum power of cellular base stations (46 dBm = 39.8 W), limited by the decisions of the State Commission on Radio Frequencies [14].

The gain of the receiver antenna G_{rx} is 0 dBi. The efficiency of converting the energy of an electromagnetic wave into DC energy η is taken as 50%. The reference distance r at which energy is collected has two options: 3 m for free frequencies and 25 m for cellular frequencies. As mentioned before, 25 meters is the restriction zone around the base station of any power, limited by the law [8].

In the calculations for each frequency, we compare two options for energy transfer: omnidirectional (isotropic) and directional. In the case of omnidirectional radiation, the transmitter antenna gain G_{tx} is 2.15 dBi (as a gain of the simplest antenna – half-wave dipole).

In terms of directional radiation of energy, the transmitter antenna gain G_{tx} is obtained by modelling the antenna array in MATLAB. It is equal to 11.4 dBi for any range due to the dependence of the size of the antenna array on the frequency. For modelling transmitting antennas, we have used the same 3×3 square antenna array consisting of half-wave vibrators (Fig. 1).

In practice, the appropriate frequency is selected based on the operating environment, the national radio frequency standards and the physical limitations of the antenna. For example, popular free frequency bands in Russia are LPD433 (433.075–434.775 MHz) [15], which is used for low-power devices, and two Wi-Fi frequencies: 2.4 GHz (range 2.400–2.4835 GHz) and 5.2 GHz (range 5.150–5.250 GHz). In modern LTE base stations, the most popular cellular frequencies among operators in Russia are 800 MHz, 1800 MHz, 2100 MHz and 2600 MHz. For the deployment of pilot zones of 5G communication networks in Russia, one of the allocated ranges is the 4.8–4.99 GHz [16].

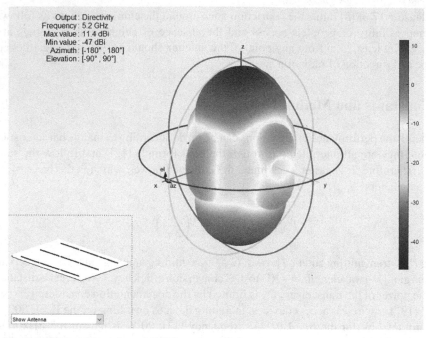

Fig. 1. Possible configuration and 3D-pattern of the square antenna array that operates on frequency 5.2 GHz (source: MATLAB Antenna Toolbox)

5 Results

The results have been obtained for two options: in Table 3, the calculations have been made for freely-used LPD433 and Wi-Fi frequencies. In Table 4, we present the calculations for the most widely-used cellular frequencies.

Table 3. Results anticipated for free frequency ranges.

	Free frequencies					
	LPD 433 MHz		Wi-Fi 2.4 GHz		Wi-Fi 5 GHz	
Center frequency, MHz	433.93		2442		5200	
Wavelength, m	0.69		0.12		0.06	
	Isotr.	Direct.	Isotr.	Direct.	Isotr.	Direct.
Transmitter power, W	0.01	0.01	0.1	0.1	0.1	0.1
P_{coll} at the reference distance, mW	0.11	23.21	0.89	7.46	0.19	1.62

The results demonstrate that the collection implemented by using the directional transmitter antenna is more effective provided that the receiver is located inside the main lobe of the radiation pattern of the transmitting antenna.

Table 4. Results anticipated for cellular frequency ranges.

	Cellular frequencies									
	791–862 MHz		1805–1880 MHz		2110–2170 MHz		2620–2690 MHz		4.8–4.99 GHz	
Center frequency, MHz	826.5		1842.5		2140		2655		4895	
Wavelength, m	0.36		0.16		0.14		0.11		0.06	
	Is.	Dir.	Is.	Dir.	Is.	Dir.	Is.	Dir.	Is.	Dir.
Transmitter power, W	20	20	20	20	20	20	20	20	20	20
P_{coll} at the reference distance, mW	22	184.3	4.4	37.1	3.3	27.5	2.1	17.9	0.6	5.3

When it comes to freely-used frequency ranges, with the restrictions established in the Russian Federation for radiated power levels, wireless energy collection is gene-rally ineffective.

Since in Table 4 we have used the same transmitter power for all frequency ranges in order to simplify the evaluation of the results, it can be concluded that using lower frequencies allows more energy to be collected.

To assess whether a nominal electronic device can be charged at the selected reference distance, we consider that its consumed power (discharge rate) P_{cons} is 15 μ W. Then from Friis formula [12] with $P_{rx} = P_{cons}$ we get the maximum charging range r_{max}, i.e. the maximum distance where collected power is more or equal to consumed device power:

$$r_{max} = \frac{\lambda}{4\pi} \sqrt{\frac{P_{tx} G_{tx} G_{rx} \eta}{P_{cons}}} \qquad (2)$$

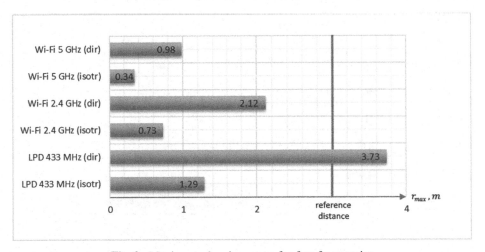

Fig. 2. Maximum charging range for free frequencies

The comparison of the maximum charging range for free frequency bands is demon-strated in Fig. 2. The most promising option there is directional energy collection in the

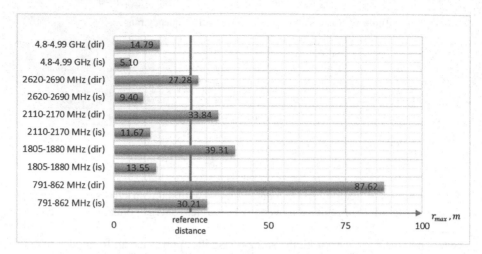

Fig. 3. Maximum charging range for cellular frequencies

LPD433 frequency range. In other cases, the device is discharged faster than it collects RF energy, even though Russian legislation permits using a more powerful antenna for Wi-Fi technology.

Figure 3 shows the comparison of the maximum charging range for cellular frequency bands. There are several options for collecting energy, where maximum charging range is greater than reference distance. For example, LTE 800 MHz band allows energy collection with both directional and omnidirectional antennas. For other LTE frequencies, only the directional energy collection is available. Finally, in the 5G range (4.8–4.99 GHz), energy collection proves to be impractical in the given conditions.

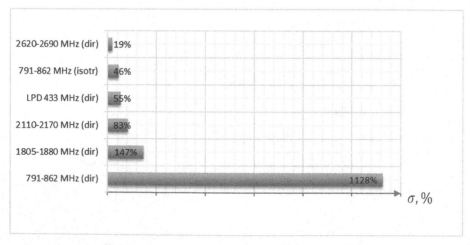

Fig. 4. Comparison of energy replenishment coefficient

To unify the results of the two previous figures and compare the efficiency of wireless charging, we enter the energy replenishment coefficient σ:

$$\sigma = \frac{P_{coll} - P_{cons}}{P_{cons}} \tag{3}$$

Figure 4 shows only those options where σ is greater than zero. According to our calculations, energy harvesting in these ranges deserves further research.

6 Conclusions

Although nowadays considerable improvement is required in many aspects of wireless power charging, we have shown that there are prospects for forming a new sustainable energy source. Based on our study, the following conclusions can be drawn:

- For wireless power harvesting in the Russian Federation, freely-used low frequency ranges could be more effective if not for the strict power restrictions imposed on transmitters emitting at such frequencies. This leads to the assumption that it is preferable to use low-frequency mobile communications, for which these restrictions are less noticeable.
- Directional energy transfer is noticeably more efficient than omnidirectional, and further technological improvements can markedly increase the efficiency of energy collection. However, even in this case, recharging devices with a relatively low power consumption is implied.
- We emphasize two promising areas for the development of wireless energy transfer: using low-frequency bands with the enhanced RF-to-DC efficiency and the wide deployment of beamforming technology in 5G networks.

In the future, RF energy collection could help the development of low-power electronic devices and significantly facilitate the life of ordinary people by their using wearable devices with frequent recharging.

Acknowledgments. The research was done at MIEM NRU HSE and supported by the Russian Science Foundation (agreement No 18-19-00580).

References

1. Van Wageningen, D., Staring, T.: The Qi wireless power standard. In: Proceedings IEEE International Power Electronics and Motion Control Conference (EPE/PEMC), Orhid, Macedonia, pp. S15-25–S15-32 (2010). https://doi.org/10.1109/EPEPEMC.2010.5606673
2. Talla, V., et al.: Powering the next billion devices with Wi-Fi. In: CoNEXT 205: Proceedings of the 11th ACM Conference on Emerging Networking Experiments and Technologies, Heidelberg, Germany, pp. 1–13 (2015). https://doi.org/10.1145/2716281.2836089
3. Freevolt. https://getfreevolt.com/. Accessed 21 May 2020
4. Barroca, N, Saraiva, H.: Antennas and circuits for ambient RF energy harvesting in wireless body area networks. In: Proceedings of IEEE International Symposium on Personal Indoor and Mobile Radio Communications (PIMRC), London, UK, pp. 532–537 (2013). https://doi.org/10.1109/PIMRC.2013.6666194

5. Nimo, A., Beckedahl, T., Ostertag, T., Reindl, L.: Analysis of passive RF-DC power rectification and harvesting wireless RF energy for micro-watt sensors. AIMS Energy 3(2), 184–200 (2015). https://doi.org/10.3934/energy.2015.2.184
6. Galinina, O., Tabassum, H., Mikhaylov, K., Andreev, S., Hossain, E., Koucheryavy, Y.: On feasibility of 5G-grade dedicated RF charging technology for wireless-powered wearables. IEEE Wirel. Commun. 23, 28–37 (2016). https://doi.org/10.1109/MWC.2016.7462482
7. Galinina, O., Mikhaylov, K., Huang, K., Andreev, S., Koucheryavy, Y.: Wirelessly powered urban crowd sensing over wearables: trading energy for data. IEEE Wirel. Commun. 25(2), 140–149 (2018). https://doi.org/10.1109/MWC.2018.1600468
8. Sanitary Epidemiological Regulations and Standards 2.1.8/2.2.4.1383-03: Hygienic requirements for the placement and operation of transmitting radio facilities, Russian Ministry of Health, Moscow (2003). (in Russian)
9. Stam, R.: Comparison of international policies on electromagnetic fields (power frequency and radiofrequency fields). The Netherlands National Institute for Public Health and the Environment, Bilthoven (2018)
10. Decision of the State Committee for Radio Frequencies under the Ministry of Telecommunications of Russia of 02.10.2012 No. 12-15-02 "On the unification of the technical cha-racteristics of communication networks of the UMTS standard and the LTE standard and its subsequent modifications" (in Russian)
11. Decision of the State Committee for Radio Frequencies under the Ministry of Telecommunications of Russia of 13.10.2014 No. 14-27-03 "On the allocation of radio frequency bands 1710–1785 MHz and 1805–1880 MHz for electronic means of communication networks of GSM, LTE standards and its subsequent modifications on the territory of the constituent entities of the Russian Federation" (in Russian)
12. Friis, H.: A note on a simple transmission formula. Proc. IRE 34(5), 254–256 (1946). https://doi.org/10.1109/JRPROC.1946.234568
13. Decree of the Government of the Russian Federation of October 12, 2004 No. 539. "On the procedure for registering radio-electronic means and high-frequency devices" (in Russian)
14. Decision of the State Committee for Radio Frequencies under the Ministry of Telecommunications of Russia of 28.12.2017 No. 17-44-07-3, Appendix No. 28. "The main tactical and technical characteristics of radio-electronic means of LTE communication networks and subsequent modifications in the radio frequency bands 880–890 MHz and 925–935 MHz" (in Russian)
15. Tuset-Peiró, P., Anglès-Vazquez, A., López-Vicario, J., Vilajosana-Guillén, X.: On the suitability of the 433 MHz band for M2M low-power wireless communications: propagation aspects. Trans. Emerg. Telecommun. Technol. 25(12), 1154–1168 (2014). https://doi.org/10.1002/ett.2672
16. The ranges for creating pilot zones of 5G are allocated (in Russian). https://digital.gov.ru/ru/events/38690/. Accessed 21 May 2020

Information Security State Analysis of Elements of Industry 4.0 Devices in Information Systems

Mikhail E. Sukhoparov[1] (ID), Ilya S. Lebedev[2] (ID), and Viktor V. Semenov[2](✉) (ID)

[1] SPbF AO «NPK «TRISTAN», 47 Nepokorennykh p., Saint Petersburg 195220, Russia
[2] SPIIRAS, 14-th Linia, VI, No. 39 St. Petersburg 199178, Russia
v.semenov@iias.spb.su

Abstract. The authors researched problematic issues of the information security state analysis of elements of Industry 4.0 devices. The type and characteristics of behavioral patterns used for the analysis were demonstrated. The authors conducted an experiment aimed at obtaining statistical information from investigated objects. During the experiment, a sample of signal trace patterns was obtained for the states under consideration. The approach based on the k-means clustering method was considered as the decisive identification rule. The approach to identifying the state of Industry 4.0 devices in information systems based on the processing of digitized sequences was proposed. The overall accuracy of the selected method was found to be 98%. The main limitations of the proposed approach are the need of formalization and selecting data groups for the formation of behavioral patterns. The basic advantage of the proposed approach is the relative ease of its implementation and minimum requirements for computing resources.

Keywords: Industry 4.0 · Behavioral patterns · State analysis · Information security

1 Introduction

The emergence of a new development paradigm of information, technological and cyber-physical systems is associated with the application of the Industrial Internet of Things and Industry 4.0. In this regard, there is a need to develop models for ensuring security, operability, sustainability and methods aimed at investigating situations resulting from the emergence of various threats.

The information security of the Industrial Internet or Industry 4.0 is associated with the introduction of digital technologies of large data analysis, secure remote access as well as interfacing of various computing, network and mechatronic devices into production systems.

The Industrial Internet is aimed at more efficient use of equipment running over different protocols, the unification of various information systems of data, the implementation of operational analysis of technological processes and improving operational management capabilities.

O. Galinina et al. (Eds.): NEW2AN 2020/ruSMART 2020, LNCS 12525, pp. 119–125, 2020.
https://doi.org/10.1007/978-3-030-65726-0_11

However, this approach initially contains multiple vulnerabilities that arise as a result of the need to run over a variety of protocols, consolidate a number of information sources as well as organize additional nodes and pre-processing storages.

The majority of attacks being conducted against IT systems and computer-aided process control systems are various modifications of relatively easy to implement DDoS attacks (different ways to saturate the bandwidth, "flood", heavy requests, etc.).

Studies related to the cyber-physical system state analysis make it possible to determine normal and abnormal behavior on the basis of external and internal characteristics and digitized traces of processes running in them.

2 Formal Problem Statement

The analysis of typical state monitoring systems shows the presence of mainly embedded solutions that has a number of disadvantages when the intruder uses exploits, logic bombs and viral infections. In most cases, the analyzed device is out of the controlled zone or difficult to access, as is proven in papers [1–3], which facilitates access to it by a potential intruder. The processes running in Industry 4.0 devices and nodes themselves must be constantly monitored and controlled to ensure operability, sustainability, functionality, and information security, according to papers [4–6].

In this regard, there is a need to obtain information not only from internal but also from external channels. The functioning of mechatronic elements is determined both by internal computing processes and network traffic and by changes in electromagnetic and sound spectra, frequencies and amplitudes of vibrations, temperature, etc. recorded by detectors and sensors.

Considering the functioning of mechatronic devices and units of Industry 4.0, each process can be identified by information from detectors, sensors, and internal control elements. A signal path S(t) is received from each sensor. Tuples of characteristics H = {S(t) I t = 1,..., M} are determined by synchronizing the values received from the various control elements in discrete moments of time. Different signatures F(H) are built on their basis.

For information security, the object state can be analyzed on the basis of data obtained through several different-type side (external) channels, as demonstrated in papers [7–9] and monograph [10].

Then the task of analyzing the state of Industry 4.0 elements can be presented as follows.

Let Z be a set of system states defined by the incoming values of signatures F(H). C is a set of state classes (in particular, normal or abnormal). The function of the distance between objects (z, z') is selected. There is a final training set of the known states $Z^k = \{z_1, \ldots, z_m\} \in Z$.

It is necessary to split the training set into subsets consisting of states close by the metric r and find the function a: $Z \to C$.

Thus, the purpose is to identify additional information from external independent sources, in the particular case calculated on the basis of external channels, through which to highlight the associated state characteristics of Industry 4.0 devices, as described in papers [11, 12].

To achieve the goal, it is necessary to develop an approach to state identification based on time-synchronized tuples of characteristics, according to works [13–15].

3 Proposed Approach

Elements of Industry 4.0 are affected by the environment and various internal situations related to the computing process, messaging, competition for resources and communication channels. The internal situations are determined by the sequence of control instructions coming to devices. The external environment brings a number of impacts related to time and physical resource constraints as well as interference.

The element is affected by control instructions and internal situations related to the operation, processes of receiving and transmitting messages between the devices, which determine the transient characteristics h(t) and depend on the current state of the external environment u(t). It gives a dynamic system, which has k inputs and d outputs, as is proven in paper [9]. A control instruction and the values of the external environment variables determining the device state are given to the input. Signals S(t) (acoustic, electromagnetic, etc.) recorded by various sensors appear at the element output.

Data received through external channels depend on the parameter of noise component v(t) associated with the properties of the measuring device, the characteristics of the received signal, etc.

In general, the state of the Industry 4.0 device is determined by the following ratio:

$$\sum_{i=1}^{k} \sum_{j=1}^{d} \int_{0}^{t} u_i(t) h_{ij}(t - \tau) d\tau - \sum_{j=1}^{d} \int_{0}^{t} f\left(s_j(t), v_j(t)\right), \tag{1}$$

where k is the number of source channels, h is the transient characteristics of the t-th channel for the j-th registering sensor values received through the channel, f is the function of the measured values.

Identification of the Industry 4.0 device state is performed based on external signals, defined in discrete instants of time $t_0, t_1,...t_n$. The signal values are calculated by the discrete function $X(t)$ and represent a sequence described by a random vector with the values of $X_0 = X(t_0)$, $X_1 = X(t_1)...X_n = X(t_n)$.

A random signal is determined from a mixture of the useful signal S(t) and the parameter $v(t)$:

$$X(t) = F[S(t), v(t)], \tag{2}$$

where vector X is the result of m mixed mutually independent signals $S(t)$ (1, 2,..., n) having distortion of the noise component $v(t)$.

The process of state monitoring is performed on the basis of calculations that implement decision making with the help of behavioral pattern databases and patterns of digitized signal traces. The calculation of deviations in the behavioral pattern of signal traces is implemented through comparisons with reference values calculated under "normal functioning" conditions.

4 Experiment

In order to identify the state, a "network bridge" type connection was implemented. Structured information was transmitted from the node A to the node B through the node C in the form of a database table.

Its processing was carried out at the node C. In the first case, information was transferred through the node C without processing (state S_1), in the second case (state S_2) filtration was performed by the predefined field of the table, in the third case (state S_3) calculations were performed, and an additional field was added to the transferred table. Identification of the state was determined through the signal trace sequences of the system monitor of the node C.

The obtained experimental data on the percentage of resource utilization are presented in the form of output vectors of time-synchronized sequences of CPU usage values, network packages, and memory resource consumption.

During the experiment, a sample of signal trace patterns was obtained for the states under consideration. The approach based on the k-means clustering method was considered as the decisive identification rule. The Euclidian distance was used as a measure of proximity:

$$r(x, \dot{x}) = \sqrt{\sum\nolimits_{\rho=1}^{n} (x_\rho - \dot{x}_\rho)^2}, \tag{3}$$

where R is the observation space $x, \dot{x} \in R^n$.

Using the values of the training set based on the k-average method, m observations are divided into k groups (or clusters)$(k \leq m)$, $S = \{S_1, S_2, \ldots, S_k\}$

$$\min\left[\sum\nolimits_{i=1}^{k} \sum\nolimits_{x} (S)_{\in S_i} \left\| x^{(j)} - \mu_i \right\|^2 \right], \tag{4}$$

where $x^{(j)} \in R^n$, $\mu_i \in R^n$, μ_i is the centroid for cluster S_i.

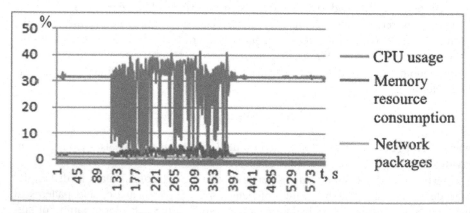

Fig. 1. Resource loading for the state S_1

The identification process is that the values are calculated by values of the incoming sequence, and calculated values are compared with the cluster centroids. Fixed sequence traces from the CPU, network packages and memory resource consumption for different states as well as state clusters with clots that are quite well distinguishable from each other, are shown in the Figs. 1, 2, 3 and 4. There is a correlation between safety of elements of Industry 4.0 devices and their information security.

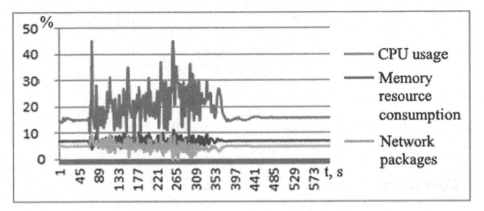

Fig. 2. Resource loading for the state S₂

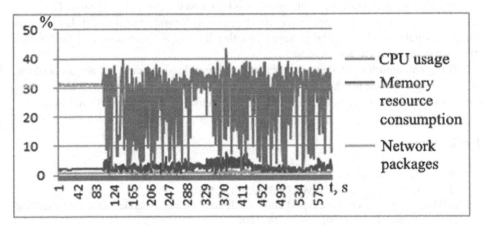

Fig. 3. Resource loading for the state S₃

By measuring the distance to the center of the cluster, the minimum value is selected. The overall accuracy of the selected method for the case of full classification was found to be 98%.

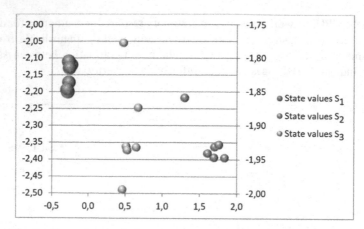

Fig. 4. Clustering results based on average value of coordinate variation

5 Conclusion

The developed approach to the identification of the state of the Industry 4.0 cyber-physical system device based on the clustering method makes it possible to identify the current state of the device. The state analysis is based on the clustering method. The main limitations of the proposed approach are the need to formalize and select data groups for the formation of behavioral patterns. Another limitation is the choice of the lengths of the considered intervals.

The combination of characteristics makes it possible to increase the accuracy of the device state estimation. The basic advantage of the proposed approach is the relative ease of its implementation and minimum requirements for computing resources.

References

1. Farwell, J.P., Rogozinski, R.: Stuxnet and the future of cyber war. Survival **53**(1), 23–40 (2011). https://doi.org/10.1080/00396338.2011.555586
2. Dit-Yan, Y., Yuxin, D.: Host-based intrusion detection using dynamic and static behavioral models. Pattern Recogn. **36**(1), 229–243 (2003)
3. Semenov, V.V., Lebedev, I.S., Sukhoparov, M.E.: Approach to classification of the information security state of elements for cyber physical systems by applying side electromagnetic radiation. Sci. Tech. J. Inf. Technol. Mech. Optics **18**(1), 98–105 (2018). https://doi.org/10.17586/2226-1494-2018-18-1-98-105
4. Gao, D., Reiter, M.K., Song, D.: Beyond output voting: Detecting compromised replicas using HMM-based behavioral distance. IEEE Trans. Dependable Secure Comput. **6**(2), 96–110 (2009)
5. Igure, V.M., Laughter, S.A., Williams, R.D.: Security issues in SCADA networks. Comput. Secur. **25**(7), 498–506 (2006)
6. Bevir, M.K., Osullivan, V.T., Wyatt, D.G.: Computation of electromagnetic flowmeter characteristics from magnetic field data. J. Phys. D Appl. Phys. **14**(3), 373–388 (2006)

7. Semenov, V.V., Lebedev, I.S., Sukhoparov, M.E., Salakhutdinova, K.I.: Application of an autonomous object behavior model to classify the cybersecurity state. In: Galinina, O., Andreev, S., Balandin, S., Koucheryavy, Y. (eds.) NEW2AN/ruSMART -2019. LNCS, vol. 11660, pp. 104–112. Springer, Cham (2019). https://doi.org/10.1007/978-3-030-30859-9_9
8. Hayashi, Y.I., Homma, N., Watanabe, T., Price, W.O., Radasky, W.A.: Introduction to the special section on electromagnetic information security. IEEE Trans. Electromagn. Compatibil. 55(3), 539–546 (2013)
9. Kocher, P., Jaffe, J., Jun, B.: Introduction to differential power analysis and related attacks. In: Proceedings CRYPTO 1998, LNCS, vol. 1109, 104–113 (1998)
10. Bendat, J., Pearsol, A.: Application of correlation and spectral analysis. Mir, Moscow, 312 p. (1983)
11. de Souza Faria, G., Kim, H.Y.: Differential audio analysis: a new side-channel attack on PIN pads. Int. J. Inf. Secur. 18(1), 73–84 (2018). https://doi.org/10.1007/s10207-018-0403-7
12. Gupta, H., Sural, S., Atluri, V., Vaidya, J.: A side-channel attack on smartphones: deciphering key taps using built-in microphones. J. Comput. Secur. 26(2), 255–281 (2018). https://doi.org/10.3233/JCS-17975
13. Spatz, D., Smarra, D., Ternovskiy, I.: A review of anomaly detection techniques leveraging side-channel emissions. In: Proceedings of SPIE – The International Society for Optical Engineering. Cyber Sensing, vol. 11011 (2019). https://doi.org/10.1117/12.2521450
14. Teilans, A.A., Romanov, A.V., Merkuryev, Y.A., Dorogov, P.P., Kleins, A.Y., Potryasaev, S.A.: Assessment of cyber physical system risks with domain specific modelling and simulation. SPIIRAS Proc. 4(59), 115–139 (2018). https://doi.org/10.15622/sp.59.5
15. Gorbachev, I.E., Glukhov, A.P.: Modeling of processes of information security violations of critical infrastructure. SPIIRAS Proc. 1(38), 112–135 (2015). https://doi.org/10.15622/sp.38.7

The State Identification of Industry 4.0 Mechatronic Elements Based on Behavioral Patterns

Mikhail E. Sukhoparov[1] (ID), Viktor V. Semenov[2,3](✉) (ID),
Kseniya I. Salakhutdinova[2] (ID), Evelina P. Boitsova[2] (ID), and Ilya S. Lebedev[2] (ID)

[1] SPbF AO "NPK "TRISTAN", 47 Nepokorennykh pr., St. Petersburg 195220, Russia
[2] SPIIRAS, 14-th Linia, VI, No. 39. St. Petersburg 199178, Russia
v.semenov@iias.spb.su
[3] ITMO University, Kronverksky pr. 49, bldg. A, St. Petersburg 197101, Russia

Abstract. Problematic questions of the state of the Industry 4.0 mechatronic elements have been considered. The prerequisites determining the need to use external monitoring systems have been revealed. The type and statistical characteristics of behavioral patterns used for the analysis have been demonstrated. The proposed approach to the analysis of the autonomous object state is based on clustering methods and allows for the identification of the current state based on the processing of digitized signal traces. An experiment aimed at obtaining statistical information on various types of movement of a mechatronic device element has been described. The obtained data were processed using the k-means method. The approach to identifying the state of Industry 4.0 mechatronic elements based on the processing of digitized sequences received through external channels has been proposed. At the minimum time of the statistical information accumulation with the use of the proposed approach, it becomes possible to reveal differences in the manoeuvres performed by the object, with the probability close to 0.7. The proposed approach to the signal information processing can be used as an additional independent element for identifying the state of Industry 4.0 mechatronic elements. The approach can be quickly adapted to achieve the specified quality of the probabilistic assessment.

Keywords: State analysis · Industry 4.0 behavioral patterns · Nodes and devices

1 Introduction

The development of technologies that combine network, computing and physical processes determines the technologies of Industry 4.0 cyber–physical systems. The shift of emphasis to the embedded software containing artificial intelligence components performing the computation, collection, and analysis of data causes the need for monitoring the processes taking place inside, as is proved in paper [1].

The implementation of Industry 4.0 cyber-physics systems tends to unify components that can be used in various devices for manufacturing, urban infrastructure, and biomedical systems, as shown in paper [2].

© Springer Nature Switzerland AG 2020
O. Galinina et al. (Eds.): NEW2AN 2020/ruSMART 2020, LNCS 12525, pp. 126–134, 2020.
https://doi.org/10.1007/978-3-030-65726-0_12

The access to such devices is carried out both remotely and physically, which considerably expands the possibilities of external destructive impacts and causes the need for the state analysis, according to paper [3].

The principal directions related to the anomaly detection are mainly focused on the analysis of internal device characteristics, network interaction, software integrity, and information availability. However, the presence of mechanical elements of cyber-physical systems (CPS) allows the development and application of methods for detecting physical impacts on remote devices using mechatronic element state analysis, according to papers [4–7].

The functioning of the devices presupposes a preprogrammed response to various external events, which includes the predefined sequence of actions described in previous papers [8–10]. Each operation is characterized by both external and internal processes, including power consumption, electromagnetic radiation, and sound, as illustrated in prior studies [11–14]. The sequence of characteristic values of external and internal processes of such actions forms a behavioral pattern for the performance of predefined commands [15]. The set of characteristic values over time provides various digitized sequences of signal traces, which can be used to identify the object's state.

To identify the state of the Industry 4.0 mechatronic devices, the digitized discrete values of the sample process traces are considered:

$$
y = \left\{ \begin{array}{c} y_0^1, \ldots, y_{k-1}^1 \\ \cdots \\ y_0^r, \ldots, y_{k-1}^r \end{array} \right\} \tag{1}
$$

The use of time synchronization processes allows for the determination of the lengths of all traces equal to K.

Thus, there exists a behavioral pattern of digitized traces of Y of the type $y = [y_0^{(1)} \ldots y_k^r]$ as well as a set of classes $C = \{C_0, \ldots, C_n\}$. There is a target dependence of c': $Y \rightarrow C$, those values are determined based on the training sample $Y^R = (y_i, c_i)_i^T = 1$. It is necessary to build the algorithm of the classification a: $Y \rightarrow C$ as well as the approximate dependence c' on the whole set of Y.

$$
A(y) = \text{argmax}_j \left| \{ r \in 1, 2, \ldots, k \} f(y^r) = j \} \right| \tag{2}
$$

The authors proposed a technique consisting of several stages and conducted a series of experiments to prove its applicability. The accuracy of the proposed approach was assessed.

2   Proposed Approach

To determine the states of mechatronic elements and nodes, a variety of object evaluation indicators are used. The amplitude, frequency, energy and other parameters of signal traces coming to the database can be considered as information channels.

Information about the object state and comparison of the corresponding values makes it possible to form a training sample, which can then be used to detect anomalies.

The proposed approach consists of the four steps.

Step 1: Database provisioning and preliminary selection of the digitized values of the signal traces.

This step involves switching over the device under a predefined operating mode as well as the collection, consolidation, integration, structuring, and organization of the database of behavioral patterns so as to ensure its readiness for the subsequent analysis.

Step 2: Preliminary data processing.

At this stage, the digitized sequences obtained through the previous step are analyzed to eliminate the various noises detected during the data collection process.

Step 3: Clustering.

This step begins with the choice of a clustering method. Clusters are created on the basis of the state data obtained from the processing of the digitized sequence traces. Further, methods are selected for the identification of the device's state and its elements.

Step 4: Identification of states on the basis of the cluster data.

This step involves the processing of incoming current data concerning the digitized sequences received from the device. The analysis is based on the metrics and procedures associated with the chosen current state clustering method.

Figure 1 illustrates the sequence of actions performed during the state identification process.

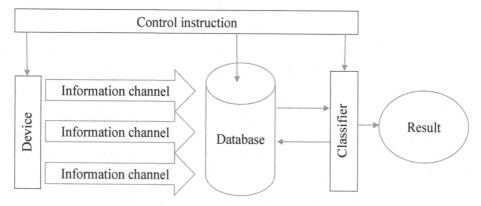

Fig. 1. The state identification sequence of actions

3   Experimentation

The performance of the experiment was based on a pattern consisting of the synchronized coordinate sequences obtained from a data accelerometer. As a result, the state of the analyzed device was identified on the basis of the recognition processes associated with the digitized signal trace values at a rate of 1000 values per each coordinate axis. The trace record times were synchronized, and they contained amplitude values when the signal states changed.

The acceleration and motion parameters were determined by an accelerometer located on the movable part of the manipulator.

The scheme of the experiment is presented in Fig. 2.

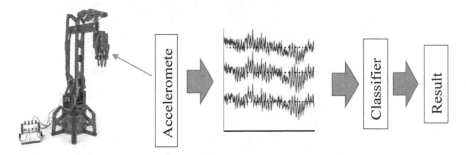

Fig. 2. The scheme of the experiment

The training and test samples contained the digitized sequences of the accelerometer's signals for the following states: S_1 for the forward and reverse manipulator movement, S_2 for the forward and left manipulator movement, and S_3 for the forward and right manipulator movement. The following two "abnormal" states were implemented in an effort to detect deviations: S_4 for the forward and left manipulator movement with interference, and S_5 for the forward and right manipulator movement with interference. The durations of the states also differed, ranging from 3.5 to 4.0 s.

The classified data are presented in the form of value tuples received through different information channels that were synchronized over time.

$$Y(t) = \{(y_0(t_0),\ y_1(t_0),\ \ldots\ y_k(t_0));\ (y_0(t_1),\ y_1(t_1),\ \ldots\ y_k(t_1));\ \ldots;\ (y_0(t_r),\ y_1(t_r),\ \ldots\ y_k(t_r))\}$$
(3)

where $Y(t)$ is a tuple of the $y_i(t_j)$ values of the digitized sequences obtained from the different information channels over time.

The digitized sequences obtained from various sources form a conventional behavioral pattern concerning the device's state. The information contained within the pattern characterizes the state of the device when receiving a typical command and also allows for the analysis of abnormal deviations.

A training sample was formed for all the different states (S_1–S_5). Figure 3 shows the information obtained when digitizing the data concerning the acceleration projections received from an accelerometer for the different states. It can be seen from the graphs that in case of performing a certain manipulation, the acceleration along the corresponding axis changes accordingly to state.

The analysis of the data obtained from the digitized trace sequences demonstrates both their homogeneity and the strongly pronounced group density. Further, the number of clusters corresponds to the number of defined states. The k–means clustering method allowed for the division of n observations of the digitized sequences of the signal traces into k non–overlapping clusters by the states.

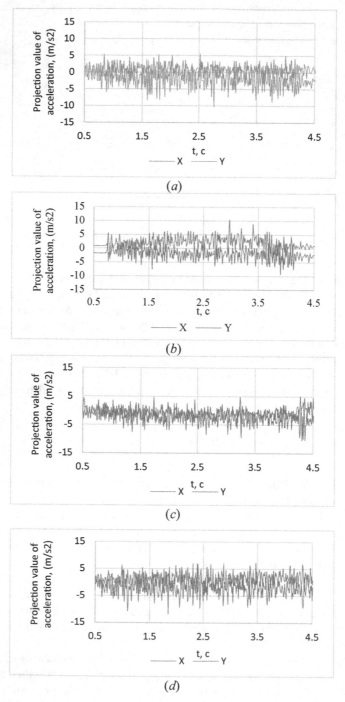

Fig. 3. The acceleration projections for the states: S_1 (a), S_2 (b), S_3 (c), and S_4 (d)

The Euclidean distance was used as a proximity measure for the numerical attributes:

$$\rho(x, y) = ||x - y|| = \sqrt{\sum_{\rho=1}^{n}(x_\rho - y_\rho)^2} \tag{4}$$

where $x, y \in R^n$, R is the observation space.

Using the training sample values obtained via the k-means clustering method, the division of m observations into k groups (or clusters) ($k \leq m$), $S = \{S_1, S_2, ..., S_k\}$ was performed in such a way as to minimize the total squared error of the cluster points from the centroids of the clusters:

$$\min\left[\sum_{i=1}^{k}\sum_{x}(S)_{\in S_i}\left|\left|x^{(j)} - \mu_i\right|\right|^2\right] \tag{5}$$

where $x^{(j)} \in R^n$, $\mu_i \in R^n$, μ_i is the centroid for the S_i cluster.

Figure 4 presents state clusters; apart from that, clots can be found that are quite well distinguished from each other and the cluster sizes are similar. This allows us to conclude that the proposed approach has a good resolution.

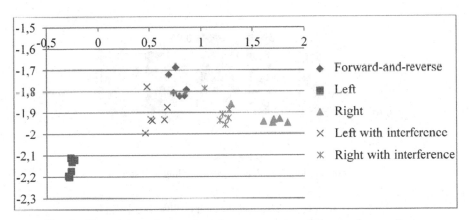

Fig. 4. Clustering results based on the average value of changes in coordinates

The occurrence of new digitized sequences is processed, and then the distance is compared to the cluster centroids. The result is the cluster with a minimum distance to its center.

The results of the state analysis are presented in Table 1. Proposed approach has shown sufficient results for multi-classification of the states of Industry 4.0 mechatronic Elements.

Table 1. Results of the state analysis based on the search of the nearest centroid of k-means clusters

		Projected state				
		S_1	S_2	S_3	S_4	S_5
Real state	S_1	421	10	5	1	12
	S_2	5	471	17	0	3
	S_3	1	11	473	13	1
	S_4	7	12	55	419	6
	S_5	20	29	7	2	430

Figure 5 illustrates the classification results in terms of the class classification accuracy, according to the check and test data.

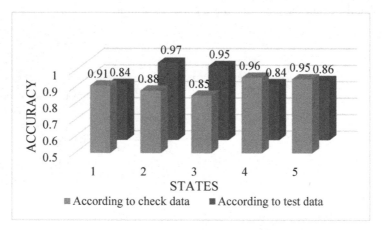

Fig. 5. The classification results

The sum of the diagonal element values demonstrates the total number of states that were correctly assigned to the corresponding cluster. The total accuracy of the selected method for the case of the full classification was found to be 0.90. The classification accuracy for most of classes is sufficient. The decrease in accuracy for some states is caused by some similarity of the portrait of the received signals in different parts of the time series.

4   Conclusion

This paper presents a method for the state identification of the mechatronic device of the Industry 4.0 cyber-physical system through information clusterization in databases of digitized signal trace sequences. The method will make it possible to determine the anomalous (in terms of function) states of devices.

The main advantage of the proposed approach is its simplicity. The method has a good operation speed. As shown in this paper, the use of five states for the recognition demonstrates the utility of the proposed method application; it should be noted that the proposed method detects anomalous states with acceptable identification accuracy values. Future directions of work are related to the development of the proposed approach in order to increase the number of identifiable states. Another direction is the research of new typical profiles of functioning for the effective application of the technique to other types of devices.

References

1. Chopra, A.: Paradigm shift and challenges in IoT security. In: Journal of Physics: Conference Series. V. 1432. First International Conference on Emerging Electrical Energy, Electronics and Computing Technologies; 30–31 October 2019, Melaka, Malaysia (2019). https://doi.org/10.1088/1742-6596/1432/1/012083
2. Teilans, A.A., Romanov, A.V., Merkuryev Yu, A., Dorogov, P.P., Kleins Ya, A., Potryasaev, S.A.: Assessment of cyber physical system risks with domain specific modelling and simulation. SPIIRAS Proceedings, 2018, vol. 4, no. 59, pp 115–139 (2018). https://doi.org/10.15622/sp.59.5
3. Gorbachev, I.E., Glukhov, A.P.: Modeling of processes of information security violations of critical infrastructure. In: SPIIRAS Proceedings, 2015, vol. 1, no. 38, pp 112–135 (2015). https://doi.org/10.15622/sp.38.7
4. Semenov, V.V., Lebedev, I.S.: Processing of signal information in problems of monitoring information security of unmanned autonomous objects. Sci. Tech. Bull. Inf.n Technol. Mech. Optics 19(3), 492–498 (2019). https://doi.org/10.17586/2226-1494-2019-19-3-492-498
5. Sukhoparov, M.E., Semenov, V.V., Lebedev, I.S.: Information security monitoring of elements of cyber-physical systems using artificial neural networks. Methods Tech. Means Inf. Saf. Provis. 27, 59–60 (2018)
6. Salakhutdinova, K.I., Lebedev, I.S., Krivtsova, I.E., Sukhoparov, M.E.: Research of the descriptor and ratio selection influence at signature formation in the task on identification of programs problems of information security. Comput. Syst. 1, 136–141 (2018)
7. Lebedev, I.S., Korzhuk, V., Krivtsova, I.E., Salakhutdinova, K.I, Sukhoparov, M.E, Tikhonov, D.: Using preventive measures for the purpose of assuring information security of wireless communication channels. In: Conference of Open Innovation Association, FRUCT 18. Series "Proceedings of the 18th Conference of Open Innovations Association FRUCT and Seminar on Information Security and Protection of Information Technology, FRUCT-ISPIT 2016, pp 167–173 (2016)
8. Devesh, M., Kant, A.K., Suchit, Y.R., Tanuja, P., Kumar, S.N.: Fruition of CPS and IoT in context of industry 4.0. In: Choudhury, S., Mishra, R., Mishra, R.G., Kumar, A. (eds.) Intelligent Communication, Control and Devices. AISC, vol. 989, pp. 367–375. Springer, Singapore (2020). https://doi.org/10.1007/978-981-13-8618-3_39

9. Page, J., Zaslavsky, A., Indrawan, M.: Countering security vulnerabilities using a shared security buddy model schema in mobile agent communities. In: Proceedings of the First International Workshop on Safety and Security in Multi-Agent Systems (SASEMAS 2004), pp 85–101 (2004)
10. Semenov, V.V., Lebedev, I.S., Sukhoparov, M.E.: The state identification of individual cyber-physical system elements based on of the external behavioral characteristics. Appl. Inform. **13**(77), 72–83 (2018)
11. Hayashi, Y.I., Homma, N., Watanabe, T., Price, W.O., Radasky, W.A. Introduction to the Special Section on Electromagnetic Information Security. IEEE Trans. Electromagnetic Compatibil. **55**(3), 539–546 (2013)
12. Kocher, P., Jaffe, J., Jun, B.: Introduction to differential power analysis and related attacks. In: Proceedings CRYPTO 1998; 1998, LNCS, vol. 1109, pp 104–113 (1998)
13. de Souza Faria, G., Kim, H.Y.: Differential audio analysis: a new side-channel attack on PIN pads. Int. J. Inf. Secur. **18**(1), 73–84 (2018). https://doi.org/10.1007/s10207-018-0403-7
14. Gupta, H., Sural, S., Atluri, V., Vaidya, J.: A side-channel attack on smartphones: deciphering key taps using built-in microphones. J. Comput. Secur. **26**(2), 255–281 (2018). https://doi.org/10.3233/jcs-17975
15. Spatz, D., Smarra, D., Ternovskiy, I.: A review of anomaly detection techniques leveraging side-channel emissions. In: Proceedings of SPIE – The International Society for Optical Engineering. Cyber Sensing 2019, vol. 11011 (2019). https://doi.org/10.1117/12.2521450

Data Mining Algorithms Parallelization in the Framework of Agent-Oriented Programming

Aleksey Malov[✉], Ivan Kholod, Sergey Rodionov, and Evgenia Novikova

Saint Petersburg Electrotechnical University "LETI", Saint Petersburg, Russia
alexeimal-2@yandex.ru, iiholod@etu.ru, sv-rodion@mail.ru,
novikova@comsec.spb.ru

Abstract. This article describes an approach to parallelization of data mining algorithms in the framework of agent-oriented programming for distributed data processing. The conversion of Naive Bayes algorithm into agent-oriented form for distributed execution and the algorithm implementation in the framework of agent-oriented programming are described as an example.

Keywords: Parallel algorithms · Distributed algorithms · Data mining · Distributed data mining · MapReduce · Agent-oriented programming

1 Introduction

Nowadays, there is an intensive growth of the amount of stored information. The volume of information from different sources and gadgets increases constantly. The set of such sources includes sensors, video cameras, mobile devices, etc. Internet of Things (IoT) is the set of such devices, united in global network. The volume of information in IoT will only increase with time [1, 2]. Currently, this kind of data is called Big data. Big data in IoT has next properties: large volumes, different storage formats and a high rate of change.

Data mining of Big data is associated with the analysis of big volume of data. It requires the usage of significant computational resources for get acceptable analysis time. Therefore, parallelization of Data mining algorithms is the actual direction in the development and implementation of such class of algorithms.

MapReduce (US patent No. 9612883) is the known method of performing data processing in a distributed and parallel processing environment.

The main disadvantages of this method are that the known method is suitable only for some tasks of Data mining. At the same time, there are Data mining algorithms, for example, Apriori, PageRank, etc., for which this method is not suitable, since the algorithms do not have a list homomorphism [3–5].

Also, this method does not show approaches to the implementation of Data mining algorithms in the framework of agent-oriented programming. Implementation and parallelization of Data mining algorithms in the framework of agent-oriented programming is

O. Galinina et al. (Eds.): NEW2AN 2020/ruSMART 2020, LNCS 12525, pp. 135–147, 2020.
https://doi.org/10.1007/978-3-030-65726-0_13

separate part of Data mining algorithm realization. This separate part appears due to the significant differences between agent-oriented approach and the traditional imperative approach. Therefore, this direction should be supported by special methods of implementing Data mining algorithms with the aim of their execution in the agent-oriented environment.

There is next main problem of parallel execution of program written in imperative programming languages (Java, C/C++, Fortran and others.). Their parallel execution is required simultaneous access to the program state from parallel branches. Therefore, there are such problems as access synchronization, blocking, race and others. Solving these problems is a difficult task at stages of development and debugging [6].

2   Agent-Oriented Programming Features and Related Works

Agent-based programming is a programming approach that assumes the design of software systems based on software agents.

In object-oriented programming, class objects interact with each other through an interface. The interface of the class object is defined in the corresponding class. A call to an object, can lead to a call to another object.

Agent-based programming assumes the interaction of a software agent with an external environment that can change rapidly. By agent is assumed a software or hardware component that can perform the tasks assigned to it. It is assumed that the agent is capable of perceiving changes in the environment, interacting with it, and performing actions that change the environment. Users and other software agents are also included in the external environment of the agent.

It can be seen from the foregoing that a program agent is a significantly more complex entity compared to a class object in object-oriented programming. Thus, the agent-based approach allows us to describe complex software and hardware systems at a new level.

For solving computational problems, program agents can be represented as computational actors. This approach assumes that a program agent has the ability to create new program agents in an agent-based programming environment, send a message to other program agents at a known address and receive messages from other program agents.

All mention capabilities allow creating universal patterns of decision for data mining algorithms [7].

There a lot of research in the field of parallelization of data mining algorithms. The biggest part of the research in focused on particular data mining algorithms and optimization of parallel structure of algorithms for execution under particular conditions. Those conditions can be different [8]. For this reason the parallel algorithms developed under particular conditions, may not be efficient under other conditions.

There are a lot of examples of realization of different types of data mining algorithms for specific types of computing systems. The set of classes of such algorithms includes decision tree algorithms, association algorithms, clustering algorithms [9–14]. All of these algorithms were implemented in imperative programming languages.

There are a lot of algorithms implementations in the framework of agent-oriented programming. However, existing decisions are intended for particular algorithm.

Thus, the most part of approaches resolve task of parallelization for particular Data Mining algorithm that requires significant effort to adopt such approach for new algorithm or create one new approach. The approach describing in this article allows converting sequential Data Mining algorithm, implemented in imperative languages into the parallel form for execution in the framework of agent-oriented programming.

3 Implementation of Data Mining Algorithm in the Framework of Agent-Oriented Programming

3.1 Data Mining Algorithm Representation as a Function

Data mining algorithm at the input receives a set of input data, and the result of if work is the final output knowledge model. Thus, each Data mining algorithm represents a function, since it receives as input a set of input data and returns the result of applying the algorithm to the input data in the form of the final output knowledge model.

During the work, Data mining algorithms analyze the data set and build an intermediate knowledge model at each step. The made intermediate knowledge model is sent to the next stage. Thus, the Data mining algorithm can be represented by a functional expression in the form of a composition of functions [15]:

$$f = fn°fn - 1°\ldots°fi°\ldots°f1$$

3.2 Data Mining Algorithm Representation in the Framework of Agent-Oriented Programming

Each function fi from previous expression represents the step of the algorithm. A data set (D) and an intermediate knowledge model are input data for each of such step. A new intermediate knowledge model (MP) is the result of the work.

Thus, the Data mining algorithm can be represented as sequential work of software agents implementing the step of algorithm.

$$D \text{->} A1 \text{->} \ldots \text{->} Ai \text{->} \ldots \text{->} An, \tag{1}$$

where Ai - a software agent implementing the i-th step of the Data mining algorithm, receives as input arguments a set of input data (D) of the Data mining algorithm and an intermediate knowledge model. In (1) the arrows indicate the transfer of the initial data (D) of the Data mining algorithm and an intermediate knowledge model from one software agent to the next.

The program agent A1, which implements the first step of the Data mining algorithm, receives only a set of input data (D) of the Data mining algorithm as input arguments.

The result of the work of each software agent is an intermediate knowledge model using in the next step. The result of the work of the software agent An is the final output knowledge model.

Hereinafter, the examples will use the notation of programming language Java [https://docs.oracle.com/javase/tutorial/]. Also, the examples will use concepts, approaches and built-in classes of the agent-oriented programming framework JADE [http://jade.tilab.com].

It is convenient to represent the set of initial data (D) of the Data mining algorithm in the form of list data structures. In Java, the source data set (D) can be represented as a class containing as a member a list of attributes (attributes_list), a list of vectors (vectors_list) and a list of all possible classes of the target attribute (class_list):

The set of initial data (D) of the Data mining algorithm can be conveniently represented in the form of list data structures. In Java, the initial data set (D) can be represented as a class containing as a members a list of attributes (attributes_list), a list of vectors (vectors_list) and a list of all possible classes of the target attribute (class_list):

```
public class D
{
    public ArrayList<ArrayList> attributes_list;
    public ArrayList<ArrayList> vectors_list;
    public ArrayList class_list;
}
```

A list consisting of K attributes (attributes_list) can be defined in the following way:

```
ArrayList<ArrayList> attributes_list =
{{
    add(attr0);
        ...
    add(attrK);
}};
```

where attr $<i>$ - list of possible values of the i-th attribute. Below is an example for attribute 0 consisting of five values:

ArrayList attr0 = new ArrayList(Arrays.asList(0.5, 3.0, 4.5, 5.4, 2.5));

A list consisting of L vectors (vectors_list) can be defined in the following way:

```
ArrayList<ArrayList> vectors_list =
{{
    add(vector0);
        ...
    add(vectorL);
}};
```

where vector $<i>$ is a list of the values of each attribute and the value of the target attribute. The value of the i-th attribute is located at the i-th place in the list. If the value of the target attribute is unknown, then in Java, it can be represented with the null character. The value of the target attribute can be placed at the end of the list. Below is an example for vector 0. First four values correspond to the attribute values, and the last value corresponds to the value of the target attribute:

ArrayList vector0 = new ArrayList(Arrays.asList(1.5, 4.0, 4.2, 5.5, 8.5));
ArrayList vector0 = new ArrayList(Arrays.asList(1.5, 4.0, 4.2, 5.5, 8.5));

The structure of the intermediate (MP) and final output knowledge model (M) depends on the algorithm that implements Data mining. Intermediate (MP) and the final output knowledge model (M) can be represented in the form of list data structures. For example, a knowledge model in the form of decision trees is often used for the algorithms of Data mining. In general, an intermediate knowledge model (MP) can be represented as structure consisting of the parameters of the current step (step_context) and the list of rules (rules_list).

```
public class MP
{
    public StepContexClass step_context;
    public ArrayList<ArrayList> rules_list;
}
```

The parameters of the current step (step_context) can contain, for example, a list of attributes that have not yet been used to build the knowledge model, and therefore should be processed in the following steps.

3.3 The Approach for the Implementation of Data Mining Algorithms in the Framework of Agent-Oriented Programming

In main case Data mining applications have data parallelism. For parallel execution of the application approach assumes adding a data partitioning features and features for merge the results obtained in software agent working simultaneously and implementing particular step of Data mining algorithm. The merge of the results should be performed in the main software agent.

In contrast to MapReduce, such approach allows to parallelize algorithms that do not have a list homomorphism. Such result is achieved because of execution in parallel mode of each individual step of Data mining algorithm, rather than the entire algorithm at once.

Mentioned features allow parallelizing of the application in an agent-oriented programming framework and a multi-agent system JADE. Properly configured JADE system installed on a set of interconnected systems, each of which has one or several processors and memory, must have functionality for

- transferring messages with data from a plurality software agents to the main software agent,
- creating of the set of software agents, in the main software agent, and the subsequent launch of the set of software agents in the systems to execute,
- receiving data in the main software agent from a plurality of software agents,
- launching the main software agent in the system for execution,
- execution of a plurality of software agents, including the main software agent, on any of the processors of the system
- reading from input files or databases source data specifying a task;

The features that need to be implemented for execution of the application in the framework of agent-oriented programming consist of:

- the feature of splitting the input data into parts for the work of a one of the set of software agents;
- the feature of merging the results of the set of software agents into a single intermediate knowledge model in the form of a set of list data structures;
- the feature of creation the final output knowledge model from the intermediate knowledge model formed at the last stage;
- the feature of receiving data in the main software agent, having the ability to receive data from a set of software agents;
- the main software agent, implemented in the agent-oriented programming environment, having next abilities

  - the creation of the set of software agents implementing a certain step of the application, and the subsequent launch of the set of software agents in the systems to execute;
  - the execution of the feature of splitting the input data into parts for the work of a one of the set of software agents;
  - the transferring of data to a set of software agents;
  - the execution of the feature of merging the results of the set of software agents into a single intermediate knowledge model in the form of a set of list data structures;
  - the execution of the feature of receiving data in the main software agent.

- form software agents, having next abilities

  - the performing of an application step;
  - the execution of the feature of transferring work results to the main software agent.

Input data D from files or databases must be read by the main software agent into a set of list data structures containing attribute lists and vector lists. The configured JADE system should have features for reading from input files or databases source data specifying a task. Since the main software agent can be executed on any machine from the system, then all machines in the system should have access to required files or databases.

4 Parallelization of Naive Bayes Algorithm in the Framework of Agent-Oriented Programming

As examples, we will consider probability algorithm Naive Bayes [16].

```
for all attributes a
  if a is not target attribute
    for all vectors w
      increment count of vectors for value of attribute a
        equaled value of the attribute a of the vector w
    end for all vectors;
  end if
end for all attributes;
for all classes c
  for all vectors w
    increment count of vectors for class of vector w;
  end for all vectors
end for all classes c
```

The input data (D) for the algorithm can be represented in the form of a table, each row of which contains the values of the input attributes and the class of the target attribute corresponding to them.

The input data (D) of the algorithm can be represented in the next form

```
public class D
{
    public ArrayList<ArrayList> attributes_list;
    public ArrayList<ArrayList> vectors_list;
    public ArrayList class_list;
}
```

where
attributes_list - a list of attributes, vectors_list - a list of vectors, class_list - a list of all possible classes of the target attribute.

The implementation of the Naive Bayes algorithm needs to be transformed in the form of software agents performing the steps of the application and the main software agent, with the purpose to run on execute the application in an agent-oriented programming environment. To implement the main program agent, it is necessary to add functionality for splitting the input data and merging the results computed in the set of software agents implementing the application step.

Below is a variant of a parallel algorithm, which performs parallel processing on vectors, implemented with usage of the offered approach. The implementation of the main agent class using the build-in classes of the JADE agent-oriented programming framework is placed below:

```
import jade.core.Agent;
import jade.core.behaviours.OneShortBehaviour;
/*the import of all required libraries */

public class AgentMainBehaviour extends OneShotBehaviour
{
    public void action()
    {
        D d;
        load_data(d);
        MP mp = new MP();

        //The initialization of software agents performing
        //the step of application and send
        //a list of vectors for calculations
        divide_vectors_parall (D);

        merge_attr_parall( mp);
        set_best_attr(mp);
        M m;

        //Build the final output model
        build_final_model(mp, m);

        // Actions with the final output model
        // M - save to database, files, etc.

        myAgent.doDelete(); //Finish the work of software agent

        return;
    }
    .....
    //Auxiliary methods of the class
}

public class AgentMain extends Agent
{
    public void setup()
    {
            addBehaviour(new AgentMainBehaviour (this));
    }
}
```

The AgentMain class is the implementation of the main software agent for parallel execution of the algorithm with parallelization by vectors in the JADE environment. The class inherits from the build-in Agent class of the JADE framework.

AgentMainBehaviour is the class of behavior. It is installed in the setup () method of AgentMain class. AgentMainBehaviour implements the behavior of a program agent in terms of the JADE environment. The AgentMainBehaviour class inherits from the build-in OneShotBehaviour class of the JADE framework.

The task performing by main software agent is implemented in the action() method of the class AgentMainBehaviour. The action() method is called once after the agent starts. When the method finishes, the agent stops execution.

The function load_data loads the source data from files or databases into an instance d of class D. The function divide_attr_parall is designed to split the source data into parts. Each part is intended for the work of a one of the set of software agents. The function is a member of the class AgentMainBehaviour. In the function before starting the set of software agents, the number of machines in the system on which agents can run is determined. Based on the mentioned number, it calculates the range of data for each of the set of software agents. Each of the set of software agents implementing the step of the application has to process its own data range. Further, in the process of the function work, a set of software agents are launched in the JADE environment and information about the running agents is stored in variable members of the class. The function also passes to each of the set of running software agents a set of vectors intended for processing by the software agent. The implementation is omitted in the example for simplicity. It should be noted that the implementation depends on the agent-oriented programming framework.

The function merge_attr_parall is designed for merging the results of the set of software agents into a single intermediate knowledge model (mp). Each of the set of software agents sends the results of the work to the main software agent at the end of work. The function merge_attr_parall receives the results of the work from each of the set of software agents implementing the step of application.

The function build_final_model forms the final output knowledge model (m).

The implementation of the class of software agent implementing the step of the application is placed below. The implementation uses the build-in classes of the agent-oriented programming framework JADE:

```
import jade.core.Agent;
import jade.core.behaviours.OneShortBehaviour;
/*the import of all required libraries */

public class AgentStepBehaviour extends OneShotBehaviour
{
    public void action()
    {
        D d;
        load_data(d);
        MP mp = new MP();

        for ( ArrayList cur_vector : receive_vector_list_for_handle() )
        {
            handle_cur_vector(cur_vector, d, mp);
        }
        send_results_to_main_agent(mp);

        myAgent.doDelete(); //Finish the work of software agent
        return;
    }
    .....
    //Auxiliary methods of the class
}

public class AgentStep extends Agent
{
    public void setup()
    {
        addBehaviour(new AgentStepBehaviour (this));
    }
}
```

Classes Agent, OneShotBehaviour are the standard classes of the JADE environment used to implement the software agent class. Those classes as well as other used concepts of the JADE environment were observed earlier. The purpose of the function load_data were observed earlier too. The receive_vector_list_for_handle method of the class AgentStepBehaviour receives from the main program agent a list of vector intended for processing by particular software agent and returns it as a result.

The function handle_cur_vector processes the vector from the parameters and adds the results to the intermediate knowledge model mp. The function send_results_to_main_agent is used to send the results of the work of the software agent to the main software agent. The implementation of the function is omitted in the example for simplicity.

Thus, the implementation of parallelization by the vectors of the Naive Bayes algorithm on the basis of the offered approach was overviewed.

5   Performance Evaluation

There were performed a series of experiments for the implemented Naive Bayes algorithms. The experiments have been performed with various input data sets (Table 1). These data sets contain various numbers of vectors. The usage of several data sets allows reaching different loading of the Naive Bayes algorithm.

Table 1. The description of input data sets

Input data set	Number of vectors	Number of attributes	Number of classes
W1	30000	50	100
W2	150000	50	100
W3	300000	50	100

The experiments were performed on a computer having several CPU cores with following configuration: CPU Intel (8 cores), 3 GHz, 16 Gb, Ubuntu 18.04 LTS, JADE 4.5. In the framework of agent-oriented programming algorithms were executed for the numbers of software agents (accordingly CPU cores) equal to 4 and 8. The experimental results are presented in Table 2.

Table 2. Results of experiments (s)

Algorithm	Cores	W1	W2	W3
Sequential form of Naive Bayes algorithm	1	2,18	44,37	170
Agent-oriented form of Naive Bayes algorithm	4	0,6	11,2	43,22
	8	0,34	6,29	24,38

According to experiments the execution times of the Naive Bayes algorithm for different data sets and parameters are different. The algorithm performs faster with grow of the count of software agents.

The coefficient of performance increasing is approximately equivalent to the count of using software agents (CPUs core), but a little bit less. Such results are observed because part of the time in the case of parallel execution consumes for data transfer between software agents. Also there is regularity described below. When the count of vectors grows, than percent of time for data transfer between software agents will decrease. Such results are observed because of the time required for computation will increase when the count of vectors grows. Accordingly computation time will consume the biggest part of entire task time, when the count of the vectors of input data sets grows.

6   Conclusion

There are a big volume and big amount of different kind of data in the word of IoT. This kind of data is called Big data. Data mining and Big data analyzing are difficult tasks requiring significant computational resources for get acceptable analysis time. For this reason parallelization of Data mining algorithms is the actual direction in the development and implementation of such class of algorithms.

Standard approaches like MapReduce are suitable only for some tasks of Data mining. This article describes an approach to implementation of data mining algorithms in the framework of agent-oriented programming. Features of the framework of agent-oriented programming for implementation Data mining algorithms were observed. The approach assumes representing an algorithm as a functional expression. Each function from the expression can be implemented in the form of software agent.

For execution of the algorithm in the framework of agent-oriented programming, according to approach it is necessary to add functionality for splitting the input data and merging the results computed in the set of software agents implementing the application step.

Using the proposed approach Naive Bayes algorithm was implemented. An experiment results showed the effectiveness of version for different data sets. Agent-oriented forms of the algorithm are more effective than sequential when several CPUs are available.

References

1. Santucci, G.: From internet to data to internet of things. In: Proceedings of the International Conference on Future Trends of the Internet (2009)
2. Tsai, C.-W., Lai, C.-F., Vasilakos, A.V.: Future internet of things: open issues and challenges. Wireless Netw. **20**(8), 2201–2217 (2014)
3. Gorlatch, S.: Extracting and implementing list homomorphisms in parallel program development. Sci. Comput. Program. **33**, 1–27 (1999)
4. Dean, J., Ghemawat, S.: MapReduce: simplified data processing on large clusters. In: Proceedings of the USENIX Symposium on Operating Systems Design & Implementation (OSDI), pp. 137–147 (2004)
5. Harmelen, F., Kotoulas, S., Oren, E., Urbani, J.: Scalable distributed reasoning using map reduce. In: Proceedings of the International Semantic Web Conference, vol. 5823, pp. 293–309 (2009)
6. Malov, A., Rodionov, S., Shorov, A.: Data mining algorithms parallelization in logic programming framework for execution in cluster. In: Galinina, O., Andreev, S., Balandin, S., Koucheryavy, Y. (eds.) NEW2AN/ruSMART -2019. LNCS, vol. 11660, pp. 91–103. Springer, Cham (2019). https://doi.org/10.1007/978-3-030-30859-9_8
7. Burgin, M.: Systems, Actors and Agents: Operation in a multicomponent environment. https://pdfs.semanticscholar.org/97bb/93c8a1850a9fcdd3e1ef9a441c491e0976da.pdf
8. Zaki, M.J.: Parallel and distributed data mining: an introduction. In: Zaki, M.J., Ho, C.-T. (eds.) LSPDM 1999. LNCS (LNAI), vol. 1759, pp. 1–23. Springer, Heidelberg (2000). https://doi.org/10.1007/3-540-46502-2_1
9. Kufrin, R.: Decision trees on parallel processors. In: Geller, J., Kitano, H., Suttner, C. (eds.) Parallel Processing for Artificial Intelligence 3. Elsevier-Science (1997)

10. Zaki, M.J., Ogihara, M., Parthasarathy, S., Li, W.: Parallel data mining for association rules on shared-memory multi-processors. In: Supercomputing 1996 (1996)
11. Cheung, D., Hu, K., Xia, S.: Asynchronous parallel algorithm for mining association rules on shared-memory multi-processors. In: 10th ACM Symposium on Parallel Algorithms and Architectures (1998)
12. Kashef, R.: Cooperative clustering model and its applications. Ph.D. thesis, University of Waterloo, Department of Electrical and Computer Engineering (2008)
13. Hammouda, K.M., Kamel, M.S.: Distributed collaborative web document clustering using cluster keyphrase summaries. Inf. Fusion 9(4), 465–480 (2008)
14. Deb, D., Angryk, R.A.: Distributed document clustering using word-clusters. In: IEEE Symposium on Computational Intelligence and Data Mining, CIDM 2007, pp. 376–383 (2007)
15. Kholod, I., Malov, A., Rodionov, S.: Data mining algorithms parallelizing in functional programming language for execution in cluster. In: Balandin, S., Andreev, S., Koucheryavy, Y. (eds.) ruSMART 2015. LNCS, vol. 9247, pp. 140–151. Springer, Cham (2015). https://doi.org/10.1007/978-3-319-23126-6_13
16. Malov, A., Rodionov, S., Kholod, I.: The realization of Naive Bayes algorithm in the logic programming framework PROLOG. In: Proceeding of 2016 IEEE North West Russia Section Young Researchers in Electrical and Electronic Engineering Conference, pp. 290–294. IEEE (2016)

The IoT and Big Data in the Logistics Development. Crude Oil Transportation in the Arctic Zone Case Study

Igor Ilin⬛, Alexandra Borremans^(✉) ⬛, and Stepan Bakhaev⬛

Peter the Great St. Petersburg Polytechnic University, Polytechnicheskaya 29, 195351 St. Petersburg, Russia
Alexandra.borremans@mail.ru

Abstract. The following contribution illustrates effects and potentials that digitalization has on the supply chain. Supply Chain Management itself is considered to be a tool for visualization, optimization and synchronization of various groups of processes within an enterprise, while its digitalization can potentially increase this influence. Such digital technologies as Big Data and Internet of Things in combination create new possibilities for a closer interlinking of participants as well as wide-ranging potentials for an optimization of supply chain planning and logistics management. Similarly, the paper aims to recognize the impacts of Big Data Analytics on information usage in a corporate and supply chain context as it is imperative for companies' logistics management to access to up-to-date, accurate, and meaningful information. Moreover, such information becomes extremely relevant when working with information that depends on constantly changing external factors, for example, severe climatic conditions. The study highlights the case of the Arctic zone, where emerging technologies allows to optimize the process of oil transportation.

Keywords: IoT · Big data · Supply chain management · Arctic zone · Big data analytics

1 Introduction

In a dynamic market environment that is characterized by a high degree of competition, companies must be able to react flexibly to permanently changing factors of influence. Consequently, the concept of supply chain management aims at optimizing business processes within the supply chain in order to reach an adaptation to dynamic market requirements. However, in this particular paper the emphasis of automizing the process the performance of which is heavily dependent on the outer environmental factors. Company's operation deployed in one of the most severe and harsh regions on the planet - the Arctic provided with the hardly manageable risks.

In order to mitigate the risks associated with the supply of oil to the developed fields, it is necessary to use the most advanced digital technologies available on the market. It

© Springer Nature Switzerland AG 2020
O. Galinina et al. (Eds.): NEW2AN 2020/ruSMART 2020, LNCS 12525, pp. 148–154, 2020.
https://doi.org/10.1007/978-3-030-65726-0_14

is necessary to exclude errors that may arise due to the human factor in order to make work processes safer and less costly [1].

Information is undoubtedly a major driver of decision making on all corporate levels: strategic, tactical, and operational. The widespread of Information and Communication Technology (ICT) has enabled the business to access massive datasets that, with the proper management, become a significant resource for enhancing strategic and business processes. However, the constant growth of the amount of data and information generated by companies sets a challenge for businesses to extract the value from it as it becomes a more complicated process of identification and application of the most relevant information.

The impact of digitalization and Industry 4.0 on the ripple effect and disruption risk control analytics in the supply chain is studied. As it is imperative for companies in the supply chain to have access to up-to-date, accurate, and meaningful information, the exploratory research provides insights into the opportunities and challenges emerging from the adaptation of Big Data Analytics in Supply Chain Management describing the operation of the oil production and transportation in the Russia's Arctic region. This description is based on an analysis of the case of Gazprom Neft, which operates throughout Russia's major oil and gas regions, including Russia's Arctic Shelf – The Prirazlomnoye Project, and Novy Port – one of the most significant oil and gas-condensate field under development in the Yamalo-Nenets Autonomous Okrug [2].

The purpose of this paper is to contribute to theory development in Supply Chain Management by investigating the potential impacts of IoT and Big Data Analytics on information usage in a corporate and supply chain context.

2 Methods

The basis of the analysis in this article was a review of the literature on the topic of supply chain management in the Arctic, application of IoT and Big Data technologies, and case study of Gazprom Neft company, as well as interviews with company representatives.

The effectiveness of the development of remote Arctic fields largely depends on how competently the oil transportation system is organized [3]. In the case of Prirazlomnoye and Novy Port hydrocarbons can only be exported by sea for several reasons. The most important one is that the fields are located at a considerable distance from the traditional oil transportation infrastructure. In such conditions, competent logistics becomes critical as any interruption occurrence in shipping increase the risks of overflowing the tank farm which leads to a limitation of the level of oil production. Hence it is fraught with financial and reputational losses to the company.

The supply chain that provides transportation of crude oil produced in Arctic oil fields includes several important links. When preparing a shipping plan, it is necessary to take into account the monthly volume of oil production, the possibility of its accumulation in tank farms, restrictions on mooring to terminals. Raw materials from assets are transported using 12 shuttle tankers that make regular round-trip movement of cargo between the floating oil storage tank in the Kola Bay near Murmansk, the platform in the Pechora Sea where two tankers operate, and the Arctic Gate terminal in the Gulf of Ob where 10 tankers operate. Despite the fact that all tankers have a reinforced ice-class that allows them to work in the Arctic, atomic icebreakers Atomflot are involved in their safe and efficient movement during the winter navigation in the Kara Sea and the Gulf of Ob [4].

The issue of uninterrupted and efficient logistics is critical for the Gazprom Neft Arctic field, which are remotely accessible from the infrastructure: production volumes are directly dependent on the timely export of hydrocarbons. Manual logistic calculation for such a number of participants and constantly growing volume of data appears to be ineffective and especially labor-consuming process.

Technologies developed for a more comprehensive and more efficient use of data have long been a significant element in Supply Chain Management, as many optimization approaches and methods only became applicable in practice with data availability and usage thereof. There are many examples for this, such as the automatized acquisition of shipping data per RFID, with which the status of shipments can be tracked via defined registration points, or the GPS-based optimization of transport routes for the minimization of transportation time and the prevention of unloaded mileage for vehicles [5]. Further developments of ERP systems have also strongly furthered cross-functional and cross-system harmonization of processes over the last few years, while simultaneously differentiating supply chains according to market-specific and product specific proper-ties. Through the further progress of digital technologies and their improved and more economical use, supply chains are becoming more transparent and more manageable through available information. Hence, the flexibility for all participants is improved, costs can be reduced further, and supply chain pace can be improved by this automatization of processes.

The attempt to make sense of this intangible growing mass of data is known as Big Data Analytics [6]. Currently, Big Data Analytics consists of the following data processes:

- Storage and data management;
- Data stripping;
- Data mining;
- Data analysis;
- Data visualization;
- Data integration;
- Data grouping [7].

All this data is collected from various processes or, for example, things from the Internet of Things network. In essence, analytics describes the application of advanced statistics to historical data in order to identify behavioral patterns that eventually enable the forecasting of future behavior to some extent [8]. Big Data is generally characterized in literature by 5Vs which are volume, variety, velocity, veracity, and value. Big Data Analysis is based on knowledge extraction from vast amounts of data, facilitating data-driven decision-making. Hence veracity and value are precisely important since data analysis evaluates the real purpose of Big Data [9].

3 Results

The analyzed company has developed and implemented a logistic scheme for year-round crude oil export. However, the use of digital technology would ensure the export of growing production volumes in the Arctic region. The main trend in the digital transformation sector is the exclusion of the human factor in those sectors of work where it seems possible. A digital Arctic logistics management system would ensure operational efficiency and safety [10]. This could be accomplished by processing data that can be gathered from various source systems and sensors installed on tankers.

The Track-and-Trace systems (T&T) aim at a timely identification of deviations or risks of deviations in supply chains, analysis of deviations and alerts about the disruptions that may occur, and elaborating control actions to recover supply chain's operability [11]. The feedback control of Track-and-Trace systems can be largely supported by RFID technology which enables supply chain event management systems for effective communication on disruptions and revision of initial schedules. In practice, the cloud-based analytics platforms such as SupplyOn Industry 4.0 Sensor Clouds enable to control the supply chain in real-time as it is a critical issue in this area to detect disruption and their scope at the actual moment. It also provides planning and processes adjustments using up-to-date information. By choosing a container type, the graphs indicate whether there has been a violation of the defined temperature or humidity limits along the time axis. The data analysis on such charts allows quick identification of all orders where the lead time was exceeded, allows for a swift identification of questionable transports.

Decision-making in terms of supply chain structural dynamics is associated with control and adaptation in different uncertainty environments where the response and recovery are needed in order to allocate scarce resources to reconnect supply chain and therefore to ensure process continuity and viability [12]. Real-time information acquiring is of vital importance for supply chain recovery planning and coordinated deployment of recovery policies [13].

The Arctic logistics management system would increase the effectiveness of analysis of the ships' movements, predict the average speed of tankers on routes, fuel consumption, calculate unit costs for oil transportation. This would allow to evaluate the effectiveness of the fleet and optimize its composition by detecting the unnecessary components of the logistics scheme. Based on the exact values of the parameters gathered from the established data streams instead of using the mean values or inaccurate predictions the system should reveal the calculations which describe the reality of the highly extreme Arctic region [14]. The information evaluated from the calculations would assist in decision-making processes on all management levels.

Gazprom Neft company has launched a digital Arctic logistics management system. The innovative project "CAPTAIN" (Complex of Automatic Planning for Interactive Transportation of Arctic Oil) was implemented to ensure year-round uninterrupted export of the entire volume of crude oil produced by ARCO and Novy Port grades and to increase the efficiency of logistics management. The system should be operating in three models: long-term and operational planning, scheduling of the Arctic fleet, and analytics using artificial intelligence based on Big Data technologies and analysis.

The system helps to solve three major problems for the company simultaneously. The first is the planning of ongoing crude oil production and shipping activities. The work result of CAPTAIN system is a schedule of ship traffic and an interconnected schedule of crude oil shipments from the terminal in the fields. The system enables user to access information on daily crude oil production for the period of interest, the amount of oil in the tanks, the exact dates, and estimated time of arrival of shuttle tankers and tanker carriers to the terminals. It also provides the up to date information on the location and movement parameters, the remaining fuel on the tankers, the icebreaker, and support ships' location and ice conditions prediction.

The CAPTAIN system is capable of current weather conditions analysis as well as forecasting in terms of planning and selection of the optimal route for the tanker following the direction and speed of the wind, air temperature, and operational ice conditions. This feature greatly increases the system's efficiency as the various weather conditions can affect the estimated time of arrival of the tanker to the terminals, and accordingly, the shipment of crude oil and the entire schedule for its production.

In order to objectively assess the existing conditions and to evaluate an accurate forecast for the nearest future event, the system is not only capable of monitoring the movement of ships in the present tense, but also comparing it with the historical data on movement and evaluating conclusions. It is provided with the functionality of predictive analytics which is based on the accumulation of a large amount of statistical data continuously processed and analyzed.

The ongoing functionality development of the CAPTAIN system consists of ice drift prediction based on images obtained from satellites using data analysis of sea conditions, wind direction, and strength. This is necessary in order to optimally calculate the routes of shuttle tankers as it its speed and travel time depends on it.

Optimizing the oil tankers fleet movement in the Arctic area increases the export of crude oil and oil products and distributes oil storage load. The volume of export shipments of Arctic oil varieties planned in the first half of 2019 was increased by 5.5 million tons, which is 10% more than in the first half of the previous year. Arctic oil marketing in foreign markets is conducted by a subsidiary Gazprom Neft Trading GmbH.

4 Conclusion

As requirements concerning supply chains and value networks continuously rise due to the influences of not only the permanently increasing complexity of business processes and collaborative manufacturing and trade processes but also the factors of the environmental nature. The significance and necessity of Supply Chain Management as a company's organizational and management instrument intensifies. The present development toward a digitalization of supply chains offers substantial impulses for mastering the requirements concerning Supply Chain Management applying Big Data and Internet of Things technologies.

The analytical system of digital logistics management CAPTAIN developed by the Russian oil and gas company Gazprom Neft and highlighted in this article uses such information streams as daily oil production volumes at the Novy Port and Prirazlomnoye fields of Gazprom Neft and oil accumulation volumes in oil storage facilities, location and parameters of vessel movement, ice conditions on routes, tidal schedules, weather conditions, the possibility of formation new standard for the market consignments of raw materials. The implementation of the system using the Big Data analysis approaches has significantly reduced the planning and coordination of oil shipping operations and optimized transportation costs [15].

The system's functionality allows real-time analysis of the fleet's operational efficiency, evaluating the speed of the route, fuel consumption, and vessel load. CAPTAIN provides online monitoring of the location and parameters of the movement of ships, cargo operations, routes, and ice-breaking assistance. Its functionality allows you to quickly create a schedule of oil shipments with a horizon of up to three years, which provides the opportunity to optimize the composition of the chartered and own fleet of the company.

This article examined only main benefits of using IoT and Big Data in Supply Chain Management. Based on modern technologies, various companies have the possibility to develop systems to monitor, plan and improve the effectiveness of organizations.

5 Discussion

Receiving telemetry data from ships is important not only for managing the Arctic logistics of the real economy industry companies. Indeed, along with information on the operation parameters of ship systems, sensors can transmit any data - for example, temperature, weather conditions, and environmental conditions. This will be an invaluable tool for experts and scientists studying the ecosystem of the Arctic. In the future, any organization or company operating in the Arctic region will theoretically be able to join CAPTAIN. Moreover, the technologies used in this system can be applied in other areas important for the Arctic zone, for example, in medicine, using IoT and Big Data Analytics for telemedicine services.

Acknowledgement. The reported study was funded by RSCF according to the research project № 19-18-00452.

References

1. Akushevich, M.: Oil without humans: how robots and the Internet of things changed the oil. https://hightech.fm/
2. Abdalla, B., Jukes, P., Eltaher, A., Duron, B.: The technical challenges of designing oil and gas pipelines in the arctic. In: OCEANS 2008, pp. 1–11. IEEE (2008)
3. Gutman, S.S., Zaychenko, I.M., Rytova, E.V.: Development strategy of Far North transport infrastructure: problems and prospects. In: Proceedings of the 29th International Business Information Management Association Conference—Education Excellence and Innovation Management Through Vision, pp. 1439–1449 (2020)
4. Agarcov, S., Kozmenko, S., Teslya, A.: Organizing an oil transportation system in the Arctic. In: IOP Conference Series: Earth and Environmental Science, p. 012011. IOP Publishing (2020)
5. Ashton, K.: That 'internet of things' thing. RFID J. **22**, 97–114 (2009)
6. Tiwari, S., Wee, H.M., Daryanto, Y.: Big data analytics in supply chain management between 2010 and 2016: Insights to industries. Comput. Ind. Eng. **115**, 319–330 (2018)

7. Rajaraman, V.: Big data analytics. Resonance **21**(8), 695–716 (2016). https://doi.org/10.1007/s12045-016-0376-7

8. Shmueli, G., Koppius, O.R.: Predictive analytics in information systems research. MIS Q. **35**, 553–572 (2011)

9. Addo-Tenkorang, R., Helo, P.T.: Big data applications in operations/supply-chain management: a literature review. Comput. Ind. Eng. **101**, 528–543 (2016)

10. Zaychenko, I.M., Ilin, I.V., Lyovina, A.I.: Enterprise Architecture as a Means of Digital Transformation of Mining Enterprises in the Arctic (2018)

11. Kelepouris, T., Da Silva, S.B., McFarlane, D.: Automatic ID Systems: Enablers for Track and Trace Performance. Aerospace-ID Technologies White Paper Series (2006)

12. Ivanov, D., Pavlov, A., Sokolov, B.: Optimal distribution (re) planning in a centralized multi-stage supply network under conditions of the ripple effect and structure dynamics. Eur. J. Oper. Res. **237**, 758–770 (2014)

13. Ivanov, D., Dolgui, A., Sokolov, B., Ivanova, M.: Literature review on disruption recovery in the supply chain. Int. J. Prod. Res. **55**, 6158–6174 (2017)

14. Maydanova, S., Ilin, I.: Problems of the preliminary customs informing system and the introduction of the Single Window at the sea check points of the Russian Federation. In: MATEC Web of Conferences, p. 04004. EDP Sciences (2018)

15. Ilin, I.V., Iliashenko, O.Y., Klimin, A.I., Makov, K.M.: Big data processing in Russian transport industry. In: Proceedings of the 31st International Business Information Management Association Conference. IBIMA (2018)

Availability of Emergency Power Supply for Voice Communications of Air Traffic Control System

Igor Kabashkin[1]($\boxtimes$) (iD) and Vadim Philippov[2] (iD)

[1] Transport and Telecommunication Institute, Lomonosov 1, 1019 Riga, Latvia
kiv@tsi.lv
[2] State Research Institute of Civil Aviation, Moscow, Russian Federation

Abstract. The reliability of the emergency power supply system for voice communications of air traffic control (ATC) systems is considered, taking into account the common set of backup batteries and their real downtime for maintenance operations. Mathematical dependability model of emergency power supply system for voice communications of ATC system on the base of batteries network is developed.

The availability of ATC controller's activity in the energy emergency for batteries network with common set of standby batteries and their maintenance is defined. The analyses of reliability model of ATC controller's functions for condition-based maintenance and periodical schedule-based maintenance of batteries of batteries is carried out.

Keywords: Availability · Power supply · Air traffic control · Battery

1 Introduction

In aviation pilot-controller voice communication is very important for air traffic control (ATC) operations. Any problems with communication in the ATC can lead to catastrophic events [1]. In such situation European organization for the safety have a special attention to communication problems as flight safety issues. This is manifested, in particular, in the architecture of the air-ground voice communications system. Duplication is widely used in such a safety critical system. Radio stations are frequently deployed in main-standby pairs with manual or automatic switch in case of radio failure [2].

The set of main ground radio stations (GRS) usually are placed at the remote center. The reliability of ground-air communication in such architecture is critically dependent on the link between radios and the controller's desk (CD) and on power supply of remote center. The standby radios (SR) are usually located directly at the workplaces of controllers. They historically have operated from both AC (alternating current) mains and a DC (direct current) battery backup supply to provide continuous operation when the mains supply has failed (it can be a frequent event in some cases).

Air traffic controllers are usually located at the air traffic control centers. The number of controllers at one center can reach several dozen, depending on the capacity of the

© Springer Nature Switzerland AG 2020
O. Galinina et al. (Eds.): NEW2AN 2020/ruSMART 2020, LNCS 12525, pp. 155–164, 2020.
https://doi.org/10.1007/978-3-030-65726-0_15

airport and the size of air traffic areas under monitoring. Each of the controllers has a specified duplicated set of communication radios and supply.

The structure of the power supply network of the ATC voice communication system is shown in Fig. 1.

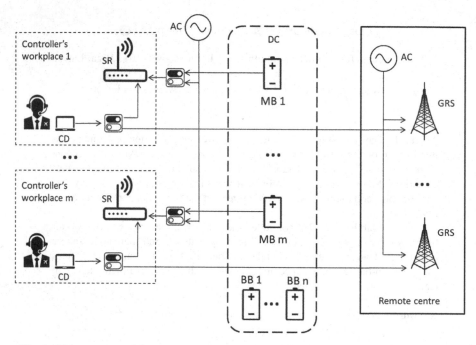

Fig. 1. The structure of the power supply network of the ATC voice communication system

To ensure the uninterrupted operation of radio stations in emergency mode from the batteries (B), there is a group of n backup batteries (BB), each of which can be used to replace any of the m main batteries (MB) installed at the controller workstations. Periodic maintenance and charging of batteries are required in real operating conditions.

The paper investigates the reliability emergency energy resources for voice communications of air traffic control system.

The structure of the paper includes four sections. Analyses of references in the area of reliability of batteries and radios of ATC systems are presented in the Sect. 2. The definitions, notation and the reliability model of study system are given in Sect. 3. The conclusion is presented in the Sect. 4.

2   Review of References

The impact of power supply is special interest critical to safety systems. Such systems with standby components and subsystems, including energy supply sources, are discussed in [3].

Electric cars and their functioning are a new area that is intensifying research on the reliability of energy supply in network structures. The approach to ensuring the fault tolerance of power supply of electric vehicles based on dynamic switching of the battery network and their optimal balancing is considered in [4]. Troubleshooting of wireless sensor networks is a separate area of research. A review of studies in this direction is contained in [5]. The study provides a classification of diagnostic methods by type of test, the nature of the test signals and the test methodology.

In the paper [6] the duplication of power supply sources as a method of dependability increasing of communication networks is discussed. The reliability model is proposed and comparative analysis of traditional and proposed method is made.

Duplication of power supplies for each of the network communication nodes increases their dependability, but at the same time requires additional resources. In article [7], a compromise solution to the problem was proposed by adopting a common set of backup energy suppliers for energy supply of network nodes.

Dependability models of multichannel network with redundant architecture of elements are proposed in [8, 9].

Battery life depends on many factors. It varies widely and depends on the operating and maintenance conditions of the batteries (Fig. 2) [10].

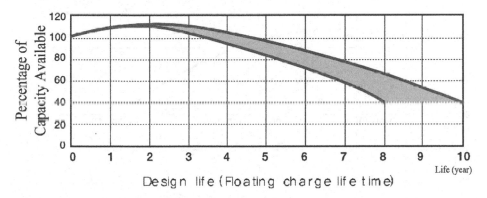

Fig. 2. The duration of the battery life cycle

Battery capacity is affected by ambient temperature and battery discharge rate. Low temperatures reduce battery capacity (Fig. 3) [10]. Depth of discharge is the most important factor for durattion of life cycle of battery. The battery capacity is depend not only on the number of charged-discharged cycles. The different discharge depth (DOD) has a great influence on final capacity that can be maintained (Fig. 4) [10].

The above dependencies indicate that the efficiency and, consequently, the reliability of the functioning of batteries significantly depends on their maintenance. At the same time, the time for maintenance operations should be taken into account when analyzing the availability of batteries for emergency use.

This paper examines the reliability of the emergency energy resources for voice communications of ATC system in real operation environment with standby set of batteries and finite downtime for their maintenance operations.

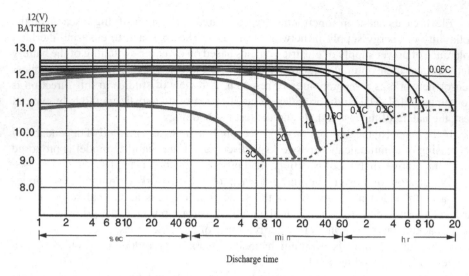

Fig. 3. Discharge characteristics of batteries

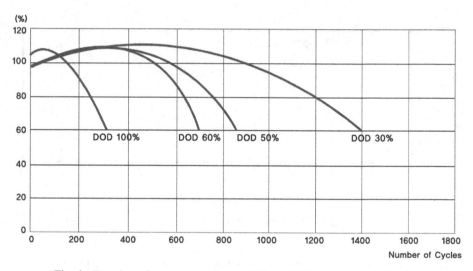

Fig. 4. Function of percentage of capacity from DOD and number of cycles

3 Model Formulation and Solution

In the paper the availability of redundant set of batteries with periodic maintenance is analyzed. The Markov model of system dependability is proposed. On the base of Kolmogorov-Chapman equations, the stationary probabilities of states for system under study are defined.

The following symbols and notations have been used in the study:

λ	- Failure Rate of batteries
μ	- Repair Rate of batteries
m	- Number of controllers in the ATC system
n	- Number of redundant batteries
A	- Availability of emergency energy resource for controller
A_M	- Availability of emergency energy resource with influence of batteries maintenance
λ_M	- Maintenance flow rate for average maintenance intervals T_M
μ_M	- The intensity of the flow of work performed during maintenance for the average time of their execution t_M
γ	$= \lambda/\mu$
ω	$= \gamma/l$

The repairable redundant emergency energy architecture of voice communication ATC system has $N = m + n$ batteries, where m are main and n are standby batteries (Fig. 1). Time of failures, repairs and maintenance operations of batteries has exponential distributions.

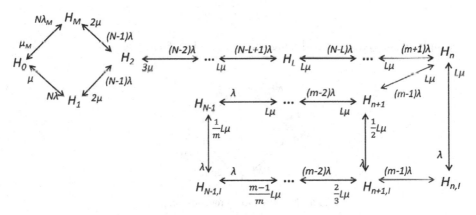

Fig. 5. Markov graph of state transitions

The Markov model can be used to identify the dependability of the system under study. The transition diagram for states of the studied system is shown in the Fig. 5. The following notation is used in this diagram: H_i is state of the system with i faulty batteries, but dedicated controller's workspace is equipped with good battery; H_{il} is state of the system with $i + 1$ faulty batteries, in the dedicated controller's workspace workable B is absent; H_M – all batteries are without failures and one B at the maintenance.

Using the state transition graph of the Markov model (Fig. 5), the Chapman – Kolmogorov system of equations can be written in accordance with the general rules [11].

In this case the availability of energy resource at dedicated controller's workspace can be presented by equation

$$A = 1 - U = 1 - \sum_{i=n}^{N-1} h_{i,I} \qquad (1)$$

Let us determine the stationary probabilities h_i of states H_i with assistance of model aggregation method proposed in [12].

In accordance with [12], the original graph (Fig. 5)

$$H = H'UH'' = \{H_0, H_M, H_1, H_2\}U\{H_{ij}, H_{j,I} : i = \overline{2, N-1}; j = \overline{n, N-1}\}$$

can be represented by two similar graphs R and S.

The graphs at the Fig. 6 and Fig. 7 are formed by states

$$R = \{R_0, R_M, R_1, R_2\};$$

$$S = \{S_{ij}, S_{jI} : i = \overline{2, N-1}; j = \overline{n, N-1}\}$$

Set of states R and S have similar configuration and parameters as the corresponding part of the original graph

$$R \equiv H'; S \equiv H''$$

Graphs of subsystems R and S are shown at the Fig. 6 and Fig. 7.

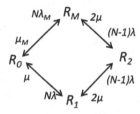

Fig. 6. Markov model for subsystem R

In accordance of [12], we can obtain

$$h_i/h_2 = r_i/r_2 : \forall i \qquad (2)$$

$$h_{\alpha\beta}/h_2 = s_{\alpha\beta}/s_2 : \forall \alpha, \beta \qquad (3)$$

$$h_2 = r_2 s_2/(r_2 + s_2 - r_2 s_2) \qquad (4)$$

where $h_i, h_{\alpha\beta}, r_i, s_{\alpha\beta}$ - stationary probabilities of states $H_i, H_{\alpha\beta}, R_i, S_{\alpha\beta}$ of related subgraphs.

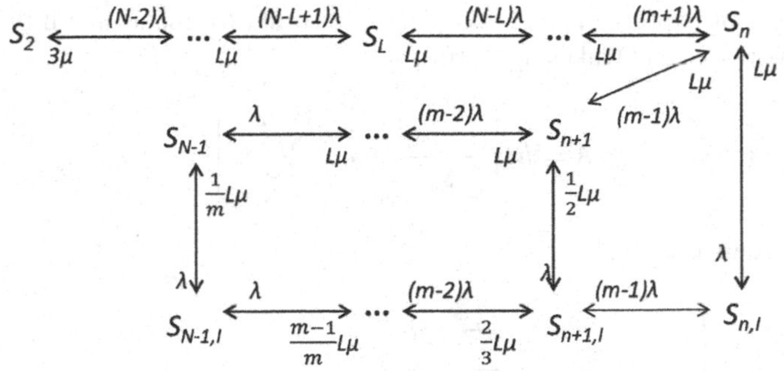

Fig. 7. Markov model for subsystem S

According to the general rules for Markov process [11] the system of Chapman-Kolmogorov equations has the form:

$$s_0'(t) = -N(\lambda + \lambda_M)s_0(t) + \mu s_1(t) + \mu_M s_M(t)$$

$$s_1' = N\lambda s_0(t) - [(N-1)\lambda + \mu]s_1(t) + 2\mu s_2(t)$$

$$s_2'(t) = (N-1)\lambda s_1(t) - 4\mu s_2(t) + (N-1)\lambda s_M(t)$$

$$s_M'(t) = N\lambda_M s_0(t) - [(N-1)\lambda + \mu_M]s_M(t) + 2\mu s_2(t)$$

Solution of this system of equation gives us opportunity to define probability s_2. Expression for s_2 in the case of highly reliable systems ($\lambda \ll \mu$) has form:

$$s_2 = \frac{N(N-1)(\lambda + \lambda_M)\gamma}{a[(N-1)\gamma\mu + 2N\lambda_M + 2\mu_M]} \tag{5}$$

where $a = \begin{cases} 1, l = 1, \\ 2, 1 < l < n, \end{cases} \quad \gamma = \lambda/\mu$

For the subgraph R the expression for probability r_2 was determined in [7] and for ideal switching can be presented by the expression

$$r_2^{-1} = 1 + \frac{2}{N(N-1)}\sum_{i=3}^{l}\binom{i}{N}\gamma^{i-2}$$

$$+ \frac{2(N-2)!l^{l-2}\omega^{N-2}}{l!}\left\{\sum_{i=m}^{N-l-1}\frac{1}{i!\omega^i} + \frac{1}{m}\left[\frac{1}{(m-1)!\omega^{m-1}} + \sum_{i=0}^{m-2}\frac{(m-i))}{i!\omega^i}\right]\right\} \tag{6}$$

The stationary probability h_2 of the system at Fig. 5 can be defined by including formulas (5) and (6) into (4).

On the base of expressions (2) and (3), the formula for the availability of selected controller's workspace (1) takes the form

$$A = h_2 \left[\frac{1 - s_2}{s_2} + r_2^{-1} \sum_{i=2}^{N-2} r_i \right] \tag{7}$$

where in accordance with [12]

$$\sum_{i=0}^{N-1} r_i = r_2 \left\{ 1 + \frac{2}{N(N-1)} \sum_{i=3}^{l} \binom{i}{N} \gamma^{i-2} \right. $$
$$\left. + 2(N-2)! l^{l-2}/l! \left[\sum_{i=l+1}^{n} \frac{\omega^{i-2}}{(N-i)!} + \sum_{i=n+1}^{N-1} \frac{\omega^{i-2}}{(N-i-1)!m} \right] \right\}$$

Thus, formulas (4)–(6) after substitution them into (7) determine the battery availability of selected controller's workspace of the initial system (Fig. 5).

Example
Effect from the loss of time due to maintenance of battery can be evaluated by using the availability reduction factor

$$V = \frac{1 - A}{1 - A_M}$$

where A – availability of emergency energy resource for controller in the model excluding the loss of time due to maintenance of battery [7], A_M – the availability in the model taking into the effect from the loss of time due to maintenance of battery.

As example, the availability reduction factor V is shown at the Fig. 8 for $m = 10$ controllers at the ATC system as function of maintenance parameter $\gamma_M = \lambda_M/\mu_M$ for n redundant batteries with reliability parameter $\gamma = 10^{-4}$.

There are two typical maintenance forms: condition-based maintenance with small value of parameter γ_M and periodical schedule-based maintenance with large value of the same parameter.

An analysis of the results of the example shows that for batteries network with first form of maintenance the availability of controller's activities weakly dependent on the parameter γ_M, but in the second case the influence of battery's maintenance downtime has a significant influence on availability of controller's activities.

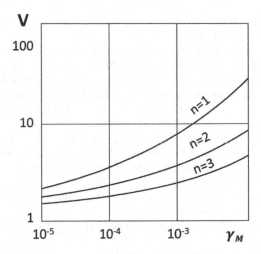

Fig. 8. The dependability degradation factor

4 Conclusions

The reliability of the emergency power supply system for voice communications of ATC systems is considered, taking into account the common set of backup batteries and their real downtime for maintenance operations.

Mathematical dependability model of emergency power supply system for voice communications of ATC system on the base of batteries network is developed.

The availability of ATC controller's activity in the energy emergency situation for batteries network with common set of standby batteries and their maintenance is defined.

The analyses of reliability model of ATC controller's functions for condition-based maintenance and periodical schedule-based maintenance of batteries of batteries is carried out.

References

1. Es, G.V.: Air-ground communication safety study. An analysis of pilot-controller occurrences. European organisation for the safety of air navigation EUROCONTROL, 2004, 50 (2004)
2. Hand, D.: The RF challenges of ATC communications, Consultant Engineer - Park Air Systems Ltd. https://www.armms.org/media/uploads/rf-challenges-of-atc-communications.pdf. Accessed 29 May 2020
3. Slovick, M.: Buck-Boost Controller Answers Call for Redundant Battery Systems, Electronic Design. https://www.electronicdesign.com/automotive/buck-boost-controller-answers-call-redundant-battery-systems. Accessed 29 Sept 2019
4. Taranovich, S.: Redundancy design solution for battery systems in autonomous vehicles. https://www.edn.com/electronics-products/electronic-product-reviews/other/4461118/Redundancy-design-solution-for-battery-systems-in-autonomous-vehicles. Accessed 29 Sept 2019
5. Mahapatro, A., Khilar, P.M.: Fault diagnosis in wireless sensor networks: a survey. IEEE Commun. Surv. Tutor. **15**(4), 2000–2026 (2013)

6. Mahajan, S., Dhiman, P.: Clustering in wireless sensor networks: a review. Int. J. Adv. Res. Comput. Sci. **7**(3), 198–201 (2016)
7. Kabashkin, I.: Reliability of cluster-based nodes in wireless sensor networks of cyber physical systems. Procedia Comput. Sci. **151**, 313–320 (2019)
8. Kabashkin, I.: Redundancy management in homogeneous architecture of power supply units in wireless sensor networks. In: Zamojski, W., Mazurkiewicz, J., Sugier, J., Walkowiak, T., Kacprzyk, J. (eds.) DepCoS-RELCOMEX 2020. AISC, vol. 1173, pp. 304–314. Springer, Cham (2020). https://doi.org/10.1007/978-3-030-48256-5_30
9. Kabashkin, I.: Dependability of multichannel communication system with maintenance operations for air traffic management. In: Zamojski, W., Mazurkiewicz, J., Sugier, J., Walkowiak, T., Kacprzyk, J. (eds.) DepCoS-RELCOMEX 2019. AISC, vol. 987, pp. 256–263. Springer, Cham (2020). https://doi.org/10.1007/978-3-030-19501-4_25
10. Missile batteries. ZENER engineering company. http://www.zenerco.com/en/products/battery/87-rocket-batteries. Accessed 29 May 2020
11. Rubino, G., Sericola, B.: Markov Chains and Dependability Theory. Cambridge University Press, Cambridge (2014)
12. Kabashkin, I.: Computational method for reliability analysis of complex systems based on the one class Markov models. Int. J. Appl. Math. Inf. **10**, 98–100 (2016)

BotSpot: Deep Learning Classification of Bot Accounts Within Twitter

Christopher Braker[1], Stavros Shiaeles[2(✉)], Gueltoum Bendiab[2(✉)], Nick Savage[2], and Konstantinos Limniotis[3]

[1] CSCAN, University of Plymouth, Plymouth PL4 8AA, UK
chris.brake@plymouth.ac.uk
[2] Cyber Security Research Group, University of Portsmouth,
Portsmouth PO1 2UP, UK
sshiaeles@ieee.org, {gueltoum.bendiab,nick.savage}@port.ac.uk
[3] National and Kapodistrian University of Athens, Athens, Greece
klimn@di.uoa.gr

Abstract. The openness feature of Twitter allows programs to generate and control Twitter accounts automatically via the Twitter API. These accounts, which are known as "bots", can automatically perform actions such as tweeting, re-tweeting, following, unfollowing, or direct messaging other accounts, just like real people. They can also conduct malicious tasks such as spreading of fake news, spams, malicious software and other cyber-crimes. In this paper, we introduce a novel bot detection approach using deep learning, with the Multi-layer Perceptron Neural Networks and nine features of a bot account. A web crawler is developed to automatically collect data from public Twitter accounts and build the testing and training datasets, with 860 samples of human and bot accounts. After the initial training is done, the Multi-layer Perceptron Neural Networks achieved an overall accuracy rate of 92%, which proves the performance of the proposed approach.

Keywords: Bot accounts · Machine learning · Spam bots · Security

1 Introduction

Twitter is currently one of the most used social media networks with over 326 million of monthly active registered users in 2019, where 46% of them are on the platform daily, together sending over 6,000 tweets every second, which corresponds to over 350,000 tweets per minute and 500 million tweets per day [1]. This social network provides a powerful micro-blogging platform where people can easily share their thoughts, feelings and opinions about a wide variety of topics in the form of tweets (a message or a post limited to 140 characters) [6,9]. Users can also share tweets created by other persons on their own Twitter feeds, which will be then visible to their friends and followers [13]. One other important

Cyber-Trust Project 2020.

feature of Twitter is the use of the hashtag, which is a word or a phrase preceded by the pound sign (#) [14]. Hashtags help users to arrange and sort their tweets and discover other Twitter users who are interested in the same subjects [14]. With this feature, Twitter creates an online social structure consisting of clusters of interconnecting people, with celebrities having huge numbers of followers [11]. The potential capability of this platform in exchanging information in the form of views, thoughts and opinions, makes it an ideal place for promoting a variety of relatively harmless tasks [9] such as targeted marketing or spreading fake news for malicious intent and manipulate the public opinion [10]. These activities are usually carried out by using fake accounts known as "bots" or "Sybils".

A bot is an automated user account controlled by a computer program that has been coded to interact with Twitters' API to perform automated tasks such as tweeting, following, unfollowing, or direct messaging other accounts. More sophisticated bots can even interact with human users, just like real people [6]. A recent study by the University of Southern California and Indiana University [12], found that up to 17% of Twitter active accounts are in fact bots rather than human users, which correspond to nearly 48 million accounts. Another study by Gartner [5] estimates that by 2020, 85% of customer requests will be handled by bots, while Inbenta estimates 1.8 billion unique customer chatbot users by 2021 [5]. Although some bot accounts such as Earthquake Bot are beneficial to the community, many are malicious. A study by Jordan Wright et al. [18] confirmed that generated bot accounts are mainly used to spread spam and malware as well as influencing online discussion and sentiment. For example, bots have been used to redirect users to particular phishing websites [5], sway political elections, manipulate the stock market and create fake followers to make some people appear more popular than they are. In this paper, we aim to address this issue by introducing a novel approach that uses Deep Learning to detect bot accounts. The proposed approach relies on the Multi-layer Perceptron Neural Network and a set of nine features that include account, tweets and graph-related features. The Neural Network is trained on a dataset that consists of 760 normal and bot twitter accounts. Similarly, it was tested on a dataset of 100 twitter accounts either bot and normal. The initial experiments show promising results with 92% accuracy.

The remainder of this paper is structured as follows. Section 2 gives an overview of existing Twitter bots detection techniques, their advantages and drawbacks. In Section 3, we present the methodology of the proposed method. Section 4 presents the results of the experiments. Finally, Sect. 5 concludes the paper and presents future work.

2   Related Work

The detection of bot accounts within Twitter has been an area of research that has gained more interest over the past few years and several approaches have been proposed to detect bots on Twitter. A recent review by Emilio Ferrara [6] classified those methods in three main categories; (a) methods based on social networks graphs, (b) systems based on crowd-sourcing and human computation, and (c) machine learning algorithms based on features of bots. In this section, we focus on the last category because our work falls in this category.

Machine learning-based approaches focus on the behavioural patterns of bot accounts that can be encoded in features and adopted with machine learning techniques to distinguish a bot account from a human one. For instance, Lin and Huang [9] proposed a method to detect bots in Twitter based on two Twitter account-related features; URL rate and interaction rate. The URL rate designs the number of tweets with URL in the total number of tweets, while interaction rate defines the ratio of the number of tweets interacting over the total number of tweets. The proposed approach was evaluated on a dataset that was collected from 26,758 public accounts with 508,403 tweets. Authors reported a precision rate between 82.9% and 88.5%, with the classification algorithm J48. In [15], Song et al. built a graph model to represent Twitter users and their relationships, where users and tweets represent the nodes of the graph and relationships represent the links between nodes. Then, distance and connectivity features are extracted from the graph and used to detect bot accounts. The distance defines the length of the shortest path between the tweet's sender and mentions, while the connectivity feature defines the strength of the connection between users. Authors claim that unlike account features, relation or graph-based features are difficult for spammers to manipulate and can be collected immediately. This approach achieved nearly 92% true positive with Bagging, LibSVM, FT, J48 and BayesNet classifiers.

In more recent work [17], Alex Hai Wang used three graph based features and three tweets-based features to facilitate spambots detection. The graph-based features (i.e. the number of friends, the number of followers and follower ratio) are extracted from the user social graph, while the tweets based features (i.e. the number of duplicate tweets, the number of HTTP links, and the number of replies/mentions) are extracted from user's most recent 20 tweets. The dataset used to evaluate this approach contains 25,847 users, around 500K tweets, and around 49M follower/friend that are collected from publicly available data on Twitter. Different classification methods are used to identify spam bots including Decision Tree (DT), Neural Network (NN), Support Vector Machines (SVM), Naive Bayesian (NB) and k-Nearest Neighbours (kNN). The NB classifier achieved the best results with 91% accuracy, 91% recall and 91% F-measure. In the same context [13], Lacopo Pozzana et al. studied the behavioural dynamics that bots exhibit for one activity session via four tweet features; mentions per tweet, the text tweet length, fraction of retweets and fraction of replies. This study found behavioural differences between human users and bot account, which can be exploited to improve bot detection techniques. For example, over the course of their online activity, humans are constantly exposed to posts and messages by other users, so their probability to engage in social interaction increases. Authors used five machine-learning algorithms (DT, Extra Trees (ET), Random Forests (RF), Adaptive Boosting (AB), kNN) with the features considered above to identify either a bot or a human produces the tweets. The dataset used in the experiments consists of more than 16M tweets posted by 2M different users. ET and RF achieved the best cross-validated average performance (86%), followed by DT and AB (83%) and kNN (81%).

In [4], Zi Chu et al. used features extracted from the tweeting behaviour, tweet content and account proprieties to classify Twitter users into three categories: human, bot and cyborg. Authors assumed that bots behaviour is less complex than that of humans. For that, they used an entropy rate to measure the complexity of a process, where low rates indicate a regular process; medium rates indicate a complex process, whereas high rates indicate a random process. The content of the tweet is used to build text patterns of known spam on twitter. Some other account-related features are also used in the classification such as external URLs ratio, link safety, account registration date, etc. The RF machine-learning algorithm is used to analyse these features and decide if a twitter account is a human, bot or cyborg. The effectiveness of the classifier is evaluated through a dataset of 500,000 different Twitter users. This approach archived an average overall true positive rate of 96.0%.

3   Proposed Approach

3.1   Approach Overview

The goal of the proposed approach is to classify a given Twitter account as a Bot or not, therefore, the bot accounts detection is considered as a binary classification problem with bot Twitter accounts belong to the positive class ("Bot") and normal accounts belong to the negative class ("Human"). As illustrated in Fig. 1, the bots detection system consists of several modules: the data crawling module, the graph database, the pre-processing module and the machine-learning module. The crawling module collects Data from the Twitter Platform and stores them in a Neo4j database. The pre-processing module uses the data stored in the Neo4j database to create the training and testing dataset and the machine-learning module uses a NN classification algorithm to detect bot Twitter accounts.

3.2   Data Collection and Processing

There is no accepted worldwide dataset that can be used in the experiments, therefore, a web crawler called "PyTrawler" is developed to collect detailed user information from public accounts. PyTrawler is a Python application that uses two Python libraries, "Tweepy" to communicate with the Twitter API's and "Py2neo" to communicate with a Neo4j database and store the collected data. PyTrawler was built to handle the issue of the limited speed of data harvesting because an application can only make a limited number of requests to Twitter's API in a certain time window. As stated in the Twitter Developer Policy[1], a host is permitted 150 requests per hour. It also handles the issue of losing the internet connectivity, which gives PyTrawler the ability to continue crawling for long period of time without

---

[1] https://developer.twitter.com/fr/developer-terms/agreement-and-policy.

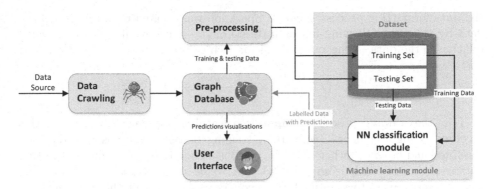

Fig. 1. Overview of the proposed approach

the need to resetting it. For each user visited, PyTrawler collected useful information about his profile, follower, friend list and posted tweets. The collected data is stored in a graph database using Neo4j technology [7]. This NoSQL database provides a browser GUI to visualise the data. The data collected and stored in the Neo4j database are formatted and normalised, then stored in a CSV file. Figure 2 illustrates the activity diagram of PyTrawler.

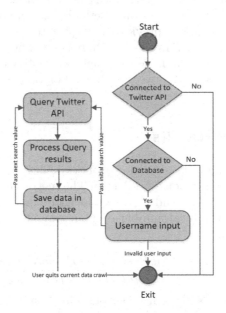

Fig. 2. Activity diagram of PyTrawler

A java application was developed to read raw data from the Neo4j and save the formatted data in the CSV file. The Apache Spark was used to speed up the data formatting process, where a Spark job was created to normalise all the data by using the following normalisation Eq. (1), which would scale each value relative to the data in the range [0, 1] for each column.

$$v(x) = log_2 \times \left(\frac{x - min}{x + min} + 1 \right) \tag{1}$$

For, the training process a supervised learning approach was chosen; this involves giving the neural network a training dataset that has already been classified and labelled either 'Human' or 'Bot'. Therefore, a training and testing datasets were created, from the CSV file, to be used by the neural network. The approach used to identify bots accounts was to look at the accounts that had high TFF Ratio (Twitter Follower-Friend Ratio), then manually evaluate the account within Twitter. This is a time-consuming process but meant that the data used to train the neural network contained genuine bot accounts. The training dataset contains 760 samples labelled either 'Human' or 'bot', while the testing dataset is composed of 100 samples (humans and bots accounts).

3.3 Features Selection

Most approaches in the literature use a large number of features. However, recent studies show that similar high performance can be achieved by using a minimal number of features [2, 8]. Thus, in our method we propose a set of nine feature that are inspired from the previous work [3, 4, 16]. The features values are gathered from the information in the NoSQL database, by examining username, account metadata, followers and friends count, description of the account, number of tweets, and content of the tweets. The explanation of the selected features is given in Table 1.

4   Experimental Results

In this section, we evaluate the efficiency of our classification system based on the datasets that have been previously collected. The metrics used in the evaluation are accuracy, precision, recall and F-score. The accuracy refers to the ratio of all correct predictions to the total number of input samples and it is computed by the following equation.

$$Accuracy = \frac{TruePositives + FalseNegatives}{TotalNumberofSamples} \tag{2}$$

Where, $TruePositives$ is the number of samples that are correctly classified as bot accounts, $TrueNegatives$ is the number of samples that are correctly classified as human accounts and $TotalNumberofSamples$ is the number of all samples (Bot and Human accounts). $FalsePositives$ refers to the number of samples incorrectly classified as bot accounts and $FalseNegatives$ notes to the number of samples incorrectly classified as humans. Precision corresponds to the

Table 1. Features explanation

Feature	Explanation
Default profile	This feature has a binary value, where true, indicates that the user has not altered the theme or background of their user profile
Statuses count	This feature presents the number of tweets and retweets issued by the user
Followers count	This feature presents the number of followers this account currently has
Listed count	This feature presents the number of Twitter lists on which this Twitter account appears
Friends count	This feature presents the number of users this account is following. Generally, Bot accounts have too many followings compared to human accounts
URLs ratio	This feature represents the frequency of included external URLs in the posted tweets by a user account. Study in [4] found that the ratio of a bot is 97%, while that of human is much lower at 29%
Verified account	This feature has a binary value, whether a user account is verified by twitter or not. It is used to establish authenticity of identities of key individuals and brands on Twitter. A true value indicates a verified account
Protected account	This feature has a binary value, which indicates if the user is protecting their tweets, and they are invisible to everyone other than its selected followers, or not. Bots are mostly unprotected accounts
Hashtags ratio	This feature represents the number of hashtags that a user account has used by the number of tweets. One tweet can include more than one hashtag

proportion of bot accounts that are correctly considered as bots, with respect to all correct prediction results (Bot and Human accounts) (Eq. 3), while recall is the proportion of bot accounts that are correctly considered as bots, with respect to all actual bot samples (Eq. 4). F-score is a weighted average between precision and recall (Eq. 5).

$$Precision = \frac{TruePositives}{TruePositives + FalsePositives} \tag{3}$$

$$Recall = \frac{TruePositives}{TruePositives + FalseNegatives} \tag{4}$$

$$F - score = 2 \times \left(\frac{Precision \times Recall}{Precision + Recall} \right) \tag{5}$$

4.1   Experiment Setup

The simulation experiments were performed on a virtual machine that is running Ubuntu 18.0.4 on Intel Core i7 CPU, 3.80 GHz, with 6 GB memory. The configuration of the Multi-Layer Perceptron (MLP) neural network is built with the DL4J (Deep Learning for Java) library. DL4J is an open-source deep-learning library written in java and includes implementations of a large number of deep learning algorithms. The layers of the MLP neural network were constructed with the 'NeuralNetConfiguration.Builder' method from DL4J. In addition, the Apache Maven tool is used to keep the list of all required dependencies for the NN in a 'pom.xml' file, which can then be altered to import or change dependencies as needed. This meant that the setup of the project on different devices was quick and easy, which sped up the development process. Finally, a java class was developed to help the NN read the data from the CSV file produced in the pre-processing step. After the neural network was configured, it was trained with 760 samples of Twitter accounts that have already been classified and labelled either Bots or Humans. Other 100 samples are used for testing the neural network. The testing set represents the unknown Twitter accounts that we want to classify as Bots or Humans.

4.2   Test Results

Using the training and testing datasets that had been previously created, several tests were carried out to evaluate the success of the detection method and determine the accuracy of the MLP neural network. In this context, several tests were performed on the initial training of the network to find a suitable learning rate for the MLP neural network. The value of this parameter has a high influence on the training process and accuracy of the neural network, large values may result in an unstable training process, whereas small values may lead to a long training process that could get stuck.

The results of these tests are illustrated in Fig. 3. From the obtained results, it was found that the optimum configuration was a learning rate of 0.02.

From the tests results, it was found that changing the number of hidden nodes or layers did not seem to influence the accuracy of the networks predictions, so it was fixed at 25 layers. Thus, the optimum configuration used in the experiments was a learning rate of 0.02, with 200 passes and 25 hidden layers. Knowing that due to the hardware limitations on the computing power the testing was restricted to 200 passes. After the optimum initial configuration was found, the neural network was reloaded and retrained on the created training dataset. Once retrained, it was assessed against the testing dataset. The MLP neural network achieved an overall accuracy rate of 92%, which is a high rate and meets the required accuracy rate in practical use. The precision is also high with a rate of 92.59%, which shows strong overall confidence in the pattern recognition process. The recall rate was lower than the precision rate (50%), knowing that in our work, precision is more important than recall because getting False Negatives (FN), when a bot account is considered as user account, cost more than False Positives (FP), when a user account is

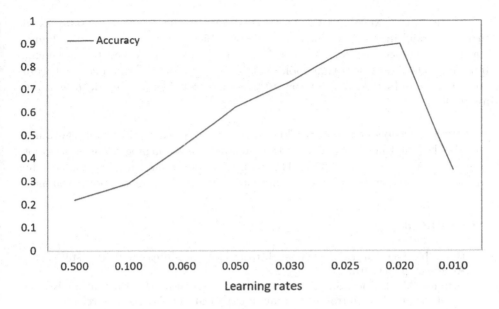

Fig. 3. Learning rate results on the accuracy

considered as bot because a bot account could be a spam bot that was created to conduct malicious activities [3]. In this context, a study conducted by Z. Chu, et al. [3] on a large Twitter dataset found that most bots include malicious URLs in tweets and that the average number of URLs in tweets sent by bots is three times higher than the number in tweets from real people accounts. The overall results of the initial test are presented in Table 2.

Table 2. Overall results of the initial test

Accuracy (A)	Precision (P)	Recall (R)	F-score (F1)
92.00%	92.59%	50.00%	64.94%

5   Conclusion

In this paper, we proposed a novel approach that utilises machine learning to solve the problem of bot accounts within Twitter. The proposed approach consists of a collection of different modules that provide functionalities to accurately and precisely detect bots within Twitter. The machine-learning module has proved that it is possible, through the analysis of account data, to detect bot accounts within Twitter by only looking at a small number of account features. Despite the neural network not being 100% accurate, it was able to learn and improve itself with minor supervision.

In the future, we plan to improve this work by the use of more samples to properly train and test the neural network, which will with no doubt enhance the predictive accuracy of the classifier. Furthermore, we intend to implement multiple neural networks that looked at different aspects of the data that were collected from Twitter and compare the results from the applied deep learning algorithms.

 Acknowledgement. This project has received funding from the European Union's Horizon 2020 research and innovation programme under grant agreement no. 786698. The work reflects only the authors' view and the Agency is not responsible for any use that may be made of the information it contains.

References

1. Blog, H.: General twitter stats. https://blog.hootsuite.com/twitter-statistics/. Accessed 19 Oct 2019
2. Brunner, M., Palmer, S., Togher, L., Dann, S., Hemsley, B.: Content analysis of tweets by people with traumatic brain injury (TBI): implications for rehabilitation and social media goals. In: Proceedings of the 52nd Hawaii International Conference on System Sciences (2019)
3. Chu, Z., Gianvecchio, S., Wang, H., Jajodia, S.: Who is tweeting on twitter: human, bot, or cyborg? In: Proceedings of the 26th Annual Computer Security Applications Conference, pp. 21–30. ACM (2010)
4. Chu, Z., Gianvecchio, S., Wang, H., Jajodia, S.: Detecting automation of twitter accounts: are you a human, bot, or cyborg? IEEE Trans. Dependable Secure Comput. **9**(6), 811–824 (2012)
5. Daniel, F., Cappiello, C., Benatallah, B.: Bots acting like humans: understanding and preventing harm. IEEE Internet Comput. **23**(2), 40–49 (2019)
6. Ferrara, E., Varol, O., Davis, C., Menczer, F., Flammini, A.: The rise of social bots. Commun. ACM **59**(7), 96–104 (2016)
7. Gong, F., Ma, Y., Gong, W., Li, X., Li, C., Yuan, X.: Neo4j graph database realizes efficient storage performance of oilfield ontology. PLoS ONE **13**(11), e0207595 (2018)
8. Kudugunta, S., Ferrara, E.: Deep neural networks for bot detection. Inf. Sci. **467**, 312–322 (2018)
9. Lin, P.C., Huang, P.M.: A study of effective features for detecting long-surviving twitter spam accounts. In: 2013 15th International Conference on Advanced Communications Technology (ICACT), pp. 841–846. IEEE (2013)
10. Margolin, D.B., Hannak, A., Weber, I.: Political fact-checking on twitter: when do corrections have an effect? Political Commun. **35**(2), 196–219 (2018)
11. Moorley, C.R., Chinn, T.: Nursing and twitter: creating an online community using hashtags. Collegian **21**(2), 103–109 (2014)
12. Newberg, M.: As many as 48 million twitter accounts aren't people says study. https://www.cnbc.com/michael-newberg/. Accessed 12 Dec 2019
13. Pozzana, I., Ferrara, E.: Measuring bot and human behavioral dynamics. arXiv preprint arXiv:1802.04286 (2018)
14. Sendible: Twitter hashtags: Guide to finding and using the right ones. https://www.sendible.com/insights/twitter-hashtags. Accessed 19 Oct 2019

15. Song, J., Lee, S., Kim, J.: Spam filtering in twitter using sender-receiver relationship. In: Sommer, R., Balzarotti, D., Maier, G. (eds.) RAID 2011. LNCS, vol. 6961, pp. 301–317. Springer, Heidelberg (2011). https://doi.org/10.1007/978-3-642-23644-0_16

16. Trinius, P., Holz, T., Göbel, J., Freiling, F.C.: Visual analysis of malware behavior using treemaps and thread graphs. In: 2009 6th International Workshop on Visualization for Cyber Security, pp. 33–38. IEEE (2009)

17. Wang, A.H.: Detecting spam bots in online social networking sites: a machine learning approach. In: Foresti, S., Jajodia, S. (eds.) DBSec 2010. LNCS, vol. 6166, pp. 335–342. Springer, Heidelberg (2010). https://doi.org/10.1007/978-3-642-13739-6_25

18. Wright, J., Engineer, P.R., Anise, O., et al.: Don't@ me: Hunting twitterbots at scale. Blackhat USA 2018 (2018)

Standardization of Road Quality Assessment by Developing Mobile Applications

Yury Klochkov[1]($\boxtimes$), Antonina Glushkova[2], Albina Gazizulina[1], and Egor Koldov[2]

[1] National Technology Initiative Center for Advanced Manufacturing Technologies Based on the Institute of Advanced Manufacturing Technologies of Peter the Great St. Petersburg Polytechnic University Polytechnicheskaya, 29, St. Petersburg 195251, Russia
y.kloch@gmail.com, albinagazizulina@gmail.com
[2] Samara University, 34, Moskovskoye Shosse, 443086 Samara, Russia
antonina.24@mail.ru, i6o6ep@gmail.com

Abstract. A significant increase in the network of roads, achieved in recent years, highlights the issues of proper repair and maintenance. Ensuring the safety of roads, improving their technical level along with the construction of new roads becomes the main task of road organizations. The solution of this problem is the ultimate goal of the road maintenance service activity and should be based on intensification of production and increasing its efficiency and quality. Among the measures aimed at improving production, a special place is occupied by the issues of timely performance of works on current repair and maintenance of highways. In these conditions, it is timely to plan the maintenance and maintenance of roads on the basis of scientifically grounded recommendations.

Due to the development of mobile applications, mobile networks, new technologies (include 5G) and communications, the timely identification of problem areas, can be solved through the development of specialized services. The article presents a new approach for improving the standardization management method using mobile applications. The analysis of the impact of mobile applications on standardization and the definition of the mechanism of such interaction is demonstrated.

Keywords: Standardization · Quality · Web-based services · Mobile services · 5G

1 Introduction

Standardization is a kind of activity aimed at establishing an optimal solution through the use of appropriate methods. The methods of standardization include:

Regulation – how the management of diversity is primarily connected with the reduction of diversity;
systematization – consists in scientifically substantiated, consistent classification and ranking of the aggregate of specific objects of standardization;

O. Galinina et al. (Eds.): NEW2AN 2020/ruSMART 2020, LNCS 12525, pp. 176–193, 2020.
https://doi.org/10.1007/978-3-030-65726-0_17

selection – the activity consisting in the selection of such specific objects that are considered expedient for further production and use;

simplification – the activity consisting in definition of such concrete objects which are recognized as inexpedient for the further manufacture and application;

typification – the activities to create typical (model) objects - structures, technological rules, forms of documentation. Unlike selection, the selected specific objects are subject to any technical changes aimed at improving their quality and universality;

optimization - finding the optimal parameters (assignment parameters), as well as the values of all other quality and economy indicators;

parametric standardization - the choice and justification of an appropriate nomenclature and the numerical value of the parameters. This problem is solved with the help of mathematical methods;

unification - the activity to rationally reduce the number of types of parts, units of the same functional purpose is called product unification. It is based on classification and ranking, selection and simplification, typing and optimization of elements of finished products;

aggregation – the method of creating machines, instruments and equipment from individual standard unified nodes, repeatedly used to create various products on the basis of geometric and functional interchangeability;

complex standardization – the establishment and application of interrelated requirements for the quality of finished products required for their production of raw materials, components and components, as well as the conditions of conservation and consumption (operation);

advanced standardization – is the establishment of higher standards and requirements for standardization objects, which are already achieved in practice, which are predicted to be optimal in the subsequent time [1, 3–7].

Today, thanks to technical progress, the modern world does not appear without the use of mobile communications (telephones, navigators, tablets), standardization must pass from passive form (when standards are on the shelf) into an active form. Mobile applications and services can successfully serve the development of active forms of standardization. Service described in this work allows you to get visual and current information about the state of roads [2, 8, 9]. The development and application of such services (which will allow standardization to pass from the passive to the active phase) at the level of the authorities of the city, region, country or union of states will help to plan the maintenance work properly.

2   Norms and Standards as an Information and Analytical Product

The modern standardization has several problems. The main reason is the orientation solely on the object or its application. At the same time, the possibility of compliance with established requirements or norms is not taken into account the established standards and norms [10–13]. The basis for improving the standardization of standard-setting procedures is the problem-oriented approach, which has proved itself in practice.

Norms and standards should be referred to information and analytical products. In this sense, they are a technical product. Based on this provision, we can assume that the methods of product development can also be used to develop information-analytical products, i.e. norms and standards [14–16]. With this method, the modularity of the content of standards, norms and requirements is achieved. Thanks to this, it is possible to develop compliance technologies in automated systems.

Separation of the process of norm development into phases or working steps. It is advisable to distinguish several different concretizing stages in the general search process of the solution. So, at first the basic interrelationships are singled out and only details and details are specified in the project being implemented [17, 18].

Based on the division of the design process into the development of appropriate elements and nodes, it is possible to apply the phases of such a process to the development of standards and norms. Methodological development of norms and standards is divided into the following phases:

- the phase of formulation of the task;
- the phase of concept creation;
- the design phase;
- the development phase;
- the testing/testing phase;
- The final phase.

The phase of the formulation of the problem.
To formulate a task, it is necessary:

- to receive a proposal for rationing;
- analyze the proposal;
- determine the functions (goals) of the valuation;
- Conduct a check on technical, economic and organizational standardization;
- approve the functions of rationing;
- Develop a sketch of the norm;
- identify professional, economic and technical requirements;
- approve the list of requirements;
- Transfer to the concept development.

Verification of technical, economic and organizational standards [19–21].

Determining the possibility of standardization is one of the most difficult tasks. Errors in this definition (either too early or late standardization) can adversely affect technical development and damage the economy [22–24]. Therefore, it is necessary to develop a methodology with unique attributes for assessing the need for standardization. Because standard or norm is a technical product, it must be evaluated according to technical and economic criteria [25]. Therefore, it is expedient to distinguish in the concept of "normability" technical, economic and organizational factors. Their relationship is shown in Fig. 1.

For standardization, which covers almost all special areas, it makes no sense to formulate general and therefore complex and voluminous criteria for estimating the normability. For this purpose, a general methodology with a number of significant features should be developed. Based on these characteristics, evaluation criteria can then

Fig. 1. Interrelation of factors of normability

be developed in accordance with the field of application. Thanks to this, they will be clear and understandable.

Technical Normability
The system is technically standardized if it has reached a certain technical level.

In doubtful cases it is necessary to take into account the opinion of specialists. The exception is the innovative industries, where the systems should be checked by market observations or studies of norms in order to understand whether rationing is necessary for subsequent technical development or not [26–28].

The normalization functions serve as the basis for the assessment.

Accounting for these functions is important, as well as the correct distribution of information on these functions, because the quality of standards depends on this.

Therefore, the rationing functions should first be checked with respect to the correctness of the content before searching for information.

With the help of the collected and evaluated information, it is possible to estimate the expected functions of the norm, i.e. Is it technically normal (state of the art) or conditionally normalized (the state of science and technology)?

In the new technology sectors, a detailed analysis is needed to establish the basis for rationing. If, for example, it is a question of stimulating development or application, which is extremely necessary for technology, standardization should be used as an incentive tool, it the system from the technical point of view should be standardized.

There is often a lack of reliable information, because enterprises, wishing to maintain their technical advantage, are reluctant to provide such information. In this case, the special efforts of the standards developers are required. An example is the standardization of machine control interfaces; these systems are prone to frequent technical changes.

Economic Normability.
Economic normability takes place if, as a result of standardization, a reduction in the cost of money is achieved.

Undeniable is the fact that standardization, among other things, is an instrument of rationalization. It is also undeniable that in some cases it is difficult to prove the cost reduction due to standardization. First of all, when it comes to the monetary expression of this reduction [29–31]. Nevertheless, it is possible to calculate the economy of the system using general and special calculation methods developed for standardization.

Organizational Normability.
On the organizational normability is the case when, as a result of checking its content for compliance with the main regulations, there are no significant contradictions [32, 33].

Integrated normability estimate.
After considering the technical, economic and organizational standardization, a general assessment should be made. Integral normability is valid if the goal-setting common elements are found in its separate types.

The system for estimating the normability using check digits is difficult because of such phenomena as copyright protection, contracts, etc. An example is the rationing of materials, because they are often protected by patents. In the general assessment, special attention should be paid to the economy.

3   An Example of the Method of Standardization Based on Compliance with the Standards Through the Use of Mobile Applications

A significant increase in the network of roads, achieved in recent years, highlights the issues of quality of their repair and maintenance. Ensuring the safety of highways, raising their technical level along with the construction of new roads becomes the main goal of standardizing road works. The solution of this problem is the ultimate goal of the road maintenance service activity and should be based on intensification of production and increasing its efficiency and quality. Among the measures aimed at improving production, a special place is occupied by the issues of timely performance of works on current repair and maintenance of highways. In these conditions, it is timely to plan the maintenance and maintenance of roads on the basis of scientifically grounded recommendations. To establish the standards of this process, it is necessary to use a method aimed at ensuring the timely detection of deviations in the established standards for the quality of the road surface.

Thus, it is necessary to adapt the established norm for the timely detection of road pavement damage areas affecting road safety on public roads at the stage of their operation and planning maintenance repairs. Such adaptation, in particular, will allow to solve the issue of reducing the impact of road services and the human factor.

Taking into account the current development of technologies and the increased number of functionalities of mobile phones, the service described in this work allows obtaining clear and up-to-date information about violations of the standards requirements. Then the standard procedure for determining the smoothness of the roadway can be replaced (supplemented) and implemented through software developed for mobile devices. This will simplify the issue of budget planning for repair work.

The roadway contains a large number of irregularities, some of them can eventually damage the running gear of the car. To such unevennesses it is possible to carry pits, "lying policemen" and ledges on the tram rails crossing the roadway. When the car hits a strong unevenness, a blow occurs, which is partly compensated by the car's suspension and tires. This blow can be fixed with. The device, allowing to measure acceleration - an accelerometer. Almost all modern mobile phones are equipped with an accelerometer that allows you to measure the acceleration of the 3-axis. The data from the phone's accelerometer can be collected with sufficient frequency to record the acceleration readings when the pit passes the car at high speed. Since the task of the project is to determine the smoothness of the roadway and its mapping, it is necessary to obtain the coordinates of the site from which the accelerometer data was collected. The coordinates are obtained from the geo-position sensor (GPS/GLONASS).

Initially, it was unclear exactly how the data from the accelerometer will look when the car passes through irregularities. Therefore, several test trips were made to get a better idea of the problem being solved. Data were collected from different types of road sections: with and without road surface irregularities. The acceleration graph on a flat section of the road can be seen in Fig. 2, and the acceleration graph with pits is shown in Fig. 3.

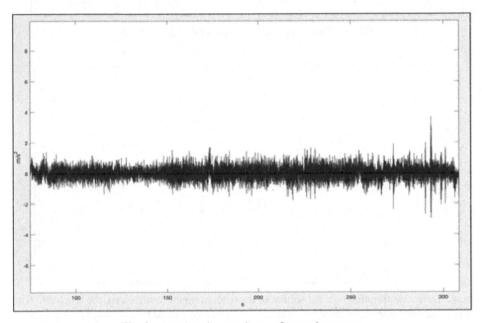

Fig. 2. Acceleration graph on a flat road segment

With a maximum purity of polling the phone's accelerometer for 1 s, about 3000 measurements are taken. Data from the geo-position sensor cannot be received at the same speed, because there will be too much error in them, so the data is obtained at the speed with which the Android platform can provide the most accurate coordinates. All measurements are decomposed into a measurement package. A package with dimensions is created each time the data from the geophone sensor changes. This approach allowed to create fewer packages for analysis when the car is at a traffic light or in a traffic jam.

When analyzing packages, it became clear that the data from the accelerometer is very noisy, because the accelerometer used in mobile phones is not a very accurate device, and also because of the small irregularities of the roadway itself. Such data is

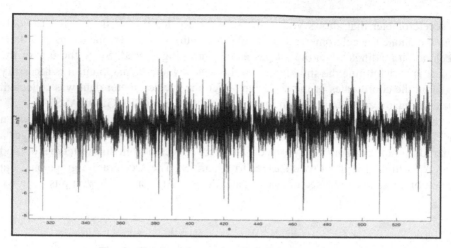

Fig. 3. Graph of the acceleration of the site with pits

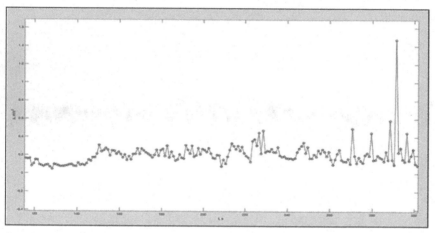

Fig. 4. Data after filtration on a flat section of the road, along the vertical axis, the acceleration in the package, along the horizontal axis, the circumference is marked by a measurement package

very difficult to interpret and a standard deviation method was used to obtain the data metric:

$$\sigma = \sqrt{\frac{1}{n}\sum_{i=1}^{n}(x_i - \bar{x})^2},$$

where $\bar{x}$ - is the standard deviation, x_i is the acceleration value in each packet, n is the number of measurements in the packet. The obtained value of σ is written as the deviation for this packet. The result of applying the algorithm to reduce the data and apply the root-mean-square deviation method on an even section of the road and on a road with pits is shown in Fig. 4 and Fig. 5.

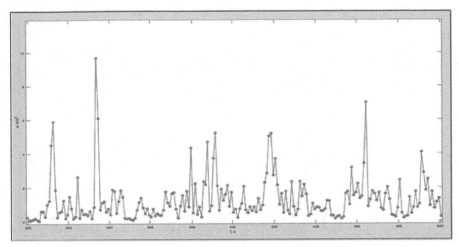

Fig. 5. Data after filtration in a section of the road with pits, along the vertical axis, the acceleration in the package, along the horizontal axis, the circumference is marked by a package of measurements

4   Classification of Uneven Roadway

To classify the data obtained, the machine learning approach was used.

Machine learning is a section of computer science that studies the construction of algorithms capable of learning. Most of the algorithms can be divided into two types:

1. Learning with the teacher, best suited to the tasks of classifying data, where classes are known in advance.
2. Learning without a teacher, algorithms that are suitable for clustering data where it is not known which classes will be, and their number.

Most of the classification tasks use the training approach with the teacher. Teaching with the teacher means that for each data instance, an answer will be provided (class, in the case of classification tasks). For the task of marking the data, a mobile data collection application was supplemented with a functional capability to mark the time for the car to pass through the unevenness. Functionality includes an additional device, with one button (mobile headset). When the button is clicked, the time is fixed and sent to the server.

A trip with marked markers is visualized in Fig. 6. The applied approach has a serious drawback - the marks marked while driving, have an error regarding the collected data, are pressed several times or simply missed. To eliminate this drawback, an additional module was written, which allows you to mark the data more accurately, relying on the tags collected during the collection of data on the car. When you click on each column, the data representing it is marked as a pit. Manually marked data are presented in Fig. 7. The use of two approaches in marking uneven road sections on data from trips made it possible to form a quality training sample for the subsequent learning of the machine learning algorithm.

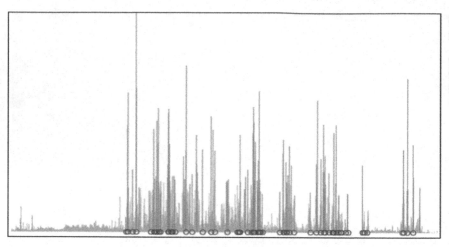

Fig. 6. Labeled data while driving, the label is marked with a circle

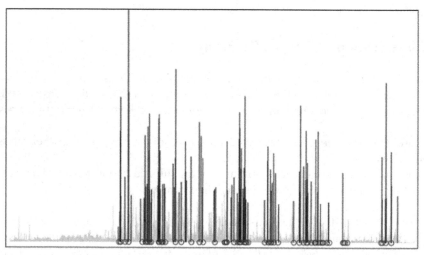

Fig. 7. Data after re-marking, gray bars indicate the columns on the flat part of the road, black marked columns with pits, circle data that was marked while driving

In order to not self-encode the algorithm of machine learning and efficiency analysis methods, Weka software was used. Weka (Waikato Environment for Knowledge Analysis) - free software aimed at analyzing and initial processing of data and their visualization. Also, "Weka" allows you to calculate how well the trained algorithm uses sliding sampling. Sliding sampling is a method in which data is divided into several samples, one part of the samples serves to classify the classifier, the other part to verify the correctness of the trained classifier (Figs. 8 and 9).

As classifiers, two algorithms were used:

```
=== Stratified cross-validation ===
=== Summary ===

Correctly Classified Instances      1045              96.8489 %
Incorrectly Classified Instances      34               3.1511 %
Kappa statistic                        0.8175
Mean absolute error                    0.0352
Root mean squared error                0.1508
Relative absolute error               19.8084 %
Root relative squared error           50.6751 %
Total Number of Instances           1079


=== Detailed Accuracy By Class ===

                 TP Rate  FP Rate  Precision  Recall  F-Measure  MCC    ROC Area  PRC Area  Class
                 0.986    0.189    0.980      0.986   0.983      0.818  0.967     0.993     not_bump
                 0.811    0.014    0.860      0.811   0.835      0.818  0.967     0.852     bump
Weighted Avg.    0.968    0.172    0.968      0.968   0.968      0.818  0.967     0.979

=== Confusion Matrix ===

   a   b   <-- classified as
 959  14 |   a = not_bump
  20  86 |   b = bump
```

Fig. 8. The result of the efficiency of the naive Bayesian classifier on a sliding sample in the special software "Weka"

```
=== Stratified cross-validation ===
=== Summary ===

Correctly Classified Instances      1045              96.8489 %
Incorrectly Classified Instances      34               3.1511 %
Kappa statistic                        0.8359
Mean absolute error                    0.0445
Root mean squared error                0.1519
Relative absolute error               25.0038 %
Root relative squared error           51.0264 %
Total Number of Instances           1079

=== Detailed Accuracy By Class ===

                 TP Rate  FP Rate  Precision  Recall  F-Measure  MCC    ROC Area  PRC Area  Class
                 0.972    0.066    0.993      0.972   0.982      0.840  0.994     0.999     not_bump
                 0.934    0.028    0.786      0.934   0.853      0.840  0.994     0.958     bump
Weighted Avg.    0.968    0.062    0.972      0.968   0.970      0.840  0.994     0.995

=== Confusion Matrix ===

   a   b   <-- classified as
 946  27 |   a = not_bump
   7  99 |   b = bump
```

Fig. 9. The effect of the K nearest neighbors method on a sliding sample in the special software "Weka"

1. Naive Bayesian classifier is a classifier based on the Bayes theorem. He makes an assumption about the object class based on the data distribution. Very often the naive Bayesian classifier shows very good results on the data.
2. The K nearest neighbors method is a classifier that classifies objects depending on the proximity of objects whose classes are known in advance.

Both algorithms showed themselves very well with a sliding test, the accuracy of correctly classified objects is about 96% in both algorithms. With equal accuracy of algorithms, I preferred a naive Bayesian classifier, because it is much faster - the method K of nearest neighbors calculates the distance from one object to another a large number of times (depends on the value of K), and on a large amount of data can show very poor performance. The class value is probably belonging to the class and takes a value from 0 to 1, the closer the value to 1, the greater the probability that the object is an unevenness.

After the data were classified, it was necessary to make their overlay on the city road map. To overlay a map, each street is divided into sections with a length of about 10 m. For correct partitioning, you need information about the geometry of the road. Unfortunately, such services as "Yandex Maps" and "Google Maps" do not provide open access to data on the geometry of the road. But they provide the service "Open Street Maps". Cartographic data in the service "Open Street Maps" is created by users of the service and the accuracy of data in cities is almost equal to commercial mapping services.

Broken sites should store information about all measurements received from mobile devices. The readings of the geology sensor have an error, and you cannot simply link the raw geological data to the broken sections on the road. To link the real coordinates to the road, the "GraphHopper" software and its "map-matching" module were used. "GraphHopper" is intended for building routes for ground movement (bicycle, motorcycle, car) in the "Open Street Maps" environment. The binding is carried out, taking into account all the data about the trip. After the coordinates are added, the classified value is added to the road section. The plot can store 10 dimensions, when the new measurement is received, the oldest dimension is deleted, and a new one is added. After that, the arithmetic mean of the plot is calculated. The chosen algorithm for averaging the value on the road segment allows to reduce the influence of false data, and allows to update the condition of the roadbed when new measurements are received.

5   The Process of Data Collection and Description of Entities

The process of collecting data begins with the receipt of the "create a trip" event, it occurs when the "start measurements" button is pressed. The event initiates a request to the server to obtain a unique trip ID, which is stored in the application memory throughout the trip. After the successful receipt of the identifier, the subscribers are registered to receive data from the sensors. If the registration process is successful, then the measurement starts. When the data is received, the "Measure collected" event is generated. This event receives a dimension handler that wraps the measurements in packets. Each package is collected within the time specified in the application settings, after that it is sent to the server. The data collection algorithm is shown in Fig. 10.

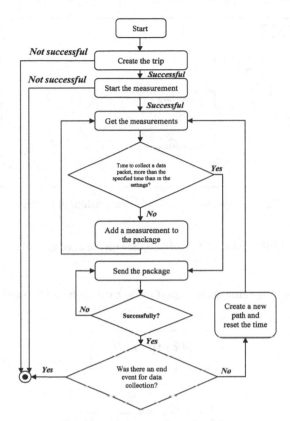

Fig. 10. Data Collection Algorithm

To present information about trips and measurements, the following entities were created:

1. The trip, stores information about the measurements, the processed measurements, the unique identifier of the device from which the collection was made.
2. Measurement, stores in itself information about the geo position, vehicle speed, data from the acceleration sensor, the measurement time.
3. The processed measurement stores the same information as the measurement, only passed through the measurement filter by the data processing module.

The relationship diagram of the entities is shown in Fig. 11.

To provide information on road roughness on the geographical map required the creation of an entity that would store information about the classification of the road. To solve this problem, we have developed the following entities:

1. Part of the road, stores ID information of the road from the service of Open Street Maps, information about classified metric plot, the coordinates of the location of the beginning and end of the segment.

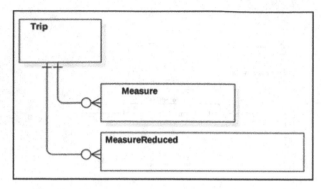

Fig. 11. Diagram of the entity relationships of the trip

2. Classified metric of the site, stores information on the classification and measurement dates.

Diagram of entity relationships related to the road segments presented in Fig. 12.

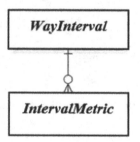

Fig. 12. Diagram of the relationship of the road section entities

The Used Technologies

The main programming language of the client application was JavaScript. JavaScript is a dynamically typed, interpreted programming language with a flexible development paradigm. It is executed on the browser side.

AngularJS is a client framework written in the JavaScript language that allows you to simplify writing a client application that is executed on the side of a web browser.

BowerJS is the package manager for the client part. It is called to simplify the receipt of dependencies and to manage their versioning.

Server Architecture

The server part consists of the following modules:

1. Web service for mobile application. Responsible for receiving requests from the mobile application and their subsequent processing. Web service methods are presented in Table 1.

Table 1. Web service methods for mobile application

The path	HTTP method	Description
/rest/trip	POST	Creates a new trip and returns its id
/rest/trip/{trip ID}/measures	PUT	Adds new dimensions to an existing trip

2. Module of interaction with the database. Provides a high abstraction at the level of business logic for performing such operations as saving, updating and deletion.
3. Data processing module. Performs processing of stored data and subsequent conversion of data for display on the map.
4. Web service for the client application. Handles requests from the client application. Web service methods are presented in Table 2.

Table 2. Methods of the web service of the client application

The path	HTTP method	Description
/web/map/	GET	Gets information about road sections

The relationship between the modules is shown in Fig. 13.

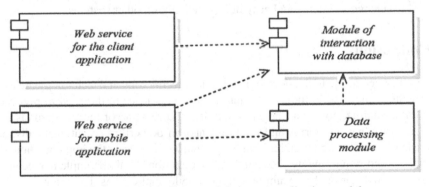

Fig. 13. Dependency diagram of the server application modules

Client Application

The client part is a web application that receives data from the server part via the HTTP protocol. The user on the client application can get information about the roughness of the roadway in the form of a map, with an additional layer that displays the state of the roadway with color markings (red color – pits, yellow for uneven coverage, green for flat sections of roads).

Graphical Interface

The graphical interface is a standard cartographic interface through which you can navigate, zoom. The screen form is shown in Fig. 14.

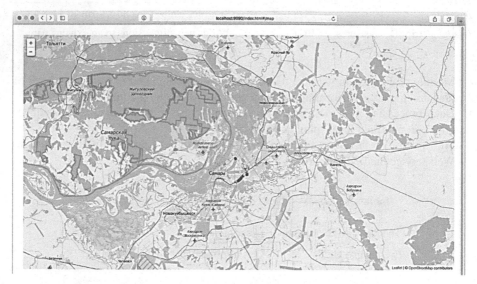

Fig. 14. Graphical user interface of the client application (Color figure online)

The loosely coupled structure of the developed modules allows you to quickly respond to new requirements and easy interpretation with other systems.

6   Conclusions

Changes that occur due to the development of new technology and technology are associated with an increase in the role of automation. This leads to the need to revise the issues of standardization in all areas of activity. The revision of the standards is necessary in order that the norms and requirements can be performed automatically, and not waste time exploring them, building a system for monitoring the implementation of these norms and requirements, etc. Thus, standardization should be implemented at the expense of active forms, for example, special mobile applications. For example, methods for measuring damage to road surfaces that affect road safety are labor-intensive and labor-intensive. They require planning work; it is always the departure of special teams for which the desired good weather conditions. As a result, the city authorities for taxpayer's money contain a large number of special brigades, which still do not have time to analyze timely the road surfaces. We propose such a passive method of monitoring norms and requirements to replace the active method by using a special mobile application. To solve the problem of ensuring the appropriate quality of the road surface at the state level, it is necessary to install this mobile application for urban vehicles and road patrol vehicles.

Acknowledgments. The research carried out with the financial support of the grant from the Program Competitiveness Enhancement of Peter the Great St. Petersburg Polytechnic University, Project 5-100-2020.

References

1. Kireeva, N., Zastupov, V.: Analysis and improvement of service quality in special purpose networks. In: 2018 International Scientific-Practical Conference on Problems of Infocommunications Science and Technology, PIC S and T 2018 – Proceedings, pp. 807–810 (2019). https://doi.org/10.1109/infocommst.2018.8632114
2. Slabko, V.V., Popov, A.K., Myslivets, S.A., Rasskazova, E.V., Tkachenko, V.A., Moskalev, A.K.: Transient processes in the parametric interaction of counter-propagating waves. Quantum Electron. **45**(12), 1151–1152 (2015). https://doi.org/10.1070/QE2015v045n12ABEH0 15840
3. Ziniakov, V.Y., Gorodetskiy, A.E., Tarasova, I.L.: Control of vitality and reliability analysis. In: Gorodetskiy, A.E. (ed.) Smart Electromechanical Systems. SSDC, vol. 49, pp. 193–204. Springer, Cham (2016). https://doi.org/10.1007/978-3-319-27547-5_18
4. Klimin, A.I., Pavlov, N.V., Efimov, A.M., Simakova, Z.L.: Forecasting the development of big data technologies in the russian federation on the basis of expert assessments. Paper presented at the Proceedings of the 31st International Business Information Management Association Conference, IBIMA 2018: Innovation Management and Education Excellence through Vision 2020, pp. 1669–1679 (2018)
5. Ianenko, M.B., Badalov, L.A., Rovensky, Y.A., Bunich, G.A., Gerasimova, E.B.: Essence, risks and control of uncertainties in the process of making investment decisions. Espacios **39**(31), 10p (2018)
6. Komkov, N.I.: Scientific and technological development: limitations and opportunities. Stud. Russian Econ. Dev. **28**(5), 472–479 (2017). https://doi.org/10.1134/S1075700717050094
7. Kolesnikov, A.M., Malevskaia-Malevich, E.D., Dubolazova, Y.A.: Peculiarities of quality management methodology for innovation projects of industrial enterprises. Paper presented at the Proceedings of the 30th International Business Information Management Association Conference, IBIMA 2017 - Vision 2020: Sustainable Economic Development, Innovation Management, and Global Growth, 2017-January, pp. 2898–2901 (2017)
8. Demidenko, D.S., Malinin, A.M., Litvinenko, A.N.: A new classification of the risks of the quality processes. Paper presented at the Proceedings of the 30th International Business Information Management Association Conference, IBIMA 2017 - Vision 2020: Sustainable Economic Development, Innovation Management, and Global Growth, 2017-January, pp. 2892–2897 (2017)
9. Krundyshev, V., Kalinin, M.: Hybrid neural network frame work for detection of cyber attacks at smart infrastructures. In: ACM International Conference Proceeding Series, paper № 3357623 (2019). https://doi.org/10.1145/3357613.3357623
10. Budanov, I.A.: Formation of an investment model of economic development of Russia. Stud. Russian Econ. Dev. **28**(1), 1–10 (2017). https://doi.org/10.1134/S1075700716060083
11. Kamenetskii, M.I.: Investment and construction activities in modern Russia: state and trends. Stud. Russian Econ. Dev. **27**(4), 390–399 (2016). https://doi.org/10.1134/S10757007160 40079
12. Kochovski, P., Drobintsev, P.D., Stankovski, V.: Formal quality of service assurances, ranking and verification of cloud deployment options with a probabilistic model checking method. Inf. Softw. Technol. **109**, 14–25 (2019). https://doi.org/10.1016/j.infsof.2019.01.003

13. Aytasova, A.S., Karpenko, P.A., Solopova, N.A.: Development the risk management system of processes in the enterprise. Paper presented at the Proceedings of the 2019 IEEE Conference of Russian Young Researchers in Electrical and Electronic Engineering, ElConRus 2019, pp. 1357–1360 (2019). https://doi.org/10.1109/eiconrus.2019.8657147

14. Nosov, S., Kuzmichev, V., Repin, S., Maksimov, S.: Methodology of ensuring road traffic safety with respect to road-building materials compaction efficiency factor. Transp. Res. Procedia **20**, 450–454 (2017). https://doi.org/10.1016/j.trpro.2017.01.073

15. Gholizadeh, H., Fazlollahtabar, H.: Production control process using integrated robust data envelopment analysis and fuzzy neural network. Int. J. Math. Eng. Manag. Sci. **4**(3), 580–590 (2019). https://doi.org/10.33889/IJMEMS.2019.4.3-046

16. Malik, P., Nautiyal, L., Ram, M.: A method for considering error propagation in reliability estimation of component-based software systems. Int. J. Math. Eng. Manag. Sci. **4**(3), 635–653 (2019). https://doi.org/10.33889/IJMEMS.2019.4.3-051

17. Siouris, G., Skilogianni, D., Karagrigoriou, A.: Post model correction in risk analysis and management. Int. J. Math. Eng. Manag. Sci. **4**(3), 542–566 (2019). https://doi.org/10.33889/ijmems.2019.4.3-044

18. Petrov, A., et al.: Broad-band fiber optic link with a stand-alone remote external modulator for antenna remoting and 5G wireless network applications. In: Galinina, O., Andreev, S., Balandin, S., Koucheryavy, Y. (eds.) NEW2AN/ruSMART-2019. LNCS, vol. 11660, pp. 727–733. Springer, Cham (2019). https://doi.org/10.1007/978-3-030-30859-9_64

19. Papic, L., Mladjenovic, M., Garcia, A.C., Aggrawal, D.: Significant factors of the successful lean six-sigma implementation. Int. J. Math. Eng. Manag. Sci. **2**(2), 85–109 (2017)

20. Bhullar, A., Gill, P.S.: Future of mobile commerce: an exploratory study on factors affecting mobile users' behaviour intention. Int. J. Math. Eng. Manag. Sci. **4**(1), 245–258 (2019)

21. Kumar, R.: Kaizen a tool for continuous quality improvement in indian manufacturing organization. Int. J. Math. Eng. Manag. Sci. **4**(2), 452–459 (2019)

22. Esmaeili, E., Karimian, H., Najjartabar Bisheh, M.: Analyzing the productivity of maintenance systems using system dynamics modeling method. Int. J. Syst. Assur. Eng. Manag. **10**(2), 201–211 (2018). https://doi.org/10.1007/s13198-018-0754-5

23. Aju kumar, V.N., Gupta, P., Gandhi, O.P.: Maintenance performance evaluation using an integrated approach of graph theory, ISM and matrix method. Int. J. Syst. Assur. Eng. Manag. **10**(1), 57–82 (2018). https://doi.org/10.1007/s13198-018-0753-6

24. Aggarwal, R., Singh, O., Anand, A., Kapur, P.K.: Modeling innovation adoption incorporating time lag between awareness and adoption process. Int. J. Syst. Assur. Eng. Manag. **10**(1), 83–90 (2019). https://doi.org/10.1007/s13198-018-00756-8

25. Nekrasova, T., Leventsov, V., Gluhov, V.: Development of infocommunications services in Russia. In: Galinina, O., Andreev, S., Balandin, S., Koucheryavy, Y. (eds.) NEW2AN/ruSMART-2019. LNCS, vol. 11660, pp. 505–514. Springer, Cham (2019). https://doi.org/10.1007/978-3-030-30859-9_43

26. Alshareet, O., Itradat, A., Doush, I.A., Quttoum, A.: Incorporation of ISO 25010 with machine learning to develop a novel quality in use prediction system (QiUPS). Int. J. Syst. Assur. Eng. Manag. **9**(2), 344–353 (2017). https://doi.org/10.1007/s13198-017-0649-x

27. Ambad, P.M., Kulkarni, M.S.: A goal programming approach for multi-objective warranty optimization. Int. J. Syst. Assur. Eng. Manag. **8**(4), 842–861 (2017). https://doi.org/10.1007/s13198-017-0674-9

28. Amrutkar, K.P., Kamalja, K.K.: An overview of various importance measures of reliability system. Int. J. Math. Eng. Manag. Sci. **2**(3), 150–171 (2017)

29. Moljevic, S.: Influence of quality infrastructure on regional development. Int. J. Qual. Res. **10**(2), 433–452 (2016). https://doi.org/10.18421/IJQR10.02-13

30. Djordjevic, A., Cvetic, T.: A business intelligence approach for choosing a optimal quality solution. Int. J. Qual. Res. **10**(2), 235–256 (2016). https://doi.org/10.18421/IJQR10.02-01

31. Ismagilova, L.A., Sukhova, N.A.: Assessment of quality of innovative technologies. Int. J. Qual. Res. **10**(4), 707–718 (2016). https://doi.org/10.18421/IJQR10.04-03
32. Nwachukwu, C., Chladkova, H., Fadeyi, O.: Strategy formulation process and innovation performance nexus. Int. J. Qual. Res. **12**(1), 147–164 (2018). https://doi.org/10.18421/IJQ R12.01-09
33. Živojinović, S., Stanimirović, A.: Support of quality management system and balanced score-card in the integration of normative, strategic and operational management. Int. J. Qual. Res. **6**(4), 389–402 (2012)

Service-Oriented Technology Architecture for Value-Based and Personalized Medicine

Igor V. Ilin⬤, Vadim V. Korablev⬤, and Anastasia I. Levina(✉)⬤

Peter the Great St. Petersburg Polytechnic University, Polytechnicheskaya 29,
195351 St. Petersburg, Russia
alyovina@gmail.com

Abstract. The current trends of the healthcare industry are value-based and personalized medicine. The requirements of compliance with the principles of value-based and personalized medicine have to be met in the architecture model of a healthcare organization – from business services to IT systems and the technology architecture. The personalized data collection is a sufficient enabler of a value-based and customer-oriented services. This paper is aimed at identifying the devices that could be used to collect and analyze personalized data, and thereby would enable the principles of value-based and personalized medicine; determining the place of such devices within the enterprise architecture; describing the existing and the target model of the technology architecture of a healthcare organization and its services; designing the architecture model of a healthcare organization that would include such devices. The research is grounded on the enterprise architecture approach which allows to describe different interdependent elements of the enterprise management system in one comprehensive model.

Keywords: Technology architecture · Personalized data collection · Healthcare device · Healthcare organization · Health 4.0

1 Introduction

Successful technological development and innovations in various industries have a significant impact on the activities of different types of enterprises, changing the very nature of their activities. The concept "Industry 4.0" connects digital and physical objects, creating an entirely new domain of scientific and practical activity that significantly influences the economy of different markets, changing the basic processes of enterprises and the life cycles of products, as well as triggering new business models and system of requirements to competencies of experts [1]. Initially, the term "Industry4.0" was coined as part of the production development process and the "Smart Factory" concept [2]. The scope of this term has changed over time, and concepts such as a "Smart City", "Smart Logistics", "Smart Home", "Smart Transport" and some others have appeared [3]. All these terms are the result of developing and implementing a sensor system that makes physical objects part of the information space of an enterprise. It also involves creating an integrated ecosystem of companies that can interact within a single space and share

O. Galinina et al. (Eds.): NEW2AN 2020/ruSMART 2020, LNCS 12525, pp. 194–204, 2020.
https://doi.org/10.1007/978-3-030-65726-0_18

the necessary data in real time, creating a maximum value for the end user, as well as making the process of delivering this value more manageable and transparent. The healthcare sector is no exception: due to the trends in the medical industry and modern digital technologies, a new type of healthcare organization appears – a "Smart Hospital» [4].

The main ideological concepts that influence the modern healthcare system are: value-based medicine, personalized medicine, the concept "Health 4.0" [5]. In general, the essence of the new stage in healthcare can be expressed as follows: due to the technological capabilities for data processing personalized collection and analysis of patient data becomes possible, which reflects the industry trend for patient-oriented and value-oriented approaches.

The requirements for compliance with the principles of value-based and personalized medicine have to be met in the architecture model of a healthcare organization. Health 4.0 technologies sets requirements for the structure of IT support and the technological infrastructure that ensures the implementation of processes. Thus, a methodology is needed to design IT and technological architectures of a healthcare organization and apply the principles of value-based and personalized medicine using devices and technologies that collect, process, analyze and store personalized data [6].

According to the concept Health 4.0, modern digital technologies (Big Data management, the Internet of Things, blockchain, telemedicine, predictive analytics, etc.) are used to improve the economic and medical efficiency as well as accessibility of medical care. Modern healthcare organizations in Russia cannot cope with the increasing data flow, because the existing management architecture, including the architecture of information systems and applications, does not provide interfaces to interact with modern digital technologies. In addition, healthcare organizations are still automated in a patchwork way, which prevents effective information exchange between the components of the information technology architecture [7–9].

Following the current trends in healthcare development, it is important to develop such a model of healthcare organization's activity that would apply the principles of value-based and personalized medicine, use the capabilities of Health 4.0 technologies, and could respond quickly and in a flexible way to the dynamically changing environmental conditions. This paper is aimed at:

- Identifying the devices that could be used to collect and analyze personalized data, and thereby would enable the principles of value-based and personalized medicine;
- Determining the place of such devices within the enterprise architecture;
- Describing the as-is and to-be models of the technology architecture of a healthcare organization and its services
- Designing the architecture model of a healthcare organization that would include such devices.

2 Materials and Methods

Materials

The leading concepts that set the trend for the development of the modern healthcare system are: value-based medicine, personalized medicine and the concept of healthcare digitalization – Health 4.0 [10].

Value-based medicine is a result-oriented approach to organizing the medical care system, which involves choosing a method of patient management that allows you to achieve better results at lower costs. Value-based medicine is defined as medical practice that includes the highest level of evidence-based medical data processing combined with assessing the effectiveness of treatment through the quality of life of a patient who has received the service [11]. At the same time, the patient is in a system in which treatment effectiveness is measured. Value-based medicine focuses on the results achieved during the time when medical services are rendered.

The following points are necessary for a healthcare organization to switch to value-based medicine:

- integrative care has to be organized, starting with prevention and primary care for each specific segment of risk populations;
- it is necessary to organize assessing the illness outcomes (in the long-term) and the cost of medical care for every patient;
- the remuneration system has to be changed so that the treatment of a pathology is paid for as a whole, not in parts;
- the participants in the process should be integrated with each other;
- an IT infrastructure and a platform for data analysis and decision-making have to be created.

According to this approach, the main goal of healthcare is the value from the patient's point of view [11]. The provider of medical services receives payment for actually helping the patient improve their health status, reducing the incidence of chronic diseases and their complications, and contributing to better public health. Of course, this approach should be used with extreme caution, since the result of healthcare has a high degree of uncertainty, and often the right approaches and techniques can be ineffective due to circumstances of force majeure or unpredictability of the patient's response.

According to the concept of personalized medicine, an individual patient treatment trajectory is selected and organized based on his or her specific features [12]. Personalized medicine is understood as a set of methods for preventing a pathological condition, diagnosing and treating a pathology considering the patient's individual characteristics. Personalized medicine is also called "precision" medicine or individualized medicine. Applying the principles of personalized medicine involves efficient collection, processing, and analysis of a large volume of primary data about every patient in real time [13].

The objectives of personalized medicine are to provide opportunities for predicting individual predisposition to diseases and developing personal tactics for preventing diseases, making an accurate diagnosis, and forming the most effective treatment tactics taking into account the individual characteristics and effects of medicinal products [14].

Using such tactics in routine clinical work is expected to bring a number of problems and constraints: it requires personalized accounting and processing of data about every patient, safe automation of such assessment and ensuring the availability of the data.

When developing solutions for the healthcare sector, the world's largest software manufacturers, such as SAP, Microsoft, Oracle etc., are guided primarily by the need to implement the ideas of value-based medicine and personalized medicine. The main goal of modern IT solutions is to maintain a balance between medical and economic efficiency of the healthcare organization. There is need for providing cost-effective care, creating a digital network for a new consumer-oriented healthcare ecosystem, and enabling real-time information exchange between health care providers and patients. It is necessary to maintain a more personalized interaction of patients with the healthcare organization at all stages of the process, from prevention and diagnostics to treatment and postoperative care.

Ensuring the availability of medical care and compliance with the principles of value-based medicine and personalized medicine are directly related to the possibility of increasing economic efficiency. Providing medical care that is appropriate, in the patient's opinion, for a particular case, creates prerequisites for the effective use of healthcare organizations' resources. Modern management technologies, including digital ones, have considerable potential and can solve a number of problems so that more affordable, cost-effective and high-quality medical care will be provided.

The described trends in healthcare are based on the capabilities of automated collection of data on the patient's condition. In this regard, it is important to identify the devices and technologies that allow such collection:

1. Smart mobile devices

This paragraph describes separate, independent devices that collect, transmit and analyze primary data on the patient's condition. Such smart devices are carried by the patient, and are often integrated into everyday things such as clothing, watches, and other accessories. The market of smart medical devices is growing every year with new, more advanced devices appearing. The production of such devices is gradually shifting towards multi-functional devices. They are very convenient and easy to use for an ordinary person, but, despite their simplicity, with their help the user can monitor their physical condition and some specific body parameters, and, if necessary, send the data received to the doctor. Table 1 shows the most popular consumer "smart" medical devices used today.

2. E-Health and m-health technologies

Mobile healthcare (mHealth, mobile health) is a branch of telemedicine that provides medical care and monitors a person's healthy lifestyle using wireless telecommunications technologies and mobile devices [15].

The goal of E-Health is to ensure the implementation of the ideas of value-based medicine and personalized medicine through the mass use of modern IT technology: cloud computing, the Internet of Things and services, the ability to process and use huge amounts of data (Big Data), machine learning, advanced mobile networks (5 g), etc. Using these technologies makes it possible to make the infrastructure of healthcare

Table 1. "Smart" medical devices

Device	Brief description
Fitness trackers	These are gadgets designed to control a person's physical activity. The main task of trackers is to encourage the owners to increase physical activity and control the resulting loads. The device has built-in sensors for monitoring heart rate, steps, burned calories, sensors for monitoring stress levels, sleep quality, travel speed and distance traveled. The information from a fitness tracker can be transferred to a smartphone or computer, which can calculate a person's activity and track the dynamics of the health indicators. The most common form of such a device is a wristband
Watches	The gadget, like a normal watch, can show the time and also collect information. The full functionality is obtained by synchronizing it with your smartphone. The main purpose is to display messages about calls and text messages received on your smartphone, updates from social media, reminders of planned events, weather forecasts, and so on. They can work as fitness trackers. Some functions such as a calculator work without connection to a smartphone
Smart clothing	Clothing that integrates with modern information technologies. It helps people with physiological abnormalities or diseases. Smart clothing is also useful when dealing with dangerous substances. Such clothing allows you to monitor your condition and control the most vital indicators. Smart clothing can conduct tests remotely and provide remote medical advice. Some models have a geolocation function
Shoes	You can track your heart rate, skin temperature, and oxygen levels using sensors built into smart socks, shoe inserts, or shoes themselves. Some models have GPS sensors
Glucose meters	A device that helps you continuously monitor your glucose levels. The sensor, attached to your body, makes measurements and transmits the data to the smartphone via wireless connection
Scales	Scales that interact with the app on your smartphone and send measurement results. The application may build a graph of changes in weight, calculate body mass index as well as other important metrics

organizations "smart", take solutions based on artificial intelligence to provide expertise and analyze huge amounts of medical data at a relatively low cost.

The Internet of Things is a large network of devices connected to the Internet. Almost any "thing" equipped with sensors can act as such a device: cars, industrial, medical and any other equipment, smartphones, tablets, oil rigs, wearable devices and many more. All these "things" collect and exchange data with the help of sensors. The Internet of Things and Machine-to-Machine technology (M2M) allow for greater transparency in any industry. In healthcare, the Internet of Things is used to remotely monitor the health status of a patient or client using wearable devices (including ECG and EEG monitors), smart sensors, and mobile applications.

Big Data refers to large amounts of data that can be structured to a various extent (well-structured, poorly-structured, or unstructured) that require special processing methods while maintaining a high level of data processing speed and quality. Healthcare, along with finance and market research, is one of the most advanced spheres using Big Data. Big Data is used in genetic analysis, clinical trial analysis, and expert systems.

Methodology

The capabilities for applying the technologies of Health 4.0 set requirements for the structure of IT support and technological infrastructure ensuring that the necessary processes are implemented. Thus, a methodology is needed to build the management system for healthcare organizations, where such elements of a healthcare organization's management system would develop as a business process system, architecture of information systems and applications as well their hardware in an integrated, interconnected manner and within a single model. In this paper an architectural approach was chosen as such a system. It is used to build management systems, including IT and technological support of activities.

The enterprise architecture is a unified whole of such elements of the management system as business processes, functional and organizational structures, material and cash flows, information systems and applications, data, document flow, and technological infrastructure facilities [16]. Reforming the operations of healthcare organizations caused by the need to implement modern management technologies, in accordance with the concept of enterprise architecture, should be carried out systematically, taking into account the interrelations and interdependencies of all elements of an organization's management system [16–20].

According TOGAF ideology [17], the enterprise architecture has the following main components:

- business architecture (a system of business processes and business services);
- data architecture (data formats, technologies for data collection, clearing, and uploading, etc.), together with application architecture often referred as IT-architecture;
- application architecture (a patient's electronic medical record, an electronic appointment with a doctor, bed occupancy, inventory of consumables in real time, etc.), together with data architecture often referred to as IT-architecture;
- technological architecture (databases, data storages, system software, network communications, etc.).

This paper focuses on IT architecture, technology architecture and the interaction between them.

3 Results

The current section describes the model of the architecture solution supporting the personalized patient data collection and processing. The technology layer of the enterprise architecture is in focus of this section as data collection capabilities refers to the functionality of this layer of the architecture.

The first step of the architecture solution modeling is to define the current state of the technology architecture model. When modeling the technological architecture of a healthcare organization, we encounter a number of limitations: the technological architecture of a healthcare organization substantially depends on the security policy adopted by the organization, as well as the general IT strategy adopted by the company. A general model of the technological architecture of a healthcare organization, which can be considered an "as is" model, can be formed only on the basis of a certain set of principles and assumptions that will form its basis. Otherwise, the technological architecture is highly variable depending on the chosen organization. The technological architecture of the "as is" model of the architecture of a healthcare organization can be based on the following principles:

- client-server application architecture (for single access to the information base from any computer in the organization);
- increased attention to data protection (to protect the personal data of patients).

It is also important to note that the medical equipment is not part of the technological architecture of the healthcare organization in an "as is" state. The integration of medical equipment is one of the stages in the development of a healthcare organization within the framework of the Industrie 4.0 paradigm.

The generalized as-is model of the technology architecture of a healthcare organization is shown on the Fig. 1.

The key part of the healthcare organization IT architecture (beside traditional for all types of companies ERP systems) is a Medical information system (hereinafter referred as MIS). It processes all the patient data and contains all the history of the patient treatment. An effective data analysis, whether of medical or economic aspects of a healthcare organization activity, requires BI functionality within the enterprise architecture [21]. The "to-be" model of the technology architecture of a healthcare organization based on the integration of the ERP, MIS and BI systems, is presented on Fig. 2. The proposed way of realization of a technology architecture provides reliable data for the data analysis services of the joint BI system, as well as to increase the accuracy and efficiency of data analysis services [22].

The personalized data collection and processing involves a patient-related IT-solutions and devices as parts of the whole architecture solution. The model of the latter, shown on the Fig. 3, is divided into two parts – healthcare organization architecture and patient-related (portable) architecture. As patient health status parameters have to be collected directly from the patient's body, there is a need to introduce a personal device for it, which is a part of the information exchange architecture. Patient data collection functionality can be performed either by a specific healthcare device or can be integrated in existing multifunctional device (like an application for a mobile phone). No matter which way is chosen, it should be integrated with a healthcare organization architecture. The specific attention should be paid to the data security aspects as the personal data is involved in the process. Depending on the type of data collected and the way it is collected, the patient can get a data analysis services via a certain interface.

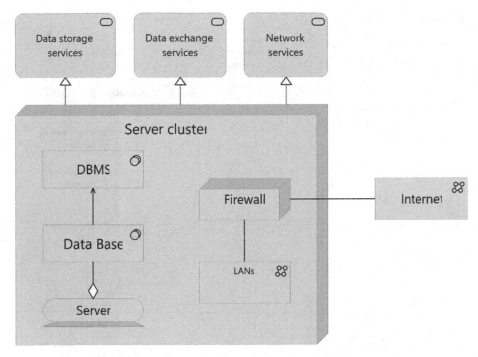

Fig. 1. As-is model of the technology architecture of a healthcare organization

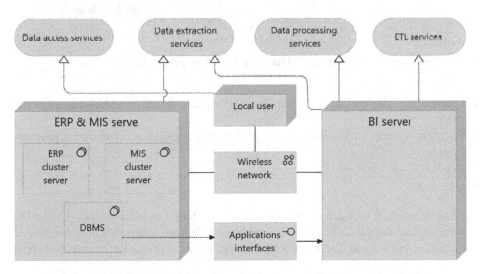

Fig. 2. To-be model of the technology architecture of a healthcare organization

The example, presented on the Fig. 3, illustrates the provision of healthcare parameters monitoring services. Another personalized services can be introduced to the corporate architecture:

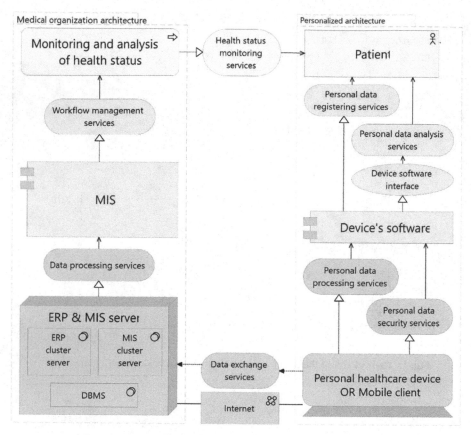

Fig. 3. Architecture solution for personalized patient data collection

- Personal account service – like an interface between a patient and his record in the MIS;
- Payment service – by means of integration of a personal account and a payment system;
- Feedback collection service;
- etc.

The mentioned services contribute to the value-based approach either. Unlike the monitoring and analysis of healthcare status service, they are not a part of the personalized architecture, but are just interfaces between a healthcare organization architecture and a patient.

4   Conclusion and Discussion

Value-based concept and customer orientation are trends of today's economy, not only of a healthcare industry. The personalized data collection is a sufficient enabler of a value-based and customer-oriented services. Services in healthcare means more than in many other industries as it is about the quality of a human life.

The paper solves the following tasks:

- Describes the role of personalized data collection for the purpose of value-based and personalized medicine;
- Describes the devices for personalized healthcare data collection;
- Analyses the as-is and to-be technology architecture of a healthcare organization;
- Describes the architecture model for patient data collection and its integration into the healthcare organization architecture.

One of the ways of further research is description of the value-based architecture models for different industries where data collection is focused not only on a person, like in healthcare case, but on other entities, e.g. houses in public utilities, vehicle in transport and logistics, etc. Authors also plan to focus on the specific digital technologies (IoT, M2M), enabling realization of value-based and personalized medicine principles for the sake of increasing medical and economic efficiency of healthcare systems.

Acknowledgement. The reported study was funded by RFBR according to the research project № 19-010-00579.

References

1. Hermann, M., Pentek, T., Otto, B.: Design principles for industrie 4.0 scenarios. In: 49th Hawaii International Conference on System Sciences (HICSS) (2016)
2. Smart Manufacturing Leadership Coalition. Implementing 21st century smart manufacturing. в Workshop summary report (2011)
3. Lepekhin, A., Borremans, A., Iliashenko, O.: Design and implementation of IT services as part of the 'smart city' concept. In: MATEC Web of Conferences, vol. 170 (2018)
4. Moosavi, S.R., et al.: SEA: a secure and efficient authentication and authorization architecture for IoT-based healthcare using smart gateways. Procedia Comput. Sci. **52**, 452–459 (2015)
5. Gkouskos, D., Burgos, J.: I'm in! Towards participatory healthcare of elderly through IOT. Procedia Comput. Sci. **113**, 647–652 (2017)
6. Lee, J., Kao, H.-A., Yang, S.: Service innovation and smart analytics for industry 4.0 and big data environment. Procedia Cirp **16**, 3–8 (2014)
7. Lee, S., Youn, B.: Industry 4.0 and prognostics and health management. Noise Vib. **25**(1), 22–28 (2015)
8. Ilin, I., Levina, A., Lepekhin, A., Kalyazina, S.: Business requirements to the IT architecture: a case of a healthcare organization. In: Murgul, V., Pasetti, M. (eds.) EMMFT-2018 2018. AISC, vol. 983, pp. 287–294. Springer, Cham (2019). https://doi.org/10.1007/978-3-030-19868-8_29
9. Zaychenko, I.M., Ilin, I.V., Dubgorn, A.: Using business model as a tool of arctic region medicine strategic development. In: Proceedings of the 31st International Business Information Management Association Conference, IBIMA 2018: Innovation Management and Education Excellence through Vision 2020, pp. 5313–5319 (2018)

10. Thuemmler, C., Bai, C.: Health 4.0: application of industry 4.0 design principles in future asthma management. In: Thuemmler, C., Bai, C. (eds.) Health 4.0: How Virtualization and Big Data are Revolutionizing Healthcare, pp. 23–37. Springer, Cham (2017). https://doi.org/10.1007/978-3-319-47617-9_2

11. Brown, M.M., Brown, G.C., Sharma, S., Landy, J.: Health care economic analyses and value-based medicine. Surv. Ophthalmol. **48**(2), 204–223 (2003)

12. Deegan, P.E.: The importance of personal medicine: a qualitative study of resilience in people with psychiatric disabilities. Scand. J. Public Health **33**(66), 29–35 (2005)

13. Estrela, V.V., Monteiro, A.C.B., França, R.P., Iano, Y., Khelassi, A., Razmjooy, N.: Health 4.0: applications, management, technologies and review. Med. Technol. J. **2**(4), 262–276 (2018)

14. Hamburg, M.A., Collins, F.S.: The path to personalized medicine. N. Engl. J. Med. **363**(4), 301–304 (2010)

15. Glasgow, R.E., Fisher, E.B., Haire-Joshu, D., Goldstein, M.G.: National institutes of health science agenda: a public health perspective. Am. J. Public Health **11**, 1936–1938 (2007)

16. Lankhorst, M.: Enterprise Architecture at Work: Modelling. Communication and Analysis. Springer, Heidelberg (2009). https://doi.org/10.1007/978-3-642-01310-2

17. Haren, V.: TOGAF Version 9.1 (2011)

18. Zachman, J.: The zachman framework for enterprise architecture. Zachman Int. **79** (2002)

19. Huemer, C., Liegl, P., Motal, T., Schuster, R., Zapletal, M.: The development process of the UN/CEFACT modeling methodology. In: Proceedings of the 10th International Conference on Electronic Commerce (2008)

20. Ilin, I.V., Iliashenko, O.Y., Levina, A.I.: Application of service-oriented approach to business process reengineering. In: в В сборнике: Proceedings of the 28th International Business Information Management Association Conference (2016)

21. Iliashenko, O.Yu., Iliashenko, V.M., Dubgorn, A.: IT-architecture development approach in implementing BI-system in medicine. In: CPSC (2019)

22. Ilin, I., Iliashenko, O., Iliashenko, V.: Approach to the choice of big data processing methods in financial sector companies. In: MATEC Web of Conferences, vol. 193, p. 05061 (2018)

SoMIAP: Social Media Images Analysis and Prediction Framework

Yonghao Shi[1], Gueltoum Bendiab[2(✉)], Stavros Shiaeles[2], and Nick Savage[2]

[1] CSCAN, University of Plymouth, Plymouth PL4 8AA, UK
syh506795003@yahoo.com
[2] Cyber Security Research Group, University of Portsmouth, Portsmouth, UK
{gueltoum.bendiab,nick.savage}@port.ac.uk, sshiaeles@ieee.org

Abstract. The personal photos captured and submitted by users on social networks can provide several interesting insights about the user's location; which is a key indicator of their daily activities. This information is invaluable for security organisations, especially for security monitoring and tracking criminal activities. Hence, we propose in this paper a novel approach for location prediction based on the image analysis of the photos posted on social media. Our approach combines two main methods to perform the image analysis; place and face recognition. The first method is used to determine the location area in the analysed image. The second is used to identify people in the analysed image, by locating a face in the image and comparing it with a dataset of images that have been collected from different social platforms. The effectiveness of the proposed approach is demonstrated through performance analysis and experimental results.

Keywords: Image analysis · Place recognition · Face recognition · Location prediction · Security · Social media

1 Introduction

The large number of personal photos shared on social media platforms presents a new opportunity to develop location prediction systems [27]. In this context, Instagram is a popular social network for sharing real-time photos with over 95 million photos uploaded each day [17]. These photos commonly contain sensitive information about the user, like places they usually go to, whether or not they are on vacation, and who are their friends and family members [27,28]. Thus, hundreds of millions of shared photos can provide several interesting insights on the locations of people [9]. This can lead to different use cases of such information, as it is a key indicator of their daily activities. Image analysis to predict and identify locations on social media could produce effective real-time monitoring systems that can be relevant to law enforcement authorities and others involved with public security to fight criminality and terrorism [13]. It may also keep track of malicious actions and threats such as the paedophile hunter activities,

© Springer Nature Switzerland AG 2020
O. Galinina et al. (Eds.): NEW2AN 2020/ruSMART 2020, LNCS 12525, pp. 205–216, 2020.
https://doi.org/10.1007/978-3-030-65726-0_19

grooming and planned criminal activities; where a person's current location could be coupled with geocoded crime statistics to predict when and where crimes will occur [13]. In this context, a recent report of the Guardian stated that complaints to police about alleged crimes linked to the use of Facebook and Twitter have increased by 780% in four years. While, in 2018, there were more than 4,908 crime reports in the UK, which involved the two sites [2]. Moreover, in the case of an emergency, incident or crisis, local authorities can achieve situational awareness in a short space of time because of the speed of social media in providing visual snapshots of the incidents that took place [9].

Motivated by the above use-cases and others, a wide array of approaches have been developed to extract the location information of users on social media [8,23]. A small number of researchers have previously exploited images submitted on those platforms to extract such information e.g. [28], by focusing on non-visual features of social media images such as geotags, descriptions, and other metadata [9,28]. Most of these approaches have limitations regarding coverage because a large number of the submitted photos may contain poor annotation, or no annotation at all [28], which affects their accuracy and raises questions about their effectiveness in real-world scenarios. In this paper, we aim to address these issues, by proposing a novel approach for predicting a user's locations through submitted photos on online social media. Our approach combines two main image analysis processes; place location and face recognition. The place location process is used to find the location area in the analysed image, by comparing it with a data set of known location images. While the face recognition technology is used to detect people in the analysed image by locating their face in the image and comparing it with a dataset of images that have been collected from different social platforms. The combination of those two techniques has the benefit of providing high accuracy and potentially complete coverage needed for security monitoring.

The rest of the paper is organized as follows. Section 2 presents the related works on the topic of identifying a user's location through social media. Section 3, provides a detailed explanation of the proposed approach. The experimental results and discussions are presented in Sect. 4. Finally, Sect. 5 reviews the content of the paper, presents the conclusions and outlines the potential future work.

2   Related Work

The prediction of a user's geographical location through social media has attracted intensive attention in recent years. In this context, a variety of information sources have been exploited for predicting locations. Some researchers have exploited a user's relationships on social networks to predict their location, such as works in [10,19,21]. These approaches are built upon the finding that friends in social media will be very likely to live in the same location. Therefore, the location of a given user can be predicted based on their relationship with other users. Most of these social-graph based approaches investigated inductive machine learning methods for making the predictions. Thus, the accuracy of the proposed approach highly depends on the samples used to train the classifier.

Another kind of approach used the content associated with a user's posts to estimate their locations [5,6,8,12,23]. These approaches generally predict a user's locations by examining words from their profile and generated posts. For example, authors in [8] used a user's tweets to extract words that are highly related to a specific geographic region and used these words to calculate the probability that this user lives at a specific location. The user profile is also applied in several content-based approaches to establish the location of users, particularly in twitter [3,15,19], where user profile is often combined with other information from message metadata such as MML (latitude and longitude geotags) [15], or other services such as Google Maps use geocoding to generate coordinates from a place name [3]. Most of these approaches face several key challenges, such as the uncertainty and heterogeneity of the generated content, which can affect the accuracy of the estimator. Study in [31] affirmed that content-based approaches have moderate coverage and low accuracy because of the lack of relationship between the user's true physical location and the mentioned one in the posts, as many users provide invalid place names. For example, on Twitter, from 46% to 77% of users provide fake location information [15].

Although a limited number of studies have focused on shared images through social media to predict a user's location, some investigative effort has been made to exploit the non-visual features of social media images such as geotags, descriptions, and other attributes to determine locations. For instance, work in [28] investigated the fusibility of geotagged photos of Flickr to examine the spatiotemporal human activities, which can be used for further location analysis. This work highlighted the potential of Volunteered Geographic Information (VGI) to examine human activities in space and time. In other recent work [9], authors introduced an image classification model to detect geotagged photos that are further analysed to determine if a fire event did occur at a particular time and place. To evaluate the proposed approach, the authors used a dataset of 114,098 Flickr photos, where 20.3% of the collected photos were geotagged and 2.5% contained GPS data in the EXIF (Exchangeable image file) header. The authors reported an average accuracy of 132 km in identifying the location of fires. However, those approaches have low coverage as only 2.5% of flicker photos have EXIF header information [27]. Furthermore, data is often noisy and photos may contain poor annotation, or no annotation at all, which affect the accuracy of these approaches.

In order to overcome the drawbacks of non-visual features-based approaches, some researchers have exploited the visual features of images to extract the location information. For example, work in [7] proposed visual features that assess the images at a low level. In this work, the authors performed image analysis of photos posted on Twitter by extracting SIFT (Scale-Invariant Feature Transform) descriptors [18] from the images. Then, the SIFT descriptors were clustered to form visual words. Authors reported an average F1-score of 70.5% of image classification using text, image and social context features. The main problem of this work is the lack of geotagged images. In prior work [14], authors proposed a data-driven scene matching approach to predict the location of social geotagged images at the global scale, they first retrieve visually similar photos and form clusters using geo-clustering. The geo-centroid of the cluster containing the most photos used for location prediction.

3   Proposed Approach

The main idea of this study is to present a visual-content-based approach that predicts a user's location from photos on social media. Our methodology comprises of two main image analysis steps. Firstly, we apply a place recognition technique on the input image to find the location area where the image was taken. This process is done by matching the input image with a data set of known-location images. In the second step, a face recognition technique is used to detect people in the input image, by locating their face in the image and comparing it with a dataset of images that have been collected from different social platforms. By combining the results of the two steps, the system outputs the location where the image is taken with the name of the person or persons shown in the image. More details are given in the following sections.

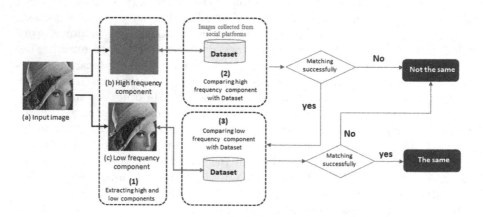

Fig. 1. Overview of the place location process.

3.1   Place Location

The location recognition step compares the input image with images of well-known locations to detect the area where the image was taken. As illustrated in Fig. 1, the place recognition process is performed by using the low and high frequency components, which are extracted from the input image. The low-frequency component provides details that describe the basic information of the input image, while the high-frequency component is very useful to find descriptive and invariant features for image matching. Firstly, the high-frequency component is compared with a dataset that contains samples of known locations images (*see* Fig. 1).

If the features matching in the first step is successful, the low-frequency component is then used to compare the basic information of the input image with the samples in the dataset. In this step, the comparison is done by using an image hashing algorithm, which is a fast method to compare the differences between the images.

3.2 Face Recognition

The face recognition process is used to identify if a person is in the input image, where his or her face is located, and who this person is. It has as input, the image to be analysed, and as output, the identity of the person that appears in this image. The procedure is separated into two main steps; face detection and face recognition.

Face Detection. In this step, a Haar classifier [30] is used to determine the existence of human faces in the input image and their locations. This classifier uses a set of Haar features [30] to capture important characteristics of human faces in the input image, and removes all the unwanted objects (e.g., building, tree, etc.). Many researches have proven the effectiveness of Haar features in building accurate classifiers with a limited number of images in training the data set [30]. The expected outputs of this step are detected faces in the input image, which will be used for further processing.

Face Recognition. The goal of this step is to automatically determine the identities of the faces in the input images. Thus, a faces dataset is required, where for each person, several images are taken and their features are extracted and stored in the dataset. In our approach, the facial images were collected from different social platforms. Then, features are extracted from each input facial image and compared with those of each face class stored in the database. For the comparison, the Fisherface method [29] is used when the facial images have large variations in illumination and facial expression. Otherwise, the Local Binary Patterns Histograms (LBPH) [1] algorithm is more suitable. Figure 2 gives an overview of the face recognition flowchart.

4 Experiments and Discussion

In this section we describe the experiments and results obtained from the methods shown in Sect. 3. First, we describe the experimental set-up and results for each step. Then we compare the performance of the proposed method with baseline methods.

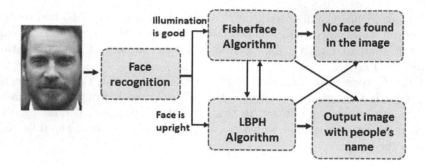

Fig. 2. Face recognition flowchart.

4.1   Location Recognition Experiment Results

In these experiments, we used the OpenCV (Open Source Computer Vision) library [20], where the three descriptors; SIFT, Speeded Up Robust Features (SURF) [4], and Oriented FAST and Rotated BRIEF (ORB) [24] were used for feature detection and collection. The hashing algorithms dhash [11] and pHash [22] were used to compare the differences between images; grayscale-images and colour images. For the training and testing, we used a dataset of 400 well-known location photos collected from social platforms: Facebook, Wechat and Tecent, with 200 similar images and 200 different images.

High-Frequency Component. Figure 3 shows comparison results for the SIFT, SURF and ORB techniques. The results illustrate the robustness and accuracy of the SURF algorithm for feature detection. While the ORB algorithm is more suitable to solve the rotation problem of image (Fig. 4). ORB provides faster image matching than the SURF, but it is less accurate.

Low-Frequency Component. For the low-frequency component experiments, four tests were carried out to determine the accuracy of the dhash and pHash algorithms. Tests were performed between similar images and different images, by using a dataset consisting of 200 similar images and 200 different images. For each test, we identified the weight hash values for the similar images test and the different images test, the threshold and the accuracy. Two tests were performed with grayscale images and the two other with colour-images. In the grayscale image tests, the hash value is computed after converting the image to the grayscale format. In the colour image tests, the hash values were calculated for each RGB colour separately. After calculated the hash value for Blue is appended to Green and finally both to Red.

As shown in the Table 1, the dhash algorithm achieved the highest accuracy with colour images (64.4%) for a threshold of 34. Whereas, the pHash algorithm reached an accuracy of 64% for the grayscale-images test with a threshold of 23, which is higher than the dHash one with approximately 7% points. Similarly,

SIFT algorithm   SURF algorithm   ORB algorithm

Fig. 3. Comparison of The SIFT, SURF and ORB algorithms.

Fig. 4. Results for rotation.

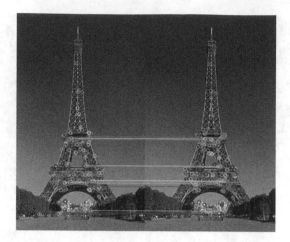

Fig. 5. Results for illumination.

it achieved the highest accuracy for the colour images test (68%) for the same threshold (23). From the results, we concluded that the pHash algorithm has higher accuracy than the dhash for grayscale-images and colour images. Also, the hashing algorithms pHash and dhash provide higher accuracy with colour images than grayscale images.

Table 1. Tests results for Dhash and Phash algorithm

Tests	Weight value		Threshold	Accuracy
	Similar images	Different images		
dhash (grayscale)	30.35	40.37	34	59.6%
dhash (colour)	32.67	40.66	36	64.4%
pHash (grayscale)	18.43	27.81	23	64%
pHash (colour)	19.83	23	23	68%

Table 2 shows the min, max and average times spend on data analysis for each test. The results reveal that for the two algorithms, the data analysis take more time for colour images than the grayscale images. Also, the pHash is a time-consuming algorithm (maximum time cost is 1.25 s) compared to the dhash (maximum time cost is 0.6 s). In summary, pHash algorithm has higher accuracy, but lower speed. While the dhash algorithm is fast but less accurate. In fact, pHash has the highest accuracy in all hash algorithms. However, it is time-consuming because of the complex calculations. Also, the two hashing algorithms provide higher accuracy with colour images but they need more computing time because the hash value calculation time is tripled.

Table 2. Speed tests results for dhash and Phash algorithm

Tests	Mean	Maximum	Minimum
Dhash (grayscale)	0.10 s	0.50 s	0.10 s
Dhash (colour)	0.10 s	0.60 s	0.10 s
Phash (grayscale)	0.30 s	0.80 s	0.15 s
Phash (colour)	0.50 s	1.25 s	0.20 s

4.2 Face Recognition Experiments Results

In the face recognition experiments, we used a Haar classifier to identify and collect front faces from the input image with rectangles (see Fig. 5). To recognize the collected front faces, we used the Fisherface, LBPH and Eigenface [29] algorithms. In these initial experiments, only 20 faces were used for testing and training. Figure 6 shows the images of three persons used for the training step.

Cai   Shi   Yuan

Fig. 6. Cai, Shi and Yuan images used for the training and testing steps.

Table 3 shows the results for the face recognition using the three algorithms Fisherface, Eigenface and LBPH. From the results we can see that the Fisherface has the highest accuracy in face recognition, while the Eigenface algorithm is the faster. Fisherface is one of the popular algorithms used in face recognition and is widely believed to be superior to Eigenface. Thus, it is more suitable for our approach. However, the LBPH algorithm is more suitable in case of upright images.

4.3 Comparison

It is not easy to conduct a fair comparison among various image and location recognition approaches due to the differences between the datasets and algorithms used. Thus, our comparison will be based on some significant features including accuracy, speed, image type, rotation and illumination. Table 4 overviews a general comparison between our approach and other approaches.

Table 3. Eigenface, Fisherface and LBPH results

	Eigenface	Fisherface	LBPH
Accuracy	40%	53.3%	79%
Speed	Fast	Normal	Normal
Colour-element	Yes	Yes	Yes
Illumination	No	No	Yes
Rotation	Less than 10°	Less than 10°	No

Firstly the hashing method is compared with other representative's approaches (*see* Table 4). Then, the proposed face recognition method is compared with previous works in the field (*see* Table 4).

As can be seen from Table 4, the hashing method in our approach has the highest accuracy with a suitable threshold for colour images. Compared to the grayscale approaches, it increased by 5% and 4% for dhash and pHash algorithms respectively, which prove the effectiveness of computing the hash values from primary colours; red, blue and green. However, the results for the face recognition step need further investigation due to the limitation of training data.

Table 4. Comparison with other methods

Hashing method, comparison with other methods					
	Accuracy	Speed	Image type	Rotation	Illumination
Zauner et al. [33]	49.6%	9.69 s	Grayscale	Yes	Not mentioned
Yang et al. [32]	60%	9.0.7 s	Grayscale	Less than 30°	Yes
Jie et al. [16]	50%	Not mentioned	Grayscale	Less than 5°	Yes
Our approach	66%	0.5 s	Colour	Yes	Yes
Face recognition method, comparison with other methods					
Nikolaos et al. [25]	40%	0.5 s	Grayscale	No	Yes
Magali et al. [26]	79%	2 s	Grayscale	No	No
Our approach	53.3%	1 s	Colour	No	Yes

5   Conclusions

This paper proposed a novel approach for location prediction based on image analysis of the photos posted on social media. This approach exploited the visual features of images to extract the location information, by using the place and face recognition techniques. From our initial experimental results, the method seems promising and being able to predict the people locations, with potentially complete coverage required for security monitoring. Future work would improve the accuracy of the face recognition process by using more samples for training and testing. Also, we intend to use other machine learning approaches such as to enhance the accuracy of this approach.

Acknowledgement. This project has received funding from the European Union's Horizon 2020 research and innovation programme under grant agreement no. 786698. The work reflects only the authors' view and the Agency is not responsible for any use that may be made of the information it contains.

References

1. Ahonen, T., Hadid, A., Pietikainen, M.: Face description with local binary patterns: application to face recognition. IEEE Trans. Pattern Anal. Mach. Intell. **28**(12), 2037–2041 (2006)
2. Press Association: Social media-related crime reports up 780% in four years. https://bit.ly/2HPQIBS. Accessed 19 July 2019
3. Baucom, E., Sanjari, A., Liu, X., Chen, M.: Mirroring the real world in social media: twitter, geolocation, and sentiment analysis. In: Proceedings of the 2013 International Workshop on Mining Unstructured Big Data Using Natural Language Processing, pp. 61–68. ACM (2013)
4. Bay, H., Ess, A., Tuytelaars, T., Van Gool, L.: Speeded-up robust features (surf). Comput. Vis. Image Underst. **110**(3), 346–359 (2008)
5. Chandra, S., Khan, L., Muhaya, F.B.: Estimating twitter user location using social interactions-a content based approach. In: 2011 IEEE Third International Conference on Privacy, Security, Risk and Trust and 2011 IEEE Third International Conference on Social Computing, pp. 838–843. IEEE (2011)
6. Chang, H.W., Lee, D., Eltaher, M., Lee, J.: @ Phillies tweeting from Philly? Predicting twitter user locations with spatial word usage. In: Proceedings of the 2012 International Conference on Advances in Social Networks Analysis and Mining (ASONAM 2012), pp. 111–118. IEEE Computer Society (2012)
7. Chen, T., Lu, D., Kan, M.Y., Cui, P.: Understanding and classifying image tweets. In: Proceedings of the 21st ACM International Conference on Multimedia, pp. 781–784. ACM (2013)
8. Cheng, Z., Caverlee, J., Lee, K.: You are where you tweet: a content-based approach to geo-locating twitter users. In: Proceedings of the 19th ACM International Conference on Information and Knowledge Management, pp. 759–768. ACM (2010)
9. Daly, S., Thom, J.A.: Mining and classifying image posts on social media to analyse fires. In: ISCRAM (2016)
10. Davis Jr, C.A., Pappa, G.L., de Oliveira, D.R.R., de L. Arcanjo, F.: Inferring the location of twitter messages based on user relationships. Trans. GIS **15**(6), 735–751 (2011)
11. dhash: dhash 1.3. https://pypi.org/project/dhash/. Accessed 19 July 2019
12. Eisenstein, J., O'Connor, B., Smith, N.A., Xing, E.P.: A latent variable model for geographic lexical variation. In: Proceedings of the 2010 Conference on Empirical Methods in Natural Language Processing, pp. 1277–1287. Association for Computational Linguistics (2010)
13. Hadjimatheou, K., Coaffee, J., De Vries, A.: Enhancing public security through the use of social media. Eur. Law Enforcement Res. Bull. **18**, 1–14 (2019)
14. Hays, J., Efros, A.A.: IM2GPS: estimating geographic information from a single image. In: 2008 IEEE Conference on Computer Vision and Pattern Recognition, pp. 1–8. IEEE (2008)
15. Hecht, B., Hong, L., Suh, B., Chi, E.H.: Tweets from Justin Bieber's heart: the dynamics of the location field in user profiles. In: Proceedings of the SIGCHI Conference on Human Factors in Computing Systems, pp. 237–246. ACM (2011)

16. Jie, Z.: A novel block-DCT and PCA based image perceptual hashing algorithm. arXiv preprint arXiv:1306.4079 (2013)
17. Lister, M.: 33 mind-boggling instagram stats & facts for 2018. https://bit.ly/2zOKGfr. Accessed 19 July 2019
18. Lowe, D.G.: Distinctive image features from scale-invariant keypoints. Int. J. Comput. Vision **60**(2), 91–110 (2004)
19. McGee, J., Caverlee, J., Cheng, Z.: Location prediction in social media based on tie strength. In: Proceedings of the 22nd ACM International Conference on Information & Knowledge Management, pp. 459–468. ACM (2013)
20. OpenCV: Opencv 4.1.1, the latest release is now available. https://opencv.org/. Accessed 19 July 2019
21. Pellet, H., Shiaeles, S., Stavrou, S.: Localising social network users and profiling their movement. Comput. Secur. **81**, 49–57 (2018)
22. pHash: phash, the open source perceptual hash library. https://www.phash.org/. Accessed 19 July 2019
23. Poulston, A., Stevenson, M., Bontcheva, K.: Hyperlocal home location identification of twitter profiles. In: Proceedings of the 28th ACM Conference on Hypertext and Social Media, pp. 45–54. ACM (2017)
24. Rublee, E., Rabaud, V., Konolige, K., Bradski, G.R.: Orb: an efficient alternative to sift or surf. In: ICCV, vol. 11, p. 2. Citeseer (2011)
25. Stekas, N., van den Heuvel, D.: Face recognition using local binary patterns histograms (LBPH) on an FPGA-based system on chip (SOC). In: 2016 IEEE International Parallel and Distributed Processing Symposium Workshops (IPDPSW), pp. 300–304. IEEE (2016)
26. Stolrasky, M.S., Jakov, N.B.: Recognition using class specific linear projection. semanticscholar.org (2015)
27. Stone, Z., Zickler, T., Darrell, T.: Toward large-scale face recognition using social network context. Proc. IEEE **98**(8), 1408–1415 (2010)
28. Sun, Y., Fan, H., Helbich, M., Zipf, A.: Analyzing human activities through volunteered geographic information: using flickr to analyze spatial and temporal pattern of tourist accommodation. In: Krisp, J. (ed.) Progress in Location-Based Services, pp. 57–69. Springer, Heidelberg (2013). https://doi.org/10.1007/978-3-642-34203-5_4
29. Turk, M., Pentland, A.: Eigenfaces for recognition. J. Cogn. Neurosci. **3**(1), 71–86 (1991)
30. Whitehill, J., Omlin, C.W.: Haar features for FACS AU recognition. In: 7th International Conference on Automatic Face and Gesture Recognition (FGR 2006), pp. 5-pp. IEEE (2006)
31. Xu, D., Cui, P., Zhu, W., Yang, S.: Find you from your friends: graph-based residence location prediction for users in social media. In: 2014 IEEE International Conference on Multimedia and Expo (ICME), pp. 1–6. IEEE (2014)
32. Yang, B., Gu, F., Niu, X.: Block mean value based image perceptual hashing. In: 2006 International Conference on Intelligent Information Hiding and Multimedia, pp. 167–172. IEEE (2006)
33. Zauner, C.: Implementation and benchmarking of perceptual image hash functions (2010). http://phash.org/

Modeling and Investigation of the Movement of the User of Augmented Reality Service

Maria Makolkina[1,2] and Alexander Paramonov[1,2(✉)]

[1] Bonch-Bruevich Saint-Petersburg State University of Telecommunications,
193232 Saint Petersburg, Russia
makolkina@list.ru, alex-in-spb@yandex.ru
[2] Peoples' Friendship University of Russia (RUDN University),
6 Miklukho-Maklaya St, 117198 Moscow, Russia

Abstract. In recent years, the use of augmented reality (AR) applications in various industries and spheres of human life has increased significantly. With the appearance of new AR devices and the development of technology, the mobility of users has increased and the possibilities of using AR have expanded. This leads to the need to develop new AR user traffic models taking into account the features of its movement. The paper presents the results of an investigation of the movement of the user of augmented reality services. Augmented reality user movement models have been developed and a detailed analysis of the influence of user behavior on AR traffic parameters and the quality of experience of AR services has been carried out. The generalized augmented reality user movement model is based on experimental data and can be used in the future for modeling and implementation of AR services.

Keywords: Augmented reality · Traffic · Quality of experience · User behavior · User movement model

1 Introduction

Augmented reality services are firmly entrenched in our everyday life in the form of many applications for smartphones, such as maps of cities and settlements, applications for paying for the metro, navigators, guides, etc. [6,15,20]. In practice, the range of such services is not limited to the provision of geographic information and mobile services. Provided that the AR service provides the appropriate quality, its various applications will find application in many fields of activity, for example, industry, medicine, transport, etc. [5,9,18,22,23].

Augmented reality terminals can serve as various devices as general purpose (smartphones, tablet computers, laptops), and specialized (augmented reality glasses, projectors, etc.). The main function of the AR service is the delivery to the consumer of information useful to him in certain conditions. The methods for identifying such conditions and methods for delivering information can be very different [10,13,19].

© Springer Nature Switzerland AG 2020
O. Galinina et al. (Eds.): NEW2AN 2020/ruSMART 2020, LNCS 12525, pp. 217–228, 2020.
https://doi.org/10.1007/978-3-030-65726-0_20

Today, augmented reality applications for smartphones are commonly called mobile augmented reality [2,3]. A lot of research is currently aimed at the application of MEC (Mobile Edge Computing) technology for the implementation of mobile augmented reality, which will allow ultra-low latency, real-time access, location-based services, and so on [1,21]. However, due to the strict latency requirements of augmented reality applications for mobile devices, the application of MEC technology is not always sufficient to provide the required quality of experience [11]. To improve the quality of the experience of AR services to mobile users, it is necessary, among other things, to take into account the speed and direction of movement of users, as well as the density of AR objects in the user's environment and the way information is displayed.

It is anticipated that AR applications will play an important role in fifth generation communications networks. Due to the great popularity of AR applications for mobile terminals, it is necessary to solve a number of technical problems in order to ensure the operation of such applications with the appropriate QoE. So investigation [8] examines the effect of network density and users on the operation of 5G networks. The authors also assess the effect of user mobility and explore the concept of dedicated radio-frequency charging. The paper [17] explores the next stage in the development of the Internet of Things, namely self-driving cars and ensuring the efficient and reliable operation of applications in them. In particular, the concept of opportunistic crowdsensing applications is proposed, which uses IoT sensors powered by vehicle-mounted mobile relays. When implementing AR applications, the use of D2D communications can significantly reduce the load on the network. In paper [16], the authors investigate the application of D2D communication in 5G networks. They believe that for the development and widespread use of D2D communications, the adoption of the concepts of trust and social-aware cooperation between end users and network operators is necessary.

Various ways of presenting information. Most AR services provide information through visual messages (text, icons, color, image brightness, etc.), although in some applications other forms of data presentation are possible (voice, sound, tactile sensations). Thus, the organization of AR services is a complex task, the solution of which is largely determined by the applied orientation [4].

Consider the services of AR intended for mass consumers, as terminals using either specialized devices (augmented reality glasses), or smartphones or tablet computers. The generalized model of AR services is shown in Fig. 1.

For the target space, we take the user's environment, where objects are located, information about which is contained in the database of the AR and can be claimed. As conditions that determine the need for this or that information, we will consider the user's position in his environment, as well as the characteristics of the movement. For example, when using a service such as a map or navigator, the user is free to move and the only characteristic of his position in the environment is the coordinates, the change of which serves as the basis for requesting data. Depending on the user's coordinates, the smartphone application downloads map data, and in the process of its movement periodically

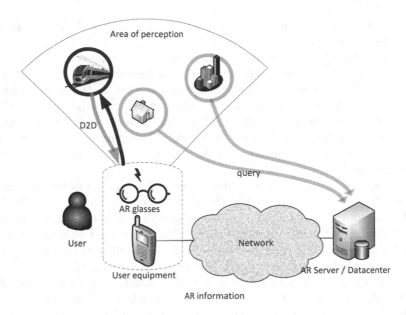

Fig. 1. The generalized model of AR services

loads the necessary data. If data loading is late, the information on the map is no longer relevant. The value of information decreases and becomes zero when the user leaves the area displayed on the map.

Obviously, the quality of user perception of the service depends on the timeliness of information delivery, and the requirements for the delivery process on the nature of the requests, i.e. from the method of its movement, which, of course, will be different for the pedestrian and for the driver of the car on the express road. To eliminate the risk of untimely data delivery, for example, by a navigator application, all map data can be pre-placed on the user's device (offline maps). However, this method is good only for one of the services, and in addition, it is applicable if the data is unchanged for a long time: it is impractical to store information, in particular, about traffic jams at the terminal. Additional information AR, which is a report on the current state (this may be, for example, a radio graph of the patient during surgery), generally not be stored. Thus, in order to organize the AR service and ensure its quality, it is necessary to take into account the traffic model, which, in turn, is determined by user behavior and the methods of generating data requests [14]. In this paper, we propose a AR traffic model based on a motion model and generating data requests.

2   Goal of Investigation

To achieve such basic goals as timely delivery and provision of AR data to the user, various mechanisms of predictive (proactive) data delivery to the user terminal can be used. To implement this mechanism, it is necessary to produce proactive data requests – the volume of transmitted traffic and the timeliness of message delivery depend on this.

Obviously, the delivery of more data to the client application increases its "autonomy", i.e. the ability to provide information for a long time. However, an increase in the volume increases the traffic intensity in the communication network and the load on the AR server, which can lead to the opposite effect, i.e. to data delivery delays and unavailability of the service. The inefficiency of such an increase in terms of the use of network and memory resources is obvious. After all, the user is rarely faced with the need for a short time to have all the cards in the terminal's memory.

Moreover, not all services, as noted above, allow you to download data in advance. Thus, the delivery of such a volume of AR data that is most likely to be in demand in the near future can be considered the best approach. And since we are talking about a future point in time, this task should be considered as a forecasting problem. The predicted value is the probability of demand for data at some, most likely, the closest point in time.

The predicted value is the probability of demand for data at some, most likely, the closest point in time. In fact, the parameters of this request are the predicted values of the state of the user's environment, on the basis of which the selection of AR data should be made. To achieve this goal, it is necessary to analyze and build a model of processes that determine the choice of forecasting method.

3   User Model

A user model is one of the most essential elements in modeling a service. Since the user is the subject for whom the service is being created, the model should reflect its basic characteristics of behavior and perception, which set the requirements for the technical parameters of the service. It is the perception of messages (information) and the behavior that determines the need for information that serve as factors in the choice of methods for organizing and providing services.

The ability to perceive various forms of presentation of messages determines the choice of means for organizing the interface (in the general case) of the human-machine [7]. Such a choice should be based on studies of the characteristics of human perception of various forms of message presentation, as well as the ability to perceive several messages in different conditions. This is a separate area of research. In this paper, we focus on user behavior, namely, on the behavior features that are associated with the nature of data requests. This component of the user model allows you to identify the features of the query traffic and data traffic services AR.

When describing the user model, we proceed from the following assumptions:

1. The user is a person, and the user terminal is AR glasses [14], a smartphone or other portable wearable device connected to the communication network and having a graphical interface (screen) with the user.

2. We consider a typical user whose behavior is determined by the most probable (typical) situations. This model does not claim to be completely general, since many special areas and situations are possible in which user behavior can differ significantly from typical. Such applications require specific models.
3. When constructing a behavior model, we study only those features that determine the nature of data requests. These include those that manifest themselves in the effect on the AR device, which can be estimated using sensors and input devices currently available.

We describe the parameters that can be measured or entered by the AR device. In general, these include:

1) sound, without recognition of the source and content;
2) sound, with recognition of the source and/or content;
3) photo or video (without object recognition);
4) photo or video (with object recognition);
5) manipulation with the input device (touch screen, etc.);
6) the position of the device in space (coordinates of GPS or other global positioning systems);
7) the orientation of the device in space (orientation in the Earth's magnetic field);
8) data on illumination;
9) temperature data.

The given data set is typical, individual devices can show a wider data set, for example fitness bracelets ("smart watches"), etc.

The AR service is provided during the interaction of the AR client application running on a mobile device and the server. Data requests are made by the client application. Moreover, the request for AR data can be as interactive, i.e. at the request of the user, and predictive – by the decision of the client application. In the first case, the user makes a request in some established manner, in particular by touching the touch screen, moving the manipulator or voice command. In the second case, the request is carried out automatically by the client program based on an analysis of user or environment actions, for example, moving to a point with other coordinates, rotating a subscriber's device, hitting a target object in the observation area, etc.

Thus, the nature of data requests can be very diverse, which significantly depends on the specifics of the service. When developing a model, we will analyze only those requests that are initiated by the application, i.e. automatically, based on the analysis of individual properties of user behavior. Consider the most characteristic properties inherent in most modern applications and services, namely: the movement of the user and the change in position of the device in space.

In such conditions, the request is initiated when the user coordinates or the position of the subscriber device in space changes. Since the data should be delivered in a timely manner (when they are supposed to be in demand), their request should be made based on some forecast. The initial data for the forecast can be parameters of user behavior until the moment the request is made. It is obvious, for example, that when a driver moves in a car on a high-speed road, it is advisable to prepare data taking into account the speed and direction of movement.

In the general case, we can say: in a particular situation, different data have different probability of being in demand. This is determined by the behavior of the user, his movement. Moreover, the movement can be characterized by the movement of both the user (change of coordinates) and the subscriber device (orientation in space).

Speaking about the user's movement (changing his coordinates in three-dimensional space), we assume that a data request is formed when the AR object enters the user's surrounding space. Such an event can be registered by the sensors of the subscriber device, if possible and if it is provided for by the service, or after accessing the AR database. In the second case, access to the AR database should be made when the user coordinates are changed. Obviously, a certain threshold value of this change should be chosen, since changes in the coordinate estimate occur not only as a result of the user's movement, but also by chance – due to the presence of an error in the functioning of the positioning system. In addition, the size of this change may depend on the density of AR objects in the space under consideration [12].

For example, if the user's environment is defined by a region bounded by a circle with radius R, then with his rectilinear and uniform movement (Fig. 2), with a random distribution of objects, the path traveled by the object in the perception area will be a random variable with a probability density equal to:

$$g(d) = \frac{1}{\pi R \sqrt{1 - \left(\frac{d}{2R}\right)^2}} \tag{1}$$

mathematical expectation

$$M[d] = \overline{d} = \frac{4}{\pi} R \tag{2}$$

When the user's speed v is the time the object stays in the perception area will also be a random variable with probability density:

$$q(t) = \frac{1}{\pi R \sqrt{1 - \left(\frac{v}{2R}\tau\right)^2}} \tag{3}$$

and mathematical expectation

$$M[t] = \overline{\tau} = \frac{4}{\pi} \frac{R}{v} \tag{4}$$

The graph of probability density (3) is shown in Fig. 3.

Expressions (3) and (4) make it possible to estimate the residence time of objects in the area accessible to the user. The task of constructing a system in this case will be to select the values of the system parameters for which condition

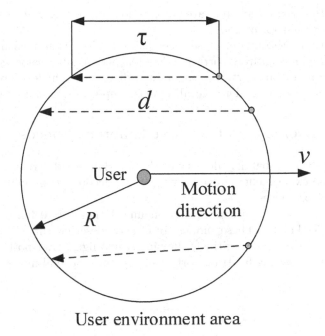

Fig. 2. User linear movement model

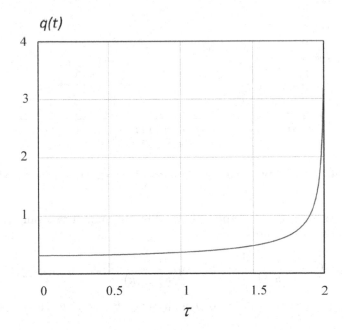

Fig. 3. The probability density of the object in the user's environment

(4) is satisfied. These parameters are the fractions of messages of each type and the methods of their formation.

Let us turn to the model of service delivery. Note that focusing only on straight traffic is not entirely correct: all users (pedestrians, passengers of various types of public transport, passengers and drivers of vehicles) have different speeds. Therefore, we consider several models of speed as a random variable.

4   User Movement Patterns at Different Speeds

In Fig. 4 shows the probability density of the speed of a pedestrian, obtained on the basis of the experiment – by analyzing traffic according to monitoring of its geographical coordinates.

The resulting histogram has three pronounced modes: 0; 0.4 m/s (1.4 km/h) and 1.4 m/s (5.0 km/h). These modes, obviously, describe three characteristic types of pedestrian traffic: waiting (allowing traffic light, transport, etc.), slow movement (while waiting for transport, walking step), normal movement (along the sidewalk).

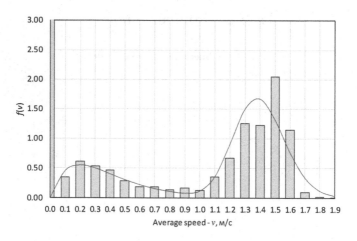

Fig. 4. Probability density of estimates of average pedestrian speed

The histogram in Fig. 4 is approximated by the sum of two gamma distributions and a delta function:

$$f(v) = \eta_1 \delta(0) + \eta_2 \frac{v^{k_1 - 1}}{\theta_1^{k_1} \Gamma(k)} e^{-\frac{v}{\theta_1}} + \eta_3 \frac{v^{k_2 - 1}}{\theta_2^{k_2} \Gamma(k)} e^{-\frac{v}{\theta_2}}, \quad \eta_1 + \eta_2 + \eta_3 = 1 \quad (5)$$

where η_1, η_2, η_3 are empirical coefficients; $k_1, k_2, \theta_1, \theta_2$ are distribution parameters.

In Fig. 5 shows an empirical histogram and the probability density of a vehicle's speed with difficulty (at rush hour). The histogram has several modes, the actual number of which is difficult to calculate. These modes are determined by the average speeds of traffic that are characteristic of the automobile flow in various states: free movement, movement when an obstacle is bypassed, an intersection travels when driving "in traffic" (acceleration, traffic and stopping in line to the intersection). There may be a different number of characteristic situations – at least in the experimental data, three modes can be distinguished.

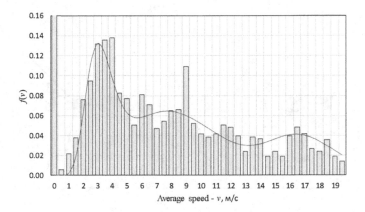

Fig. 5. Probability density of estimates of average vehicle speed in difficult traffic

According to the selected modes, we construct a probability density function. As in the previous case, we will consider the situations described above, which determine the different nature of the movement of random and independent events. Then the probability density function can be represented as a weighted sum of the probability densities of each of the considered types of motion. The probability density in this case is:

$$g(v) = \eta_1 \delta(0) + \eta_2 \frac{v^{k_1-1}}{\theta_1^{k_1} \Gamma(k)} e^{-\frac{v}{\theta_1}} + \eta_3 \frac{v^{k_2-1}}{\theta_2^{k_2} \Gamma(k)} e^{-\frac{v}{\theta_2}} + \eta_4 \frac{v^{k_3-1}}{\theta_3^{k_3} \Gamma(k)} e^{-\frac{v}{\theta_3}} \qquad (6a)$$

$$\eta_1 + \eta_2 + \eta_3 + \eta_4 = 1 \qquad (6b)$$

where $\eta_1, \eta_2, \eta_3, \eta_4$ are empirical coefficients; $k_1, k_2, k_3, \theta_1, \theta_2, \theta_3$ are distribution parameters.

Summarizing the two cases considered, we can assume that the probability density of the movement of a pedestrian, car or passenger of public transport is determined by the expression:

$$h(v) = \eta_0 \delta(0) + \sum_{i=1}^{N} \eta_i \frac{v^{k_i-1}}{\theta_i^{k_i} \Gamma(k)} e^{-\frac{v}{\theta_i}}, \sum_{i=0}^{N} \eta_i = 1 \qquad (7)$$

where η_i are empirical coefficients; k_i, θ_i – parameters distributions; N – number of mods.

In Fig. 6 shows the coordinate changes during the observation time. Each point corresponds to one sample, samples taken at intervals of 1 s. Neighboring samples are connected by lines. Figure 6b illustrates the main directions of motion that occurred during the observations. The data obtained are divided into three clusters (indicated by ovals in the figure), for each of which a vector is constructed, formed by averaging in direction and distance.

(a)   **(b)**

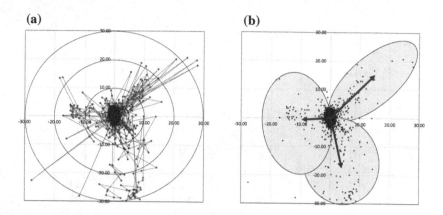

Fig. 6. Change of coordinates during observations: a - sequence of changes in coordinate, b - main directions of movement

The clusters obtained are characterized by the proximity of both the readings and the time for which they were obtained, i.e. Each vector can be associated with a continuous time interval during observations. From the analysis of Fig. 6 it follows that the most probable transitions occur in the direction of movement of the object.

5   Conclusion

The growing number and variety of augmented reality applications in recent years has attracted an increasing number of users of this technology. To date, a number of training programs have been developed in the field of education, the military industry and production. AR is actively used to create Smart Cities, in the field of tourism, city navigation, visualization of historical objects, in museums, theaters, etc. The possibilities of the augmented reality itself are expanding. Today it is not necessary to buy expensive specialized devices, just download the application on your smartphone. With an increase in the number of users, difficulties can arise with the timely delivery and display of augmented reality data to the user, which will have a significant impact on the quality of experience of the service as a whole.

When implementing and providing augmented reality services, it is necessary to take into account the main factors affecting the quality of its experience by the user. These factors are different for different services; they determine the main parameters of the interaction of client equipment with AR servers. Key features include user behavior.

The paper presents a generalized AR service model, a AR user model, and an analysis of the movement of AR users. The proposed model of user movement is based on experimental data and takes into account the peculiarities of the movement of a pedestrian and passenger in a urban environment. The model can be used both for modeling services (modeling the movement of users), and in the process of its implementation (in the formation of data request parameters).

Acknowledgment. The publication has been prepared with the support of the "RUDN University Program 5-100".

References

1. Al-Shuwaili, A., Simeone, O.: Energy-efficient resource allocation for mobile edge computing-based augmented reality applications. IEEE Wirel. Commun. Lett. **6**(3), 398–401 (2017). https://doi.org/10.1109/lwc.2017.2696539

2. Chatzopoulos, D., Bermejo, C., Huang, Z., Hui, P.: Mobile augmented reality survey: from where we are to where we go. IEEE Access **5**, 6917–6950 (2017). https://doi.org/10.1109/access.2017.2698164

3. Chen, H., Dai, Y., Meng, H., Chen, Y., Li, T.: Understanding the characteristics of mobile augmented reality applications. In: 2018 IEEE International Symposium on Performance Analysis of Systems and Software (ISPASS). IEEE, April 2018. https://doi.org/10.1109/ispass.2018.00026

4. Chen, H., Dai, Y., Xue, R., Zhong, K., Li, T.: Towards efficient microarchitecture design of simultaneous localization and mapping in augmented reality era. In: 2018 IEEE 36th International Conference on Computer Design (ICCD). IEEE, October 2018. https://doi.org/10.1109/iccd.2018.00066

5. Ellejmi, M., Bagassi, S., Persiani, A.: Evaluation of augmented reality tools for the provision of tower air traffic control using an ecological interface design. In: 2018 Modeling and Simulation Technologies Conference. American Institute of Aeronautics and Astronautics, June 2018. https://doi.org/10.2514/6.2018-2939

6. Ferrer, L., Garcia-Mancilla, J., Gonzalez, V.M., Bermudez, S., Bleier, P., Prieto, C.: Using augmented reality in urban context: georeferenced system for business localization using Google glass. In: 2015 IEEE First International Smart Cities Conference (ISC2). IEEE, October 2015. https://doi.org/10.1109/isc2.2015.7366157

7. Futahi, A., Paramonov, A., Koucheryavy, A.: Wireless sensor networks with temporary cluster head nodes. In: 2016 18th International Conference on Advanced Communication Technology (ICACT). IEEE, January 2016. https://doi.org/10.1109/icact.2016.7423362

8. Galinina, O., Tabassum, H., Mikhaylov, K., Andreev, S., Hossain, E., Koucheryavy, Y.: On feasibility of 5G-grade dedicated RF charging technology for wireless-powered wearables. IEEE Wirel. Commun. **23**(2), 28–37 (2016). https://doi.org/10.1109/mwc.2016.7462482

9. Kaklauskas, A., Krutinis, M., Petkov, P., Kovachev, L., Bartkiene, L.: Housing health and safety decision support system with augmented reality. InImpact: J. Innov. Impact **6**(1), 131 (2016)

10. Koucheryavy, A., Makolkina, M., Paramonov, A.: Applications of augmented reality traffic and quality requirements study and modeling. In: Vishnevskiy, V.M., Samouylov, K.E., Kozyrev, D.V. (eds.) DCCN 2016. CCIS, vol. 678, pp. 241–252. Springer, Cham (2016). https://doi.org/10.1007/978-3-319-51917-3_22
11. Li, W., Zhao, Y., Lu, S., Chen, D.: Mechanisms and challenges on mobility-augmented service provisioning for mobile cloud computing. IEEE Commun. Mag. 53(3), 89–97 (2015). https://doi.org/10.1109/mcom.2015.7060487
12. Makolkina, M., Koucheryavy, A., Paramonov, A.: The models of moving users and IoT devices density investigation for augmented reality applications. In: Galinina, O., Andreev, S., Balandin, S., Koucheryavy, Y. (eds.) NEW2AN/ruSMART/NsCC -2017. LNCS, vol. 10531, pp. 671–682. Springer, Cham (2017). https://doi.org/10. 1007/978-3-319-67380-6_64
13. Makolkina, M., Vikulov, A., Paramonov, A.: The augmented reality service provision in D2D network. In: Vishnevskiy, V.M., Samouylov, K.E., Kozyrev, D.V. (eds.) DCCN 2017. CCIS, vol. 700, pp. 281–290. Springer, Cham (2017). https:// doi.org/10.1007/978-3-319-66836-9_24
14. Makolkina, M., Koucheryavy, A., Paramonov, A.: Investigation of traffic pattern for the augmented reality applications. In: Koucheryavy, Y., Mamatas, L., Matta, I., Ometov, A., Papadimitriou, P. (eds.) WWIC 2017. LNCS, vol. 10372, pp. 233–246. Springer, Cham (2017). https://doi.org/10.1007/978-3-319-61382-6_19
15. de Oliveira, L.C., Andrade, A.O., de Oliveira, E.C., Soares, A., Cardoso, A., Lamounier, E.: Indoor navigation with mobile augmented reality and beacon technology for wheelchair users. In: 2017 IEEE EMBS International Conference on Biomedical & Health Informatics (BHI). IEEE (2017). https://doi.org/10.1109/bhi.2017.7897199
16. Ometov, A., et al.: Toward trusted, social-aware D2D connectivity: bridging across the technology and sociality realms. IEEE Wirel. Commun. 23(4), 103–111 (2016). https://doi.org/10.1109/mwc.2016.7553033
17. Petrov, V., et al.: Vehicle-based relay assistance for opportunistic crowdsensing over narrowband IoT (NB-IoT). IEEE Internet Things J. 5(5), 3710–3723 (2018). https://doi.org/10.1109/jiot.2017.2670363
18. Qiu, H., Ahmad, F., Govindan, R., Gruteser, M., Bai, F., Kar, G.: Augmented vehicular reality. In: Proceedings of the 18th International Workshop on Mobile Computing Systems and Applications. ACM, February 2017. https://doi.org/10. 1145/3032970.3032976
19. Quandt, M., Knoke, B., Gorldt, C., Freitag, M., Thoben, K.D.: General requirements for industrial augmented reality applications. Procedia CIRP 72, 1130–1135 (2018). https://doi.org/10.1016/j.procir.2018.03.061
20. Rashid, Z., Melià-Seguí, J., Pous, R., Peig, E.: Using augmented reality and internet of things to improve accessibility of people with motor disabilities in the context of smart cities. Future Gener. Comput. Syst. 76, 248–261 (2017). https://doi.org/ 10.1016/j.future.2016.11.030
21. Tran, T.X., Hajisami, A., Pandey, P., Pompili, D.: Collaborative mobile edge computing in 5G networks: new paradigms, scenarios, and challenges. IEEE Commun. Mag. 55(4), 54–61 (2017). https://doi.org/10.1109/mcom.2017.1600863
22. Chen, X., Liu, X., Xu, P.: IOT-based air pollution monitoring and forecasting system. In: 2015 International Conference on Computer and Computational Sciences (ICCCS). IEEE, January 2015. https://doi.org/10.1109/iccacs.2015.7361361
23. Younes, G., et al.: Virtual and augmented reality for rich interaction with cultural heritage sites: a case study from the Roman Theater at byblos. Digit. Appl. Archaeol. Cult. Herit. 5, 1–9 (2017). https://doi.org/10.1016/j.daach.2017.03.002

Audio Interval Retrieval Using Convolutional Neural Networks

Ievgeniia Kuzminykh[1,5](✉) ⓘ, Dan Shevchuk[2], Stavros Shiaeles[3] ⓘ,
and Bogdan Ghita[4] ⓘ

[1] King's College London, Strand, London WC2R 2LS, UK
ievgeniia.kuzminykh@kcl.ac.uk
[2] Blekinge Institute of Technology, Campus Grasvik, 371 41 Karlskrona, Sweden
[3] University of Portsmouth, Portsmouth PO1 3RR, UK
stavros.shiaeles@port.ac.uk
[4] University of Plymouth, Drake Circus, Plymouth PL4 8AA, UK
bogdan.ghita@plymouth.ac.uk
[5] Kharkiv National University of Radio Electronics, Nauky av. 14, Kharkiv 61166, Ukraine

Abstract. Modern streaming services are increasingly labeling videos based on their visual or audio content. This typically augments the use of technologies such as AI and ML by allowing to use natural speech for searching by keywords and video descriptions. Prior research has successfully provided a number of solutions for speech to text, in the case of a human speech, but this article aims to investigate possible solutions to retrieve sound events based on a natural language query, and estimate how effective and accurate they are. In this study, we specifically focus on the YamNet, AlexNet, and ResNet-50 pre-trained models to automatically classify audio samples using their respective melspectrograms into a number of predefined classes. The predefined classes can represent sounds associated with actions within a video fragment. Two tests are conducted to evaluate the performance of the models on two separate problems: audio classification and intervals retrieval based on a natural language query. Results show that the benchmarked models are comparable in terms of performance, with YamNet slightly outperforming the other two models. YamNet was able to classify single fixed-size audio samples with 92.7% accuracy and 68.75% precision while its average accuracy on intervals retrieval was 71.62% and precision was 41.95%. The investigated method may be embedded into an automated event marking architecture for streaming services.

Keywords: Deep learning · Intervals retrieval · Natural language query · Audio classification · Convolutional neural network

1 Introduction

Natural language search is becoming more and more popular among users, with an increasing number of mobile and embedded devices providing the feature either included in the operating system or as part of a streaming services. This is evidenced by the sale of devices that support this feature. Due to this increased market interest, recent years

© Springer Nature Switzerland AG 2020
O. Galinina et al. (Eds.): NEW2AN 2020/ruSMART 2020, LNCS 12525, pp. 229–240, 2020.
https://doi.org/10.1007/978-3-030-65726-0_21

have witnessed a significant amount of research on factors influencing engine rankings during voice search [1]. In early 2019, Amazon released device sales data for which it sold over 100 million devices that support the voice assistant applications [2]. Demand for these devices exceeded supply by several times, therefore, some models are currently impossible to purchase. Other studies from WARC, Dynata and PwC also confirms the popularity of voice searches [3, 4]. According to their research, 60% of the mobile device users actively use voice search, and mobile advertising reached 62.4% of the user population. More than half of users (53%) who make a request from a smartphone are looking for information about a product, 50% find answers to questions of interest, 42% use navigation and 41% look for information about brands.

The usability and convenience of voice search subsequently led to an expansion of the scope of this function, with searching for a video fragment by description being a very popular choice. Most of the time people can describe verbally what they are looking for but, given the lack of metadata associated with the timeline and content of the video, this option is currently mostly unavailable. however, currently there is no publicly available efficient way of searching through multimedia content to identify and label an audio event or sound.

Numerous studies have been conducted in the area of audio recognition over the past few decades [5–9]. Most of the traditional approaches require handcrafted features to provide metadata. This situation improved significantly with the use of modern deep neural network architectures that rely on convolutional layers [10]. While up until recently it was possible to achieve a reasonable level of feature extraction from images, now it is also possible to effectively recognise patterns in videos using deep neural networks. The most recent research [6] achieves a very reliable result. However, it aggregates features from 3 sources: individual frames, an array of frames at once (continuous snippets) and subtitles. Its success can further be improved by extracting the features from the soundtrack, which the paper does not do. To exemplify one should consider a scene where the actor stays silent and only the sound of an airplane can be heard in the background, but the aircraft is not visible in the scene. Querying video or subtitles for "sound of a flying airplane while the actor is standing still" cannot yield any helpful result because the required input is not present either in the video or in the subtitles. Another example is a generic nature scene with an arbitrary song in the background. The user can remember the song but we would need to also search through the soundtrack to use it for query. Such examples demonstrate that this result can be improved by also including the soundtrack as one of the input parameters. In this context, the biggest challenge is the lack of technology to allow interval retrieval from sound data based on semantic input, in order to replicate and support the existing technology for video interval retrieval.

The aim of this study is to identify and investigate models capable of retrieving intervals from an audio sample based on a natural language query. To benchmark their efficiency, the models will be trained on the AudioSet [11] database that consists of an expanding ontology of 632 audio event classes and a collection of 2,084,320 human-labeled 10-s sound clips drawn from YouTube videos. The ontology is specified as a hierarchical graph of event categories, covering a wide range of human and animal sounds, musical instruments and genres, and common environmental sounds.

2 Related Works

There have been a few studies conducted in different areas that relate to the challenges of audio information retrieval based on semantic input. A significant subset of this body of research proposed a number of methods for querying an audio file by the semantic description of its class [12–16]. These can be considered partial solutions when compared to the aim of this study, which is not only to identify the class of the given audio but also to convert its semantic description into an abstraction that can be matched to the extracted features of the given audio file of an arbitrary length.

Aside from actual querying, research also aimed to provide a better, more distinctive input through data pre-processing, analyse the features of the audio data to be fed into the models, and identify the best approaches for one of the intermediate data segmentation and classification steps. From this line of research, the approach from Qazi et al. involved segregating the audio intervals of interest (such as music and speech) from noisy data [17]. This may provide a useful and necessary pre-processing step to clear up the audio input before starting to extract features that can be matched to the semantic description, thus improving the accuracy of the resulting model. Along the same direction, a number of studies [18–21] sought to investigate the most useful features of the audio data, which would subsequently allow them to analyse and retrieve information from it more accurately. Others research [22–25] redesigned the audio data classification process to allow searching for an audio file or to automatically label existing audio clips.

On the wider societal context, Pfeiffer et al. sought to automate the process of audio data analysis with different applications such as music indexing and retrieval as well as violence detection in the sound track of videos [26]. Foote J. has studied the process of audio information retrieval in general to give insights into the process that can be valuable for any kind of further research in this area [27].

In terms of the core method used, Shawn Hershey et al. have compared the VGG, AlexNet, ResNet-50, Inception V3, and Fully-Connected architectures on their performance on audio data. Based on a 17 million samples dataset, the study identified ResNet-50 as the best performing model [10]. However, the analysis focused exclusively on the performance of the models on sound classification. The evaluation can be extended by using the models for audio interval retrieval based on the natural language query and comparing the models' performance in terms of accuracy, precision etc.

All of the studies that are mentioned above provide either a partial solution to the problem of audio-interval retrieval based on a semantic description, which we are seeking to solve with this study, or provide a useful information that will help address this thesis' aim faster and more accurately.

Though there are reliable methods of event retrieval based on semantic input, they are all based solely on the visual data, like individual frames or motion features. To the best of our knowledge, none of the related work papers we surveyed employ the soundtrack for increasing the accuracy of the interval retrieval. Therefore, studying the best performing methods for audio-based interval retrieval would improve the existing technology of content-based video and audio classification and searching in a unified approach and would enable further analysis of audio data.

3   Method

This study investigates the effectiveness of deep learning models within the convolutional neural networks of sound classification. To benchmark the performance of such algorithms, the experiment involved three models: AlexNet, ResNet-50 and YamNet. Both AlexNet and ResNet-50 are known to be well-suited for image classification, as highlighted in the previous section. In order to exploit their ability to discriminate visual input, the input audio data used for training and testing the models was converted into melspectrograms, providing them with the necessary input [10, 18]. YamNet model is an already pretrained model provided by TensorFlow team. YamNet takes in a waveform of the given sound data sample and predicts the probability of each of its 521 classes; it was chosen for the study due to the fact that it is pretrained on the same dataset used for this study.

3.1   Performance Metrics

In order to evaluate the performance of the models and comparatively benchmark them, we followed the procedure outlined in previous studies [28, 29] and calculated Accuracy, Precision, F-1 score, MCC, and ROC AUC.

The metrics operate with true and false positives and negatives measurements to be calculated. The nature of true and false positives and negatives is explained in Table 1.

Table 1. True and false negatives and positives.

	NO (prediction)	YES (prediction)
NO (actual)	True Negative (TN)	False Positive (FP)
YES (actual)	False Negative (FN)	True Positive (TP)

The first metric used to compare the models is the receiver operating characteristic area under curve (ROC AUC). The ROC curves are constructed by plotting the false positive rate (FPR) on the x-axis against the true positive rate (TPR) on the y-axis at various threshold settings. After calculating the ROC curves, the area under the curve (AUC), is computed for each ROC curve. The area under the curve is equal to the probability that a classifier will rank a randomly chosen positive instance higher than a randomly chosen negative one (assuming 'positive' ranks higher than 'negative') [29].

The Matthews correlation coefficient (MCC) is used in machine learning as a measure of the quality of binary (two-class) classifications. The metric is generally regarded as a balanced measure that can be used even if the classes are of different sizes [29].

$$\mathrm{MCC} = \frac{\mathrm{TP} \cdot \mathrm{TN} - \mathrm{FP} \cdot \mathrm{FN}}{\sqrt{(\mathrm{TP} + \mathrm{FP}) \cdot (\mathrm{TP} + \mathrm{FN}) \cdot (\mathrm{TN} + \mathrm{FP}) \cdot (\mathrm{TN} + \mathrm{FN})}} \tag{1}$$

Accuracy is closeness of the measurements to a specific reference value.

$$Accuracy = \frac{TP + TN}{TN + FP + TP + FN}. \tag{2}$$

The precision of a model is defined as the number of True Positives divided by the sum of all positive predictions.

$$Precision = \frac{TP}{TP + FP}. \tag{3}$$

A F measure (or sometimes F1 score) is a statistic that tries to combine the concerns of precision and recall in the same metric. F measure is calculated using the following Equation:

$$F1 = \frac{2 \cdot (recall \cdot precision)}{recall + precision}. \tag{4}$$

The above parameters provide a full statistical overview of the accuracy of the method, beyond its ability to discriminate individual events.

3.2 Data

The dataset used for evaluation is based on the AudioSet [11] database that consists of an expanding ontology of 527 audio event classes and a collection of 2,084,320 human-labelled 10-s sound clips drawn from YouTube videos. The ontology is specified as a hierarchical graph of event categories, covering a wide range of human and animal sounds, musical instruments and genres, and common everyday environmental sounds. Every video has on average 5 event labels. A combination of metadata (title, description, comments, etc.), context, and image content for each video were used to generate the labels automatically. It is worth noting that, in the dataset, the labels apply to the entire video and the labels are generated automatically, hence they are not 100% accurate [10].

The AudioSet database contains links to Youtube videos, labels and time frames for the correct segments from distinct videos. But not all links are available in the moment, therefore, a subset of 16902 samples was used for evaluation. The resulting number of items from the training dataset was 19614 items. We have decided to use only 6 out of 527 audio classes due to simplification of the experiment, and due to time and computational constraints. The selected classes are: "Rapping", "Cheering", "Gunshot, gunfire", "Radio", "Cat" and "Helicopter".

The reduced dataset is balanced. The downloaded evaluation and training datasets were merged and only audio samples that have one of the selected classes as labels were picked for the experiment as the final training and evaluation dataset. For the purpose of obtaining a higher degree of accuracy, all the entries from both training and evaluation dataset were merged and then randomly split 80/20 for as the training and testing subsets.

Each of 6 classes has approximately 120 audio samples linked to them in the training data had been picked and then another 11266 augmentations had been generated so that each class is represented by approximately 2000 samples in the training dataset. Totally, 12000 were used for training, of which 734 are 10 s raw samples in wave format.

After the last layers of AlexNet and ResNet-50 models were fitted, an additional classifier, Random Forest, was trained for each model, including YamNet.

3.3 Interval Retrieval

To understand the performance of the models on a fixed-size length audio samples, 184 audio samples out of 16902 from the evaluation dataset of AudioSet [11] were used. The selection criteria for this data was that an audio sample contains keyword(s) belonging to one or more tested classes. Each sample gets split into fixed-size non-overlapping patches and fed into the classifiers. The evaluation dataset does not contain any augmentations, only raw original data. For each model, the output was fed into the instance of the Random Forest classifier trained for that specific model and the final output was evaluated against the target. The type of classification in this experiment is also binary multilabel classification.

In order to evaluate the performance of the models, a new audio file was created. The file is 41 s long and it contains samples from 3 audios, each of which is present in the evaluation dataset for the classification problem. The audio file is constructed in a way presented on Fig. 1 that has distinct intervals of sounds that are easily recognizable by a human listener and has intervals without any sound as well. This melspectrogram is fed into all the models that have been already trained with the data. Since the evaluation audio file was handcrafted, it is labeled with a high degree of accuracy. The predicted intervals were compared against the handmade labels.

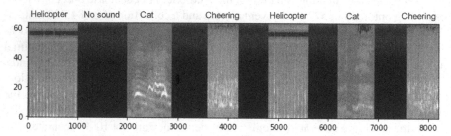

Fig. 1. A melspectrogram obtained by transforming the handcrafted evaluation audio file.

Comparing the predicted intervals with the handmade labels involves creating binary arrays for both predicted intervals and for hand-made ones. The binary array is an output in the binary multilabel classification, whereby the interval is retrieved using the user-provided keyword that should match one of the classes in the fixed term (in this case a fixed size of 0.01 s). Each patch is an array of length 6 but in the case of our audio file from Fig. 1 three out of six elements in the array will be 0. Each element of the output arrays is a float number in range [0, 1] and represents the probability of each of the predicted classes.

3.4 Models

YamNet. It is a deep neural network that, following training predicts 521 audio event classes based on the AudioSet-YouTube corpus, and employing the Mobilenet_v1 depthwise-separable convolution architecture [30]. Six classes out of 527 were omitted based on the recommendations from reviewers [10].

The MobileNet structure is built on depthwise separable convolutions except for the first layer which is a full convolution. All layers are followed by a batchnorm and ReLU nonlinearity with the exception of the final fully connected layer, which has no nonlinearity and feeds into a softmax layer for classification. Down sampling is handled with strided convolution in the depthwise convolutions as well as in the first layer. A final average pooling reduces the spatial resolution to 1 before the fully connected layer. Counting depthwise and pointwise convolutions as separate layers, MobileNet has 28 layers.

As mentioned above, the model normally outputs 521 classes. However, for the purposes of the experiment, the output has been filtered and the array of 521 elements was replaced with a 6-element array, each of which represents the probability of each of the 6 classes picked for the study.

The output is then fed into another classifier - Random Forest. The final output is the one used for intervals retrieval since the model performs better together with the classifier than on its own.

AlexNet. It contains eight layers - five convolutional and three fully-connected [31]. The original model was modified for this task, with the last layer changed to output an array of 6 classes instead of the default 1000. We used the pretrained version of the model, which was trained to classify natural images. We decided to use the deep features of the model as well retrain it so that the model fits the problem better. The Random Forest classifier was also used on top of the output of AlexNet.

ResNet-50. The original ResNet-50 is a residual neural network which consists of 50 layers, most of which are convolutional [32]. The model was altered similarly to AlexNet, with the last layer set to output an array of 6 classes instead of the default 1000. The pretrained version of the model was used, which is pretrained to classify natural images. We decided to use deep features of the model as well retrain nine last layers. We also used a Random Forest classifier on top of the ResNet-50's output.

4   Results and Analysis

To understand the performance of the models on fixed-size audio samples, they were applied on the evaluation dataset. Table 2 shows the result value of the measured metrics in percentage for all three models. For comparison purposes, the YamNet model was implemented without the additional Random Forest classification in the experiment.

The best performing model overall is a combination of YamNet and Random Forest. However, comparing to the pure YamNet model, without Random Forest, the other models with additional classifier in form of Random Forest showed better results. To be more specific, the reason for the difference in performance lies in the fact that YamNet was trained on 2084320 human-labeled 10-s sound clips drawn from YouTube videos, while AlexNet and ResNet-50 were trained on 12000 samples, 11266 of which were automatically generated from the original 734.

The next experiment was conducted in order to see the performance of the model on the classification of a single sample correlated with the performance on retrieving the

Table 2. Models' performance on classifying audio samples.

	YamNet without RF	YamNet	AlexNet	ResNet-50
ROC AUC	62.5	92.5	87	88
MCC	24.9	81.53	65.8	67.6
Accuracy	79.16	92.7	88.7	88.85
Precision	37.5	68.75	61.74	63.11
F1 score	42.85	75.25	71.4	72.63

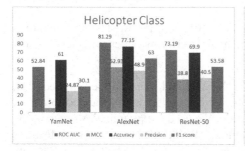
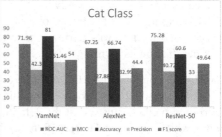
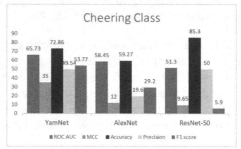

Fig. 2. Comparison of the metrics on the intervals retrieval by keywords.

intervals by querying the specific classes. As input the hand-crafted file was used. The performance of the models for three classes is presented on the Fig. 2.

The best performing model for class "Helicopter" was AlexNet which outperforms the other models on every single metric. The performance of AlexNet in this case is far from perfect, with an accuracy of 77.15% and a precision of 48.9%. In addition, the values of the other metrics suggest that it could be possible to achieve a reliable result with more training data. YamNet yielded a very low value for MCC even though the model had been trained on more examples than the others. This is possibly due to the fact that YamNet was trained to recognize 521 classes and its output was just filtered and the 6 classes were used to construct the final output while the other two models were fitted for these specific 6 classes.

The best performing model for class "Cat" was YamNet with accuracy of 81% and precision of 51.46%. AlexNet and ResNet-50 yielded a similar result, but ResNet-50 still performed better, yielding higher values for both ROC AUC (75.28%) and F1 score (49.64%).

The best performing model for class "Cheering" was YamNet, with accuracy of 72.86% and precision of 49.54%. ResNet-50 yields an even higher accuracy and precision, however, a low value of F1-score suggests that the high values of some of the other metrics are a result of the model not activating the queried class on a disproportionately large part of the audio sample rather than a result of good performance.

As we can see from Table 3, the aggregated values of the models' performance metrics are comparable. However, we know from examining the classes one by one that some of the values are too high on some classes and too low on the others just like in case of ResNet-50. Having examined the performance of the models on a single class case by case we can say that the best performing model overall is YamNet, yielding a mean accuracy of 71.62% and a mean precision of 41.95%. The model also yields stable values for most of the other metrics.

Table 3. Mean performance on three queried keywords.

	YamNet	AlexNet	ResNet-50
ROC AUC	67	69	66.59
MCC	27.4	30	29.72
Accuracy	71.62	67.72	71.93
Precision	41.95	33.83	41.16
F1 score	45.95	45.53	36.37

5 Discussion

In order to find the most suitable matching method to retrieve an audio of an arbitrary length via a natural language query input, two experiments have been conducted. Since the data that needs to be classified is audio and the features that were extracted from the data are melspectrograms, we have picked the models that perform well on image classification [10, 30]. The selected models are AlexNet and ResNet-50. All models have been pretrained to classify audio samples.

Two sets of tests were conducted to find the best performing model. The first test evaluated the performance of the models on the fixed-size audio samples classification problem. The best performing model turned out to be YamNet with accuracy of 92.7% and precision of 68.75%.

The purpose of the second test was to evaluate the performance on the intervals retrieval problem. The best performing model is still YamNet, but it is worth noting that the aggregated value of the metrics is similar for all the models. Evaluation of the models' performance on a single class at a time gave us a more clear picture of how the models actually perform. Both YamNet and AlexNet had a relatively stable performance, while ResNet-50 showed evidence of being biased towards certain classes.

None of the models was able to match the natural language query to the corresponding interval with a reliable degree of accuracy and precision. However, there are a few factors that might have affected the experiment negatively. Firstly, YamNet, the best performing model, could have performed better on the classes that had more examples in the original training dataset because had been trained originally with more samples. Secondly, the models might have misclassified the audio samples and it is possible that retrieving the intervals for related classes as well and aggregating that into a single array of intervals would have yielded a more reliable result. However, picking the relevant classes for the audio samples is beyond the scope of the study and could be the baseline for future research.

6 Conclusions

The experimental study has compared the performance of three models Yam-Net, AlexNet and ResNet-50 on two different but related problems: a classification problem and interval retrieval based on natural language query. The result was evaluated using the following metrics: ROC AUC, MCC, accuracy, precision and F-1 score. The motivation behind this study was to discover which classifiers are able to solve this problem and to what degree (performance-wise) the classifiers are able to retrieve intervals based on a natural language query.

We used transfer learning for all the three models evaluated by training instances of Random Forest, each of which used the pretrained high level features of the models. The original dataset contains samples that are labelled with 527 classes, however, we used only 6 classes during the experiment to compensate for the lack of the computational capacity and to be able to analyse the result more clearly.

The study established that the tested models were not capable of retrieving intervals from an audio of an arbitrary length based on a natural language query; however, the degree to which the models are able to retrieve the intervals varies depending on the queried keyword and other underlying learning parameters, such as the value of the threshold that is used to filter the audio patches that yield too low probability of the queried class.

The results showed that YamNet was able to classify single fixed-size audio samples with 92.7% accuracy and 68.75% precision, while its average accuracy on intervals retrieval was 71.62% and precision was 41.95%. AlexNet classified the single fixed-size audio samples with 88.7% accuracy and 61.74% precision, while its average accuracy on intervals retrieval was 67.72% and precision was 33.83%. ResNet-50 classified the single fixed-size audio samples with 88.85% accuracy and 63.11% precision. Its average accuracy on intervals retrieval was 71.93% and precision was 41.16%. ResNet-50 yielded an unreliable result on two of the tested classes and displayed a significant difference in the average activation strength of different classes.

Acknowledgement This project has received funding from the European Union Horizon 2020 research and innovation programme under grant agreement no. 833673 and no. 786698. This work reflects authors view and Agency is not responsible for any use that may be made of the information it contains.

References

1. Market Research Report: Fortune Business Insights (2018). https://www.fortunebusiness insights.com/industry-reports/natural-language-processing-nlp-market-101933. Accessed 26 June 2020
2. Exclusive: Amazon says 100 million Alexa devices have been sold—what's next? The verge interview. https://www.theverge.com/2019/1/4/18168565/amazon-alexa-devices-how-many-sold-number-100-million-dave-limp. Accessed 26 June 2020
3. The Dynata global trends report. Dynata (2019)
4. Consumer Intelligence Series: Prepare for the voice revolution. PwC report (2019)
5. Kim, K., Heo, M., Choi, S., Zhang, B.: DeepStory: video story QA by deep embedded memory networks. In: Proceedings of the 26th International Joint Conference on Artificial Intelligence (IJCAI), Melbourne, Australia, pp. 2016–2022 (2017)
6. Lei, J., Yu, L., Berg, T.L., Bansal, M.: TVR: a large-scale dataset for video-subtitle moment retrieval. arXiv:2001.09099 (2020)
7. Brindha, N., Visalakshi, P.: Bridging semantic gap between high-level and low-level features in content-based video retrieval using multi-stage ESN–SVM classifier. Sādhanā 42(1), 1–10 (2016). https://doi.org/10.1007/s12046-016-0574-8
8. Smeaton, A.F., Wilkins, P., et al.: Content-based video retrieval: three example systems from TRECVid. Int. J. Imaging Syst. Technol. 18(2–3), 195–201 (2008)
9. Araujo, A., Girod, B.: Large-scale video retrieval using image queries. IEEE Trans. Circ. Syst. Video Technol. 28(6), 1406–1420 (2018)
10. Hershey, S., et al.: CNN architectures for large-scale audio classification. In: IEEE International Conference on Acoustics, Speech and Signal Processing (ICASSP), New Orleans, LA, pp. 131–135 (2017)
11. Gemmeke, J.F., et al.: Audio set: an ontology and human-labeled dataset for audio events. In: IEEE International Conference on Acoustics, Speech and Signal Processing (ICASSP), New Orleans, LA, pp. 776–780 (2017)
12. Dogan, E., Sert, M., Yazici, A.: A flexible and scalable audio information retrieval system for mixed-type audio signals. Int. J. Intell. Syst. 26(10), 952–970 (2011)
13. Guggenberger, M.: Aurio: audio processing, analysis and retrieval. In: Proceedings of the 23rd ACM International Conference on Multimedia (MM 2015), pp. 705–708 (2015)
14. Sundaram, S., Narayanan, S.: Audio retrieval by latent perceptual indexing. In: IEEE International Conference on Acoustics, Speech and Signal Processing, Las Vegas, NV, pp. 49–52 (2008)
15. Wan, C., Liu, M.: Content-based audio retrieval with relevance feedback. Pattern Recogn. Lett. 27(2), 85–92 (2006)
16. Kim, K., Kim, S., Jeon, J., Park, K.: Quick audio retrieval using multiple feature vectors. IEEE Trans. Consum. Electron. 52(1), 200–205 (2006)
17. Qazi, K.A., Nawaz, T., Mehmood, Z., Rashid, M., Habib, H.A.: A hybrid technique for speech segregation and classification using a sophisticated deep neural network. PLoS ONE 13(3), e0194151 (2018)
18. Mäkinen, T., Kiranyaz, S., Raitoharju, J., Gabbouj, M.: An evolutionary feature synthesis approach for content-based audio retrieval. EURASIP J. Audio Speech Music Process. 2012(1), 1–23 (2012). https://doi.org/10.1186/1687-4722-2012-23
19. Patel, N.P., Patwardhan, M.S.: Identification of most contributing features for audio classification. In: International Conference on Cloud & Ubiquitous Computing & Emerging Technologies, Pune, pp. 219–223 (2013)
20. Lostanlen, V., Lafay, G., Andén, J., Lagrange, M.: Relevance-based quantization of scattering features for unsupervised mining of environmental audio. EURASIP J. Audio Speech Music Process. 2018(1), 1–10 (2018). https://doi.org/10.1186/s13636-018-0138-4

21. Lu, G.: Indexing and retrieval of audio: a survey. Multimed. Tools Appl. **15**(3), 269–290 (2001). https://doi.org/10.1023/A:1012491016871
22. Richard, G., Sundaram, S., Narayanan, S.: An overview on perceptually motivated audio indexing and classification. Proc. IEEE **101**(9), 1939–1954 (2013)
23. Pinquier, J., André-Obrecht, R.: Audio indexing: primary components retrieval: robust classification in audio documents. Multimed. Tools Appl. **30**(3), 313–330 (2006). https://doi.org/10.1007/s11042-006-0027-1
24. McLoughlin, I., Zhang, H., Xie, Z., Song, Y., Xiao, W.: Robust sound event classification using deep neural networks. IEEE/ACM Trans. Audio Speech Lang. Process. **23**(3), 540–552 (2015)
25. Xie, L., et al.: Pitch-density-based features and an SVM binary tree approach for multi-class audio classification in broadcast news. Multimed. Syst. **17**(2), 101–112 (2011). https://doi.org/10.1007/s00530-010-0205-x
26. Pfeiffer, S., Fischer, S., Effelsberg, W.: Automatic audio content analysis. In: Proceedings of the Fourth ACM International Conference on Multimedia (MULTIMEDIA 1996), pp. 21–30 (1997)
27. Foote, J.: An overview of audio information retrieval. Multimed. Syst. **7**(1), 2–10 (1999). https://doi.org/10.1007/s005300050106
28. Catal, C.: Performance evaluation metrics for software fault prediction studies. Acta Polytech. Hung. **9**(4), 193–206 (2012)
29. Boughorbel, S., Jarray, F., El-Anbari, M.: Optimal classifier for imbalanced data using Matthews Correlation Coefficient metric. PLoS ONE **12**(6), e0177678 (2017)
30. Andrew, G., et al.: MobileNets: efficient convolutional neural networks for mobile vision applications. Computer Vision and Pattern Recognition arXiv:1704.04861 (2017)
31. Krizhevsky, A., Sutskever, I., Hinton, G.E.: ImageNet classification with deep convolutional neural networks. Commun. ACM **60**(6), 1097–1105 (2017)
32. He, K., Zhang, X., Ren, S., Sun, J.: Deep residual learning for image recognition. Computer Vision and Pattern Recognition arXiv:1512.03385 (2015)

Modeling the NB-IoT Transmission Process with Intermittent Network Availability

Nikita Stepanov[1]($\boxtimes$) (iD), Dmitri Moltchanov[2]($\boxtimes$) (iD), and Andrey Turlikov[1]($\boxtimes$) (iD)

[1] State University of Aerospace Instrumentation, Saint-Petersburg, Russia
{nstepanov,turlikov}@k36.org
[2] Unit of Electrical Engineering, Tampere University, Tampere, Finland
dmitri.moltchanov@tuni.fi

Abstract. Standardized by 3GPP, Narrowband Internet-of-Thing (NB-IoT) technology operating in licensed bands is nowadays widely deployed and utilized for static deployments of IoT communications services. The recent trend to equip large complex inherently nomadic systems such as trains and ships with advanced sensory capabilities call for mobility support in NB-IoT technology. Such systems entering and leaving the NB-IoT coverage periodically could lead to synchronized behavior of sensor nodes resulting in occasional spikes in the number of sensors simultaneously accessing the NB-IoT random access channel. In this study, we develop a model capturing behavior of nomadic systems roaming between coverage of NB-IoT technology. The metrics of interest are mean message transmission delay as well as the message loss probability. Our numerical results illustrate that these metrics are mainly affected by the duration of the outage interval and fraction of time systems spends in outage conditions. At the same time, the loss and delay performance only insignificantly affected by the number of sensors implying that NB-IoT random access procedure may efficiently handle sporadic loads.

Keywords: NB-IoT · Massive MTC · Random access · Mobile sensors

1 Introduction

Standardized as a part of 3GPP Release 13 Narrowband Internet-of-Things (NB-IoT) technology quickly became the de-facto standard for commercial IoT systems [14]. The NB-IoT technology utilizes much narrower channels of only 200 KHz by enabling the devices having about 10% complexity of that for LTE Cat-1. As a result, it offers unprecedented coverage of up to 30 km with over 50 thousand of networked devices per cell and much longer battery lifetimes [4, 10]. Similarly to its predecessor, LTE-M, NB-IoT is deployed over the LTE infrastructure, which makes it possible to provide enhanced security features as well as deployment options via software updates [6, 13].

NB-IoT technology is designed to mainly target those applications generating data periodically over constant or random time intervals, e.g., environment and medium monitoring services. However, dealing with event driven applications, especially, those that might be triggered by events affecting large territories, e.g., disaster use-cases,

© Springer Nature Switzerland AG 2020
O. Galinina et al. (Eds.): NEW2AN 2020/ruSMART 2020, LNCS 12525, pp. 241–254, 2020.
https://doi.org/10.1007/978-3-030-65726-0_22

public protection and disaster relief (PPDR) applications, may lead to sub-optimal performance of NB-IoT technology as a result of congestion events at the random access stage [17,18].

Recently, the scope of NB-IoT technology is enhanced to target vehicle mounted sensors [3,15]. The new use-cases include container tracking systems mounted at large moving systems such as trains or vessels sailing near-the-shore [9]. Featuring thousands of sensors these systems move between the areas with NB-IoT coverage naturally causing random access "storms" just after entering coverage areas of NB-IoT base stations (BS). To develop efficient access barring schemes accurate models characterizing on-off service process of sensors in such systems are needed.

In this paper, we formulate an accurate model of the service process of sensors deployed at the large object (e.g., train or vessel) moving across the area with intermittent NB-IoT connectivity. Explicitly accounting for both random access and data transmission phases by capturing the essentials of NB-IoT technology we represent the transmission process of data messages from a large number of sensors as a multidimensional Markov chain. The key performance indicators include the mean message transmission delay and message loss probability. The latter include losses as a result random access and data transmission. The developed model can be utilized for developing access barring schemes for novel applications of NB-IoT technology for large nomadic systems.

The paper is organized as follows. The system model is formulated in Sect. 2. The model of the service process is introduced in Sect. 3. Numerical results are provided in Sect. 4. The conclusions are drawn in the last section.

2 System Model

In this section we introduce our system model by specifying its parts. We successively characterize deployment and connectivity, sensor behavior and traffic, NB-IoT random access and data transmission models. Finally, we introduce the considered metrics of interest.

2.1 Deployment and Connectivity

We consider a large complex object such as vessel or train with N NB-IoT sensors deployed on-board moving across a certain area, see Fig. 1. A part of the area is covered with NB-IoT technology. We assume that the coverage and outage duration are geometrically distributed with parameters λ_{ON} and λ_{OFF}. These parameters can be found analyzing a special use-case of interest, see, e.g., [9] for container vessel example.

2.2 Sensor Behavior and Traffic

We assume that all the sensors operate independently of each other, i.e., their transmissions are not globally synchronized or, alternatively, intentionally de-synchronized. The inter-message generation time is assumed to be geometrically distributed with the

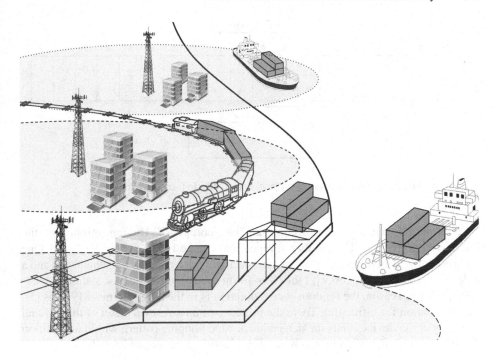

Fig. 1. Potential scenario with intermittent NB-IoT connectivity.

parameter λ. Once message is generated, the sensor is assumed to test network availability. If there is NB-IoT coverage the message is scheduled for transmission by initiating the NB-IoT random access procedure. If the network is unavailable, sensor enters the waiting phase. During this phase, the network availability is tested or regular time intervals. Once the network becomes available the random access procedure is immediately initiated. The message lifetime is assumed to be limited and geometrically distributed with the parameter T_l.

2.3   The Captured NB-IoT Mechanisms

NB-IoT Random Access Phase.   Following NB-IoT specification [1] user equipment (UE) is assumed to determine NB-IoT carrier by measuring the power of the received synchronization signals, see Fig. 2 on the downlink direction. The time interval between synchronization information repetition may vary between 24 and 2604 ms [2]. Once synchronized, UE can configure the NPRACH resource so that the number of repetitions and the transmit power is sufficient.

Next, the NPBCH carries the master information block (MIB) for 640 ms transmission time interval (TTI). Also, overhead information about the cell characteristics is transmitted to the SIB1-NB for 2560 ms and other SIB2-NB information from the base station. More details can be found in [11].

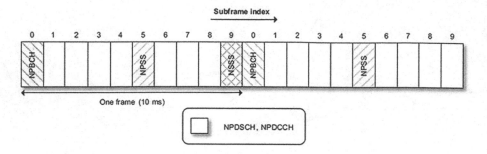

Fig. 2. Downlink physical channels on an NB-IoT anchor carrier [11]

After the DL message transmission has been completed, UL transmission on the NPRACH is performed. The number of repetitions can be 1, 2, 4, 8, 16, 32, 64, 128. One preamble consists of 4 groups of characters, each of which consists of 5 characters and a circle prefix (66.67 μs or 266.7 μs for 10 or 40 km of distance to the base station, respectively). For this reason, the random access duration is in the range 5.6 ms–819.2 ms [5]. The base station for estimating TA in the presence of an unknown offset of the residual frequency of the device exists the deterministic tone hopping pattern within a repetition unit. NB-IoT specifies the minimum number of orthogonal preambles to be 12.

NB-IoT Data Transmission Phase. The data transfer phase is initiated in NPDCCH channel. Repetitions of this signal can be 1, 2, 4, 8, 16, 32, 64, 128, 256, 512, 1024, 2048 times. This is utilized to transmit the Downlink Control Information (DCI).

Figure 3 illustrates the full PSM cycle without any activity followed by an activation to transmit data is shown. DL signals are represented on the Y axis as RX. DL signals use 15 kHz Subcarrier spacing. The code modulation scheme is provided only by QPSK. NPDSCH serves for transmitting service data in DL including broadcast information for SI transmission. It is possible to use sequentially 1, 2, 3, 4, 5, 6, 8, 10 SF and the same number of repetitions as for NPDCCH. To transmit data to UL, the NPUSCH channel is used. UL typically uses either 3.75 kHz or 15 kHz Subcarrier spacing. For this reason, NPUSCH has two formats and has various combinations of RU duration of 1, 2, 4, 8, 32 ms. A detailed relationship is presented in Table 1.

2.4   Metrics of Interest

The metrics of interest include the mean message delay and message loss probability. In the next section, we proceed analyzing the specified system model.

3   Mathematical Model

In this section, we formalize and solve our mathematical model. First, we outline the basic structure of the model and then proceed specifying the Markov chain framework and then solve it using numerical algorithms.

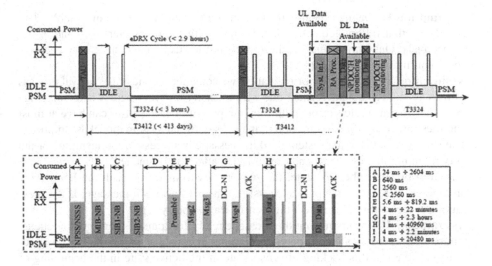

Fig. 3. Life cycle and related power levels of an NB-IoT UE [2,5].

3.1 Approach at the Glance and Assumptions

The core of the proposed modeling approach is on application of two-dimensional Markov chain, where we explicitly differentiate between two large set of states: connectivity (ON) and outage (OFF) subspaces. Sensor nodes are assumed to follow the same rules message generation rules in both subsets of states with the only exception that transmission is only possible in connectivity subspace. Thus, in the OFF states the number of sensors having a message ready for transmission grow creating the backlog of messages to be transmitted at the beginning of the ON state. However, the lifetime of the message might be expired leading to the loss of messages.

In the connectivity subset of states, UEs are assumed to compete for access to the system according to NB-IoT access rules. We assume that the time is discrete with the time slot duration coinciding with frame duration in NB-IoT technology. The following additional assumptions are accepted:

Table 1. RU values specified by NPUSCH format and subcarrier spacing

NPUSCH format	Subcar. spacing	No. of subcar	Number of slots	Length of RU	Modulation scheme
Format 1	3.75 kHz	1	16	16 ms	BPSK/QPSK
	15 kHz	1	16	8 ms	BPSK/QPSK
		3	8	4 ms	QPSK
		6	4	2 ms	QPSK
		12	2	1 ms	QPSK
Format 2	3.75 kHz	1	4	8 ms	BPSK
	15 kHz	1	4	2 ms	BPSK

- **Assumption 1:** The time spent in the ON and OFF states are a random variables T_{ON} and T_{OFF}, that follow geometric distributions with the parameters q_{ON} and q_{OFF}, respectively. One may determine these probabilities using the connectivity and outage sojourn times, see, e.g., [9].
- **Assumption 2:** To simplify formalization we consider the messages arrival process from N sensors as the aggregated one with intensity of $N\lambda$, where λ is the message intensity from a single sensor. With this interpretation each sensor can have at most one message ready for transmission that agrees with our system model assumptions. The sensor remains in the system until its message is successfully transmitted or the maximum number of access and transmission attempts is reached.
- **Assumption 3:** In the *ON* state, the sensor tries to associate with the BS using l preambles. If access attempt is successful, sensor transmits a message. If the message is successfully transmitted, this sensor leaves the system.
- **Assumption 4:** Sensors having the message ready for transmission forms a queue, where all the sensors are considered to be simultaneously active. If the ON (connectivity) state ends, this backlog of sensors are in the active state in the beginning of the next ON period.

3.2 Markov Model

Empowered with the introduced assumptions, the system evolution can be represented using the Markov chain illustrated in Fig. 4. Let $\{S^t, N_{act}^t, t = 0, 1, \dots\}$ be stochastic process, where S^t describes the connectivity state of the system with ON state corresponding to 1 and OFF states denoted by 0, N_{act} is the number of active sensors in the systems having message ready of transmission that have not received access to NB-IoT system yet. Thus, the process is defined over the state space $\mathbb{Z} \in \{0, 1\} \times \{0, 1, \dots, N\}$, Recalling our assumptions, it is easy to see that the choice of the next state depends only on the current one implying that the process $\{S^t, N_{act}^t, t = 0, 1, \dots\}$ is Markov in nature.

The number of active UEs at the time slot $t + 1$ is related to the number of active UE in the time slot t as follows

$$N_{act}^{t+1} = N_{act}^t - T(N_{act}^t, S^t) + V^t(N_{act}^t), \tag{1}$$

where $T(N_{act}^t, S^t)$ is number of successful transmissions when the system is in the state S^t and the system has N_{act}^t active subscribers.

Denote by $V^t(N_{act}^t)$ number of sensors that have become active in slot t, provided that N_{act}^t was active subscribers to the beginning of slot t. Since the number of active sensors coincides with the number of messages, we have

$$S^t = \begin{cases} 0 & \text{if the system is in OFF state} \\ 1 & \text{if the system is in ON state} \end{cases}, \tag{2}$$

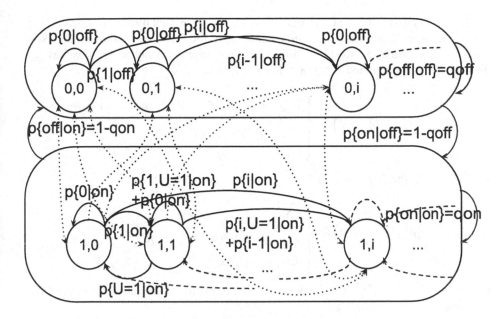

Fig. 4. Markov Chain

Table 2. Principal structure of transition probability matrix.

	0,0	0,1	⋯	0,i	⋯		1,0	1,1	⋯	1,i	⋯
0,0			⋯		⋯	**0,0**			⋯		⋯
0,1	0		⋯		⋯	**0,1**	0		⋯		⋯
⋮	⋮	⋮	⋮	⋮	⋮	⋮	⋮	⋮	⋮	⋮	⋮
0,i	0	0	⋯		⋯	**0,i**	0	0	⋯		⋯
1,0			⋯		⋯	**1,0**			⋯		⋯
1,1			⋯		⋯	**1,1**			⋯		⋯
⋮	⋮	⋮	⋮	⋮	⋮	⋮	⋮	⋮	⋮	⋮	⋮
1,i			⋯		⋯	**1,i**			⋯		⋯
⋮	⋮	⋮	⋮	⋮	⋮	⋮	⋮	⋮	⋮	⋮	⋮

implying that the component S^{t+1} takes the following form

$$
S^{t+1} = \begin{cases}
0 & \text{with probability } q_{OFF} \text{ if } S^t = 0 \\
0 & \text{with probability } 1 - q_{ON} \text{ if } S^t = 1 \\
1 & \text{with probability } q_{ON} \text{ if } S^t = 1 \\
1 & \text{with probability } 1 - q_{OFF} \text{ if } S^t = 0
\end{cases}
\tag{3}
$$

Using (1)–(3), one can calculate the transition probabilities of $\{S^t, N^t_{act}, t = 0, 1, \ldots\}$. Figure 4 illustrates the generic structure of the proposed Markov model. Note that the associated transition probability matrix is sparse with only non-zero values, see Table 2. They are obtained as follows. For $i > j$ we have

$$
p\{j, S^{t+1} \mid i, S^t\} = \begin{cases} s \sum\limits_{m=i-j}^{N-j} C^{m-(i-j)}_{N-i} q^{m-(i-j)} \times & S_t = 1 \\ \times (1-q)^{N-j-m} Pr\{T = m \mid i\} \\ s C^{i-j}_{N-i} q^{i-j}(1-q)^{N-j} & S_t = 0 \end{cases}
$$

while for $i \leq j$ the following holds

$$
p\{j, S^{t+1} \mid i, S^t\} = \begin{cases} s \sum\limits_{m=0}^{N-j} C^{j-i+m}_{N-i} q^{j-i+m} \times & S_t = 1 \\ \times (1-q)^{N-j-m} Pr\{T = m \mid i\} \\ s C^{j-i}_{N-i} q^{j-i}(1-q)^{N-j} & S_t = 0 \end{cases}
$$

where i is N^t_{act}, j is N^{t+1}_{act}, s is the probability of transition from state ON to state OFF accounting for the following

$$
s = \begin{cases} q_{on}, & S^t = 1, S^{t+1} = 1 \\ 1 - q_{on}, & S^t = 1, S^{t+1} = 0 \\ q_{off}, & S^t = 0, S^{t+1} = 0 \\ 1 - q_{off}, & S^t = 0, S^{t+1} = 1 \end{cases}, \tag{4}
$$

$Pr\{T = m \mid i\}$ is the probability that there are T UEs with message ready for transmission in the system. This quantity takes on when $S^t = 0$. Otherwise, we have

$$
Pr\{T = m \mid i\} = \sum_{k=0}^{i} C^k_i p^k (1-p)^{i-k} P(l, k, m) \tag{5}
$$

where p is the probability that the active sensor transmits in the current slot.

$$
p = \begin{cases} 0 & \text{if } i = 0 \\ \min(l/i, 1) & \text{else,} \end{cases} \tag{6}
$$

and $P(l, k, m)$ is the probability of the distribution of k messages over l channels, such that m channels are selected by exactly one UE. Following [16] this probability is given by

$$
P(l, k, m) = \begin{cases} \dfrac{(-1)^m l! k!}{l^k m!} \sum\limits_{f=m}^{\min(l,k)} \dfrac{(-1)^f (l-f)^{k-f}}{(f-m)!(l-f)!(k-f)!} & m \leq k \\ 0 & m > k \end{cases}. \tag{7}
$$

3.3 Performance Metrics

Having obtained the transition probability matrix, one can solve it finding stationary probabilities using standard methods, e.g., by solving a system of linear equations [7, 12].

Having the stationary probabilities at our disposal characterizing the number of active UEs in the system in the steady-state we may now derive the metrics of interest. Applying the Little result to a system with a limited number of waiting positions, the average delay is calculated as

$$E[d] = \frac{E[N_{act}]}{\lambda_{out}},$$ (8)

where λ_{out} is the intensity of the output stream, i.e.,

$$\lambda_{out} = (N - E[N_{act}]) \cdot (1 - e^{\frac{-\lambda}{N}}).$$ (9)

Combining (8) and (9), the mean delay value is given by

$$E[D] = \frac{E[N_{act}]}{(N - E[N_{act}]) \cdot (1 - e^{\frac{-\lambda}{N}})},$$ (10)

To calculate the message loss probability, we first determine the sensor transmission probability. The latter is given by the ratio of the number of transmitted messages obtained in (9) and the total number of messages λ_{inp},

$$\lambda_{inp} = N \cdot (1 - e^{\frac{-\lambda}{N}}).$$ (11)

Now, the transmission probability reads as

$$P_{tran} = 1 - \frac{E[N_{act}]}{N}.$$ (12)

immediately leading to the message loss probability in the following form

$$P_{loss} = \frac{E[N_{act}]}{N}.$$ (13)

4   Numerical Results

In this section, we elaborate our numerical results. We start assessing accuracy of the developed model and then proceed illustrating the system response to input parameters, including mean delay and message loss probability.

4.1   Accuracy Assessment

We start assessing the accuracy of model developed in the previous section. To this aim, we specifically develop an accurate simulation environment capturing all the details of the system model and specifics of NB-IoT access procedure. The simulation is written in Mathlab using multi-threaded optimization allowing to scale well for realistic values on the number of sensors and ON and OFF period duration. To gather statistics we have utilized the method of replications with sampling technique. To deliver the statistics of interest, each replication consisted of 100 ON and OFF periods. The number of replications was set to 10. For this reason, in what follows, we illustrate the point estimates of considered metrics.

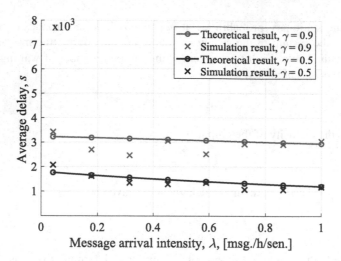

Fig. 5. Comparison with computer simulations.

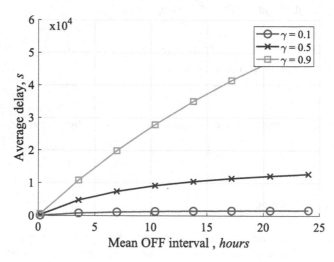

Fig. 6. Mean delay as a function of γ for $\lambda = 0.2$ msg/h.

The comparison of model results and the ones obtained using the simulator is illustrated in Fig. 5 for different values of the fraction of time the system in outage, γ. Furthermore, as one may observe, the analytical data coincides with the simulation ones very well across the considered range of message arrival intensity. Thus, in what follows, to study system response to various input parameters we utilize the developed model. Additionally, we emphasize that for considered range of message arrival intensity the mean delay decreases. We discuss this effect in detail in the rest of this section.

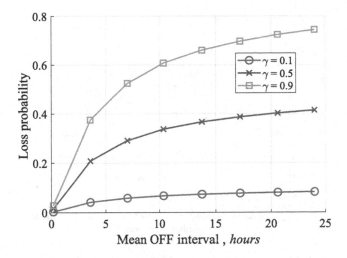

Fig. 7. Message loss probability as a function γ for $\lambda = 0.2$ msg/h

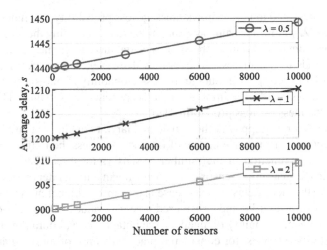

Fig. 8. Mean delay for $\gamma = 0.5$ and $1/\lambda_{OFF} = 1$ h.

4.2 System Performance

We start studying the system response by considering the mean delay as a function of mean outage period, $1/\lambda_{OFF}$ for different values of the fraction of time in outage, γ, illustrated in Fig. 6. First of all, we stress that in the considered system the message delay may reach extreme values of 3×10^4 s. Still these values might be tolerable in practical use-cases as no real-time communications is expected. This time is mainly induced by the outage interval duration with NB-IoT infrastructure. Expectedly, the increase in the fraction of time in outage increases the mean message delay for a given values of $1/\lambda_{OFF}$. Similar effect is also observed when increase the mean outage interval.

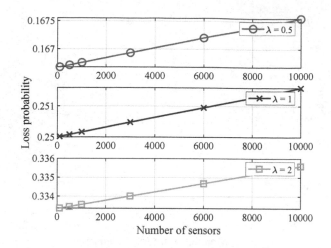

Fig. 9. Message loss probability for $\gamma = 0.5$ and $1/\lambda_{OFF} = 1$ h.

The results presented in Fig. 7 shows message loss probability as a function of mean outage period, $1/\lambda_{OFF}$, for the same system parameters. Analyzing the results, one may observe that the main trends remain the same, i.e., the increase in the values of γ as well as in $1/\lambda_{OFF}$ leads to higher loss probabilities. However, it is interesting to observe that for just 10% of time spent in outage the loss probability remains less than 10% for all considered values of $1/\lambda_{OFF}$ implying that the system even satisfies ITU-R M.2412 constraints on the message loss probability [8].

Number of sensors equipped at the considered large nomadic system is expected to drastically affect the performance metric of interest. To assess their effect, Fig. 8 shows the mean delay as a function of the number of sensors for three considered message arrival intensities from a single sensor, $\gamma = 0.5$ and mean outage interval of one hour. As one may observe the mean delay first decrease in response to higher number of equipped sensors. The reason is that for the considered practical values of time out-of-coverage the delay performance is mainly dictated by the outage interval duration. Indeed, during the connectivity intervals, for considered practical values of message arrival intensity per single sensor, sensors experience almost no competition for resources. Thus, increasing the number of sensors the effect of outage intervals dominates. However, when the number of sensors further increases and thus the traffic intensity increases the delay increases as well.

Figure 9 shows the message loss probability as a function of the number of sensors for the same system parameters. Here, the effect of the number of sensors is much more profound. The increased message loss probability is explained by the fact that sensors having a message ready for transmission tend to accumulate during the outage period and start competing together at the same time when connectivity period begins. Still this effect is not as drastic as one may expect implying that the random access procedure of NB-IoT technology may efficiently handle sporadic loads of up to 2000 UEs. Similarly to delay performance, message loss probability drastically increases when per-sensor load increases.

5 Conclusions

The intermittent connectivity in mobile massive IoT use-cases may lead to various undesirable effects such as sensor synchronization once entering the service area mMTC technology. In this paper, we have proposed an analytical model for NB-IoT technology serving a nomadic system equipped with a large number of sensors, e.g., ship or train, roaming between coverage areas of NB-IoT BSs. The model is based on the Markov chain theory and allows to consider realistic values of outage and non-outage periods as well as message arrival intensities. The metrics of interest are the message loss probability and mean message delay.

Our numerical results demonstrate that the developed model captures the simulation results well across a wide range of message arrival intensities and fraction of time in outage. Further, we have revealed that performance metrics of interest are mainly affected by the outage interval duration and fraction of time system spends in outage state. We have also observed that the even very long outage intervals with the infrastructure do not drastically increase the message loss probability meaning that the capacity of NB-IoT random access channel is sufficient to efficiently handle sporadic loads of up to thousands UEs.

Acknowledgement. The research of A. Turlikov and N. Stepanov was supported of the Ministry of Science and Higher Education and of the Russian Federation, grant agreement No. FSRF-2020-0004, "Scientific basis for architectures and communication systems development of the onboard information and computer systems new generation in aviation, space systems and unmanned vehicles". The work of Dmitri Moltchanov has been supported by 5G Force project.

References

1. 3GPP: LTE; Evolved Universal Terrestrial Radio Access (E-UTRA); LTE physical layer; TS 36.201 V14.1.0, April 2017
2. Adhikary, A., Lin, X., Wang, Y.P.E.: Performance evaluation of NB-IoT coverage. In: 2016 IEEE 84th Vehicular Technology Conference (VTC-Fall), pp. 1–5. IEEE (2016)
3. Ayoub, W., Samhat, A.E., Nouvel, F., Mroue, M., Prévotet, J.C.: Internet of mobile things: overview of LoRaWAN, DASH7, and NB-IoT in LPWANs standards and supported mobility. IEEE Commun. Surv. Tutor. 21(2), 1561–1581 (2018)
4. Begishev, V., et al.: Resource allocation and sharing for heterogeneous data collection over conventional 3GPP LTE and emerging NB-IoT technologies. Comput. Commun. **120**, 93–101 (2018)
5. Feltrin, L., et al.: Narrowband IoT: a survey on downlink and uplink perspectives. IEEE Wirel. Commun. **26**(1), 78–86 (2019)
6. Flore, D.: 3GPP standards for the Internet-of-Things. Recuperado el **25** (2016)
7. Häggström, O., et al.: Finite Markov Chains and Algorithmic Applications, vol. 52. Cambridge University Press, Cambridge (2002)
8. ITU-R: Guidelines for evaluation of radio interface technologies for IMT-2020. M.2412-0, July 2017
9. Kavuri, S., Moltchanov, D., Ometov, A., Andreev, S., Koucheryavy, Y.: Performance analysis of onshore NB-IoT for container tracking during near-the-shore vessel navigation. IEEE Internet Things J. **7**, 2928–2943 (2020)

10. Lauridsen, M.: Studies on mobile terminal energy consumption for LTE and future 5G. Aalborg University (2015)
11. Liberg, O., Sundberg, M., Wang, E., Bergman, J., Sachs, J.: Cellular Internet of Things: Technologies, Standards, and Performance. Academic Press, Cambridge (2017)
12. Meyer, C.D.: Matrix Analysis and Applied Linear Algebra, vol. 71. SIAM (2000)
13. Ometov, A., Orsino, A., Militano, L., Araniti, G., Moltchanov, D., Andreev, S.: A novel security-centric framework for D2D connectivity based on spatial and social proximity. Comput. Netw. **107**, 327–338 (2016)
14. Petrov, V., et al.: When IoT keeps people in the loop: a path towards a new global utility. IEEE Commun. Mag. **57**(1), 114–121 (2018)
15. Petrov, V., et al.: Vehicle-based relay assistance for opportunistic crowdsensing over narrowband IoT (NB-IoT). IEEE Internet Things J. **5**(5), 3710–3723 (2017)
16. Szpankowski, W.: Statistic analysis of multiaccess systems with random access and feedback. Ph.D. thesis, University of Gdansk (1980)
17. Zhang, H., Li, J., Wen, B., Xun, Y., Liu, J.: Connecting intelligent things in smart hospitals using NB-IoT. IEEE Internet Things J. **5**(3), 1550–1560 (2018)
18. Zhou, C., Zhao, J., Liu, H.: Adaptive status report with congestion control in NB-IoT. In: 2019 Sixth International Conference on Internet of Things: Systems, Management and Security (IOTSMS), pp. 1–5. IEEE (2019)

Evaluation of Routing Protocols for Multi-hop Communication in LPWAN

Van Dai Pham[1]([✉])[iD], Duc Tran Le[3], and Ruslan Kirichek[1,2]

[1] Bonch-Bruevich Saint-Petersburg State University of Telecommunications,
193232 Saint Petersburg, Russia
fam.vd@spbgut.ru, kirichek@sut.ru
[2] V.A. Trapeznikov Institute of Control Sciences of Russian Academy of Sciences,
117997 Mosscow, Russia
[3] The University of Danang - University of Science and Technology, Danang,
Vietnam
letranduc@dut.udn.vn

Abstract. Nowadays, the low-power long-range networks are required for the Internet of Things applications, in which devices can transmit data over long distances and consume low energy. Low-Power Wide-Area Networks (LPWANs) have emerged to focus on a group of networks providing solutions for long-range communication and saving power consumption. However, most such networks rely on star topology networks, where the end nodes send data directly to the gateway, which leads to an issue when many nodes are far from the gateway. Aiming for no need for additional gateways, we consider multi-hop communication in LPWANs in this paper. Routing protocols are used to help some nodes that can become relay nodes and find the optimal route to forward the data to the gateway. In the simulated LoRa network, we evaluated the routing protocols in considering the delivery latency and packet loss ratio in varying the network size and number of nodes. Also, the results bring an insight into the future design of a multi-hop communication supported in LPWANs.

Keywords: IoT · Mesh network · Routing protocols · Delay · Packet delivery ratio · LPWAN · LoRa · Smart city

1 Introduction

Nowadays, communication technologies play an important role in connecting things and people. A lot of applications have been developed to bring our lives more modern and convenient. In recent years, a topic called the Internet of Things (IoT) has emerged and became a basis for recent development towards the industrial revolution 4.0. In most IoT applications, there are lots of sensor devices used to collect data that can be about the weather as temperature, humidity, etc. By using sensors we can monitor how our health is and how plants are growing. The collected sensor data are transmitted via communication technologies via the Internet to a remote server, where we can access the data anytime. The IoT

© Springer Nature Switzerland AG 2020
O. Galinina et al. (Eds.): NEW2AN 2020/ruSMART 2020, LNCS 12525, pp. 255–266, 2020.
https://doi.org/10.1007/978-3-030-65726-0_23

paradigm has led to the emergence of other types of communication networks as well as communication technologies.

Moreover, working with most sensor devices requires low power consumption and the ability to transmit data over long distances. There are long-range technologies such as LoRa, Sigfox proposed for IoT applications which can transmit data in the long distances and save energy consumption. The LoRa technology developed by Semtech Corporation is considered one of the promising technologies for building energy-effective long-range networks in both urban and rural environments. On the other hand, there are technologies such as IEEE 802.11, IEEE 802.15.4, or BLE (Bluetooth Low Energy) are also widely used in the IoT applications. However, these technologies have a short communication range. To construct the long-range sensor networks, we consider development to expand the network coverage by supporting both star and multi-hop or mesh topology.

In the context of developing applications of Smart Sustainable Cities, the communication networks are deployed to bring the connectivity ability to the devices [2]. However, some problems emerged in ensuring the connectivity of devices in the network in the urban environment. A group of Low-Power Wide Area Networks (LPWANs) has emerged to group the technologies used for long-range communication and saving energy consumption. As known well, there are several proposed technologies such as LoRa with LoRaWAN, Sigfox, NB-IoT, or Ingenu, etc. LPWANs connect IoT devices or telemetry devices located over long distances to the gateway or the base station.

In most of the solutions for organizing networks, we can see that the devices are connected in various topologies such as a star, mesh, multi-hop, or point-to-point. Depending on the requirements of the application, a topology can be chosen to build a network between devices. Initially, the networks based on the LoRa technology were proposed in work with the star topology, where many devices are connected to the external network via a base station or a gateway. Moreover, other wireless sensor networks such as ZigBee or Z-wave support mesh and multi-hop topology. Although these networks also have low-power consumption, the devices can communicate with the other over a short distance.

Thus, it becomes the idea of using a long-range mesh network as a LoRa network in star and mesh topology, which provide the devices that are far away from the gateway can transmit the data via the other devices. However, there is a low data rate in such networks. Therefore, when developing routing protocols, it is necessary to consider changes to adapt to such networks. In this paper, we consider evaluating the well-known routing protocols used in the wireless mesh networks that we can simply modify to adapt to the LPWANs.

2   Low Power Wide Area Networks

LPWANs represent a group of low-power wide-area networks. Such networks connect sensors and devices covering wide areas while consuming a little energy consumption. LPWANs have been developed to enable long-range communication at a low data rate. There are emerging and promising technologies proposed to build LPWANs. As well-known and popular in the market and also in scientific research, it can be called LoRa technology from Semtech, ultra-narrow band (UNB) technology from Sigfox, and random phase multi-access (RPMA) technology from Ingenu.

LoRaWAN. One of the most promising networks is used for IoT devices. LoRaWAN has been developed based on the LoRa technology, which was launched by Semtech Corporation in 2012. The LoRaWAN Alliance groups companies, developers to focus on the development of a low-power wide-area network LoRaWAN. As mentioned, most LPWANs use unlicensed frequency ISM to transmit data. In LoRaWAN, the frequency ranges of 868 MHz, 912 MHz, 433 MHz are used in Europe, North America, and Asia, respectively. The key parameters provided by the LoRa technology are: modulation, bandwidth (BW), spreading factor (SF), coding rate (CR), which can be chosen to achieve the required data rate. At the physical layer, the chirp spread spectrum modulation is used to provide an increased channel budget and better noise immunity. Moreover, the data date is varying from 0.3 to 50 kbps depending on the BW, SF, and CR, to transmit the payload with a length of up to 200 bytes. [14].

Sigfox. This technology reduces the spectrum to increase the data transmission range. The data are transmitted at a very low data rate with a modulation scheme to ensure minimal spectrum used. The advantage of this method is that the perceived noise (after filtering the signal) is reduced since it linearly depends on the occupancy of the signal spectrum. In the Sigfox network, the payload length is defined to 12 bytes and can be transmitted with a low bit rate up to 100 bps. [15].

Ingenu. The difference between this network and others in LPWANs is using a higher frequency range. The 2.4 GHz frequency band is used, therefore this technology can provide a higher throughput than the others, which work in sub-GHz band. However, the higher frequency may lead to propagation losses and constraints of the transmission range. Besides, using the RPMA technology enables a higher data rate than LoRaWAN or Sigfox. The data can be transmitted with hundreds of kps. Ingenu also enables effective bidirectional data exchange by synchronizing the gateway and the end nodes [18].

In most solutions of LPWANs, the star topology is used to communicate between end nodes and the base station or the gateway, as shown in Fig. 1. In a single-hop connection, the end nodes send the data directly to the gateway that forwards received data to the server. A single gateway can cover a large coverage area. However, with some nodes located far from the gateway, there could be challenges in transmission power. The gateway requires higher energy to transmit data to these nodes. That means that the further a node is away from the gateway, the more energy it has to expend relaying a message. That is a critical issue when the end nodes require to send the data to the gateway. Besides, most of the end nodes are powered by batteries, therefore there is a limitation in energy consumption.

Another alternative solution that can be combined with the star topology is to use the multi-hop or mesh topology in LPWANs. As shown in Fig. 2, we

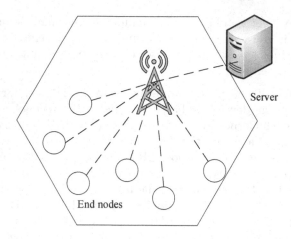

Fig. 1. Star topology

can see that some nodes are out of the coverage area of the gateway. Thus, to deliver the data to the gateway, the other nodes can become the transit nodes relaying the data via more than a single hop to the gateway. In some cases, LoRa devices may still be unable to communicate wirelessly with a nearby gateway due to physical obstacles that can attenuate wireless signal strength and result in data losses and communication errors [8]. In wireless sensor networks, the mesh and multi-hop networks are often deployed based on technologies such as ZigBee, WirelessHART, 6LoWPAN. And recently, Bluetooth Low Energy 5.0 also supports relaying data via nodes in multi-hop connection. It can be seen that most of the existing technologies, nowadays, are supporting mesh and multi-hop communication [4], included the single-hop or star topology. In addition to the end nodes, there are different types of nodes, which have the functionality to forward data to the other nodes.

Based on this approach, we consider deploying a LoRa network, in which the data can be relayed via several nodes to the gateway. Moreover, to construct a mesh or multi-hop network, the routing protocols are the important elements to find the optimal path delivering the data packets to the destination. As known that the LPWANs have a low data rate and require small energy consumption. Developing and using the routing protocols in such networks may differ from others. An overview of routing protocols is presented in the next section. Network simulation is considered to evaluate the routing protocols in the LoRa network.

3   Routing Protocols

Designing and developing routing protocols in wireless mesh networks is a challenging issue that should cover multiple performance metrics such as minimum hop count, preventing disruption of the service methods according to robustness concepts, using mesh infrastructure to perform routing processes as efficient as

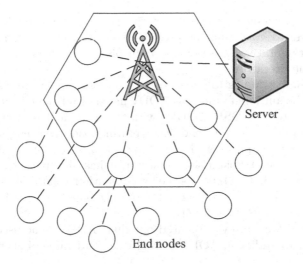

Fig. 2. Multi-hop topology

it possible, and increasing the scalability of routing protocols to install or maintain routing paths in a mesh network with large capacity [5]. To implement the idea of building a LoRa mesh network model we need to choose an appropriate routing protocol.

Typically, ad-hoc routing protocols are divided into three categories, based on the network topology information used for route discovery: proactive, reactive, or hybrid.

- Proactive routing protocols: This kind of protocol periodically exchanges the topology information between all the network nodes. Therefore, proactive routing protocol has no route discovery since the destination route is saved and maintained within a table. The tables usually must be updated. These protocols are used where the route requirements are frequent. However, the drawback of this protocol is that it gives low idleness to constant application [10]. DSDV (Destination Sequenced Distance Vector), OLSR (Optimized Link State Routing) are examples.
- Reactive routing protocols: These routing protocols choose routes to other nodes only when they are needed. A route discovery process is launched when a node wants to communicate with another station for which it does not possess any route table access. AODV (Ad-hoc On-Demand Distance Vector routing protocol), DSR (Dynamic Source Routing) are examples.
- Hybrid routing protocols: Hybrid Routing joining nearby proactive routing protocols and global reactive routing protocols together to reduce routing overhead and delay due to route disclosure process. The advantages of these protocols are higher efficiency and scalability. However, the disadvantage is high latency for locating new routes [3]. Examples of these protocols are ZRP (Zone Routing Protocol).

Within each of these three categories, there are many protocols, and as such, a comprehensive review cannot be provided here. We will instead examine and evaluate a representative selection of protocols that are commonly used and referenced in the literature.

There are many studies focused on the comparison of protocols mentioned above. In [6,7] the authors found that AODV has shown better performance than other routing protocols (DSR, DSDV) with the increment of nodes number in all performance metrics (end-to-end delay, routing load, received packets, packet delivery ratio, dropped packets). In [16] Singh et al. showed that although DSR performs well in quick transmission, however, it has high packet loss. Jogendra Kumar in [9] proved that AODV has the best execution as far as normal jitter and end-to-end delay in comparison with DYMO (Dynamic MANET On-Demand Routing Protocol), DSR, OSLR, ZRP.

In [12] Makodia et al. even pointed out that, AODV is advised for secured communication. In addition, AODV also gives a good value of average throughput [17].

In addition to those evaluations, we can see that, due to its characteristics, OSLR is well-suited to large and dense networks with random and sporadic traffic. However, we need a few gateways to cover even a large area in the LoRa network. As such, the added overhead of choosing relays and updating topology information is unnecessary in our case [11].

Since reactive protocols require sharing of topology information only when routes fail or a new route needs to be established, they allow for a reduced control overhead, and thus energy cost, in comparison to proactive protocols [13].

DSR protocol is designed for a network with potentially high mobility. Therefore it does not suit our case [11].

As most nodes' positions are fixed in the LoRa network, the proactive protocols could be used for routing problems. Besides, the reactive protocols also could be combined with the proactive protocols to establish routes from the end nodes to the gateway when adding or removing nodes from the network.

4   Network and Simulation Model

Typically, LPWAN networks consist of the following elements [1]:

- end node – the low-performance device that used to interact with sensors and/or actuators connected to them;
- switch – the device that acts as routers in the LPWAN networks;
- gateway – the device that receives and extracts useful data from packets of the LPWAN network format and then encapsulates them and sends it to the target network (usually the IP).

And in typical IoT applications, the network can be divided into several fragments from end devices to remote cloud servers. Communication technology provides communication networks between devices. In wireless sensor networks, there are several methods for implementing a mesh topology between nodes.

Mesh networks can be built between end devices, between cluster head nodes, or between gateways. Application of LoRa technology makes it possible to transmit data over long distances, which can use to ensure communication of network fragments located far away from the base station.

An example of the simulated network in OMNET++ is shown in Fig. 3, in which there are several nodes around the gateway. Some of the nodes, which are far from the gateway, will need to assistance of the other nodes to deliver the data to the gateway. In practice, there are a lot of nodes deployed in a large deployed area. However, the nodes send data with a low intensity to the gateway. Although there is a limitation of the number of nodes in the network in the simulation model, the data send intensity will be higher. Since the data rate is low up to 37.5 kbps in the LoRa network, we chose to consider the mean interval between sending packets equals to 120 s.

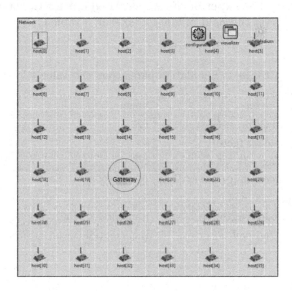

Fig. 3. A simulated network in OMNET++

Based on the OMNET++ and inet frameworks, we have developed a simulated network based on LoRa technology. At the physical layer of the network, the parameters such as $SF = 8$, $BW = 125$ kHz, $CR = 4/5$ are configured for the LoRa radio modules. Using these parameters, the node can receive a radio signal up to -127 dBm that is a high reception sensitively [14]. However, the data rate is low in this case (3.125 kbps). Therefore, the intensity of message generation is considered small to avoid network overload. The interval between sending messages is a random variable according to the exponential distribution with a mean value of 120 s. The payload length of each message is also randomly generated in a range from 20 to 150 bytes.

We considered the network that is deployed in a square field, on which the position of nodes is evenly distributed. Where there is a node as a gateway connected to the server is located in the center of the simulation field and the rest of the nodes transmit messages at a random time to the gateway. When considering the routing protocols for the given network, we evaluate the quality of service parameters such as delivery delay and packet delivery ratio to the gateway from the other nodes. The analysis of network simulation results is carried out in two cases:

- A network with the same number of nodes is deployed on a field of various sizes. A series of computer experiments were carried out with a network of 25 nodes distributed on the fields with sizes of 1000×1000, 1500×1500, and $2000 \times 2000 \, \mathrm{m}^2$.
- A network is simulated with a different number of nodes distributed on a field of the same size. The experiments were carried out for the network with 16, 25 and 36 nodes on the field of $2000 \times 2000 \, \mathrm{m}^2$ (Table 1).

Table 1. Simulation parameters and value.

Parameter	Value
Bandwidth, kHz	125
Spreading factor	8
Coding rate	4/5
Transmission power, dBm	14
Antenna, dBi	5
Payload length, B	Randint (20, 150)
Sent interval, s	Exponential (mean $= 120\,\mathrm{s}$)

5   Simulation Results

5.1   Analysis in Varying the Network Size

In the network of 25 nodes, we have received a distribution of packet delivery delays to the gateway in Fig. 4 when using the AODV protocol (Fig. 4a and the DSDV protocol (Fig. 4b). As we can see that the latencies in the LoRa network are distributed up to several seconds. For example, when using the AODV protocol in the network size of 1500×1500 the delay in the interval (0, 2.5) s has a probability equal to $2.5 \times 0.25 = 0.875$, i.e. about 87% of messages are transmitted to the gateway with the delivery latency in the interval to 2 s. On the other hand, the size of the network field does not greatly affect the delivery latency when using the DSDV protocol. In this case, the delay distribution is similar to the exponential distribution that was set for the interval of sending messages at the source nodes. When using the DSDV protocol, the routing table between senders and the gateway is saved after the routes are found after the first request. After that, the table is updated if there is information about changing the network topology. Therefore, the delivery time does not take much when searching for routes in this case. However, the routing table is temporarily stored for a duration when using AODV. The delivery delay, in this case, can be longer compared to using DSDV (Fig. 5), since the timeout for finding routes after the time when the routing table saved in memory was deleted.

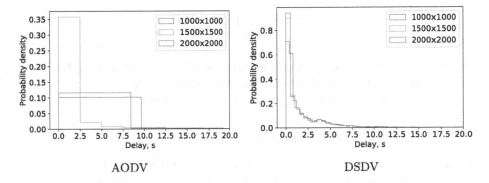

AODV   DSDV

Fig. 4. Histograms of delays in different sizes of network

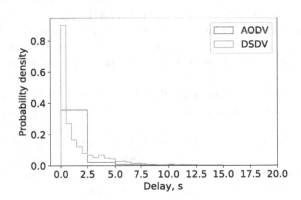

Fig. 5. Comparison of delay distribution in the network of 25 nodes in 1500×1500

However, the probability of successful packet delivery using AODV is greater than using DSDV (Fig. 6a). Since the route search is repeated in the AODV protocol, messages are sent via relay nodes after the routes were found. Moreover, the size of the network field does not affect the packet delivery ratio. The

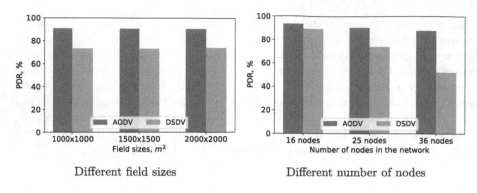

Fig. 6. Packet delivery ratio

percentage of received packets in the network with sizes of 1000×1000 and 2000×2000 is approximately the same. Thus, with the fixed number of nodes in the network, we can deploy the network in different field sizes.

5.2 Analysis in Varying Number of Nodes

On the other hand, in the network with a size of 2000×2000, we consider the effect of changes in the number of nodes on the latency distribution and the packet delivery ratio. A comparison of the delays when using AODV and DSDV protocols is presented in Fig. 7 with a different number of nodes in the network. Increasing the number of nodes in the network changes delivery delays. In the case of using DSDV, there is more probability of longer latency while increasing the number of nodes. However, when using the AODV protocol, a network of 36 nodes has delays less than the networks with 16 and 25 nodes. But the network of 25 nodes has delays greater than the network of 16 nodes. This can be explained by the fact that the network of 36 nodes has more options for choosing routes between source nodes and the gateway. Therefore, the packet forwarding latency can be less than with the network of 25 nodes in the given field size.

Moreover, the packet delivery ratio decreases as the number of nodes in the network increases (Fig. 6b). The loss coefficient increases more in the case of using DSDV protocol, which in the network of 16 nodes, the delivery ratio is more than 80%, and in the network of 36 nodes, less than 60% of messages were successfully delivered. Besides, the delivery ratio also decreases when using the AODV protocol, but there was a small change value.

6 Conclusion

In this paper, we have considered the multi-hop communication supported for LPWAN networks, in particular for the LoRa network. By using the simulation model we have evaluated routing protocols AODV and DSDV used for solving routing problems in the proposed network. The results have shown how high

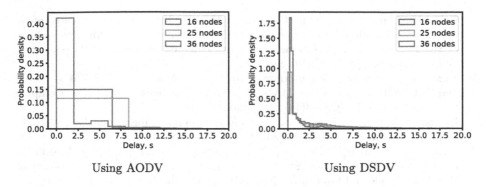

Using AODV   Using DSDV

Fig. 7. Distribution of delays with different number of nodes in the network

is the latency when transmitting data via several nodes. However, the delivery delay in using the AODV protocol is higher than in using DSDV. Therefore, the combination of these protocols should be taken into account at the next stage of development. Besides, the packet delivery ratio may be considered acceptable in such networks. Thus, multi-hop communication may be an additional functionality for the nodes in the LPWANs.

Acknowledgment. The publication has been prepared with the support of the grant from the President of the Russian Federation for state support of leading scientific schools of the Russian Federation according to the research project HШ-2604.2020.9.

References

1. LoRa Alliance: Lorawan specification. LoRa Alliance, pp. 1–82 (2015)
2. Ben Dhaou, S., Lopes, N., Meyerhoff Nielsen, M.: Connecting cities and communities with the sustainable development goals (2017)
3. Chandra, A., Thakur, S.: Qualitative analysis of hybrid routing protocols against network layer attacks in MANET. Int. J. Comput. Sci. Mob. Comput. 4(6), 538–543 (2015)
4. Devalal, S., Karthikeyan, A.: Lora technology-an overview. In: 2018 Second International Conference on Electronics, Communication and Aerospace Technology (ICECA), pp. 284–290. IEEE (2018)
5. Eslami, M., Karimi, O., Khodadadi, T.: A survey on wireless mesh networks: architecture, specifications and challenges. In: 2014 IEEE 5th Control and System Graduate Research Colloquium, pp. 219–222. IEEE (2014)
6. Ferreiro-Lage, J.A., Gestoso, C.P., Rubiños, O., Agelet, F.A.: Analysis of unicast routing protocols for VANETs. In: 2009 Fifth International Conference on Networking and Services, pp. 518–521. IEEE (2009)
7. Haerri, J., Filali, F., Bonnet, C.: Performance comparison of AODV and OLSR in VANETs urban environments under realistic mobility patterns. In: Proceedings of the 5th IFIP Mediterranean Ad-Hoc Networking Workshop, pp. 14–17 (2006)

8. Ke, K.H., Liang, Q.W., Zeng, G.J., Lin, J.H., Lee, H.C.: A LoRa wireless mesh networking module for campus-scale monitoring: demo abstract. In: Proceedings of the 16th ACM/IEEE International Conference on Information Processing in Sensor Networks, pp. 259–260 (2017)
9. Kumar, J.: Comparative performance analysis of AODV, DSR, DYMO, OLSR and ZRP routing protocols in MANET using varying pause time. Int. J. Comput. Commun. Netw. (IJCCN) **3**(1), 43–51 (2012)
10. Kumar, R., Dave, M.: A comparative study of various routing protocols in VANET. arXiv preprint arXiv:1108.2094 (2011)
11. Lundell, D., Hedberg, A., Nyberg, C., Fitzgerald, E.: A routing protocol for LoRa mesh networks. In: 2018 IEEE 19th International Symposium on "A World of Wireless, Mobile and Multimedia Networks" (WoWMoM), pp. 14–19. IEEE (2018)
12. Makodia, B., Patel, T., Parmar, K., Hadia, S., Shah, A.: Implementing and analyzing routing protocols for self-organized vehicular adhoc network. In: 2013 Nirma University International Conference on Engineering (NUiCONE), pp. 1–6. IEEE (2013)
13. Pandey, K., Swaroop, A.: A comprehensive performance analysis of proactive, reactive and hybrid MANETs routing protocols. arXiv preprint arXiv:1112.5703 (2011)
14. Semtech Corporation: Datasheet SX1276/77/78/79 LoRa Transciever (2019)
15. Sigfox, S.: Sigfox technical overview (2017)
16. Singh, P.K., Lego, K., Tuithung, T.: Simulation based analysis of adhoc routing protocol in urban and highway scenario of VANET. Int. J. Comput. Appl. **12**(10), 42–49 (2011)
17. Talooki, V.N., Ziarati, K.: Performance comparison of routing protocols for mobile ad hoc networks. In: 2006 Asia-Pacific Conference on Communications, pp. 1–5. IEEE (2006)
18. IoT Technology: RPMA technology for the Internet of Things (2017)

Deep Learning with Long Short-Term Memory for IoT Traffic Prediction

Ali R. Abdellah[1,2(✉)] and Andrey Koucheryavy[2]

[1] Electronics and Communications Engineering, Electrical Engineering Department,
Al-Azhar University, Qena, Egypt
alirefaee@azhar.edu.eg
[2] The Bonch-Bruevich Saint-Petersburg
State University of Telecommunications, St. Petersburg, Russia
akouch@mail.ru

Abstract. 5G network is new wireless mobile communication technology beyond 4G networks. These days, many network applications have been emerged and have led to an enormous amount of network traffic. Numerous studies have been conducted for enhancing the prediction accuracy of network traffic applications. Network traffic management and monitoring require technology for traffic prediction without the need for network operators. It is expected that each of the 5G networks and the Internet of things technologies to spread widely in the next few years. On the practical level, 5G uses the Internet of Things (IoT) for working in high-traffic networks with multiple sensors sending their packets to a destination simultaneously, which is an advantage of IoT applications. 5G presents wide bandwidth, low delay, and extremely high data throughput. Predicting network traffic has a great influence on IoT networks which results in reliable communication. A fully functional 5G network will not occur without artificial intelligence (AI) that can learn and make decisions on its own. Deep learning has been successfully applied to traffic prediction where it promotes traffic predictions via powerful fair representation learning. In this paper, we perform the prediction of IoT traffic in time series using LSTM - deep learning, the prediction accuracy has been evaluated using the RMSE as a merit function and mean absolute percentage error (MAPE).

Keywords: 5G network · IoT · AI · Deep learning · Prediction · LSTM

1 Introduction

The 5G network will require powerful smart algorithms to adapt network protocols and manage resources for different services in different scenarios. Artificial intelligence (AI), which is defined as any process or device that is aware of its environment and takes actions that maximize the chances of success to achieve a predetermined goal, is a practical solution for designing an emerging complex communications system. Recent developments in deep learning, convolutional neural networks, and reinforcement learning hold important promise for the solution of extremely complex problems that have considered intractable until now [1, 2].

© Springer Nature Switzerland AG 2020
O. Galinina et al. (Eds.): NEW2AN 2020/ruSMART 2020, LNCS 12525, pp. 267–280, 2020.
https://doi.org/10.1007/978-3-030-65726-0_24

It is now suitable for adding AI technology to 5G wireless communications to address the optimal design of the physical layer, complex decision making, network management, and resource optimization tasks in these networks. Moreover, the emerging big data technology has provided us with an excellent chance to study the basic characteristics of wireless networks and to help us to get more clear and deep knowledge of the behavior of 5G wireless networks.

The Internet of Things (IoT) [3–5] enables communication of various devices. Vehicles, buildings, etc. built-in sensors are connected via the Internet of Things, and data can be collected and shared over the Internet. In the next decade, the service targets of IoT for users in various industries will be improved, and the number of machines to machine (M2M) terminals will be greatly increased, and applications will be widespread.

IoT devices communicate with each other and collect a massive amount of data every day. As the device's number increases, the collected data amount increases as well. In many applications, IoT devices can also be programmed to raises some actions based either on some predefined conditions or some responses from the collected data. However, to analyze the collected data and extract significant information and make smart applications, human intervention is required. IoT devices require not only to collect data, and the connection with other devices. They need to be able to make decisions and learn from their collected data. This need resulted in the creation of Cognitive IoT. Also, smart IoT devices are needed, that can create automated smart applications with automatic resource allocation, communication, and network operation and management.

The deployment of ML algorithms in an IoT framework can introduce significant improvements in the applications or the infrastructure, itself. ML can be applied for network management improvement, avoiding congestion, and optimization of resource allocation, but also for real-time or offloading data analyzing and decision making. There are many ML algorithms like Artificial Neural Networks (ANN) that can help to deal efficiently with big data [6].

Traffic prediction using a deep learning approach has great importance due to its ability to learn from large data and to learn patterns more accurately compared to other approaches. Besides, it is necessary for providing high-quality communication through the network. predicting possible traffic will enable solutions for improving QoS before it drops. Deep neural network learning can be applied for prediction analysis since it will utilize historical data to make better decisions and hence fulfill higher accuracy. Additionally, expecting a possible massive flow occurrence at uncommon times which can most probably be labeled as a flow-based intrusion, will provide a more secure network. In addition to that, the prediction of such large flows can also delete the risk which can spoil the IoT system working [7, 8, 10].

The Network Traffic prediction allows traffic operators to take early actions to control the traffic load and improve network performance. Also, long-term traffic forecasting gives detailed predicting of traffic models to assess future capacity requirements and thus allows for more accurate planning and better decisions. Short period prediction (milliseconds to minutes) is related to the dynamic resource. Fast and accurate traffic prediction is an important technique to enable better efficiency [9].

In this work, we perform the IoT traffic prediction using deep neural network learning (DNN) with the LSTM network. we predict the IoT traffic with time series prediction.

The prediction accuracy is evaluated using root mean square error (RMSE) as a merit function and mean square error percentage error (MAPE). We proposed three deep learning models according to the number of hidden units in the LSTM layer to verify the influence of changing the number of hidden units in LSTM- deep leaning in optimizing the prediction accuracy.

2 Literature Review

Many researchers have devoted their studies on traffic modeling, analysis, and prediction, using machine learning and in the field of IoT technology. Our focus in this paper is on predicting the IoT traffic using deep learning approaches, and therefore, in the rest of this section, we review the notable works related to our focus area in this paper.

Ali R. Abdellah et al. [10] presented an approach to time series prediction of IoT traffic using a multi-step ahead prediction with Time Series NARX feedback Neural Networks, he assessed the prediction accuracy using MSE, SSE, and MAE performance functions, in addition to another measure of prediction accuracy is mean absolute percentage error (MAPE). Ateeq et al. [11] implemented the prediction of delay in IoT using DNN: a multiparametric approach, DNN is adopted for predicting delay in IEEE 802.15.4 based applications in IoT.

Tuli et al. [12] focused on prediction analysis of the delay in packet delivery in ad-hoc networks on the regression graph. Also, he tried to compare the predictions done by the time series prediction model of ANN for three routing schemes. G. White et al. [13] focused on QoS prediction in IoT environments. The predictions include service response time and throughput. However, the approach used depends on the matrix factorization technique and is limited to missing value predictions in the data matrix that contain values for both latency and throughput.

Yuhan Jia et al. [14] studied the traffic speed prediction using deep learning method, he made the prediction using deep belief network (DBN) which consists of a stack of Restricted Boltzmann Machine (RBMs) and a Back Propagation Neural Network (BPNN) output layer. B. Karthika et al. [15] focused on the research of traffic prediction using deep learning technique. He discussed the rich mobility data and deep learning about urban traffic predictions.

Loan N. N. et al. [16] discussed Survey of various NN-based approaches for short-term traffic state prediction, the depth discussion is conducted to demonstrate how various types of NNs have been used for different aspects of short-term traffic state prediction. Also, they proposed research directions for additional applications of NN models, particularly the use of deep architectures, to address the dynamic nature of complex transport networks.

Yang Zhang et al. [17] studied the development of a graph deep learning to predict network traffic flow at a large-scale with high accuracy and efficiency. Specifically, modeling traffic flow dynamics on a road network as an irreducible and aperiodic Markov chain on a directed graph.

Yanyun Tao et al. [18] proposed a multitask learning neural network (MLNN). MLNN performs the speed prediction task for three short-terms by combining the convolution neural network (CNN) and the gated recurrent units' network (GRU) and accomplishes the task of estimating the confidence at the expected speed with the confidence network.

3   IoT Model Simulation

In this paper, the proposed model is the IoT system we simulated the model the Anylogic simulation system, which allows building a simulation model of a discrete event.

Figure 1 shows the structure of an IoT model for generating traffic and simulating the process of one or a set of IoT devices. The traffic generator of conventional communication services and TI traffic which is implemented as H2H + TI (H2H - Human to Human, TI - tactile Internet). The executed incoming traffic moves to node connection and the model is introduced as a queuing system with the combined service discipline (with delay-basis and failure-basis system). The average service time of a packet (message) is equal to $\bar{t}$.

IoT traffic arrival rate is denoted by λ_{IoT}, H2H traffic $-\lambda_{h2h}$, combined stream $\lambda = \lambda_{h2h} + \lambda_{IoT}$. Assuming probability p, a packet arrives at the input of the system where all positions in the queue are occupied and get a service denial (losses occur). The combined traffic stream at the system output has a total intensity of λ. The properties of both streams define the collected traffic stream at the system input therefore, in general, it varies from the properties of both conventional traffic and Internet of Things traffic.

The queue system (QS) model described above can be performed as a G/G/1/k system. For this system, there are no precise analytical models to estimate the probability of packet loss and delivery delay (waiting time in the queue). In [19], the propagation approximation method is utilized to estimate the probability of packet losses with known distribution parameters describing the traffic at the input and the packet servicing process, and the following expression is obtained for an approximate estimation.

$$p = \frac{1 - \rho}{1 - \rho^{\frac{2}{C_a^2 + C_s^2} n_b + 1}} \rho^{\frac{2}{C_a^2 + C_s^2} n_b} \tag{1}$$

where C_a^2 and C_s^2 quadratic coefficients of distributions variation of the incoming stream and service time, respectively; n_b – buffer size, ρ - system load. Approximate estimation of the average package delivery time can be obtained using the below expression [20]:

$$T = \frac{\rho \bar{t}}{2(1 - \rho)} \left(\frac{\sigma_a^2 + \sigma_s^2}{\bar{t}^2} \right) \left(\frac{\bar{t}^2 + \sigma_s^2}{\bar{a}^2 + \sigma_s^2} \right) + \bar{t} \tag{2}$$

For designing the IoT model we proposed the AnyLogic simulation system [10, 20], which enables establishing discrete event simulation models. For simulating a self-similar stream, we used a generator for a series of independent events, the time intervals are random and have a Pareto distribution.

$$f_X(x) = \begin{cases} \dfrac{k x_m^\alpha}{x^{\alpha+1}} & x \geq x_m \\ 0 & x < x_m \end{cases} \tag{3}$$

where x_m and α are distribution parameters.

Expected value and variance of the random variable are determined according to

$$E(x) = \frac{\alpha x_m}{\alpha - 1}, \quad D(x) = \left(\frac{x_m}{\alpha - 1}\right)^2 \frac{\alpha}{\alpha - 2} \tag{4}$$

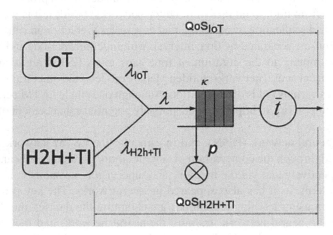

Fig. 1. Service model of aggregated traffic

4 LSTM Deep Learning

There is a need for a mechanism for improving the network traffic prediction accuracy and in turn, avoid deteriorating the system QoS. The visual mechanism must be proactive to avoid weak interactive solutions; thus, it requires a traffic prediction solution. Many ML techniques have been proposed so far to improve traffic prediction accuracy. one of the best techniques is Deep learning Neural Network (DNN) which relies on neural networks technique, where the algorithm was observed and tested aiming at predicting the upcoming traffic load. Deep learning (DL) is a special type of multi-layer neural networks.

These networks are better than the traditional neural network in continuing the information from the preceding event. Recurrent neural network (RNN) is one of these machines that have a set of networks in the loop. Loop networks allow the information to continue also, each network in the loop picks input and information from the previous network, performs the specified process, and produces output while passing the information to the next network. Some applications only need new information while others may require more from past information. The popular recurrent neural networks are lagging in learning as the gap between the preceding required information and the key requirement increases dramatically. But fortunately, Long Short-Term Memory (LSTM) Networks, is a deep learning model, it is a kind of RNN can learn such scenarios. These networks are precisely designed to get away the long-term dependency case of recurrent networks. LSTMs are good at keeping information for a long time. Since greater preceding information may affect the accuracy of the model, LSTMs become a natural choice to use [21].

LSTM network is universal in the sense that, with an adequate number of network elements, it can perform any calculation according to a regular computer capability, which requires a suitable weight matrix that can be considered as a program. the LSTM network differs from traditional recurrent neural networks; besides, it is well suited for learning on task classification, processing, and time series prediction in situations where significant events are separated by time intervals with indefinite periods and boundaries. The relative immunity to the duration of time gaps gives LSTM an advantage over alternative recurrent neural networks, hidden Markov models, and other training methods for sequences in various fields of application. Although one single LSTM cell unit might handle the memory issue, to implement the possibly potential enhancement of prediction accuracy [7, 8].

In a deep neural network (DNN), and in particular the LSTM network, the neuron can be activated through the contribution of several inputs simultaneously and receiving the inputs respectively and via the memory and supervision mechanism, it manages to save traffic patterns, as it has also appeared in several works. The key procedures for traffic prediction using learning techniques are obtaining the dataset, the data format, implementing the neural network, training the neural network, and then started predicting (or testing your network). Each step is important to get the best accuracy for prediction compared to real values. The key to prediction using deep learning is the dataset. Nowadays, operators can easily collect this data as they own their infrastructure and have a clear idea of the evolution of the load on their network [21].

The traditional LSTM unit consists of a cell, an input gate, an output gate and a forget gate. After the inputs go in the LSTM structure, some memory has been preserved for further use. We can use the labels of input data to do classification, regression, or prediction. The primary component of LSTMs is cell state, which is a line runs from Memory from preceding block (C_{t-1}) to Memory from actual block (C_t), it allows the information to stream directly down the line. The network can decide the amount of preceding information to flow. The first step that of the LSTM cell state this layer is represented by a sigmoid layer called the "forget gate layer", and the operation carried out in this layer is given in Fig. 2, function f_t is defined as follows:

$$f_t = \sigma\left(W_f.[h_{t-1}, x_t] + b_f\right) \tag{5}$$

where h_{t-1} and x_t first go through a linear transformation and then input into a sigmoid transformation to get the output between 0 and 1 for each number in the cell state C_{t-1}. The forget gate decides to accept the contribution of the cell state from the past time step C_{t-1} then the following step is to decide whether the input of the current time step will contribute to the cell state or not. Based on the key idea of recurrent neural networks, must take into account the output of the previous time step. Therefore, current input x_t and former output h_{t-1} should be combined. In Fig. 1, function i_t and $\widetilde{C}_t$ are defined as follows:

$$i_t = \sigma\left(W_i.[h_{t-1}, x_t] + b_i\right) \tag{6}$$

$$\widetilde{C}_t = tanh(W_c.[h_{t-1}, x_t] + b_c) \qquad (7)$$

$$C_t = f_t \times C_{t-1} + i_t * \widetilde{C}_t \qquad (8)$$

At the final stage of the LSTM cell, we shall derive the result of the output from the cell unit. In Fig. 1, o_t and h_t are defined as follows:

$$o_t = (W_o.[h_{t-1}, x_t] + b_o) \qquad (9)$$

$$h_t = o_t \times tanh(C_t) \qquad (10)$$

where o_t represents which parts of inputs will be selected as a composition of outputs and h_t is derived by determining how much affect cell state will work on those selected inputs. The basic LSTM cell structure is shown in Fig. 2.

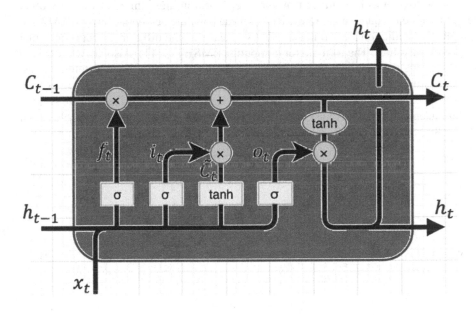

Fig. 2. Basic structure of LSTM cell

5 Training LSTM - Deep Learning

Deep learning-LSTM units can be trained in a supervised manner, on a set of training sequences, using an optimization algorithm, such as gradient descent, integrated with backpropagation through the time needed in computing the gradients over the optimization process, for changing each weight of the LSTM network in proportion to the derivative of the error (at the output layer of the LSTM network) according to the corresponding weight.

The gradient descent algorithm usage for the RNNs is that error gradients disappear quickly with the size of the time lag between important events. LSTM units, while the error values are backpropagated from the output layer, the error remains in the LSTM unit's cell. This continuously returns this error to all LSTM gates until they learn to cut off the value.

Input and output time series prediction depends on predicting the future value of one time-series is given another time-series. The past values of both series (for best accuracy), or only one of the series (for a simpler system) may be used to predict the target series.

The prediction error values are typically evaluated by deep learning algorithms. error is a kind for a poor prediction, more specifically, the error value will be zero, if the model's prediction is perfect. Hence, the aim is to minimize the error values through obtaining a set of weights and biases that help in minimizing the error. In addition to loss, which is utilized by the deep learning algorithms, researchers often use the root mean square error (RMSE) and mean absolute percentage error (MAPE) to evaluate the prediction performances. RMSE measures the differences between actual and predicted values. The formula for computing RMSE Eq. (11). Also, MAPE Eq. (12) (mean absolute percentage error) is a relative error measure that utilizes absolute values. MAPE has two advantages. First, the absolute values retain the positive and negative errors from canceling each other. Second, since relative errors do not rely on the scale of the dependent variable, this measure allows you to compare forecast accuracy between differently scaled time-series data.

$$RMSE = \sqrt{\frac{1}{N} \sum_{t=1}^{nn} (y_t - \hat{y}_t)^2} \tag{11}$$

$$MAPE = \frac{1}{N} \sum_{t=1}^{n} \left| \frac{y_t - \hat{y}_t}{y_t} \right| \tag{12}$$

Where N is the total number of observations, y_t is the actual value, whereas $\hat{y}_t$ is the predicted value.

Algorithm: Prediction using LSTM network
load example (IoT traffic datasets)

1. **Inputs:**
   Time series training data $D = \{D_1, D_2, ..., D_t\}$
2. **Outputs:**
   RMSE and MAPE of the predicted data
3. **Initialize:**
   A pre-trained model
4. **Split data into:**
   70% training and 30% testing data
5. **size** ← length(series) * 0.70
6. **Train** ← series[0...size]
7. **Test** ← series[size...length(size)]
8. Normalize the dataset (Di) into values from 0 to 1
9. Select training window size (tw) and organize Di accordingly
10. **Define:**
    LSTM Network Architecture
11. **for** n epochs and batch size do
    a.   Train the Network (LSTM)
12. **end for**
13. Run Predictions using LSTM
14. Calculate the performance
15. Calculate RMSE
16. Calculate MAPE

6   Simulation Results

In this paper, the simulation was performed on the Intel (R) Core(TM) I5-3210 M processor of 2.40 GHz clock speed having 6 GB of memory. We used Matlab R2020a for implementation and simulations of the prediction of IoT traffic using LSTM deep learning. We examined the performance in three cases according to the number of hidden units in the LSTM network. we opted for the prediction in three cases according to the numbers of hidden units, 500, 100, 50, respectively. The datasets were generated from the IoT model besides, we simulated the IoT data generator using AnyLogic simulator. After gathering and preparation of the dataset, we divided it into 70%, 30% for training, and testing, respectively. For evaluating the prediction accuracy for traffic data, we used the RMSE and MAPE as shown in Eq. (11), (12). Table 1 shows the prediction accuracy for the IoT throughput using RMSE and MAPE.

Table 1 illustrates the prediction accuracy of IoT throughput by utilizing LSTM deep learning in three cases according to the number of hidden units in LSTM layer, we opted 500, 200, 50 hidden units for verifying the ability of the LSTM deep learning in for optimizing the IoT traffic prediction in different cases. For evaluating the error of prediction, we use the RMSE and another measure for performance accuracy MAPE with MSE as performance function.

Table 1. The measure of prediction accuracy for the predicted model validation using RMSE and MAPE

LSTM's hidden units	Performance function	RMSE	MAPE
500	MSE	0.0298	2.12
200		0.1029	7.35
50		0.1694	13.86

Looking at the tabulate results, the model predicted in the case of number hidden units 500 has the best prediction accuracy with RMSE value equal to 0.0298, and MAPE equals 2.12% in comparison to the other cases. The maximum average prediction accuracy improvement in the case of 500 hidden units is 11.74%. Also, the prediction accuracy in the case of 200 hidden units has dropped to RMSE value 0.1029 and the MAPE decreased to 7.35%, the maximum average improvement in prediction accuracy, in this case, is 5.23%.

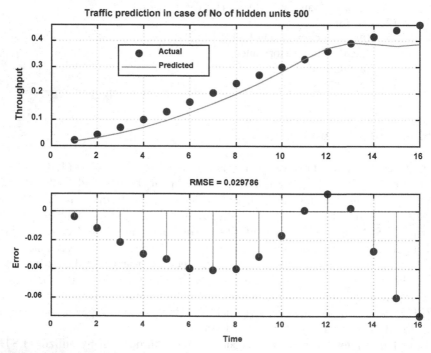

Fig. 3. The response of output element for time series in case of the number of hidden units in LSTM layer 500

On the other hand, the model predicted in the cases of hidden layers 50 has the least prediction accuracy with RMSE value 0.1694 and MAPE dropped to 13.86% comparison of them.

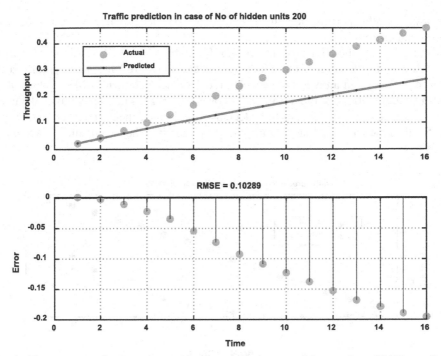

Fig. 4. The response of output element for time series in case of the number of hidden units in LSTM layer 200

Figure 3, Fig. 4 and Fig. 5 illustrates the predicted model based on the IoT throughput prediction using the LSTM network with deep learning. We chose different models based on the number of hidden units in the LSTM layer to verify the ability of the LSTM deep learning in for optimizing the IoT traffic prediction. Every figure contains two curves, the first curve indicates the relation of the throughput (actual and predicted models) vs the time however the second curve indicates the relation between the prediction error and time.

From Fig. 3 the model predicted using the LSTM approach with deep learning in the case of the number of hidden units 500 has the best prediction accuracy with RMSE value equal 0.0298 and the improvement is 11.74% in comparison to its peers. The consumed time during the prediction process is 16. By looking at the figure, we notice that the predicted model performance approximately equal to the actual model. Also, the predicted model increases gradually starting from time 1 then at time 13 the prediction becomes a little constant until time 16 which gives the best prediction accuracy in this case.

Looking at Fig. 4 the prediction of IoT traffic in the case of the number of hidden units 200. The model predicted has prediction less than the accuracy in case of the model predicted using 500 hidden units, where RMSE value dropped to 0.1029 and the improvement was 5.23% in comparison to the others. Also, As shown in Fig. The consumed time during the prediction process is 16 in this case. By looking at the first curve you found that the predicted model is similar to the actual model until the time 3 then deviate gradually from the actual until the time 16 which provides the best prediction accuracy in this case.

Figure 5 shows the prediction accuracy of IoT traffic using the LSTM approach with deep learning in the case of the number of hidden units 50. The model predicted in the case of 50 hidden units has the lowest prediction accuracy with RMSE value equal 0.16939 in comparison with its peers. As shown in Fig. 1 the predicted model deviates from the actual model besides, its little decreases until time 2 then become constant until time 5.2 then increases gradually until time 16 which gives the best prediction accuracy in this case.

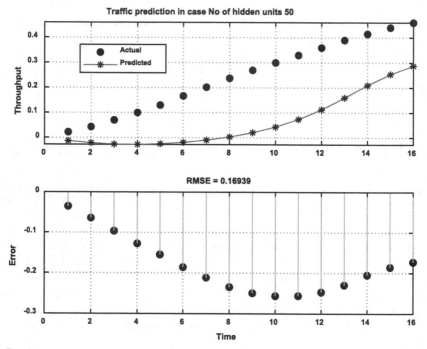

Fig. 5. The response of output element for time series in case of the number of hidden units in LSTM layer 50

7   Conclusion

This paper addresses the prediction approach for IoT traffic prediction using deep learning with the LSTM network. This approach has the advantage to remember the previous state of time point and give a more accurate estimation of future time points. Besides, it has an advantage over traditional time series prediction models because it helps in optimizing the learning process accuracy during the iteration of training. Moreover, by providing more data into the model, the model will be intelligent and better evaluate the traffic volume, which is important in real-time traffic prediction. The prediction accuracy of the deep learning model has been evaluated in terms of RMSE also, another measure for accuracy is MAPE. Simulation results show that the model predicted in case of the number of hidden units 500 has the best prediction accuracy in comparison to its peers and the predicted model is approximately equal to the actual model. On the other hand, the model predicted in the case of the number of hidden units 50 has the lowest prediction accuracy in comparison to others and the predicted model deviates from the actual model.

References

1. Abdellah, A., Koucheryavy, A.: Survey on artificial intelligence techniques in 5G networks. J. Inf. Technol. Telecommun. **8**(1), 1–10 (2020). SPbSUT, Russia http://www.sut.ru/doci/nauka/1AEA/ITT/2020_1/1-10.pdf
2. Morocho-Cayamcela, M.E., Lee, H., Lim, W.: Machine learning for 5G/B5G mobile and wireless communications: potential, limitations, and future directions. IEEE Access **7**, 137184–137206 (2019)
3. Solomitckii, D., Gapeyenko, M., Semkin, V., Andreev, S., Koucheryavy, Y.: Technologies for efficient amateur drone detection in 5G millimeter-wave cellular infrastructure. IEEE Commun. Mag. **56**(1), 43–50 (2018). Art. no. 8255736
4. Petrov, V., et al.: Vehicle-based relay assistance for opportunistic crowdsensing over narrowband IoT (NB-IoT). IEEE Internet Things J. **5**(5), 3710–3723 (2018). Art. no. 7857676
5. Ometov, A., et al.: Feasibility characterization of cryptographic primitives for constrained (wearable) IoT devices. In: 2016 IEEE International Conference on Pervasive Computing and Communication Workshops, PerCom Workshops 2016 (2016). Art. no. 7457161
6. Jagannath, J., Polosky, N., Jagannath, A., Restuccia, F., Melodia, T.: Machine learning for wireless communications in the Internet of Things: a comprehensive survey. Ad Hoc Netw. **93**, 1–46 (2019). Art. no. 101913. ISSN 1570-8705. https://doi.org/10.1016/j.adhoc.2019.101913
7. Crivellari, A., Beinat, E.: LSTM-based deep learning model for predicting individual mobility traces of short-term foreign tourists. Sustainability **12**(1), 1–14 (2020)
8. Du, X., Zhang, H., Van Nguyen, H., Han, Z.: Stacked LSTM deep learning model for traffic prediction in vehicle-to-vehicle communication. In: IEEE 86th Vehicular Technology Conference (VTC-Fall), Toronto, ON, Canada, pp. 1–5, September 2017
9. Joshi, M., Hadi, T.H.: A review of network traffic analysis and prediction techniques, July 2015. https://arxiv.org/abs/1507.05722
10. Abdellah, A.R., Mahmood, O.A.K., Paramonov, A., Koucheryavy, A.: IoT traffic prediction using multi-step ahead prediction with neural network. In: IEEE 11th International Congress on Ultra-Modern Telecommunications and Control Systems and Workshops (ICUMT) (2019)
11. Ateeq, M., Ishmanov, F., Afzal, M.K., Naeem, M.: Predicting delay in IoT using deep learning: a multiparametric approach. IEEE Access **7**, 62022–62032 (2019). https://doi.org/10.1109/ACCESS.2019.2915958
12. Tuli, H., Kumar, S.: Prediction analysis of delay in transferring the packets in ad-hoc networks. In: Proceedings of the 3rd International Conference on Computing for Sustainable Global Development (INDIACom), pp. 660–662, March 2016
13. White, G., Palade, A., Cabrera, C., Clarke, S.: IoTPredict: collaborative QoS prediction in IoT. In: IEEE PerCom, pp. 1–10, March 2018
14. Jia, Y., Wu, J., Du, Y.: Traffic speed prediction using deep learning method. In: IEEE 19th International Conference on Intelligent Transportation Systems (ITSC), pp. 1–5, November 2016. https://doi.org/10.1109/itsc.2016.7795712

15. Karthika, B., UmaMaheswari, N., Venkatesh, R.: A research of traffic prediction using deep learning techniques. Int. J. Innov. Technol. Explor. Eng. (IJITEE) **8**(9S2), 725–728 (2019). ISSN 2278-3075. https://doi.org/10.35940/ijitee.I1151.0789S219
16. Do, L.N.N., Taherifar, N., Vu, H.L.: Survey of neural network-based models for short-term traffic state prediction. WIREs Data Min. Knowl. Discov. 1–24 (2018). https://doi.org/10.1002/widm.1285
17. Zhang, Y., Cheng, T., Ren, Y.: A graph deep learning method for short-term traffic forecasting on large road networks. Comput.-Aided Civ. Infrastruct. Eng. **34**(10), 877–896 (2019)
18. Tao, Y., Wang, X., Zhang, Y.: A multitask learning neural network for short-term traffic speed prediction and confidence estimation. In: Tetko, I.V., Kůrková, V., Karpov, P., Theis, F. (eds.) ICANN 2019. LNCS, vol. 11728, pp. 434–449. Springer, Cham (2019). https://doi.org/10.1007/978-3-030-30484-3_36
19. Iversen, V.B.: Teletraffic engineering and network planning. DTU Fotonik (2015)
20. Mahmood, O.A., Khakimov, A., Muthanna, A., Paramonov, A.: Effect of heterogeneous traffic on quality of service in 5G network. In: Vishnevskiy, V.M., Samouylov, K.E., Kozyrev, D.V. (eds.) DCCN 2019. LNCS, vol. 11965, pp. 469–478. Springer, Cham (2019). https://doi.org/10.1007/978-3-030-36614-8_36
21. Huang, C., Chiang, C., Li, Q.: A study of deep learning networks on mobile traffic forecasting. In: 2017 IEEE 28th Annual International Symposium on Personal, Indoor, and Mobile Radio Communications (PIMRC), pp. 1–6 (2017). http://dx.doi.org/10.1109/PIMRC.2017.8292737

VANET Traffic Prediction Using LSTM with Deep Neural Network Learning

Ali R. Abdellah[1,2(✉)] and Andrey Koucheryavy[2]

[1] Electronics and Communications Engineering, Electrical Engineering Department,
Al-Azhar University, Qena, Egypt
alirefaee@azhar.edu.eg
[2] The Bonch-Bruevich Saint-Petersburg
State University of Telecommunications, St. Petersburg, Russia
akouch@mail.ru

Abstract. Vehicular ad hoc networks (VANETs) are a promising technology that enables the communication between vehicles on roads. It becomes an emerging topic that integrates the capabilities of new generation wireless networks for vehicles. Network traffic prediction allows Intelligent Transport Systems (ITS) for proactive response to events before they happen. With the rapid increase in the amount, quality, and detail of traffic data, there is a need for new techniques that can use the information in the data to provide better results while they can scale and cope with increasing amounts of data and growing cities. In this paper, we purpose (Long Short-Term Memory) LSTM deep learning for the prediction of VANET network traffic. We have trained the models using traffic data collected from the VANET network. The prediction accuracy has been evaluated using RMSE as a merit function and another measure of prediction accuracy is the mean absolute percentage error (MAPE).

Keywords: Traffic prediction · VANET · Deep learning · AI · LSTM

1 Introduction

Vehicular Ad hoc Networks (VANETs) special category of traditional Mobile Ad hoc Networks (MANETs). The main characteristic of VANETs is that each vehicle operates as a mobile node equipped with advanced onboard components, Moving on dedicated paths. VANET provides the exchange of information about the other vehicles through a wireless medium via Vehicle-to-Vehicle (V2V) communication protocols, as well as between vehicles and fixed road-side units (i.e., wireless and cellular network infrastructure), in case of Vehicle-to-Infrastructure (V2I) communications [1, 2].

The term VANET is used to describe the assigned ad hoc network formed between the moving vehicles on the road. Vehicular networks are rapidly emerging to develop and deploy new and traditional applications. More details, VANETs are characterized by high mobility, frequent and very fast-changing topology, and transient. VANETs have paved the way to several road safety applications where Internet access is considered as

© Springer Nature Switzerland AG 2020
O. Galinina et al. (Eds.): NEW2AN 2020/ruSMART 2020, LNCS 12525, pp. 281–294, 2020.
https://doi.org/10.1007/978-3-030-65726-0_25

their indisputable support [3, 4]. VANETs share some similarities with MANETs like the movement and self-organization of the nodes (i.e., vehicles in the case of VANETs). However, due to the driver behavior, and High-speed, VANETs features differ from the typical MANETs. VANETs are characterized by rapid topology changes but slightly predictable, with frequent fragmentation, a small effective network diameter, and redundancy that is limited temporally and functionally [5, 6].

The network traffic prediction [7, 8] is one of the most promising areas of artificial intelligence (AI) research for data networks. It has applications in wide fields and has recently attracted many studies. Several types of research are conducted to identify various problems in current computer network applications. Predicting network traffic is a proactive approach to ensuring safety, reliability, and specific network connectivity. It is proposed and tested various techniques for predicting the traffic of the network including techniques based on the neural network to data mining techniques. Likewise, many Linear and non-linear models are proposed to predict network traffic. Several interesting combinations of network prediction techniques are implemented to achieve efficient and effective results.

To implement the prediction, it is necessary to make an estimated time, using time slots to collect traffic. Once traffic is collected and estimated in slots, the prediction consists of predicting traffic volume for the next slot (simple prediction) or the earliest future slots in the future (k-ahead prediction). Depending on the application, intervals can be seconds, minutes, and hours, Application of statistical analysis methods to forecast traffic has been the usual trend, but the trend has recently moved to ML methods. From the ML model, traffic volume forecasting can be considered as a regression problem where a regression function performs a simple prediction (a single output regression) or prediction of k-ahead (multi-output regression), using the previous volumes of traffic volume or external variables, all of that is model features [7–10].

Artificial intelligence (AI) [11–14] is the major component needed in understanding the vast amount of data collected these days and increase its value to businesses. Also, it will be useful in analyzing IoT data in the following areas: data preparation, data discovery, visualizing flow data, the accuracy of time series data, predictive and advanced analytics, and real-time geospatial and location (logistical data AI has become an integral part of almost every technology sector. It has an impact on applications, development tools, computing platforms, database management systems, middleware, management, and monitoring tools almost everything in the IT field.

In this work, we implemented the time series prediction approach using LSTM with deep neural networks learning for VANET traffic. we made the prediction in cases of the number of packets sent 4 pckts/s, 6 pckts/s, 8 pckts/s, 10 pckts/s, 12 pckts/s, and 14 pckts/s.

We proposed the LSTM network because of its ability in optimizing the prediction accuracy better than the traditional time series also, it is more efficient and faster to fit data compared to traditional time series models, besides, they deal with larger data sets better than traditional time series models. the prediction accuracy is evaluated using RMSE as a merit function and MAPE.

This paper is organized as follows: Sect. (1) Introduction; Sect. (2) discusses Deep learning; Sect. (3) discusses LSTM network; Sect. (4) discusses VANET simulation using Matlab; Sect. (5) discusses gives our experimental result; Sect. (6) gives Sect. (6) conclusion.

2 Deep Learning

Deep learning, a class of machine learning (ML), which uses the hierarchical structure of artificial neural networks for the implementation of the machine learning process. The artificial neural networks mimic the human brain, are built with neuron nodes connected like a web. However, the traditional programs analyze data linearly, the hierarchical function of deep learning systems help machines to process data with a nonlinear approach. Deep learning is the function of the artificial intelligence that simulates the functions of the human brain in processing data for use in decision making. Deep learning AI can learn from data that is both unstructured.

Deep neural networks take the fundamental type of the MLP and with multiple hidden layers within the middle of the model. So rather than there being an input layer, one hidden layer, and an output layer, there are several hidden layers within the middle and therefore the outputs of one hidden layer become the inputs for the following hidden layer until the data has created it through the network and been returned.

The multiple hidden layers of a deep neural network can interpret more complex patterns than the traditional multilayer perceptron. Various layers of the deep neural network learn the patterns of various parts of the data. For example, if the input data consists of images, the first part of the network may explain the brightness or darkness of pixels while the subsequent layers will choose shapes and edges that can be used to recognize objects in the image [15].

There is a necessity for a mechanism for improving the accuracy network traffic prediction and thus avoid deteriorating the system performance. The visual mechanism must be proactive to avoid weak interactive solutions; thus, it needs a traffic prediction solution. Several ML techniques have been proposed so far to improve traffic prediction accuracy. one of the best techniques is Deep learning Neural Network (DNN) which depends on neural networks technique, where the algorithm was observed and tested aiming at predicting the upcoming traffic load [16].

Some networks are better than the traditional neural network in persisting the information from the past event. Recurrent neural network (RNN) is one of these networks that have a set of networks in the loop. The loop networks allow the information to go on also, each network in the loop pick input and information from the past network and carry out specific process and produces output with passing information to the next network.

Some applications only need new information while others may require more from the preceding information. The popular recurrent neural networks are lagging in learning as the gap between the past required information and the key requirement increases dramatically. But fortunately, Long Short-Term Memory (LSTM) Networks [17], is a deep learning model, it is a kind of RNN that can learn such scenarios. These networks are precisely designed to get away the long-term dependency case of recurrent networks. LSTMs are good at keeping information for a long time. Since greater preceding information may affect the accuracy of the model, LSTMs become a natural choice to use.

3   LSTM Neural Network

Long Short-Term Memory network (LSTM) [17–19] is a special type of artificial recurrent neural network (RNN), having the ability to learn long-term dependencies. It has gained popularity by many people in the field of the machine learning community. LSTM is used in the field of deep learning, it differs from the traditional feedforward neural networks (FFNNs), that LSTM has feedback connections. It can not only process individual data points (such as images) but also complete data sequences (such as speech or video). They work very well on several problems and are now widely used. the operation of LSTM enables a network to understand the long-term dependencies between time steps in both data and time series.

It is designed to avoid the long-term dependency problem. Preserving information for long periods is practically their default behavior, not something they struggle to learn. Traditional recurrent neural networks (RNNs) contain the form of a series of repeating modules of a neural network and the repeated modules will have a very simple structure, like a single tanh layer.

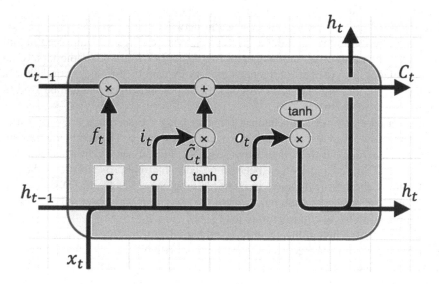

Fig. 1. Basic structure of LSTM cell

The basic concept behind LSTM is to transfer the cell state from the former time step to the current time step. We can define a simple linear transformation of the cell state as well as add the gate structure to manipulate it. The LSTM can eliminate or add information to the cell state, carefully organized by structures called gates. The traditional LSTM unit consists of a cell, an input gate, an output gate and a forget gate. The cell reminds the values of random periods and the three gates regulate the information stream into and out of the cell. LSTM networks are Perfectly suited for classifying, processing, and making predictions based on time series data where there may be a delay of unknown duration between important events in a time series.

LSTMs have been developed to deal with the problems of explosive and fading gradient that can be encountered when training traditional RNNs. LSTM is characterized by the Approximate insensitivity to gap length which differentiates it over RNNs, hidden Markov models (HMMs), and other methods of sequence learning in several applications. One simple way is to use the sigmoid function as follows:

$$\sigma(x) = 1/(1 + e^{-x}) \tag{1}$$

which outputs a value between 0 and 1, followed by the multiplication of the process for determining whether the past information must be remembered or forgot. Like a structure called the forget gate and is widely used in LSTM to implement speech recognition, robot control, and many other prediction tasks. Besides, the forget gate, the percentages of the input contribution must be measured. The measurement uses a *tanh* function as follows:

$$\tanh(x) = \frac{e^x - e^{-x}}{e^x + e^{-x}} \tag{2}$$

Since the value of tanh will fall between -1 and 1, so it is a good activation function to describe the contribution, both active and negative. And the tanh layer is a contribution gate in the LSTM cell structure in general, the inputs (tensors) go through the LSTM in the following procedure. Firstly, according to Fig. 2, function f_t is defined as follows:

$$f_t = \sigma\left(W(h_{t-1}, X_t) + b_f\right) \tag{3}$$

where h_{t-1} and X_t first go through a linear transformation and then input into a sigmoid transformation to get the binary result between 0 and 1, which can be utilized to decide whether the information from the former time step is going to contribute to the next cell state. This is a basic forget gate structure. After the forget gate decides to accept the contribution of the cell state from the former time step C_{t-1} the next step is to determine whether the input of the current time step will contribute to the cell state or not. According to the basic idea of recurrent neural networks, the output of the former time step should be taken into consideration. Therefore, current input X_t and former output h_{t-1} should be combined. In Fig. 1, function i_t and $\sim \tilde{C}_t$ are defined as follows:

$$i_t = \sigma(W(h_{t-1}, x_t) + b_i) \tag{4}$$

$$\tilde{C}_t = \tanh(W(h_{t-1}, x_t) + b_c) \tag{5}$$

$$C_t = f_t \times C_{t-1} + i_t * \tilde{C}_t \tag{6}$$

At the last stage of the LSTM cell, we shall derive the result of the output from the cell unit. In Fig. 2, o_t and h_t are defined as follows:

$$o_t = (W(h_{t-1}; X_t) + b_o) \tag{7}$$

$$h_t = o_t \times \tanh(C_t) \tag{8}$$

where o_t represents which parts of inputs will be selected as a composition of outputs and h_t is derived by determining how much affect cell state will work on those selected inputs.

Although one single LSTM cell unit may address the memory issue, to implement the possibly potential enhancement of prediction accuracy.

After the inputs (tensors) go through the LSTM structure, some memory has been kept for further use. We can use the labels of input data to do classification, regression, or prediction. The basic LSTM cell structure is shown in Fig. 1.

4 VANET Simulation

In this section, the simulation of VANET in Urban City is performed as follow:

We used Matlab for the creation of a realistic mobility model for VANETs. Routing protocols AODV was designed via the generated realistic mobility model to analyze & evaluate their behavior and performance.

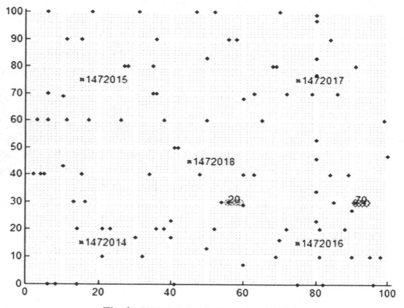

Fig. 2. VANET simulation using Matlab

To create a mobility map, you must first create the road network. It contains three main modules: City Size, Nodes & RSU's. Here the size of the city must be specified, where the nodes will travel in random directions for the AODV implementation. A maximum city size and large number nodes will be needed to show the AODV action. Likewise, a greater number of RSU's are required to be installed. If the city size is greater than the simulation time it is automatically extended. According to the work, we assumed the size of the city is 100 m concerning X-axis and Y-axis.

The urban city will be designed so that the desired nodes can travel in random directions on the designated routs. Figure 2 shows the nodes (vehicles) with a dot and the RSU's locations along with their ID numbers that are specified to them by the network architecture or topology designer. The source and destination nodes in this model are indicated by node number 20 and node number 70, respectively.

This module is responsible for designing the number of nodes, the flow of nodes that will allocate the groups of nodes movements that flow over the simulation and turn ratio that will determine the probability of directions on each intersection. The simulation module is used to visualize the network structure, as well as determine the start time, and end time for the simulation.

The RSU's (Roadside Unit) location in the urban city map to help the nodes moving in a random direction for communication with other nodes that are far from other nodes domain. An RSU provides communication and information exchange with passing vehicles, including safety warnings and traffic information. RSUs can also communicate with each other directly or via multihop. Figure 2 shows the VANET Simulation in an Urban city.

5   Simulation Results

In this work, we perform VANET traffic prediction approaches using LSTM. The prediction accuracy was evaluated using the RMSE as a merit function and another measure is the mean absolute percentage error (MAPE).

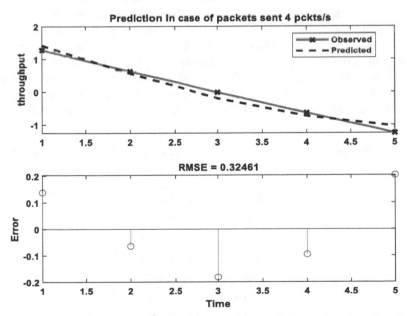

Fig. 3. The response of output element for time series in case of the number of packets 4 pckts/s

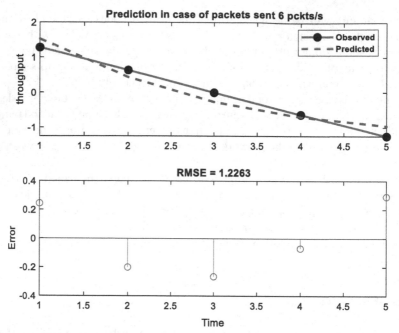

Fig. 4. The response of output element for time series in case of the number of packets 6 pckts/s

The input-output time series is based on predicting the next value of one time series given another time series. The previous values of both series (for best accuracy), or only one of the series (for a simpler system) may be used to predict the target series.

The dataset can be used to demonstrate how LSTM with deep learning can be trained to make predictions. The datasets are obtained from VANET traffic the model was simulated using Matlab, after the collection and preparation of the data set that was divided into 70%, 30% for training, and testing, respectively. The implementation of the feedback neural network to predict the performance accuracy of VANET traffic.

Table 1. The measure of prediction accuracy for the predicted model validation using RMSE and MAPE

Packets/s	MAPE	RMSE
4 Pckts/s	1.3155	0.3246
6 Pckts/s	6.4529	1.2263
8 Pckts/s	5.9316	1.1113
10 pckts/s	2.2314	0.4670
12 pckts/s	6.4529	1.2263
14 pckts/s	10.1508	0.5983

Table 1 shows the prediction accuracy for the VANET throughput using RMSE and MAPE.

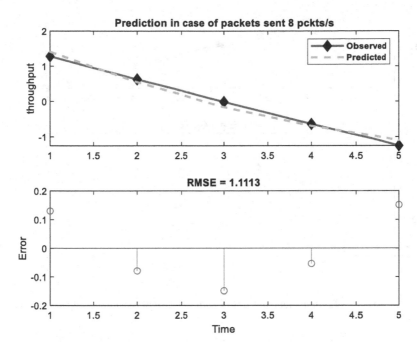

Fig. 5. The response of output element for time series in case of the number of packets 8 pckts/s

Table 1 displays the prediction accuracy of VANET traffic in case of the number of packets sent 4 pckts/s, 6 pckts/s, 8 pckts/s, 10 pckts/s, 12 pckts/s, and 14 pckts/s respectively to estimate the error of prediction we use the RMSE and another measure for performance accuracy MAPE.

From the tabulated results, the model predicted in the case of the number of a packet sent 4 pckts/s has the best prediction accuracy with RMSE value equal 0.3246 and MAPE equal 1.3155% in comparison to its peers. The maximum average prediction accuracy improvement in the case of 4 pckts/s up to 8.8353%. Also, the models predicted in the cases of 10 pckts/s and 14 pckts/s have a prediction accuracies that are approximately equal to the accuracy in the case of 4 pckts/s with RMSE values are 0.4670, 0.5983 respectively, and in the case of 10 pckts/s has dropped the maximum average prediction accuracy of MAPE up to 2.2314%, while in the case of 14 pckts/s the MAPE has large drop up to 10.1508% compared with the others.

On the other hand, the models predicted in the cases of a number of packets sent 6 pckts/s and 12 pckts/s have the lowest and identical prediction accuracy and the model predicted using the number of packets 8 pckts/s has semi equal accuracy in comparison of them.

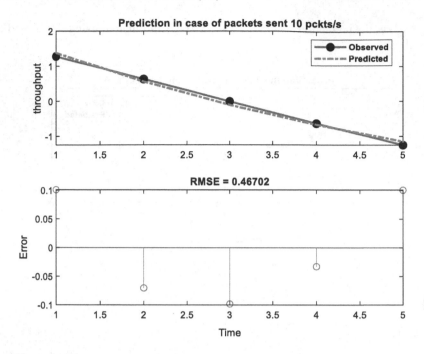

Fig. 6. The response of output element for time series in case of the number of packets 10 pckts/s

Figure 3 shows two curves the first curve observes the prediction for VANET through-put with time and the second curve observes the prediction error with time. The prediction time 6 which to verify the ability of the LSTM deep learning in for improving the VANET traffic load prediction in the cases of the number of a packet sent 4 pckts/s. as shown in Fig. 3 the throughput with time for the observed and predicted models we notice from that figure that the predicted model similar to the observed model also, we notice that the predicted model increase at time 1 then decreases gradually until the time 6 which gives the best prediction accuracy.

Figure 4 illustrates two curves the first curve observes the prediction for VANET throughput with time and the second curve observes the prediction error with time. The prediction time 5 which to verify the ability of the LSTM deep learning in for improving the VANET traffic load prediction in the cases of the number of a packet sent 6 pckts/s. as shown in Fig. 4 the throughput with time for the observed and predicted models we notice from that figure that the predicted model semi-similar to the observed model, also, we notice that the predicted model increase at time 1 then decreases gradually until the time 5 which gives the best prediction accuracy.

It is clear from Fig. 5 that it contains two curves the first curve the plot of VANET throughput prediction with time for the observed and predicted models and the second curve illustrates the prediction error with time. The prediction time 5 for proving the ability of the LSTM deep learning in for improving the VANET traffic load prediction in the cases of the number of a packet sent 8 pckts/s. Looking at Fig. 5 we notice that the predicted model semi equal to the observed model also, we notice that the predicted model increase at time 1 then decreases gradually until time 5 which gives the best prediction accuracy.

By looking at Fig. 6 that it contains the plot of VANET throughput prediction with time for the observed and predicted models in the cases of the number of a packet sent 10 pckts/s. The prediction time 5 to confirm the ability of the LSTM deep learning in for improving the VANET throughput prediction. Looking at Fig. 6 we notice that the predicted model equal to the observed model, besides, as shown in Fig. 6 the predicted model increases at time 1 then decreases until time 5 which gives the best prediction accuracy.

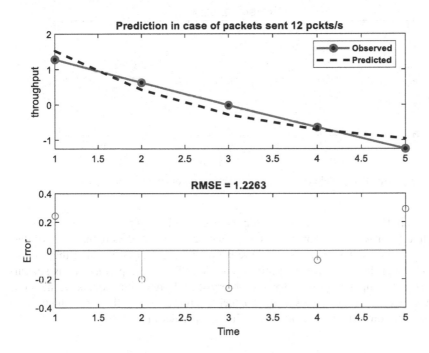

Fig. 7. The response of output element for time series in case of the number of packets 12 pckts/s

Figure 7 observes the plot of prediction for VANET throughput with time besides, the prediction error with time for the observed and predicted models in the cases of the number of a packet sent 12 pckts/s. The prediction time 5 which to confirm the ability of the LSTM deep learning in for improving the VANET traffic prediction. as shown in Fig. 7 the throughput with time for the observed and predicted models we notice from that figure that the predicted model slightly deviates from the observed model also, we notice that the predicted model increase at time 1 then decreases gradually until the time 6 which gives the best prediction accuracy.

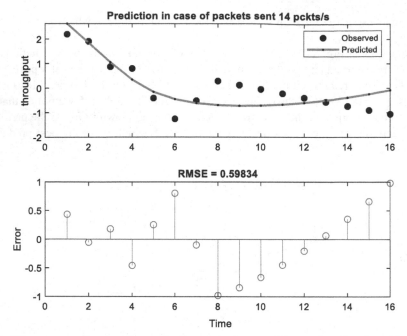

Fig. 8. The response of output element for time series in case of the number of packets 14 pckts/s

As shown in Fig. 8 the plot of prediction for VANET throughput with time, besides, the prediction error with time for the observed and predicted models in the cases of the number of a packet sent 14 pckts/s. The prediction time 16 for confirming the ability of the LSTM deep learning in for improving the VANET traffic prediction. as shown in Fig. 8 the throughput with time for the observed and predicted models we noticed that the predicted model increases at time 1 then decreases gradually until time 6 then increases slightly until time 16 which gives the best prediction accuracy.

6   Conclusion

In this paper, we implement a Long Short-Term Memory (LSTM) with a deep learning model to predict the VANET traffic the LSTM model can show its advantage to remember the preceding state of time point and give a more accurate estimation of next time points. This learning model has its advantage over traditional time series prediction models such that learning accuracy will increase during the iteration of training. Furthermore, with more data fed in the model, the model will be smarter and estimate the traffic volume better, which is important in the real-time prediction of traffic volume. The prediction accuracy of the deep learning model has been evaluated in terms of RMSE besides, another measure for accuracy is MAPE. Simulation results show that the model predicted in case of the number of packets 4 pckts/s has the best prediction accuracy with both measure of accuracy RMSE and MAPE in comparison to its peers and the models predicted using and 6 6 pckts/s and 12 pckts/s have the least RMSE value, while the model predicted in case of the number of packets 14 pckts/s has the lowest MAPE in comparison to others.

References

1. Abdellah, A.R., Muthanna, A., Koucheryavy, A.: Robust estimation of VANET performance-based robust neural networks learning. In: Galinina, O., Andreev, S., Balandin, S., Koucheryavy, Y. (eds.) NEW2AN/ruSMART -2019. LNCS, vol. 11660, pp. 402–414. Springer, Cham (2019). https://doi.org/10.1007/978-3-030-30859-9_34
2. Abdellah, A.R., Muthanna, A., Koucheryavy, A.: Energy estimation for VANET performance based robust neural networks learning. In: Vishnevskiy, V.M., Samouylov, K.E., Kozyrev, D.V. (eds.) DCCN 2019. CCIS, vol. 1141, pp. 127–138. Springer, Cham (2019). https://doi.org/10.1007/978-3-030-36625-4_11
3. Petrov, V., et al.: Vehicle-based relay assistance for opportunistic crowdsensing over narrowband IoT (NB-IoT). IEEE Internet Things J. 5(5), 3710–3723 (2018). Art. no. 7857676
4. Pyattaev, A., Johnsson, K., Andreev, S., Koucheryavy, Y. Proximity-based data offloading via network assisted device-to-device communications. In: IEEE Vehicular Technology Conference (2013). Art. no. 6692723
5. Solomitckii, D., Gapeyenko, M., Semkin, V., Andreev, S., Koucheryavy, Y.: Technologies for efficient amateur drone detection in 5G millimeter-wave cellular infrastructure. IEEE Commun. Mag. 56(1), 43–50 (2018). Art. no. 8255736
6. Vegni, A.M., Biagi, M., Cusani, R.: Smart vehicles, technologies and main applications in vehicular ad hoc networks. In: Vehicular Technologies - Deployment and Applications. INTECH Open Access Publisher (2013). https://doi.org/10.5772/55492
7. Boutaba, R., Salahuddin, M.A., Limam, N., et al.: A comprehensive survey on machine learning for networking: evolution, applications, and research opportunities. J. Internet Serv. Appl. 9 (2018). Article number: 16 https://doi.org/10.1186/s13174-018-0087-2
8. Abdellah, A.R., Mahmood, O.A.K., Paramonov, A., Koucheryavy, A.: IoT traffic prediction using multi-step ahead prediction with neural network. In: IEEE 11th International Congress on Ultra-Modern Telecommunications and Control Systems and Workshops (ICUMT) (2019)
9. Lopez-Martin, M., Carro, B., Sanchez-Esguevillas, A.: Neural network architecture based on gradient boosting for IoT traffic prediction. Future Gener. Comput. Syst. 100, 656–673 (2019)
10. https://www.obitko.com/tutorials/neural-network-prediction/prediction.html
11. Zahra, M.M., Essai, M.H., Abd Ellah, A.R.: Performance functions alternatives of MSE for neural networks learning. Int. J. Eng. Res. Technol. (IJERT) 3(1), 967–970 (2014)
12. Abd Ellah, A.R., Essai, M.H., Yahya, A.: Robust backpropagation learning algorithm study for feed forward neural networks. Thesis, Al-Azhar University, Faculty of Engineering (2016)
13. Essai, M.H., Abd Ellah, A.R.: M-estimators based activation functions for robust neural network learning. In: The IEEE 10th International Computer Engineering Conference (ICENCO 2014), 29–30 December 2014, Cairo, Egypt, pp. 76–81 (2014)
14. Abd Ellah, A.R., Essai, M.H., Yahya, A.: Comparison of different backpropagation training algorithms using robust M-estimators performance functions. In: The IEEE 2015 Tenth International Conference on Computer Engineering &Systems (ICCES), 23–24 December, Cairo, Egypt, pp. 384–388 (2015)
15. Schmidhuber, J.: Deep learning in neural networks: an overview. Neural Netw. 61, 85–117 (2015)
16. Alawe, I., Ksentini, A., Hadjadj-Aoul, Y., Bertin, P.: Improving traffic forecasting for 5G core network scalability: a machine learning approach. IEEE Netw. 32(6), 42–49 (2018). https://doi.org/10.1109/MNET.2018.1800104

17. Huang, C., Chiang, C., Li, Q.: A study of deep learning networks on mobile traffic forecasting. In: 2017 IEEE 28th Annual International Symposium on Personal, Indoor, and Mobile Radio Communications (PIMRC), pp. 1–6 (2017). http://dx.doi.org/10.1109/PIMRC.2017.8292737

18. Du, X., Zhang, H., Van Nguyen, H., Han, Z.: Stacked LSTM deep learning model for traffic prediction in vehicle-to-vehicle communication. In: IEEE 86th Vehicular Technology Conference (VTC-Fall), Toronto, ON, Canada, pp. 1–5, September 2017

19. Crivellari, A., Beinat, E.: LSTM-based deep learning model for predicting individual mobility traces of short-term foreign tourists. Sustainability **12**(1), 1–14 (2020)

Modelling Medical Devices
with Honeypots

Jouni Ihanus[1(✉)] and Tero Kokkonen[2]

[1] Huld Oy, Kuopio, Finland
`jouni.ihanus@huld.io`
[2] Institute of Information Technology, JAMK University of Applied Sciences,
Jyväskylä, Finland
`tero.kokkonen@jamk.fi`

Abstract. Cyber security is one of the key priorities in the modern digitalised and complex network totality. One of the major domains of interest is the healthcare sector where a cyber incident may cause unprecedented circumstances. In the healthcare domain there are abundant networked systems, software and hardware, which may be vulnerable for a cyber intrusion or incident. For cyber resilience, it is important to know the status of the valuable assets under attention. Sensor information has a significant role for achieving the comprehension of the valuable assets in the cyber domain. While networked medical devices form an important asset group in healthcare environment, one interesting solution to gather sensor information are the honeypots. In this paper, honeypot technology is studied for the healthcare domain. Especially typical characteristics of medical devices are considered from the perspective of modelling the medical devices with honeypots. The technical priorities are studied and concluded with the discovered future research topics.

Keywords: Honeypots · Cyber security · Situation awareness ·
Intrusion detection

1 Introduction

Cyber domain is an extremely complex entity. For realising the status of the valuable assets in the cyber domain, sensor based Situation Awareness (SA) is required. The Endsley's well-known definition of SA is recognized as follows: *"Situation awareness is the perception of the elements in the environment within a volume of time and space, the comprehension of their meaning, and the projection of their status in the near future"* [9]. By reflecting on the Endsley's definition of SA, it can be comprehensively seen that technical visibility gained by sensor information has a fundamental role for achieving the relevant SA in the complex cyber domain. For understanding the current situation and for making decisions based on that understanding, the relevant SA is required. That can

© Springer Nature Switzerland AG 2020
O. Galinina et al. (Eds.): NEW2AN 2020/ruSMART 2020, LNCS 12525, pp. 295–306, 2020.
https://doi.org/10.1007/978-3-030-65726-0_26

be appreciated by considering the two classical decision-making models, OODA-loop (Observation-Orientation-Decision-Action) [25] and Gartner's four stages of an adaptive security architecture (Predict-Prevent-Detect-Respond) [18].

One of the typical approaches for technical visibility is the Intrusion Detection System (IDS). IDSs are used for guarding the traffic by detecting possible illicit activity. In general, IDSs are classified as follows: anomaly-based detection (anomaly detection) and signature-based detection (misuse detection). Anomaly detection is capable of detecting unknown attack patterns; however, the shortcoming of anomaly detection is its high false detection rate as it generating a large amount of false positive indications. Misuse detection has the capability to detect predefined known attacks with a high detection accuracy; however, it cannot detect undefined unknown attacks [24,26].

For tackling the infirmities of IDSs the honeypots can be used. As stated in [13], honeypots are an advanced concept to gain information about intrusions. If an attacker is capable of intruding into the network, there is a honeypot resembling the asset under protection that will be assaulted by the attacker, and the original asset under protection remains safe behind the honeypot under attack [37]. Honeypots can be used for luring and alerting about intrusions or attacks and gathering beneficial technical information about the used techniques and methods of attacks [21]. Ordinarily honeypots are capable to be used for server-type systems [2].

Honeypots are widely used in different domains. Authors of [38] used honeybot for attack capture in Software Defined Networking (SDN), while Djanali et al. introduced a honeypot for emulating vulnerabilities for XSS and SQL injection attacks with the capability of exposing attacker's identity [8]. Study [29] proposed honeypots for a power grid against Advanced Persistent Threads (APT). Anwar et al. proposed an algorithm for honeypot allocation over attack graphs [3], while Mayorga et al. used honeypots for detection and prevention tool in a network through attack patterns [17]. Honware is a honeypot framework capable of emulating Customer Premise Equipment (CPE) and Internet of Things (IoT) devices for detecting earlier unknown vulnerabilities, so called zero day vulnerabilities [36]. In the study [5] honeybots were implemented for Direct Digital Controls (DDCs) of building automation systems. A five-year analysis of honeybots concluded the capability to avoid the majority of the attacks made by both humans and bots [16].

In the healthcare domain, honeybots are used for example in the mobile health concept [4] and for the security of Electronic Health Record (EHR) based big data [6]. When focusing on the healthcare sector and especially the medical devices, the main contributions of this paper are: what are the typical technical characteristics of the networked medical devices and how can the medical devices be modelled with honeypots?

The paper is organised as follows. First, in Sect. 2, the overview of healthcare environment with common technical elements and threats is presented. After that, in the Sect. 3, modelling of medical devices is described. Lastly, the study is concluded with found future research topics in Sect. 4.

2   Overview of Networked Medical Devices

The honeypots tend to imitate a defined information system service to invite illicit users to interact with them [19]. In order to model the medical devices with the honeypots, it is important to understand how to masquerade the honeypot as an authentic system. For this conclusion, understanding of the information system under review should be reached.

2.1   Healthcare Environment

Medical devices are widely used at different levels of medical treatment. To comprehend the security challenges of the medical devices, it is significant to understand the architecture. The network model proposed by Yaqoob et.al states a three-tiered model as presented in Fig. 1. *Tier 1* presents a considerable number of different medical devices for diagnosis, treatment and monitoring of medical conditions. These devices include wearable, implantable and on-site medical devices. *Tier 2* depicts the gateway level which is responsible for transmitting and processing data received from tier 1. *Tier 3* presents systems utilized to store and analyse the gathered data. These elements form highly interconnected information systems with multiple attack vectors [40].

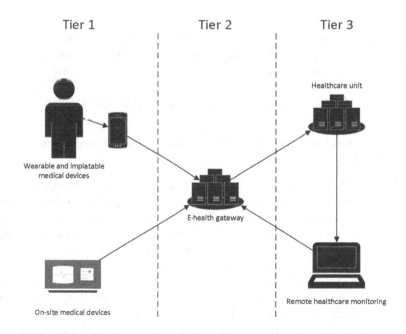

Fig. 1. Tiers [40]

The structure is presented in Fig. 2 on a more practical level. This example presents concretely some of the assets on Tiers 1 and 3. The example aims to emphasize the connection between medical devices and interconnected information systems. Previous studies present that these assets are seen as the most critical ones in the context of smart hospital environment [28].

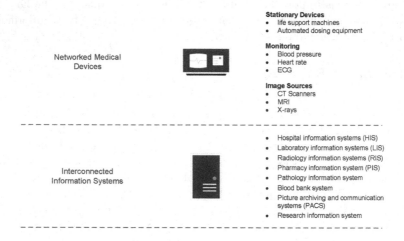

Fig. 2. Structure [28]

When estimating the number of devices, the per-patient devices emerge from the data. Study by [12] states that these devices form the majority of the healthcare devices in a typical healthcare environment. As analysis presents, this is logical, as per-patient devices track and monitor patients on a 1:1 ratio while devices such as CT scanners are shared with multiple patients.

2.2 Restrictions on the Implementation of Technical Security Controls

Medical devices make a crucial contribution in diagnosing, preventing, monitoring, treating illness as well as overcoming disabilities. This role places demands for the safety and efficacy of the medical devices. The domain is highly regulated. [10, 34] Medical device manufacturers are under exact regulations to establish and maintain procedures to validate the device design. Changes in device design have to go through appropriate verification procedures for approval before their implementation [34]. These regulations also affect how cybersecurity updates and controls can be implemented to medical devices. In certain cases, even routine updates and patches require reporting to authorities [33]. While [22] states that many medical devices are sold without typical security controls, implementing security controls to a medical device can cause challenges and/or design changes. For example, [32] present a severe incident occurred during the medical procedure. In this case, the misconfiguration of antivirus software caused the crashing of patient monitoring system. The root cause behind this incident was that the instructions delivered by the medical device manufacturer were not followed. In another example presented by [31], one healthcare professional expressed challenges to follow given instructions, as antivirus software version validated by manufacturer was no more available for purchase.

2.3   Common Technical Characteristics

According to study of [28], networked medical devices are seen as critical assets by 67% of responders. At the same time maintaining the cyber security of these devices has proven challenging: the analysis presented in [12] indicates that in 2019, 70% of the medical devices were running operating system versions that will have been unsupported during the first quarter of 2020. The data set under review included 75 healthcare deployments. According to [23], the situation seems particularly bad for medical imaging systems, as 83 percent of all of them run an end-of-life operating system with known vulnerabilities. The problematics of outdated operating systems relating to the medical devices has also been recognized in other studies [7,12,23,30,35]. While patching these devices is clearly challenging, the study by [39] presents a steady increase in the number of vulnerabilities related to the medical devices. These devices can form a prominent risk to the hospital assets if compromised. As an example, some of the identified cases show that the medical devices were used to enable backdoors into the hospital networks. In these cases, this channel was further utilized for lateral movement and for exfiltration of the confidential hospital data [30]. One of the reasons behind the threats relating to lateral movement is insufficient network segmentation. The analysis by [23] states that 72% of healthcare VLANs contained a mix of a wide variety of different devices, also including medical devices.

On the operating system level, the data set analysed in the study of [12] states that most of the devices in medical networks were running the Windows operating system. The rest of the devices detected included Linux, Unix and embedded systems. The emphasis of Windows systems on medical devices can also be observed in other studies [23]. Many of these devices were running high-risk services. The most common Windows services relating to medical device networks presented in the study by [12] are as follows: SMB, RDP, FTP, SSH, Telnet, and DICOM Imaging Protocol.

It should be noted that SMB and RDP implementations have both been lately exploited by modern automated threats: In 2017 WannaCry ransomware was used in a massive attack, which infected systems in over 150 countries. WannaCry worm component used SMB vulnerability for initial infection [1]. In 2019 similar wormable vulnerability concerning RDP was found [20].

Another key observation is that some unencrypted protocols such as Telnet and FTP are still present. Unencrypted traffic, especially while concerning medical data, poses a great threat to cyber security [12]. At the same time encrypted traffic poses a challenge for network IDS systems as the detection capabilities are limited [11,15].

2.4 Typical Threats

Threat modelling can be seen as a practical discipline to use different techniques to find security problems [27]. Regarding the medical devices, multiple reports have addressed this issue [12,23,30,35]. In this study this information is used as a motivation for defining key use cases for the honeypot usage.

By reflecting the studies above, following challenges can be observed:

- Most of the medical devices use an outdated Windows operating system
- There is a significant challenge to patch medical devices
- There is a challenge in sufficient network segmentation in healthcare environments
- Technical visibility to medical devices is limited

By reflecting the studies above, the following threats have materialized:

- Malware infections in medical devices
- Utilization of a medical device in lateral movement
- Utilization of a medical device as a backdoor to hospital network
- Utilization of a medical device as a pivot device in cyber attack

In summary, a considerable part of the medical devices are running outdated and insecure operating systems, which may pose several threats to the operating environment. At the same time the visibility to these devices can be limited due to restrictions to implement security controls on them.

3 Construction

A typical use case for using honeypot technology is to gain more technical visibility. Honeypots are used as a source of sensor data, which supports perceiving elements in cyber environment. In this chapter honeypot specific features are correlated with typical characteristics of healthcare environment and medical devices to support technical visibility. The main contribution of this study is summarized in the form of a construction model.

3.1 Technical Definition

To understand possibilities to reduce the threats presented above with honeypots, challenges relating to technical visibility should be summarized. Based on the studies presented above, the key challenges to gain the needed technical visibility are presented as follows.

1. Host level visibility

   (a) Challenges to implement host based security controls
   (b) Challenges to implement host based security monitoring

2. Network level visibility

   (a) Usage of encrypted protocols
   (b) Insufficient network segmentation – Visibility relating to lateral movement

To model devices with honeypots, the operational elements of the sensor need to be taken into account. From the technical point of view, a networked medical device appears as a rather typical device in a healthcare network. However, there are individual characteristics that can be noted. These characteristics can be divided into following levels:

1. Operating system level
   (a) Most commonly older versions of Windows operating system
2. Service level
   (a) Quite typical service profile with healthcare specific services like DICOM
3. Network level
   (a) Mixed networks with low segmentation profile.

3.2 Model

In the chapters presented above, following elements relating to networked medical devices have been discussed:

- Threats relating to networked medical devices
- Challenges relating to technical visibility
- Individual characteristics of networked medical devices

Combining these elements with a modified construction model based on [14], refined cyber situation awareness can be reached. The construction presented in Fig. 3 leans heavily to **risk management**. The actual need for situation awareness together with **technical visibility** should be defined through an organization's risk management functions. From a technical point of view, the defined need should be fulfilled with appropriate sensor technology, which in this case is the honeypot technology. **Sensor elements** relating to honeypot should be defined with the emphasis on typical characteristics of the operating environment. When a need for technical visibility encounters capabilities of sensor technology, the wanted refinements for situation awareness can be reached.

Honeypots have certain unique technical **capabilities** which can be used to gain the technical visibility observed in this study: Honeypot architecture is based on emulating the target system on an adequate level. Thereby, on the network level the honeypot appears as a rather typical networked medical device. While using encrypted protocols, a honeypot operates as one of the endpoints. For this reason, there is no need for additional decryption methods. Honeypots can also be used to detect lateral movement, when located in the same network segment with the primary assets. This architecture also offers visibility to new tactics as the methods used against device can be highly monitored. It should be noted that the restrictions relating to the original system do not inherit to

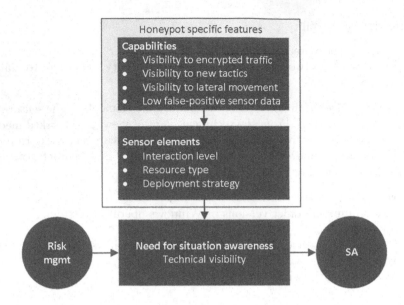

Fig. 3. Construction model [14]

the honeypot system, as the original system is left untouched. On the host level, this offers possibilities to implement security controls and monitoring features for the required purpose. This architectural model also affects the liability of the sensor data received from the honeypot. As the system has no real legit function from users' point of view, all interaction can be defined as illicit action with high certainty.

Sensor elements present how honeypots operate on a more detailed level: Interaction level defines how deeply a system emulates the target system, which also affects the monitoring capabilities that a sensor can offer. For example, the capability to detect new tactics and methods might be affected by this feature. The resource type defines the type of information system resource emulated by the honeypot. The resource type can be defined on protocol level, which in this use case can include typical protocols used in medical devices. To support the effectiveness of the honeypot sensor, also the deployment strategy should be considered. This feature indicates the tactics of deploying honeypots in a defined operating environment. A wide variety of approaches can be selected to support priorities of technical visibility.

4   Conclusion

This study proposes a new construction model to specify how medical devices can be modelled with honeypots. The main attributes identified behind this model are threats facing the healthcare environment, typical technical characteristics of the medical devices and challenges in technical visibility. Sensor technology based on the honeypots can offer added value by gaining technical visibility in areas that are typically challenging in a defined operating environments. It can be concluded that the honeypots can be used to model the assets under review.

For future research, the effectiveness of this model should be demonstrated in production. Additionally, a deeper technical specification of protocol level modelling should be defined. While a plethora of different resource type specific honeypots are available, appropriate ones should be selected. Additionally, it should be noted that the usability of sensor data is dependent on capabilities to process this data. This phase supports the comprehension of the elements which have been perceived from the cyber environment. Hence, future research topics should also include cooperation with technologies such as security information and event management (SIEM). The usability of honeypot sensor data in terms of SIEM use cases should be evaluated.

Acknowledgement. This research is partially funded by the Regional Council of Central Finland/Council of Tampere Region and European Regional Development Fund as part of the *Health Care Cyber Range (HCCR)* project of JAMK University of Applied Sciences the Institute of Information Technology.

References

1. Akbanov, M., Vassilakis, V.: Wannacry ransomware: analysis of infection, persistence, recovery prevention and propagation mechanisms. J. Telecommun. Inf. Technol. **1**, 113–124 (2019). https://doi.org/10.26636/jtit.2019.130218
2. Anagnostakis, K.G., Sidiroglou, S., Akritidis, P., Xinidis, K., Markatos, E., Keromytis, A.D.: Detecting targeted attacks using shadow honeypots. In: Proceedings of the 14th Conference on USENIX Security Symposium - vol. 14, p. 9. SSYM 2005, USENIX Association, USA (2005)
3. Anwar, A.H., Kamhoua, C., Leslie, N.: Honeypot allocation over attack graphs in cyber deception games. In: 2020 International Conference on Computing, Networking and Communications (ICNC), pp. 502–506, February 2020. https://doi.org/10.1109/ICNC47757.2020.9049764
4. Basnet, R., Mukherjee, S., Pagadala, V.M., Ray, I.: An efficient implementation of next generation access control for the mobile health cloud. In: 2018 Third International Conference on Fog and Mobile Edge Computing (FMEC), pp. 131–138, April 2018. https://doi.org/10.1109/FMEC.2018.8364055
5. Bauer, J., Goltz, J., Mundt, T., Wiedenmann, S.: Honeypots for threat intelligence in building automation systems. In: 2019 Computing, Communications and IoT Applications (ComComAp), pp. 242–246, October 2019. https://doi.org/10.1109/ComComAp46287.2019.9018776
6. Bhargavi, U., Gundibail, S., Manjunath, K., Renuka, A.: Security of medical big data images using decoy technique. In: 2019 International Conference on Automation, Computational and Technology Management (ICACTM), pp. 310–314, April 2019. https://doi.org/10.1109/ICACTM.2019.8776696
7. Davé, N.: Cyberattacks on medical devices are on the rise–and manufacturers must respond. https://spectrum.ieee.org/the-human-os/biomedical/devices/cyber-attacks-on-medical-devices-are-on-the-riseand-manufacturers-must-respond (2019). Accessed 29 April 2020

8. Djanali, S., Arunanto, F.X., Pratomo, B.A., Baihaqi, A., Studiawan, H., Shiddiqi, A.M.: Aggressive web application honeypot for exposing attacker's identity. In: 2014 The 1st International Conference on Information Technology, Computer, and Electrical Engineering, pp. 212–216, November 2014. https://doi.org/10.1109/ICITACEE.2014.7065744

9. Endsley, M.: Toward a theory of situation awareness in dynamic systems. Hum. Factors **37**(1), 32–64 (1995). https://doi.org/10.1518/001872095779049543

10. European Commission: Medical Devices. https://ec.europa.eu/growth/sectors/medical-devices_en (2020). Accessed 17 May 2020

11. Fadlullah, Z.M., et al.: Combating against attacks on encrypted protocols. In: 2007 IEEE International Conference on Communications, pp. 1211–1216 (2007)

12. Forescout Technologies Inc: putting healthcare security under the microscope. https://www.forescout.com/company/resources/forescout-healthcare-report/ (2019). Accessed 20 April 2020

13. Fraunholz, D., Zimmermann, M., Schotten, H.D.: An adaptive honeypot configuration, deployment and maintenance strategy. In: 2017 19th International Conference on Advanced Communication Technology (ICACT), pp. 53–57, February 2017. https://doi.org/10.23919/ICACT.2017.7890056

14. Ihanus, J.: Expanding Cyber Situation Awareness with Honeypots in Corporate Environment. M. eng. thesis, Jyväskylä University of Applied Sciences, Finland (2019)

15. Kovanen, T., David, G., Hämäläinen, T.: Survey: intrusion detection systems in encrypted traffic, vol. 9870, pp. 281–293, September 2016. https://doi.org/10.1007/978-3-319-46301-8_23

16. Lihet, M., Dadarlat, V.: Honeypot in the cloud five years of data analysis. In: 2018 17th RoEduNet Conference: Networking in Education and Research (RoEduNet), pp. 1–6, September 2018. https://doi.org/10.1109/ROEDUNET.2018.8514128

17. Mayorga, F., Vargas, J., Álvarez, E., Martinez, H.D.: Honeypot network configuration through cyberattack patterns. In: 2019 International Conference on Information Systems and Computer Science (INCISCOS), pp. 150–155, November 2019. https://doi.org/10.1109/INCISCOS49368.2019.00032

18. van der Meulen, R.: Build adaptive security architecture into your organization. https://www.gartner.com/smarterwithgartner/build-adaptive-security-architecture-into-your-organization/, Jun 2017. Accessed 3 April 2020

19. Mokube, I., Adams, M.: Honeypots: concepts, approaches, and challenges, pp. 321–326, January 2007. https://doi.org/10.1145/1233341.1233399

20. Myllykangas, T.: You need to patch the bluekeep rdp vulnerability (CVE-2019-0708).https://blog.f-secure.com/patch-bluekeep-rdp-vulnerability-cve-2019-0708/ (2019). Accessed 29 April 2020

21. Nagpal, B., Singh, N., Chauhan, N., Sharma, P.: Catch: comparison and analysis of tools covering honeypots. In: 2015 International Conference on Advances in Computer Engineering and Applications, pp. 783–786, March 2015. https://doi.org/10.1109/ICACEA.2015.7164809

22. Nelson, R., Staggers, N.: Health Informatics - E-Book: An Interprofessional Approach. Elsevier Health Sciences (2016). https://books.google.fi/books?id=eROwDQAAQBAJ

23. Palo Alto Networks, Unit 42: 2020 Unit 42 IoT Threat Report. https://unit42.paloaltonetworks.com/iot-threat-report-2020/ (2020). Accessed 3 May 2020

24. Puuska, S., Kokkonen, T., Alatalo, J., Heilimo, E.: Anomaly-based network intrusion detection using wavelets and adversarial autoencoders. In: Lanet, J.-L., Toma, C. (eds.) SECITC 2018. LNCS, vol. 11359, pp. 234–246. Springer, Cham (2019). https://doi.org/10.1007/978-3-030-12942-2_18

25. Rogova, G.L., Ilin, R.: Reasoning and decision making under uncertainty and risk for situation management. In: 2019 IEEE Conference on Cognitive and Computational Aspects of Situation Management (CogSIMA), pp. 34–42 (2019). https://doi.org/10.1109/COGSIMA.2019.8724330

26. Sahu, A., Mao, Z., Davis, K., Goulart, A.E.: Data processing and model selection for machine learning-based network intrusion detection. In: 2020 IEEE International Workshop Technical Committee on Communications Quality and Reliability (CQR), pp. 1–6 (2020)

27. Shostack, A.: Threat Modeling: Designing for Security. John Wiley and Sons Inc, BoulevardIndianapolis (2014)

28. The European Union Agency for Network and Information Security (ENISA): smart hospitals, security and resilience for smart health service and infrastructure, November 2016. https://doi.org/10.2824/28801

29. Tian, W., et al: Prospect theoretic study of honeypot defense against advanced persistent threats in power grid. IEEE Access, pp. 1–1 (2020). https://doi.org/10.1109/ACCESS.2020.2984795

30. TrapX Labs - A Division of TrapX Security Inc: ANATOMY OF AN ATTACK: MEDJACK (Medical Device Hijack). https://trapx.com/trapx-labs-report-anatomy-of-attack-medical-device-hijack-medjack/ (2015). Accessed 29 April 2020

31. U.S Food and Drug Administration: MAUDE Adverse Event Report: GE HEALTHCARE MACLAB. https://www.accessdata.fda.gov/scripts/cdrh/cfdocs/cfMAUDE/Detail.CFM?MDRFOI_ID=3239402 (2013). Accessed 21 May 2020

32. U.S Food and Drug Administration: MAUDE Adverse Event Report: MERGE HEALTHCARE MERGE HEMO PROGRAMMABLE DIAGNOSTIC COMPUTER. https://www.accessdata.fda.gov/scripts/cdrh/cfdocs/cfmaude/detail.cfm?mdrfoi_id=5487204 (2016). Accessed 21 May 2020

33. U.S Food and Drug Administration: Postmarket Management of Cybersecurity in Medical Devices. https://www.fda.gov/media/95862/download (2016). Accessed 15 May 2020

34. U.S Food and Drug Administration: Department of health and human services, Medical Devices, Part 820, Quality System Regulation. https://www.accessdata.fda.gov/scripts/cdrh/cfdocs/cfcfr/CFRSearch.cfm?CFRPart=820&showFR=1&subpartNode=21:8.0.1.1.12.3 (2019). Accessed 21 May 2020

35. Vectra: 2019 Spotlight Report: Healthcare's legacy infrastructure of unmanaged devices exposes a vulnerable attack surface. https://www.vectra.ai/download/spotlight-report-on-healthcare-2019#form-download (2019). Accessed 16 May 2020

36. Vetterl, A., Clayton, R.: Honware: a virtual honeypot framework for capturing CPE and IoT zero days. In: 2019 APWG Symposium on Electronic Crime Research (eCrime), pp. 1–13, November 2019. https://doi.org/10.1109/eCrime47957.2019.9037501

37. Wafi, H., Fiade, A., Hakiem, N., Bahaweres, R.B.: Implementation of a modern security systems honeypot honey network on wireless networks. In: 2017 International Young Engineers Forum (YEF-ECE), pp. 91–96, May 2017. https://doi.org/10.1109/YEF-ECE.2017.7935647

38. Wang, H., Wu, B.: SDN-based hybrid honeypot for attack capture. In: 2019 IEEE 3rd Information Technology, Networking, Electronic and Automation Control Conference (ITNEC), pp. 1602–1606, March 2019. https://doi.org/10.1109/ITNEC.2019.8729425
39. Xu, Y., Tran, D., Tian, Y., Alemzadeh, H.: Poster abstract: analysis of cybersecurity vulnerabilities of interconnected medical devices. In: 2019 IEEE/ACM International Conference on Connected Health: Applications, Systems and Engineering Technologies (CHASE), pp. 23–24 (2019)
40. Yaqoob, T., Abbas, H., Atiquzzaman, M.: Security vulnerabilities, attacks, countermeasures, and regulations of networked medical devices–a review. IEEE Commun. Surv. Tutorials **21**(4), 3723–3768 (2019). https://doi.org/10.1109/COMST.2019.2914094

High Density Internet of Things Network Analysis

Alexander Paramonov[1,2]([✉]), Evgeny Tonkikh[3], Andrey Koucheryavy[1],
and Tatiana M. Tatarnikova[4]

[1] St. Petersburg State University of Telecommunication,
22 Prospekt Bolshevikov, St. Petersburg, Russia
`alex-in-spb@yandex.ru`
[2] Peoples' Friendship University of Russia (RUDN University),
6 Miklukho-Maklaya St., Moscow 117198, Russia
[3] Radio Research and Development Institute (NIIR),
Bolshoi Smolensky pr., D. 4, St. Petersburg, Russia
[4] Russian State Hydrometeorological University,
Voronezhskaya ulitsa, 79, St. Petersburg, Russia

Abstract. This article presents results of Internet of things network modeling as an ad hoc network. The main attention is paid to the features of the functioning of such a network in high density conditions, up to 1 device per square meter. The paper presents the results of evaluations of the basic operating conditions, namely, the level of interference from neighboring network nodes and the signal-to-noise ratio. The results obtained show that such a network can remain connected, but construction of relatively long routes is required. The developed models make it possible to express the dependence of the noise level and signal-to-noise ratio on the network density, produced traffic, and transmitter power.

Keywords: Internet of things · High density · Interference · Signal to noise ratio · Attenuation · Traffic · Routing

1 Introduction

Today various estimates and forecasts are known regarding the growth rate and the number of Internet things [1–7], however, they all agree that the number of Internet things will grow steadily and will significantly exceed the number of subscriber terminals and people in general. It should be expected that the IoT network will have a high density of devices, which is estimated as such as 1 device per 1 m^2 [8]. It is also intended to use wireless technologies for building IoT networks, at least at the access level.

In the general case, the functioning of such a network depends on the location of its nodes and on the environment, which affect the propagation of the signal between the nodes. It is worth noting that most often they operate with such forecasts and estimates in the context of a flat model, i.e. speaking of the density of devices (Internet of things) as the quantity per unit area. Such a model is not always convenient, especially if the

© Springer Nature Switzerland AG 2020
O. Galinina et al. (Eds.): NEW2AN 2020/ruSMART 2020, LNCS 12525, pp. 307–316, 2020.
https://doi.org/10.1007/978-3-030-65726-0_27

communication zone of the network nodes is not large, and the network itself is located in multi-storey buildings, i.e. takes up some volume. In this case, it is not entirely clear what is meant by density per unit area: a "flat" model with a given density of devices on each floor of a building, or the total density of devices as a result of their projection from all floors to the base of the building. The difference between these models can be quite significant.

Also, the capabilities of such a network are largely determined by the choice of its structure. With a star-shaped network structure, for example, when devices are connected to base stations of a mobile network, their number in the coverage area of the base station, according to the forecasts, can be close to a million or even several million (depending on coverage area). Serving such a number of devices may either be impossible at all or create problems for the communication network.

It should also be noted that along with the indisputable advantages of a centralized network, it also has a number of disadvantages, one of which is that its survivability is determined by the survivability of the base station and the network equipment associated with it, as well as with the possibility of its congestion in case of uncontrolled traffic growth.

Based on the foregoing, it can be noted that the construction of the IW network as an ad hoc network [9] allows us to solve a number of problems related to the problems noted above. This presupposes the construction of the IW network as a self-organizing network capable of delivering traffic over considerable distances using only the communication capabilities of the nodes of the IW network [10–12]. Typically, these networks are decentralized and use random access technologies. This leads to mutual interference produced by the network nodes during data transmission. Naturally, the level of this interference depends on the power of the node transmitters, the conditions of signal propagation, the number of network nodes (network density) and the intensity of the traffic they produce [13, 14].

Let us evaluate the potential capabilities of such a network depending on the traffic intensity, radiated signal power, and node density. To do this, we first consider a "flat" model in which network nodes are randomly distributed within the service area. We assume that the power of the emitted signal is the same for all nodes of the network.

2   Network Modeling

Due to the additive nature, the interference power p_{0I} at any point o of the served territory is the sum of the powers of all signal sources, taking into account attenuation in the propagation medium p_{oj}

$$p_{0I} = \sum_{j=1}^{n} p_{oj} \, \text{W} \tag{1}$$

It is obvious that the signal sources located near the receiving node can create a level of interference at which reception of the target signal will be impossible. In this case, the separation of the channel resource by time is used. We assume that the transmission and reception of the target signal is not performed when the receiving node receives one or more signals, the level of each of which exceeds a certain threshold value p_m.

In this case, the interference at the receiving point is created only by signals, each of which does not exceed a given threshold level. In the case of a homogeneous propagation medium and equal power of all signal sources and a circular antenna pattern, the nodes that create interference will be located outside the circle (Fig. 1) or sphere in a 3-dimensional model with a center at the receiving point and a radius defined as

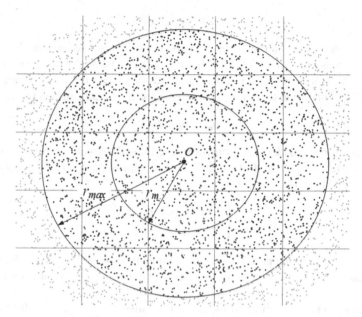

Fig. 1. Signal and interference areas.

$$r_m = \arg\{p_0 - a(r) = p_m\} \tag{2}$$

where p_0 is the radiated signal power level (dBm), p_m is the threshold power level (dBm), $a(r)$ is the attenuation introduced by the propagation of the signal over a distance r (dB).

Let us give the conditional names to the regions inside the circle and outside it as the signal region and the interference region, respectively.

To select a damping model, consider the model recommended in P.1411–10 [15]

$$a(r) = 10\gamma \lg f + 10\alpha \lg r + \beta \text{ dB} \tag{3}$$

where f is the frequency (GHz), r is the distance (m).

The numerical values of the parameters of these models depend on the conditions of their application. γ - corrects the dependence of the attenuation in the propagation medium on the signal frequency, α - determines the attenuation growth with distance, β - a constant coefficient. When modeling, we take $\alpha = 2.12$, $\beta = 29.2$, $\gamma = 2.11$.

Then the interference power at an arbitrary point o can be determined as

$$p_{oI} = \sum_{j=1}^{n} I_j p_{oj} \tag{4}$$

where $I_j = \begin{cases} 1 & p_{oj} \leq p_m \\ 0 & p_{oj} > p_m \end{cases}$ is the indicator function,

$$p_{oj} = \tilde{p}_o - a(r_{oj}) \, \text{dBm}, \tag{5}$$

r_{oj} the distance between the observation point and the j-th network node.

The value $\tilde{p}_o$ is random, we assume that it is equal to the power of the emitted signal p_0 when the node transmits data and is equal to zero when there is no transmission. Transitions from one state to another are determined by the transmitted traffic. Then

$$\tilde{p}_o = p_0 \mu(t) \tag{6}$$

where $\mu(t)$ is a binary random time function describing the stream of frames transmitted by the transmitter of the node. In fact, this is formal representation of the binary random stream generated by node. It can be described as

$$\mu(t) = \begin{cases} 1 & t_0 + \alpha < t \leq t + \tau \\ 0 & \text{in other case} \end{cases},$$

where t_0 is the initial moment of time, α is a random time interval between the moments of frame transmission, τ is a random time interval equal to the time of transmission of the frame.

Properties $\mu(t)$ are determined by the laws of distribution α and τ. In the general case, model (5) should accurately describe the traffic produced by the node. For this purpose, it is necessary to choose the appropriate laws of α distribution and τ. However, in the framework of this problem, the value of interference (4) is more important, which is the sum of signals from a large number of sources and represents an aggregated stream. According to [16], the properties of this flow will be close to the properties of the simplest flow. The distribution of the average value p_{oI} depends on the distribution of distances to the signal sources and the dependence of the attenuation on the distance, i.e. from the assumptions made in the model.

The average value of traffic intensity ρ determines the fraction of the time during which the node transmits a signal. We assume that it is the same for all network nodes.

3　Modeling Results

Obviously, under the conditions of the accepted restrictions, the intensity of the traffic produced by each of the network nodes will be limited by the number of nodes located in the signal area, i.e. threshold value pm.

$$\rho\text{max} = \frac{1}{\pi r_m^2 d} \tag{7}$$

where d is the device density $1/m^2$, r_m is the radius of the signal region, according to (2).

For example, under the assumptions made and $p_0 = 20$ dBm (0.1 W), $p_m = -70$ dBm, the radius of the signal zone is $r_m \approx 63$ m, and $\rho_{max} \approx 8 \cdot 10^{-5}$. The value ρ_{max} only demonstrates the upper limit, which occurs when the channel is fully occupied, which is practically unattainable. In a real network, traffic intensity should be significantly less.

For modeling, a network was selected in the area of 200×200 m, with random placement of network nodes. Threshold value $p_m = -70$ dBm. As the results of simulation modeling showed, the distribution of the interference power level at an arbitrary point in the service area with the accepted model parameters can be quite accurately described by the normal distribution, Fig. 2.

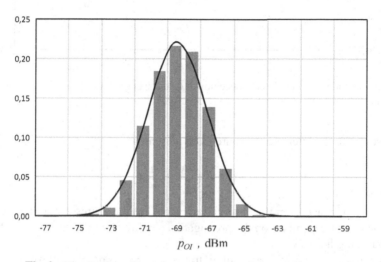

Fig. 2. Distribution of interference power level at an arbitrary point.

In Fig. 3 shows the dependence of the average interference power at an arbitrary point on the intensity of traffic produced by network nodes. The traffic intensity is understood as the fraction of the time the channel uses the node. In this case, the power of each of the network nodes is $p_0 = 0.1$ W or 0.01 W (level 20 and 10 dBm, respectively).

The analytical formation of the interference signal model is described by the following expression

$$p_{OI} = d_0 \iint\limits_C k(x, y)dxdy \qquad (8)$$

where d_0 is the interference power produced per unit area W/m^2,

$k(x, y)$ -coefficient determining the dependence of the interference power at point O on the coordinates of the interference source,

C is the area under consideration.

With some approximation, based on model (3), and also taking into account the network model under consideration, Fig. 1, the dependence can be expressed in terms

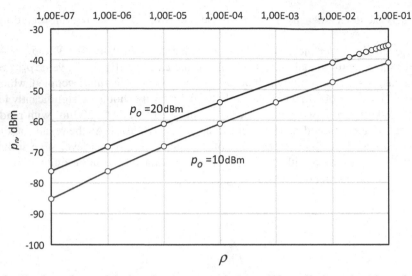

Fig. 3. The dependence of the interference power on the specific traffic intensity (channel use by one device) at a power level of each device of 20 dBm.

of the distance to the interference source and presented

$$k(r) = \left(\frac{\lambda}{4\pi}\right)^2 \frac{1}{r^\alpha} \qquad (9)$$

where r is the distance from the observation point O to the source of interference,

α - coefficient depending on the propagation conditions of the signal ($\alpha \geq 2$),

λ - wavelength (m).

Taking into account (9), according to model (8), using the transition to polar coordinates, we can calculate

$$p_{OI} = \int_{r_m}^{r_{max}} rk(r)dr \int_0^{2\pi} d\phi = 2\pi \left(\frac{\lambda}{4\pi}\right)^2 \int_{r_m}^{r_{max}} r^{1-\alpha}dr \qquad (10)$$

r_m is the radius of the signal region, according to (2), r_{max} is the radius of the interference region, $k(r)$ is the dependence of signal attenuation on distance (9).

Finally, the dependence of the interference power at a point on the parameters of the region under consideration can be expressed as

$$p_{OI} = \begin{cases} \frac{d_0\lambda^2}{8\pi} \ln \frac{r_{max}}{r_m}, & \alpha = 2 \\ \frac{d_0\lambda^2}{8\pi(\alpha-2)} \left(r_m^{2-\alpha} - r_{max}^{2-\alpha}\right), & \alpha > 2 \end{cases} \text{W}, \qquad (11)$$

r_m is the radius of the signal region, according to (2), r_{max} is the radius of the interference region, $k(r)$ is the dependence of signal attenuation on distance.

The value of r_{max} is determined by the actual size of the zone of reception of signals from surrounding sources. In practice, this is a line of sight. Under urban conditions, this zone is probably determined by the distance to the nearest buildings. In the simulation, it was taken equal to 500 m.

Figure 4 shows the dependences of the average interference power at an arbitrary point on the network density (the number of nodes per m^2) obtained by simulation (black curve) and analytical model (11).

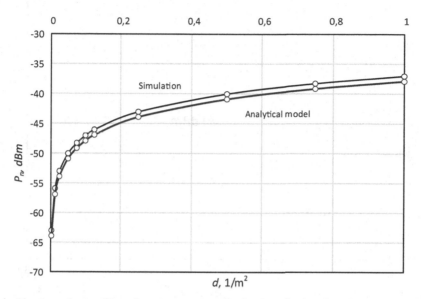

Fig. 4. The dependence of interference power on the density of network nodes at a power level of each device of 20 dBm.

As can be seen, the results of both models are quite close. The difference between them is due to slightly different modeling conditions (the shape and size selected in the simulation of the region).

To establish communication with neighboring nodes in the IV network, it is required to provide some level of signal-to-noise ratio (SNR). Here, the noise level should be understood as the total power of the interference signals and other non-target signals at the input of the receiver. However, given that the interference signal from the network nodes significantly exceeds the level of natural interference, we will consider in relation to SNR, only the interference signal. Let us evaluate the dependence of SNR on the distance between network nodes using the attenuation model mentioned above.

$$SNR(r) = p_0 - a(r) - P_{OI} \text{ dB} \tag{12}$$

where P_{OI} is the interference power level generated by the network nodes at the considered point (dBm), p_0 is the power of the signal radiated by the network node (dBm), $a(r)$ is the distance attenuation (dB).

Figure 5 shows the dependence of SNR on distance for various threshold levels p_m. Naturally, for different levels, different traffic intensities are acceptable, as noted above. When modeling was adopted intensity $\rho = \rho_{\max}/2$.

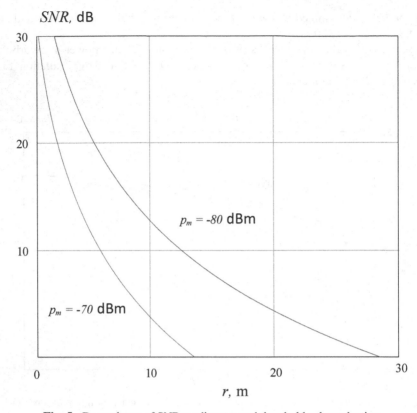

Fig. 5. Dependence of SNR on distance and threshold value selection.

We assume that the acceptable SNR is more than 5 dB, then the distance between the nodes of the receiver and transmitter should be no more than 20 m at $p_m = -80$ dBm and 10 m at $p_m = -70$ dBm.

Thus, it can be noted that the real values of the distances when transmitting traffic between network nodes with a node density of 1 1/m^2 in the route will be no more than 20 m, and the traffic intensity is about $1 \cdot 10^{-5}$.

The distance values from Fig. 5 can be interpreted as the expected communication radius of the node taking into account interference, then the potential connectivity of the network can be estimated.

4   Conclusions

The proposed models make it possible to evaluate the dependence of the level of mutual interference of nodes and the signal-to-noise ratio on the density of nodes and the intensity of the traffic of the IoT network. This allows us to draw conclusions about the length of routes in the ad hoc network.

The study of the obtained models showed that an increase in the density of the IoT network leads to an increase in mutual interference between nodes and a decrease in the signal-to-noise ratio. This leads to the need to reduce the distance between nodes included in the data delivery route, i.e. to increase its length. On the one hand, this leads to an increase in data delivery delays, but on the other hand, it ensures network connectivity in difficult conditions.

The results are obtained for conditions of random placement of nodes in a homogeneous signal propagation medium. The choice of other signal propagation models will influence the results of numerical estimates, however, general trends are likely to continue.

In the framework of further research, modeling of an inhomogeneous signal propagation environment, which may take place in urban conditions, as well as the study of dependencies for various wavelengths, is of interest. It is probably possible to reduce the mutual influences of network nodes with increasing signal frequency due to greater attenuation in an inhomogeneous propagation medium.

Acknowledgement. The publication has been prepared with the support of the "RUDN University Program 5–100".

References

1. Wortmann, F., Flüchter, K.: Internet of Things. Telecommunication **57**(3), 221–224 (2015). https://doi.org/10.1007/s12599-015-0383-3
2. Borodin, A.S., Kucheryavy, A.E.: Communication networks of the fifth generation as the basis of the digital economy. Telecommunication **5**, 45–49 (2017)
3. Kucheryavy, A.E., Borodin, A.S., Kirichek, R.V.: Communication networks 2030. Telecommunication **11**, 52–56 (2018)
4. Solomitckii, D., Gapeyenko, M., Semkin, V., Andreev, S., Koucheryavy, Y.: Technologies for efficient amateur drone detection in 5G millimeter-wave cellular infrastructure. IEEE Commun. Mag., **56**(1), 43–50 (2018). Art. no. 8255736
5. Galinina, O., Tabassum, H., Mikhaylov, K., Andreev, S., Hossain, E., Koucheryavy, Y.: On feasibility of 5G-grade dedicated RF charging technology for wireless-powered wearables. IEEE Wireless Commun. **23**(2), 28–37 (2016). Art. no. 7462482
6. Petrov, V., et al.: Vehicle-based relay assistance for opportunistic crowdsensing over narrowband IoT (NB-IoT). IEEE Internet Things J. **5**(5), 3710–3723 (2018). Art. no. 7857676
7. Ometov, A., et al.: Feasibility characterization of cryptographic primitives for constrained (wearable) IoT devices. In: 2016 IEEE International Conference on Pervasive Computing and Communication Workshops, PerCom Workshops 2016, Art. no. 7457161 (2016)
8. Borodin, A.S., Kucheryavy, A.E., Paramonov, A.I.: Features of the use of D2D technologies depending on the density of users and devices. Telecommunication **10**, 40–45 (2018)
9. Barbeau, M., Kranakis, E.: Principles of Ad-hoc Networking, p. 254. Wiley, Hoboken (2007)
10. Hussein, O.A., Paramonov, A.I., Kucheryavy, A.E.: Analysis of the clustering of D2D devices in fifth-generation networks. Telecommunications. **9**, 32–38 (2018)
11. Nurilloev, I.N., Paramonov, A.I., Kucheryavy, A.E.: A method for assessing and ensuring the connectivity of a wireless sensor network. Telecommunications, **7**, 39–44 (2017)
12. Buzyukov, L.B., Okuneva, L.B., Paramonov, A.I.: Problems of building wireless sensor networks. Proc. Educ. Inst. Commun. **3**(1), 5–12 (2017)
13. Borodin, A.S., Kucheryavy, A.E., Paramonov, A.I.: Features of the use of d2d-technology depending on the density of users and devices. Telecommunications **10**, 40–45 (2018)

14. Borodin, A.S., Kucheryavy, A.E., Paramonov, A.I.: A method for constructing a communication network based on D2D technologies using additional routers. Telecommunications **4**, 20–26 (2019)
15. Recommendation ITU-R P.1411-10, Propagation data and prediction methods for the planning of short-range outdoor radiocommunication systems and radio local area networks in the frequency range 300 MHz to 100 GHz, Geneva (2019)
16. Raygorodsky, A.M.: Models of random graphs and their applications. WORKS OF MIPT, vol. 2, no. 4, pp. 130–139 (2010)
17. Bollobás, B.: Random Graphs, 520 c. Cambridge University Press, Cambridge (2001)
18. Nurilloev, I.N., Paramonov, A.I.: Effective connectivity of the wireless sensor network. Telecommunications **3**, 68–74 (2018)

Dynamic Programming Method for Traffic Distribution in LoRaWAN Network

Mohammed Saleh Ali Muthanna[1,2], Ping Wang[3], Min Wei[3(✉)],
Waleed Al-mughalles[1], and Ahsan Rafiq[1]

[1] School of Computer Science and Technology, Chongqing University of
Posts and Telecommunications, Chongqing, China
muthanna@mail.ru, waleedalmoghales@gmail.com,
asn_rafiq@hotmail.com
[2] Department of Automation and Control Processes Saint Petersburg, Electrotechnical
University "LETI" Saint Petersburg, St. Petersburg, Russia
[3] School of Automation,
Chongqing University of Posts and Telecommunications, Chongqing, China
{wangping,weimin}@cqupt.edu.cn

Abstract. Internet of things (IoT) allows millions of devices to be connected, measured, monitored to automate processes, and support better decision making. On the other hand, these IoT devices demand cost-effective, long-range, and power-efficient sensors and actuators. LoRaWAN can be considered as a promising way to overcome these issues. By leveraging LoRaWAN protocol into IoT systems, it will help to optimize energy consumption, capacity, cost, and coverage of the system. This study proposes a scheme for modeling the LoRAWAN network based on the availability of several independent radio frequency channels. As part of this approach, we also offer a model and calculation method. Numerical results show the efficacy of our proposed scheme.

Keywords: IoT · LoRaWAN · Radiofrequency · Traffic distribution

1 Introduction

Internet of Things (IoT) applications [1] are required more technologies that can offer low-power operation, low-cost and low-complexity end devices that will be able to communicate over large distances wirelessly. As in most cases, the IoT end devices are battery-powered sensor nodes, and the power usage profile should be carefully designed to extend the battery lifetime. The communication range needs to go from different hundreds of meters up to different kilometers, as end devices are distributed over a large area of operation. Considering all the characteristics mentioned above, this can be only be realized by using a low power wide area network (LPWAN) technologies. Various LPWAN technologies are already present in the market: SigFox [2], NB-IoT [3], or LoRaWAN [4].

LoRaWAN is one of the media access control (MAC) protocol for broad area network. It aims to allow low powered devices to interact with Internet-connected applications

© Springer Nature Switzerland AG 2020
O. Galinina et al. (Eds.): NEW2AN 2020/ruSMART 2020, LNCS 12525, pp. 317–325, 2020.
https://doi.org/10.1007/978-3-030-65726-0_28

over long-range wireless connections. This protocol can be scheduled to the second and third layers of the OSI model and performed on top of Frequency Shift Keying (FSK) modulation or LoRa in scientific, industrial, and medical (ISM) radio bands. Also, the protocol is defined via the LoRa Alliance and formalized in the LoRaWAN Specification and Regional Parameters [5, 6].

LoRaWAN technology allows us to implement a cheap and fairly high-quality way to deliver data from points receiving data to the gateway using a wireless channel. In this case, various modes of operation end devices and the gateway can be used [7], which allow selecting different transmission rates and energy consumption of sources modes depending on the requirements of specific applications. Existing LoRAWAN specifications [8, 9] for various countries regulate the use of different frequency bands and different sets of radio frequency channels within these ranges. All specifications provide for several disjoint radio frequency channels that can be used for uplink and downlink connections (uplink and downlink channels). The availability of independent channels allows us to implement various mechanisms for servicing traffic. For example, data transmission using frequency-hopping or simultaneous operation of neighboring stations on different channels can be achieved, which allows improving the quality of communication and system capacity.

We can say that the set of available radio frequency channels is a resource that can be used in a way that is preferable to the solution of a particular application problem. Surprisingly, and to the best of our knowledge, there is limited published works discussing channel access methods for LoRa [10–12]. In this paper, we propose an approach to modeling the LoRaWAN network based on the availability of several independent radio frequency channels. As part of this approach, we also offer a model and calculation method.

The main contribution of this work is to develop a method of optimal traffic distribution between access points, which increases the efficiency of the LoRaWAN network functioning. The method allows for close to the optimal distribution of users between access points. The organization of the paper will be as follows: In Sect. 2, the model and problem formulation. Section 3 provides the methods of distribution Radio Frequency channels. And the conclusion will be given in Sect. 4.

2 Model and Problem Formulation

For more generality, we will not get attached to the specific LoRaWAN specification. Still, we will assume that there are a certain number of radio-frequency channels N connected from each end node to the gateway.

The network structure represents a star topology in the center locate the gateway, as shown in Fig. 1. We will also assume that the communication zone of the gateway is a disk of radius R. A network node located at any point on this disk can transmit or receive data from the gateway.

We assume that all network nodes, the number of which is equal to n, are in the communication zone of one gateway. We also assume that each of the network nodes n_i, $i = 1 \ldots n$, has in its composition one transceiver, i.e., can simultaneously transmit or receive data on only one radio frequency channel. We suppose that the gateway includes

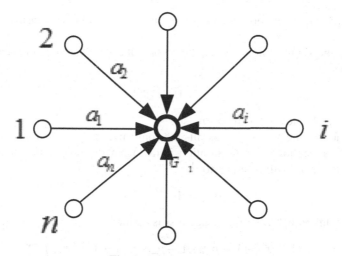

Fig. 1. Network structure

several transceivers, which allows it to transmit or receive simultaneously on any of the available radio frequency channels. It should be noted that the compatibility issue when using several transceivers, was already considered in [9].In this paper, we assume that such an operation is possible. We assume that simultaneous reception or simultaneous transmission on different frequency channels is possible, but not both reception and transmission. Otherwise, the gateway can only receive simultaneously on all channels or simultaneously transmit data on all channels.

Each of the network nodes generates traffic with the intensity of ai messages per unit time, and all nodes of the network generate traffic with the intensity of A messages per unit time. Simultaneous transmission of messages by two or more nodes in one radio frequency channel leads to a collision; as a result, frame loss may occur. Note that the frame loss probability in case of collision is less than unity, both due to different conditions for receiving signals from different nodes and because of the possibilities of the transmission and reception methods used by LoRa technology. In this paper, we consider the estimate of the probability of frame loss from above; i.e., we will assume that the frame is lost in any case when a collision occurs.

Along with collision probability, and delivery probability is also affected by the probability of errors in the frame p_E. This probability depends on the transmission method and propagation conditions of the signal. In general cases, it can be different for different frequency channels.

Note also that if the acknowledged transmission mode is used, then all frames whose transmission began during the transmission of the confirmation message by the gateway will be lost.

Define the overall probability of message loss as

$$p\_m = 1 - (1 - p\_c)(1 - p\_R)(1 - p\_E) \tag{1}$$

The probability of collisions in the channel will be determined as

$$p\_C = p_{\geq 1}(2\tau) = 1 - p\_0(2\tau) \tag{2}$$

Where $p_0(2\tau)$ - is the probability that in interval 2 not begin transmission of any frames.

Assuming the simplest flow model, the probability of collision will be described by the expression

$$p_C = 1 - e^{-a2\tau} \tag{3}$$

Where a – is the flow intensity, frames/s.

We assume that the gateway transmits the confirmation message immediately after the end of the reception, and its duration is tR. Then the probability of losing p_R messages, in this case, will be equal to

$$p_R = 1 - e^{-at_R} \tag{4}$$

Then the total probability of message loss is defined as

$$p_m = 1 - (1 - p_C)(1 - p_R)(1 - p_E) = 1 - (1 - p_E)e^{-a(2\tau + t_R)} \tag{5}$$

In this case, a is the message intensity in one considered channel.

The different frequency channels cannot provide the same transmission conditions in each particular case, for example, due to interference from extraneous radio transmitters, industrial interference, barriers to the distribution signal, the mutual influence between different networks built using the same technology, and other factors.

It means that $p_E^{(i)} \neq p_E^{(j)}$, $i, j = 1 \ldots n$, $i \neq j$. Dependence packet loss probability determined according to (5) is shown in Fig. 2 for different values of pEand tR.

Figure 2 shows that both of these parameters significantly affect the probability of frame delivery, and as showen in Table 1 summarizes all the results with the averaging values between our proposed work and the previous ones. Concerning p_m will also be different for different channels $p_m^{(i)} \neq p_m^{(j)}$, $i, j = 1 \ldots n$, $i \neq j$.

To provide the most efficient use of the radio frequency spectrum (channels), a certain control of the radio frequency resource is required, which will provide the highest quality of traffic service for all network nodes. This can be achieved by redistributing the traffic produced by the network nodes over the available communication channels, taking into account their quality.

3   Methods of Distribution Radio Frequency Channels

The channel distribution task, under the conditions described above, can be formulated as follows. Required to find a display of the set of network nodes n into a plurality of channels C, which performs a specific criterion O

$$f : N \to C \tag{6}$$

$$O = true \tag{7}$$

In this case, f – is some process (function) that allows us to select radio frequency channels to serve the traffic of the network nodes. Criterion O is a condition that determines the desired network status.

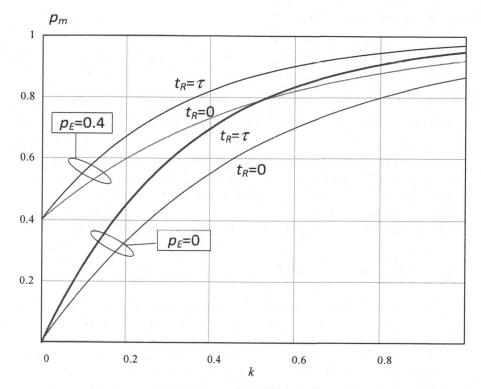

Fig. 2. Dependence of packet loss probability

Table 1. Comparison between proposed and previous works.

Performance Metric	Variables	Number of nodes
		300
	Existing Work	
Average frame loss probability	[10]	0.72 %
	[11]	0.67 %
	[12]	0.57 %
	[Proposed]	0.52 %

We assume that the purpose of the task is to minimize frame loss that can occur, in the general case, due to three reasons: collisions, data transmission by the network node at the moment when the gateway is in a transmission confirmation state, and errors in channel. Then, taking into account (5), we can formulate the optimization problem as the problem of minimizing the number of lost frames with a constant traffic intensity and a constant number of channels.

$$\{k_i\} = \arg\min_{k_i}\left\{\sum_{i=1}^{N} k_i A p_m^{(i)}(k_i)\right\}, \quad i = 1\ldots N, \quad 0 \le k_i \le 1, \quad \sum_{i=1}^{N} k_i = 1 \quad (8)$$

Where N – is the number of radiofrequency channels; A–is the total amount of traffic; Produced by network nodes $A = \sum_{i=1}^{n} a_i, k_i$ - is the share of traffic served by the i-m channel $k_i = a_i/A$.

Formulation (9) means that it is necessary to find such values of ki, i = 1...n, at which the minimum value of the number of lost (per unit time) frames is achieved.

The analytical solution (9) is not expressed in elementary functions. But it can be obtained by numerical methods.

The objective function, taking into account the above, can be written as

$$\{k_i\} = \arg\min_{k_i} \sum_{i=1}^{N} k_i A\left(1 - \left(1 - p_{\_E}^{(i)}\right)e^{-k_i A(2\tau + t_R)}\right), \quad i = 1\ldots N, \quad 0 \le k_i \le 1, \quad \sum_{i=1}^{N} k_i = 1 \quad (9)$$

As an example, we will choose the following parameters $a_i = a = 1$, $i = 1\ldots n$, $n = 100$, $N = 2, p_{\_E}^{(1)} = 0.1, p_{\_E}^{(2)} = 0.5$ we will also assume that $t_R = \tau$.

Solution (10) can be illustrated by the graph shown in Fig. 3.

The solution was obtained by the conjugate gradient method in Mathcad. The point corresponding to the solution of the problem is at a minimum curve formed by the intersection of two surfaces. For the given values k1 = 0,597, k2 = 0,403.

For the practical implementation of the solution to this problem, in our opinion, it is more convenient to make several assumptions and apply the dynamic programming method. We will assume that all nodes of the network generate traffic of the same intensity and that only an integer number of traffic flows can be distributed over frequency channels. Then we slightly modify the objective function (9)

$$L = \sum_{i=1}^{N} \eta_i\left(1 - \left(1 - p_{\_E}^{(i)}\right)e^{-\eta_i a(2\tau + t_R)}\right), \quad i = 1\ldots N, \quad \eta_i \in [0\ldots n], \quad \sum_{i=1}^{N} \eta_i = n \quad (10)$$

Where η_i - is the number of network nodes (traffic flows) served by the i-th channel. To solve this problem, we proposed the following algorithm:

1. Input source data, initialization.

    The number of channels N, the number of nodes n;
    cnt = n – counter of the number of nodes;
    c1, c2, cN– the number of nodes served by the corresponding channel.
    L1, L2,.., LN– values of the objective function.
    The initial number of serviced nodes $\eta_i = 0, \quad i = 1\ldots N$

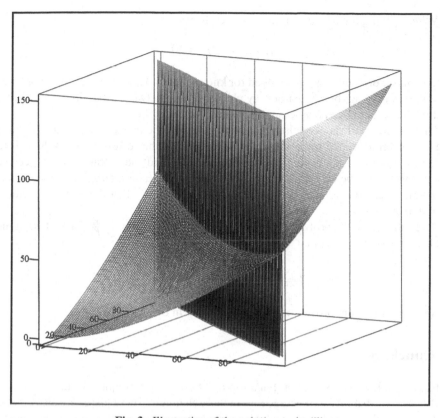

Fig. 3. Illustration of the solution tasks (9)

2. We attempt to increase the number of nodes in each of the channels, and for each of these options, we calculate the value of the objective function: $c_i = \eta_i + 1,\quad L_i = L(c_i),\quad i = 1\ldots N$

We find i for which the value of the objective function is minimal

$$imin = \min_i\{L_i\},\quad i = 1\ldots N$$

We increase per unit the number of serviced nodes for this channel

$$\eta_{imin} = \eta_{imin} + 1,$$

We decrease the node counter
cnt = cnt-1.

3. If cnt = 0, then the values found $\eta_i,\quad i = 1\ldots N$ are a solution to the problem. Stop.

If cnt > 0, then go to step 2.

When solving the above example, we get the values

$$\eta_1 = 60, \quad \eta_2 = 40$$

The above problem has been solved for known values $p^{(i)}_{\_E}$, $i = 1 \ldots N$. In practice, these values may not be known or may change during network operation. Therefore, it is advisable to organize an assessment of these values in the gateway.

One of the methods of such an assessment can be the collection of statistics about received and transmitted frames calculating based on it the corresponding values. If for some time interval T in channel i frames were transmitted and r_i frames were received, then the value can be estimated as follows. If for some time interval T in the channel iK_i frames were transmitted and r_i frames were received, then the value $p^{(i)}_{\_E}$ can be estimated as follows.

The estimate of the probability of frame loss is equal to $\hat{p}^{(i)}_{\_E} = \frac{r_i}{K_i}$. Then, taking into account (5), we can write that

$$p^{(i)}_{\_E} = 1 - \frac{1 - \hat{p}_{\_m}}{e^{-A_i(2\tau + t_R)}}, \quad A_i = \frac{K_i}{T} \tag{11}$$

This measurement procedure can be organized in the gateway.

4 Conclusion

Different conditions of signal propagation in different radio frequency channels lead to the different probability of message loss in these channels. These losses are also affected by the probability of collisions, which depends on the traffic intensity in the channel. Given the unequal properties of the channel, there is such a distribution of traffic on these channels that provides a minimum of lost frames, i.e., optimal distribution. The paper presents an approach to the formation of the problem of traffic distribution over radio frequency channels as optimization problems, and also describes approaches to its solution. In particular, a solution method using the dynamic programming approach is described. Also described is a method of obtaining source data to solve the problem of optimal traffic distribution.

Acknowledgment. This paper is supported by The National Key Research and Development Program of China (2017YFE0123000) and Technology Innovation and Application Development Project of Chongqing (cstc2019jscx-fxydX0018).

References

1. Lin, J., Yu, W., Zhang, N., Yang, X., Zhang, H., Zhao, W.: A survey on internet of things: architecture, enabling technologies, security and privacy, and applications. IEEE Internet Things J. **4**(5), 1125–1142 (2017)
2. Zuniga, J.C., Ponsard, B.: "Sigfox system description," LPWAN@ IETF97, Nov 14th (2016)

3. Wang, H., Fapojuwo, A.O.: A survey of enabling technologies of low power and long range machine-to-machine communications. IEEE Commun. Surv. Tutorials **19**(4), 2621–2639 (2017)
4. Haxhibeqiri, J., De Poorter, E., Moerman, I., Hoebeke, J.: A survey of LoRaWAN for IoT : From Technology to Application. SENSORS 2018 18, 3995:38
5. LoRa Alliance. LoRaWAN Specifications, v1.1, LoRa Alliance: Fremont, CA, USA (2017)
6. Petajajarvi, J., Mikhaylov, K., Roivainen, A., Hanninen, T., Pettissalo, M.: LoRaWAN^{TM} Specifications, V1.0; LoRa Alliance: San Ramon, CA, USA, 2015. On the coverage of lpwans: Range evaluation and channel attenuation model for lora technology. In Proceedings of the 2015 14th International Conference on ITS Telecommunications (ITST), Copenhagen, Denmark, 2–4 December 2015, pp. 55–59 (2015)
7. LoRa Alliance. LoRaWAN Specifications v1.1; LoRa Alliance: Fremont, CA, USA (2017)
8. Bankov, D., Khorov, E., Lyakhov, A.: On the limits of LoRaWAN Channel Access. In: Engineering and Telecommunication, International Conference, pp. 10–14 (2016)
9. Muthanna, M.S.A., Wang, P., Wei, M., Ateya, A.A., Muthanna, A.: Toward an zultra-low latency and energy efficient LoRaWAN. In: Galinina, O., Andreev, S., Balandin, S., Koucheryavy, Y. (eds.) NEW2AN/ruSMART -2019. LNCS, vol. 11660, pp. 233–242. Springer, Cham (2019). https://doi.org/10.1007/978-3-030-30859-9_20
10. Reynders, B., Meert, W., Pollin, S.: Range and coexistence analysis of long range unlicensed communication. In: 2016 23rd International Conference on Telecommunications, ICT, pp. 1–6 (2016)
11. Ferré, G.: Collision and packet loss analysis in a LoRaWAN network. In: 25th European Signal Processing Conference, EUSIPCO2017, vol. 4, pp. 2586–2590 (2017)
12. Casares-Giner, V., Martinez-Bauset, J., Portillo, C.: Performance evaluation of framed slotted ALOHA with reservation packets and successive interference cancelation for M2M networks. Comput. Netw. **155**, 15–30 (2019)

Study of the Accuracy of Determining the Location of Radio Emission Sources with Complex Signals When Using Autocorrelation and Matrix Receivers in Broadband Tools for Analyzing the Electronic Environment

Vladimir P. Likhachev[1], Alexey S. Podstrigaev[2(✉)], Nguyen Trong Nhan[2],
Vadim V. Davydov[3,4,5], and Nikita S. Myazin[3]

[1] Zhukovsky-Gagarin Air Force Academy, Voronezh, Russia
[2] Saint Petersburg Electrotechnical University "LETI", St. Petersburg, Russia
ap0d@ya.ru
[3] Peter the Great Saint Petersburg Polytechnic University, St Petersburg 195251, Russia
[4] The Bonch-Bruevich Saint - Petersburg State University of Telecommunications,
Saint Petersburg 193232, Russia
[5] All-Russian Research Institute of Phytopathology, 143050 Moscow Region, Russia

Abstract. The article presents a study of the accuracy of determining the location of radio emission sources when using autocorrelation and matrix receivers in the spectrum management systems for the reception and processing of complex broadband signals. The ratio of the root mean square errors of determining the location of the radio emission sources using the autocorrelation and matrix receivers is calculated. In addition, the article establishes the feasibility of using an autocorrelation and matrix receivers for various methods for determining the position of a radio emission source. Results of the studies are presented.

Keywords: Autocorrelation receiver · Matrix receiver · Autocorrelation function · Source of radio emission · Location accuracy · RMS location error

1 Introduction

To assess and monitor the correct use of the radio frequency spectrum, spectrum management systems are used. In these systems, an important component is the determination of the position of unauthorized radiation sources. This is especially true for determining the distances between moving objects. [1, 2]. In addition, this is particularly important if there is no direct connection between the two objects since it is necessary to determine the optimal number of intermediate stations and ensure maximum efficiency of information transfer [2, 3]. Recently, complex signals (such as linear frequency

© Springer Nature Switzerland AG 2020
O. Galinina et al. (Eds.): NEW2AN 2020/ruSMART 2020, LNCS 12525, pp. 326–333, 2020.
https://doi.org/10.1007/978-3-030-65726-0_29

modulated (LFM) signals and phase-shift keying (PSK) signals) have been increasingly used to transmit information. It is necessary to improve both interference immunity and covert of operation [4–6]. However, their use creates several difficulties in solving problems of determining the coordinates of the source of radio emission (SRE) [9–12]. Broadband electronic environment analysis tools include, among other things, a multi-stage multi-channel receiver (matrix receiver) [7–10, 13] and an autocorrelation receiver (ACR) [14–17] for recording complex wideband signals and solving these problems.

The matrix receiver contains several stages. When entering the first stage, the input signal is split into several channels and converted to a single intermediate frequency range (IFR) for all channels in the first stage. After that, the signal in the IFR goes to the next stage, in which it is again divided by frequency and converted to the second IFR (single for all channels in the second stage) and so on until the last stage. Each frequency channel in all stages is supplemented by an indicator of the number of the triggered channel. Using a set of triggered indicators, it is possible to determine the frequency of the received signal with an accuracy of half the channel width of the last stage. When calculating the fast Fourier transform (FFT) of the intermediate frequency signal from the last stage output, the original frequency is specified with an accuracy of fewer than 1 MHz. The type of complex signal (LFM and PSK signals) is determined by the width and nature of spectrum change after the FFT made over time samples of the signal. In practice, a matrix receiver with two stages and an output processing unit is often used. This type of receiver will be discussed in this article.

In the autocorrelation receiver, a frequency scan is performed with conversion to a fixed IFR and calculation of the autocorrelation function. To determine the type (LFM, PSK, and simple signals) of modulation of the received signal, additional mathematical operations are performed. In particular, after multiplying the received signal and its delayed copy, the low-frequency component is isolated, and its spectrum is obtained. The same is done with a signal at double frequency. Thus, four spectra are obtained: low-frequency and high-frequency components after autocorrelation of the signal at the initial and doubled frequencies. Then, for each of the four spectra, the width and amplitude of the spectrum are compared with threshold values.

The task of determining the location of the SRE using radio engineering methods on a plane or in space is reduced to measuring geometric quantities that unambiguously characterize the desired location. However, the difference between real and ideal conditions of radio wave propagation, as well as instrumental measurement errors due to the type of receiver, lead to errors in determining the location.

In this regard, the aim of the article is to study the accuracy of determining the location of SRE with complex signals using devices with autocorrelation or matrix receivers, as well as to compare the results obtained.

2   The Ratio of the Root Mean Square Errors of Determining the Location of the Radio Sources Using the Autocorrelation and Matrix Receiver

Consider methods for determining the location of an SRE based on calculating the coordinates of the point of intersection of position lines [11, 12, 18–21]:

- The direction-finding method (Fig. 1): the signal is received at two reception points (points A and B). Then the lines of the position of the radiation source (straight line) are found.

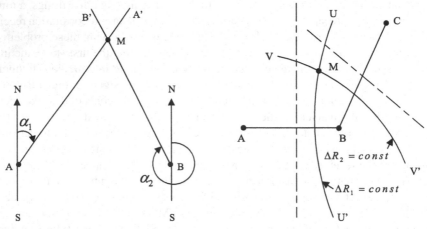

Fig. 1. Angular method for locating a target   **Fig. 2.** Range-difference method for locating a target

- The range-difference method (Fig. 2): the signal is received at the control point (point B) and two reception points (points A and C). Then position lines of the radiation source (hyperbolas) are found.

Although the ellipse of errors of a given probability gives the most complete idea of the accuracy of the location on the plane, a root mean square (RMS) error is used along with it. It is equal to the root of the square covariance error matrix of location errors.

When calculating coordinates using two position lines, the expression for location RMS error is defined as follows [16–19]:

$$R_{sk} = \frac{\sqrt{\sigma_{lp1}^2 + \sigma_{lp2}^2 + 2\rho\sigma_{lp1}\sigma_{lp2}\cos(\gamma)}}{\sin(\gamma)}, \tag{1}$$

where σ_{lp1} and σ_{lp2} are the RMS errors in determining the first and second position lines; ρ is the correlation coefficient of errors in determining position lines; γ is the cross angle (angle between position lines).

RMS error in calculating the line (bearing) is determined as $\sigma_{lp} = R\sigma_\theta$, where R is the distance between SRE and the receiver; $\sigma_\theta = \theta_{0,5}/\sqrt{\pi q_{out}^2}$ is RMS bearing error measured in radians; $\theta_{0,5}$ is the half-power beamwidth measured in radians, q_{out} is the signal to noise ratio (SNR) at the output of the receiver.

For a hyperbolic line of position, the formula is determined as $\sigma_{lp} = \sigma_{\Delta R}/(2\sin(\varphi/2))$, where $\sigma_{\Delta R} = c\sigma_\tau$ is the RMS of the distance difference; c is the speed of light; $\sigma_\tau = 1/\left(\pi\sqrt{q_{out}^2}\Delta f_s\right)$ is the RMS error of the delay time estimating, Δf_s is the signal spectrum width; φ is the angle between focal radius vectors.

In order to compare the RMS location errors of direction-finding (Fig. 1) and range-difference (Fig. 2) methods when using autocorrelation R_{skA} and matrix R_{skM} receivers, let's assume the following:

- the bandwidth Δf_I of the first stage of the matrix receiver is equal to the bandwidth Δf_{HF} of the high-frequency filter of the ACR;
- $\rho = 0$ (the random errors of the position lines are independent);
- $\sigma_{lp1} = \sigma_{lp2} = \sigma_{lp}$;
- SNR at the input q_{in} is the same as the low noise amplifier gain K_u and the same as the radiation pattern width $\theta_{0.5}$;
- The receivers search for SRE that have the same characteristics and are located at the same distance.

With the direction-finding method, the RMS location error is determined as follows:

$$R_{sk} = \frac{\sqrt{2}R\theta_{0.5}}{\sqrt{\pi q_{out}^2 \sin\gamma}}, \tag{2}$$

Notice that SNR at the matrix receiver output $q_{outM} \approx K_u m_1 m_2 q_{in}$, where m_1, m_2 is the amount of the channels of the first and second stages, which is determined by the requirement for the determination accuracy of the SRE signal frequency. Meanwhile, at the output of the ACR $q_{outA} = K_u q_{in}^2 \sqrt{\Delta f_{HF}/\Delta f_{LF}}/\sqrt{1 + 2q_{in}^2}$, where Δf_{LF} is the bandwidth of the low-frequency filter.

Therefore, the relationship takes the following form:

$$\frac{R_{skA}}{R_{skM}} = \frac{\sqrt{q_{outM}^2}}{\sqrt{q_{outA}^2}} = m_1 m_2 \sqrt{\frac{1 + 2q_{in}^2}{q_{in}^2}}\sqrt{\frac{\Delta f_{LF}}{\Delta f_{HF}}}. \tag{3}$$

With the range-difference method, the RMS location error is determined as follows:

$$R_{sk} = \frac{c}{\sqrt{2}\pi\sqrt{q_{out}^2}\Delta f_s \sin(\gamma)\sin(\varphi/2)}. \tag{4}$$

In general, for a matrix receiver, the signal spectrum is divided between channels, one of which is switched to a processing device. Therefore, the width of the band entering the processing is equal to $\Delta f_{sM} = \Delta f_I/(m_1 m_2)$; while for the ACR signal spectrum width $\Delta f_{sA} = \Delta f_{HF}$.

Therefore, the relationship takes the following form:

$$\frac{R_{skA}}{R_{skM}} = \frac{\sqrt{q_{outM}^2}}{\sqrt{q_{outA}^2}}\frac{\Delta f_{sM}}{\Delta f_{sA}} = \sqrt{\frac{1 + 2q_{in}^2}{q_{in}^2}}\sqrt{\frac{\Delta f_{LF}}{\Delta f_{HF}}}. \tag{5}$$

3   Results of the Studies

By changing SNR and the processing bandwidth, let us study the ratio of the RMS location errors of the autocorrelation and matrix receivers when using direction-finding and range-difference methods. Let us set the following initial parameter values: $\Delta f_{LF} = 10\,\text{MHz}$, $m_1 = 6$, $m_2 = 10$. Figures 3 and 4 are correspond to the following parameters: $q_{in} = 0\ldots20\,\text{dB}$ and $\Delta f_{HF} = 500\,\text{MHz}$. Figures 5 and 6 are correspond to the following parameters: $\Delta f_{HF} = 300\ldots500\,\text{MHz}$ and $q_{in} = 0, 5, 10\,\text{dB}$.

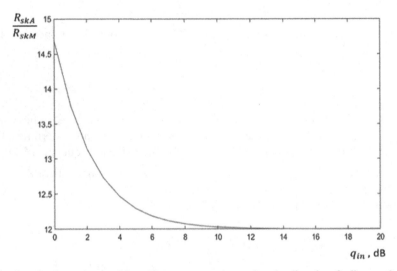

Fig. 3. The dependence of R_{skA}/R_{skM} on q_{in} when using the direction-finding method

Figures 3 and 5 show that with the direction-finding method and $\Delta f_{HF} = 500\,\text{MHz}$, the ACR provides $12.5\ldots14.5$ times better location accuracy at low signal-to-noise ratios ($q_{in} = 0\ldots4\,\text{dB}$) than the matrix receiver. If $q_{in} > 4\,\text{dB}$, the improvement changes slightly and the accuracy tends to be about 12 times better.

When Δf_{HF} decreases from 500 to 300 MHz (at $q_{in} = 0$ dB) the ratio R_{skA}/R_{skM} increases from 14.8 to 19 times. When Δf_{HF} decreases to 300 MHz and $q_{in} = 10\,\text{dB}$, the ratio R_{skA}/R_{skM} increases from 12 to 15.5 times. Further increase of q_{in} practically does not lead to changes in the ratio R_{skA}/R_{skM}.

Figures 4 and 6 show that the autocorrelation receiver has 4–5 times worse SRE location accuracy than the matrix one when using a range-difference method and the

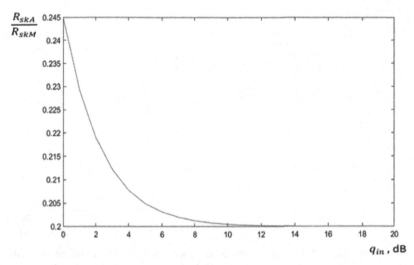

Fig. 4. The dependence of R_{skA}/R_{skM} on q_{in} when using the range-difference method

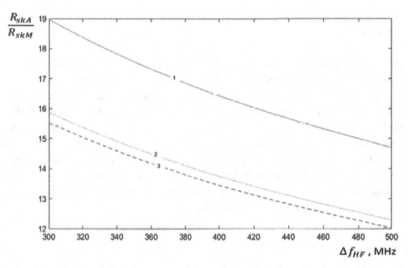

Fig. 5. The dependence of R_{skA}/R_{skM} on Δf_{HF} when using the direction-finding method for different q_{in} values. 1 corresponds to $q_{in} = 0$ dB, 2 corresponds to $q_{in} = 5$ dB, 3 corresponds to $q_{in} = 10$ dB

next set of parameters: $\Delta f_{LF} = 10$ MHz, $\Delta f_{HF} = 500$ MHz, $m_1 = 6$, $m_2 = 10$. In other cases, the nature of the dependencies is preserved. Namely, for $q_{in} > 4$ dB, the ratio R_{skA}/R_{skM} tends to a constant value, and with a decrease in the band Δf_{HF} the ratio R_{skA}/R_{skM} increases. However, at low SNR $q_{in} = -10 \ldots - 5$ dB, $\Delta f_{LF} = 50$ MHz, $\Delta f_{HF} = 500$ MHz, $m_1 = 6$, $m_2 = 10$, improvement of the accuracy of determining the position of the SRE is provided by 1,1 ... 3,2 times.

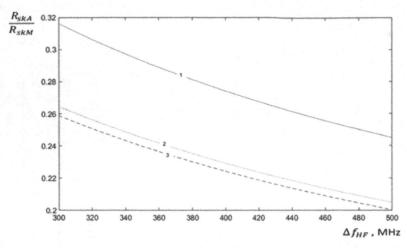

Fig. 6. The dependence of R_{skA}/R_{skM} on Δf_{HF} when using the range-difference method for different q_{in} values. 1 corresponds to $q_{in} = 0$ dB, 2 corresponds to $q_{in} = 5$ dB, 3 corresponds to $q_{in} = 10$ dB

4   Conclusion

The accuracy of the SRE location for the ACR is higher when using the direction-finding method. Improving the accuracy of the SRE of the ACR in comparison with the matrix receiver when using the range-difference method depends on the SNR and the passband of the low-pass filter. When the SNR decreases, the difference between the RMS errors of the methods increases. The difference also increases with a decrease in the processing bandwidth. The main advantage of a matrix receiver compared to an ACR is the instant overview of the entire bandwidth. This eliminates the possibility of skipping the signal from the source (provided the availability of the signal). At the same time, when receiving wideband signals in the matrix receiver, ambiguity in determining the frequency may occur, while in an ACR this drawback is absent.

References

1. Ateya, A.A., Muthanna, A., Vybornova, A., Darya, P., Koucheryavy, A.: Energy - aware offloading algorithm for multi-level cloud based 5G system. In: Galinina, O., Andreev, S., Balandin, S., Koucheryavy, Y. (eds.) NEW2AN/ruSMART -2018. LNCS, vol. 11118, pp. 355–370. Springer, Cham (2018). https://doi.org/10.1007/978-3-030-01168-0_33
2. Simonov, A., Fokin, G., Sevidov, V., Sivers, M., Dvornikov, S.: Polarization direction finding method of interfering radio emission sources. In: Galinina, O., Andreev, S., Balandin, S., Koucheryavy, Y. (eds.) NEW2AN/ruSMART -2019. LNCS, vol. 11660, pp. 208–219. Springer, Cham (2019). https://doi.org/10.1007/978-3-030-30859-9_18
3. Pirmagomedov, R., Blinnikov, M., Kirichek, R., Koucheryavy, A.: Wireless nanosensor network with flying gateway. In: Chowdhury, K.R., Di Felice, M., Matta, I., Sheng, B. (eds.) WWIC 2018. LNCS, vol. 10866, pp. 258–268. Springer, Cham (2018). https://doi.org/10.1007/978-3-030-02931-9_21

4. Garnaev, A., Trappe, W., Petropulu, A.: A prospect theoretic look at a joint radar and communication system. In: Galinina, O., Andreev, S., Balandin, S., Koucheryavy, Y. (eds.) NEW2AN/ruSMART -2018. LNCS, vol. 11118, pp. 483–495. Springer, Cham (2018). https:// doi.org/10.1007/978-3-030-01168-0_43

5. Podstrigaev, A.S., Smolyakov, A.V., Davydov, V.V., Myazin, N.S., Slobodyan, M.G.: Features of the development of transceivers for information and communication systems considering the distribution of radar operating frequencies in the frequency range. In: Galinina, O., Andreev, S., Balandin, S., Koucheryavy, Y. (eds.) NEW2AN/ruSMART -2018. LNCS, vol. 11118, pp. 509–515. Springer, Cham (2018). https://doi.org/10.1007/978-3-030-01168-0_45

6. Podstrigaev, A.S., Davydov, R.V., Rud, V.Yu., Davydov, V.V.: Features of transmission of intermediate frequency signals over fiber-optical communication system in radar station. In: Galinina, O., Andreev, S., Balandin, S., Koucheryavy, Y. (eds.) NEW2AN/ruSMART -2018. LNCS, vol. 11118, pp. 624–630. Springer, Cham (2018). https://doi.org/10.1007/978-3-030-01168-0_56

7. Anderson, G.W., Webb, D.C., Spezio, A.E., Lee, J.N.: Advanced channelization technology for RF, microwave, and millimeterwave applications. Proc. IEEE **79**(3), 355–388 (1991)

8. Grover, R.K.: Disrupting the Net. ECM against Advanced Radars. Signal, no. 3, pp. 10–13 (1978)

9. Tsui, J.: Special Design Topics in Digital Wideband Receivers (2010)

10. Tsui, J.: Digital Techniques for Wideband Receivers (2004)

11. Poisel, R.: Electronic Warfare Target Location Methods. Artech House, Norwood (2005)

12. Zekavat, R., Michael Buehrer, R.: Handbook of Position Location: Theory, Practice, and Advances, 1376 p. Wiley-IEEE Press, Hoboken (2019)

13. Poisel R. Electronic Warfare Receivers and Receiver Systems-Artech (2014)

14. Helton, J., Chen, C.-I.H., Lin, D.M., Tsui, J.B.Y.: FPGA-based 1.2 GHz bandwidth digital instantaneous frequency measurement receiver. In: 9th International Symposium on Quality Electronic Design (2008)

15. Darvin, Ch.R., Paranjape, H., Mohanan, S.K., Elango, V.: Analysis of autocorrelation based frequency measurement algorithm for IFM receivers. In: 2014 IEEE International Conference on Electronics, Computing and Communication Technologies (CONECCT) (2014)

16. Mahlooji, S., Mohammadi, K.: Very high resolution digital instantaneous frequency measurement receiver. In: 2009 International Conference on Signal Processing Systems (2009). https://doi.org/10.1109/icsps.2009.43

17. Lee, Y.-H.G., Helton, J., Chen, C.-I.H.: Real-time FPGA-based implementation of digital instantaneous frequency measurement receiver. In: 2008 IEEE International Symposium on Circuits and Systems (2008). https://doi.org/10.1109/iscas.2008.4541962

18. Friedlander, B.: A passive localization algorithm and its accuracy analysis. IEEE J. Ocean. Eng. **12**(1), 234–245 (1987)

19. Jorrieri, D.J.: Statistical theory of passive location system. IEEE Trans. Aerosp. Electron. Syst. **AES-20**(2), 183–198 (1984)

20. Chen, C.K., Gardner, W. A.: Signal selective time-difference-of-arrival estimation for passive location of manmade signal sources in highly corruptive environments Part II: algorithms and performance. IEEE Trans. Sig. Process. **40**, 1185–1197 (1992)

21. Kupper, A.: Location-based Services: Fundamentals and Operation. Wiley, Hoboken (2005)

Electromagnetic Compatibility Research of Non-standard LTE-1800 TDD Base Stations for Railway Applications and Base Stations LTE-1800 FDD

Sergey Terentyev[3], Mikhail Shelkovnikov[3]($\boxtimes$), Valery Tikhvinskiy[1,2]($\boxtimes$), and Evgeny Deviatkin[2]

[1] Moscow Technical University of Communications and Informatics (MTUCI), Moscow, Russia
vtniir@mail.ru
[2] FSUE Radio Research and Development Institute (NIIR), Moscow, Russia
[3] OJSC GlobalInformService (GIS), Moscow, Russia
s.ter@mail.ru

Abstract. The subject of this article is the study of electromagnetic compatibility (EMC) conditions of LTE-1800 TDD base stations for railway technological communication in a non-standardized frequency band 1785–1805 MHz and LTE-1800 FDD base stations of traditional mobile operator networks for sharing utilization in adjacent band. Research actuality is due to the future deployment of railway technological communication network based on LTE-1800 TDD with the mobile operator networks of LTE-1800 FDD operating in contiguous frequency bands 1710–1785 MHz/1805–1880 MHz and the needs to requirements for sharing spectrum in common location places of such base stations. Provided result of the study allowed to solve EMC problem based on calculated norms of spatial - territorial spacing between LTE-1800 TDD and LTE-1800 FDD base stations.

Keywords: Electromagnetic compatibility · Non-standard LTE-1800 TDD band · Spektrum emission mask · Out of band emission · Spatial - territorial spacing · Inter-band filter

1 Introduction

The band 1710–1885 MHz is allocated by the Radio Regulations to the mobile service on a worldwide basis and can be allocated by national communications administrations for use by any radio technologies included in the IMT family [1]. A part of this frequency band 1785–1805 MHz is allocated by the Russian Communications Administration [2] for the construction technological communication network of LTE standard with time-duplex mode (hereinafter LTE-1800 TDD) for railway transport. However, this frequency band is not part of the frequency bands standardized by the 3GPP Partnership Project for LTE networks with TDD duplex mode. According to the European common allocation (ECA) of frequency bands and national tables in the radio frequency bands

O. Galinina et al. (Eds.): NEW2AN 2020/ruSMART 2020, LNCS 12525, pp. 334–350, 2020.
https://doi.org/10.1007/978-3-030-65726-0_30

1710–1785 MHz and 1805–1880 MHz, mobile communication operators using networks with IMT technology, including LTE-1800 with FDD duplex mode. The task of sharing use ensuring for LTE FDD and LTE TDD networks in adjacent frequency bands was solved for the 2.6 GHz band and conditions for their operation with frequency spacing of adjacent channels of 5 MHz were determined [3]. The Russian communications administration has established 5 MHz frequency spacing requirement to provide an EMC between technological railway network of LTE-1800 TDD (1785–1805 MHz) and traditional mobile networks of LTE-1800 FDD (Band 3). The frequency guard intervals (1785–1790 MHz and 1780–1805 MHz) were established, which do not allow the use of LTE-1800 TDD for the transmission and reception of radio signals.

Moreover, the national regulatory documents do not specify requirements to spectrum emission mask (SEM) and unwanted emission levels of transmitters of base stations(eNB) and user equipment (UE) operating in a non-standardized frequency band 1785–1805 MHz by Partnership project 3GPP to provide EMC. Therefore, the development of requirements for SEM and permissible level of out-of-band emissions (OOB) for LTE-1800 TDD base station transmitters of railway networks are relevant issues of EMC research, as well as development of norms of spatial and territorial separation (STS) between these LTE-1800 TDD with non-standard frequency bands and standard base stations LTE-1800 FDD (Band 3).

2   EMC-Scenarios for Study of LTE-1800 TDD and LTE-1800 FDD Network Sharing

EMC-scenarios of these research can be divided into two groups depending on whether the BS or AS is source of harmful interference (aggressor) as is shown in Fig. 1.

The first group of these scenarios includes EMC- scenarios in which the transmitting devices of the LTE-1800 TDD railway communication network are the source of harmful interferences (Fig. 1 a). The second group includes EMC-scenarios in which the transmitters (TX UE and TX eNB) LTE-1800 FDD are the sources of harmful interference (Fig. 1 b).

The most difficult scenarios for providing EMC of LTE networks and developing norms STS are scenarios with indices 1.1.1 and 2.2.2 for mutual influences of LTE-1800 TDD and LTE-1800 FDD base stations. These scenarios for the assessment of EMC and the development of norms STS are determined by the values of acceptable levels of unwanted emissions, which characterize BS or AC transmitters emissions in outside of BS or AC spectrum bands, which interfere with operation of receivers BS and AC of other networks. In these scenarios are two types of unwanted emissions: out-of-band and spurious emissions. The requirements for these types of transmitter emissions of eNB base stations are established in Technical Specification 3GPP TS 36.104 [4] and in Recommendation ITU-R SM.329 [5].

Out of band emissions (OOB) are unwanted transmitter emissions at frequencies directly adjacent to the left and right part of the emission band of LTE frequency channel (excluding spurious emissions), which are the result of modulation and non-linearity of the processes on transmitter. In accordance with Technical Specifications 3GPP, the OOBs are defined as [4]:

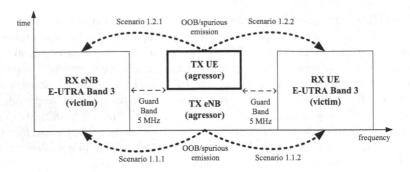

a) BS and UE Transmitters LTE-1800 TDD network as source harmful interferences.

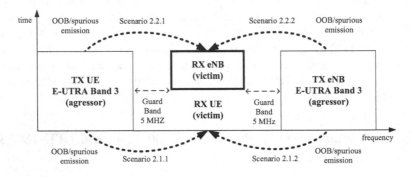

b) BS and UE Transmitters LTE-1800 FDD network as source harmful interferences.

Fig. 1. EMC-scenarios for LTE-1800 TDD и LTE-1800 FDD networks.

- Operating band unwanted emissions define all unwanted emissions in each supported downlink operating band plus the frequency ranges 10 MHz above and 10 MHz below the band 3.
- Radiation of the part of power of the useful signal at the frequencies of the adjacent channel, the level of which is determined by the ACLR (Adjacent Channel Leakage Power Ratio).

Spurious emissions of transmitter in accordance with 3GPP Technical Specifications are unwanted emissions from the transmitter at frequencies outside the border of out-of-band emissions that result of carrier frequency formation. Spurious emissions include harmonic emissions, spurious emissions, intermodulation products, and frequency conversion products.

The arrangement of the frequency bands occupied by OOB and spurious emissions relatively on the band of the main emission of BS transmitter is shown in Fig. 2 [5].

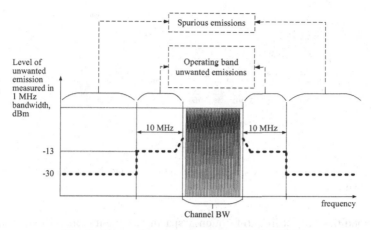

Fig. 2. Types of unwanted emissions TX eNB [4].

3   Conditions of EMC Providing for LTE-1800 FDD Radio Access Networks

Analysis of the 3GPP Technical Specifications for the LTE-1800 FDD BS (Band 3) made it possible to determine norms of frequency separation (FS) and requirements for the levels of spurious emissions [4]:

1. The frequency spacing of the DL and UL lines is 20 MHz.
2. The spacing of the center carriers of the transmitter (TX) and the receiver (RX) of Base station for a given channel is 95 MHz.
3. The level of unwanted (spurious) emissions of the base station transmitter in the frequency band of its own receiver is no more than minus 96 dBm in the measurement range of 100 kHz [4, Table 6.6.4.4.1-1].
4. The level of unwanted (spurious) emissions of the base station transmitter in the frequency band of receiver Base station eNB Band 3 is no more than minus 96 dBm in the measurement range of 100 kHz [4, Table 6.6.4.2-1].
5. The level of unwanted (spurious) emissions of the eNB base station transmitter of other frequency bands in the frequency band of receiver Base station eNB Band 3 is no more than minus 49 dBm in the measurement range of 1 MHz [4, Table 6.6.4.3.1-1].
6. The level of unwanted (spurious) emissions of the eNB base station transmitter of other frequency bands in the frequency band of receiver UE Band3 is no more than minus 52 dBm in the measurement range of 1 MHz [4, Table 6.6.4.3.1-1].
7. The level of unwanted (spurious) emissions of the eNB base station transmitter eNB Band3 category «B» in frequency band 1-12,75 GHz is no more than minus 30 dBm in the measurement range of 1 MHz, excluding p. 3–6 [4, Table 6.6.4.1.2.1-1].

Limits to provide EMC conditions which defined in items 1, 3, 4 and 5 (Fig. 1) for EMC-scenarios 1.1.1 and 2.2.2, requirements for frequency spacing and also requirements to level of unwanted (spurious) emissions in band of receiver base station eNB (Band 3) are shown in Fig. 3.

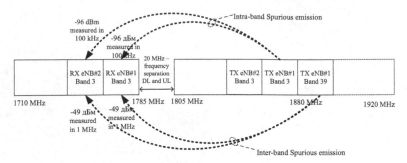

Fig. 3. Requirements to frequency spacing and level of unwanted (spurious) emissions in band of RX eNB Band 3.

EMC conditions according to frequency spacing norms in items 3 and 4 require the introduction of an additional selectivity in filter of transmitting path of EMC conditions according to the standards given in clauses 3 and 4 require the introduction of an additional filter selectivity of the transmitting path of the base station eNB LTE-1800 FDD. This additional selectivity provides attenuation of the power level of spurious emission in the frequency band of its own receiver of base station eNB LTE-1800 FDD and receivers of others eNB. $P_{se_{own}}$, in the measurement range of 100 kHz up to level:

$$P_{se_{own}} = -96\,\text{dBm} \tag{1}$$

Taking into account the requirements of item 5 of frequency spacing norms for the power level of spurious emissions from transmitters of base stations eNB for other frequency bands on input of RX eNB (Band 3) $P_{se_{in-band3}}$, in the measurement range of 100 kHz, has to be not more than:

$$P_{se_{in-band3}} = -49\,\text{dBm} + 10\lg(100\,\text{kHz}/1\,\text{MHz}) = -59\,\text{dBm}. \tag{2}$$

From the given values (1) and (2) it follows that the power level of spurious emissions of transmitters of base stations eNB, operating in a different frequency range and not placed co-located with eNB (Band 3), can be higher than -96 dBm in measuring band 100 kHz. Reduced requirements for spurious emissions due to their attenuation by spatial territorial separation or the use of inter-band filters. Thus, to provide EMC of eNB base stations of different frequency bands, spatial territorial separation of eNB antennas is requested, or utilization of inter-band filters in eNB, which attenuate spurious (spurious) emissions in the measuring band of 100 kHz by an amount:

$$L_1[dB] = P_{se_{in-band3}} - P_{se_{own}} = -59\,\text{dBm} + 96\,\text{dBm} = 37\,\text{dB}. \tag{3}$$

4   Conditions of EMC Providing Between Base Stations LTE-1800 TDD and LTE-1800 FDD

In accordance with the requirements of Technical Specifications 3GPP [4] for EMC-scenarios 1.1.1 and 2.2.2 to ensure normal operation of the RX eNB Band 3 (in Fig. 1a for the eNB Band 3) and the RX eNB LTE-1800 TDD (in Fig. 1 b for RX eNB TDD) are required following conditions of EMC providing:

1. The level of unwanted (spurious) emissions from co-located base station transmitters in the frequency band of receiver (any from consider receivers) is no more than minus 96 dBm in the measurement range of 100 kHz.
2. The interference signal level from co-located TX eNB is no more than the set value of the receiver selectivity requirements given in the Table 1 [4, Table 7.6.1.1-1].

Table 1. RX eNB LTE (Band 3) selectivity requirements for macro cells [4, Table 7.6.1.1-1].

Wanted Signal		Interfering Signal				
E-UTRA channel bandwidth, MHz	Wanted Signal mean power, dBm	Type of interfering signal	Centre Frequency of Interfering Signal, MHz		Interfering signal centre frequency minimum offset to the lower/upper eNB RF Bandwidth edge, MHz	Interfering Signal mean power, dBm
			From	To		
1,4	−100,8	1.4 MHz E-UTRA	1690 (F_{UL_low} − 20)	1805 (F_{UL_high} + 20)	±2,1	−43
3	−97	3 MHz E-UTRA			±4,5	
5	−95,5	5 MHz E-UTRA			±7,5	
10	−95,5	5 MHz E-UTRA			±7,5	
15	−95,5	5 MHz E-UTRA			±7,5	
20	−95,5	5 MHz E-UTRA			±7,5	
20	−95,5	20 MHz E-UTRA			±30	
1.4/3/5/ 10/15/20	Sensitivity + 6 dB		1	1690	–	−15
			1805	12750		

The fulfillment of the first condition requests the analysis of the characteristics of the spectrum signals masks of the LTE-1800 FDD (Band 3) and -LTE-1800 TDD. The spectrum signal masks of LTE-1800 FDD transmitters (Band 3) for European countries and the Russian Federation correspond to category "B" option 2 and are shown in Fig. 4 [4, Table 6.6.3.2.2-1, 4].

As shown in Fig. 4, for EMC - scenario 2.2.2, unwanted emissions from eNB LTE-1800 FDD (Band 3) transmitters of railway communication network, which operating

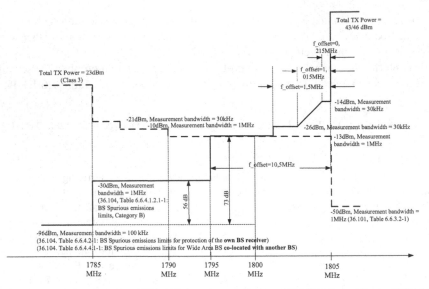

Fig. 4. Spectrum signal masks of TX eNB (continuous line) and TX UE (dashed line) of LTE-1800 FDD (Band 3).

in frequency band of 1785–1805 MHz, exceed the maximum permissible level of minus 96 dBm in two frequency bands:

- in frequency band 1790–1795 MHz (spurious emissions) on 56 dB

$$
\begin{aligned}
L_2[dB] &= P_{se} - P_{se_{own}} \\
&= -30\,\text{dBm} + 10\lg(100\,\text{kHz}/1\,\text{MHz}) + 96\,\text{dBm} = 56\,\text{dB};
\end{aligned}
\tag{4}
$$

- in frequency band 1795–1800 MHz (OOB) on 73 dB

$$
\begin{aligned}
L_3[dB] &= P_{OOB} - P_{se_{own}} \\
&= -13\,\text{dBm} + 10\lg(100\,\text{kHz}/1\,\text{MHz}) + 96\,\text{dBm} = 73\,\text{dB}.
\end{aligned}
\tag{5}
$$

Mathematical expressions (4) and (5) determine norms of spatial and territorial separation that provide the attenuation of unwanted emissions without utilization of Inter-band Filters inside base stations.

When using Inter Band filters that providing attenuate unwanted emissions to 49 dBm (in measurement band 1 MHz), norms of spatial and territorial separation are defined by mathematical expression (3) to attenuate spurious (secondary) emissions of $L1 = 37$ dB.

Fulfillment of these requirements for attenuation of unwanted emissions and attenuation of spurious (spurious) emissions will provide, respectively, EMC conditions for both scenario 2.2.2 and scenario 1.1.1.

Given the additional requirements for the level of spurious (secondary) radiations indicated in item 5 and item 6 (see Sect. 2), it is proposed to provide EMC with the aim of eliminating the effect of unwanted emissions by following measures:

- have use inter-band filters in RX eNB (Band 3) which attenuate unwanted emissions in the frequency band 1790–1800 MHz to the level of minus 49 dBm (in the measurement band 1 MHz);
- have use the spectrum signal mask of TX eNB LTE-1800 TDD in the frequency band 1785–1805 MHz as shown in Fig. 5.

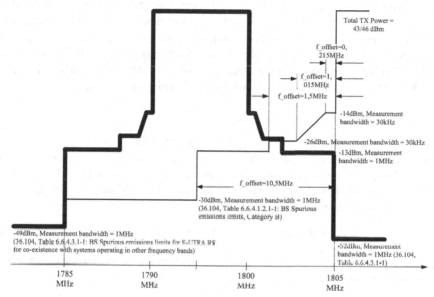

Fig. 5. Spectrum signal mask of TX eNB LTE-1800 TDD (thick line) and eNB LTE-1800 FDD (Band 3, thin line).

If consider the second condition (see Fig. 1) of providing EMC for scenarios 1.1.1 and 2.2.2, then take into account that the receiver selectivity means its ability to receive a minimum power useful signal in the presence of interference signal. In this case, throughput of LTE channel should not be lower than 95% relative to reference channel, which is understood as a channel with an input signal at the sensitivity level but without of interference [4, п. 7.6.1.1].

As can be seen from Table 1 which contains of selectivity requirement to RX eNB LTE (Band 3) for a macro cell [4, Table 7.6.1.1-1], 3GPP considers cases when the interfering signal has a frequency channel width of 1.4, 3, 5, and 20 MHz and in the frequency band 1690–1805 MHz, its power should not exceed minus 43 dBm.

In addition, when the upper border of the spectrum of the useful uplink signal of the LTE-1800 FDD network is $F_{UL\_high} = 1785$ MHz, and the frequency channel of the interfering signal from the eNB TDD is 5 MHz, the center frequency of interfering signal can be within the frequency band 1792,5–1805 MHz with an acceptable power level of Base station as source of interference up to 43 dBm. In this case, the frequency band of 1792.5–1805 MHz of base station-source of interference, can intersect with the frequency range of the railway communication network of 1790–1800 MHz.

Thus, in accordance with receiver selectivity requirements (Table 1), the power of the interfering signal from the TX eNB LTE-1800 TDD at input of RX eNB (Band 3) should not exceed minus 43 dBm. If interfering signal power from TX eNB LTE-1800 TDD exceeds this level minus 43 dBm, then it is considered that the requirements of the Communications Administration [2] Are violated and there will be an interfering effect on LTE receivers of mobile networks operators in frequency bands 1710–1785 MHz and 1805–1880 MHz. To eliminate this interference effect, it is necessary to provide norms of spatial-territorial separation for antennas TX eNB LTE-1800 TDD and RX LTE-1800 FDD (Band 3), which give attenuation of the interference signal is equal to:

$$P_{TX_{iterf}} + 43 \, \text{dBm},$$

where $P_{TX_{iterf}}$ – interfering signal power from TX eNB LTE-1800 TDD.

In the case of using TX eNB LTE-1800 TDD with an interference signal power of $P_{TX_{iterf}} = 40 \, \text{W} (46 \, \text{dBm})$ and frequency channel with bandwidth of 10 MHz (for example, the radio module has two RF ports of 20 W each), the EMC condition determinates by amount of attenuation of interfering signal equal to:

$$L_4[dB] = 46 \, \text{dBm} - 3 \, \text{dB} + 43 \, \text{dBm} = 86 \, \text{dB}. \tag{6}$$

In expression (6) for L_4, the term equal to minus 3 dB is determined due to converting the power to bandwidth of 5 MHz.

5   Definition and Providing of Norms of Spatial and Territorial Separation for LTE Base Stations

EMC conditions presented in expressions (3)–(6) are determined by the levels of unwanted emissions of the transmitters (out-of-band and spurious) at the input of the eNB receivers. In accordance with the specifications of Partnership Project 3GPP these levels are measured at points shown in Fig. 6. [2, p. 6.1 и p. 7.1]. Measurement point "A" is used in case when there are no external amplifiers and filters in eNB, and point "B" in case when there are any.

If in EMC scenarios 1.1.1 and 2.2.2 interaction between transmitter of one eNB and receiver of another eNB is considered, then required resulting coefficient of unwanted emissions level attenuation can be calculated by the formula as the sum of the following coefficients [5–8]:

$$L_\Sigma[\text{дБ}] = - G_{TX}(\Delta\varphi_{TX}, \Delta\theta_{TX})[dBi] + L_{Fider_{TX}}[dB] + L_{FS}[dB] + L_{CL}[dB]$$
$$- G_{RX}(\Delta\varphi_{RX}, \Delta\theta_{RX})[dBi] + L_{Fider_{RX}}[dB], \tag{7}$$

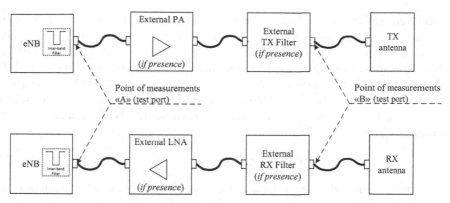

Fig. 6. Measurement points of unwanted emission and interference signal power for evaluating the eNB EMC determined by 3GPP [2].

where:

- $L_{Fider_{TX}}[dB]$ и $L_{Fider_{RX}}[dB]$ – attenuation (loss) coefficients of signal in feeders of transmission and reception paths of eNB, respectively (in dB);
- $G_{TX}(\Delta\varphi_{TX}, \Delta\theta_{TX})[dBi]$ and $G_{RX}(\Delta\varphi_{RX}, \Delta\theta_{RX})[dBi]$ – gain coefficients of TX and RX eNB antenna depending on the angles of deviation from the maximum pattern in the azimuthal plane $\Delta\varphi_{TX(RX)}$ and the angular plane $\Delta\theta_{TX(RX)}$ (see Fig. 7);

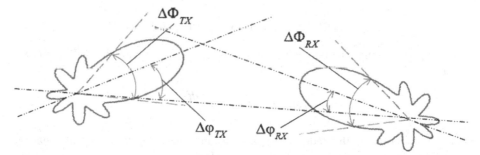

Fig. 7. Beam orientation with main lobe TX and main lobe RX antennas of eNBs relative to direction of line of sight in azimuth plane.

- $L_{FS}[dB]$ – coefficient of attenuation radio waves in free space without taking into account features of propagation in communication link (in dB);
- $L_{CL}[dB]$ – coefficient of attenuation radio waves with taking into account features of propagation in communication link (in dB).

Expression (7) shows that for given characteristics of eNBs, the resulting attenuation in TX path will largely depend on spatial orientation of TX and RX eNB antenna beams of the relative to line of sight of base stations location. In Fig. 7 shows an example of such beam orientation with main lobe TX width $\Delta\Phi_{TX}$ and main lobe RX width $\Delta\Phi_{RX}$

at 3 dB level, respectively, relative to direction of line of sight (transmission - reception) in azimuth plane. By analogy with Fig. 7, easy to imagine a scenario of antenna beams orientation relative to direction of line of sight for eNB base stations in elevation plane.

Norms of spatial territorial separation are determined based on fulfillment of EMC conditions provided in expressions (3)–(6). The most critical are norms of spatial territorial separation which defined by expression (6), since these norms require more highest level of attenuation (suppression) of unwanted emissions TX eNB in comparison with conditions for providing EMC (3)–(5):

$$L_\Sigma[dB] \geq L_4[dB] = 86 \, \text{dB}. \tag{8}$$

Obviously, if the EMC conditions are met expression (8), norms of spatial territorial separation defined by expressions (3)–(5) will also to be done.

The providing possibility of EMC conditions in expression (8) is determined by values of attenuation level of unwanted emissions coefficients in expression (7). Technical characteristics of transmitting and receiving antennas eNB [6–8], limit the values of gain antennas coefficients:

$$G_{TX}(\Delta\varphi_{TX}, \Delta\theta_{TX})[dBi] \leq 18 \, \text{dBi}, \quad G_{RX}(\Delta\varphi_{RX}, \Delta\theta_{RX})[dBi] \leq 18 \, \text{dBi}. \tag{9}$$

Typical RF Jumpers used in eNBs are 2, 4, 6, 8 or 10 meters long. The specific attenuation in feeder and attenuation in connector of eNB feeder, as a rule, are 0.147 dB/m and 0.1 dB, respectively. For the most commonly used feeder length of 2 m, values of signal attenuation coefficients (losses) in feeders of transmission and reception paths of eNB are

$$L_{Fider_{TX}}[dB] = 0,494 \, \text{dB}, \text{L}_{Fider_{RX}}[dB] = 0,494 \, \text{dB}. \tag{10}$$

Free space attenuation coefficient calculated in accordance with ITU-R Recommendation [11]:

$$L_{FS}[dB] = 20 \lg\left(\frac{4\pi \, df}{c}\right), \tag{11}$$

where c - velocity of the radio wave, d - distance between receiving antenna and transmitting antennas $(m), f$ - carrier frequency (Hz).

As radio propagation models for predicting the path loss coefficient LCL [dB] for mobile communications is usually used Okamura-Hata, COST231-Hata and COST231-Walfisch-Ikegami empirical models [10–12]. The last two models are applicable for 1500–2000 MHz and 800–2000 MHz bands and are used directly for propagation loss calculations in LTE networks [11]. Application of the COST231-Hata model is limited by communication distances from 1 to 20 km [11, 12].

To study EMC scenarios 1.1.1 and 2.2.2 under consideration (see Fig. 1), it can be considered more better to use the COST231-Walfisch-Ikegami model, which is designed to calculate a signal level in small cells with radiuses from 0.02 to 5 km subject to flat earth surface [11]. In scope of a solved task conditions for providing EMC can be considered as some restrictions on eNB permissible placement from each other not exceeding limits of line of sight (LOS). In this case, re-reflected waves from the earth's surface and buildings with arbitrary amplitudes and phases, as well as changes in polarization of interfering signal, are added to direct waves of interfering signal. The attenuation coefficient of radio waves for these conditions can be determined in accordance with the expression [13–15].

$$L_{CL}[dB] = 6\lg(0,05d). \tag{12}$$

Based on the expressions (11) and (12), the sum $L_{FS}[dB] + L_{CL}[dB]$ can be represented as:

$$L_{FS}[dB] + L_{CL}[dB] = 20\lg(d) + 20\lg(f) + 20\lg\left(\frac{4\pi}{c}\right) + 6\lg(d) + 6\lg(0,05) \tag{13}$$
$$= 26\lg(d) + 20\lg(f) - 155,4.$$

Substituting the value (13) into expression (7) limitations of necessary territorial separation between the transmitter and receiver antennas for different eNBs has determine for corresponding EMC condition (expression 6):

$$d(\Delta\varphi_{TX}, \Delta\theta_{TX}, \Delta\varphi_{RX}, \Delta\theta_{RX}, f) \geq 10^{(L_4[dB]-L(\Delta\varphi_{TX},\Delta\theta_{TX},\Delta\varphi_{RX},\Delta\theta_{RX}f))/26}, \tag{14}$$

where $L(\Delta\varphi_{TX}, \Delta\theta_{TX}, \Delta\varphi_{RX}, \Delta\theta_{RX}, f)$ - resulting attenuation function

$$L(\Delta\varphi_{TX}, \Delta\theta_{TX}, \Delta\varphi_{RX}, \Delta\theta_{RX}, f)$$
$$= -G_{TX}(\Delta\varphi_{TX}, \Delta\theta_{TX})[dBi] - G_{RX}(\Delta\varphi_{RX}, \Delta\theta_{RX})[dBi] \tag{15}$$
$$+L_{Fider_{TX}}[dB] + L_{Fider_{RX}}[dB] + 20\lg(f) - 155,4dB.$$

When determining antenna separation range of different eNBs for EMC conditions which given in expressions (3), (4) and (5), it is necessary to substitute $L_1[dB]$, $L_2[dB]$ and $L_3[dB]$ respectively, in to expression (14) instead of $L_4[dB]$.

Based on the conditions for providing EMC in expressions (14)–(15), determining factor for providing EMC in scenarios 1.1.1 and 2.2.2 is a mutual orientation of beams for separated TX and RX eNB antennas. Separation on distance between eNBs in expression (14) determines territorial separation, and difference in angular orientation of eNBs antennas in expression (15) determines conditions of spatial separation.

It possible to evaluate requirements of spatial territorial separation norms taking into account expressions (6), (14), (15) for providing EMC by utilization of typical TRX antenna feeder patches of eNB LTE-1800 TDD and eNB LTE-1800 FDD (Band 3), the technical parameters of these eNBs correspond to coefficients values obtained in expressions (9) and (10).

If antennas are used for transmission and reception in eNB base stations with a maximum gain of 18 dBi, then it is possible to determine the parameters of such radiation patterns of eNB antennas. Such directional patterns of eNB antennas should be symmetrical with respect to the direction of the maximum of the main lobe and have a width of minus 3 dB:

- in azimuth plane $\Delta\Phi_{TX} = \Delta\Phi_{RX} = 65°$;
- in angular plane $\Delta\Theta_{TX} = \Delta\Theta_{RX} = 5°$.

For a typical antenna pattern used in LTE networks, one can obtain graphical dependences of minimum eNBs territorial separation to ensure the EMC condition (6) for different angular positions of the antenna pattern maximums of their TX and RX antennas and with "equal "sign (=) in expression (13).

Obtained distances make it possible to estimate spatial territorial separation parameters taking into account an angular position of antennas relative to each other. In this case, EMC provision of base stations on place of location depends on an orientation of beams in the azimuthal plane, i.e., on the difference in angles $\Delta\varphi_{TX}$ and $\Delta\varphi_{RX}$.

A variant of a such dependence for above indicated characteristics of antenna and carrier frequency of 1780 MHz, at which TX eNB LTE-1800 TDD interference signal is attenuated to the least extent shown in Fig. 8. The orientation of the antenna pattern in the elevation plane is selected along the LOS direction with the parameters: $\Delta\theta_{TX} = \Delta\theta_{RX} = 0°$.

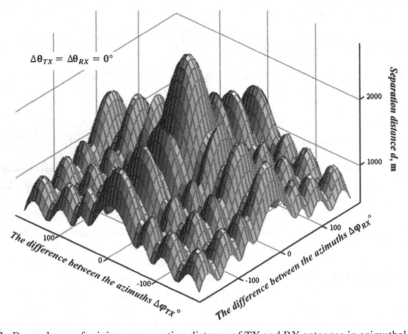

Fig. 8. Dependence of minimum separation distance of TX and RX antennas in azimuthal plane on angles difference.

Figure 8 shows that maximum separation distance providing EMC between TX and RX antennas of base stations were in case when maximums of antenna beams are oriented at each other with following parameters: $\Delta\varphi_{Tx} = 0°$, $\Delta\theta_{Tx} = 0°$, $\Delta\varphi_{Rx} = 0°$, $\Delta\theta_{Rx} = 0°$. An increase angular position difference of maximums of TX and RX base stations antennas leads to a decrease in value of required separation distances eNBs. The minimum separation distances between eNBs will be in case when antennas orientation at each other by back beams of antennas with minimums gains.

A significant reduction of territorial spacing for ensuring EMC of LTE base stations can be achieved by changing the position of the maximum of TX and RX antenna of eNBs in elevation plane [6]. If antennas patterns are symmetric in vertical plane relative to maximum of the main antenna lobe with a width of 5o, then the orientation of the antennas on location place for the values $\Delta\theta_{TX}$ and $\Delta\theta_{RX}$ can be estimated corresponding to the condition:

$$|\Delta\theta_{TX} - \Delta\theta_{RX}| \leq 10°.$$

A dependence graph of relative values of required separation distance of antennas eNBs on antennas orientation relative to line of sight in the elevation angles plane has determined by the difference $|\Delta\theta_{TX} - \Delta\theta_{RX}|$ as shown in Fig 9. d_{max} –parameter is the maximum value of the territorial separation between the TX and RX antennas of the base stations for the given EMC conditions.

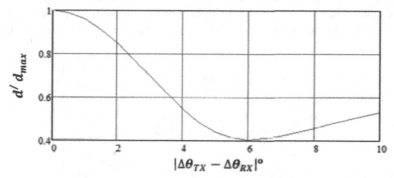

Fig. 9. Dependence graph of the relative values of the necessary territorial separation to ensure the EMC TX and RX antennas of eNBs from different orientations of antenna beam in the elevation plane.

An analysis of the graph (Fig. 9) shows that by changing the position of antenna pattern in elevation plane can receive a significant decrease of territorial spacing which shown in Fig. 8. For example, when $|\Delta\theta_{TX} - \Delta\theta_{RX}| \approx 6°$ it allows to decreases d/d_{max} by 2.5 times for required of territorial spacing.

The graphs shown in Fig. 8 and 9 are determined by characteristics and type of antennas used eNBs. Therefore, for a specific type of antenna pattern, recommendations can be developed on implementation of norms of spatial territorial separation between eNB LTE-1800 TDD and eNB LTE-1800 FDD (Band 3). The characteristics of antenna pattern and antenna gain depend on frequency range, nature of underlying surface, terrain and other factors that must also be taken into account.

Range of minimum values possible changes of territorial separation of base stations eNB under given conditions, as follows from (13)–(14), is determined by sum of values of the functions $G_{TX}(\Delta\varphi_{TX}, \Delta\theta_{TX})$ and $G_{RX}(\Delta\varphi_{RX}, \Delta\theta_{RX})$. The values of these functions, based on the characteristics of antennas used, can vary in the range from minus 15 dBi to 18 dBi (see restriction (9)) depending on the specified parameters. The minimum value of minus 15 dBi is conditionally set, since it is difficult to strictly determine it due to constant change in levels of antenna side lobes and dips (minima) of the radiation pattern depending on communication and propagation conditions.

In Fig. 10 shows the dependences of the minimum territorial separation providing EMC between eNB LTE-1800 TDD and LTE-1800 FDD (Band 3) on the values of resulting antenna gains of TX and RX base stations, which are calculated taking into account the expression:

$$L_{TX-RX}(\Delta\varphi_{TX}, \Delta\theta_{TX}, \Delta\varphi_{RX}, \Delta\theta_{RX})[dBi]$$
$$= G_{TX}(\Delta\varphi_{TX}, \Delta\theta_{TX})[dBi] + G_{RX}(\Delta\varphi_{RX}, \Delta\theta_{RX})[dBi].$$

The dependencies shown in Fig. 10 correspond to the smallest values of the territorial separation of antennas, i.e., when using the equal sign in expression (14). The values of the resulting antenna gain of 36 dBi and range of territorial separation between antennas min = 20 m limit the area of analysis. These values do not establish a fundamental limitation for obtaining estimates of the diversity ranges outside this area of analysis. The maximum values of the territorial spacings of the antennas of the base station for providing EMC are determined in Fig. 10 how $d_{max1}, d_{max2}, d_{max3}$ и d_{max4} consequently.

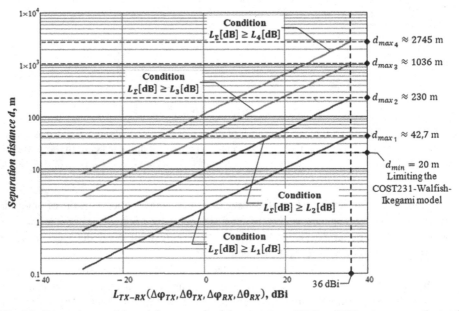

Fig. 10. Dependence of the minimum territorial separation of TX and RX antennas on the total gain of these antennas.

6 Conclusion

The research results showed that for the joint use of base stations eNB LTE-1800 TDD for railway communications with a non-standard frequency range and eNB LTE-1800 FDD

(Band 3) and ensure EMC, it is necessary to limit unwanted emission levels through use of inter-band filters and due to utilization developed spectrum signal mask for eNB LTE-1800 TDD. The use of inter-band filters changes the requirements of norms of spatial and territorial separation for the considered base stations depending on the relative orientation of antennas beam and urban conditions (Urban and Dense Urban) or rural areas (Rural).

Depending on power level of spurious emissions from base station transmitters, the required values of territorial separation may be:

- 10–40 m provided that inter-band filters are used at eNB LTE-1800 TDD for railway communications and eNB LTE-1800 FDD (Band 3) base stations, which is feasible in Urban and Dense Urban areas;
- 50–230 m for the frequency range 1790–1795 MHz without the use of inter-band filters at base stations eNB LTE-1800 TDD and eNB LTE-1800 FDD (Band 3), which is acceptable in urban areas and rural areas;
- 250–1000 m for frequency band 1795–1800 MHz without the use of inter-band filters at base stations eNB LTE-1800 TDD for railway communications and eNB LTE-1800 FDD (Band 3), which is permissible only in rural areas.

To completely eliminate the influence of interference from the eNB LTE 1800 TDD for railway communications and the eNB FD-LTE (Band 3), territorial separation norms have to be 650–2700 m, which is difficult to do in urban areas and rural areas.

References

1. Radio Regulations, ITU, Geneve (2019)
2. Decision SCRF № 18-46, September 2018
3. ECC Report 119. Coexistence between mobile systems in the 2.6 GHz. Frequency band at the FDD/TDD boundary. Kristiansand, June 2008
4. GPP TS 36.104 Evolved Universal Terrestrial Radio Access (E-UTRA); Base Station radio transmission and reception
5. Recommendation ITU-R SM.329-12, September 2012. Unwanted emissions in the spurious domain. SM Series. Spectrum management
6. Tikhvinskiy, V.O., Terentyev, S.V., Vysotsin, V.P.: Mobile networks LTE/LTE Advanced: т 4G Technologies, Applications, Architecture, p. 342. Media Publisher (2014)
7. Sklyar, B.: Digital communication: theoretical foundations and practical application. In: Sklyar, B., Thunderstorm, E.G. et al. (transl. from English), 2nd edn. Williams Publishing House, 1104 p. (2003)
8. Shorin, O.A., Bokk, G.O., Sukhatsky, S.V.: Methods of improving intersystem EMC for fourth-generation mobile communication systems. Commun. Netw. 2, 35–41 (2016)
9. Shorin, O.A., Bokk, G.O.: Analysis of electromagnetic compatibility of fourth-generation standards. Wireless. First mile. 1, 44–52 (2016)
10. Shorin, O.A., Bokk, G.O.: On the issue of electromagnetic compatibility of fourth-generation standards. Econ. Qual. Commun. Syst. 2, 51–59 (2016)
11. Recommendation ITU - R P.525-2. Calculation of free-space attenuation (1978–1982–1994)
12. Recommendation ITU- R 1546-6. Method for point-to-area predictions for terrestrial services in the frequency range 30 MHz to 4 000 MHz. ITU, Geneve (2019)

13. Svistunov, A.S.: Empirical models of radio wave propagation for analysis of intra-system electromagnetic compatibility and security of cellular networks with microcellular structure. J. Belarusian State University Phys. **2**, 107–116 (2018)
14. Dvornikov, S.V., Balykov, A.A., Kotov, A.A.: A simplified model for calculating signal loss in a radio line, obtained by comparing Vvedensky quadratic formula with existing empirical models. Control Commun. Secur. Syst. **2**, 87–99 (2019)
15. Vladimirov, S.S.: Wireless data networks. In: Practical Exercises, p. 58. SPbSUT, St. Petersburg (2016)

Elimination of Carrier Frequency Offset of Local Oscillator to Improve Accuracy of GNSS Positioning

Igor Petrov$^{(\boxtimes)}$ ⓘ, Aleksandr Gelgor ⓘ, and Timur Lavrukhin

Peter the Great St. Petersburg Polytechnic University, St. Petersburg, Russia
{petrov_ia,agelgor}@spbstu.ru, lavruhin2.t@edu.spbstu.ru

Abstract. The article proposes a technique for algorithmic estimation and compensation the inaccuracy of the tuning local oscillator in GNSS chip to the carrier frequency. With this technique the carrier tracking loop provides more accurate calculations of integrated Doppler. Then the code tracking loop including carrier aiding provides more accurate code synchronization. As the result the accuracy of GNSS positioning improves. We observed the records of GPS signals with precise zero carrier frequency offset (CFO) and synthetically included nonzero CFO to them. The using of the proposed technique provided almost the same accuracy of positioning as with precise zero CFO.

Keywords: GNSS · Signal tracking · Loop filters · Integrated Doppler shift · Carrier aiding

1 Introduction

In recent years, the use of GNSS (Global Navigation Satellite System) chips for determination of the coordinates and speed of a receiver has become extremely widespread. About twenty years ago, GNSS chips were used only in specialized equipment. Now they are installed almost everywhere: in each smartphone, in public transport vehicles, in drones, in car sharing service etc. However, it doesn't mean that all GNSS chips provide the same functionality.

The quality of positioning depends on many factors, such as: the number of satellites that the receiver can track simultaneously, the number of systems that the receiver can process, whether the receiver processes satellite signals at only one carrier frequency or at two frequencies, whether the receiver has an ability to receive and process the information from external systems [1–3].

In equipment that has GNSS chip, most hardware focuses on targets that is unrelated to navigation signal processing. Moreover, in the simple civilian GNSS receivers the cheap elements can be used. It leads to significant decrease of the positioning accuracy [4]. This raises the question of whether it is possible to overcome the imperfections of

This work was supported by the Academic Excellence Project 5-100 proposed by Peter the Great St. Petersburg Polytechnic University.

© Springer Nature Switzerland AG 2020
O. Galinina et al. (Eds.): NEW2AN 2020/ruSMART 2020, LNCS 12525, pp. 351–360, 2020.
https://doi.org/10.1007/978-3-030-65726-0_31

the element base by using sophisticated algorithms and to improve positioning accuracy even using the elements with not ideal characteristics.

In the case of positioning with using pseudoranges the most important problem is precisely tracking of time synchronization with the received signal. The synchronization process is usually performed by using a Delay Locked Loop (DLL) in code tracking block [5, 6].

On the one hand, the smaller dynamics in receiver-satellite system, the narrower bandwidth of the loop filter can be set in DLL to obtain greater accuracy of the time synchronization. On the other hand, the greater dynamics in receiver-satellite system, the wider loop filter band should be set in order to keep tracking, i.e. to remain tracking in synchronism mode. However, the increase of the filter band leads to the increase of the noise power. In turn to, it leads to the reduction of the time synchronization accuracy. Therefore, positioning accuracy highly depends on the dynamics of the receiver [7].

There is the method which allows increasing the accuracy of the time synchronization even for receivers with high dynamics [8, 9]. It uses information from the carrier tracking loop to adjust the time synchronization. This method is based on the fact that the value of the integrated Doppler frequency shift is proportional to the shift of the time synchronization during the integration interval. However, the feature of the Doppler shift integration is inability to determine absolute time synchronization. This way only synchronization changes are tracked.

Carrier tracking block estimates phase and frequency of GNSS signal using Phase Locked Loop (PLL) and Frequency Locked Loop (FLL). Relatively to pseudoranges, these measurements converted to several orders more accurate than the measurements from DLL [1, 3]. Therefore, the using of relatively large values for the loop filter band in PLL and FLL results in more accurate measurements for the time synchronization shift than in case of using single DLL.

The idea of combining code tracking block with carrier tracking block is that carrier loop aiding removes virtually all of the Line of Sight (LOS) dynamics from the delay loop. That is why the filter order in delay loop can be set smaller, its update rate slower, and its bandwidth narrower than for unaided case. In fact, the delay loop only tracks the dynamics of ionosphere delay plus noise and compensates bias of the time synchronization error.

This approach is widely described [1, 3, 8, 9], but it has one significant disadvantage. If relatively cheap local oscillator is used, then signal is demodulated to CFO, rather than to zero frequency [4]. In this case, the carrier tracking loop doesn't track the true Doppler shift. It tracks the Doppler shift with a systematic error equal to the CFO. It leads to the fact that in case of using carrier aiding for code tracking block, DLL is forced to track false dynamics provided by the carrier loop. Depending on the parameters of DLL it either increases inaccuracy of the time synchronization error or, in the worst case, it causes the breakdown of tracking. That's why carrier aiding technique is either used in expensive professional equipment with a precisely tuned local oscillator, or not used at all.

In this paper, we propose an algorithm, which can be applied to estimation and compensation of the CFO thus providing ability of using carrier aiding technique even in cheap equipment with a poorly tuned local oscillator. It is performed before switching on carrier aiding to code tracking block. The proposed technique is tested both on a simulation model and on the real GPS signal recordings.

2 The Idea

The idea of calculation the value of CFO is to compare the Doppler shift determined by the carrier tracking loop, $f_{D,Track}$, with the Doppler shift calculated by the real speeds of the receiver and the satellite, $f_{D,V}$. The calculation of the receiver speed $\mathbf{v_u} = \{v_{u,x},$ $v_{u,y}, v_{u,z}\}$ can be performed by differentiating the receiver coordinates [1]. Similarly, the calculation of the satellite speed $\mathbf{v_s} = \{v_{s,x}, v_{s,y}, v_{s,z}\}$ can be performed either by differentiating the satellite coordinates or by processing of the ephemeris values [10].

Note that the satellite speed must be calculated for the time of the signal transmission t_s, and the receiver speed must be calculated at the time t_u when signal transmitted at the time t_s was received. The LOS connects the satellite coordinates at the time t_s and the receiver coordinates at the time t_u.

Consider the algorithm of calculation the projection V_s of the satellite speed $\mathbf{v_s}$ on the LOS:

1. At first, we need to calculate coordinates of the satellite (x_s, y_s, z_s) at the time t_s and coordinates of the receiver (x_u, y_u, z_u) at the time t_u. From these coordinates we can obtain the radius-vector of LOS:

$$\mathbf{r_{su}} = \{x_s - x_u, y_s - y_u, z_s - z_u\}. \tag{1}$$

2. At second, we should calculate the satellite velocity $\mathbf{v_s}$ at the time t_s.
3. Finally we can calculate the V_s which is the projection of $\mathbf{v_s}$ on $\mathbf{r_{su}}$ (equal to $|v_{s,LOS}|$):

$$V_s = -|\mathbf{v_s}| \cos(\alpha) = \frac{\mathbf{r_{su} v_s}}{|\mathbf{r_{su}}|}. \tag{2}$$

Evidently, calculation of the projection V_u can be performed analogously.

Once the projections of the receiver velocity V_u and the satellite velocity V_s on the LOS were determined, the Doppler shift can be calculated as follows [11]:

$$f_{D,V} = \frac{V_u - V_s}{c} f_0, \tag{3}$$

where V_u is positive for the receiver moving towards the satellite and the same for V_s when the satellite moving from the receiver, f_0 is the central frequency of the signal transmitted from the satellite. For example, for GPS, depending on the choice of the L1 or L2 band, we have respectively $f_0 = 1575.42$ MHz and $f_0 = 1227.60$ MHz (Fig. 1).

The essence of our approach is that the receiver, once it turned on, should perform switching from one operating mode to another according to the scheme in Fig. 2. When

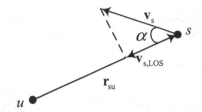

Fig. 1. To the calculation of the projection of the satellite speed on the LOS

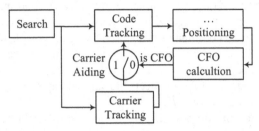

Fig. 2. A simple block diagram for CFO compensation to provide stable processing while code tracking is in carrier aiding mode

it switches from the satellite acquisition to the tracking mode, ordinary satellite tracking starts, i.e. without carrier aiding for code tracking loop.

Once the receiver obtain own coordinates, it is possible to estimate the CFO. We suggest using all the satellites for which tracking is performed (loops are in synchronism mode) and all ephemeris are read from signal. As the value of CFO we suggest to consider the averaged over satellites difference between the values of $f_{D,V}$ and $f_{D,Track}$. The obtained value of CFO should be aided to DLL as the auxiliary information from the carrier tracking loop.

When the carrier aiding is turned on, it is possible to reduce the bandwidth of DLL filter and thereby increase the accuracy of the pseudoranges calculation and, consequently, the accuracy of the receiver positioning.

One can assume that the local oscillator can be not only inaccurately tuned to the carrier frequency but also can be unstable. Then it is advised to regularly check the estimation of CFO. Moreover, it is possible to perform continuous adjustment of such estimate in the loop. However, it requires frequent calculations of receiver and satellite speed, what can be difficult for low-cost receivers.

3 Modeling

We used simulation modeling to investigate the dependence of efficiency of code tracking aided with carrier on the value of CFO.

3.1 Carrier Aiding

DLL scheme with carrier aiding in our model is based on the generalized scheme from [1] and is presented in Fig. 3.

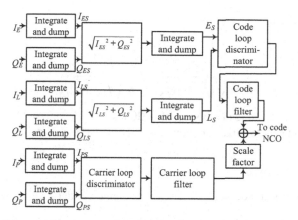

Fig. 3. Scheme of the tracking time synchronization using DLL with carrier aiding. I and Q are real and imaginary parts of the E, P, and L values which in turn are correlations of local copy of CA-code with the signal. For E value the signal is taken one sample earlier than the expected time of CA-code beginning in signal, for P value the exact time of beginning is used, and for L value the delay of one sample is used.

3.2 Model Description

The model simulates the signal processing of the one satellite. The core of the model is a block calculating the correlation of signal with the C/A-code. This block takes into account the continuous drifting of the time and frequency synchronization, as well as the value of the Doppler shift.

For carrier tracking we used PLL assisted (aided) by FLL (FLL-Assisted-PLL) which is denoted further as FPLL [8]. The FLL loop filter has the second order; the PLL loop filter has the third order. The filter bands are 1 and 10 Hz for FLL and PLL respectively. In DLL, we used the first order filter with the band of 0.1 Hz in the case of carrier aiding and the second order filter with the band of 1 Hz in the absence of aiding.

The FLL discriminator works according to four-quadrant arctangent algorithm:

$$\frac{ATAN2(dot/cross)}{(t_2 - t_1)}, \tag{4}$$

$$dot = I_{PS1}I_{PS2} + Q_{PS1}Q_{PS2},$$
$$cross = I_{PS1}Q_{PS2} - I_{PS2}Q_{PS1},$$

where t_2 and t_1 is time samples forming the interval from which the values come to the FLL discriminator.

The PLL discriminator works according to Costas algorithm:

$$\tan^{-1}(Q_{PS}/I_{PS}). \tag{5}$$

Before bit synchronization, the FPLL is turned off. After bit synchronization, it turns on with the integration period of 20 ms, i.e. the duration of one bit.

DLL uses non-coherent discriminator:

$$\frac{1}{2}\frac{E-L}{E+L},\tag{6}$$

$$E = \sqrt{I_{ES}^2 + Q_{ES}^2}, \ L = \sqrt{I_{LS}^2 + Q_{LS}^2},$$

and the integration period is always equal to 20 ms.

Performing bit synchronization requires analysis of 100 C/A-codes, i.e. it takes 0.1 s.

3.3 Simulation Results

This section presents and describes the results obtained under the following conditions:

1. The receiver is stationary.
2. The value of V_s is equal to -450 m/s that is the average absolute value of the projection of the satellite's speed on the LOS [1].
3. The carrier-to-noise ratio (CNR) is equal to 45 dB·Hz, that is the average value for visible satellites [1].
4. The oversampling factor is equal to 2, i.e. the signal sampling rate is twice greater than the chip rate.
5. In practice, with a "cold" start of the receiver, it takes from 18 to 36 s to get the first coordinates [1], and the switching-on of carrier aiding for DLL is possible only after the coordinates are calculated. Nevertheless, for the convenience of the results presentation we performed carrier aiding after 10 s, when DLL entered the synchronism mode. It doesn't limit the generality of the obtained results.

Note that the second order filters are able to track motions caused by the constant velocity. Therefore, in order to avoid the influence of the motions caused by the acceleration on the results we considered the acceleration of the receiver and satellite to be equal to zero during the simulation.

Figure 4 shows that the GNSS signal tracking loop has entered the synchronism mode, i.e. time synchronization error is practically zero. The values of FLL and PLL discriminators in the synchronism mode are very close to zero. At the same time DLL discriminator generates the saw-shaped error signal. It happens because the time adjustment is carried out by taking into account the sampling frequency resolution of the signal.

From Fig. 5a, b it follows that the using of DLL with carrier aiding can significantly improve the accuracy of the time synchronization. At Fig. 5b the variation of the time synchronization error seems to be at least one order smaller than at Fig. 5a. From Fig. 5b, c it follows that the presence of non-zero CFO significantly degrades the results. Despite the small variance of the time synchronization error, it is biased. This bias is explained by the fact that an estimate of the time synchronization error from the carrier tracking block contains incorrect dynamics. The greater the value of CFO, the greater the value of the excess dynamics. For example, from Fig. 5d it follows that the time synchronization was lost after 10 s for the case of CFO equal to 500 Hz. Note that a 1-chip time synchronization error means that satellite was lost.

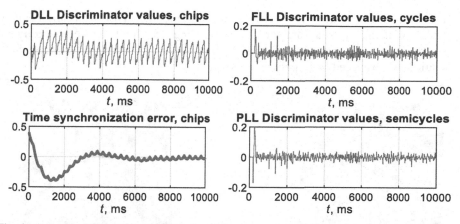

Fig. 4. Outputs of DLL, PLL, and FLL discriminators and the time synchronization error for the case of ordinary DLL processing, i.e. without carrier aiding.

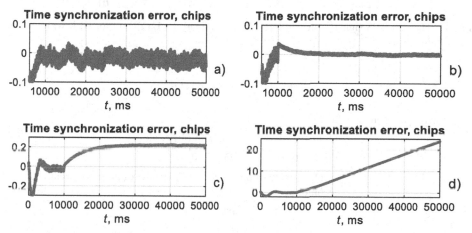

Fig. 5. Time synchronization error for ordinary DLL (a), for DLL with precise carrier aiding, i.e. CFO = 0 Hz (b), for DLL with unprecise carrier aiding and CFO = 10 Hz (c), and for DLL with unprecise carrier aiding and CFO = 500 Hz (d).

4 Results

We have implemented a model in MATLAB, which allows to perform all stages of GNSS signals processing up to positioning. In this model, it is possible to use carrier aiding for code tracking block. Using this model, the processing of the real GPS signal recordings was performed. Recordings were made with a high-precision local oscillator and for the case of stationary receiver. The heterodyne inaccuracy, i.e. non-zero value of CFO, was modeled in MATLAB.

From Fig. 6 it follows that in the case of zero CFO the use of DLL with carrier aiding significantly increases the accuracy of the positioning, the cloud of receiver positions seems to be simply the point. From Table 1 it follows that the standard deviation (SD) of positioning is reduced by 5 times.

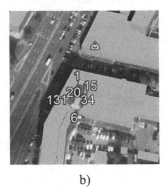

a)   b)

Fig. 6. The real GPS signal positioning results for ordinary DLL (a), and for DLL with precise carrier aiding (b)

Table 1. SD of Coordinates

Geometric parameter	SD, m			
	Ordinary DLL		DLL with carrier aiding	
	CFO = 0 Hz		CFO = 10 Hz	
	Without using of proposed technique		With using of proposed technique	
Latitude	6.8	1.3	302.1	1.3
Longitude	12.7	2.9	132.6	2.9
Altitude	35.4	2.8	872.7	2.8

From Fig. 7a it follows that in the case of non-zero CFO and for DLL with carrier aiding, the positioning results are greatly distorted, that is imaginary movement of the receiver appears. In Fig. 7b it is shown that the using of our proposed technique provides compensating of the CFO. From Table I it follows that the results of Fig. 6b and Fig. 7c are practically coincided. That means that our proposed algorithm is virtually eliminating CFO.

a)   b)

Fig. 7. The real GPS signal positioning results for DLL with carrier aiding and CFO = 10 Hz without (a) and with (b) using of proposed technique

5 Conclusions

In this paper, the method for estimating and compensating the carrier frequency offset was proposed. This method improves the stability of code tracking with carrier aiding. Carrier aiding is used to significantly improve the accuracy of the receiver positioning.

The idea of calculation of the CFO is based on evaluation of the Doppler frequency shifts difference. The first one Doppler shift is obtained in the carrier tracking loop and the second one is calculated based on the analysis of the receiver and the satellite positions and speeds.

By means of simulation, it was demonstrated that the CFO leads to a bias in the time synchronization estimate or even to a failure of tracking when DLL is aided with carrier tracking loop.

By analyzing the real GPS signal recordings, it was shown that the proposed technique almost removes the influence of CFO. As a result, it ensures the accuracy of positioning close to that, which can be obtained using a local oscillator with precise tuning.

References

1. Kaplan, E.D., Hegarty, C.J.: Understanding GPS. Principles and Applications, 3rd edn. Artech House (2017)
2. Borre, K., Akos, D.M., Bertelsen, N., Rinder, P., Jensen, S.H.: A Software-Defined GPS and Galileo Receiver. A Single-Frequency Approach. Birkhauser (2007)
3. Betz, J.W.: Engineering Satellite-Based Navigation and Timing: Global Navigation Satellite Systems, Signals, and Receivers, pp. 480–481. Wiley-IEEE Press, Hoboken (2016)

4. Barth, C.: Subsampling GPS Receiver Front-end. A Dissertation submitted to the dep. of electrical engineering and the committee on graduate studies of Stanford University in partial fulfillment of requirements for the Degree of Doctor of Philosophy, pp. 11–19, August 2011
5. Divya, J., Irulappan, M., Radhamani, N., Jeeva, B.: Evaluating the performance of GPS signals acquisition and tracking. In: IEEE 2nd International Conference on Recent Trends in Electronics, Information & Communication Technology (RTEICT), pp. 791–795, January 2018
6. Tu, Z., Lu, T., Chen, Q.: A novel carrier loop based on unscented Kalman filter methods for tracking high dynamic GPS signals. IEEE 18th International Conference on Communication Technology (ICCT), pp. 1007–1012, January 2019
7. Petrov, I.A.: A study of the influence of DLL parameters on the GNSS positioning accuracy. J. Phys.: Conf. Ser. **1326**, 012041 (2019)
8. Phillip, W.Ward.: Performance comparisons between FLL, PLL and a novel FLL-assisted-PLL carrier tracking loop under RF interference conditions. In: Proceedings of the 11th International Technical Meeting of the Satellite Division of the Institute of Navigation, pp. 783–795, September 1998
9. Chen, X., Wang, W., Meng, W., Zhang, Z.: High dynamic GPS signal tracking based on UKF and carrier aiding technology. In: International Conference on Communications and Mobile Computing, pp. 476–480, May 2010
10. Zhang, J., Zhang, K., Grenfell, R., Deakin, R.: GPS satellite velocity and acceleration determination using the broadcast ephemeris. J. Navigat. **59**, 293–305 (2006)
11. Hugh, D.Y., Freedman, R.A.: University Physics with Modern Physics. Sears & Zemansky's, 14th edn. pp. 468–505 (2016)

Modified Direct Positioning Method in Satellite Geolocation

Pavel Kistanov[1]($\boxtimes$), Elizaveta Shcherbinina[2]($\boxtimes$) (ORCID), Alexander Titov[1]($\boxtimes$),
Oleg Tsarik[1]($\boxtimes$), and Igor Tsikin[2]($\boxtimes$)

[1] Ltd. Special Technology Center, Saint-Petersburg, Russia
pakistanov@gmail.com, altv7@mail.ru, ovtzar@mail.ru
[2] Peter the Great St. Petersburg Polytechnic University, Saint-Petersburg 195251, Russia
lizspbstyle@gmail.com, tsikin@mail.spbstu.ru

Abstract. The paper presents features of direct positioning method application in satellite geolocation for radio source with unknown signal waveform. This method is used in terrestrial radio monitoring systems along with the widespread two-step method. The paper proposes a modification of the satellite geolocation direct method. The modified direct method reduces computational costs for implementation of signal processing on the satellite geolocation ground station and increases the radio source positioning accuracy. The accuracy benefit of the modified direct method increases when attenuation increases in the channels of adjacent satellites of the satellite geolocation system and signal to noise ratio decreases. The paper analyzes the efficiency of the direct method and its modification with an arbitrary ratio between the frequency band of the radio source signal and the analyzed frequency band of the satellite geolocation ground station. This analysis showed the advantage of the modified direct method in a wide range of analysis bandwidths, signal-to-noise ratios, and attenuation in the adjacent channels.

Keywords: Satellite geolocation · Modified direct positioning method · Direct positioning method · Two-step TDOA-based positioning method · Signal bandwidth · Analysis bandwidth

1 Introduction

Radio frequency resource monitoring of geostationary satellite transponders is an important component of the satellite communication systems (SCS) operation [1–3]. In particular, ground station with a priory unknown form and frequency band of any other SCS operator can operate incorrectly and utilize in an unauthorized way the free frequency band of the satellite transponder [1, 2, 4]. Satellite geolocation systems (SGS) are used for the determination of the such radio source coordinates [1, 2, 4]. The SGS ground station receives signals from primary (Sat_1) and adjacent satellites (Sat_2, Sat_3) on physically separated antennas (Fig. 1). The primary satellite is a satellite whose frequency resource is used incorrectly. The adjacent satellites re-transmit the same RS signal, have been received due to the existence of the RS antenna pattern side lobes [1, 5].

O. Galinina et al. (Eds.): NEW2AN 2020/ruSMART 2020, LNCS 12525, pp. 361–369, 2020.
https://doi.org/10.1007/978-3-030-65726-0_32

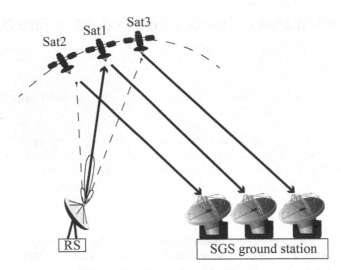

Fig. 1. Satellite geolocation principle

RS coordinates can be estimated by joint processing of the signals, received on SGS ground station.

In satellite geolocation, the two-step time difference of arrival-based (TDOA-based) method is widely used, when the RS coordinates are calculated (second step) using differences in the propagation time delay of signals from the satellites, measured at the first step [1–3, 6, 7]. On the other hand, in terrestrial radio monitoring systems the Direct Positioning (DP) method is used to determine the RS coordinates in addition to the two-step TDOA-based method [8–11]. The DP method also involves the joint processing of signals from the same RS, incoming with different delays to different processing points. This method provides a significant accuracy benefit before the two-step TDOA-based method for small signal-to-noise ratios (-17 dB and below) [11] in the conditions of ground-based systems, when the RS signal levels at different processing points are approximately the same. A problem arises about the possibility and effectiveness of using such a method in satellite geolocation, where a typical attenuation of the received signals from Sat_2 and Sat_3 is 50 dB or more compared with the signal from Sat_1 [2]. At the same time, it is important to take into account the actual operating conditions of the SGS, when not only the waveform, but also the frequency band of the RS signal are unknown. So, the situations are possible where the analysis frequency band is both greater and less than the frequency band of the RS signal.

The goal of this article is to analyze the effectiveness of the use of DP method and the possible modification of this method in the SGS under conditions of an arbitrary ratio of the analysis frequency band and the RS signal frequency band.

2   Positioning Methods

The two-step TDOA-based method in the satellite geolocation system involves obtaining at least two estimates $\hat{\delta}t_{12}$, $\hat{\delta}t_{13}$ of the differences δt_{12}, δt_{13} in the propagation time of the RS signal over the primary (through Sat_1) and adjacent (through Sat_2 and Sat_3) channels at the first step [2, 3]. These values estimations by maximum likelihood results to maximization of the functions:

$$L(\delta t_{1i}) = \left| \int_0^{T_a} X_1(t) X_i^*(t - \delta t_{1i}) e^{-j(\Delta\omega_1 - \Delta\omega_i)t} dt \right|, \ i = 2, 3,$$

where $X_i(t)$ – complex envelope of analyzed process $r_i(t) = \delta A_i \cdot s(t - \delta t_i; \Delta\omega) + n_i(t)$, $i = 1,2,3$, $s(t)$–unknown radio source signal, δA_i and δt_i – attenuation and propagation time in channel from RS to Sat_i and from Sat_i to SGS ground station, $\Delta\omega_i$ – sum of frequency shifts, caused by the instability of RS, satellites and SGS ground station local oscillators and by the Doppler effect during signal propagation through the uplink and downlink satellite channels, $n_i(t)$ – random process, characterizing the total effect of additive noise, when receiving an RS signal on Sat_i and on the SGS ground station, T_a – analysis interval, sign * denotes complex conjugation operation. As $n_i(t)$, we then consider a normal random process with zero mathematical expectation and an average power spectral density $N_0/2$. We assume the steps of signal detection and frequency shifts elimination are pre-completed.

The second step of the two-step TDOA-based method is reduced to solving a system of equations $\|\mathbf{p}_{RS} - \mathbf{p}_{SV_1}\| - \|\mathbf{p}_{RS} - \mathbf{p}_{SV_i}\| + \Delta d_{SV-SGS}^{1i} - \hat{\delta t}_{1i} \cdot c = \varepsilon_{1i}, i = 2, 3,$ where $\mathbf{p}_{RS} = [x_{RS}, y_{RS}, z_{RS}]^T$ – unknown RS coordinates vector (sign T denotes transpose operation); $\mathbf{p}_{SV_i} = [x_{SV_i}, y_{SV_i}, z_{SV_i}]^T$, $i = 1, 2, 3$ – coordinates vector of Sat_i; Δd_{SV-SGS}^{1i} – difference between distances $\|\mathbf{p}_{SGS} - \mathbf{p}_{SV_1}\|$ and $\|\mathbf{p}_{SGS} - \mathbf{p}_{SV_i}\|$; $\mathbf{p}_{SGS} = [x_{SGS}, y_{SGS}, z_{SGS}]^T$ – coordinates vector of the SGS ground station; ε_{1i} – error, caused differences between $\hat{\delta t}_{1i}$ and δt_{1i}; c – light speed in a vacuum. The values Δd_{SV-SGS}^{1i} can be considered known, if the SGS ground station coordinates are precisely known and satellites coordinates are obtained on the basis ephemeris and refined using the signals of the reference stations [3, 12–14]. The solution of such a non-linear system of equations is carried out on the basis of various numerical methods, such as Gauss-Newton [7], Nelder-Mead [15, 16] and others.

In contrast to the two-step TDOA-based method, the direct positioning method, used in ground-based radio monitoring systems, carries out joint processing of input process realizations (received on the SGS ground station) without an intermediate step of estimating the parameters of these realizations. Scientists in [8, 11] obtain algorithm of such direct positioning method analyzing joint likelihood function (LF) of the complex envelopes $X_i(t)$ of the analyzed processes $r_i(t)$ in form $\prod_{i=1}^{3} W(X_i(t)/\mathbf{p}_{RS}, S(t), \delta t_i, \delta A_i, \Delta\omega_i)$, where conditional probability density $W(X_i(t)/\mathbf{p}_{RS}, S(t), \delta t_i, \delta A_i, \Delta\omega_i)$ of process $X_i(t)$ with the desired (estimated) vector $\mathbf{p}_{RS}$ and unknowns $S(t), \delta t_i, \delta A_i, \Delta\omega_i$ is proportional to the value:

$$l(X(t)/\mathbf{p}_{RS}, S(t), \delta t_i, \delta A_i, \Delta\omega_i) = \exp\left(-\frac{1}{2\sigma_i^2} \int_0^{T_a} |X_i(t) - \delta A_i \cdot S(t - \delta t; \Delta\omega_i)|^2 dt\right).$$

In this case, $S(t)$ is the complex envelope of the signal, σ_i^2 is the variance of additive noise in the analyzed frequency band at the input of the antenna. As shown in [8, 11, 17, 18], by eliminating the "interfering" parameters based on the generalized maximum likelihood criterion [19], as well as compensating the frequency shifts at the preliminary step, the search for the maximum of the considered LF corresponds to maximizing a function of the form:

$$
L_{DP}(\mathbf{p}_{RS}) = \left| \int_0^{T_a} X_1(t)X_2(t - \tau_{12}(\mathbf{p}_{RS}))dt \right| + \left| \int_0^{T_a} X_1(t)X_3(t - \tau_{13}(\mathbf{p}_{RS}))dt \right| +
$$

$$
+ \left| \int_0^{T_a} X_2(t)X_3(t - \tau_{23}(\mathbf{p}_{RS}))dt \right|,
$$

where values $\tau_{12}, \tau_{13}, \tau_{23}$ are calculated according to the equation:

$$
\tau_{ij} = \frac{\|\mathbf{p}_{RS} - \mathbf{p}_{SV_i}\| + \|\mathbf{p}_{SGS} - \mathbf{p}_{SV_i}\| - \|\mathbf{p}_{RS} - \mathbf{p}_{SV_j}\| - \|\mathbf{p}_{SGS} - \mathbf{p}_{SV_j}\|}{c}; i = 1, 2, 3; j = 1, 2, 3; i \neq j
$$

It is interesting to find out whether DP method has the above-mentioned accuracy benefit in terms of SGS over the two-step TDOA-based positioning method. Moreover, the DP method has the high computational complexity of the function $L_{DP}(\mathbf{p}_{RS})$ maximization procedure [9, 10] and it is interesting to consider any modifications of the DP method, aimed at reducing computational costs without significantly reducing (or even without losing) the accuracy of the RS coordinates estimates. Note that the DP method based on maximization $L_{DP}(\mathbf{p}_{RS})$ is the optimal for direct estimation of the RS coordinates in the conditions of arbitrary relations between the RS signal levels in the considered realizations at the inputs of the various SGS ground station antennas. At the same time, the effectiveness question of such DP method remains open in the real-world conditions of the SGS, when the RS signal levels in realizations $X_2(t), X_3(t)$ always turn out to be 30... 50 dB lower than in $X_1(t)$. In addition, the role of the third term in maximization $L_{DP}(\mathbf{p}_{RS})$ is the least important. It is interesting to consider a modified direct positioning (MDP) method of the form, where: $\hat{\mathbf{p}}_{RS} = \arg\max\{L_{MDP}(\mathbf{p}_{RS})\}$, where:

$$
L_{MDP}(\mathbf{p}_{RS}) = \left| \int_0^{T_a} X_1(t)X_2(t - \tau_{12}(\mathbf{p}_{RS}))dt \right| + \left| \int_0^{T_a} X_1(t)X_3(t - \tau_{13}(\mathbf{p}_{RS}))dt \right|.
$$

3   Simulation

We carried out statistical simulation in the Matlab environment of radio source positioning methods. We consider the ground station of a satellite communications system emitting a QPSK signal as RS. In the simulation the satellite Yamal 601 (longitude $\lambda_{Sat_1} = 49°$) [20] is Sat_1, and satellites Express AM6 [20] and Express AM7 [20] with longitude values $\lambda_{Sat_2} = 53°$, $\lambda_{Sat_3} = 40°$ are Sat_2 and Sat_3 respectively. In the simulation, the incoming realizations are processed by three methods: the two-step TDOA-based positioning method, the direct positioning method, and the modified direct positioning method. We determine the accuracy of each method by root mean square error (RMSE) $\sqrt{\frac{1}{N}\sum_{i=1}^{N}\left\|\hat{\mathbf{p}}_{RSi}-\mathbf{p}_{RS}^{0}\right\|^{2}}$, where $\hat{\mathbf{p}}_{RSi}$ – estimations of RS coordinates vector. We choose the true RS coordinates $\mathbf{p}_{RS}^{0}$ are near the city Saint-Petersburg in Russia and the SGC ground station coordinates – near the city Krasnodar in Russia.

The simulation was carried out for different attenuation values on adjacent channels with respect to the primary one (the attenuation values on two adjacent channels were assumed the same) in the signal-to-noise ratio range $SNR_{in} = 10\ldots 20$ dB [2, 3] on the primary channel, which is of practical interest. The value SNR_{in} is given as the ratio of the average signal power to the average noise power in the RS signal band $B_s = 2$MHz.

Figure 2 shows RMSE for the direct and the two-step TDOA-based positioning methods in the attenuation range $att = -30\ldots -70$dB on adjacent channels and two values of the signal-to-noise ratio on primary channel $SNR_{in} = 10$dB, 20dB. These dependencies are given for the cases: analysis interval duration $T_a = 5\,s$, equality between analysis frequency bandwidth B_a and RS signal frequency bandwidth B_s.

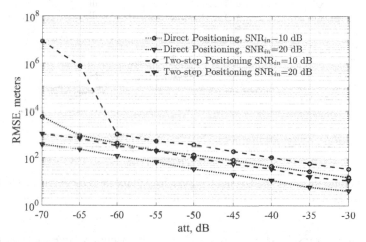

Fig. 2. Positioning RMSE of the DP and the two-step TDOA-based methods for varying attenuation and two values of signal-to-noise ratio 10 dB and 20 dB ($T_a = 5\,s$, $B_a = B_s = 2$MHz)

As shown on Fig. 2, DP method provides higher accuracy in RS positioning over the entire considered range of the attenuation values in the adjacent channels and besides starting from $att = -50$dB and below positioning accuracy increase reaches hundreds of meters. The accuracy benefit of the direct method increases substantially with decreasing SNR_{in}. An increase in attenuation ($att < -60$ dB) leads to the predominance of abnormal errors in the operation of the two-step TDOA-based positioning method. Further simulation was carried out for the direct positioning method with various simulation parameters.

Dependencies similar to Fig. 2 were obtained for the direct method and its modification for $SNR_{in} = 10, 20$ dB and $T_a = 5$ sec.

Table 1 shows the difference in values for the direct method and its modification in accordance with the Fig. 3.

Table 1. Differences between RMSE of the DP and the modified DP methods

att, dB	$RMSE_{DP} - RMSE_{MDP}$ в метрах, $SNR_{in} = 20$ dB	$RMSE_{DP} - RMSE_{MDP}$ в метрах, $SNR_{in} = 10$ dB
−50	1	4
−55	2	8
−60	10	16
−65	15	21
−70	18	1843

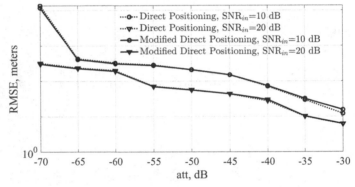

Fig. 3. Positioning RMSE of the DP and the modified DP methods for varying attenuation and two values of signal-to-noise ratio 10 dB and 20 dB ($T_a = 5\,s$, $B_a = B_s = 2$MHz)

The simulation results (Fig. 3, Table 1) show the accuracy benefit of the modified direct method with an attenuation increase in, starting from a value of −50 dB or lower.

We also compare the effectiveness of the direct method and its modification in conditions of an arbitrary ratio of the analyzed frequency band B_a and the RS signal frequency band B_s. Such analysis is important in view of the fact that the RS signal frequency bandwidth is unknown, when solving the problem of the RS coordinates determination. Figure 4 shows the dependences of the RMSE positioning versus the analysis bandwidth B_a, when we processed incoming realizations by the direct positioning method and its modification for the $B_s = 2$ MHz and fixed signal-to-noise ratio over the primary channel in the frequency band B_s ($SNR_{in} = 10$dB, 20dB).

Thus, in the case when the analysis bandwidth is greater than the RS frequency bandwidth, the positioning accuracy reduces, when using both the direct positioning

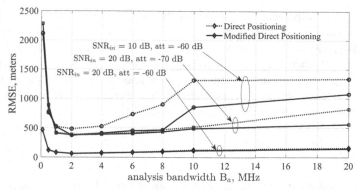

Fig. 4. Positioning RMSE of the DP and the modified DP methods for varying analysis frequency bandwidth, two values of signal-to-noise ratio 10 dB and 20 dB, two values of attenuation -60 dB and -70 dB ($T_a = 5\,s$, $B_a = B_s = 2$MHz)

method and its modification. This is explained by the fact that while keeping the signal-to-noise ratio SNR_{in} in the RS signal frequency band, shown on Fig. 4, the analysis bandwidth spread leads to a decrease in the signal-to-noise ratio at the input of the signal processing block. Nevertheless, the modified direct positioning method has the accuracy benefit of the obtained estimates with respect to the direct positioning method for all considered values of the analysis bandwidth, signal-to-noise ratios, and attenuation (Fig. 4).

In the region of large excesses of the analysis frequency band over the RS signal frequency band a decrease in the value SNR_{in} leads to a significant decrease in positioning accuracy, regardless of whether direct or modified direct positioning methods are used to measure the RS coordinates. For example, at the maximum of the considered value of the analysis bandwidth (20 MHz), a decrease SNR_{in} of 10 dB at the same adjacent channels attenuation leads to a decrease in positioning accuracy of almost 1 km. Under the same conditions, an increase in adjacent channels attenuation of by 10 dB leads to a decrease in accuracy by about 300 m.

4   Conclusions

The direct method of RS coordinates determination (DP method), used in terrestrial radio monitoring systems, shows a significant accuracy benefit compared with the widely used two-step TDOA-based positioning method in typical conditions of the satellite geolocation system operation, where the signal attenuation in the adjacent channels reaches $-30\ldots -70$ dB compared with the primary channel.

The modification of the satellite geolocation direct method, considered in the paper (modified direct method, MDP method), allows to reduce computational costs (for implementation of signal processing on the SGS ground station) and to increase the RS positioning accuracy. In this case, the accuracy benefit of the MDP method increases with increasing attenuation in the adjacent channels compared with the DP method.

When the analyzed frequency band of the incoming processes on the SGS ground station exceeds the RS signal frequency band, a comparative analysis of the considered methods still shows the accuracy benefit of the MDP method compared with the DP method at the same level of attenuation in the adjacent channels. At the same time, an increase in the analysis frequency band compared with the signal frequency band leads to a decrease in the accuracy of both considered methods. In this case, an attenuation increase in the primary channel (keeping the attenuation value in the adjacent channels) leads to greater accuracy loss than an attenuation increase in the adjacent channels relative to the primary channel.

References

1. Chan, M.: Application of a dual satellite geolocation system on locating sweeping interference. World Acad. Sci. Eng. Technol. **6**, 1029–1034 (2012)
2. Haworth, D., Smith, N., Bardelli, R., Clement, T.: Interference localization for EUTELSAT satellites–the first European transmitter location system. Int. J. Satell. Commun. **15**, 155–183 (1997)
3. Griffin, C., Duck, S.: Interferometric radio-frequency emitter location. IEE Proc.-Radar, Sonar Navig. **149**, 153–160 (2002)
4. Yan, H., Cao, J.K., Chen, L.: Study on location accuracy of dual-satellite geolocation system. In: IEEE 10th International Conference on Signal Processing Proceedings, pp. 107–110. IEEE (2010)
5. Wu, R., Zhang, Y., Huang, Y., Xiong, J., Deng, Z.: A novel long-time accumulation method for double-satellite TDOA/FDOA interference localization. Radio Sci. **53**, 129–142 (2018)
6. Ho, K.C., Chan, Y.T.: Solution and performance analysis of geolocation by TDOA. IEEE Trans. Aerosp. Electron. Syst. **29**, 1311–1322 (1993)
7. Ho, K.C., Chan, Y.T.: Geolocation of a known altitude object from TDOA and FDOA measurements. IEEE Trans. Aerosp. Electron. Syst. **33**, 770–783 (1997)
8. Weiss, A.J., Amar, A.: Direct geolocation of stationary wideband radio signal based on time delays and doppler shifts. In: 2009 IEEE/SP 15th Workshop on Statistical Signal Processing, pp. 101–104. IEEE (2009)
9. Ma, F., Liu, Z.-M., Guo, F.: Direct position determination for wideband sources using fast approximation. IEEE Trans. Veh. Technol. **68**, 8216–8221 (2019)
10. Ma, F., Guo, F., Yang, L.: Low-complexity TDOA and FDOA localization: a compromise between two-step and DPD methods. Digital Signal Process. **96**, 102600 (2020)
11. Vankayalapati, N., Kay, S., Ding, Q.: TDOA based direct positioning maximum likelihood estimator and the Cramer-Rao bound. IEEE Trans. Aerosp. Electron. Syst. **50**, 1616–1635 (2014)
12. Zhou, P., Zhang, Q., Lin, H., Yu, P.: The influence of sampling mode on the accuracy of satellite interference geolocation. In: 2017 IEEE International Conference on Signal Processing, Communications and Computing (ICSPCC), pp. 1–5. IEEE (2017)
13. Zheng-bo, S., Shang-Fu, Y.: Analysis on parameter error of satellite interference location. In: Proceedings of 2004 Asia-Pacific Radio Science Conference, pp. 265–268. IEEE (2004)
14. Севидов, В., Чемаров, А.: Определение координат спутников-ретрансляторов в разностно-дальномерной системе геолокации. РОССИИ **3**, 41 (2015)
15. Nelder, J.A., Mead, R.: A simplex method for function minimization. Comput. J. **7**, 308–313 (1965)
16. Martinez, A., Aguado Agelet, F., Alvarez-Vázquez, L., Hernando, J., Mosteiro, D.: Optimal transmitter location in an indoor wireless system by Nelder-Mead method. Microwave Opt. Technol. Lett. **27**, 146–148 (2000)

17. Tsikin, I.A., Melikhova, A.P.: Direct signal processing for GNSS integrity monitoring. In: Galinina, O., Andreev, S., Balandin, S., Koucheryavy, Y. (eds.) NEW2AN/ruSMART/NsCC -2017. LNCS, vol. 10531, pp. 635–643. Springer, Cham (2017). https://doi.org/10.1007/978-3-319-67380-6_60
18. Tsikin, I., Shcherbinina, E.: Algorithms of GNSS signal processing based on the generalized maximum likelihood criterion for attitude determination. In: 2018 25th Saint Petersburg International Conference on Integrated Navigation Systems (ICINS), pp. 1–4. IEEE (2018)
19. Van Trees, H.L., Bell, K.L.: Detection Estimation and Modulation Theory. Wiley, United States (2013)
20. Celestrak orbit visualization. http://www.celestrak.com/NORAD/elements/geo.txt. Accessed 01 Jun 2020

Offset Generation and Interlayer Network Architecture for 5GNR LDPC Parallel Layered Decoder with Variable Lifting Factor Support

Aleksei Krylov[1,2]($\boxtimes$), Andrey Rashich[1,2], Chao Zhang[1,2], and Kewu Peng[1,2]

[1] Peter the Great St. Petersburg Polytechnic University, St. Petersburg, Russia
{krylov_ae,rashich}@cee.spbstu.ru
[2] Tsinghua University, Beijing, China
{z_c,pengkewu}@tsinghua.edu.cn

Abstract. Technical specification of 5G New Radio uses QC-LDPC code as forward error correction coding scheme in data channel for eMBB scenario. The specification gives tough requirements of performance, latency and throughput in addition to code rate flexibility. In this paper we propose a modified parallel layered decoder architecture that is able to support all the mentioned in-standard codeblock lengths in a natural and extendible way. Also we provide estimates on the hardware resources consumption and decoder throughput.

Keywords: 5G · Belief propagation decoder · Parallel layered decoder · Layered scheduling · LDPC · Flexible code rate

1 Introduction

Gallager [4] proposed LDPC codes in 1962, but they found wide applications only in the current century. Fifth generation new radio (5G-NR) wireless systems expands the channel coding of LDPC codes compared to previous generation (4G-LTE). 5G-NR LDPC codes [8] are Quasi-Cyclic (QC-LDPC) codes and support two base graphs, 51 different lifting factors, puncturing and shortening [1] for rate matching and flexible applications.

Also there are high requirements for decoding latency, throughput and performance. These metrics vary for different scenarios (eMBB, URLLC or mMTC), but the most challenging one is 1 ms for latency and 20 Gbps throughput. Thus the potential decoder architecture should be flexible enough to fulfill all supported check matrices and also have efficient hardware implementation in terms of hardware resources.

Though there are already many architectures and hardware implementations of LDPC decoders in previous works, most of them are designed for Wi-Fi,

This research work was supported by Peter the Great St. Petersburg Polytechnic University in the framework of the Program "5-100-2020".

© Springer Nature Switzerland AG 2020
O. Galinina et al. (Eds.): NEW2AN 2020/ruSMART 2020, LNCS 12525, pp. 370–380, 2020.
https://doi.org/10.1007/978-3-030-65726-0_33

WiMax, DVB-S2, S2x, etc., but not for 5G-NR. Techniques that performed well for previous systems might become non-profitable or even non-applicable in 5G systems due to both large and embedded base graphs and lifting sizes. Thus in this paper we attempt to propose an effective hardware architecture for 5G-NR LDPC decoder and estimate its throughput and computational complexity.

Classical solution for LDPC decoding is Belief Propagation Algorithm (BPA). This algorithm has quite complex hardware implementation since its product operations involved, thus there are several simplified alternative algorithms, the well-known one is Min-Sum Algorithm (MSA) [3]. Further evolutions of MSA are Offset MSA (OMSA) and Normalized MSA (NMSA), these algorithms provide better performance close to that using BP-decoding.

The normalization factors in NMSA should be adjusted for different SNR values, channel conditions and checknode degrees, which could give near-BP performance. In previous work we proposed enhanced adaptive NMSA (EANMSA) [6], with look-up tables for different check-node degrees and the check ratios in the iterative decoding process, which is the evolution of adaptive NMSA (ANSMA) [5].

BP decoder implementation could have different scheduling schemes – layered [7] or conventional flooded. Layered scheduling is more preferable since its fast convergence rate, thus the decoder requires less iterations and achieves higher throughput accordingly. Layered scheduling also has straightforward implementation for QC LDPC codes since each row in base graph is simply considered as one layer. For large base graphs layered decoder has another advantage over the flooded one, because the interconnection network in flooded decoder rapidly grows and becomes more complicated, and even congested.

High latency is the main drawback of classical layered decoding, if all layers are processed sequentially. Parallel layered decoder (PLD) [10] was proposed to overcome this drawback for WiMax LDPC decoding. The architecture in paper [10] though has difficulty to support variable lifting sizes of check matrices.

In this paper we propose a flexible PLD architecture for 5G base graph 2 that supports all 51 possible lifting sizes with adaptive normalization factor. The proposed architecture is implemented in bit-accurate and cycle-accurate model in Simulink and thus can be easily moved to hardware implementation in FPGA or ASIC. Also we provide the estimates of resource usage. The EANMSA features are all applicable to this architecture and though this gives performance gain at the cost of slightly improved computational complexity.

This paper is organized as follows. Brief description of PLD algorithm is presented in Sect. 2. Proposed architecture of LDPC decoder is presented in Sect. 3. Performance and resources estimates are provided in Sect. 4. Final conclusions are drawn in Sect. 5.

2   Parallel Layered Decoder

Parallel layered architecture is presented in [10], here we give a short reference for better understanding of the following sections.

2.1 MS Loosely Coupled Algorithm

MSA can be considered as an approximation of BPA that avoids product operation and thus much more appropriate for hardware implementation. First we give the following definitions: let $r_{mn}[k]$ be the check-to-variable (CV) message from check node m to variable node n on the kth decoder iteration, let $q_{mn}[k]$ be the variable-to-check (VC) message from variable node m to check node n, let p_n be the input LLR for n_{th} variable node (codeword bit) and $\Lambda_n[k]$ is aposteriori LLR (APLLR) for n_{th} variable node on k_{th} iteration.

Also let $N(m)$ be the set of variable nodes connected (in terms of connections in Tanner graph that represents check matrix) to m^{th} check nodes and $M(n)$ is the set of check nodes, connected to n^{th} variable node. $K(x) \backslash y$ means that we use a set of nodes that are connected to x^{th} node except y^{th} node in that set.

With these definitions the decoding algorithm goes as follows: p_n is set to decoder input LLRs, and at the k_{th} iteration decoder calculates VC messages according to "(1)" and CV messages according to "(3)". Decoder uses APLLRs "(2)" to calculate hard decision vector and do the parity check according to check matrix.

$$q_{mn}[k] = p_n + \sum_{m' \in M(n) \backslash m} r_{m'n}[k-1]. \tag{1}$$

$$\Lambda_n[k] = p_n + \sum_{m' \in M(n)} r_{m'n}[k-1]. \tag{2}$$

$$r_{mn}[k] = (\prod_{n' \in N(m) \backslash n} sign(q_{mn'}[k])) \times (\alpha \min_{n' \in N(m) \backslash n} |q_{mn'}[k]|). \tag{3}$$

In Eq. (3) α is a normalization factor that helps to approximate BP and turns MSA into NMSA.

Loosely coupled algorithm [9] simplifies interconnections between check nodes and variable nodes since no variable messages are sent (and thus there are no explicit variable node processing units in the design). This is possible when each check node stores check node messages $r_{mn}[k-1]$ which is sent on previous iteration. In this case check nodes receive messages with APLLRs Λ_n, modify it using "(4)", "(5)" and send it the to following check node involving that particular LLR.

$$q_{mn}[k] = \Lambda_{n,in}[k] - r_{mn}[k-1]. \tag{4}$$

$$\Lambda_{n,out}[k] = q_{mn}[k] + r_{mn}[k]. \tag{5}$$

In this case aposteriori LLRs Λ_n are initialized with input decoder LLRs, and CV messages $r_{mn}[k]$ are calculated according to "(3)".

2.2   Adaptive Normalized MS Algorithm

Normalization factor α in "(3)" in NMSA is selected before the decoder architecture design and henceforth remains fixed. This lowers implementation cost as usually product with constant is much "cheaper" operation than complicated product of two variables, especially if we could select some "good" constants like 0.75, etc.

On the other hand, since the channel conditions change (signal-to-noise ratio - SNR could be a channel characteristic), the optimum α value changes too. So in [6] and [5] we proposed an adaptive normalization MSA. It uses some Monte-Carlo simulations to generate a table of α values that are optimal for different check-node decoding conditions. Thus during decoding we can track check-node decoding conditions and use appropriate value of α and get better decoder performance.

2.3   Layered and Parallel Layered Decoders

Layered decoder [7] uses less iterations for decoding than the flooded one, all other parameters being comparable. This is achieved because most layers (all except the first one in the queue) use LLRs that were updated by some previous layers within the same iteration. This means faster belief propagation and lower number of iterations.

There are many ways to separate check matrix into layers, but one layer is always limited to have no more than one 1 in each column (or, equivalently, each bit could be used in at most one parity check within one layer). If we use QC LDPC codes we can always consider each row of base matrix as a layer and this limitation would be fulfilled due to structure of QC code check matrix.

The only drawback of this scheduling scheme is high latency if layers are processed sequentially and each layer has to wait until the previous ones which share the codeword bits provide up-to-date APLLRs. PLD [10] solves this problem with reordering of calculations within a layer, thus different layers could perform their calculations in parallel and without cross-layer interference.

Basic idea of PLD decoder is explained in Fig. 1. It shows some dummy check matrix, its base matrix has only 3 rows, thus the decoder has 3 layers. Each entry of base graph is already replaced with square matrices of size $z \times z$ (z–lifting factor) with ones lying on depicted cyclic shifted diagonal and zeros elsewhere. Due to sparse and systematic structure of submatrices of check matrix it is obvious that layers 1 and 2 could work in parallel without interfering. Both these layers start processing from the first rows and move row by row to the bottom of the layer, and the updated aposteriori values from each processed layer could be used instantly in the following layers.

But layers 2 and 3 collide in the first column of base graph, since the diagonal with ones has the same shift in these layers (in this case zero shift). In this case we need to add an offset to the third layer to prevent collision. Offset adding means that we cyclic-shift the diagonal in all columns of the layer by the same

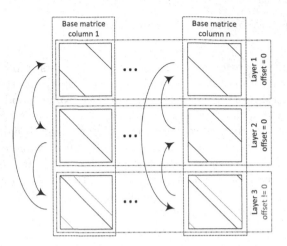

Fig. 1. Check matrix inter-layer dataflow example

number of positions (Fig. 1, solid black lines in layer 3 refer to shifted diagonals). Equivalently this means this layer starts processing from row $k_3 = $ offset.

It is important to notice that the row-permutation of the check matrix due to offset-adding will not change the encoding and the decoding of the underlying LDPC codes. Resulting dataflow between layers is shown in Fig. 1 with arrows. It is worth noticing that the dataflow for different columns can vary as for columns 1 and n. Also the offset value should be selected in a way to prevent collisions in all non-zero columns after offset-addition to a layer.

PLD as described above could be applied only to QC codes, and the true parallelism and pipelining is achievable only if one row calculation delay is less then minimum distance between layers. Obviously it becomes more complicated or even impossible to find appropriate offsets for layers when the number of layers increases and/or lifting size decreases rapidly.

3   Proposed Decoder Hardware Architecture

In this section we describe the proposed architecture for PLD of 5G-NR LDPC base graph 2 for further FPGA or ASIC implementation.

3.1   Overall Decoder Architecture

Since decoder architecture highly depends on base graph (BG) structure, we make some definitions on base graph parameters and provide their maximum values for 5G BG 2. Let N be the number of layers in decoder, in our case it is equal to number of rows in BG – 42. Let k_i be the number of non-zero elements in i^{th} row of BG. For 5G BG 2 we have $\max\limits_{i \in [1,42]} k_i = 10$, but mean value is about 5.

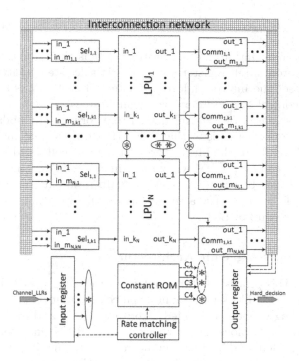

Fig. 2. Parallel layered decoder overall architecture

Each row in BG has some non-zero elements, and there could be some non-zero elements in the same columns in other layers. In this case layers "share" this column and APLLRs from this column move cyclically between these layers (see Sect. 2.3). If we consider i^{th} row of BG and j^{th} non-zero element in that row, than let $m_{i,j}$ be the number of non zero elements in same column but in other rows. In this case for t^{th} row we have $i = 1 \ldots N$ and $j = 1 \ldots k_t$, for BG 2 $\max m_{i,j} = 23$.

Decoder overall architecture is presented in Fig. 2. It consists of N Layer Processing Units (LPU), one for each layer in the decoder. The ith LPU has k_i input and k_i output ports for APLLRs being sent from and to other layers. For rate matching flexibility each of LPU inputs and outputs are connected to corresponding Selector (Sel) and Commutator (Comm) block. Those blocks are connected to Interconnection Network (IN), consisting of data buses that connect different layers. IN has rigid structure and does not change during decoding.

PLD uses pre-calculated set of offsets to provide inter-layer parallelism. But since in 5G-NR LDPC there are different lifting sizes z, there is a set of different offsets for different z. This means different data sequencing order between the layers and therefore a set of commutators and selectors accompany each LPU. Also there is a ROM that stores all constant values for mode switching of different z. In hardware implementation no check matrices are stored, instead it stores pre-calculated constants which determine the order for layers to send data and offsets between the layers and input/output registers to fix up communication between layers.

ROM stores following arrays of constants: $C1$ is the number of LLRs that each layer takes from input register during the first decoder iteration, $C2$ is a set of offsets to preset the internal address counters of each. $C4$ is a set of output addresses that control all the inter-layer commutators.

Commutators consist of a demultiplexer that forward the updated APLLRs to one needed layer and a register that stores the address for demultiplexer. The address value depends on the lifting size z for current codeword and need to be updated from the constant ROM when each time z changes. This means that on the inputs of Selector blocks there is always data from only one of other layers. Therefore the selectors just use a set of bitwise OR operations upon all inputs and provide the results to LPU.

3.2   Layer Processing Unit Architecture

Each layer in PLD is processed with one Layer Processing Unit (LPU) presented in Fig. 3. The main subblock is check node processing unit (CNPU) that updates APLLRs according to loosely coupled algorithm (Eqs. 4 and 5).

LPU has two RAM block, one is check message RAM that stores check messages $r_{mn}[k-1]$, calculated in this layer at previous decoder iteration. This RAM contents is set to zeros before the first iteration. The other RAM is aposteriori LLR RAM (APLLR RAM), its content is filled with input channel LLRs before the first iteration and then is updated by other layers through Selector blocks, depicted in Fig. 2.

Updated APLLRs are forwarded to other layers' APLLR RAMs with corresponding auxiliary information (writing address and data valid). LPU also has control logic block that handles row counters and controls whether data in APLLR RAM is up-to-date (see Sect. 3.3).

3.3   Layer Sequencing Optimizations

In PLD LTUs can perform their calculations in truly concurrent way only if minimum inter-layer distance is $\min d_{inter-layer} \geq Z_{CNPU}$, where Z_{CNPU} is check node processing unit delay (in clock cycles) and the minimum is taken over all rows and columns of check matrix with added offsets. In this case CNPU operates in pipeline mode and the whole decoder throughput increases notably. Thus the offsets should be pre-calculated in a way to minimize $\min d_{inter-layer}$.

5G uses LDPC codes with two BGs and a broad set of lifting sizes $z = 2\ldots384$. However, the number of rows in BGs is 42 and 46, so it is obvious for $z = 2$ there is no way to get $\min d_{inter-layer} > 0$ for any set of offsets. The same statement is true for many lifting sizes and it is obvious that PLD is not applicable for these cases. Anyway, these lifting sizes are used when information blocks are small and the required throughput is usually low. Thus we propose to use the PLD with some extra control elements for these lifting sizes as well. Thus

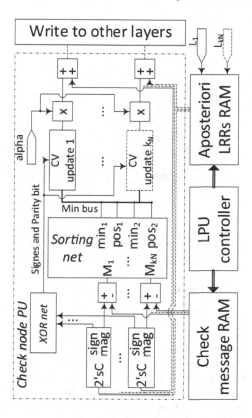

Fig. 3. Layer processing unit architecture

PLD would have the worst case latency and throughput same as classical layered decoder, but it also supports higher zs and would switch between different z modes through its operation.

We made several optimizations using Genetic Algorithm (GA) to find offset sets for different zs that minimize $\min d_{inter-layer}$. Optimization results are presented in Fig. 4. Histogram shows number of lifting factors that lead to $\min d_{inter-layer} = 0, 1, 2, 3$. Offset values for cases $\min d_{inter-layer} > 1$ are presented in Table 1.

In order to use pipeline mode in as many as possible z cases we set number of pipeline stages in CNPU to 2. This will cause quite long maximum combinatorial path through this block and CNPU will become the bottleneck for clock frequency used for the decoder.

Unfortunately 44 most small values of z cause the pipeline to break and the LPUs sometimes have to pause their calculations and thus the decoder throughput decreases. Decoder uses special flags that are stored in a register along with all values in APLLR RAMs that prevent irrelevant data usage. If the needed APLLRs are not available at the moment, then LPU waits until other layers update those values.

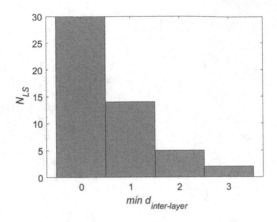

Fig. 4. Minimum distances optimization results

Table 1. Offset array values

z	Offset array
256	104 98 147 153 158 241 79 186 161 226 202 195 178 112 238 198 69 109 134 239 143 150 119 119 156 103 103 24 93 179 164 233 125 111 171 235 136 102 70 90 143 157
384	364 374 29 87 89 371 222 295 29 378 316 238 243 172 29 262 363 345 295 9 134 296 281 301 277 142 169 7 354 63 297 104 38 57 311 38 286 69 240 12 177 350
320	117 154 66 192 234 151 14 235 256 208 295 100 90 56 10 74 35 204 220 160 55 146 42 278 74 77 169 89 68 282 201 130 231 197 44 253 275 152 17 112 292 111
224	221 60 210 184 38 93 180 100 182 62 59 176 3 80 35 38 145 55 163 208 123 4 214 46 24 79 172 73 181 207 99 176 113 183 93 121 60 185 159 105 82 103
288	91 97 145 56 178 236 196 131 143 177 82 142 267 187 191 186 26 134 91 181 278 165 164 78 155 195 33 99 197 133 29 51 246 121 172 76 104 106 126 79 173 32
352	101 326 254 82 146 309 128 153 73 72 159 156 105 285 70 185 201 113 256 147 112 237 180 110 293 188 184 320 84 165 247 227 213 165 282 166 129 71 144 258 158 84
240	101 35 107 135 181 150 55 66 197 119 126 82 150 52 189 186 19 95 67 193 107 13 3 39 128 202 145 170 117 94 145 56 9 149 117 157 29 68 143 148 17 150

4   Decoder Throughput and Resources Estimates

Proposed decoder architecture is implemented and verified in Simulink bit-accurate and cycle accurate model. This approach both simplifies further ASIC implementation and helps to estimate resources usage, since all functional blocks like multiplexers, adders etc. could be counted.

Table 2 shows the number of gates required respectively for different important decoder subblocks as well as the summation of the numbers. The number of gates could be transformed to chip area estimate using an average gate density in TSMC 28 nm technology $d_{28nm} = 4.5 \times 10^6 \frac{gates}{mm^2}$ [2]. Number of bits per channel and aposteriori LLR values $B_{LLR} = 6$, clock frequency is $f_{clk} = 300$ MHz.

Table 2. PLD resources estimates

Subblock name	Gates, 10^3	Overall Area, mm^2	Overall percent
CNPUs	116	0.026	2.4
APLLR RAMs	1815	0.403	37.5
CM RAMs	1815	0.403	37.5
Constant ROM	83	0.018	1.7
In-and-out registers	958	0,213	20
Commutation	16	0.003	0.3
Overall PLD	*4836*	*1.075*	*100*

We also estimate the throughput of PLD for two cases: when PLD operates in parallel mode and the LPUs do not interfere, and in non-parallel mode and PLD works similar to the conventional layered decoder. We provide area efficiencies for both modes, for better comparison. The estimate for $z = 384$ (parallel mode) is $A_{384} = 1451 \frac{Mbps}{mm^2}$ and for $z = 2$ (non-parallel mode) – $A_2 = 186 \frac{Mbps}{mm^2}$.

Proposed architecture also satisfies the 1 ms delay demand from 5G standard requirements. The decoding process itself, not considering the data preload, takes time $t_{dec} = N_{iter} t_{iter}$. Here N_{iter} is the average number of iterations that decoder uses and value of 20–30 iterations gives reasonable performance. The t_{iter} factor is one iteration time. This value varies a little for different lifting factors, for example for $z = 384$ we have $t_{iter} = N_{ps} z / f_{clk} = 2.56 \, \mu s$. It is obvious that such a small iteration duration will cause negligible overall decoder delay.

5   Conclusion

Parallel Layered decoder has a structure that is able to easily support different lifting sizes, since it only uses a set of commutators and ordering sequences in the ROM. These blocks together occupy only 2% of the chip (Table 2) and show no implementation problems. Generated with GA, the layer offsets provide desired order and parallel layer processing for a subset of most high-throughput demanding z–s. However, there is no way to support fully-parallel mode for all the lifting sizes and the decoder throughput and latency suffers greatly in modes with small lifting sizes. That is not a big problem, though, since high throughput always means long codeword length and large lifting size.

PLD BER performance analysis and simulation results are not presented in this paper, but the PLD algorithm changes nothing compared to the software model of layered decoder [10], except the order in which rows inside one given layer are processed. Thus the LLR update algorithm remains the same as in the classical layered decoder and the performance remains the same too.

References

1. 5G;NR; Multiplexing and channel coding, document TS 38.212, V15.04.0,3GPP, December 2018
2. MegaChips ASIC Process Technology Comparison. http://www.megachips.com/products/asic/process-technology. Accessed 06 Mar 2020
3. Fossorier, M.P.C., Mihaljevic, M., Imai, H.: Reduced complexity iterative decoding of low-density parity check codes based on belief propagation. IEEE Trans. Commun. **47**(5), 673–680 (1999). https://doi.org/10.1109/26.768759
4. Gallager, R.: Low-density parity-check codes. IRE Trans. Inf. Theory **8**(1), 21–28 (1962). https://doi.org/10.1109/TIT.1962.1057683
5. Liu, Y., Peng, K., Pan, C., Fan, L.: Genie-aided adaptive normalized min-sum algorithm for LDPC decoding. In: 2015 International Wireless Communications and Mobile Computing Conference (IWCMC), pp. 221–225, August 2015. https://doi.org/10.1109/IWCMC.2015.7289086
6. Liu, Y., Peng, K., Pan, C.Y., Fan, L.: Adaptive normalized min-sum algorithm for LDPC decoding. In: 2013 9th International Wireless Communications and Mobile Computing Conference (IWCMC), pp. 1081–1084 (2013)
7. Mansour, M.M., Shanbhag, N.R.: High-throughput LDPC decoders. IEEE Trans. VLSI Syst. **11**, 976–996 (2003)
8. Richardson, T., Kudekar, S.: Design of low-density parity check codes for 5G new radio. IEEE Commun. Mag. **56**(3), 28–34 (2018). https://doi.org/10.1109/MCOM.2018.1700839
9. Kang, S.-H., Park, I.-C.: Loosely coupled memory-based decoding architecture for low density parity check codes. IEEE Trans. Circ. Syst. I Regular Papers **53**(5), 1045–1056 (2006). https://doi.org/10.1109/TCSI.2005.862181
10. Zhang, K., Huang, X., Wang, Z.: High-throughput layered decoder implementation for quasi-cyclic LDPC codes. IEEE J. Sel. Areas Commun. **27**(6), 985–994 (2009). https://doi.org/10.1109/JSAC.2009.090816

Bitstreams Multiplexing with Trellis-Coded Modulation and the Fixed Point LDPC Decoding Procedure for Centralised Wireless Networks

Igor A. Pastushok$^{(\boxtimes)}$ (iD), Nikita A. Boikov(iD), and Nikita A. Yankovskii(iD)

Saint Petersburg State University of Aerospace Instrumentation,
Saint Petersburg, Russia
i.pastushok@k36.org

Abstract. This article is a continuation of the study of enhanced Mobile BroadBand and Ultra-Reliable and Low Latency communication multiplexing methods in the downlink of fifth-generation wireless networks. Based on a previous study, the following approach to multiplexing eMBB and URLLC data streams based on Trellis-Coded Modulation using LDPC codes for fifth generation networks in soft decision mode using different quantization levels is proposed.

Keywords: URLLC · eMBB · Trellis-coded modulation · Fixed point LDPC decoding · 5G

1 Introduction

Currently, the task of multiplexing eMBB and URLLC streams is one of the priority tasks in 5G networks. Some authors have already managed to achieve great successes in this subject area. For example, there are many works related to the evaluation of the coexistence of two flows in mmWave systems. In [1], it was found that to provide URLLC with high-speed wireless access, it is desirable to seamlessly integrate the reliability of μW networks with high bandwidth mmWave networks and the authors presented the first comprehensive mmWave-μW integrated communications tutorial. This proposed integrated design will allow new wireless networks to take advantage of the best features from each of the networks. To achieve this goal, the authors discuss key concepts and solutions that include new architectures for the radio interface, URLLC-based frame structure, and resource allocation methods along with mobility management to realize the

The paper was prepared with the financial support of the Ministry of Science and Higher Education and of the Russian Federation, grant agreement No. FSRF-2020-0004, "Scientific basis for architectures and communication systems development of the onboard information and computer systems new generation in aviation, space systems and unmanned vehicles".

© Springer Nature Switzerland AG 2020
O. Galinina et al. (Eds.): NEW2AN 2020/ruSMART 2020, LNCS 12525, pp. 381–392, 2020.
https://doi.org/10.1007/978-3-030-65726-0_34

potential of mmWave-µW integrated communications. In [2], dynamic resource planning of URLLC and eMBB services is proposed. Resource planning took place over a time interval with multiplexed eMBB and URLLC traffic to protect eMBB users while maintaining strict URLLC latency requirements. For this purpose, the authors use the method of puncturing URLLC traffic on planned resources and consider a sequential planning scenario for excluded eMBB users in the following time interval. The simulation result shows the gain in planning based on priorities. In [3], a joint scheduler for eMBB and URLLC is proposed, which allows one to take into account the parameters of both streams. In [4], the authors propose a zero-space spatial proactive scheduler for shared URLLC and eMBB traffic for densely populated 5G networks. The proposed scheduler structure aims at cross-objective optimization, where critical URLLC QoS is guaranteed when extracting the maximum possible ergodic capacity eMBB.

Authors [5] present a punctured scheduling scheme for efficiently transmitting low latency (LLC) traffic multiplexed on an enhanced mobile broadband (eMBB) downlink shared channel. This allows you to plan eMBB traffic on all shared channel resources without first reserving transmission resources for periodically arriving LLC traffic. When LLC traffic arrives, it is immediately scheduled with a short transmission by puncturing part of the current eMBB transmissions. In [6], the authors present a dynamic puncturing scheme that allows URLLC data to occupy the part of the radio resource that was planned for the current eMBB transmission. The authors also introduce a signal diversity scheme (SSD) in the proposed dynamic puncturing scheme. Thus, the decoding efficiency of eMBB data over a fading channel is improved by interleaving components and modulating rotation. The paper [7] proposes to reach a QoS compromise between eMBB and URLLC in 5G networks. This is achieved by allocating URLLC user bandwidth and traffic using a deep deterministic policy gradient algorithm that monitors channel changes and URLLC traffic arrivals. The authors of the paper [8] propose a dynamic multiconnection-based collaborative planning framework with traffic management for eMBB and URLLC. EMBB and URLLC are deliberately separated from each other to avoid the URLLC queue. Thus, the task of joint scheduling and multiplexing of eMBB and URLLC traffic is a priority in 5G systems. The goal of this work is to create methods for multiplexing eMBB and URLLC streams, which allow to ensure stream separation and not degrade eMBB channel characteristics.

2   The 5G mmWave

2.1   Description of Purpose

The incredible demand for wireless data shows no signs of slowing down soon. At the same time, the mobile data experience for users continues to expand and develop, putting an increasing burden on the use of the available wireless spectrum network. Given this expected increase, the mobile industry has paid attention to other frequency groups that can be used in the development of new 5G wireless technologies. High-frequency groups in the spectrum over 24 GHz had to have the potential to support large amounts of bands and high data rates, ideal for increasing the width of wireless networks. These high-frequency groups are often called "mmvava" because of short waves that can be measured in millimeters. Although mvvv groups range up to 300 GHz, there are groups from 24 GHz to 100 GHz, which should be used for 5G. MMWA groups up to 100 GHz can support bandwidth up to 2 GHz, without having to join groups together for higher data streams.

The study of mvvva groups available in the US provides a good example of the spectrum that can be used for 5G networks. The FCC has made great efforts to expand the spectrum available for 5G, and has reported that the most authorized groups will be open for use (Fig. 1).

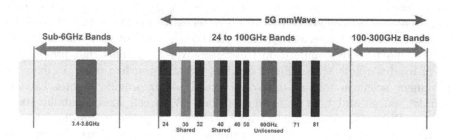

Fig. 1. 5G mmWave bands.

Previously, the use of frequency bands much higher than 6 GHz was considered unsuitable for mobile communication due to high propagation losses and the ease with which signals are blocked not only by building materials and foliage but also by the human body. While these challenges pose limitations to mmWave implementations, new antenna technologies, along with a better understanding of Channel properties and signal propagation, allow a range of distribution scenarios to be considered.

High penetration losses and blocking mean that mmWave implementations will cover outdoor or indoor environments, but will not provide outdoor-to-indoor connectivity. Therefore, the dimensions of the mmWave cells will be smaller and denser. Besides, mmWave can be expected to coexist in close integration with 5G implementations below 6 GHz and 4G LTE. Rapid adaptation to changing channel conditions allows you to change internal and internal cells to maintain performance and coverage. Also, it is almost certain that there will be a key role for software-defined networks (SDN) and Network Function Virtualization (NFV) in how networks work and provide seamless connectivity for users.

At the heart of 5G mmWave core technology is a new interface based on time Division Duplex and robust orthogonal frequency division multiplexing (OFDM) methods similar to those used in LTE and Wi-Fi networks. With maximum performance speeds of 10 Gbps or more and the ability to support a large number of devices, 5G mmWave has performance targets that will provide a transformation in the way wireless communications are used. The smaller cell sizes of 5G mmWave not only provide high performance but also allow efficient use of the spectrum, as frequencies can be reused at relatively small distances. An important part of mmWave 5G performance depends on signal propagation and antenna line of sight (LOS) and non-line of sight (NLOS) design.

To outline the requirements for 5G services, the International Telecommunication Union (ITU) has identified three main categories for the 5G NR architecture; enhanced mobile broadband (eMBB) for higher capacity ultra-reliable and low latency mobile communications (uRLLC) for mission-critical services and massive Machine communications (MMTC) for a large number of devices these large areas offer many early deployment possibilities for mmWave 5G, such:

Wireless fixed Internet access. 5G mmWave gigabit data rates could completely replace several hybrid fiber internet access technologies and wireless networks that connect subscribers' homes. Although it is not really a mobile system, it could provide competition to existing Wi-Fi systems that provide this type of fixed wireless access. Small outdoor urban/suburban cells. An expected deployment scenario for 5G mmWave would be to provide greater capacity in public spaces and high demand locations. With cell sizes of about 100 m, small mmWave 5G access points can be placed on poles or buildings to provide the required coverage. Mission-critical control applications. Autonomous vehicles, vehicle-to-vehicle communications, drone communications, and other high-reliability latency-sensitive applications provide other possible deployment scenarios for mmWave 5G with a projected network latency of less than one millisecond. The internal access point. Shopping malls, offices, and other indoor areas that require a high density of microcells, mmWave 5G. These small cells, potentially supporting download speeds of up to 20 Gbps, providing seamless access to data in the cloud, and the ability to support multiple applications, as well as various forms of entertainment and media. Internet of things. General connectivity of objects, sensors, devices, and other devices for data collection, control, and analysis. It could cover intelligent home applications, security, energy management, logistics and monitoring, medical care, and a multitude of other industrial operations.

2.2   Description of the Channel Structure and Numerologies

The 5G-NR standard implies the use of a different number of templates with different network parameters (Table 1). Each template allows you to adaptively configure the physical layers of the system. Such templates are called numerology and in this paper, we use the numerology parameters under number 3. The structure of the frame is presented in Fig. 2. In this work, a channel with additive white Gaussian noise is used as a channel. In real systems, a decoding approach using a fixed point is used, where the number of bits for representing values in the decoding procedure is artificially limited to a certain value, thus achieving the possibility of a guaranteed decoding rate of LDPC code blocks. This approach is most relevant for mmWave systems in TDD mode, since big data is used, and time is limited. Therefore, this work takes into account the real specifics, namely the LLR quantization (likelihood-ratio).

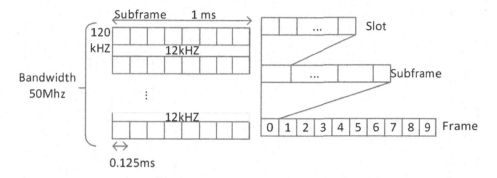

Fig. 2. 5G-NR Numerology 3 frame structure.

Table 1. 5G - NR numerology

Numerology	0(LTE)	1	2	3
Subcarrier width, kHz	15	30	60	120
Num of slots in subframe	1	2	4	8
Slot duration, ms	1	0.5	0.25	0.125
Symbol duration	66.7	33.3	16.6	8.33

2.3   Description of 5G LDPC

5G uses LDPC channel coding to provide the best transmission performance (Fig. 3).

LDPC codes are linear block codes defined using a verification matrix H, which contains mostly zeros and a relatively small number of ones. LDPC codes are characterized by a relatively high decoding speed, which led to their choice for use on high-speed traffic channels of 5G networks. LDPC codes replaced turbo encoders used for encoding traffic channels in 4G-LTE networks. This is mainly because turbo encoders compared to LDPC have higher complexity of decoder implementation and a lower speed of its operation. Also, LDPC allows you to use lower-speed encoding schemes and therefore has greater capabilities for restoring distorted signals.

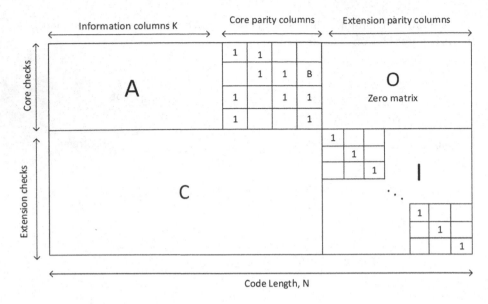

Fig. 3. 5G LDPC check matrix

3   System Model

3.1   Common System

The general system model consists of eMBB and URLLC message sources, base stations, and users. The information from the sources is fed to the fifth generation base station. The base station serves the subscribers of its network, among the subscribers there can be both eMBB users and URLLC users. The task of the base station is to select the multiplexing method and ensure the efficient transmission of messages of both streams (Fig. 4).

3.2   KPI

The system performance criteria are:

1. Error probability per codeword for the eMBB stream bits
2. URLLC channel capacity
3. Complexity of separating eMBB and URLLC streams.

3.3   Basic Scenario of Bitstream Multiplexing

Let's consider a reference data transfer scenario when there is an eMBB stream within the transmission of a single data transfer time frame. In the system, there is one sender (the base station) and one data receiver. In one report, m bits are sent from the output of the eMBB stream encoder to the modulator input. Based

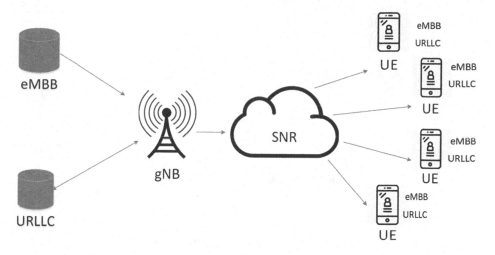

Fig. 4. System model

on the received bits, the modulator selects a point of the modulating constellation that will be transmitted over the communication channel without memory as a signal. An incoming signal with an additive Gaussian noise component distributed according to the normal law with mathematical expectation equal to zero and sigma deviation is observed at the receiver. The received signal goes through a demodulation procedure, where the received signal will be converted to m bits at the minimum Euclidean distance. The output from the demodulator goes to the input of the decoder (Fig. 5).

3.4   Scenario with Two Streams

This article extends the result of the previous articles [9,10] in which a modulation scheme was proposed that allows for the multiplexing of URLLC and eMBB streams without loss according to the BER criterion due to the complexity of the signal demodulation procedure at the receiving side. The expansion occurs by adding LDPC codes on the sender side. As in the previous article, the simultaneous transmission of data for different recipients from one sender is considered. The sender is the 5G-NR standard base station. At one point in time, 2 different messages appear on it, which, after adding the CRC-16 checksum, are sent to independent encoders. In each time sample from the outputs of the URLLC encoder and the eMBB encoder, l and m bits respectively arrive at the input of the modulation encoder. The modulator selects a modulation dimension that enables the simultaneous transmission of $(l + m)$ bits to two user devices within a single modulation symbol. The selected modulation symbol is transmitted over the communication channel, after passing through the receivers of the URLLC and eMBB streams, the transmitted modulation symbol with its unique noise component will be observed. Then, on each device, independent demodulation, and decoding of a specific stream will be performed (see Fig. 6).

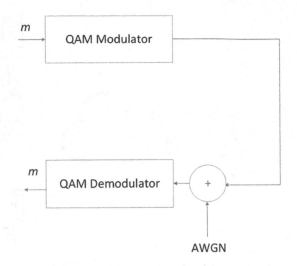

Fig. 5. Basic scenario

Fig. 6. The general scheme of the scenario of simultaneous transmission of eMBB and URLLC streams in the downlink (r is the number of redundant bits in the modulation symbol).

We use the following assumptions in the work.

1. We are considering a channel with additive white Gaussian noise.
2. We consider the downlink in TDD mode.
3. Viterbi algorithm decoder works in trunk mode.
4. We used a fixed-point decoding algorithm. We used only log_2Q high bits of $min(\lfloor LLR \rfloor, 127)$ if LLR is above zero, and $max(\lfloor LLR \rfloor, -128)$ otherwise.
5. The belief propagation algorithm was used as the LDPC decoding algorithm.

4   Numerical Examples

The MatLab 5g toolbox was used to simulate our algorithm. This toolbox provides standard-compliant functions and reference examples for the modeling, simulation, and verification of 5G New Radio (NR) communications systems. The toolbox supports link-level simulation, golden reference verification, conformance testing, and test waveform generation.

For the baseline scenario, the key performance parameter is the error rate per codeword for the eMBB data stream. In this scenario, the channel capacity for URLLC traffic is equal to zero. And the decoding complexity is determined by LDPC decoding with fixed-point for 5G-NR. Figure 7 shows figures of the dependence of the error probability per codeword on the signal-to-noise ratio in the channel for the baseline scenario at different quantization levels ($Q = 2$, 4, 8, 16).

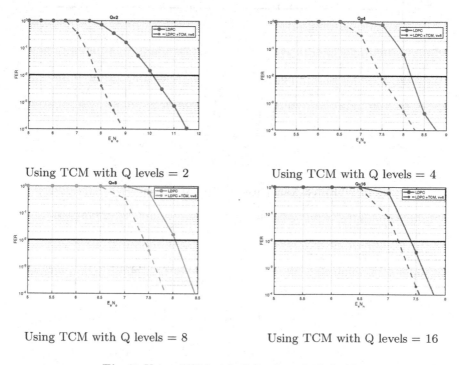

Using TCM with Q levels = 2   Using TCM with Q levels = 4

Using TCM with Q levels = 8   Using TCM with Q levels = 16

Fig. 7. Using TCM with Q levels = 2, 4, 8, 16

In Fig. 8, we can compare all the options for using different levels of quantization among themselves.

For the scenario of multiplexing streams, the key performance indicators are the error probability per codeword for the eMBB stream bits, the URLLC channel capacity, and the complexity of separating eMBB and URLLC streams. The complexity of the partition can be estimated as:

$$O(T \times S^2), \tag{1}$$

where T is a length of message in bit and S is a number of states in hidden Markov chain. The decoding complexity is also determined by LDPC decoding with fixed-point for 5G-NR.

It is also important to note the parameters of TCM that were used in the simulation. The convolutional encoder is shown in Fig. 9. Using it, you can get

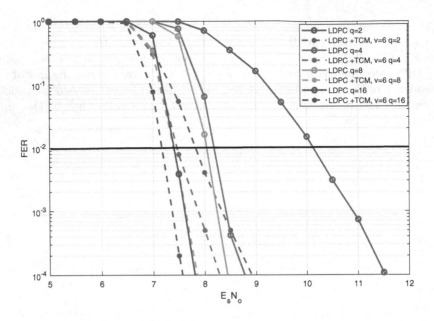

Fig. 8. Comparison all TCM variants

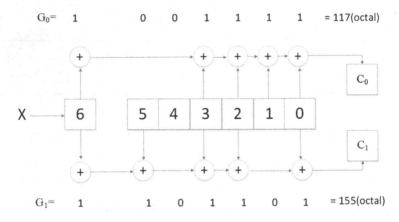

Fig. 9. Convolutional coder

information about the input and output sequences. Polinom with memory 6 is used.

In the paper, a modified partition of the Ungerboeck is used. Recall that a modification of the Ungerboeck approach allows introducing uneven bit protection in the modulation constellation. URLLC stream bits will be less secure compared to eMBB stream bits. This is achieved because the first l levels of partitioning will determine the bits of the URLLC stream, the last m levels of partitioning will determine the bits of the eMBB stream. Using polynomial with memory 6 a simulation was carried out that demonstrates the effect of using LDPC codes and the complexity of the soft decoding procedure in the problem of stream multiplexing. As a result of the simulation, figures were obtained. As can be seen from the Fig. 8, the use of soft decoding with different quantization levels for the Trellis coded modulation method is superior to the scenario when using only channel coding according to the FER criterion. Also in the work [10], a graph of the probability of non-transmission of a URLLC message for 1 subframe was obtained. Based on it, we can conclude about the capacity of the URLLC channel and that the proposed multiplexing method provides the transmission of 1000 URLLC messages of 40 bits each in 1 ms, with a probability greater than 99%.

5 Conclusion

In this paper, we presented the results of modeling such a method of multiplexing bit streams as Trellis Coded modulation in a 5G-NR system. The results obtained in the previous work were expanded due to the use of soft decoding with quantized input. Different quantization levels were used to obtain FER plots. On the graphs, you can clearly understand how the quantization levels affect the proposed method in the 5G-NR system.

References

1. Semiari, O., Saad, W., Bennis, M., Debbah, M.: Integrated millimeter wave and sub-6 GHz wireless networks: a roadmap for joint mobile broadband and ultra-reliable low-latency communications. IEEE Wirel. Commun. **26**(2), 109–115 (2019)
2. Pandey, S.R., Alsenwi, M., Tun, Y.K., Hong, C.S.: A downlink resource scheduling strategy for URLLC traffic. In: 2019 IEEE International Conference on Big Data and Smart Computing (BigComp), Kyoto, Japan, pp. 1–6 (2019)
3. Anand, A., de Veciana, G., Shakkottai, S.: Joint scheduling of URLLC and eMBB traffic in 5G wireless networks. IEEE/ACM Trans. Netw. **28**(2), 477–490 (2020)
4. Esswie, A.A., Pedersen, K.I.: Opportunistic spatial preemptive scheduling for URLLC and eMBB coexistence in multi-user 5G networks. IEEE Access **6**, 38451–38463 (2018)
5. Pedersen, K.I., Pocovi, G., Steiner, J., Khosravirad, S.R.: Punctured scheduling for critical low latency data on a shared channel with mobile broadband. In: IEEE 86th Vehicular Technology Conference (VTC-Fall), Toronto, ON, pp. 1–6 (2017)
6. Wu, Z., Zhao, F., Liu, X.: Signal space diversity aided dynamic multiplexing for eMBB and URLLC traffics. In: 2017 3rd IEEE International Conference on Computer and Communications (ICCC), Chengdu, pp. 1396–1400 (2017)
7. Li, J., Zhang, X.: Deep reinforcement learning based joint scheduling of eMBB and URLLC in 5G networks. IEEE Wirel. Commun. Lett. **9**, 1543–1546 (2020)
8. Zhang, K., Xu, X., Zhang, J., Zhang, B., Tao, X., Zhang, Y.: Dynamic multiconnectivity based joint scheduling of eMBB and uRLLC in 5G networks. IEEE Syst. J.

9. Pastushok, I.A., Boikov, N.A.: Investigation of methods for multiplexing EMBB and URLLC streams in a downlink. In: Wave Electronics and its Application in Information and Telecommunication Systems (WECONF), Saint-Petersburg, Russia, pp. 1–4 (2019)
10. Pastushok, I.A., Boikov, N.A., Yankovskii, N.A.: Bit stream multiplexing in 5G networks. In: Wave Electronics and its Application in Information and Telecommunication Systems (WECONF), Saint-Petersburg, Russia, pp. 1–4 (2020)

About Burst Decoding
for Block-Permutation LDPC Codes

Andrei Ovchinnikov[ID] and Anna Fominykh[(✉)][ID]

Saint-Petersburg State University of Aerospace Instrumentation,
B.Morskaya 67, 190000 Saint-Petersburg, Russia
mldoc@ieee.org, aawat@ya.ru

Abstract. Hard-decision decoders are considered for burst error correction for low-density parity-check codes. The decoder for block-permutation construction of low-density parity-check proposed. Experiments on complexity and error probability are conducted with burst lengths both within and beyond the burst error correction capability. Also simulation results for Gilbert model are presented.

Keywords: LDPC codes · Burst-error correcting codes · Channels with memory

1 Introduction

Nowadays, data transmission is widespread. Data is transmitted over the noisy channels that may introduce errors. To reduce the errors that appear during the transmission over the channel error correcting codes are used. One of the most promising type of error correcting codes that are widely used in modern standards are low-density parity-check (LDPC) codes [5,12] based on the block-permutation construction [15].

Errors that appear during the transmission are not independent, but most standards design codes in an assumption of errors being independent. This problem is solved during the transmission routine using the interleaving technique. One of the most important properties of LDPC codes is that they are less vulnerable to error probability decreasing when the errors tend to group in comparison, for example, to cyclic codes.

Apart from the channel transmission there are a lot of other processes, for example, processing, storing and protection during which the information may be distorted, that can be described as an artificial transmission channel that is also not free of errors grouping.

The paper was prepared with the financial support of the Ministry of Science and Higher Education and of the Russian Federation, grant agreement No. FSRF-2020-0004, "Scientific basis for architectures and communication systems development of the onboard information and computer systems new generation in aviation, space systems and unmanned vehicles".

O. Galinina et al. (Eds.): NEW2AN 2020/ruSMART 2020, LNCS 12525, pp. 393–401, 2020.
https://doi.org/10.1007/978-3-030-65726-0_35

The paper is organized as follows. Section 2 describes the simplest channel models with memory. Section 3 gives important notations about LDPC codes. Section 4 introduces decoding of error bursts for block-permutation LDPC codes. Section 5 presents the simulation results and Sect. 6 concludes the paper.

2   Channel Models with Memory

2.1   Data Transmission

When the data is transmitted over the real communication channels the influence on a signal may be described by a probability model, where the distortions of separated symbols are not independent. The simplest model that may describe such a channel is a finite state channel (Fig. 1) [6]. Through this base model several derivations may be described, including Markov model [13], Gilbert model [7] and Gilbert–Elliott model.

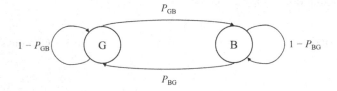

Fig. 1. Finite state channel model.

The finite state channel model describes each state as a binary symmetric channel each one with its own crossover probability that may differ. In state G (good) this probability is very low and in state B (bad) may be different depending on the channel model. In general, channel influence on the transmitted data may be described as an additive model with a received vector pointed as $\mathbf{b} = \mathbf{a} + \mathbf{e}$, where $\mathbf{a}$ is a transmitted vector, $\mathbf{e}$ is an error vector. Channel models that are under consideration describe the error vector that contains error bursts which are the areas in error vector that begin and end with one.

2.2   Information Storing

Although data transmission is a typical scenario of errors appearing, other processes are also subject to errors, moreover, such errors are not independent, and this problem can be solved by an error correcting coding. For example, distributed information storage systems allow to store data in multiple spatial distributed devices that may be organized in many different ways and may contain failures and hidden errors [11]. When such failures and errors appear, due to the system architecture the errors are more likely to form fixed length error bursts (which lengths depend on the architectural properties) rather than to spread uniformly.

2.3   Information Security

Post-quantum public-key cryptosystems become more and more relevant, most of them are based on error-correcting codes. In [10] cryptosystem based on error correcting codes that are able to correct error bursts is observed. The paper describes the encryption process that contains the generation of fixed length error burst that the legal user must be able to correct afterwards. Since the error vector is constructed in an artificial manner, the task of information protection also uses fixed length error bursts.

3   Low-Density Parity-Check Codes

Low-density parity-check (LDPC) codes were proposed by R. G. Gallager in 1962 [5], but due to the computing limitations in implementing the encoder and decoder for such codes, LDPC codes were ignored for almost 30 years. LDPC codes were rediscovered by D. Mackay [12] in the 1990s and subsequent development of computing power arose a new wave of interest to LDPC codes [14, 16], which deserve attention due to the near-Shannon-limit error-correcting capability and effective procedures of encoding and decoding. These properties of LDPC codes made them desirable candidates for many communication standards [1–3]. LDPC codes are specified by a parity-check matrix that due to its sparseness may be graphically represented by means of a bipartite graph (Tanner graph). The length of the shortest cycle in the Tanner graph is called the girth. Since cycles, especially short cycles, degrade the performance of LDPC decoders, codes with large girth should be constructed.

The most popular construction of LDPC codes that allows compact representation and flexible way of code construction is a block-permutation construction [8]. A special case of block-permutation construction is Gilbert codes and their modifications which burst error correcting capability was analyzed in [9, 11]. A Gilbert code is defined by a parity-check matrix $\mathbf{H}_l$,

$$\mathbf{H}_l = \begin{bmatrix} \mathbf{I}_m \ \mathbf{I}_m \ \mathbf{I}_m \ \cdots \ \mathbf{I}_m \\ \mathbf{I}_m \ \mathbf{C} \ \mathbf{C}^2 \ \cdots \ \mathbf{C}^{l-1} \end{bmatrix}, \tag{1}$$

where $\mathbf{I}_m$ is $(m \times m)$-identity matrix, $\mathbf{C}$ is $(m \times m)$-matrix of cyclic permutation:

$$\mathbf{C} = \begin{bmatrix} 0 & 0 & 0 & \cdots & 0 & 1 \\ 1 & 0 & 0 & \cdots & 0 & 0 \\ 0 & 1 & 0 & \cdots & 0 & 0 \\ \multicolumn{6}{c}{\dotfill} \\ 0 & 0 & 0 & \cdots & 1 & 0 \end{bmatrix}, \tag{2}$$

and $\ell \leq m$. Ensembles of block-permutation codes with small amount of blocks $(3 \times 6, 4 \times 8)$ were analyzed in [4] for information security tasks. The analysis showed that for block-permutation constructions with a block size of m maximum correctable length of the error burst is $b \leqslant m - 1$ and in the case of codes that have no cycles of length 4 the maximum correctable burst length is distributed in the range of $[m/2, m - 1]$ and is more likely to become closer to $m - 1$. Moreover, it was shown that the determination of burst error correction capability has polynomial complexity and its computation may be done in an acceptable time for the codes of length up to several thousands of bits.

4   Decoding of Error Bursts for Block-Permutation LDPC Codes

In general, LDPC codes decoding methods are iterative procedures that operate on each symbol separately. Algorithms are also described as message passing between the nodes along the edges of the Tanner graph that proceeds until the predefined amount of iteration is reached or the codeword is found. For LDPC codes both hard decision and soft decision decoding algorithms may be used. The most common among them are bit flipping (BF) algorithm and belief propagation (BP) algorithm, respectively. These algorithms are able to provide low error probabilities, but do not guarantee error correction and burst error correction within the code error correction capability, that is an unacceptable scenario for many applications (for instance, data storage and data protection). Since the models that are observed in this article are discrete, only hard decision decoders will be further in consideration. It was shown in [17] that BF can't provide an acceptable error probability level in case of burst error correction, but shows better results if the windowed BF is applied instead of the original BF.

The original bit flipping algorithm for the received vector $\mathbf{y}$ and parity-check matrix $\mathbf{H}$ proceeds as follows [15]:

1. Compute syndrome $\mathbf{s} = \mathbf{y}\mathbf{H}^T$ (over $\mathbb{F}_2$), if $\mathbf{s} = \mathbf{0}$, stop, since $\mathbf{y}$ is a codeword.
2. Compute vector $\mathbf{f} = \mathbf{s}\mathbf{H}$ (over $\mathbb{Z}$).
3. Identify values of $\mathbf{f}$ that are greater than some predefined threshold (that may be chosen depending on the channel conditions), flip the corresponding bits in $\mathbf{y}$.
4. If the maximum amount of iteration is not reached, go to step 1.

The windowed version of bit flipping algorithm tries to correct burst locally if it is covered by the window. The decoder in a consequent manner considers all possible locations of burst and tries to correct errors in the currently observed window. Then, at each decoding iteration, step 3 of the original bit flipping algorithm is performed for the positions in the current window of length b. However the optimal size of the window for different channel models is an open question. It should be mentioned that when the block-permutation matrix is used BF algorithm may be modified taking into account the matrix structure. This modification includes a preprocessing step where all of nonzero syndrome elements that may be uniquely matched to the columns of $\mathbf{H}$ are eliminated. More precisely, the preprocessing step performs the following procedure: for currently observed window the syndrome elements are viewed from the first to the last.

If the currently observed syndrome element s_j is nonzero and the corresponding row in **H** on the window positions contains exactly one nonzero element, then the corresponding syndrome position is eliminated using the column of **H** that has the position of that single nonzero element in a row. After that the same procedure starts again from the first syndrome element. The preprocessing step ends, when all of syndrome positions are observed.

After such preprocessing step a situation that is shown in Fig. 2 may appear: for a given nonzero syndrome entry there is more than one nonzero element in a row, so there is more than one possible option for a specific nonzero syndrome value. Then it was proposed in [17] to switch after the preprocessing to BF within the same window. Conducted experiments showed that for block-permutation matrices all bursts with length within the code error correction capability are corrected.

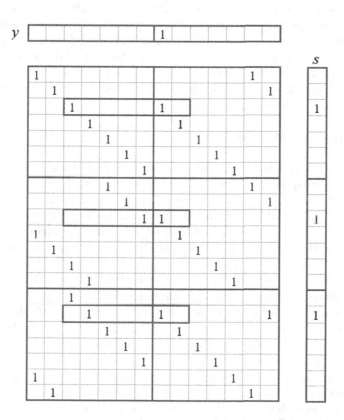

Fig. 2. After preprocessing case.

The preprocessing procedure may be followed not by BF, but by the selection from the possible variants of elements in a row. The selection procedure is described as follows: first nonzero element in the row matching to the first nonzero position in syndrome is chosen and the corresponding column is added to the syndrome, then the first nonzero element of the row that is matched to the next nonzero syndrome position is taken and the first one is taken from that row and its column is added to the syndrome. The same is done for the rest of the nonzero positions of the syndrome. The algorithm ends when all-zero syndrome vector is reached. During the process some choices may be made wrong, so the selection process has to follow some steps back and modify the choice of some of the previously observed rows. That describes the tree like procedure that leads to time increasing, to overcome which the algorithm should be optimized. The optimization may be done as follows: selection of an element in a row should be determined by the most coincidence of one of the columns that correspond to nonzero positions in a row and syndrome. Considering such an optimization the selection process observes all the positions of the syndrome in a more efficient way. Suppose syndrome entry s_j is nonzero and the row contains more than one nonzero element. The choice of an element in a row is dictated by the most inter-sections of the corresponding column with a syndrome, in other words, that row element is chosen which corresponding column sum modulo two with a syndrome makes the recomputed syndrome closer to all zero vector. If several elements in a row lead to the same syndrome weight, then for each of them the recursive procedure begins that repeats previously described selection step switching to the next nonzero position in syndrome.

5   Simulation Results

The point of experiments is to determine if the observed algorithms are able to correct bursts with a length over burst error correction capability. Experiments are performed for the random block-permutation matrix with no cycles of length 4 that consists of 4×8 blocks with the block length of $m = 59$, which burst error capability $b = m - 1$ has been determined following the algorithm presented in [9]. During the experiments to perform the comparison the burst length is set to the values $b = m - 1$, $b = m + 2$ and $b = 2m + 2$. The experimental results contain time per iteration and frame error rate (FER) comparison of three algorithms. The compared algorithms are: BPBF (block-permutation bit-flip) is an algorithm with preprocessing and bit flipping, BPT (block-permutation tree) contains preprocessing and one selection, WBF (windowed bit-flip) with 1, 5 and 10 iterations. The burst of length b for an error vector is constructed in an artificial way: at first, the random start position is generated, then ones are put on the first and the last indices and the probability of one inside is p_1. The horizontal axis represents the probability of one inside burst.

It may be seen that for all burst lengths b iteration time of BPT is greater than the BPBF. BPT and BPBF are correcting every possible variant of bursts whilst $b = m-1$ and $b = m+2$, that is depicted in Fig. 3 and Fig. 5, but erroneous frames appear with $b = 2m + 2$ (Fig. 7) and FER curves of both algorithms are nearly equal. WBF frame error probability is the worst for all considered b, but it requires the smallest time to complete the iteration.

Also the experiments for the Gilbert channel model were conducted. In such experiments generating of the burst is following the next procedure: a probability

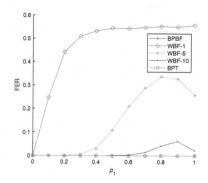

Fig. 3. FER for $b \leqslant m - 1$.

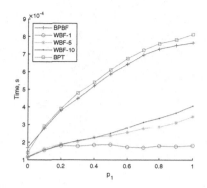

Fig. 4. Time for $b \leqslant m - 1$.

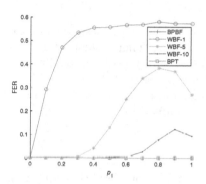

Fig. 5. FER for $b = m + 2$.

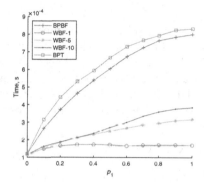

Fig. 6. Time for $b = m + 2$.

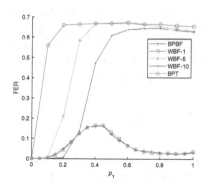

Fig. 7. FER for $b = 2m + 2$.

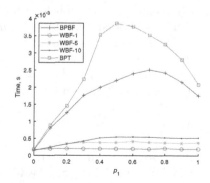

Fig. 8. Time for $b = 2m + 2$.

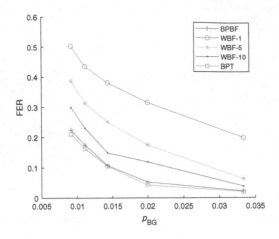

Fig. 9. Algorithm comparison for Gilbert model.

p_{BG} is determined so the mean of the length of the burst was less or equal to b (b values were chosen from the interval $[m/2; 2m + 2]$). Then random start burst position is generated, and each one inside the burst appears with probability that is set to 0.5. The modeling results are shown in Fig. 9. It may be concluded that the BPBF and BPT algorithms tend to behave similarly under the Gilbert model conditions and have a smaller error probability than WBF (Figs. 4, 6 and 8).

6   Conclusion

Hard-decision decoders were considered for burst error correction for block-permutation matrices. The modification of decoder based on optimized selection procedure is proposed. The hypothesis about the guaranteed burst error correction using the decoder with block-permutation matrices analysis is not disproved. Experiments on comparing the frame error probability were conducted with burst error correction length beyond the error correction capability. The experiments showed that for $b = m - 1$ and $b = m + 2$ the proposed algorithm (BPT) corrects all possible bursts with no much loss in time, whereas for $b = 2m + 2$ BPT serves no worse than the BPBF with a small iteration time gap. Also the modeling for Gilbert model were conducted that showed the tendency of BPBF and BPT to behave similarly.

References

1. IEEE 802.11n/d1.0 Part 11: Wireless LAN Medium Access Control (MAC) and Physical Layer (PHY) Specifications. http://www.techstreet.cpm/standards/ieee-802-11n-2005. Accessed 10 June 2020
2. IEEE 802.16e-2005. Part 16: Air Interface for Fixed and Mobile Broadband Wireless Access Systems. http://www.techstreet.cpm/standards/ieee-802-16e-2005. Accessed 10 June 2020

3. Multiplexing and channel coding, 3GPP Technical Specification 38.212 V15.2.0. https://panel.castle.cloud/view_spec/38212-f11. Accessed 10 June 2020
4. Bakay, K.A., Ovchinnikov, A.A., Ilina, D.V.: About burst-correction capability of block-permutation LDPC codes ensembles. In: 2019 Wave Electronics and its Application in Information and Telecommunication Systems (WECONF), pp. 1–4 (2019). https://doi.org/10.1109/WECONF.2019.8840134
5. Gallager, R.: Low-density parity-check codes. IRE Trans. Inf. Theory **8**(1), 21–28 (1962). https://doi.org/10.1109/TIT.1962.1057683
6. Gallager, R.: Information Theory and Reliable Communication. Wiley, New York (1968)
7. Gilbert, E.N.: Capacity of a burst-noise channel. Bell Syst. Tech. J. **39**(5), 1253–1265 (1960). https://doi.org/10.1002/j.1538-7305.1960.tb03959.x
8. Kozlov, A., Krouk, E., Ovchinnikov, A.: An approach to development of block-commutative codes with low density of parity check, vol. 8, pp. 9–14. Izvestiya vuzov, Priborostroenie (2013). https://doi.org/10.15217/issn1684-8853.2017.2.58
9. Krouk, E., Ovchinnikov, A.: Exact burst-correction capability of Gilbert codes. Informatsionno-upravliaiushchie sistemy **1**, 80–87 (2016). https://doi.org/10.15217/issn1684-8853.2016.1.80
10. Krouk, E., Ovchinnikov, A.: Code-based public-key cryptosystem based on bursts-correcting codes. In: AICT 2017: The Thirteenth Advanced International Conference on Telecommunications, pp. 90–92 (2017)
11. Krouk, E., Ovchinnikov, A.: 2-stripes block-circulant LDPC codes for single bursts correction. In: De Pietro, G., Gallo, L., Howlett, R.J., Jain, L.C. (eds.) Intelligent Interactive Multimedia Systems and Services 2016. SIST, vol. 55, pp. 11–23. Springer, Cham (2016). https://doi.org/10.1007/978-3-319-39345-2_2
12. MacKay, D.J.C., Neal, R.M.: Near Shannon limit performance of low density parity check codes. Electron. Lett. **33**(6), 457–458 (1997). https://doi.org/10.1049/el:19970362
13. Proakis, J., Salehi, M.: Digital Communications, vol. 5. McGraw-Hill, New York (2008)
14. Richardson, T.J., Urbanke, R.L.: The capacity of low-density parity-check codes under message-passing decoding. IEEE Trans. Inf. Theory **47**(2), 599–618 (2001). https://doi.org/10.1109/18.910577
15. Ryan, W., Lin, S.: Channel Codes: Classical and Modern. Cambridge University Press, Cambridge (2009)
16. Chung, S.-Y., Forney, G.D., Richardson, T.J., Urbanke, R.: On the design of low-density parity-check codes within 0.0045 dB of the Shannon limit. IEEE Commun. Lett. **5**(2), 58–60 (2001). https://doi.org/10.1109/4234.905935
17. Veresova, A.M., Ovchinnikov, A.A.: About one algorithm for correcting bursts using block-permutation LDPC-codes. In: 2019 Wave Electronics and its Application in Information and Telecommunication Systems (WECONF), pp. 1–4 (2019). https://doi.org/10.1109/WECONF.2019.8840580

Estimation of the Possibility of PAPR Reduction for Optimal Signals

Aleksandr V. Zhila, Anna S. Ovsyannikova(✉) [iD], and Sergey V. Zavjalov [iD]

Peter the Great St. Petersburg Polytechnic University, Saint Petersburg, Russia
aleksandr.zhila@mail.ru, {ovsyannikova_as,zavyalov_sv}@spbstu.ru

Abstract. The method of optimizing single frequency signals with a predetermined reduction rate of the level of the energy spectrum and restrictions on the energy and peak-to-average power ratio (PAPR) is presented in this paper. The method of numerical solution of the optimization problem is shown. The effect of restrictions on the solution of the optimization problem is considered. Obtained signals provide the gain in PAPR up to 4.3 dB compared to the case without corresponding restriction.

Keywords: Spectral efficiency · Single frequency signals · Optimization · PAPR · Restrictions

1 Introduction

Improving the efficiency of radio systems for various purposes, including data transmission systems, has been and remains one of the main tasks facing the developers of transceiver devices.

The increase in efficiency is associated with an increase in the transmission rate with an acceptable reliability of reception. Moreover, the higher the spectral efficiency $R/\Delta F$ (R is the data transfer rate, ΔF is the occupied bandwidth) and the lower the energy loss ΔSNR in bit error rate (BER) performance, the higher the total system efficiency. Out-of-band (OOB) emissions, which can be expressed in terms of the decay rate of the energy spectrum, are also a key parameter. In radio systems, filters are used to limit OOB emissions. For filters of small orders, the selectivity is low, and the frequency band is quite high. When using high-order filters on transmitting devices, it is possible to reduce the occupied frequency band, that is, to obtain higher values of spectral efficiency. However, it leads to intersymbol interference and, as a result, to deterioration in the quality data transmission [1–5].

Data transmission systems use single-frequency and multi-frequency signals. For example, the most widespread in existing wireless data transmission systems (Wi-Fi, LTE, DVB-T2) are multi-frequency signals with orthogonal frequency division multiplexing (OFDM) [6, 7]. There are also modifications of these signals with non-orthogonal frequency multiplexing, which allows achieving higher spectral efficiency compared to OFDM signals: N-OFDM (non-orthogonal frequency division multiplexing) signals

O. Galinina et al. (Eds.): NEW2AN 2020/ruSMART 2020, LNCS 12525, pp. 402–414, 2020.
https://doi.org/10.1007/978-3-030-65726-0_36

[8–11] or SEFDM (Spectrally efficient frequency division multiplexing) signals [12–14]. We are interested in single-frequency signals with smoothed envelopes. A common problem of such signals is the great value of the peak-to-average power ratio of the emitted oscillations [6, 15, 16]. The PAPR (peak-to-average power ratio) is the ratio of the peak power to the average power of the emitted oscillations. A high value of the signal PAPR leads either to the underutilization of power amplifiers and, as a result, to a decrease in the average signal power and BER performance, or to an increase in the level of nonlinear distortions in the signal [17–21], which, in turn, leads to an increase in the level of radiation, as well as to reducing the BER performance [22].

Much attention to the study of the possibilities of reducing PAPR of oscillations. It is due to the fact that this parameter of signals significantly limits the scope of their application, especially in portable transmitting and receiving devices with low power consumption.

There are various methods for reducing the PAPR of signals:

- Methods based on block coding (codes based on Golay sequences, Reed-Muller codes, methods for adding subcarriers in multi-frequency signals).
- Methods based on the amplitude limitation of signals (clipping, companding, filtering).
- Probabilistic method.

Block coding based PAPR reduction techniques have the potential to solve the problem of constructing signals with relatively low PAPR, high coding rate, and moderate algorithm complexity. The main idea of block coding to reduce PAPR is to introduce a relatively small redundancy in the transmitted message, to display the entire set of input combinations in the set of words with PAPR not exceeding the specified one. When using excessive block coding, the data rate is reduced [23–25].

The amplitude limitation method is based on signal clipping. This method is the simplest. Using clipping, it is possible to obtain almost any given value of the PAPR signal. However, when the clipping threshold is reduced, the degree of signal distortion increases and the frequency band occupied by the signal increases. Distortion introduced into the signal reduces the BER performance [26, 27].

In probabilistic methods, for a single set of information symbols, several signals are generated and one with the lowest PAPR is selected. In this case, additional information about the choice made must be transmitted to the transmitting device. The main disadvantage of the probabilistic methods for reducing PAPR is their high complexity, which is determined by the number of transformations necessary for the formation of several (usually 4–10) signal implementations at once [16, 28–30].

There are also methods to reduce PAPR, based on a combination of methods of different classes. The disadvantages of these approaches can be minimized by using optimal signals. Such signals can be obtained as a solution to an optimization problem with given restrictions on the spectral and temporal characteristics, as well as on the BER performance [31, 32].

The optimal signals are characterized by smooth amplitude-phase trajectories, which allows one to obtain a high degree of compactness of the spectrum, i.e., high values of spectral efficiency, and the use of effective (optimal or suboptimal) reception algorithms allows one to obtain acceptable values of energy losses [33–36]. In addition, various optimal envelope shapes were obtained for such signals, taking into account restrictions on the decay rate of OOB emissions. However, the issue of obtaining waveforms with a controlled PAPR value is little studied.

In the synthesis of optimal signals, a function $a(t)$ is searched for, which describes the envelope of signals of duration T_s and provides a minimum of the following functional:

$$\arg\left\{\min_{a(t)}(J)\right\}, \quad \text{Where} \quad J = \frac{1}{2\pi} \int_{-\infty}^{+\infty} g(f) \left| \int_{-T_s/2}^{T_s/2} a(t) \exp(-j2\pi ft) dt \right|^2 df \quad (1)$$

The specific form of the functional J is determined by the optimality criterion. In this article, we will consider a criterion for ensuring a given rate of decay of OOB emissions. The function $g(f)$ is the weighting function, which determines the decay rate of the resulting energy spectrum.

The function $g(f)$ in the general case can be any increasing function satisfying the conditions of the optimization problem. In this article, we restrict ourselves to the quadratic form of the function:

$$g(f) = f^{2n}, \quad (2)$$

where parameter n determines the necessary decay rate of OOB emissions. Note that analytical solutions to problems of this class can be found only for a small set of input parameters without additional restrictions. The issues of reducing PAPR lead to a complication of the task and the addition of additional restrictions.

The objective of the work is the analysis of the possibility of obtaining optimal waveforms in the presence of restrictions on the PAPR of the emitted oscillations.

2 Optimization Problem

When solving the problem of minimizing functional (1), it is required to find the shape of the optimal signal $a(t)$ that is finite over a given time interval T_s and has a given rate of decrease in the level of the energy spectrum outside the occupied bandwidth ΔF, subject to various restrictions. To solve this problem numerically, we can use the expansion of the function $a(t)$ in a limited Fourier series. Then the optimization problem may be reduced to the problem of searching for expansion coefficients $\{a_k\}_{k=1}^{m}$ which minimize the function of many variables:

$$\arg\left\{\min_{\{a_k\}_{k=1}^{m}}(J)\right\}, \quad J\left(\{a_k\}_{k=1}^{m}\right) = \frac{T_s}{2} \sum_{k=1}^{m} \left(\frac{2\pi}{T_s}k\right)^{2n} a_k^2 \quad (3)$$

To fix the definiteness of the problem, the condition for normalizing the energy E_a of the signal is used, which can be set as follows:

$$\int_{-T_s/2}^{T_s/2} a^2(t) dt = E_a = 1 \quad (4)$$

The following restriction provides a maximum decay rate of OOB emissions of at least $1/f^{2(n+1)}$:

$$a^{(k)}|_{t=\pm T_s/2} = 0, \quad k = 1 \ldots (n-1) \quad (5)$$

We introduce a limiting condition on the PAPR oscillations, which is conveniently considered as the following inequality (6):

$$PAPR \ < \ (PAPR^* - \Delta PAPR). \tag{6}$$

Here PAPR* is the initial value of the PAPR of the emitted oscillations. As a result of solving the optimization problem with this restriction, an envelope shape will be obtained that provides ΔPAPR less than that of the original signal.

2.1 Method for Solving the Optimization Problem

Figure 1 shows a graphical view of the procedure for solving the optimization problem. On it, along the axes of the two-dimensional graph, the decay rate of the energy spectrum level $|S(f)|^2$ and the restriction on PAPR are plotted. The parameter n included in the expression for the decay rate of OOB emissions of the energy spectrum $1/f^{\,2(n+1)}$ is plotted along the abscissa. The initial approximation for solving the optimization problem is the rectangular shape of the envelope, which corresponds to the PAPR value of the emitted oscillations at a high frequency of 3 dB. At the first step of the optimization problem, restrictions on the decay rate of the energy spectrum level $|S(f)|^2$ outside the occupied frequency band ΔF are introduced. In this case, the shape of the envelope $a(t)$ changes. As parameter n increases, the PAPR value of the emitted oscillations also increases. In the second step, a restriction on the PAPR oscillation is introduced. The result of solving the optimization problem by the numerical method will be m expansion coefficients of the envelope $a(t)$ in the Fourier series $\{a_k\}$. As parameter n increases, the PAPR value of the emitted oscillations also increases.

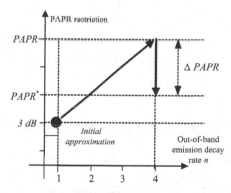

Fig. 1. A graphical representation of the optimization procedure.

The sequence of solutions to the optimization problem is presented in Fig. 2. Initially, the required accuracy of the solution is set and the initial approximation is set. It should be noted that the choice of the initial approximation can significantly affect the final result of the algorithm. The required accuracy of the solution is determined by the choice of the number of expansion coefficients m of the envelope $a(t)$ in a limited Fourier series. The value of m, the initial approximation, and the constraints of the optimization problem are the input parameters of the optimization algorithm (Fig. 2). At the output of the optimization block, the coefficients of the expansion of the envelope $a(t)$ in a limited Fourier series are calculated. The resulting accuracy of the solution is estimated. If necessary, an increase in the value of m and a restart of the optimization algorithm are performed.

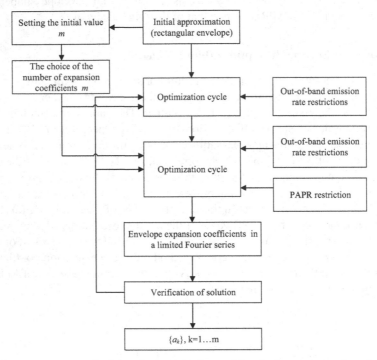

Fig. 2. The sequence of solving the optimization problem in the presence of restrictions.

3   Examples of Solutions of the Optimization Problem

Let's move on to solving the optimization problem. When checking, we will consider the parameter of the decay rate of the OOB emission level and the PAPR value. The duration $T_s = T$ was also selected. When calculating the PAPR of the emitted oscillations, a signal at a high frequency is considered.

To begin with, consider the case without restrictions on PAPR (Fig. 3). The main lobe of the energy spectrum increases with increasing parameter n. So, for $n = 2$, this value at the -30 dB level is $3.5/T$, with $n = 12$ it is already equal to $8.6/T$.

The PAPR values are 7 dB at $n = 2$ and 10.5 dB at $n = 12$. This fact is explained by the following reason. With an increase in the decay rate of the OOB emission level, the energy falling on the frequency range outside the main lobe of the energy spectrum decreases, which, in turn, leads to an increase in the energy falling on the main lobe.

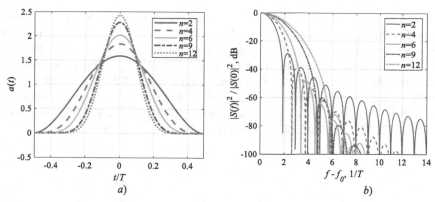

Fig. 3. The results of the solution for the case without restriction on the values of PAPR and the corresponding energy spectra.

Therefore, the wider the main lobe of the spectrum, the narrower the main lobe of the time function, since the frequency and time regions are opposite. It follows that the higher will be the PAPR.

Let us consider the case when there is a limit on the PAPR value of the emitted oscillations (Fig. 4). In this case, we fix the value of the decay rate of OOB oscillations $n = 2$. Without restriction, the PAPR value is 7 dB. Figure 4, a) shows examples of optimal envelopes when restricting the PAPR value to 6, 5.5, 5 dB. It can be noted that when the restriction on PAPR is tightened, the envelope expands and tends to a rectangular shape. In this case, the band of occupied frequencies expands (Fig. 4, b). With an increase in the restriction on PAPR, the occupied bandwidth at the –30 dB level in the spectrum decreases from $3.1/T$ at PAPR $= 6$ dB to $2.7/T$ at PAPR $= 5$ dB.

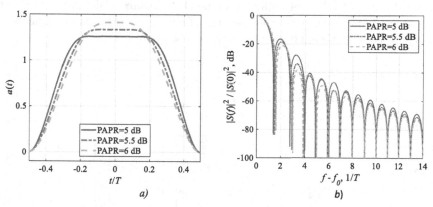

Fig. 4. The results of the solution for the case with restrictions on the values of PAPR and the corresponding energy spectra.

As can be seen (Fig. 5), with an increase in the parameter n, the occupied frequency band at the −30 dB level expands from $\Delta F_{-30 \text{ dB}} = 3.5/T$ for $n = 2$ to $\Delta F_{-30 \text{ dB}} = 6.8/T$ for $n = 8$ for the case without restrictions. For cases with a restriction on PAPR with a 4-fold increase in the decay rate of OOB emissions, $\Delta F_{-30 \text{ dB}}$ will change from 5.4/T to 6.8/T for PAPR = 6 dB, from 5.38/T to 6.3/T for PAPR = 5.5 dB. If PAPR is limited by 5 dB, the parameter n can be increased only to 6, while $\Delta F_{-30 \text{ dB}}$ will change from 5.2/T to 5.7/T (Fig. 5). The more stringent the restriction on the PAPR of the emitted oscillations ΔPAPR, the lower the growth rate of the $\Delta F_{-30 \text{ dB}}$ value.

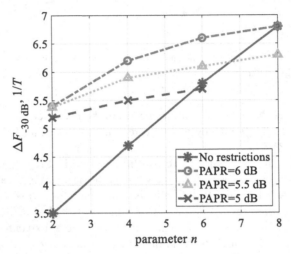

Fig. 5. The occupied frequency band for various options of the optimization task.

Consider the possibility of finding a solution by maximizing the ΔPAPR value for each n value. In this case, we fix the number of envelope expansion coefficients in a Fourier series $m = 9$. Figure 6 shows examples of solutions for $n = 2, 4, 6$.

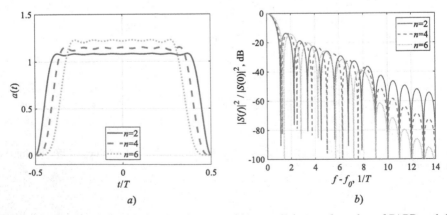

Fig. 6. The results of the solution for the case with a restriction on the value of PAPR and the corresponding energy spectra.

Let's consider Fig. 7, *a*). With an increase in the value of the parameter *n*, which is responsible for the decay rate of OOB emissions, by a factor of 3, the PAPR value changes by 0.9 dB (from 3.7 dB to 4.8 dB) in the case of limiting the PAPR value in the optimization problem. Accordingly, in the case of no restrictions, the PAPR increases by 2 dB (from 7 to 9 dB). Consider the dependence of the occupied frequency band on the value of *n* (Fig. 7, *b*). At the –30 dB level, the frequency band expands with increasing parameter *n* from 2 to 6, both with a restriction on PAPR (ΔF becomes wider by 25%) and without limitation (ΔF becomes wider by 24%). When measuring the frequency band at a level of –60 dB, ΔF decreases by 1.76 times and 1.71 times with and without limitation on the PAPR value correspondingly.

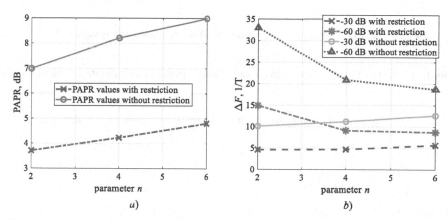

Fig. 7. Dependence of the PAPR value and occupied bandwidth on a change in parameter *n*.

We proceed to consider the estimates of the solutions of the optimization problem depending on the number of used coefficients of the expansion of the envelope in a Fourier series. It is worth noting that for the optimization problem under consideration, the choice of the number of expansion coefficients *m* is a non-trivial task. Due to the nature of the problem, if a small value of *m* is chosen, no solution will be found. The threshold value *m* from which the solution will be found is determined by both the target decay rate of OOB emissions and the limitation on the PAPR of the emitted oscillations. As the value of *m* increases, the time required for the solution increases sharply. However, on the other hand, an increase in the value of *m* potentially makes it possible to obtain more accurate solutions.

In solving the optimization problem, we take the number of coefficients of expansion of the envelope function in the Fourier series *m* equal from 9 to 60. Thus, the nature of the change in the accuracy of the representation of the function *a*(*t*) and the resulting parameters (PAPR of the emitted oscillations, band of occupied frequencies) will be shown. An example of the results obtained for *n* = 2 is shown in Fig. 8.

It can be seen that an increase in the value of *m* at a fixed value of *n* = 2 allows one to achieve lower PAPR values of the emitted oscillations. In other words, an increase in the number of taken into account coefficients of the expansion of the envelope in the Fourier series allows us to find more and more accurate solutions corresponding

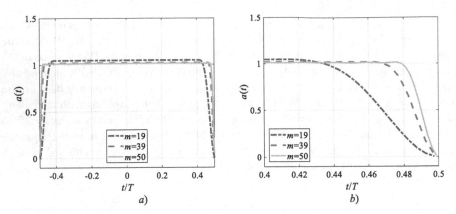

Fig. 8. An example of envelopes obtained with $n = 2$ and various values of m.

Table 1. Characteristics of solutions to the optimization problem with different values of m and n.

n	m	PAPR$_{min}$, dB	Occupied bandwidth at the level −30 dB, $1/T$	Occupied bandwidth at the level −60 dB, $1/T$
2	9	3.70	12	35
	19	3.42	16	47
	29	3.26	18	67
	39	3.15	20	85
	50	3.07	21	109
	60	3.06	19	119
4	9	4.24	11	21
	19	3.54	17	39
	29	3.40	18	59
	39	3.29	18	77
	50	3.19	18	97
	60	3.14	20	109
6	9	4.81	13	19
	19	3.77	17	38
	29	3.48	19	57
	39	3.42	20	72
	50	3.34	20	84
	60	3.28	20	94

to the envelopes of the signals with restrictions on the decay rate of OOB emissions and PAPR of emitted oscillations. However, as mentioned earlier, with increasing m, the complexity of finding solutions significantly increases. Also, the rate of decrease in target indicators slows down asymptotically. Consider this fact as an example of the value of PAPR (Table 1).

As we can see, for the decay rate of OOB emissions $n = 2$, the transition from $m = 9$ to $m = 19$ leads to a decrease in the PAPR of the emitted oscillations by 8%, and the transition from $m = 50$ to $m = 60$ leads to a decrease only 0.3%. The nature of the dependences is observed for $n = 4$ and $n = 6$. We emphasize that the lowest asymptotic limit for decreasing the PAPR value of the emitted oscillations at a high frequency is 3 dB. When solving practical problems, it is necessary to maintain a balance between the resulting parameters of the signals and the complexity of their synthesis.

4 Conclusion

The optimization technique for single-frequency signals having a given rate of decline of the energy spectrum level outside the occupied frequency band is considered, if there is a restriction on the PAPR of the emitted oscillations. Using this technique, it is possible to solve optimization problems for a wide class of spectrally effective signals.

The influence of restrictions on the solution of the optimization problem is shown. In particular, it was shown that when the value of the parameter n, which is responsible for the decay rate of the OOB emission level, increases by a factor of 3, the main lobe of the energy spectrum expands by 20%, and outside the main lobe, the occupied band decreases by more than 40%. It is also shown that with an increase in the decay rate of OOB emissions and a decrease in the number of used envelope expansion coefficients in the Fourier series, the PAPR increases. It was possible to synthesize signals with a gain of 4.2 dB compared with the case without restrictions with the parameter $n = 6$.

In addition, a change in the estimation of solutions to the optimization problem was considered, depending on the number of used Fourier series expansion coefficients. With the parameter value $n = 2$ and $m = 60$, the minimum PAPR value of the emitted oscillations was obtained, equal to 3.06 dB, differing from the minimum possible value only by 0.06 dB.

Acknowledgment. The results of the work were obtained under the grant of the President of the Russian Federation for state support of young Russian scientists (agreement MK1571.2019.8 №075-15-2019-1155) and used computational resources of Peter the Great Saint-Petersburg Polytechnic University Supercomputing Center (http://www.scc.spbstu.ru).

References

1. Anderson, J.B., Rusek, F., Öwall, V.: Faster-Than-Nyquist signaling. Proc. IEEE **101**(8), 1817–1830 (2013). https://doi.org/10.1109/JPROC.2012.2233451
2. Rodrigues, M.R.D., Darwazeh, I.: A spectrally efficient frequency division multi-plexing based communications system. In: Proceeding of 8th Int OFDM-Workshop (InOWo), pp. 70–74 (2003)

3. Kanaras, I., Chorti, A., Rodrigues, M., Darwazeh, I.: An overview of optimal and sub-optimal detection techniques for a non orthogonal spectrally efficient FDM. Proc. London Commun. Symp. (2009). http://www.ee.ucl.ac.uk/lcs/previous/LCS2009/LCS/lcs09_21.pdf

4. Xu, T., Darwazeh, I.: Spectrally efficient FDM: spectrum saving technique for 5G? In: Proceeding of 1st International Conference 5G Ubiquitous Connectivity (5GU), pp. 273–278, November 2014

5. Isam, S., Darwazeh, I.: Characterizing the intercarrier interference of non-orthogonal spectrally efficient FDM system. In: Proceeding of 8th International Symposium on Communication System Network and Digital Signal Processing (CSNDSP), pp. 1–5, July 2012

6. Gelgor, A., Nguyen, V.P.: Outperforming conventional OFDM and SEFDM signals by means of using optimal spectral pulses and the M-BCJR algorithm. In: 2019 26th International Conference on Telecommunications (ICT), Hanoi, Vietnam, pp. 130–134 (2019). https://doi.org/10.1109/ict.2019.8798793

7. Rashich, A., Kislitsyn, A., Gorbunov, S.: Trellis demodulator for pulse shaped OFDM. In: 2018 IEEE International Black Sea Conference on Communications and Networking (BlackSeaCom), Batumi, pp. 1–5 (2018). https://doi.org/10.1109/blackseacom.2018.8433690

8. Sliusar, I., Voloshko, S., Smolyar, V., Slyusar, V.: Next generation optical access based on N-OFDM with decimation (2017). In: 2016 3rd International Scientific-Practical Conference Problems of Infocommunications Science and Technology, PIC S and T 2016 - Proceedings, art. № 7905378, pp. 192–194 (2016). https://doi.org/10.1109/infocommst.2016.7905378

9. Sliusar, V., Smoliar, V., Stepanets, A., Sliusar, I.: Method for frequency-division multiplexing of narrow-band information channels, UA Patent 47918 A. IPC8 H04J1/00 H04L5/00, July 2002

10. Slyusar, V.: Neortagonalnoe chastotnoe multipleksirovanie (N-OFDM) signalov. Chast 1[The non-orthogonal frequency division multiplexing (N-OFDM) signals. Part 1.]. Tehnologii I sredstva sviazi [Communication Technologies & Equipment Magazine] **5**, 61–65 (2013)

11. Slyusar, V.: Neortagonalnoe chastotnoe multipleksirovanie (N-OFDM) signalov. Chast 2 [The non-orthogonal frequency division multiplexing (N-OFDM) signals. Part 2.]. Tehnologii I sredstva sviazi [Communication Technologies & Equipment Magazine] **6**, 60–65 (2013)

12. Darwazeh, I., Ghannam, H., Xu, T.: The first 15 years of SEFDM: a brief survey. In: 2018 11th International Symposium on Communication Systems, Networks & Digital Signal Processing (CSNDSP), Budapest, pp. 1–7 (2018). https://doi.org/10.1109/CSNDSP.2018.8471886

13. Gelgor, A., Gorlov, A., Nguyen, V.P.: The design and performance of SEFDM with the Sinc-to-RRC modification of subcarriers spectrums. In: 2016 International Conference on Advanced Technologies for Communications (ATC), Hanoi, pp. 65–69 (2016). https://doi.org/10.1109/ATC.2016.7764831

14. Kislitsyn, A.B., Rashich, A.V., Tan, N.N.: Generation of SEFDM-Signals using FFT/IFFT. In: Balandin, S., Andreev, S., Koucheryavy, Y. (eds.) NEW2AN 2014. LNCS, vol. 8638, pp. 488–501. Springer, Cham (2014). https://doi.org/10.1007/978-3-319-10353-2_44

15. Isam, S., Darwazeh, I.: Peak to average power ratio reduction in spectrally efficient FDM systems. In: 2011 18th International Conference on Telecommunications, Ayia Napa, pp. 363–368 (2011). https://doi.org/10.1109/cts.2011.5898951

16. Kholmov, M., Fadeev, D.: The effectiveness of active constellation extension for PAPR reduction in SEFDM systems. In: 2018 IEEE International Conference on Electrical Engineering and Photonics (EExPolytech), St. Petersburg, pp. 116–118 (2018). https://doi.org/10.1109/eexpolytech.2018.8564432

17. Jin, Q., Ruan, X.: Switch-linear hybrid envelope-tracking power supply with multilevel structure. In: IECON Proceedings (Industrial Electronics Conference), art. № 6699324, pp. 1325–1330 (2013). https://doi.org/10.1109/iecon.2013.6699324

18. Pergushev, A.: The analytical model for calculating distortions in the envelope tracking power supply. In: 2019 IEEE International Conference on Electrical Engineering and Photonics (EExPolytech), St. Petersburg, Russia, pp. 72–75 (2019). https://doi.org/10.1109/eexpol ytech.2019.8906813

19. Yousefzadeh, V., Alarcón, E., Maksimovic, D.: Efficiency optimization in linear-assisted switching power converters for envelope tracking in RF power amplifiers. In: Proceedings - IEEE International Symposium on Circuits and Systems, art. № 1464834, pp. 1302–1305 (2005). https://doi.org/10.1109/iscas.2005.1464834

20. Pergushev, A., Sorotsky, V., Ulanov, A.: Criteria for selection envelope tracking power supply parameters for high peak-to-average power ratio applications. In: 2019 IEEE International Conference on Electrical Engineering and Photonics (EExPolytech), St. Petersburg, Russia, pp. 13–16 (2019). https://doi.org/10.1109/eexpolytech.2019.8906793

21. Zudov, R.I.: Efficiency of a class DE power amplifier for RF signals with high peak-to-average power ratio. In: 2019 IEEE International Conference on Electrical Engineering and Photonics (EExPolytech), St. Petersburg, Russia, pp. 28–30 (2019). https://doi.org/10.1109/ eexpolytech.2019.8906856

22. Fadeev, D.K., Rashich, A.V.: Optimal input power backoff of a nonlinear power amplifier for SEFDM system. In: Balandin, S., Andreev, S., Koucheryavy, Y. (eds.) ruSMART 2015. LNCS, vol. 9247, pp. 669–678. Springer, Cham (2015). https://doi.org/10.1007/978-3-319-23126-6_60

23. Idris, A., MohdSapari, N.L., Syarhan Idris, M., Sarnin, S.S., Norsyafizan Wan Mohamad, W., Naim, N.F.: Reduction of PAPR using block coding method and APSK modulation techniques for F-OFDM in 5G system. In: TENCON 2018 – 2018 IEEE Region 10 Confer-ence, Jeju, Korea (South), pp. 2456-2460 (2018)

24. Krongold, B.S., Jones, D.L.: An active-set approach for OFDM PAR reduction via tone reservation. IEEE Trans. Signal Process. 52(2), 495–509 (2004)

25. Antonov, E.O., Rashich, A.V., Fadeev, D.K., Tan, N.: Reduced complexity tone reservation peak-to-average power ratio reduction algorithm for SEFDM signals. In 2016 39th International Conference on Telecommunications and Signal Processing (TSP), Vienna, pp. 445–448 (2016). https://doi.org/10.1109/tsp.2016.7760917

26. Han, S.H., Lee, J.H.: An overview of peak-to-average power ratio reduction techniques for multicarrier transmission. IEEE Wireless Comm. Mag. 12, 56–65 (2005)

27. Nguyen, D.C., Zavjalov, S.V., Ovsyannikova, A.S.: The effectiveness of application of multi-frequency signals under conditions of amplitude limitation. In: Galinina, O., Andreev, S., Balandin, S., Koucheryavy, Y. (eds.) NEW2AN/ruSMART-2019. LNCS, vol. 11660, pp. 681–687. Springer, Cham (2019). https://doi.org/10.1007/978-3-030-30859-9_59

28. Reinoso-Chisaguano, D.J., Urquiza-Aguiar, L., Paredes-Paredes, M.C.: Effect of constellation-shaping-based PAPR reduction methods over the capacity of OFDM systems. In: 2019 IEEE Fourth Ecuador Technical Chapters Meeting (ETCM), Guayaquil, Ecuador, pp. 1–6 (2019). https://doi.org/10.1109/ETCM48019.2019.9014868

29. Zhang, M., Liu, M., Zhong, Z.: Neural network assisted active constellation extension for PAPR reduction of OFDM system. In: 2019 11th International Conference on Wireless Communications and Signal Processing (WCSP), Xi'an, China, pp. 1–6 (2019). https://doi.org/10.1109/wcsp.2019.8928056

30. Mounir, M., El_Mashade, M.B.: Performance evaluation of hybrid ACE-TRNS PAPR reduction technique. In: 2018 International Japan-Africa Conference on Electronics, Communications and Computations (JAC-ECC), Alexandria, Egypt, pp. 29–34 (2018). https://doi.org/10.1109/jec-ecc.2018.8679561

31. Lavrenyuk, I.I., Ovsyannikova, A.S., Zavjalov, S.V., Volvenko, S.V., Makarov, S.B.: Improving energy efficiency of finite time FTN pulses detection by choosing optimal envelope shape. In: 2019 26th International Conference on Telecommunications (ICT), Hanoi, Vietnam, pp. 289–294 (2019). https://doi.org/10.1109/ict.2019.8798830

32. Zavjalov, S.V., Ovsyannikova, A.S., Lavrenyuk, I.I., Volvenko, S.V.: The efficiency of detection algorithms for optimal FTN signals. In: Galinina, O., Andreev, S., Balandin, S., Koucheryavy, Y. (eds.) NEW2AN/ruSMART -2019. LNCS, vol. 11660, pp. 670–680. Springer, Cham (2019). https://doi.org/10.1007/978-3-030-30859-9_58

33. Rashich, A., Urvantsev, A.: Pulse-shaped multicarrier signals with nonorthogonal frequency spacing. In: 2018 IEEE International Black Sea Conference on Communications and Networking (BlackSeaCom), Batumi, pp. 1–5 (2018). https://doi.org/10.1109/blackseacom.2018.843 3714

34. Gelgor, A., Gelgor, T.: New pulse shapes for partial response signaling to outper-form faster-than-nyquist signaling. In: 2019 IEEE International Conference on Electrical Engineering and Photonics (EExPolytech), St. Petersburg, Russia, pp. 144–148 (2019). https://doi.org/10.1109/eexpolytech.2019.8906884

35. Smirnova, E.N., Ovsyannikova, A.S., Zavjalov, S.V., Dong, G.: On features of implementation of SEFDM-transmitter with optimal shape of envelope. J. Phys. Conf. Ser. **1236**(1), art. № 012067, 1–7 (2019). https://doi.org/10.1088/1742-6596/1236/1/012067

36. Gelgor, A., Gorlov, A., Nguyen, V.P.: Performance analysis of SEFDM with optimal subcarriers spectrum shapes. In: 2017 IEEE International Black Sea Conference on Communications and Networking (BlackSeaCom), Istanbul, pp. 1–5 (2017). https://doi.org/10.1109/blackseacom.2017.8277680

Study of Detection Characteristics in Recognition of Simple Radio Pulses and Signals with LFM and PSK in the Autocorrelation Receiver

Nguyen Trong Nhan[1], Alexey S. Podstrigaev[1(✉)], Vladimir P. Likhachev[2],
Alexey A. Veselkov[2], Vadim V. Davydov[3,4,5], Nikita S. Myazin[3],
and Sergey S. Makeev[3]

[1] Saint Petersburg Electrotechnical University "LETI", St. Petersburg, Russia
ap0d@ya.ru
[2] Zhukovsky-Gagarin Air Force Academy, Voronezh, Russia
[3] Peter the Great Saint Petersburg Polytechnic University, St. Petersburg 195251, Russia
[4] The Bonch-Bruevich Saint-Petersburg State University of Telecommunications,
Saint Petersburg 193232, Russia
[5] All-Russian Research Institute of Phytopathology, 143050 Moscow Region, Russia

Abstract. The article offers both method and device for signal detection with recognition of modulation type. Using simulation methods, the detection characteristics of the developed device in case of simple and complex signals are obtained. Complex signals are signals with linear-frequency modulation or binary phase-shift keying. In addition, the article compares the sensitivity of the device when detecting and recognizing signals of various types.

Keywords: Detector · Autocorrelator · Linear-frequency modulated signal · Binary phase-shift keying signal · Simple radio pulse · Detection characteristics

1 Introduction

Complex signals are widely used in modern radio-electronic equipment to improve both interference immunity and covert operation [1–6]. The quality of their detection depends on how well the characteristics of the receiving devices and registration systems are matched [6–15]. However, *a priori* information about the type and parameters of the received signal is usually not available in broadband environment analysis tools. Therefore, the sensitivity in broadband analysis tools when receiving complex signals is significantly lower than that of a receiver with a matched detector.

It is known that in the absence of *a priori* signal data, the autocorrelation detector has the highest sensitivity [16–26]. However, such a detector cannot recognize the type of signal modulation.

Therefore, this article aims to develop a detector that allows determining the following types of signal modulation during the detection: linear-frequency modulation (LFM), phase-shift keying (PSK), and simple pulse (SP) signals. A comparative analysis of the detection characteristics is made for these types of signals.

O. Galinina et al. (Eds.): NEW2AN 2020/ruSMART 2020, LNCS 12525, pp. 415–423, 2020.
https://doi.org/10.1007/978-3-030-65726-0_37

2   Method for Determining the Types of Radar Signals in an Autocorrelation Receiver

The method for processing LFM signals in a traditional autocorrelation detector consists in determining the pulse duration τ_i (by determining the number of counting pulses during the existence of the signal) and determining the signal spectrum width Δf using the following relation:

$$\Delta f_s = \frac{f_{df} \cdot \tau_i}{\tau_d}, \tag{1}$$

where f_{df} is the differential frequency of the signal at the output of the autocorrelator, τ_d is the signal delay duration.

To recognize the modulation type in the proposed detector, the following steps are performed:

1. Multiply the signal with its delayed copy.
2. Extract the low-frequency component and component at the differential frequency in the resulting spectrum (for the initial frequency).
3. Double the frequency of the received signal.
4. Multiply the signal at the double frequency with its delayed copy.
5. Extract the low-frequency component and component at the differential frequency in the resulting spectrum (for the double frequency).
6. Compare the amplitudes of the four spectrum components obtained in steps 2 and 5 with the given threshold values and decide on the type of the detected signal.

The amplitudes of the low-frequency component and the component at the differential frequency are determined by the type of modulation of the original signal [16–26]. The amplitudes of the signal components at a double frequency after multiplication with its delayed copy are also determined by the type of modulation of the original signal.

A simple signal is characterized by low-frequency components at the differential frequency, which is close to zero frequency due to the constant carrier frequency. The same is true for the original simple signal at double frequency. The original LFM signal is characterized by the presence of a component at the differential frequency due to changes in the instantaneous frequency of the signal during the delay. The low–frequency components of the LFM signals are close to zero. The same is true for the original LFM signal at double frequency. As for the binary phase–shift keying signal, his component at the differential frequency after doubling the frequency is close to zero. Thus, by checking the presence or absence of components, it is possible to determine the modulation type of the received signal.

The block diagram of a detector that implements the described detection process with recognition is shown in Fig. 1.

During the simulation of the device operation (Fig. 1), it was assumed that the received signal $S_{input}(t)$ is fed to the input of a band-pass filter with a bandwidth Δf_{HF} (PF HF) determined by the maximum width of the signal spectrum in a given frequency analysis range [27, 28]. The extracted signal is delayed in the delay line (DL1) for a

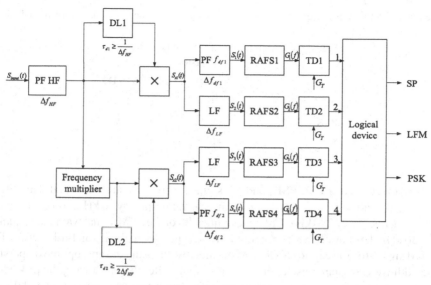

Fig. 1. Structural scheme device.

certain time τ_{d1} and multiplied with its delayed copy. The time τ_{d1} is defined as follows: $\tau_{d1} \geq \frac{1}{\Delta f_{HF}}$. A band-pass filter extracts a component of the signal $S_{x1}(t)$ at a differential frequency f_{df1}.

In case of a simple signal, the level of this component is close to zero. The signal $S_{x1}(t)$ is fed to the input of the low-pass filter, where the low frequency component of the signal is extracted. The level of this component is close to zero in the case of receiving LFM signals. For both signals $S_1(t)$ and $S_2(t)$, the spectrum components are obtained and compared in threshold devices (TD1 and TD2). The threshold value G_T is determined by the Neumann-Pearson criterion for given false alarm probabilities and correct detection [29–31].

Additionally, signal at the output of the band-pass filter with a specified bandwidth Δf_{HF} is fed to the input of frequency multiplier, which doubles the signal frequency. After delaying the signal for a time $\tau_{d2} \geq \frac{1}{2\Delta f_{HF}}$, it multiplies with its delayed copy. A component at the differential frequency f_{df2}, which is close to zero for signals with binary phase-shift keying, is extracted from the signal $S_{x2}(t)$ by a band-pass filter. A low-pass filter extracts the low-frequency component of the signal $S_{x2}(t)$, which is close to zero for LFM signals. For both signals $S_3(t)$ and $S_4(t)$, the spectrum components are obtained and compared in threshold devices (TD3 and TD4).

Based on the decisions made in threshold devices (Table 1), the modulation type of the received signal is determined.

3   Simulation of the Process of Detecting Radar Signals in an Autocorrelation Receiver

To determine the probability of correct detection of complex signals of different types, a simulation of the device operation was performed (Fig. 1).

Table 1. Determination of the signal modulation type based on the solutions of threshold devices.

Signal modulation type	Threshold device decisions			
	TD1	TD2	TD3	TD4
LFM	1	0	0	1
PSK	1	1	1	0
SP	0	1	1	0

Digital records of LFM, PSK, and SP signals were generated as initial data. Pulse parameters: duration $\tau_{i1} = 13$ ms, $\tau_{i2} = 26$ ms; carrier frequency 10 kHz; equal amplitude at sampling frequency 200 kHz. The spectrum width of the LFM signal was taken equal to $\Delta f_s = 30$ kHz. The law of PSK phase rotation corresponded to the 13-bit Barker code. The required signal-to-noise ratio (SNR) was ensured by choosing the appropriate dispersion of the additive Gaussian noise at the detector input. After that, following the procedure described above, a computational experiment was conducted on the processing of digital signal records at $\tau_d = 0.1$ ms and $\Delta f_{HF} = 100$ kHz. The number of FFT points in the calculation of the spectrum was taken equal to 1024. Threshold values were calculated based on the levels of false alarm $P_{F0} = 0.001$ and $P_{F0} = 0.0005$, and the probability of correct detection was estimated using the following formula:

$$P_{D0} = \frac{N_1}{N},$$ (2)

where N_1 is the number of simulations with correct signal detection, N is the total number of simulations with a fixed value of noise dispersion.

The results of calculations at $N = 1000$ are shown in Figs. 2 and 3.

Thus, the obtained characteristics allow to quantitatively estimating the values of the signal/noise ratio, at which the given probability of correct detection is achieved at different values of probability of false alarm (Table 2).

In addition, digital records of single LFM pulses were generated and processed. Pulse parameters: duration $\tau_{i2} = 26$ ms, carrier frequency 50 kHz, spectrum width $\Delta f_s = 30$, 60 and 90 kHz. Thresholds are calculated for the probability $P_{F0} = 0.001$. The simulation results are shown in Fig. 4 and Table 3.

Comparative analysis of the probability of correct detection of LFM, PSK, and SP signals with a duration of 13 to 26 ms has shown that the proposed scheme when detecting modulated signals (at $P_{D0} = 0.8$) gives a gain:

- of about 1.5...2.0 dB at $P_{F0} = 0.001$ and of about 1.8...3.2 dB at $P_{F0} = 0.0005$ over PSK signal;
- of about 5.5...6.0 dB at $P_{F0} = 0.001$ and of about 1.8...3.2 dB at $P_{F0} = 0.0005$ over SP signal.

Obviously, when receiving modulated signals with a longer duration, the gain will increase. In addition, it is guaranteed to determine the type of LFM and PSK signals at

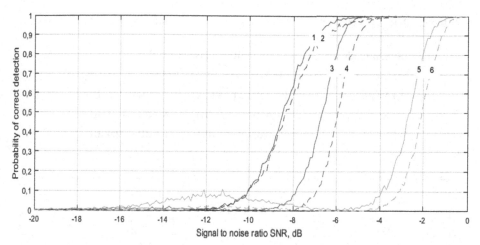

Fig. 2. Detection characteristics of LFM, PSK and simple pulses. The pulse duration is $\tau_{i1} = 13$ ms. Graph 1 corresponds to LFM pulse, $P_{F0} = 0.001$; Graph 2: LFM pulse, $P_{F0} = 0.0005$; Graph 3: PSK pulse, $P_{F0} = 0.001$; Graph 4: PSK pulse, $P_{F0} = 0.0005$; Graph 5: simple pulse, $P_{F0} = 0.001$; Graph 6: simple pulse, $P_{F0} = 0.0005$.

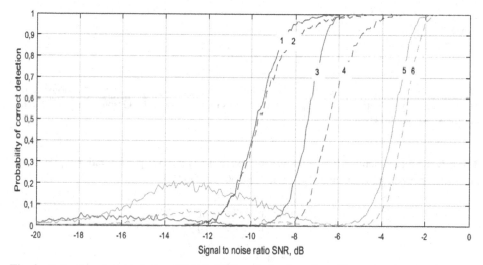

Fig. 3. Detection characteristics of LFM, PSK and simple pulses. The pulse duration is $\tau_{i1} = 26$ ms. Graph 1 corresponds to LFM pulse, $P_{F0} = 0.001$; Graph 2: LFM pulse, $P_{F0} = 0.0005$; Graph 3: PSK pulse, $P_{F0} = 0.001$; Graph 4: PSK pulse, $P_{F0} = 0.0005$; Graph 5: simple pulse, $P_{F0} = 0.001$; Graph 6: simple pulse, $P_{F0} = 0.0005$.

SNR in the range of $-2...-3$ dB. The probability of determining the type of a simple radio pulse is $0.6...0.8$ at $\tau_i = 13$ ms and SNR $= -2$ dB and at $\tau_i = 26$ ms and SNR $= -3$ dB.

Table 2. SNR at which the $P_{D0} = 0.8$ is achieved at pulse duration $\tau_{i1} = 13$ ms (26 ms).

Signal modulation type	Probability of false alarm P_{F0}	
	0,001	0,0005
LFM	−7.5 dB (−8.9 dB)	−7.1 dB (−8.6 dB)
PSK	−6 dB (−6.9 dB)	−5.3 dB (−5.4 dB)
SP	−2 dB (−2.9 dB)	−1.4 dB (−2.4 dB)

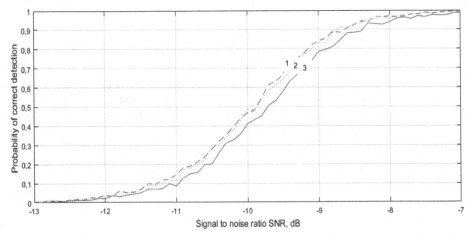

Fig. 4. Characteristics of detection of LFM pulses with a duration of $\tau_{i1} = 26$ ms at various values of the frequency deviation Δf_s. Graph 1 corresponds to $\Delta f_s = 60$ kHz; Graph 2: $\Delta f_s = 90$ kHz; Graph 3: $\Delta f_s = 30$ kHz.

Table 3. SNR at which the $P_{D0} = 0.8$ is achieved for LFM pulse at pulse duration $\tau_{i1} = 26$ ms and different frequency deviation Δf_s values (30, 60 and 90 kHz).

Δf_s, kHz	Probability of false alarm P_{F0}	
	0.001	0.0005
30	−8.9 dB	−8.6 dB
60	−9.1 dB	−8.9 dB
90	−9.1 dB	−8.8 dB

The analysis of dependencies presented in Fig. 4 shows that an increase in the ratio $\Delta f_s / \Delta f_{HF}$ from 0.3 to 0.6 provides an increase in the probability P_{D0} from 0.80 to 0.86. In the meantime, an increase in the ratio $\Delta f_s / \Delta f_{HF}$ from 0.6 to 0.9 does not provide a noticeable increase in the P_{D0}. Obviously, when the condition $\Delta f_s \leq \Delta f_{HF}$ is met and the value Δf_{df1} is fixed, the probability P_{D0} increases when receiving LFM signals with a larger spectrum width.

4 Conclusion

The highest sensitivity (the lowest SNR) of the developed detector under equal conditions is achieved for an LFM radio pulse. With fixed probabilities of correct detection and false alarms, the SNR at the detector's input should be higher by approximately 3 dB for the PSK signal and higher by 6 dB for the simple pulse signal.

References

1. Tsui, J., Cheng, C.-H.: Digital Techniques for Wideband Receivers, p. 608. SciTech Publishing Inc., New York, United States (2015)
2. Makolkina, M., Pham, V.D., Kirichek, R., Gogol, A., Koucheryavy, A.: Interaction of AR and IoT applications on the basis of hierarchical cloud services. In: Galinina, O., Andreev, S., Balandin, S., Koucheryavy, Y. (eds.) NEW2AN/ruSMART -2018. LNCS, vol. 11118, pp. 547–559. Springer, Cham (2018). https://doi.org/10.1007/978-3-030-01168-0_49
3. Zaugg, E.C., Edwards, M.C., Margulis, A.: The SlimSAR: a small, multi-frequency, synthetic aperture radar for UAS operation. In: 9th IEEE International Radar Conference, pp. 277–282 (2010)
4. Bystrov, V.V., Likhachev, V.P., Ryazantsev, L.B.: Experimental check of the coherence of radiolocation signals from objects with nonlinear electrical properties. Meas. Tech. 57(9), 1073–1076 (2014). https://doi.org/10.1007/s11018-014-0582-1
5. Duersch, M.I.: BYU MICRO-SAR: A Very Small, Low-Power LFM-CW SAR. A thesis submitted to the faculty of Brigham Young University in partial fulfillment of the requirements for the degree of Master of Science (2004)
6. Simonov, A., Fokin, G., Sevidov, V., Sivers, M., Dvornikov, S.: Polarization direction finding method of interfering radio emission sources. In: Galinina, O., Andreev, S., Balandin, S., Koucheryavy, Y. (eds.) NEW2AN/ruSMART-2019. LNCS, vol. 11660, pp. 208–219. Springer, Cham (2019). https://doi.org/10.1007/978-3-030-30859-9_18
7. Kirichek, R., DInh, T.D., Pham, V.D., Le, D.T., Koucheryavy, A.: Positioning methods based on flying network for emergencies. In: 22nd International Conference on Advanced Communications Technology (ICACT 2020). Phoenix ParkPyeongchang (South Korea), 9061217, pp. 245–250 (2020)
8. Koucheryavy, A., Vladyko, A., Kirichek, R.: State of the art and research challenges for public flying ubiquitous sensor networks. In: Balandin, S., Andreev, S., Koucheryavy, Y. (eds.) ruSMART 2015. LNCS, vol. 9247, pp. 299–308. Springer, Cham (2015). https://doi.org/10.1007/978-3-319-23126-6_27
9. Al-Bahri, M., Ruslan, K., Aleksey, B.: Integrating internet of things with the digital object architecture. In: Galinina, O., Andreev, S., Balandin, S., Koucheryavy, Y. (eds.) NEW2AN/ruSMART -2019. LNCS, vol. 11660, pp. 540–547. Springer, Cham (2019). https://doi.org/10.1007/978-3-030-30859-9_47
10. Podstrigaev, A.S., Smolyakov, A.V., Davydov, V.V., Myazin, N.S., Grebenikova, N.M., Davydov, R.V.: New method for determining the probability of signals overlapping for the estimation of the stability of the radio monitoring systems in a complex signal environment. In: Galinina, O., Andreev, S., Balandin, S., Koucheryavy, Y. (eds.) NEW2AN/ruSMART -2019. LNCS, vol. 11660, pp. 525–533. Springer, Cham (2019). https://doi.org/10.1007/978-3-030-30859-9_45

11. Pirmagomedov, R., Kirichek, R., Blinnikov, M., Koucheryavy, A.: UAV-based gateways for wireless nanosensor networks deployed over large areas. Comput. Commun. **146**, 55–62 (2019)

12. Podstrigaev, A.S., Smolyakov, A.V., Davydov, V.V., Myazin, N.S., Slobodyan, M.G.: Features of the development of transceivers for information and communication systems considering the distribution of radar operating frequencies in the frequency range. In: Galinina, O., Andreev, S., Balandin, S., Koucheryavy, Y. (eds.) NEW2AN/ruSMART-2018. LNCS, vol. 11118, pp. 509–515. Springer, Cham (2018). https://doi.org/10.1007/978-3-030-01168-0_45

13. Al-Bahri, M., Yankovsky, A., Kirichek, R., Borodin, A.: Smart system based on DOA IoT for products monitoring anti-counterfeiting. In: 4th MEC International Conference on Big Data and Smart City (ICBDSC-2019). Muscat (Oman), pp. 8645610 (2019)

14. Dinh, T.D., Le, D.T., Tran, T.T.T., Kirichek, R.: Flying Ad-Hoc network for emergency based on IEEE 802.11p multichannel MAC protocol. In: Vishnevskiy, V.M., Samouylov, K.E., Kozyrev, D.V. (eds.) DCCN 2019. LNCS, vol. 11965, pp. 479–494. Springer, Cham (2019). https://doi.org/10.1007/978-3-030-36614-8_37

15. Zakharov, M., Kirichek, R., Makolkina, M., Koucheryavy, A.: Signal transmitting in pheromone networks. In: Galinina, O., Andreev, S., Balandin, S., Koucheryavy, Y. (eds.) NEW2AN/ruSMART-2019. LNCS, vol. 11660, pp. 534–539. Springer, Cham (2019). https://doi.org/10.1007/978-3-030-30859-9_46

16. Helton, J., Chen, C.I.H., Lin, D.M., Tsui, J.B.Y.: FPGA-based 1.2 GHz bandwidth digital instantaneous frequency measurement receiver. In: 9th International Symposium on Quality Electronic Design (2008)

17. Darvin, Ch.R., Paranjape, H., Sarath, K.M., Elango, V.: Analysis of autocorrelation based frequency measurement algorithm for IFM receivers. In: 2014 IEEE International Conference on Electronics, Computing and Communication Technologies (CONECCT) (2014)

18. Mahlooji, S., Mohammadi, K.: Very high resolution digital instantaneous frequency measurement receiver. In: 2009 International Conference on Signal Processing Systems (2009)

19. Lee, Y.H.G., Helton, J., Chen, C.I.H.: Real-time FPGA-based implementation of digital instantaneous frequency measurement receiver. In: 2008 IEEE International Symposium on Circuits and Systems (2008)

20. Liang, Z., Dong, X., Yang, X., Song, H.: Digital weighted autocorrelation receiver using channel characteristic sequences for transmitted reference UWB communication systems. In: 2016 IEEE Wireless Communications and Networking Conference (2016)

21. Pausini, M., Janssen, G.J.M.: Analysis and comparison of autocorrelation receivers for IR-UWB signals based on differential detection. In: IEEE International Conference on Acoustics, Speech, and Signal Processing (2004)

22. Leus, G., Van Der Veen, A.-J.: A weighted autocorrelation receiver for transmitted reference ultra-wideband communications. In: IEEE 6th Workshop on Signal Processing Advances in Wireless Communications (2005)

23. Mohammed, M.S., Singh, M.J., Abdullah, M.: New TR-UWB Receiver Algorithm Design to Mitigate MUI in Concurrent Schemes. Wireless Pers. Commun. **97**(3), 4431–4450 (2017). https://doi.org/10.1007/s11277-017-4732-z

24. Liang, Z., Zhang, G., Dong, X., Huo, Y.: Design and analysis of passband transmitted reference pulse cluster UWB Systems In The Presence Of Phase Noise. IEEE Access **6**, 14954–14965 (2018)

25. Liu, J., Luo, Z., Xiong, X.: Low-resolution ADCs for wireless communication: a comprehensive survey. IEEE Access **7**, 91291–91324 (2019)

26. Rogozhnikov, E.V., Savenko, K.V., Movchan, A.K., Dmitriyev, E.M.: The study of correlation receivers. In: 2019 20th International Conference of Young Specialists on Micro/Nanotechnologies and Electron Devices (EDM) (2019)

27. Levanon, N., Mozeson, E.: Radar Signals, New Work, IEEE Press, John Wiley & Sons (2004)
28. Skolnik, M.I.: Introduction to Radar Systems, 3rd edn. McGraw-Hill, New York (2001)
29. Neyman, J., Pearson, E.S.: On the problem of the most efficient tests of statistical hypotheses. Phil. Trans. Roy. Soc. London **231**, 289–337 (1933)
30. Conte, E., De Maio, A., Galdi, C.: Signal detection in compound-Gaussian noise: Neyman-Pearson and CFAR detectors. IEEE Trans. Signal Process. **48**(2), 419–428 (2000)
31. Maria-Pilar, J.A., de David la, M.M., Roberto, G.P., Manuel, R.Z.: Radar detection with the Neyman–Pearson criterion using supervised-learning-machines trained with the cross-entropy error. EURASIP J. Adv. Signal Process. **2013**, 44 (2013)

Wideband Tunable Delay Line for Microwave Signals Based on RF Photonic Components

Alexey S. Podstrigaev[1]([⊠]), Alexander S. Lukiyanov[2], Alina A. Galichina[2],
Alexander P. Lavrov[3], and Mikhail V. Parfenov[3]

[1] Saint Petersburg Electrotechnical University "LETI", St. Petersburg, Russia
ap0d@ya.ru
[2] Scientific-Research Institute "Vector" OJSC, St. Petersburg, Russia
[3] Peter the Great Saint Petersburg Polytechnic University, St. Petersburg, Russia

Abstract. The principle of operation of the wideband tunable delay line for microwave signals is presented. Delay is performed after the transfer of the microwave signal to the optical frequency domain. The configuration of the delay line model is described. Bandwidth, losses, and distortion characteristics of the delay line model are experimentally determined.

Keywords: Wideband delay line · Tunable delay line · RF photonics · Optical fiber · Microwave signal delay · Delay control

1 Introduction

Microwave (MW) delay lines are being widely used in a big variety of devices for reception, processing, and generation of signals, in particular, in beamforming elements of phased arrays [1–12].

Nowadays the most widespread types of delay lines are cable, strip, ultrasound delay lines, delay lines based on ferrite waveguides, and other types.

Each of them has its advantages, but none of them has at the same time large bandwidth, low losses, small weight and size, and, in addition, the possibility to tune delay time within a wide range.

The variant of the MW delay line presented in this work satisfies from our point of view all the above-mentioned requirements. To confirm its advantages the delay line model was developed. The main characteristics of the delay line model were experimentally investigated.

2 State of the Art Review

The closest technical solutions that meet the requirements are presented in [13–16].

In [13] the controlled optical delay line is made in the form of an optical fiber wound around a coil. The delay control is realized by changing the temperature of the liquid surrounding the fiber.

© Springer Nature Switzerland AG 2020
O. Galinina et al. (Eds.): NEW2AN 2020/ruSMART 2020, LNCS 12525, pp. 424–431, 2020.
https://doi.org/10.1007/978-3-030-65726-0_38

In the device described at [14], a multicore optical fiber is used. In it, the input signal enters all the cores simultaneously, and at the output of the optical fiber in different cores, it acquires a different delay. Different cores have different group refractive index of modes and, accordingly, different group delay values. The disadvantage is the large dimensions of the used fiber sections needed for controlling the delay.

In [15, 16], the delay line is based on a plurality of switched fiber sections. The segments have different electrical lengths and can be connected either individually or in various combinations. The disadvantage of such a device is the need to use optical switches.

So, when using optical MEMS switches, the switching time is approximately 0.5 to 1 ms [17]. Accordingly, when adjusting the microwave signal delay, the device will not be able to provide delay discreteness less than the switching time. The lower limit of the delay variation range also cannot be less than the switching time. For switching the optical signal, it is also possible to use switches based on solid-state crystals, the switching time of which is approximately up to 300 ns [18]. But such switches have a higher cost, which significantly increases the cost of the delay line if we need to achieve a high discreteness of the delay change.

A comprehensive description of the issue is given in the review article [12].

3   MW Signal Delay Line Operating Principle

The delay line that satisfies the pointed above requirements can be developed based on a fiber optic segment usage. The operating principle of such a delay line is based on the multiple cyclic passages of the signal through an optical fiber. After each cycle, the signal is sent through a "feedback loop" to device input again (to increase the delay) or to device output (if no more delay is necessary). Note that conversion of an MW signal to an optical one and vice versa can be performed one time–after all N delay cycles–or many times–in every delay cycle.

In the first case signal switching (and subsequent signal passages through the fiber optic segment) should be performed in the optical domain. However, available solid-state fiber-optic switches have low isolation between their outputs. Typical values of isolation range from 20 to 50 dB [19, 20]. If using many cycles, insufficient isolation leads to signal spectrum distortion. Isolation can be increased by the use of several subsequent optical switches, but this leads to size, cost, and complexity increases of the system.

Therefore, the second case was chosen, i.e., the delay line with conversions in every cycle during signal passage through the delay loop included in the delay line.

The block diagram of the delay line is presented in Fig. 1. An input MW signal comes through switch S1 and amplifier A1, after which it is transferred by VD1 laser modulator to an optical carrier frequency. The optical signal is delayed in the fiber optic segment, and then the delayed signal is converted back to the MW frequency range by photodiode VD2. Then the MW signal comes through amplifier A3 and output switch S2. Amplifiers A1 and A3 are used to obtain the transmission coefficient of the delay line close to 1. From the output switch S2 MW signal comes to the device output or the input switch S1 again. If the MW signal is sent to the input switch again, its power is controlled by amplifier A4 and attenuator A2. Thus, the device has a "feedback loop", i.e. a loop with the possibility to pass a signal many times. Depending on the necessary delay time value the signal is passed through the delay line desired number of times.

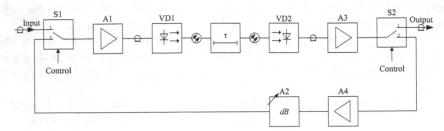

Fig. 1. Block diagram of tunable delay line

The minimum delay time of the considered device can be calculated as $\tau_1 = (L \cdot n)/c$, where L is the length of the fiber, n is the effective refractive index of an optical fiber mode, c is the light velocity in vacuum. In addition, the delay can't be longer than the switching time of switches S1, S2. The typical switching time of an MW switch is 10 ns [21].

The delay time of the device τ_{DL} for MW signal is regulated discretely: $\tau_{DL} = N \cdot \tau_1$ and is defined by a number of optical signal passages through the loop. The maximum delay time is limited in practice by the degree of distortion of an MW signal, caused during signal passages through the loop.

Electro-optic (modulator) and optoelectronic (photodetector) converters, as well as optical fiber, should be matched by wavelength and optical power level.

4   Delay Line Model

According to the block diagram (Fig. 1), a delay line model was developed. The model consists of four devices (modules) (Fig. 2, 3):

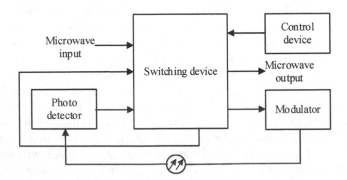

Fig. 2. Block diagram of the delay line model

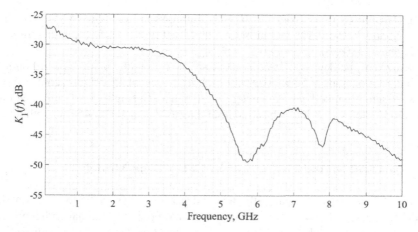

Fig. 3. Response characteristic of modulator and photodetector modules $K_1(f)$

- switching device;
- modulator;
- photodetector;
- control device.

All MW components (switches, amplifiers, and attenuator) are placed in the switching device. Signal input and output are also included in this module.

Previously we investigated analog optical lines for transmission of MW signals, which consisted of microwave photonic units available on the telecom market [22]. In this model of s delay line, easier and cheaper solutions are used.

The modulator is based on Xiamen's GTLD-3-DF-W-4-P-FA-V-10G laser diode. In addition to the laser diode itself, this modulator includes a supply unit and a wideband matching circuit to a standard 50-Ω MW line.

In usual optical delay lines, the SMF-28 fiber optic segment placed between the transmitter and the photodetector defines the time delay. In this delay line model, the fiber optic segment of the length L is placed between the modulator and photodetector and provides time delay $\tau_1 = 7.45$ μs.

The photodetector is based on Xiamen's GTPD-InGaAs-10G-R-1 photodiode, also including a supply unit and wideband matching circuit to a standard 50-Ω MW line.

The switching device is designed to control the number of cycles of signal passage N through the delay loop using switches S1 and S2.

Another function of this device is to support the fixed transmission coefficient using units A2 and A4 (see Fig. 1).

Modulator, photodetector, and matching MW circuits are developed for operating in the frequency range up to 10 GHz. The response characteristic of the modulator and photodetector $K_1(f)$, when they used in a single MW transmission line, is presented in Fig. 3. The value of the pass-through transmission coefficient obtained for the model is about −30 dB, which is typical for optical delay lines. Response characteristic measurement was performed using the Planar C1220 vector network analyzer.

In the frequency range from 1 to 10 GHz transmission coefficient K_1 is in the range from −49.5 to −30.0 dB. The transmission coefficient flatness $\Delta K_1(f)$ in this frequency range is about ±10 dB.

The sizes of the developed testing units are the following: modulator and photodetector have dimensions of 50 × 20 mm, switching device, of 45 × 6 mm, control device, of 65 × 20 mm, fiber coil has a diameter of 230 mm and a height of 300 mm. Therefore, the developed delay line model has maximal dimensions of 180 × 45 mm without fiber coil.

5   Losses and Signal Distortion in Delay Line Model

For the FRC $K(f)$ measurement of the whole delay line, the switches S1, S2 was set to provide one passage ($N = 1$) of a MW signal. A harmonic MW signal with a power of 0 dBm was sent to the delay line input with frequency tuned in the range from 100 MHz to 10 GHz. The response characteristic of the delay line model is presented in Fig. 4.

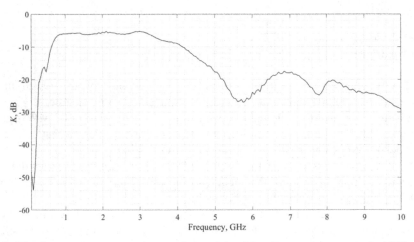

Fig. 4. The frequency response characteristic of the delay line model at a single MW signal passage

The response characteristic of the delay line model in the frequency range 0.1–10 GHz, as shown in Fig. 4, is in the range from −29.0 to −3.0 dB (transmission coefficient flatness $\Delta K_1(f)$ is ±13 dB).

Note that $K(f)$ of the whole device is higher than $K_1(f)$ of the optical line itself due to the amplification in switching device (as in Fig. 3 and Fig. 4). However, the model has a 1 dB larger flatness of response characteristic $\Delta K(f)$ than the flatness of basic RF photonic units included in it.

It is obvious that after multiple electro-optic and optoelectronic conversions, the distortion grade of MW signals can be significantly increased. For the investigation of the dependence of the distortion grade on the number of passages through the optical loop inside the delay line the following experiment was carried out.

The continuous signal with the frequency $fs = 3$ GHz and power of 0 dBm was sent to the delay line input. The number of passage cycles N was controlled using the control device in the range from 1 to 1000, which corresponds to delay times τ_{DL} range from 7.45 μs to 7.45 ms. The delay line caught the MW signal, delayed it for 7.45 μs, and then the MW signal was sent to the Anritsu MS2726C spectrum analyzer.

During one passage cycle ($N = 1$, delay of 7.45 μs) signal power on the device output is 13 dBm. When transmitted through the delay line several times the "feedback" line is used, which leads to an increase of the response characteristic of the delay line model (due to units A2, A4, see Fig. 1).

Therefore, if the number of cycles increases, signal power stays on the level of −10 dBm and doesn't depend on the number of cycles.

As expected, an increase of the number of cycles leads to an increase of noise in the signal spectrum. The MW spectrum at different passage cycles (1, 15, 100, and 1000 times) through the feedback loop of the delay line is presented in Fig. 5.

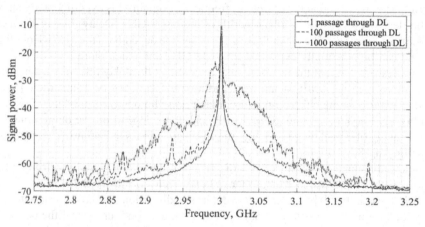

Fig. 5. Signal spectrum at different numbers of passage cycles through the loop of the delay line

Results of experiments, which were performed for different numbers of cycles N, have shown the following dependence of noise increase (in dBc) on frequency shift Δf from signal frequency fs: (see Table 1).

Presented signal distortions were probably caused by the following main reasons:

1. Multiple conversions from microwaves to the optical frequency domain and vice versa.
2. Nonlinear distortion of signals because of excessive amplification in microwave domain (units A2 and A4, see Fig. 1), which is necessary for the support of constant transmission coefficient.
3. Influence of switches jitter on signal fronts.

Table 1. Noise level (in dBc).

Number of cycles N	Frequency shift Δf, MHz				
	25	50	75	100	125
15	−55...−45	−57...−50	−60...−55	−58...−57	−63...−60
30	−53...−47	−58...−55	−60...−58	−60...−59	−65...−60
100	−50...−45	−55...−50	−60...−59	−62...−60	−65...−64
500	−40...−39	−55...−53	−60...−56	−65...−64	−66...−65
1000	−40...−34	−48...−40	−48...−55	−60...−55	−62...−60

6 Conclusion

The model of the MW delay line is developed. Time delay is realized after the transfer of the input microwave signal to the optical frequency domain. It is experimentally shown that the developed model has a bandwidth of at least 9 GHz. Delay time is discretely tunable in a wide range. The bandwidth of the delay line depends on the used RF photonic units and can be potentially expanded up to 18 GHz and much more – up to 40 GHz. The significant flatness of the response characteristic of the delay line (in the developed model: more than ±7.5 dB in the bandwidth of 9 GHz) can be compensated using matching circuits in the electro-optic modulator and photodetector modules. Losses in the delay line model are from 10 to 13 dB and don't depend on the delay time. The experimentally obtained range of delay times is from 7.45 µs to 7.45 ms. The model has dimensions of 180 × 45 mm.

The disadvantage of the device is a distortion of the output signal spectrum, which increases with an increase of the number of delay cycles inside the delay line.

Further research will be carried out to determine distortion grounds, to estimate them strictly, and to predict distortion grade. In addition, the configuration of the delay line will be improved to obtain larger bandwidth and decrease a flatness of the response characteristic. Beyond that, the work of the delay line should be investigated in the time domain and, in particular, by the passage of short pulses through the delay line, which duration is significantly shorter than the delay time discrete.

Acknowledgments. A. P. Lavrov and M. V. Parfenov have used funding provided by RFBR to participate in the research of this microwave delay line possibilities (project number 20-07-00928).

References

1. Skolnik, M.I.: Radar Handbook, 3rd edn. The McGraw-Hill Companies, New York (2008)
2. Tsui, J.B.: Microwave Receivers with Electronic Warfare Applications. SciTech Publishing Inc., Raleigh (2005)
3. Poisel, R.A.: Electronic Warfare Receivers and Receiver Systems, 3rd edn. Artech House, New York (2014)

4. Wang, L., Guo, Y.X., Lian, Y., Heng, C.-H.: 3-to-5 GHz 4-channel UWB beamforming transmitter with 1° phase resolution through calibrated vernier delay line in 0.13 μm CMOS. IEEE J. Solid-State Circuits **47**(12), 3145–3159 (2012). https://doi.org/10.1109/jssc.2012.2216704

5. Abielmona, S., Gupta, S., Caloz, C.: Compressive receiver using a CRLH-based dispersive delay line for analog signal processing. IEEE Trans. Microw. Theor. Tech. **57**(11), 2617–2626 (2009). https://doi.org/10.1109/TMTT.2009.2031927

6. Toughlian, E.N., Zmuda, H.: A photonic variable RF delay line for phased array antennas. J. Lightwave Technol. **8**(12), 1824–1828 (1990). https://doi.org/10.1109/50.62877

7. Ortega, B., Cruz, J.L., Capmany, J., Andres, M.V., Pastor, D.: Variable delay line for phased-array antenna based on a chirped fiber grating. IEEE Trans. Microw. Theor. Tech. **48**(8), 1352–1360 (2000). https://doi.org/10.1109/22.859480

8. Ryazantsev, L.B., Likhachev, V.P.: Assessment of range and radial velocity of objects of a broadband radar station under conditions of range cell migration. Meas. Tech. **60**(11), 1158–1162 (2018). https://doi.org/10.1007/s11018-018-1334-4

9. Liu, Y., Yao, J., Yang, J.: Wideband true-time-delay unit for phased array beamforming using discrete-chirped fiber grating prism. Optics Commun. **207**(1–6), 177–187 (2002). https://doi.org/10.1016/S0030-4018(02)01529-8

10. Ivanov, S.I., Lavrov, A.P., Saenko, I.I., Filatov, D.L.: Chirped fiber grating beamformer for linear phased array antenna. In: Galinina, O., Andreev, S., Balandin, S., Koucheryavy, Y. (eds.) NEW2AN/ruSMART -2018. LNCS, vol. 11118, pp. 594–604. Springer, Cham (2018). https://doi.org/10.1007/978-3-030-01168-0_53

11. Reindl, L., Ruppel, C.C.W., Berek, S., et al.: Design, fabrication, and application of precise SAW delay lines used in an FMCW radar system. IEEE Trans. Microw. Theor. Tech. **49**(4), 787–794 (2001). https://doi.org/10.1109/22.915465

12. Shahoei, H., Yao, J.: Wiley encyclopedia of electrical and electronics engineering. In: Webster, J. (ed.) Delay Lines. John Wiley & Sons, Inc., Hoboken (2014)

13. Patent RU2620763C1 (2016)

14. Patent WO2013178847 (2013)

15. Egorova, O.N., Belkin, M.E., Klushnik, D.A., Zhuravlev, S.G., Astapovich, M.S., Semojnov, S.L.: Microwave signal delay line based on multicore optical fiber. Phys. Wave Phenom. **25**(4), 289–292 (2017). https://doi.org/10.3103/S1541308X17040082

16. Egorova, O.N., Astapovich, M.S., Belkin, M.E., Semenov, S.L.: Fiber-optic delay line using multicore fiber. Bull. Lebedev. Phys. Inst. **44**(1), 5–7 (2017). https://doi.org/10.3103/S10683 3561701002X

17. https://www.thorlabs.de/newgrouppage9.cfm?objectgroup_id=1553

18. https://agiltron.com/category/fiber-optic-switches/nanospeed-fiber-optical-switches/

19. NanoSpeed 1 × 2 series fiber optical switch datasheet. https://agiltron.com/PDFs/NS_1x2_switch_All.pdf

20. PM series fiber optic switch datasheet, https://agiltron.com/PDFs/CL%201x2%20PM%20Series%20Switch.pdf

21. Switch HMC347ALP3E datasheet, https://www.analog.com/en/products/hmc347alp3e.html

22. Ivanov, S.I., Lavrov, A.P., Saenko, I.I.: Main characteristics study of analog fiber-optic links with direct and external modulation in transmitter modules. In: Proceedings IEEE International Conference on Electrical Engineering and Photonics (EExPolytech), pp. 264–267 (2018). https://doi.org/10.1109/eexpolytech.2018.8564391

BER Performance of SEFDM Signals in LTE Fading Channels with Imperfect Channel Knowledge

Valentin Salnikov[1], Andrey Rashich[1(✉)], Viet Them Nguyen[1], and Wei Xue[2]

[1] Radio and Telecommunication Systems Department, Peter the Great St. Petersburg Polytechnic University, St. Petersburg, Russia
valyentin129@gmail.com, rashich@cee.spbstu.ru,
vietthembk@gmail.com
[2] College of Information and Communication Engineering, Harbin Engineering University, Harbin, China
xuewei@hrbeu.edu.cn

Abstract. The paper considers the BER performance of Spectral Efficient Frequency-Division Multiplexing (SEFDM) signals in LTE fading channels with imperfect channel knowledge. Analysis of the effect of channel estimation errors on the BER performance is carried out regardless of the selected estimation method. Demodulation is done using ZF-equalizer and trellis demodulator. The analysis is done for perfect synchronization and perfect knowledge of noise power.

Keywords: Fading channels · Equalizer · Multicarrier FTN · NOFDM · OFDM · SEFDM · LTE

1 Introduction

Orthogonal multicarrier signals (OFDM, orthogonal frequency division multiplexing) are widely used in modern wireless telecommunication systems (LTE, WiFi, DVB–T2). The today demand from telecommunications is to increase the spectral efficiency for next generation wireless systems. The promising approach is based on non-orthogonal multicarrier signals known as SEFDM (Spectrally Efficient Frequency-Division Multiplexing) [1]. Due to non-orthogonality of subcarriers, the occupied bandwidth is reduced by $1/\alpha$ times, where α is a frequency compression coefficient.

The ancestor of SEFDM – OFDM – shows good BER performance in frequency selective channels using simple 1-tap equalizer in frequency domain. Channel estimation for SEFDM systems is covered in [2–4]. The papers [2, 3] introduces Partial Channel Estimator (PCE) with interpolation and Full Channel Estimator (FCE) using pilot symbols and Least Squares (LS) solution. In paper [4] Maximum Likelihood principle is

This research work was supported by Peter the Great St. Petersburg Polytechnic University in the framework of the Program "5-100-2020".

© Springer Nature Switzerland AG 2020
O. Galinina et al. (Eds.): NEW2AN 2020/ruSMART 2020, LNCS 12525, pp. 432–439, 2020.
https://doi.org/10.1007/978-3-030-65726-0_39

used. These papers are mainly focused on channel estimation accuracy and pilot symbols positioning. In the current work we focused on BER performance of SEFDM signals with distorted channel estimates regardless of channel estimation methods.

Non-orthogonality of subcarriers complicates the reception and demodulation of SEFDM signals. There is a number of works offering several approaches for SEFDM demodulation such as successive interference cancellation [5], sphere decoder [6], and trellis demodulator [7]. In this paper we use trellis demodulator because it provides acceptable BER performance for high number of subcarriers ($\sim 10^3$-10^4). We also apply ZF equalizer in frequency domain [8] to reduce the overall complexity of the receiver.

In this paper SEFDM BER performance is analyzed for typical LTE fading channels (EPA-5, EVA-70, ETU-300) with imperfect channel knowledge for different subcarrier numbers and compression coefficients. The system model is described in Sect. 2, proposed channel estimation and equalization is described in Sect. 3, in Sect. 4 there are simulation results and in Sect. 5 is the conclusion.

2 System Model

The baseband SEFDM-signal in time domain can be written as:

$$s(t) = \sum_{k=-N/2}^{N/2-1} C_k e^{j2\pi k \Delta f t} \tag{1}$$

Here $\omega_k = k\omega_1 = 2\pi k \Delta f$ is k-th subcarrier cyclic frequency, C_k is a complex modulation symbol for k-th subcarrier. For OFDM signals frequency spacing is $\Delta f_{\text{OFDM}} = 1/T$, and $\Delta f = \alpha/T$ for SEFDM signals, where $\alpha = \Delta f / \Delta f_{\text{OFDM}} < 1$.

Denoting sampling frequency as $F_s = 1/\Delta t = N\Delta f$ we can see that discrete-time SEFDM-symbol has α times less samples than OFDM symbol with the same number of subcarriers and symbol duration. A discrete-time SEFDM-symbol with N subcarriers and symbol duration T is expressed as:

$$s_n = \sum_{k=-N/2}^{N/2-1} C_k e^{j2\pi k \Delta f n / F_s} = \sum_{k=-N/2}^{N/2-1} C_k e^{j2\pi k n / N} \tag{2}$$

Here $n = 0,\ldots(L-1)$, L is the number of time samples in one SEFDM-symbol, $L = F_s T = N\alpha$.

Equation (1) can be rewritten in matrix form:

$$s = F_{L \times N}^{-1} \times C \tag{3}$$

Here $s = \{s_k\}_{k=0}^{L-1}$ and $C = \{C_k\}_{k=-N/2}^{N/2-1}$ are column vectors, $F_{L \times N}^{-1}$ is a $L \times N$ inverse Fourier matrix with elements $F_{k,n}^{-1} = e^{j2\pi k n / N}$. The generation of SEFDM symbol is done using the N_{FFT}-point IFFT ($N_{FFT} = N$) followed by discarding the last $N - L$ samples at the IFFT output.

The received signal in case of fading channel is the sum of convolution of SEFDM signal with channel impulse response (CIR) and AWGN samples:

$$r_i = \sum_{j=0}^{J-1} s_{i-j} h_j + w_i \tag{4}$$

Here h_j is the complex sample of CIR, J is the CIR length in samples, w_i is the AWGN sample.

If CIR considered to be static for the duration of one SEFDM-symbol and intersymbol interference is fully neglected due to usage of cyclic prefix, then in matrix notation one received SEFDM-symbol can be written as following:

$$r = H_{L \times L} \times F_{L \times N}^{-1} \times C + w \tag{5}$$

Here $H_{L \times L}$ is $L \times L$ matrix containing circularly shifted impulse response $h = \{h_j\}_{j=0}^{L-1}$ on main diagonal, r – is the column vector of received samples of length L.

The main task of receiver is to make estimates $\hat{C}_k$ of transmitted symbols C_k (or to provide their LLR values).

The system model is shown in Fig. 1. SEFDM transmitter consists of random generated bits, QPSK mapper, SEFDM modulator based on IFFT and cyclic prefix insertion block. The generated SEFDM signal goes through LTE fading channel and sums up with AWGN. The Channel Estimation block computes distorted CIR. Estimations are imperfect due to the AWGN in channel. The equalizer applies these estimations to the received SEFDM signal in frequency domain. Then SEFDM signal is demodulated in the iterative demodulator.

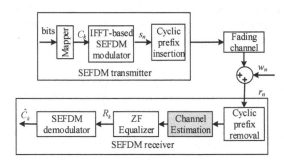

Fig. 1. System model

3   Channel Estimation and Equalization

As described in [9], N-subcarrier SEFDM signal can be represented as equivalent L-subcarrier OFDM signal. Then the equivalent OFDM-symbol complex modulation symbols are linear combinations of original symbols C_k. The channel estimation and

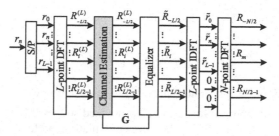

Fig. 2. Channel estimation and equalization scheme

equalization is produced in this L-point DFT domain. This structure is presented on Fig. 2.

Received SEFDM symbol after removing cyclic prefix and L-point DFT can be expressed as:

$$R^{(L)} = F_{L\times L} \times H_{L\times L} \times F_{L\times L}^{-1} \times C + F_{L\times L} \times w = G \times C + W, \tag{6}$$

where diagonal matrix $G = F_{L\times L} \times H_{L\times L} \times F_{L\times L}^{-1}$ is the channel transfer function and $W = F_{L\times L} \times w$ is the column vector of AWGN samples in frequency domain.

In [2, 3] was shown, that channel estimation can be represented by the sum of CIR and a Gaussian distributed random variable $\mathbf{Q}$ caused by AWGN:

$$\tilde{G} = G + Q,$$

$$MSE = \mathrm{E}\left\{\left[\tilde{G} - G\right]^H \times \left[\tilde{G} - G\right]\right\} = Q. \tag{7}$$

Here MSE is mean square error, $\mathrm{E}\{\cdot\}$ is expectation, $\cdot^H$ is Hermitian transpose operator. In general the error may be of non-additive nature due to nonlinear interpolation or other reasons.

Using the channel estimation, one tap ZF-equalizer for informational SEFDM signal can be used. As shown in [10] the equalizer output in N-point DFT domain is

$$R = (F_{N\times L} \times \mathcal{F}_{L\times L}^{-1}) \times \tilde{R} =$$
$$(F_{N\times L} \times F_{L\times L}^{-1}) \times \tilde{G} \times F_{L\times L} \times (H_{L\times L} \times F_{LxN}^{-1} \times C + W) \tag{8}$$

The equalizer output samples $\tilde{R}_k$ go to the demodulator input.

4 Simulation Results

As the example of CIR estimation distortion, in this paper we obtain channel estimations using L-subcarrier OFDM pilot symbols. As pilot modulation symbols C^{pilot} are known on the receiver side the k-th element of the channel transfer function can be estimated as:

$$\tilde{G}_k = \frac{R_k}{C_k^{pilot}} = \frac{G_k C_k^{pilot} + W_k}{C_k^{pilot}} = G_k + \frac{W_k}{C_k^{pilot}} \tag{9}$$

Mean square error (MSE) of this estimation equals:

$$MSE = \mathrm{E}\left\{ \frac{W^H \times W}{(C^{pilot})^H \times C^{pilot}} \right\} = \frac{\sigma^2_{AWGN}}{P^{pilot}_{avr}} \tag{10}$$

Here σ^2_{AWGN} is noise dispersion and P^{pilot}_{avr} is average power of pilot modulation symbols. Pilot modulation symbols can be normalized so that $P^{pilot}_{avr} = 1$.

Simulation was done for QPSK subcarriers modulation, perfect synchronization and perfect knowledge of noise power. The confidence probability for all simulations is 0.95 and confidence interval is 0.1. Sampling frequency used in simulations can be obtained using the following equation:

$$F_s = 30.72 \cdot 10^6 \cdot \alpha \cdot N_{FFT}/2048 \tag{11}$$

The trellis demodulator uses three neighbor subcarriers on each side of the demodulated subcarrier to compensate intercarrier interference.

The BER performance of the proposed SEFDM reception scheme with imperfect channel estimation for various compression coefficients α is shown on Fig. 3. The energy loss is increasing with decreasing compression coefficient. The energy loss for the $\alpha = 1/2$ case compared to the $\alpha = 7/8$ case is about 5 dB. The energy difference between $\alpha = 3/4$ and $\alpha = 7/8$ cases is about 2 dB.

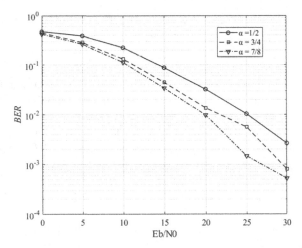

Fig. 3. BER performance of SEFDM signals for various α, EPA channel and $N_{used} = 300$

The same results for EVA and ETU channels presented on Fig. 4 and Fig. 5 respectively. For EVA channel the energy loss for the $\alpha = 1/2$ case compared to the $\alpha = 7/8$ case is about 5 dB for $BER = 10^{-1}$ and more than 10 dB for $BER = 4 \cdot 10^{-2}$. The energy difference between $\alpha = 3/4$ and $\alpha = 7/8$ cases is about 2 dB.

For ETU channel and $\alpha = 1/2$ case the curve is saturated for $E_b/N_0 \geq 20$ dB. The energy loss between $\alpha = 7/8$ and $\alpha = 3/4$ cases is 4 dB for $BER = 0.2$. BER does not exceed 10^{-1} value.

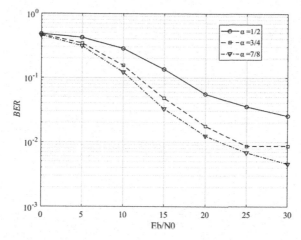

Fig. 4. BER performance of SEFDM signals for various α, EVA channel and $N_{used} = 300$

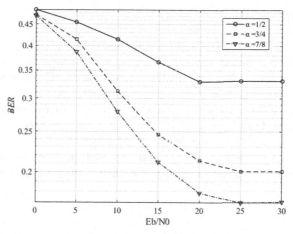

Fig. 5. BER performance of SEFDM signals for various α, ETU channel and $N_{used} = 300$

The BER performance for EPA, EVA, ETU multipath channels with maximum Doppler shifts 5 Hz, 70 Hz and 300 Hz respectively is shown on Fig. 6. The energy difference between EPA and EVA channel does not exceed 5 dB. For ETU channel, the proposed reception scheme provides very poor BER performance, BER does not exceed 10^{-1}.

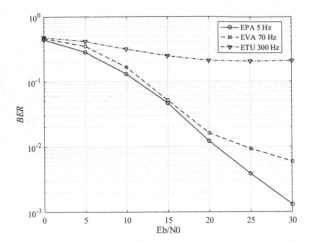

Fig. 6. BER performance of SEFDM signals for various channels, $\alpha = 3/4$, $N_{used} = 300$

5 Conclusion

The BER performance of SEFDM signals with imperfect channel knowledge was analyzed for typical LTE fading channels (EPA, EVA, ETU) with non-zero Doppler shifts. The best performance was obtained for EPA channel, and for ETU channel the proposed reception scheme provided very poor BER performance.

The performance degrades as frequency compression coefficient α decreases. For EVA and ETU channels and $\alpha = 1/2$ BER does not exceed 10^{-1} value. The energy loss between $\alpha = 3/4$ and $\alpha = 7/8$ varies between 2 and 5 dB.

The drawback of proposed channel estimation analysis is that it does not consider non-Gaussian channel estimation errors, which can be caused by interpolation.

References

1. Kanaras, I., Chorti, A., Rodrigues, M., Darwazeh, I.: Spectrally efficient FDM signals: bandwidth gain at the expense of receiver complexity. In: IEEE International Conference on Communications ICC 2009 Proceedings, June 2009
2. Ahmed, S.I.A.: Spectrally efficient FDM communication signals and transceivers: design, mathematical modelling and system optimization. Doctoral thesis, UCL (University College London) (2011)
3. Ghannam, H., Darwazeh, I.: Robust channel estimation methods for spectrally efficient FDM systems. In: 2018 IEEE 87th Vehicular Technology Conference (VTC Spring), Porto, pp. 1–6 (2018)
4. Wang, X., Ho, P., Wu, Y.: Robust channel estimation and ISI cancellation for OFDM systems with suppressed features. IEEE J. Sel. Areas Commun. 23(5), 963–972 (2005)
5. Zavjalov, S.V., Makarov, S.B., Volvenko, S.V., Balashova, A.A.: Efficiency of coherent detection algorithms nonorthogonal multifrequency signals based on modified decision diagram. In: 15th International Conference on Next-Generation Wired/Wireless Advanced Networks and Systems, NEW2AN 2015 and 8th Conference on Internet of Things and Smart Spaces, ruSMART 2015 (2015)

6. Kanaras, I., Chorti, A., Rodrigues, M., Darwazeh, I.: Analysis of suboptimum detection techniques for a bandwidth efficient multi-carrier communication system. In: Proceedings of the Cranfield Multi-Strand Conference, Cranfield University, pp. 505–510, May 2009

7. Rashich, A., Kislitsyn, A., Fadeev, D., Ngoc Nguyen, T.: FFT-based trellis receiver for SEFDM signals. In: 2016 IEEE Global Communications Conference (GLOBECOM), Washington DC, pp. 1–6 (2016)

8. Rashich, A., Gorbunov, S.: Computational complexity analysis of SEFDM time and frequency domain equalizers. In: 2019 IEEE International Conference on Electrical Engineering and Photonics (EExPolytech), St. Petersburg, Russia, pp. 94–97 (2019)

9. Gorbunov, S., Rashich, A.: BER performance of SEFDM signals in LTE fading channels. In: 2018 41st International Conference on Telecommunications and Signal Processing (TSP), Athens, pp. 1–4 (2018)

10. Rashich, A., Gorbunov, S.: ZF equalizer and trellis demodulator receiver for SEFDM in fading channels. In: 2019 26th International Conference on Telecommunications (ICT), Hanoi, Vietnam, pp. 300–303 (2019)

Sensitivity of Energy Spectrum Shape and BER to Variation of Parameters Used in Constraint on Correlation Coefficient During FTN Pulse Optimization

Anna S. Ovsyannikova[1]([⊠]) (iD), Sergey V. Zavjalov[1] (iD), Sergey B. Makarov[1] (iD), Ilya I. Lavrenyuk[1] (iD), and Xue Wei[2] (iD)

[1] Peter the Great St. Petersburg Polytechnic University, Polytechnicheskaya 29, St.Petersburg 195251, Russia
{ovsyannikova_as,zavyalov_sv}@spbstu.ru, makarov@cee.spbstu.ru, knaiser@mail.ru
[2] Harbin Engineering University, Nantong Street 145-1, Harbin 150001, China
xuewei@hrbeu.edu.cn

Abstract. Optimal signals, the shape of which is the result of solving an optimization problem, may provide high spectral efficiency without significant energy losses. The parameters of optimization constraints such as the value of the correlation coefficient and the number of signals considered in the constraint on bit error rate (BER) performance define the shape of the energy spectrum of signals and their correlation properties. In this work sensitivity of energy spectrum and BER performance to variation of parameters of the constraint on correlation coefficient during optimization of FTN pulse shape according to the criterion of maximum energy concentration within occupied frequency bandwidth is estimated. It is shown that the lower the correlation coefficient, the less the energy spectrum changes when the number of signals considered in the constraint on BER performance varies. At the same time, for a rather high value of correlation coefficient increasing the number of signals considered in the constraint on BER performance leads to widening of occupied frequency bandwidth by 7% and reducing the level of emissions by 40 dB at a fixed frequency offset. Besides, energy gain may reach 7 dB. The results obtained during this research allow numerically estimating the possibilities of achieving high spectral and energy characteristics at transmission rates higher than the Nyquist limit.

Keywords: Optimization problem · Maximum band energy concentration criterion · Faster than Nyquist signaling

1 Introduction

One of the development directions of telecommunication systems and communication networks of 5G and 6G generation is achieving high spectral efficiency (more than 2 bps/Hz) with minimal energy losses [1–4]. FTN signals based on RRC (root-raised

© Springer Nature Switzerland AG 2020
O. Galinina et al. (Eds.): NEW2AN 2020/ruSMART 2020, LNCS 12525, pp. 440–448, 2020.
https://doi.org/10.1007/978-3-030-65726-0_40

cosine) pulses have become widespread [5]. FTN signaling provides overcoming the Nyquist limit for binary alphabet with transmission rate $R \geq 1/T$ (T is transmission time of one bit). FTN signals based on RRC pulses are formed via low-pass filter with frequency response $|H(f)|^2$ of raised cosine shape with roll-off factor $0 < \alpha < 1$ [6]. The drawback of such signals is a low reduction rate of the level of energy spectrum $G(f)$ outside occupied frequency bandwidth ΔF. The energy efficiency of detection is determined by correlation properties of transmitted FTN signals based on RRC pulses which in turn depend on $|H(f)|^2$ shape.

Application of optimal $s_{opt}(t)$ FTN signals [7, 8] deserves significant attention. The shape of optimal pulses is obtained as a result of solving the problem of synthesis according to various criteria. For instance, the criterion of providing the given reduction rate of energy spectrum level (the level of out-of-band emissions) [1, 9, 10] or the criterion of maximizing energy concentration of signals within occupied (given) frequency bandwidth may be used [8, 11].

Using the method of optimizing pulse shape allows obtaining such shapes of $s_{opt}(t)$ which meet technical and economic requirements and cannot be obtained with the help of linear filter with frequency response $|H(f)|^2$.

The complexity of the problem of searching for optimal pulse shape depends on the parameters used in optimization constraints. These parameters also influence the energy spectrum and correlation properties of signals.

That is why in this work an attempt to estimate the sensitivity of energy spectrum shape and bit error rate (BER) to variation of parameters used in the optimization constraint on the correlation coefficient is made. Pulse optimization is done according to the criterion of maximum energy concentration within given frequency bandwidth.

2   Optimization Problem

Let us assume that optimal signal $s_{opt}(t)$ with arbitrary pulse shape $a(t)$, amplitude A_0, carrier frequency f_0 has duration $T_s = LT$ ($L > 1$). Then $s_{opt}(t)$ looks as follows:

$$s_{opt}(t) = A_0 a(t) c_j^{(0)} \cos(2\pi f_0 t). \tag{1}$$

The value of the modulation symbol on transmission time interval T of one bit is equal $c_j^{(n)} = (M - 2j + 1)/(M - 1)$, $j = 1 \ldots M$, where M is the volume of the channel alphabet. For binary phase shift keying (BPSK) $c_j^{(0)} = \pm 1$. Signal energy may be presented the next way (E_b is bit energy):

$$\int_{-T_s/2}^{T_s/2} s_{opt}^2(t)dt = \frac{A_0^2}{2} \int_{-T_s/2}^{T_s/2} a^2(t)dt = E_{opt} = E_b$$

The optimization problem of searching for pulse shape $a(t)$ at the time interval of signal existence $T_s = LT$ with the constraint on constant signal energy may be formulated in the following way. The criterion of maximizing energy concentration within occupied frequency bandwidth ΔF (*BEC* – band energy concentration) is written by this expression [8, 9]:

$$\arg\left\{\max_{a(t)} BEC(W)\right\}, \ BEC(W) = \int_{-\Delta F/2}^{\Delta F/2} |F_a(f)|^2 df. \tag{2}$$

In (2) function $F_a(f)$ is Fourier transform from $a(t)$:

$$F_a(f) = \int_{-T_s/2}^{T_s/2} a(t) \exp(-j2\pi ft)dt.$$

We will choose the value of maximum energy concentration within an occupied frequency bandwidth to be equal to 99% of the whole energy of the finite-time signal in infinite bandwidth. Then optimization problem (2) may be presented by (3):

$$\arg\left\{\min_{a(t)} J\right\}, \ J = |BEC(W) - 0.99|. \tag{3}$$

The functional (3) is calculated until the deviation of *BEC* from 0.99 is not more than the given value of calculation accuracy Λ. Here $\Lambda = 5\cdot10^{-4}$.

During solving optimization problem the list of constraints is introduced:

- the constraint on the signal energy (1) may be reduced to (4):

$$\int_{-T_s/2}^{T_s/2} a^2(t)dt = 1; \tag{4}$$

- the constraint on cross-correlation coefficient K_0 of optimal FTN signals depends on information transmission rate R. For $R = 1/T$ intersymbol interference takes place at duration $T_s = LT$ from $(L - 1)$ previous signals and $(L - 1)$ following signals. Then this constraint looks this way:

$$\max_{i=1...(L-1)} \left| \int_{-LT/2}^{LT/2} c_j^{(k)} a(t) [A_j + B_j] dt \right| < K_0, \tag{5}$$

where $A_j = \sum_{i=1}^{L-1} c_j^{(k+i)} a(t - (k + i - 1)T)$, $B_j = \sum_{i=1}^{L-1} c_j^{(k-i)} a(t + (k + i - 1)T)$.

If we take into account not all $(L - 1)$ signals but only N_{acc}, then (5) may be presented as:

$$\max_{i=1...(L-1)} \left| \int_{-LT/2}^{LT/2} c_j^{(k)} a(t) \left[A_j^{(acc)} + B_j^{(acc)}\right] dt \right| < K_0,$$

where $A_j^{(acc)} = \sum\limits_{i=1}^{N_{acc}} c_j^{(k+i)} a(t - (k+i-1)T)$, $B_j^{(acc)} = \sum\limits_{i=1}^{N_{acc}} c_j^{(k-i)} a(t + (k+i-1)T)$.

- the constraint on the symbol transmission rate R for binary channel alphabet. Here $R = 1/T$. This parameter is used in the constraint (5) and influences the cross-correlation coefficient.

Let us estimate the influence of parameters used in constraint (5) on the shape of the energy spectrum and BER of optimal FTN signal (1).

3   Illustration of Optimization Procedure with Varying Parameters of Constraint Taken into Account

This section contains a description of the procedure of minimizing the functional (3) with constraints (5). As an initial approximation we will use the rectangular pulse shape $a(t)$ with duration $T_s = T$.

In Fig. 1 a three-dimensional plot which illustrates the procedure of solving the optimization problem is given. Optimization parameters such as pulse duration, occupied frequency bandwidth, and cross-correlation coefficient are plotted along the axes. The reference point corresponds to the position of initial approximation at the three-dimensional plot: the original signal with a rectangular pulse shape has duration $T_s = T$ and occupied frequency bandwidth $\Delta F_{99\%}^{(0)}\big|_{T_s=T}$. For such signals cross-correlation coefficient $K_0 = 0$.

The optimization procedure starts with increasing duration T_s to the value $2T$. In this case intersymbol interference takes place that leads to the growth of the cross-correlation coefficient (in Fig. 1 $K_0 < 0.5$). Due to increasing pulse duration occupied frequency bandwidth decreases to the value $\Delta F_{99\%}^{(1)}\big|_{T_s=2T}$. An obtained pulse shape is used in further calculations as an initial approximation.

At each step the search for pulse shape of slightly lower value of frequency band containing 99% of energy $\Delta F_{99\%}^{(i)}\big|_{T_s=2T} < \Delta F_{99\%}^{(i-1)}\big|_{T_s=2T}$, $i = 2 \dots n$ is done iteratively until at n-th step certain value $\Delta F_{99\%}^{(n)}\big|_{T_s=2T}$ is achieved. During functional minimization the pulse shape obtained at each $(i-1)$-th step is used as an initial approximation at each i-th step. The required value of the cross-correlation coefficient $K_0 = 0.1$ ($K_0 = 0.01$) is achieved the same way after several iterations. For better stability of solution the value of constraint on frequency band needs to be increased at each iteration $\Delta F_{99\%}^{(n+i)}\big|_{T_s=2T} > \Delta F_{99\%}^{(n)}\big|_{T_s=2T}$, $i = 1, 2, \dots$ Finally we get the required value of cross-correlation coefficient and minimal achievable band under these conditions $\Delta F_{99\%}^{min}\big|_{T_s=2T}$.

For signals with pulse duration $T_s = 2T$ transmitted at the rate $1/T$ only one previous and one following signal are taken into account in constraint (5). The number of signals considered in constraint (5) is denoted by numbers above the arrows in plane $T_s = 2T$,

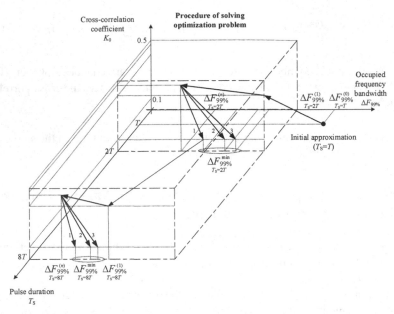

Fig. 1. The procedure of solving the optimization problem with a variation of constraint parameters

$T_s = 8T$ in Fig. 1 and affects the expanding of occupied frequency bandwidth while target value of cross-correlation coefficient is achieved. After optimal pulse shape with duration $T_s = 2T$ which occupies the minimum possible frequency band $\Delta F_{99\%}^{\min}{}_{T_S=2T}$ with target K_0 is obtained, the same sequence (increasing pulse duration, reducing bandwidth, reducing cross-correlation coefficient while increasing bandwidth) is done to obtain optimal pulse shape with duration $T_S = 4T$, $6T$ and so on until desired pulse duration and cross-correlation coefficient for this duration is achieved.

The result of the iterative process of minimizing the functional (3) is the expansion coefficients into limited Fourier series a_k, where $k = 0, 1, \ldots, m - 1$. Then optimal FTN signal has duration $T_S = LT$, cross-correlation coefficient $K_0 = 0.1$ ($K_0 = 0.01$) with N_{acc} considered signals and occupied the minimum possible under these constraints bandwidth containing 99% of signal energy $\Delta F_{99\%}^{\min}{}_{T_S=LT}$.

4 Results of Solving the Optimization Problem with Different Constraint Parameters

In Fig. 2-7 the results of numerical solving the optimization problem of searching for finite-time optimal FTN signals are presented. Figure 2, a-7, a show pulse shapes $a(t)$ with duration $T_S = 8T$. During the optimization procedure the symbol rate was chosen as $R = 1/T$. In Fig. 2, b-7, b you can see the shapes of normalized energy spectrum $G(f)/G(0) = |F_a(f)|^2/|F_a(0)|^2$ of random sequence of optimal FTN signals.

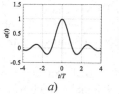
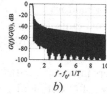

Fig. 2. Optimal pulse shape $a(t)$ and energy spectrum $G(f)/G(0)$ for $N_{\mathrm{acc}} = 1$ ($K_0 = 0.1$, $\Delta F_{99}\% = 0.96/T$)

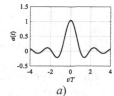
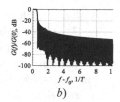

Fig. 3. Optimal pulse shape $a(t)$ and energy spectrum $G(f)/G(0)$ for $N_{\mathrm{acc}} = 1$ ($K_0 = 0.01$, $\Delta F_{99}\% = 1.08/T$)

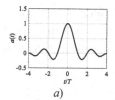
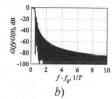

Fig. 4. Optimal pulse shape $a(t)$ and energy spectrum $G(f)/G(0)$ for $N_{\mathrm{acc}} = 2$ ($K_0 = 0.1$, $\Delta F_{99}\% = 1.03/T$)

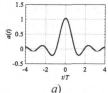
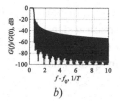

Fig. 5. Optimal pulse shape $a(t)$ and energy spectrum $G(f)/G(0)$ for $N_{\mathrm{acc}} = 2$ ($K_0 = 0.01$, $\Delta F_{99}\% = 1.085/T$)

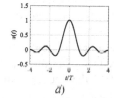
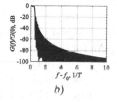

Fig. 6. Optimal pulse shape $a(t)$ and energy spectrum $G(f)/G(0)$ for $N_{\mathrm{acc}} = 3$ ($K_0 = 0.1$, $\Delta F_{99}\% = 1.03/T$)

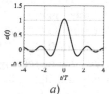
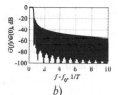

Fig. 7. Optimal pulse shape $a(t)$ and energy spectrum $G(f)/G(0)$ for $N_{\mathrm{acc}} = 3$ ($K_0 = 0.01$, $\Delta F_{99}\% = 1.086/T$)

As it can be noticed from dependencies in Fig. 2, b, Fig. 4, b, Fig. 6, b, for cross-correlation coefficient $K_0 = 0.1$ increasing constraint parameter (5) from $N_{\mathrm{acc}} = 1$ to $N_{\mathrm{acc}} = 3$ leads to reducing the level of out-of-band emissions. For instance, when the offset from carrier frequency is equal to $\Delta f = 10/T$, the level of energy spectrum changes from -55 dB to -95 dB. At the same time frequency bandwidth becomes wider by 6.8%. For $K_0 = 0.01$ such variation of parameters (5) does not lead to a significant reduction of energy spectrum level. Actually, in this case the level of $G(f)/G(0)$ at the offset $\Delta f = 10/T$ decreases only by 5 dB (see Fig. 3, b, and Fig. 7, b). Besides, the change in bandwidth is less than 1%. It can be explained by the fact that higher requirements for BER cause lower sensitivity of energy spectrum shape to variation of parameters used in constraint on cross-correlation coefficient during optimizing pulse shape.

Analysis of the energy spectrum shape of random optimal FTN signals (Fig. 2, b–Fig. 7, b) shows that the level of out-of-band emissions varies depending on constraint parameters in (5) while the reduction rate of $G(f)/G(0)$ level remains constant and proportional to $1/f^2$.

Let us consider the influence of parameters in constraint (5) on BER performance of coherent detection of signals (1). The packet of N optimal FTN signals which needs to be detected looks as follows:

$$x(t) = A_0 \sum_{k=0}^{N-1} a(t - kT)c_r^{(k)} \cos(2\pi f_0 t) + n(t), \tag{6}$$

where $n(t)$ is the realization of additive white Gaussian noise (AWGN) with power spectral density $N_0/2$. The algorithm of coherent detection [12] at each k-th interval may be described the next way. The decision in favor of symbol $c_r^{(k)}$ is made if the next inequality held:

$$\int_{-T_s/2+kT}^{T_s/2+kT} x(t)a(t - kT) \cos(2\pi f_0 t)dt \underset{c_2^{(k)}}{\overset{c_1^{(k)}}{\gtrless}} \frac{\cdot}{\cdot}. \tag{7}$$

The simulation model [9] includes the calculation of bit error rate depending on signal-to-noise ratio E_b/N_0. For each value E_b/N_0 error probability is averaged over 10^6 bits. We use signals based on optimal pulses from Fig. 2,a, Fig. 4,a, Fig. 6,a with cross-correlation coefficient $K_0 = 0.1$ and transmitted at symbol rate $R = 1/T$.

In Fig. 8 the relationships of BER and E_b/N_0 for different constraint parameters (5) are presented. It can be seen that increasing the number of considered signals from $N_{acc} = 1$ to $N_{acc} = 3$ leads to reducing BER. For error probability 10^{-4} the energy gain provided by using $N_{acc} = 3$ instead of $N_{acc} = 1$ reaches about 7.5 dB.

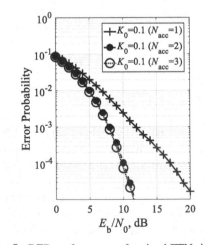

Fig. 8. BER performance of optimal FTN signals

5   Conclusions

In this work the sensitivity of energy spectrum shape and BER to variation of parameters used in constraint on cross-correlation coefficient K_0 during optimizing pulse shape according to the criterion of maximum energy concentration within occupied frequency bandwidth is estimated. If $K_0 = 0.1$, the sensitivity of the energy spectrum shape turns to be rather high. When the number of considered signals in (5) increases from $N_{acc} = 1$ to $N_{acc} = 3$, the level of out-of-band emissions decreases. At the offset from carrier frequency $\Delta f = 10/T$ the level of the energy spectrum reduces by 40 dB, while the frequency band widens by 6.8%. With the transition to $K_0 = 0.01$ the energy spectrum becomes less sensitive to the variation of parameters: its level reduces only by 5 dB at the same frequency offset.

It is also shown that for $K_0 = 0.1$ application of $N_{acc} = 3$ instead of $N_{acc} = 1$ results in better BER performance. The energy gain at error probability 10^{-4} reaches 7.5 dB.

The research allows numerical estimating the prospects of achieving high spectral and energy characteristics at the rates higher than the Nyquist limit.

Acknowledgements. The results of the work were obtained under the grant of the President of the Russian Federation for state support of young Russian scientists (agreement MK-1571.2019.8 №075-15-2019-1155) and used computational resources of Peter the Great Saint-Petersburg Polytechnic University Supercomputing Center (http://www.scc.spbstu.ru).

References

1. Rashich, A., Urvantsev, A.: Pulse-shaped multicarrier signals with nonorthogonal frequency spacing. In: 2018 IEEE International Black Sea Conference on Communications and Networking (BlackSeaCom), Batumi, pp. 1–5 (2018). https://doi.org/10.1109/blackseacom.2018.843 3714
2. Vasilyev, D., Rashich, A.: SEFDM-signals euclidean distance analysis. In: 2018 IEEE International Conference on Electrical Engineering and Photonics (EExPolytech), St. Petersburg, pp. 75–78 (2018). https://doi.org/10.1109/eexpolytech.2018.8564439
3. Gelgor, A., Gorlov, A., Nguyen, V.P.: Performance analysis of SEFDM with optimal subcarriers spectrum shapes. In: 2017 IEEE International Black Sea Conference on Communications and Networking (BlackSeaCom), Istanbul, pp. 1–5 (2017). https://doi.org/10.1109/blacks eacom.2017.8277680
4. Kholmov, M., Fadeev, D.: The effectiveness of active constellation extension for PAPR reduction in SEFDM systems. In: 2018 IEEE International Conference on Electrical Engineering and Photonics (EExPolytech), St. Petersburg, pp. 116–118 (2018). https://doi.org/10.1109/ eexpolytech.2018.8564432
5. Liveris, A.D., Georghiades, C.N.: Exploiting faster-than-Nyquist signaling. IEEE Trans. Commun. **51**(9), 1502–1511 (2003). https://doi.org/10.1109/TCOMM.2003.816943
6. Anderson, J.B.: Bandwidth Efficient Coding. John Wiley & Sons, Incorporated, Hoboken (2017)
7. Gelgor, A., Gelgor, T.: New pulse shapes for partial response signaling to outperform faster-than-Nyquist signaling. In: 2019 IEEE International Conference on Electrical Engineering and Photonics (EExPolytech), St. Petersburg, Russia, pp. 144–148 (2019). https://doi.org/10. 1109/eexpolytech.2019.8906884

8. Said, A., Anderson, J.B.: Bandwidth-efficient coded modulation with optimized linear partial-response signals. IEEE Trans. Inf. Theory **44**(2), 701–713 (1998). https://doi.org/10.1109/18.661514

9. Ovsyannikova, A.S., Zavjalov, S.V., Volvenko, S.V.: Influence of correlation coefficient on spectral and energy efficiency of optimal signals. In: 2018 10th International Congress on Ultra Modern Telecommunications and Control Systems and Workshops (ICUMT), Moscow, Russia, pp. 1–4 (2018). https://doi.org/10.1109/icumt.2018.8631218

10. Xue, W., Guo, L.-L., Zhang, X.-L., Ma, W.-Q.: Analysis of the impact of intersymbolic interference and symbol cross correlation on characteristics of signals. Harbin Gongcheng Daxue Xuebao/J. Harbin Eng. Univ. **31**(1), 109–114 (2010). https://doi.org/10.3969/j.issn.1006-7043.2010.01.019

11. Gelgor, A., Gorlov, A.: A performance of coded modulation based on optimal faster-than-Nyquist signals. In: 2017 IEEE International Black Sea Conference on Communications and Networking (BlackSeaCom), Istanbul, pp. 1–5 (2017). https://doi.org/10.1109/blackseacom.2017.8277678

12. Proakis, J.G., Salehi, M.: Digital Communications, 5th edn. McGraw-Hill Higher Education, New York (2008)

Author Index

Printed in the United States
By Bookmasters